The Law-Making Process

Law in Context

Editors: William Twining (University College, London) and
Christopher Mc Crudden (Lincoln College, Oxford)

Ashworth: *Sentencing and Criminal Justice*
Barton & Douglas: *Law and Parenthood*
Bercusson: *European Labour Law*
Birkinshaw: *Freedom of Information: The Law, the Practice and the Ideal*
Cane: *Atiyah's Accidents, Compensation and the Law*
Collins: *The Law of Contract*
Cranston: *Legal Foundations of the Welfare State*
Davies & Freedland: *Labour Law: Text and Materials*
Detmold: *Courts and Administrators: A Study of Jurisprudence*
Doggett: *Marriage, Wife-Beating and the Law in Victorian England*
Dummett & Nicol: *Subjects, Citizens, Aliens and Others: Nationality and Immigration Law*
Elworthy & Holder: *Environmental Protection: Text and Materials*
Fortin: *Children's Rights and the Developing Law*
Goodrich: *Languages of Law*
Hadden: *Company Law and Capitalism*
Harlow & Rawlings: *Law and Administration*
Harris: *An Introduction to Law*
Lacey & Wells: *Reconstructing Criminal Law: Text and Materials*
Lewis: *Choice and the Legal Order: Rising above Politics*
Moffat: *Trusts Law: Text and Materials*
Norrie: *Crime, Reason and History*
Oliver & Drewry: *The Law and Parliament*
Page & Fergusson: *Investor Protection*
Palmer & Roberts: *Dispute Processes – ADR and the Primary Forms of Decision Making*
Picciotto: *International Business Transaction*
Ramsay: *Consumer Protection: Text and Materials*
Richardson: *Law, Process and Custody*
Snyder: *New Directions in European Community Law*
Stapleton: *Product Liability*
Turpin: *British Government and the Constitution: Text, Cases and Materials*
Twining & Anderson: *Analysis of Evidence*
Twining & Miers: *How to do Things with Rules*
Ward: *A Critical Introduction to European Law*
Zander: *Cases and Materials on the English Legal System*

The Law-Making Process

Fifth Edition

Michael Zander QC

Emeritus Professor of Law
London School of Economics

Butterworths
London Edinburgh Dublin
1999

United Kingdom	Butterworths, a Division of Reed Elsevier (UK) Ltd, Halsbury House, 35 Chancery Lane, LONDON WC2A 1EL and 4 Hill Street, EDINBURGH EH2 3JZ
Australia	Butterworths, a Division of Reed International Books Australia Pty Ltd, CHATSWOOD, New South Wales
Canada	Butterworths Canada Ltd, MARKHAM, Ontario
Hong Kong	Butterworths Asia (Hong Kong), HONG KONG
India	Butterworths Asia, NEW DELHI
Ireland	Butterworth (Ireland) Ltd, DUBLIN
Malaysia	Malayan Law Journal Sdn Bhd, KUALA LUMPUR
New Zealand	Butterworths of New Zealand Ltd, WELLINGTON
Singapore	Butterworths Asia, SINGAPORE
South Africa	Butterworths Publishers (Pty) Ltd, DURBAN
USA	Lexis Law Publishing, CHARLOTTESVILLE, Virginia

© Michael Zander 1999

A CIP Catalogue record for this book is available from the British Library.

First published 1980 (reprinted 1983); Second edition 1985 (reprinted 1986, 1987); Third edition 1989 (reprinted 1990); Fourth edition 1994

ISBN 0 406 90409 X

Printed and bound by William Clowes Ltd, Beccles & London

Visit us at our website: http://www.butterworths.co.uk

Preface to the Fifth Edition

A new edition was needed as it was five years since the last. There are no major changes but some 30 pages of new material have been added, mainly to bring the material up to date. The topics covered by new material include: the Tax Law Rewrite; Special Public Bill ('Jellicoe') Committees in the House of Lords; Second Reading Committees in the House of Commons; the Report on the Legislation Process of the Select Committee on Modernisation of the House of Commons; latest views regarding the impact of *Pepper v Hart*.

The effects of implementation of the Human Rights Act 1998 are explored in regard to the fast track procedure for 'remedial' legislation, Ministerial statements of compatibility, statutory interpretation and the doctrine of precedent. There is a new section on the retrospective effect of common law decisions. The section on European Union law has been strengthened.

The manuscript was revised up to March 1999.

Michael Zander

Preface to the First Edition

The chief purpose of this book is to improve the understanding of the law-making process. For many years I have taught the English Legal System course at the London School of Economics and an equivalent course taken by non-law students. Experience has suggested to me that there is a great gap in the existing literature which this book attempts to fill. It is something between a book of cases and materials, on the one hand, and a textbook on the other. It presents a large number of original texts from a variety of sources – cases, official reports, articles, books, speeches and surveys. It also, however, contains a good deal of the author's own reflections on the subject-matter. The book deals only with the official forms of law-making on a national scale and therefore says nothing about 'private' law-making by lawyers for their clients or by organisations such as trade unions, clubs or companies for their members or shareholders. The book is intended as a companion to the author's *Cases and Materials on the English Legal System* [8th edn, 1999]. There is no overlap between the two books. They are intended to complement each other and together to provide the basic reading required for a university or equivalent course on the legal system. It is hoped that the book will also be of value to anyone concerned to understand how the law-making process actually operates.

January 1980   *Michael Zander*

Acknowledgments

The materials excerpted here are included with the kind permission of those who hold the copyright. A book of this kind would be impossible without their help and I am most indebted to all those who consented to this use of their material. They may be divided into four main groups. There are, first, those who hold copyright over official publications and law reports – the Controller of Her Majesty's Stationery Office, and the Incorporated Council of Law Reporting for England and Wales in relation to the *Law Reports* and the *Weekly Law Reports*, and Butterworths in relation to the *All England Law Reports*. The second group are the publishers and editors of journals from which extracts have been taken – *Australian Law Journal, British Tax Review, Canadian Bar Review, Current Legal Problems, International and Comparative Law Quarterly, Israel Law Review, Journal of the Society of Public Teachers of Law, Law Quarterly Review, Law Society's Gazette, Michigan Law Review, Modern Law Review, New Law Journal, New Society, New Zealand Law Review, Parliamentary Affairs, Public Law, Statute Law Review, The Lawyer* and *William and Mary Law Review*. The third group are publishers of extracts in books: Oceana Press, for the extracts from Karl Llewellyn's *Bramble Bush*; the Yale University Press, for extracts from Benjamin Cardozo's *The Nature of the Judicial Process*; the BBC, for extracts from a broadcast on the background to the Criminal Justice Bill which was later published in *Beyond Westminster*, edited by Anthony King and Anne Sloman; the Institute of Criminology, Cambridge, for extracts from a paper by Mr Michael Moriarty published in a Cropwood booklet; Hamish Hamilton Ltd, for extracts from the late Lord Radcliffe's book *Not in Feather Beds*, and Hamish Hamilton and Jonathan Cape Ltd, for an extract from *Diaries of a Cabinet Minister* by the late Richard Crossman. Fourthly there are the individual authors themselves: the late Professor Brian Abel-Smith, Mr E. Angell, Dame Mary Arden, Professor Patrick Atiyah, Mr G. W. Bartholomew,

Mr Francis Bennion, Mr Mark Carlisle QC, MP (now Lord Carlisle), Professor J. A. Clarence Smith, Professor Stephen Cretney, the late Sir Rupert Cross, Sir William Dale, Mr Edmund Dell MP, Lord Devlin, Professor Aubrey Diamond, Lord Elwyn-Jones, Sir George Engle, Professor M. D. A. Freeman, Ms G. Ganz, Mr James Goudie QC, Professor J. A. G. Griffith, Dr H. R. Hahlo, the late Professor Delmar Karlen, Sir Harold Kent, Sir Michael Kerr, Professor Anthony King, Mr G. Kolts, Professor H. K. Lücke, Professor Norman Marsh, Mr Timothy Millett, Mr Michael Moriarty, Dr R. J. C. Munday, Mr Andrew Nicol, Dr Peter North, Lord Russell of Killowen, Mr Alec Samuels, Lord Scarman, Professor Robert Stevens, Mr I. M. L. Turnbull, Mr D. A. S. Ward, Professor J. Willis, and Mr William Wilson. I am extremely grateful to all those listed, and finally to Mrs Soia Llewellyn for permission to use extracts from her late husband's work, *The Bramble Bush*.

Books, pamphlets, memoranda and articles excerpted

Contents

CHAPTER 4

Binding precedent – the doctrine of stare decisis 194

Table of cases

PAGE

O

P

PAGE

PAGE

Decisions of the European Court of Justice are listed below numerically. These
decisions are also included in the preceding alphabetical list.

CHAPTER I

Legislation — the Whitehall stage

I. THE PREPARATION OF LEGISLATION

The dominant form of law-making is legislation in that legislation is superior to everything other than European Community law (see pp. 374–383 below).

In an average session Parliament produces something between 60 and 80 statutes. The number of statutes per session has not changed greatly but the length of statutes has been growing considerably in recent years as may be seen from the table below:

Volume of all Public General Acts, 1901—1991[1]

Year	No. of Acts	Pages	No. of Sections[2] and Schedules
1901	40	247	400
1911	58	584	701
1921	67	569	783
1931	34	375	440
1941	48	448	533
1951	66	675	803
1961	65	1048	1087
1971	81	2107	1963
1981	72	2276	2026
1991	69	2222[3]	1985

1 Source: Report of Hansard Society, note 12, p. 7 below, at p. 11.
2 The number of sections and Schedules do not tell the whole story as they can be of greatly differing importance and length. (In the Broadcasting Act 1990, s. 191 is four lines long, whereas Schedule 12 is 16 pages long. But each is counted once in the table.) Also the table takes no account of the extent to which provision is made for delegated legislation.
3 Printed on A4 paper which was larger than the size previously used, so requiring fewer pages.

The figures in the table are however somewhat distorted by the inclusion of consolidation statutes which bring together into a new statute what was previously found in several earlier statutes. The second table shows the volume of legislation in recent years when consolidation Acts are excluded:

Volume of all Public General Acts 1985–1991, showing effect of excluding consolidation Acts[4]

Year	No. of Acts	Pages	No. of Acts excluding cons. Acts	Pages excluding Cons. Acts
1985	76	3233	65	1860
1986	68	2780	64	2310
1987	57	1538[5]	56	1269
1988	55	3385	49	2047
1989	46	2489	43	2399
1990	46	2391	42	1743
1991	69	2222	61	2012

Legislation takes the form either of public or private bills. Most Acts are public general Acts which affect the whole public. Private Acts (see further p. 70 below) are for the particular benefit of some person or body of persons such as an individual or company, or local inhabitants. (They must not be confused with Private Members' bills – for which see p. 67 below.) Private Acts sometimes deal with the affairs of local authorities and are then called Local Acts. But, to confuse matters, Local Acts are sometimes the result of public bills but any public bill which affects a particular private interest in a manner different from that of other similar private interests is technically called a hybrid bill (see further p. 73 below). The significance of the difference between public bills, private bills and hybrid bills lies in the parliamentary procedure adopted in each case. This book concerns itself primarily with public bills.

In addition to Acts of Parliament there are also very large numbers of statutory instruments (see further pp. 91–9 below). In the early years of this century the number of statutory instruments was in the hundreds, since the Second World War it has been in the thousands, and again the number of pages has been increasing greatly. Thus in 1951 there were 2,335 statutory instruments running to 3,523 pages. In 1995 there were 3,345 running to 9,688 pages.

---

4   Source: Report of Hansard Society, note 12, p. 7 below.
5   As noted above, the statute book from 1987 onwards has been printed on A4 paper which is larger than the size previously used, so requiring fewer pages.

(a)   The sources of legislation

The belief that most bills derive from a government's manifesto commitments is mistaken. It has been estimated that only 8 per cent of the Conservative Government's bills in the period from 1970 to 1974 came from election commitments and that in the 1974–9 Labour Government the proportion was only a little higher at 13 per cent[6]. The great majority of bills originated within government departments, with the remainder being mainly responses to particular and unexpected events such as the Prevention of Terrorism (Temporary Provisions) Act 1974 in response to the Birmingham IRA bombings, or the Drought Act 1976.

A surprising number of bills derive from the recommendations of independent advisory commissions or committees. Some of these are ad hoc – such as Royal Commissions, Departmental and Inter-Departmental Committees. Others are standing bodies, such as the Law Reform Committee which advises the Lord Chancellor on civil law reform and the Criminal Law Revision Committee which advises the Home Secretary on reform of the criminal law. The most important standing body is the Law Commission.[7]

Analysis has shown that as many as a quarter to a third of all statutes that could have been preceded by the report of an independent advisory committee or commission were the result of such a report. Dr Helen Beynon of the Law Department of Reading University studied all the public bills which received the Royal Assent between 1951 and 1975 (a total of 1,712 statutes). She excluded (1) legislation which did not change the law, such as consolidation or statute law revision legislation, or re-enactment legislation; (2) emergency legislation rushed through to deal with some unexpected crisis; (3) certain financial legislation such as the Appropriation Act which authorises the bulk of annual expenditure and the Consolidated Fund Acts authorising interim and supplementary expenditure; (4) legislation concerning the Civil List which pays for the monarchy; and (5) statutes to give effect to treaties and other international commitments. When all of these were eliminated, there remained 1,335. In 380 cases (28 per cent) the statute was preceded by a report of an independent advisory committee or commission.[8]

Very little has been written about the process of preparing legislation from Whitehall's perspective. One rare instance, however, was a paper by a senior Home Office official speaking at a Cambridge conference on penal policy-making in December 1976.

6   Richard Rose, *Do Parties Make a Difference?* (2nd edn, 1984), pp. 72–3.
7   On law reform bodies, and the Law Commission in particular, see further Chapter 8 below.
8   H. Beynon, *Independent Advice on Legislation*, 1982, unpublished Ph.D. thesis, Oxford University, Table 11, p. 21.

Michael Moriarty, 'The Policy-Making Process: How It Is Seen from the Home Office', in *Penal Policy-Making in England*, ed. Nigel Walker, Cropwood Conference, Institute of Criminology, Cambridge (1977), pp. 132–9

In general it is unusual for an incoming government to bring with it anything approaching a detailed blueprint of penal policy. This is not really surprising. Although the maintenance of law and order remains a basic task of any government, the methods of performing it are simply not of great political importance in comparison with the major economic and social issues of the day which rightly preoccupy the political parties and other organs of society. Nor is there, among those in the political parties who concern themselves in depth with penal questions, any fundamental difference of approach towards them (though this statement would certainly need some qualification if it were applied to the active rank-and-file members of the parties)... .

The absence, usually, of a strong and detailed Party programme on penal matters does not mean that an incoming Home Secretary (or other Home Office Minister) may not have its own well-formed objectives and priorities. A recent example is the Ministerial commitment, since March 1974, to improving bail procedures and developing the parole system. But time and again the Ministerial contribution to penal policy-making, at least as it appears to the observer and participant within the Home Office, lies not in the Minister's bringing in his own fresh policy ideas, but in his operating creatively and with political drive upon ideas, proposals, reports etc, that are, so to speak, already to hand, often within the department but sometimes in the surrounding world of penal thought.

Sources of the Criminal Justice Act 1972
The year 1970 was notable for a sharp rise in the prison population to what was then a peak of 40,000, which gave rise to intensified policy discussions within the Department of ways of developing alternative measures. The Report of the Advisory Council on the Penal System (ACPS) on Non-Custodial Measures (the 'Wootton Report')[9] contained a number of relevant proposals, notably a proposal that offenders should carry out community service. The Department instituted an urgent study of the practicalities by a working group with substantial probation service representation. Two other working groups were set up at the same time: one on use of probation resources, the other on residential accommodation for offenders. The main production of the first of these was a proposal to establish experimentally some day training centres, on a model originating in the United States, interest in which had been stimulated by the Howard League for Penal Reform among others. The other group developed ideas for running probation hostels: a substantial adult hostel building programme was established in 1971, following a small-scale experiment promoted by the Department in extending this method of treatment to those over 21. Detailed work on the proposals in the ACPS report on Reparation – the 'Widgery Report'[10] – was also going on.

9   Non-custodial and Semi-custodial Penalties (1970).
10 Reparation by the Offender (1971).

Thus the Criminal Justice Bill of 1971/2 could be said to be born from a fusion of a Ministerial desire to be active in the criminal justice field, along lines which were identified but not too rigidly pre-determined by them, with a supply of departmental and other raw material that was lying ready or in process of being worked up. Much of the Widgery Report was in tune with a political objective that offenders should recompense their victims. From the Wootton Report, the community service proposal appealed partly for its reparatory element, partly because it was a non-custodial penal measure (Ministers were already well aware of the need to try to bring down the prison population) that would appeal to those who were suspicious of 'softness'. The form in which the community service proposals appeared in the Bill owed something to the specific intention of Ministers that the new measure should be seen as a credible alternative to custodial sentences.

In fact recommendations from the two ACPS reports made up much of the 'core' of the Bill – Part I entitled 'Powers for Dealing with Offenders'. In the form in which it received Royal Assent, Part I comprised 24 sections (and one linked Schedule) which related to the main sources of the Bill roughly as follows:

Section	Subject	Origin
1–6	Compensation	Widgery Report
7–10	Criminal Bankruptcy	– do –
11–14	Suspended prison sentences etc.	Ministerial/ Departmental (s. 12 from Wootton Report)
15–19	Community Service	Wootton Report
20	Day Training Centres	Departmental
21	Breach of Probation	Departmental
22	Deferment of Sentence	Wootton Report
23	Forfeiture of Property	– do –
24	'Criminal' driving disqualification	– do –

Not all the sections listed above were in the original 'core': the origin of some of the later starters is illustrative of how penal policy is formed. What became section 14, extending the principle of the First Offenders Act to a wider range of adult offenders, was devised during the preparatory stage as a counterweight to the ending of mandatory suspension of sentence. Other provisions owed their origin, or final form, to the Parliamentary proceedings on the Bill.

However, the bulk of the Bill was devoted to provisions aptly described as Miscellaneous and Administrative Provisions (sections 28 to 62). Some of these supported Part 1 provisions (e.g. administrative aspects of community service) or were otherwise related to its main themes (e.g. probation hostel provision; legal aid before first prison sentence). Others covered a wide range of topics of varying importance. In source they were hardly less diverse. At least one – increase in penalties for firearms offences – was a 'core provision'; some came from organisations close to the Home Office such as the Justices' Clerks. The provision giving 'cover' for the police to take drunks to a detoxification centre (section 34) had its origin in the report of the Working Party on Habitual Drunken Offenders.[11] Others came from the famous pigeon holes of Whitehall – and these in turn can be sub-divided into, on the one hand, tidying up and, on the other, more substantial though minor changes – for example simplification of parole procedure (section 35).

... In 1970–1 much detailed work was done on community service and criminal bankruptcy in particular, but to a lesser degree on the other major Bill proposals in working parties by the Home Office which brought into consultation others whose advice and co-operation were needed. The community service working group included representatives of the probation service, magistracy and voluntary service movement; the criminal bankruptcy group included lawyers of both the Home Office and Lord Chancellor's Office and officials from the Bankruptcy Inspectorate of the (then) Board of Trade.

Beyond this area of activity there was (to move on to a second point) a wider and continuing process of consultation, on particular proposals and on ways of giving effect to them, with many official and non-official interests. A number of Bill proposals affected other Government departments – for instance, Transport and Health and Social Security – in addition to those already mentioned. On any penal policy it is necessary to keep the Scottish and Northern Ireland Offices in close touch. The Director of Public Prosecutions was closely involved in the criminal bankruptcy scheme and other Bill matters, at least one of which owed much to his suggestion. Consultation also went on with the police and probation services (the prison service was not greatly affected by the Bill, except as a hopeful beneficiary), the judiciary, magistrates and justices' clerks. The various representative organisations of course play an active part in the consultation process; and the burden on them can be a heavy one, especially as the pace quickens. The task of keeping the consultation process on the move while doing all the other preparatory work also makes considerable demands on the small team of officials working on a Bill.

(b)   The consultative process

The government department with responsibility for the legislative project will need to decide how much, if at all, to consult during the gestation process leading to the introduction of a bill in Parliament. Obviously, if the proposed legislation impinges on the responsibilities of other government departments or govermental agencies they will have to be consulted. But there is also the question whether and, if so, to what extent persons or bodies outside the governmental machine should be consulted.

The traditional Whitehall view has been that outside persons and bodies should not normally be consulted at this stage – that the time for consultation is later when the bill has been introduced in Parliament. The effect of this is that consultation only starts when it is generally too late to influence the basic shape of the legislation and all that can be achieved is

11 HMSO, 1971.

adjustment at the margins. But in recent years consultation has become more common.

In an important and wide-ranging Report on the Legislative Process (*Making the Law*)[12] issued in 1992 the Hansard Society said that many organisations in their evidence to the Society emphasised the fundamental importance of consultation. Some (English Heritage, the Bank of England, the Institute of Directors, the Association of Chief Police Officers) thought that it worked tolerably well. Some (such as the CBI, the Institute of Chartered Accountants and the National Consumer Council) said it worked better than in the past. Others (the Consumers' Association, the BMA, the TUC, local authority associations) were very critical of the lack of consultation. The Independent Television Commission said that the absence of any open inquiry before the introduction of the Broadcasting Bill in 1989 led to many late changes.[13]

Many organisations complained that when there was consultation the time allowed was frequently inadequate. The Consumers' Association said that six weeks was a reasonable time but that of 100 consultation documents in 1990, 10 per cent had allowed three weeks or less and another 20 per cent allowed only four weeks.

Some organisations regretted that Royal Commissions or committees of inquiry were no longer appointed. (Mrs Thatcher appointed no Royal Commission during the thirteen years of her premiership.) The local authority associations regretted a decline in the use of Green Papers and White Papers (see below). Also it regretted a change in the style of White Papers which it said had become glossy booklets promoting the government's policy without reference to alternatives and with less discussion of issues than in former years.[14] The consultation procedures of the Law Commission (pp. 412–414 below) were commended as a model.

12 The report was the work of a 'Commission' appointed by the Society. Its prestigious membership included a former Permanent Secretary to the Home Office, a former First Parliamentary Counsel, a former Director-General of the Royal Institute of Public Administration, a former Clerk of Committees of the House of Commons, the Director of Legal Affairs of the Consumers' Association, the General Secretary of the Association of First Division Civil Servants and a sitting Law Lord. The chairman was Lord Rippon. The report, which will be referred to as the Report of the Hansard Society, is available, price £16, from the Hansard Society, St Philips Building, Sheffield Street, London WC2A 2EX. For a review of the Report see 14 Statute Law Review, 1992, pp. 75–83.

13 There were 58 government amendments in Committee in the Commons and 503 on Report. In the Lords a further 359 government amendments were agreed in Committee, 285 on Report and 117 on Third Reading. The number of clauses increased from the original 167 to 204 and the Schedules from 11 to 22.

14 They contrasted the 'Rates' White Paper of 1983 (Cmnd 9008) which gave a great deal of background information and discussed the pros and cons of the options, with the 1991 White Paper on 'Education and Training for the 21st Century' (Cm 1536) which they said was made up of assertions without relevant statistics or reasoning.

The Report concluded that 'the overwhelming impression from the evidence is that many of those most directly affected are deeply dissatisfied with the extent, nature, timing and conduct of consultation on bills as at present practised' (p. 30).

The Report recommended (pp. 29–40) that government should so far as possible consult those with relevant interests or experience at the policy information stage. Consultative documents should be as precise as possible. Wherever possible, clauses, or even whole bills, should be published in draft for comment before introduction in Parliament.[15] Government should draw up and publish guidelines to government departments about consultation.

(c) Green and White Papers

Sometimes a bill is preceded by a Green or a White Paper setting out the government's plans in advance. The difference between those two forms of government statement, and a discussion of their function in the context of tax legislation, appeared in the *British Tax Review* in 1980:

Cedric Sandford, 'Open Government: The Use of Green Papers', *British Tax Review*, 1980, p. 351

WHAT COLOUR OF PAPER?

Green Papers were invented by the Labour Government in 1967. White Papers are of much earlier vintage. It is generally held that 'White Papers announce firm government policy for implementation. Green Papers announce tentative proposals for discussion.'[16]

Sir Harold Wilson wrote: 'A White Paper is essentially a statement of government policy in such terms that withdrawal or major amendment, following consultation or public debate, tends to be regarded as a humiliating withdrawal. A Green Paper represents the best that the government can propose on the given issue, but, remaining uncommitted, it is able without loss of face to leave its final decision open until it has been able to consider the public reaction to it.'[17]

As applied to taxation these distinctions are at best over-simplifications. Where Green Papers were not issued, the proposals of the White Paper were often subject to change on major issues. Thus, with selective employment tax

15 This has been done on occasion. There was extensive consultation on the clauses of the Copyright, Designs and Patents Bill 1987–88. The Child Support Bill 1990–91 was first issued in draft for consultation. The Inland Revenue has consulted key financial and industrial bodies on clauses of tax bills. Twenty-two clauses of the 1992 Finance Bill were for instance circulated in draft for consultation.

16 John E. Pemberton, 'Government Green Papers,' Literary World, Vol. LXXI, No. 830, August 1969.

17 Harold Wilson, *The Labour Government 1964–70* (1971), p. 380.

the treatment of charities, agriculture and mining was all changed within a fortnight of the publication of the White Paper, whilst with capital transfer tax a lower rate of tax for life-time gifts was adopted during the passage of the Finance Act in direct contradiction to the White Paper. On the other hand, important elements in some of the Green Papers have been presented as 'hard'. As Grant Gordon puts it: 'One believes that one knows the difference between White Papers, Green Papers and their kin, but under close examination they often tend to merge to a uniform grey.'[18]

The 1992 Report of the Hansard Society[19] stated the number of Green Papers in recent years varied from 3 in 1982 to 15 in 1980 and 1985. 'Other consultative documents' issued by govern·ment departments had gone from under 100 in each of the years between 1976 and 1982, to 100–200 between 1983 and 1986, to 200–300 in each of the years from 1987 to 1991.

(d) Cabinet control

To what extent is the process of the preparation of legislation controlled or supervised by the Cabinet and its sub-committees? Little is known of this. But a rare glimpse of some of what goes on behind the scenes was given in a lecture in 1951 by the then First Parliamentary Counsel in charge of the office of parliamentary draftsmen (see below).

Sir Granville Ram, 'The Improvement of the Statute Book', *Journal of the Society of Public Teachers of Law*, N.S., 1951, pp. 442, 447–9

> Under present arrangements the opening of a new session of an old Parliament normally takes place at the end of October or beginning of November; and about six weeks after the beginning of each session the Cabinet Office asks Departments to send in lists of the Bills likely to be required for introduction in the *next* session, together with their observations as to the urgency of any Bill included in the lists, an estimate of its magnitude, and a forecast of the date on which instructions to Parliamentary Counsel can be ready.
>
> I must make it plain that all these proposals, observations and forecasts relate not to the session that has just begun but to the next one which will begin nearly eleven months later. When they have been received from Departments they are collated and submitted to a Cabinet committee, known as the Future Legislation Committee, which always includes in its membership the Leaders of both Houses and the Chief Whip, because the drawing up and control of the legislative programme must be closely related to the arrangement of Parliamentary business. Soon after Christmas the Committee examines the Department's proposals in detail, and draws up a tentative list of Bills for discussion with the Ministers who have put forward the proposals. The Committee then holds a meeting at which those Ministers are present, and

18 Grant Gordon, 'Grey Papers' (1977) 48 Political Quarterly No. 1.
19 See note 12, p. 7 above, Appendix 8.

after consultation with them and with the First Parliamentary Counsel, draws up a provisional list of Bills for the session due to begin in the following autumn. This list is prepared with careful regard to the amount of time likely to be available for legislation during the session and, in drawing it up, the Committee makes allowances for the subsequent inclusion of Bills the need for which has not yet been foreseen, and for annual Bills (such as Finance Bills, Army and Air Force (Annual) Bills and Expiring Law Continuance Bills).[20]

The Bills recommended for inclusion in the programme are placed in order of priority, having regard to the dates when instructions to Parliamentary Counsel can be ready, to the time that drafting may be expected to take, and to the Chief Whip's estimate of the approximate dates on which the Bills must, respectively, be introduced in order to pass through their successive stages under the arrangements he will have to make for the Parliamentary business of the session. The list is then submitted to the Cabinet, and when the Cabinet has approved the recommendations of the Committee, with or without alterations, the Bills remaining in the list become the Government's provisional programme of legislation for the following session.

The need for determining the lines of a session's programme so long before the session starts is obvious because Bills take time to draft, but there remains much for the Future Legislation Committee to do before the programme is finally completed and its main features are announced in the King's Speech at the opening of the new session. Between Easter and the summer recess the Committee reviews the progress of the Bills decided upon, and considers any proposals made by Ministers for the addition to the programme of Bills that have not been previously foreseen. Early in June Departments will be asked by the Cabinet Office for particulars of any such Bills, but the Departments anticipate this request whenever possible by giving information to the Cabinet Office as soon as it becomes reasonably clear that any Bill not already included in the provisional programme is likely to be wanted. During this period between Easter and the end of July the Future Legislation Committee also controls the flow of instructions to Parliamentary Counsel so as to secure, so far as possible, that it shall conform to the order of priority approved by the Cabinet. Finally after the summer recess the Future Legislation Committee presents to the Cabinet, when they are considering the King's Speech for the opening of Parliament, a complete classified programme.

Upon the opening of a new session, control of the programme for that session passes to another Cabinet committee called the Legislation Committee. That Committee performs functions in relation to the examination of draft Bills which I will describe later, but it also exercises control over the programme for the current session, much in the same way as the Future Legislation Committee controls the programmes for future sessions. In this capacity it reviews every month the progress of all Bills in the programme for the current session, and regulates both the flow of instructions to Parliamentary Counsel and the flow of Bills to the two Houses according to the progress made. Applications for the admission of new Bills to the programme are made to this Committee through the Cabinet Office, and any necessary adjustments, whether

20 Today there are no annual bills apart from the Finance Bill. The Army, Navy and Air Force Acts are now continued from year to year by Order in Council. An Armed Forces Bill is required every five years (ed.).

by way of changes in priority or of addition to, or deletions from, the programme are authorised by the Committee.

This machinery for obtaining a place in the programme is the product of many years of experience and has proved far more effective than anything previously devised. The simple requirements it imposes on Ministers and their Departments are necessary to prevent a return to the chaotic conditions which existed before it was invented, but it is designed to deal with ordinary cases, and like most human institutions, it would be capable of abuse if it were too rigidly applied to cases that are not ordinary. A sudden emergency or an unexpected change of circumstances may necessitate the production of a Bill at such short notice that some deviation from the usual procedure is essential. Circumstances do, therefore, sometimes arise in which the normal procedure may have to be either anticipated or short-circuited, and in such cases strict compliance with it may be dispensed with by the Chairman of the Future Legislation Committee or of the Legislation Committee, as the case may be … .

When the Bill is ready for presentation it becomes necessary to submit the latest draft of it with a covering memorandum initialled by the Minister to the Legislation Committee. That Committee is presided over by a senior Cabinet Minister, and its membership normally includes the Lord Chancellor, the Leaders of the two Houses of Parliament, the Law Officers, and the Chief Whip. The meetings of the Committee are attended by any Ministers who may be concerned with items on the agenda, and papers for the Committee are circulated to all Departments, so that any Ministers who may not have been expressly invited may have an opportunity to attend. The Parliamentary Counsel are in attendance, and any departmental officials whose presence is necessary accompany their Ministers. As has been said, the Legislation Committee has control of the legislative programme for the current session, and holds a special meeting once a month to review its progress, but at the ordinary weekly meetings the main business of the Committee is to go through the draft Bills submitted to it. This it does in some detail, and any points that have occurred to the Ministers present, the Law Officers, or the Chief Whip are raised and discussed with the Minister in charge of the Bill.

When the Legislation Committee has considered the Bill it decides whether it may be presented to Parliament, and if so, in which House. The choice of House is often a matter of convenience depending on the state of parliamentary business and the time of year, but Bills which contain many clauses providing for fresh expenditure and Bills which consist largely of provisions imposing 'charges on the people', whether by way of rates or taxes, may not be introduced in the House of Lords because, although there are various expedients for enabling that House to avoid questions of privilege where such provisions appear only as minor and subsidiary features of a Bill, legislation which is substantially of that character cannot be dealt with by the Lords without infringing the privileges of the Commons.[1] The Committee also decides the date of presentation, which

---

1   The class of bills capable of being started in the Lords was enlarged in 1972 to include bills authorising fresh expenditure or imposing 'charges on the people' – other than a bill of aids and supplies (e.g. the Finance Bill: see House of Commons Standing Order No. 61). But most bills of this kind are in fact still started in the Commons.

will depend partly on the Chief Whip's plans, and, of course, upon the amount of redrafting that may be necessary as a result of the Committee's deliberations. The Committee sometimes gives provisional approval to a draft Bill subject to questions of law or of drafting being settled by the Lord Chancellor and the Law Officers in consultation with the Parliamentary Counsel, or subject to minor points raised by Ministers being adjusted by subsequent discussion; but if differences arise on major points of policy, the issues are referred to the Cabinet and the Legislation Committee postpones a decision as to the presentation of the Bill.

But the formal recital of the stages of the process gives little clue as to whether the process functions effectively. How much control does the Cabinet, either itself or through its committees, actually exert over the details of legislation? On this almost the only source of information is the late Richard Crossman's *Diaries of a Cabinet Minister*. (Crossman was successively Minister of Housing, Lord President of the Council and Leader of the House of Commons, and Secretary of State for Social Services. Previously he had been both a journalist and an Oxford don.) The impression that Crossman conveys is that neither the Cabinet nor the Future Legislation Committee actually exercise much real scrutiny.

Lord Simon of Glaisdale, speaking with experience as a former Minister, Law Officer and judge, told the Hansard Society's inquiry into the legislative process that he would like to see the Legislation Committee 'giving closer attention to the way bills were drafted'. According to him, the Committee used to be chaired by the Lord Chancellor and acted as a scrutiny committee, 'looking carefully at constitutional points as well as drafting' but now it was chaired by the Leader of the House of Commons 'and operated more as a business management committee'.[2]

For further reading on the stages leading to the formulation of legislative proposals, see especially W. J. Braithwaite, *Lloyd George's Ambulance Wagon* (1957), a detailed 'inside' account of the preparation of the National Insurance Act 1911 by one of the chief civil servants involved; M. J. Barnett, *The Politics of Legislation: the 1957 Rent Act* (1969); K. Hindell, 'The Genesis of the Race Relations Bill', *Political Quarterly*, 1965, p. 390; J. J. Richardson, 'The Making of the Restrictive Trade Practices Act, 1956', *Parliamentary Affairs*, 1967, p. 101; Victor Bailey and Sheila Blackburn, 'The Punishment of Incest Act 1908: A Case Study of Law Creation', 1979, *Criminal Law Review*, p. 708. See also Sir Noel Hutton, 'Mechanics of Law Reform', 24 *Modern Law Review*, 1961, pp. 18–23.

---

2   Report of the Hansard Society, note 12, p. 7 above at p. 47.

2.   THE DRAFTING PROCESS

The great majority of statutes are introduced by the government of the day. Government bills are drafted by parliamentary counsel to the Treasury acting on the instructions of the government department responsible for the legislation. The Office of Parliamentary Counsel was established in 1869. Its members can be either barristers or solicitors. They number currently 39, of whom five are on permanent attachment to the Law Commission (see pp. 406–14 below).

The head of the office is First Parliamentary Counsel, who is directly responsible to the Chairman of the Future Legislation Committee of the Cabinet (currently the Leader of the House of Commons) for delivering the government's programme of legislation.

Parliamentary counsel normally work in pairs in close collaboration with the civil servants who instruct them. (By convention the responsible minister rarely sees the Instructions sent from his department to the draftsmen.) Substantial bills may go through many drafts before being published. The work is often done under intense pressure of time. Parliamentary counsel also draft government amendments moved during the passage of legislation. This involves a great amount of work. It has been estimated that between 1979 and 1983 an average of 1,106 government amendments were moved in the Lords alone. Between 1983 and 1987 the average was 1,609 and between 1987 and 1989 it rose to 2,668. Government amendments may add very considerably to the length of Acts. For example the total length of five key bills introduced in the 1987–88 session was 714 pages but by the time they reached Royal Assent the five Acts were 1,084 pages long – an increase of 53 per cent. In session 1988–89, eight key bills totalling 1,160 pages on introduction increased in length by 43 per cent to 1,663 pages on enactment.[3]

Parliamentary counsel also frequently redraft amendments offered by back-benchers which the government is prepared to accept in principle. Where the government offers support for a bill introduced by a Private Member, it will often be redrafted by parliamentary counsel. Indeed parliamentary counsel will generally look at any Private Member's Bill that is likely to become law and advise the relevant Minister whether drafting amendments are necessary.

The workload of this small band of draftsmen may be judged from the fact that in the three decades from 1943 to 1972 they added a total of 45,000 pages to the statute book. In the ten years from 1974 to 1984 alone, a total of 20,686 pages were added – though it has to be noted that nearly one-fifth of the statutes (123 out of 664) passed in those ten years were

3   Statistics produced by Lord Howe in a speech to the Statute Law Society, May 1991, quoted in the Report of the Hansard Society, note 12, p. 7 above at pp. 45–46.

consolidation Acts (p. 63 below) and that they accounted for one-third of the pages.[4] In his 1951 lecture Sir Granville Ram said that they were regarded as an elite in Whitehall:

> As to the standard required I should be misleading you if I allowed any false modesty to prevent me from saying that only men and women of first-class ability can do the work. Among past and present members of the Office there have been a few who have not taken their university degrees with first-class honours, but the great majority have done so, and I may say that my three immediate predecessors in the Office of First Parliamentary Counsel all had the distinction of being Fellows of All Souls. As a result of the standard that has been maintained I can say without fear of contradiction that the members of the Office are unquestionably recognised by the Civil Service Legal Departments as a *corps d'élite*; if it were not so, satisfactory relations between them and the Office would be impossible. [*Journal of the Society of Public Teachers of Law*, N.S., 1951, pp. 442, 444.][5]

He continued by reflecting on the way the draftsmen did their work (ibid., at pp. 449–52):

> I now come to the drafting stage. After a Bill has been given a place in the programme by the appropriate Cabinet Committee (the Future Legislation Committee) it is for that Committee to decide when instructions for the Bill may be sent to Parliamentary Counsel, and when the Committee have so decided the Treasury send to the First Parliamentary Counsel a formal letter desiring him to put himself into communication with the Department concerned with a view to drawing the Bill.
>
> The First Parliamentary Counsel then receives the Department's written instructions and when he has informed the Department which Counsel will be responsible for the Bill the officials of the Department get into touch with him. Then together they will, if the Bill is a big one, embark upon a strenuous joint adventure entailing laborious days – and nights – for all concerned. Much will depend upon the care and skill with which the original instructions to Counsel are drawn. Here again, as in the case of memoranda submitted to the Cabinet, it is above all things necessary to avoid anything in the nature of a 'rough draft Bill'. The professional draftsman will rightly insist on building his own edifice stone by stone, and if he is presented with 'sectional units' or ready-made façades, he will only have to waste time in picking them to pieces before he can use them as building material. He should of course, be given the whole of the

4   See D. Miers, 'Legislation, Linguistic Adequacy and Public Policy', *Statute Law Review*, Summer 1986, p. 103, Table 1.

5   For a rather less favourable view, see the caustic conclusion of R. T. Oerton, who after twelve years working as a Senior Solicitor with the Law Commission said of the breed of parliamentary counsel: 'One could say that they are, taking them by and large, the rudest, most arrogant, most vain and most self-satisfied group of people inside (and, so far as I know, outside) the Civil Service' (R. T. Oerton, *A Lament for the Law Commission* (1987), p. 51) (ed.).

legislative proposals in full detail, and should be candidly informed about so much of the background of what is proposed as is relevant... .

When the draftsman has had time to digest his instructions and inform himself as to the existing law relating to the subject in hand he usually begins by asking for a conference with the department officials in charge of the Bill, and this will be the beginning of many close interchanges between them. At this point it is desirable to define their respective responsibilities. The departmental staff are responsible to their Minister for the substance of the Bill and for any questions of policy that may arise. The draftsman is responsible to the Minister, to the Treasury, to the Cabinet, and to Parliament, for producing the desired result in the correct form and in language that is aptly chosen to produce the legal effect intended. He also carries responsibility for the integration and coherence of the Statute Book itself. But substance, form, policy and law, are almost inextricably mixed up. Fortunately on the one hand the draftsman will be not altogether unversed in administrative and political ways, and on the other hand the departmental staff will generally have had previous experience in the preparation of Bills. Moreover they, and especially their departmental legal adviser, will also have an intimate knowlege of such particular aspects of the law as concern their daily work. It is important that the departmental officials who confer with the draftsman should be of sufficient standing to give, or obtain speedily, authoritative answers to the many questions which he will have to put, for the process of drafting invariably throws up difficulties that have until then lain hidden below the surface. It will not be a surprise to you as lawyers, but it seems constantly to surprise laymen, to discover that, even with the most carefully thought out schemes, there are almost always innumerable points which are found to require further consideration when drafting begins. It is largely for this reason that a Parliamentary draftsman requires years of training and experience... .

As soon as the draftsman, with the help of the departmental officials, has sufficiently clarified the situation to enable him to prepare the first draft of the Bill he does so and sends them as many copies of it as they have asked for. There then ensues a series of conferences,[6] telephone calls, and letters, which often call for much hard thought, many late hours, and a great deal of work on the part of all concerned. Eventually, probably after many further drafts have been prepared, criticised, and revised, the time comes when the draft Bill is in a fit state to be shown to the Minister. If the Minister interests himself closely in the preparation of his Bill, he will at this stage hold conferences upon it, which his own officials and the draftsman will be required to attend, either in his office or at the House. Time and effort devoted by a Minister to all points of importance that are thrown up in the course of the drafting is usually more than repaid to him during the passage of the Bill through Parliament.

Not infrequently, while a Bill is being drafted, some point of policy or political tactics arises of such importance that reference to the Cabinet or to a Cabinet committee is necessary. Whether this step should be taken or not is, of course, a question for the Minister and one on which he may very likely seek advice from the Cabinet Office. It often saves delay to make such a reference as

6   Conferences always take place in Parliamentary Counsel's Office (ed.).

soon as the point emerges rather than have questions raised at the last moment when the drafting of the Bill is by way of being completed.

If this picture of the labours of those engaged upon the drafting of a Bill has given the impression that the process is as leisurely as it ought to be it is indeed a false one. The drafting of a Bill is essentially a task that *ought* to be carried out under conditions which allow sufficient time for deliberate thought and research upon the innumerable points that invariably arise, but unfortunately such work has almost always to be done under exactly the opposite conditions.[7] To those who devote their lives to the business it is a constant source of wonder how it is that even the most experienced Ministers and civil servants never seem to appreciate that drafting always takes longer than was expected. I can say little to suggest a remedy. I can only regret that, despite many efforts, I have so often failed to impress Ministers and others with the simple fact that the drafting of a Bill does take a considerable time. How much time depends, of course, upon the length and difficulty of the Bill as well as upon the preparedness of the Department in whose charge it is. A Bill of moderate length will take several months to draft and even the shortest Bills often give rise to many difficulties and the need for much research and consultation. It is true that, in emergencies, Bills are sometimes produced with astonishing speed, but a *tour de force* of this kind disturbs the progress of other Bills in the programme, and involves an almost intolerable strain upon all who are called upon to co-operate in achieving it. Unfortunately the more experienced a Minister is the more likely it is that he will have seen Bills spring into being in this way and – well – watching a conjurer produce rabbits out of a hat is not the best training in midwifery.

The process of drafting was also described by Sir Harold Kent, a former parliamentary draftsman, in his autobiography:

Sir Harold Kent, *In on the Act* (1979), pp. 43–5

It starts with the arrival of some sort of instructions from the department responsible for the Bill. In the case of the Gas Undertakings Bill these consisted of two reports of a Departmental Committee with an accompanying letter from Tommy Barnes, the Solicitor to the Board of Trade. He said that the Government broadly accepted the recommendations of the Committee and had authorised the preparation of a Bill; he did not propose to comment on those recommendations in writing but would gladly come over for a talk if that would help.

This was fairly typical of the way a Bill starts, a combination of written material generated inside or outside the department and oral discussions. It was rare in my experience for a formal and comprehensive 'Instructions for a Bill' to be prepared by the department.[8] Indeed, it was quite common for the

---

7   Normally there is a deadline in the form of a date by which the bill is required to be ready for consideration by the Legislation Committee (ed.).

8   Nowadays formal instructions appear to be the norm (ed.).

draftsman's brief to be entirely the product of oral discussions, and for him to take a hand in the policy-making, especially when a Bill arose suddenly out of a political or economic crisis.

Stainton[9] liked, if possible, to get a first print of a Bill circulated to the officials concerned before holding his first big conference. Draft Bills were always printed in widely spaced type with wide margins, and were ideal documents on which to make notes and amendments. So Barnes' offer of a talk was not taken up and a first draft was soon sent off to the printer, based largely on my own effort. The Office had a marvellous contract with Eyre & Spottiswoode, the Government printer, whose presses at Drury Lane would work all night in order to deliver our draft Bills first thing in the morning[10]. Stainton ordered twenty copies, twelve for the Board of Trade, six for us, and two spares. That first print contained twenty-six clauses and one Schedule and was twenty-six pages long; a medium-sized Bill of a useful and non-political kind.

The team from the Board of Trade consisted of Tommy Barnes with a clever young barrister called Rupert Sich, who was the latest recruit to his office, and an Assistant Secretary from the Gas division of the department. They were a good team and we discussed the Bill from beginning to end, perhaps for a whole day or more. A few days later the Bill, heavily amended, went off to the printer for a second edition, followed by another conference and another print. During a period of four months, before the Bill was ready for introduction, it went through seven prints, interspersed with conferences, telephone calls and correspondence. This was a shade over the average for a Bill of this kind; it reflected the Staintonian method of non-stop amendment and fair-copying. In the last print there were two more clauses, two more Schedules and eleven more pages than in the first, an increase in bulk of nearly forty-five per cent... .

There is a certain conflict of interest between the draftsman and the department. The former seeks to confine the Bill strictly to matters requiring an alteration of the law. The department is conscious that the Minister would like to make a Parliamentary splash; it also knows that administration is sometimes helped by being able to refer to an Act of Parliament; so it wants to put as much as possible into the Bill. The issue is confused by the fact that even when a new government activity does not need statutory powers, the expenditure involved may, under the rules of the House of Commons, require statutory sanction.

Other occasions of conflict are when the Minister wants a clause to look as attractive politically as possible, and is impatient of the detail needed for precision; or when the department wants its administrative powers drawn up widely, or even obscurely, so as to avoid risk of legal challenge, an attitude which hardly pleases a self-respecting draftsman. I remember a clause of mine receiving the dubious compliment of 'nice and vague' from a bureaucrat of seasoned experience.

9   Then Kent's superior in the office. (Ed.)
10 Nowadays drafts of Bills are produced by the draftsman on the word processor rather than being printed (ed.).

Ram[11] was fond of saying that a Bill was hammered out by the operation of the departmental hammer on the anvil of the draftsman's table... . I would call the process a creative partnership in which tensions might arise but a considerable team spirit could be generated. The theory is that the department has the last word on matters of policy, and the draftsman on matters of form or of law, but both parties poach freely on each other's preserves.

There has been some writing on the actual problems faced by the parliamentary draftsman. One example is a paper written by F. A. R. Bennion, himself for many years a draftsman.[12] In his paper Bennion identified the parameters within which the draftsman had to work:

Legal effectiveness The draftsman must express the government's intentions in such a way that the statute will have its desired effect.

Procedural legitimacy The bill must comply with the procedural requirements of each House of Parliament. Parliamentary procedure governs the form of the bill. It decrees, for instance, that a bill have a long title and be divided into clauses. It allows a preamble and Schedules but no other type of formulation. It requires amendments to be in a certain form.

Timeliness The Future Legislation Committee of the Cabinet is responsible for the government's timetable of legislation. Usually this is such as to create serious pressure on the draftsman. The pressure of time exists not merely in the period before first publication of a bill but equally after publication for the preparation of amendments.

Certainty It is usually desired that the text have one construction only. But sometimes it is intended to leave things deliberately somewhat vague – often because those responsible for the bill were themselves unable to agree as to how it should be handled.

Comprehensibility Most statute-users are lawyers or experts, but most politicians are non-lawyers and non-experts. The bill must be comprehensible to both categories.

Acceptability The language must not excite opposition; the prose style is flat; traditional and often verbose forms are normally preferred. (Bennion described how he incurred considerable criticism when he once used the phrase 'tried his best' instead of the more familiar 'used his best endeavours'.)

11 Sir Granville Ram, First Parliamentary Counsel. (Ed.)
12 'Statute Law Obscurity and the Drafting Parameters', 5 *British Journal of Law and Society,* 1978, p. 235.

Brevity Draftsmen are encouraged to be as brief as possible. In particular they are desired to keep down the number of clauses because MPs have the right to debate each clause if they wish.

Debatability The bill must be so framed as to allow the main points of policy to be debated. ('If they are buried in confused verbiage, it becomes difficult for Members to perceive what they are and deploy argument.')

Legal compatibility The bill when it becomes law should fit as well as possible with existing law. The language used in one statute should be the same as that used in other statutes to describe the same subject-matter. ('Contrary to most people's beliefs, however, there are no books of precedents in the Parliamentary Counsel's Office in Whitehall. Draftsmen vary in their willingness to spend time hunting for models in earlier legislation. They are discouraged by the knowledge that if they carry out this search it will throw up a variety of examples, not one of which may appear any better than the others.')[13] The draftsman should also indicate in his bill what its effect is on other statutory provisions – by way of repeal or amendment. ('His task is greatly hampered by the chaotic state of the statute book, the lack of arrangement under titles, delays in printing updated official texts, and the absence of computerised search and retrieval systems.') Another consideration is who is the audience for the statute? The draftsman needs to have in mind whether the statute is likely to be read by other than specialists. That the statute is aimed mainly at persons familiar with the subject matter does not mean that it be drafted badly. But there is a difference if the reader may be completely innocent of any knowledge of the subject.[14]

In an address in autumn 1981 Sir George Engle, First Parliamentary Counsel, said that there were three main restraints on the preparation of bills: 'the fact that they were legal documents, shortage of time and the impracticability of continuous design'.

Sir George Engle, 'Bills are made to pass as razors are made to sell: Practical constraints in the preparation of legislation', 1983 *Statute Law Review*, pp. 7, 10–15

---

13 See, however, C. M. Campbell and J. McGurk, 'Revising Statutes with Computer Support', *Statute Law Review*, Summer 1987, p. 104, on a project in Northern Ireland to promote the use of computers by the draftsmen.
14 See Francis Bennion, 'If it's not broke don't fix it: A review of the New Zealand Law Commission's proposals on the format of legislation' 15 *Statute Law Review*, 1994, pp. 165–67.

ACTS OF PARLIAMENT ARE LEGAL DOCUMENTS

The fact that Acts of Parliament are legal documents marks them off from other kinds of writing with which they are sometimes unfavourably compared, such as works of literature, text-books, political manifestos and journalism. Their special character is well described by Sir Bruce Fraser in his revision of Gowers' *The Complete Plain Words:*

'The legal draftsman', he says, '… has to ensure to the best of his ability that what he says will be found to mean precisely what he intended, even after it has been subject to detailed and possibly hostile scrutiny by acute legal minds… .

'Legal drafting must therefore be unambiguous, precise [and] comprehensive… . If it is readily intelligible, so much the better; but it is far more important that it should yield its meaning accurately than that it should yield it on first reading, and the legal draftsman cannot afford to give much attention, if any, to euphony or literary elegance. What matters most to him is that no one will succeed in persuading a court of law that his words bear a meaning he did not intend, and, if possible, that no one will think it worth while to try.'

Our statute book goes back to the year 1235. A great deal of the dead wood has been cleared away; but over the centuries there is hardly a topic that has not attracted its share of legislation. Once there has been legislation on a given topic, it is only a matter of time before a further round of legislation on the same topic is found to be necessary; and the nearer one gets to the present, the shorter is the interval between one round and the next.

This proliferation of statute law on every topic means that each new change in the law has to be meticulously knitted into the existing fabric; and this in turn means that the draftsman's room for manoeuvre is more often than not severely limited by the need to make what he has to say fit in with, and match, the structure and language of existing statute law. In my experience it is comparatively rare for the draftsman to be entirely free of this particular form of constraint for more than a few lines at a time.

SHORTAGE OF TIME

For reasons which I hope to explain, much of the work of the Parliamentary Counsel, and of the departmental lawyers and administrators who instruct them, is done under considerable pressure of time. This is apt to be the case at all stages in the preparation of a piece of legislation, from the initial working out of the details of policy, through the preparation of drafting instructions and the production and consideration of successive drafts of a Bill, to the stage of amendment in Parliament. This pressure basically results from the fact that the period of up to five years for which a Parliament is elected is in practice broken up into a succession of roughly year-long sessions each of which is, legislatively speaking, entirely self-contained.

A normal session of Parliament starts at or soon after the end of October, and continues until the end of the following July, with short adjournments at Christmas, Easter and Whitsun. As often as not, a backlog of legislative business makes it necessary for both Houses to sit again for a short spillover period in October, after which the session is terminated by prorogation. Bills which have not received Royal Assent by the end of the session in which they were introduced lapse.

The number of days on which the House of Commons sits in a normal session varies between 160 and 180. Of the 30 sessions from 1952–53 to 1980–81, 20 were of normal length in this sense. For those 20, the average number of days on which the House of Commons sat was 167; and of those 167 days, an average of 87 (over half) were unavoidably spent on matters other than government legislation, the actual number of days varying between 96 at one extreme and 60 at the other. However an average of 18 (or nearly a quarter) of those 80 days were necessarily devoted to proceedings on the unavoidable Finance and Consolidated Fund Bills, including proceedings on the Budget and the financial resolutions on which these Bills are brought in. So the average number of days available to the government for what I may call optional or 'programme' Bills turns out to have been only 62. This comparatively meagre ration of (on average) 62 days per session for all proceedings on the floor of the House on programme Bills severely limits the number of such Bills which any government can in practice hope to get through Parliament in a normal session. For the same 20 normal sessions from 1952–53 onwards, the average number of government Bills of all kinds which received Royal Assent was 54. But if one subtracts from this figure the average of four unavoidable Finance and Consolidated Fund Bills, and further subtracts an average of 8 consolidation and Statute Law Revision Bills per session, one is left with an average of only 42 programme Bills per session, occupying the 62 days which, as we have seen, were on average available for such Bills. And of these 42, a varying proportion will have had to be brought in at short notice in the course of the session, whether in response to unforeseeable circumstances or because some recognised contingency did not in fact materialise. So on average a government is unlikely to be in a position to include more than some 30 to 35 programme Bills in its legislative programme for a normal session, as originally planned. Into the 60-odd days available for programme Bills there have to be fitted all those proceedings on these Bills which fall to be taken on the floor of the House, namely Second Reading, Committee of the whole House, Report, Third Reading and, for Bills amended by the Lords after they have left the Commons, Consideration of Lords' Amendments. In practice the Committee stage of nearly all programme Bills takes place 'upstairs' in one of the standing committees rather than on the floor of the House; and since 1965 it has been possible for the government, with the agreement of the Opposition, to arrange for the Second Readings of a number of non-controversial government Bills to be taken upstairs in a Second Reading Committee, thus saving some time in the House itself. Even so, when it comes to deciding how many Bills can sensibly be included in the legislative programme for a given session, the primary constraint is the number of days on the floor of the House that they may be expected to occupy. This is a matter on which the views of the Ministers responsible for the management of the government's Parliamentary business naturally carry great weight. The more controversial the Bill, the more time it will eat up… .

The process of settling the legislative programme for a given session of Parliament may take, from start to finish, anything up to five months; and the fact that it only starts around Christmas, after the preceding session has been got under way, means that the final details will probably not be decided until some time in May – though it may be clear before then that certain Bills will almost certainly be included. This period of uncertainty coincides with the main period of Parliamentary activity on the current session's Bills, when departmental lawyers and administrators may have little or no time to spare for new work. So until a sponsoring department knows for certain that a particular Bill proposed by it has obtained a firm place in the next session's programme, it will in the nature of things be reluctant to devote too much of the time of its hard-pressed officials to the detailed working out of the policy, let alone to the all-important but onerous task of preparing drafting instructions – something which, in any case, cannot be taken very far until the details of the policy have been settled.

The result of all this is that, for too many Bills, the time left for serious work on their preparation is less, and for large and difficult Bills often far less, than the minimum time needed to do the job satisfactorily. Instructions may have to be sent before the policy is finally settled. Drafting too often has to begin on the basis of partial or incomplete instructions. And if the requirements of the Parliamentary timetable make it necessary for a particular Bill to be introduced at the earliest practicable moment in the session, the draftsman may find himself hard put to it to produce a Bill at all in the time, and is most unlikely to be allowed the luxury of a period of calm in which to consider how the drafting could be improved. Given time, the draftsman of a Bill can nearly always perceive ways in which its structure and wording could be bettered; but this is not something that can be done in a rush. And once a Bill has been introduced and published, Ministers are understandably reluctant to prolong the proceedings on it – and especially those proceedings which take up time on the floor of the House – by moving amendments which are not strictly necessary. Most large or controversial Bills – and many Bills are both – are more or less heavily amended in the course of their passage. These amendments are partly accounted for by changes of policy, mainly in response to criticisms made in or outside Parliament, and partly by the necessity of making such corrections and additions as are needed to remedy defects and omissions in the Bill which there was no time to deal with, and perhaps not even time to detect, in the run-up to introduction. Thus shortage of time in Parliament militates against the moving of amendments whose only purpose is to cure infelicities of structure and wording.

THE IMPRACTICABILITY OF CONTINUOUS REDESIGN

The third and last of the constraints I mentioned earlier is what I have chosen to call the impracticability of continuous redesign. By this I mean the practical difficulty of altering the basic structural and conceptual elements of a Bill, as originally designed, so as to enable it to accommodate and present in a satisfactory way all sorts of additional provisions, late changes of policy and other afterthoughts which could not be foreseen when the Bill was originally designed. One of the skills of the experienced draftsman is to make some allowance in his original design for this sort of proliferation. But there is a limit to what he can cater for, sight unseen.

On receipt of a set of drafting instructions, the draftsman's first task is to study them and make sure that he fully understands what those instructing him wish to achieve. To arrive at this understanding he may need to discuss particular aspects of the instructions with the department concerned; and these discussions may result in immediate modification of details of the proposals. When he is reasonably clear about what is wanted, the draftsman must at a fairly early stage decide on a suitable set of concepts in which to embody the basic ideas with which the Bill is concerned, and must work out an appropriate legislative structure for the Bill as a whole. This 'design' aspect of the drafting process is concerned not only with the overall arrangement of what may be a large and complex body of material, but also with the internal organisation of each particular clause or schedule; and it is not too much to say that good design, in this sense, is the essence of a well-drafted Bill. The trouble is, of course, that a conceptual and legislative structure designed to fit a particular set of detailed legislative proposals ought, in principle, to be reconsidered and, where necessary, redesigned each time the proposals it was designed for are altered or added to… . Each successive draft of a Bill is apt to cause the instructing department to have second thoughts about some aspects of the detailed policy; and major shifts of policy are not unusual.

If something has to be done it nearly always calls for more detail in the next draft. In the early stages it may be comparatively easy to redesign each successive draft to fit the latest version of what is wanted; but as each successive draft embodies a larger proportion of material that has been seen and commented on by the various departments interested in the Bill, it becomes more and more difficult, in the time available before introduction, to make radical changes in the way the Bill is drafted, since to do so would mean taking to pieces many provisions which have been generally agreed.

Once the Bill has been introduced, there is little enthusiasm for redesign for redesign's sake. Yet, in the case of nearly all complex or controversial Bills, the process of amendment goes relentlessly on; and though the draftsman can sometimes achieve a measure of redesign in the course of preparing government amendments to the Bill, his ability to do anything radical in this line is limited by the fact that it is usually not until the Bill is nearing the end of its course that its ultimate content becomes settled in substance – and by then Ministers are not only reluctant to disturb provisions which have emerged from earlier stages of the Bill, but are also, as I have already mentioned, unwilling to devote valuable time on the floor of the House to amendments which are not strictly necessary.

3. CRITICISM OF THE QUALITY OF DRAFTING OF ENGLISH STATUTES

Criticism of the quality of drafting goes back a long way. The Report of the Renton Committee (*The Preparation of Legislation*, 1975, Cmnd 6053)[15] said that such criticism had been common centuries ago:

---

15 Reprinted by Sweet & Maxwell Ltd, 1981.

2.8 As long ago as the 16th and 17th centuries there were in England many expressions of dissatisfaction with, and projects for reforming, the drafting of statutes and the shape of the statute book. These early critics included Edward VI ('I would wish that … the superfluous and tedious statutes were brought into one sum together, and made more plain and short, to the intent that men might better understand them'), Lord Keeper Sir Nicholas Bacon ('a short plan for reducing, ordering, and printing the Statutes of the Realm'), James I ('divers cross and cuffing statutes … [should] be once maturely reviewed and reconciled; and … all contrarieties should be scraped out of our books'), and Sir Francis Bacon, when Attorney General ('the reducing of concurrent statutes, heaped one upon another, to one clear and uniform law').

In recent years, however, such criticism has been mounting significantly.[16] In May 1973 the government set up the committee under the chairmanship of Sir David Renton (as he then was) whose terms of reference were: 'With a view to achieving greater simplicity, and clarity in statute law to review the form in which Public Bills are drafted, excluding consideration of matters relating to policy formulation and the legislative programme; and to consider any consequential implications for Parliamentary procedure.'

The Report of the Renton Committee on the *Preparation of Legislation* said that it had received evidence from judges, bodies representing the legal and other professions, from non-professional bodies and from prominent laymen, that much statute law lacked simplicity and clarity. The complaints, it said (p. 27), fell into four main categories:

(a) Language It was said that the language used was obscure and complex, its meaning elusive and its effect uncertain. The Statute Law Society criticised the language of the statutes as: 'legalistic, often obscure and circumlocutious, requiring a certain type of expertise in order to gauge its meaning. Sentences are long and involved, the grammar is obscure, and archaisms, legally meaningless words and phrases, tortuous language, the preference for the double negative over the single positive, abound'. One type of problem for instance was the piling of one hypothetical provision on another, as in a provision of the National Insurance Act 1946: 'For the purpose of this Part of the Schedule a person over pensionable age, not being an insured person, shall be treated as an employed person if he would be an insured person were he under pensionable age and would be an employed person were he an insured person'.

(b) Over-elaboration It was said that the desire for 'certainty' in the application of legislation leads to over-elaboration. The parliamentary draftsman tried to provide for every contingency. The committee said that

---

16 See, for instance, Statute Law Society, *Statute Law Deficiencies* (1970), and *Statute Law: the Key to Clarity* (1972) both published by Sweet and Maxwell.

this was because of concern on the part of the legislature to ensure against the possibility that the legislation will be construed by someone, in some remote circumstances, so as to have a different effect from that envisaged by those preparing the bill in question. As one parliamentary draftsman had put it: 'The object is to secure that in the ultimate resort the judge is driven to adopt the meaning which the draftsman wants him to adopt. If in so doing he can use plain language, so much the better. But this is often easier said than done!' (p. 29).

(c) Structure The internal structure of, and sequence of clauses within, individual statutes was considered to be often illogical and unhelpful to the reader:

> Each Act has, or should have, an inherent logic, and its provisions should be arranged in an orderly manner according to that underlying logic. But this ideal, it is said, is not always realised. From a logical point of view, the main purpose of a Bill should be made clear early on. This statement of intent, whether it takes the form of the enunciation of general principles or otherwise, is desirable both for the legislators to help them to understand what they are being asked to pass into law, and for the courts to help them to understand the intention of Parliament when they are interpreting the legislation. Statements of intent would also assist those who must obey and advise on the legislation. The intention is now, however, rarely spelt out in the statute itself, although in continental and EEC legislation this is often done in the form of a preamble or in other ways …
>
> Many of the witnesses have said that more attention should be paid to the logical sequence of the provisions of statutes, and that there should be a consistent approach to such questions as what kind of provision should go in the main body of the Act and what in the Schedules, so that people could more easily find their way about them. There is also the criticism that sentences are sometimes too long, and complicated by too many subordinate phrases, and that there should be greater readiness to break up clauses into separate subsections. [pp. 30–1.]

(d) Arrangement and amendment The chronological arrangement of the statutes and the lack of clear connection between various Acts bearing on related subjects were said to cause confusion and made it difficult to ascertain the current state of the law on any given matter. This confusion was increased by the practice of amending an existing Act, not by altering its text (and reprinting it as a new Act) but by passing a new Act which the reader had to apply to the existing Act and work out the meaning for himself:

> It is said that among the new statutes which are added to the statute book year by year there are many which are more or less intimately connected with existing statutes and that insufficient assistance is given to the reader in the

task of collation which results from the purely chronological arrangement. It becomes increasingly difficult to locate the relevant Acts on any given topic; and, more seriously, once the relevant Acts have been located they may well be found to be distributed among three or four separate volumes, so that reading them together becomes – physically as well as mentally – a formidable task [p. 31].

... But there is another problem. New laws frequently amend existing statutes. Such amendment, however, by no means always takes the form of substituting a fresh and amended text in the statute which is being amended. The 'non-textual' amendment of legislation has been criticised by many of our witnesses, though some of them conceded that its use may be unavoidable. Amendments drafted non-textually have been described as being:

> 'Drafted in a narrative or discursive style producing an inter-woven web of allusion, cross-reference and interpretation which effectively prevents the production of a collection of single Acts each relating to a particular subject, otherwise than by the legislative processes of consolidation and repeal. Often Act is heaped upon Act until the result is chaotic and almost completely unintelligible. Indeed much of the confusion existing in the Statute Book today is directly attributable to referential legislation'.[17]

The other method of amending previous legislation which several witnesses have commended to us is the system of 'textual amendment'. By using this method new statutes which alter the provisions of earlier Acts give effect to such alterations by enacting fresh portions of text which are then added to or substituted for the earlier version.

The committee gave an example of each form of amendment drawn in both cases from the Town and Country Planning Act 1968. Section 149 of the principal Act, the Town and Country Planning Act 1962, was amended *non-textually* by section 37(3) of the 1968 Act, which reads as follows:

> For a person to be treated under section 149(1) or (3) of the principal Act (definitions for purposes of blight notice provisions) as owner-occupier or resident owner-occupier of a hereditament, his occupation thereof at a relevant time or during a relevant period, if not occupation of the whole of the hereditament, must be, or, as the case may be, have been occupation of a substantial part of it.

A corresponding *textual* amendment of section 149 of the principal Act was effected by section 38 of the 1968 Act (with Schedule 4):

> *Section 149*
> In subsection (1)(*a*), (1)(*b*), (3)(*a*) and (3)(*b*), for the words 'the whole or part' (wherever occurring) there shall be substituted the words 'the whole or a substantial part'.

17   H. H. Marshall and N. S. Marsh, *Case Law, Codification and Statute Law Revision* (1965).

The non-textual form of amendment was better for MPs in that it was easier to see the effect of the amendment. But it was more difficult for the ordinary user since it not only required reference to earlier legislation but often left considerable doubt as to how the two provisions should be read together (conflated). By contrast, the textual form of amendment enabled the reader to see exactly how the old law had been amended, providing only he had both the old and the new before him. The Committee said it accepted that textual amendments were generally preferable. The needs of MPs could be met by an accompanying memorandum which could show how the amended legislation would look if the proposals being considered for enactment became law (p. 79). For strong support for textual amendment, see the evidence of F. A. R. Bennion to the Renton Committee in *Renton and the Need for Reform*, published on behalf of the Statute Law Society (1979), pp. 27–60.[18]

In his evidence to the Renton Committee Mr Bennion argued for an even better form of official document which would restate the law after amending legislation, taking into account statutory instruments as well as statutes. The reader would then have everything set out in a connected sequence. The work of organising the material would have been done for him and by lay-out and other visual means it could be made easier to read than is normally the case with statutory materials – see F. A. R. Bennion, 'Statute Law Processing: The Composite Restatement Method'. *Solicitors' Journal*, 1980, pp. 71 and 92.[19]

The Renton Committee said (para. 6.21) that there was no intention to reflect upon the skill and dedication of the parliamentary draftsmen. They had to work under pressure and constraints which made it very difficult for them, with the best will in the world, to produce simple and clear legislation. They were inadequately staffed and were often given gigantic tasks to perform in a race against time. Many statutes were in fact well drafted. 'Nevertheless, after making all due allowance, there remains cause for concern that difficulty is being encountered by the ultimate users of statutes, and this difficulty increases as the statute book continues to grow' (ibid.).

A senior lawyer-civil servant, Sir William Dale, subsequently published a study in which he compared the approach to legislative drafting in France, Germany, Sweden and the United Kingdom. Sir William, a former legal adviser to the Commonwealth Office, concluded that our system was the least satisfactory:

18 The placing of textual amendments is considered in an article by a Canadian draftsman – A. C. Lövgren, 'The Location of Textual Amendments in Bills', *Statute Law Review*, Spring 1988, p. 27.
19 Mr Bennion's book *Consumer Credit Control* (1978) is an example of this method of presenting the material.

Sir William Dale, *Legislative Drafting — a New Approach* (1977),
pp. 331–3

[Sir William summarised the features that appeared to make for obscurity or
length or both in United Kingdom statutes:]

(*a*) long, involved sentences and sections;
(*b*) much detail, little principle;
(*c*) an indirect approach to the subject-matter;
(*d*) subtraction – as in 'Subject to ...', 'Provided that ...';
(*e*) centrifugence – a flight from the centre to definition and interpretation
       clauses;
(*f*) poor arrangement;
(*g*) schedules – too many and too long;
(*h*) cross-references to other Acts – saving space, but increasing the vexation.

In contrast, lucid and often succinct drafting is to be found in the countries
on the European continent, represented in this study by France, Germany and
Sweden. The continental lawmakers, influenced by their heritage of codes,
think out their laws in terms of principle, or at least of broad intention, and
express the principle of intention in the legislation. This is the primary duty of
the legislator – to make his general will clear. An orderly unfolding of the
concepts and rules follows; and whenever it is necessary to give the meaning of
a term, it is done when that term first makes its appearance.

The characteristics of French drafting are clarity of principle, of form and of
word, a logical development, economy of expression, and a resultant brevity.
The French, as their President has observed, 'like things to be said and done
clearly, on the basis of an overall concept'.

In Sweden the laws are drafted in layman's language, often with some
generality of expression and even greater brevity. Technical terms are likely to
be in the legislative material, the *Proposition*, to which recourse is constantly
had. In some laws in the social field the policy is to use general language, set up
special courts, and leave them to develop the law in the light of varying
circumstances and changing conditions.

In Germany the practice is to state a principle, and then to fill in the detail
with, very often, great thoroughness. There is necessarily some length, but a
systematic arrangement. At times one finds thick clusters of sentences. Some
contain matter which in the United Kingdom would be put into regulations:
German statutes rarely contain a regulation-making power.

Sir William Dale identified one problem as being the lack of any adequate
process of revision or review of draft legislation (pp. 334–5):

In France all draft laws are examined and revised as necessary by the Conseil
d'Etat; in Sweden many are referred to the Law Council; in Germany there is
no similar body, the Ministry of Justice performing an examining and co-
ordinating role for all Federal draft laws.

Parliamentary committees then closely scrutinise all draft Bills, in round-
the-table discussions attended by ministers and civil servants, and report on

the Bills, with draft amendments proposed, to the House. In Germany the scrutiny by the committees of the Bundesrat, the second Chamber, to which the Government *must* under the Constitution first send all its Bills, is particularly efficacious.

See to same effect Sir William Dale, 'A London Particular', *Statute Law Review*, Spring 1985, p. 11. Similar thoughts on the contrast between English and continental methods were expressed by Professor Clarence Smith of the University of Ottawa.

J. A. Clarence Smith, 'Legislative Drafting: English and Continental', *Statute Law Review*, 1980, pp. 14–22

Certain differences of attitude are pervasive. They may be arranged in four groups: the civilian's preference for generality over particularity; his desire to be easily understood as opposed to the common law draftsman's anxiety not to be misunderstood; the common law draftsman's obsession with judicial hostility; the common law unquestioning assumption that legal drafting requires a legal draftsman.

I

On the first point, between generality and particularity there is in practice a difference only of degree. If a common law draftsman wishes to hit a particular situation he will always dress his provisions up as directed at situations of that kind in general; and on the other side the civilian is perfectly aware that if a principle is too general it is more appropriate to philosophy than to legislation… .

It is not entirely a comparison of civilian ideal with common law falling short of the ideal to say that a French mind holds in horror the catalogue which apparently gives the common law draftsman so much aesthetic pleasure: 'Any judge, notary public, justice of the peace, police or stipendiary magistrate, recorder, mayor or commissioner authorised to take affidavits to be used either in the provincial or federal courts, or any functionary authorised by law to administer an oath in any matter,' the whole of which would be reduced by a civilian to 'any person authorised by law to record a statement on oath.' The common lawyer's preference for this sort of precision – as opposed to concision – is due to his aim not to be misunderstood, a legitimate aim even if it is put in terms of being certain that a particular group of persons shall not 'get away with it'. There are two questions to be considered here: first, whether the object is in fact secured by this method, and secondly, whether, even if it is, it is worth the countervailing inconvenience.

First, it is impossible in the nature of things to avoid a *casus omissus*. One cannot think of all the situations one wishes to cover, or all the manoeuvres one wishes to checkmate. A statement of principle however will catch the *casus omissus* as well as the situations actually in mind; and it is infinitely shorter, therefore easier to bear in mind. But it takes a special type of intellect to penetrate to underlying essentials and then formulate them in terms of general principle, and both simply and precisely; and apart from the *casus omissus* it is true that if the situation described in the statute arises one knows where one is without having to think whether a more generally stated principle will be attracted to it. In that case time is saved, once one has unearthed the passage dealing with the circumstance – but unearthing may take a good deal of time. The common lawyer would add that his type of precision has the advantage of certainty, implying that if he merely enunciates a principle the judge will find a way – or will endorse a way found by the ingenuity of counsel – to avoid its application to the particular circumstances which he, the legislator, desired to catch. The usual form of the complaint relates to findings by the courts that the words of the statute describe particular circumstances (perhaps only slightly different) and do not state an inclusive principle …

II

It is the civilian's ideal that his meaning – his master's meaning – shall be not only understood but easily understood, so far as the subject matter permits.... . This ideal finds practical expression in the rule that if there is a great deal to say it must be broken down into grammatically self-contained sentences, eliminating even subordinate clauses so far as possible. If some provisions are by way of being qualifications, the general rule will be stated first, unqualified, and then the qualifications, each separately. The common lawyer prefers to have everything dealing with the same point together in one grammatical sentence, broken down if necessary into indented paragraphs, sub-paragraphs – and sub-subparagraphs – but not separated by full stops.

Professor Clarence Smith gave as an example the provisions of the Sale of Goods Act as against the equivalent provisions of the French Civil Code:

Sale of Goods Act

41 (1) Subject to the provisions of this Act the unpaid seller of goods who is in possession of them is entitled to retain possession of them until payment or tender of the price in the following cases, namely:

(*a*)   where the goods have been sold without any stipulation as to credit;

(*b*)   where the goods have been sold on credit, but the term of credit has expired;

(*c*)   where the buyer becomes insolvent.

(2) The seller may exercise his right of lien notwithstanding that he is in possession of the goods as agent or bailee.

Civil Code

1612. The seller is not bound to deliver the property if the buyer does not pay the price for it, unless the seller has granted him time for payment.

1613. He shall also have no duty of delivery, even if he shall have granted time for payment, if after the sale the buyer has become bankrupt or insolvent so that the seller is in imminent danger of losing the price, unless the buyer gives him security for payment on the due date.

The common lawyer does lighten his long sentences to some extent by separately defining some of the key words. His definition section, a source of pride and satisfaction to himself, is an object of wonderment to the civilian, to whose style (if pure) definitions are mostly unnecessary. His sentences do not need to be lightened, and a word once used with a particular meaning should bear the same meaning elsewhere; but it should be added that it is against the civilian's principles to use any word in a specialised sense for which reference to a definition is necessary… .

The civilian also finds unnecessary another favourite of the common law draftsman, the beginning of so many sections with 'subject to the provisions of this Act' – again in the illustration – still more the tautologous 'subject to any *contrary* provision.' For him the matter is governed by the principle that the special derogates from the general; but it must be confessed that there are occasions where it is not too clear which of two conflicting provisions is general and which special.

These common law practices are aimed, as is the civilian's staccato brevity, at facilitating understanding, but not at being easily understood by ordinarily intelligent people. For the common law draftsman it is enough that a lawyer can understand his text, be it with difficulty, so long as he (and even more the judge) can after diligent concentration find no excuse for misunderstanding… .

The common law style has undoubted merit, and is not unknown to civilians in other contexts: it is the style universally employed in lecture notes, whether by learner or by teacher, and not only in the law. Civilians use it happily in legal text books, where it is the Anglo-Saxon's turn to be irritated by the 'technicity' of the subdivision indicated by letters and figures – and sub-letters and sub-figures – even though there they do not break up continuous sentences. True, the possibility of an ordinary word being defined elsewhere with a special meaning does constitute a trap for the unwary in common law drafting; but this is hardly a serious objection, for it could easily be avoided typographically by an initial capital, or inverted commas, or italics. Apart from that, the long but complete sentence makes sure that everything is read, and (if it is expertly done) the careful and attentive reader will still not have lost the thread by the time he gets to the end… .

The choice is perhaps finely balanced as between the two styles viewed ideally; but there is the further consideration that in practice draftsmen do not on either side live up to their ideas, and in the world of real life they cannot be expected to do so. The departure of the civilian from his ideal does not usually have the effect of rendering his draft unintelligible, while it very often has that effect on a common law draft. There is no need to emphasise at this time of day that many English statutes are frankly incomprehensible even in England: a Frenchman will usually be too exasperated to persevere with his reading, and this is a result to be avoided in the common market. The reason for the Delphic obscurity is usually the exaggeration of the tendencies described above which, if they had been kept within limits, might have been tolerable… .

Professor Clarence Smith ascribes the English problem with statutory drafting to the establishment of a separate office of Parliamentary Counsel which has over years developed its own distinctive house-style. In France, by comparison, drafting meant writing simply and clearly – a skill that was traditionally mastered by the intelligentsia.

The English draftsman objected that simplicity of expression and certainty were incompatible. But English drafting, he suggests, did not achieve certainty. In fact its undue particularity created uncertainty at the margins.

In an article in the *Statute Law Review* of Autumn 1986, Mr Timothy Millett, Legal Secretary at the Court of Justice of the European Communities, analysed the differences between the English and French Nationality Acts as an illustration of the national styles of legislative drafting. Having devoted over sixteen pages to his basic presentation he then turned to analysis and discussion of the differences.

Timothy Millett, 'A Comparison of British and French Legislative Drafting (with particular reference to their respective Nationality Laws)', *Statute Law Review*, Autumn 1986, pp. 130, 158–60

CONCLUSIONS

The scheme of the legislation is easy to grasp. The provisions of the Code are laid out in a logical expository order, and elements that do not fit into the pattern are left to be dealt with by separate primary or subordinate legislation. That legislation is not, however, voluminous. The Code has no schedules, and its articles are short and simple in structure. The sentences are short and simple. They use normal syntax and give words their ordinary meaning. References to extraneous provisions are rare. Using the Code de la Nationalité requires little more than reading and understanding in the ordinary way. It is easy to use, because it was designed to be easy to use. It was obviously designed as a statement of the law to the citizen, and it is evident that considerable effort has gone into making that statement as clear and simple as possible. As the worked example above demonstrates, that effort has been successful.

Comparison with the British legislation in the field brought a number of features to light. First, the volume of different pieces of subordinate and primary legislation is large and unmanageable. The texts are not published together in one place, although initiatives by private publishers might change that. It is mainly thanks to private sector initiatives that it is possible to track down all the various texts, and even when found they remain voluminous and heterogeneous.

Secondly, the habit of fixing a commencement date at a different time from the actual passing of the Act is an inconvenience, particularly when different commencement dates are fixed for different parts of the Act.

Thirdly, there is a habit of splitting up relatively simple propositions into several pieces, putting them into separate provisions and then making cross references from one provision to another, greatly increasing volume and unnecessarily increasing complexity. The effect is moderately damaging where the various fractions are contained within one provision, as is the case with the four subsections of section 2 of the Act, some of which at least could well be stated in a single provision. The effect is much worse where related matters are split up and placed in quite different parts of the Act, as with section 2 and section 14 on nationality by descent. Instead of being an autonomous statement, section 2 of the Act tells half the story and is only intelligible by reference to section 14. The user therefore has to keep jumping between one section and the other, each time assembling for himself a complete statement of what the law actually is.

Fourthly, the Act fails to make its overall scheme clear. On the contrary, there appears to be a deliberate effort to obscure the principal policy in the Act (*i.e.* linking the right of abode in the United Kingdom to British citizenship) by putting the key provision towards the end of the Act at section 39 under the heading 'Miscellaneous and Supplementary', instead of incorporating it in the beginning of the Act where it would explain the scheme of everything that is to follow. Another important policy of the Act is similarly obscured by the placing of section 14 late in the Act instead of alongside (or indeed fused with) section 2 so as to give a coherent statement of what is meant by British citizenship 'by descent'. This failure to make the scheme of the Act apparent is compounded by the ellipsis which has been noted in section 2(1)(*a*) and is all the more remarkable as the rest of the Act is prolix.

Fifthly, there is a tendency to legislate by reference to extraneous provisions. Kept within limits this is only a moderate disadvantage, but left unchecked it robs certain provisions of almost all inherent meaning. The contrast with the French Code de la Nationalité is striking: in that text, almost all the provisions consist of words which have a meaning of their own and are therefore free-standing. Legislation by reference to extraneous provisions means that the user has to go and find those provisions, read them, and fit them into the scheme of the Act in order to endow the provision concerned with meaning. The problem is aggravated where the reference is to legislation existing before the Act but now repealed. Thus section 1(1) of the Act is almost as clear as Article 23 of the Code, but that advantage is cancelled out because it uses a term ('British citizen') which, for the lifetime of any parent born before 1 January 1983, will require reference to section 11, which requires the ascertainment of the situation prevailing under both the British Nationality Act 1948 and the Immigration Act 1971. This is a serious defect in any country's legislation. As a general principle a legislator should, it is submitted, try to make his text autonomous and not refer the user back to pre-existing law and require him to apply to no longer valid rules which become more and more remote from current reality with every year that passes.

Sixthly, by comparison with the Code de la Nationalité, the British Nationality Act 1981 makes very extensive use of technical terms. The length of the 'glossary' provided in section 50 of the Act gives some idea of how many are used, but the problem is even worse for technical terms not defined within the Act. A related, but slightly different problem is that the Act uses certain definitions which distort the natural meaning of the words in the operative sections. This is true in particular of the phrase 'by descent', which is not used in its ordinary sense: whenever the Act says 'a British citizen by descent', what is actually meant is 'a British citizen in one of the categories defined in section 14'. The practical consequence is that whenever the phrase is encountered in a provision of the Act, the user has to run through the list in section 14 and ascertain its effect in the case which he is studying. This practice is particularly prone to mislead the user and, given the richness of the English language, is hard to justify.

Seventh, the prolixity of British legislative drafting is in itself a source of obscurity. The extra volume of material requires to be organised, which the British Nationality Act 1981 largely fails to do. Many sentences in the Act are too long to be read normally. Comparison between the Act and the Code demonstrates that brevity is conducive to clarity whereas prolixity is conducive to obscurity. Long sections have correspondingly complex structure, with subsections, paragraphs and sub-paragraphs.

Eighth, long sentences have unnaturally complicated syntax. Highly complicated clause structures are overloaded with adjectival and adverbial phrases of all sorts. Doubtless very hard to write, such sentences are also extremely hard for the user to unravel. They are far from being normal English, and certainly cannot be read like ordinary prose.

These defects are cumulative, and as a result the process of extracting the law from the British Nationality Act 1981 goes beyond the simple act of reading and understanding a serious piece of written prose; it requires a far more complicated series of intellectual exercises. From the cumulative effect of all the difficulties noted it is apparent that, whatever else he may be aiming at, the British legislator is not aiming at stating the law in a way readily intelligible to most users of the statute. The result is legislation which is hard to use; and the worked example above demonstrates that the British legislation imposes much heavier burdens on the user than the French.

The basic difference between the drafting of the Code and that of the Act is that the draftsman of the Code clearly appears to attach paramount importance to making himself readily intelligible to the citizen whereas the British legislator is at best heedless of the user and at times even seems deliberately obscure (as in the placing of section 39 or the wording of section 2(1)(*a*)). The comparison prompts the question: if another civilised country, our close neighbour, can adequately regulate its nationality in a clear and straightforward manner, what reason is there for our country to shroud its nationality law in obscurity? The British legislator has a fine drafting tool in the English language. It has been refined and enriched over centuries; he has a highly developed legal system to draw on; and he has the institutions of one of the world's longest-standing parliamentary democracies to rely on. He has all the means to draft clear and intelligible legislation if he chooses to. The preservation of the rule of law in a democratic society demands that he should choose to do so. What emerges from the comparison with French legislation is not that the British legislator is failing in French terms but that he is failing in his own terms as the legislator in a democratic country. It is high time that he chose to legislate in a clear and straightforward manner with the user in mind.

See further *British and French Statutory Drafting: Proceedings of the Franco-British Conference, April 1986* (Institute of Advanced Legal Studies, 1986) and F. A. R. Bennion, 'How they do things in France', 16 *Statute Law Review*, 1995, pp. 90–97. See also Sir William Dale, 'The European Legislative Scene', 13 *Statute Law Review*, 1992, pp. 79–96.

For some reflections on the differences between the United States and the United Kingdom in regard to drafting of statutes – rather to the advantage of the latter – see Reed Dickerson, 'Legislative Drafting in London and Washington', *Cambridge Law Journal*, 1959, p. 49.

4. PROPOSALS FOR IMPROVING THE QUALITY OF THE STATUTE BOOK

Sir William Dale offered a number of possible remedies for the condition of the statute book:

(1) Changes in drafting technique 'We need at least to reduce the verbal impedimenta; to be less fussy over detail, to be more general and concise; and to situate each rule where it belongs, in an orderly and logical development. On this level, the question is largely a matter of style and arrangement. A more profound change is also desirable: a determination to seek the principle, to express it, and to follow up with such detail, illuminating and not obscuring the principle, as the circumstances require' (ibid., p. 335).

(2) The establishment of a Law Council To advise the government on draft bills. It would include judges, practising lawyers, academics, lay authors, members of consumer councils, etc. 'Its duty would be to examine [draft bills] from the point of view of coherent and orderly presentation, clarity, conciseness, soundness of legal principle, and suitability for attaining the Government's objective' (p. 336). It would report to the Minister responsible. The role of the Law Council would be similar to that played in France by the Conseil d'Etat, which reviews all draft legislation in discussion with an official of the initiating department. If the ministry is not prepared to accept an amendment proposed by the Conseil d'Etat, it states its reasons and the matter is determined by the Council of Ministers. Sir William Dale recognised, however, that it would not be realistic to expect that the Law Council could match the authority and prestige of the Conseil d'Etat overnight. For some further explication of the role of the Conseil d'Etat, see *British and French Statutory Drafting: Proceedings of the Franco-British Conference, April 1986* (Institute of Advanced Legal Studies, 1986), pp. 79–80. For a fuller account of the role of the Conseil d'Etat see a twenty-page article by Bernard Ducamin, 'The Role of the Conseil d'Etat in Drafting Legislation', *International and Comparative Law Quarterly*, 1981, 882–901. The article makes clear that the Conseil d'Etat concerns itself with both form and substance. It addresses style, language, conciseness, clarity and presentation. In regard to substance, attention is paid to the cost of the proposals, difficulties of control, or

conflict with some part of France's international obligations or the Constitution.

Technically, the government is not bound to submit to views put by the Conseil d'Etat but in practice it normally does so, especially on matters of form. In regard to substance the government also normally follows the advice given when it concerns legal points. If the matters raised concern policy, the government may or may not follow the advice given.

Also the fact that everyone knows that the Conseil d'Etat has to be brought in at the end of the process before it goes to parliament means that there are indirect effects. Civil servants will obviously try to anticipate objections that may be made and so avoid them in advance. According to M. Ducamin, the fact that the Conseil d'Etat is there as a check is a matter of security for both civil servants and ministers. The power is exercised in a restrained and responsible manner and is generally highly respected.

(3) A greater hand in the drafting process to be given to experts in the subject-matter rather than experts in drafting Instead of all drafting being done by parliamentary counsel, at least some should be done within departments, as was the case in continental countries and is the case in the UK for delegated legislation.

(4) Improved system for parliamentary examination of legislation 'A legislative body is wise to arm itself with the means of criticising and revising the draft Bills laid before it; and this the continental system of parliamentary working parties provides' (p. 340). The report of such a committee, reflecting discussions with ministers and civil servants and setting out amendments, would be a helpful guide to the House when the bill came to be debated.

Dr Peter North, a former Law Commissioner, suggested in a lecture in 1984 that bills should be available to expert scrutiny and comment in draft – as was the case in West Germany and Switzerland.[20]

The Renton Committee also made many proposals for possible reforms. Most of its proposals related to matters too detailed to consider here (such as the layout of statutes, punctuation, internal cross-referencing, the use of definitions, etc.). The Committee thought, however, that consideration should be given to providing a training course for legislative drafting (para. 8.16), and that more draftsmen should be recruited 'as a matter of high priority' (para. 8.22). The use of statements of principle should be encouraged – where detailed guidance was called for in addition, it should be given in Schedules (para. 10.13). More use might be made of examples in Schedules to show how a bill was intended to work in particular

---

20 See P. North, 'Is Law Reform Too Important to be Left to Lawyers?', *Legal Studies*, vol. 5, no. 2, 1985, 119, pp. 125–6.

situations (para. 10.07). Long un-paragraphed sentences should be avoided (para. 11.12). Statements of purpose should be used when they are the most convenient method of clarifying the scope and effect of legislation (para. 11.8).

The Committee considered but rejected the idea that there should be some form of prior scrutiny of draft bills. It concluded that 'it must be left to Government departments themselves to decide what advice they should seek before presentation [of legislation] from advisory bodies on the drafting' (para. 18.29, p. 130). Nor was the Committee persuaded that there should be such scrutiny machinery after a bill had been published. ('Having weighed the arguments on both sides, we do not think that there is any practical scope for introducing a new scrutiny stage during the Parliamentary process. This would in our opinion impose strain on a Parliamentary machine which is already under great pressure, and would also add to the labours of the draftsmen who have more than enough to do as it is to keep pace with the legislative programme' (para. 18.33, p. 131).)

The Committee did propose, however, that there should be two new procedures for scrutinising after the completion of the parliamentary process. One would be to tidy up defects in drafting before the Royal Assent by giving the Speaker and the Lord Chancellor, on application of the sponsor of legislation, the power to certify that amendments were of a purely drafting nature. Parliament would then be given the chance of accepting or rejecting them en bloc without debate. Secondly, even after Royal Assent there should be the possibility of redrafting obscure or otherwise badly drafted bills (in whole or part). The method would be to introduce a bill 'to re-enact with formal improvements [section ... of] the [...] Act'. Such bills would be introduced in the House of Lords and would automatically be referred to a joint committee of both Houses, which would report either that they were satisfied that the bill contained only formal improvements or that they were not so satisfied. If the joint committee reported favourably, the bill would enjoy the expedited parliamentary procedure now available for bills which simply consolidate existing law and add nothing new (pp. 17–18).

In addition, the Renton Committee proposed that there should be continuing review of the condition of the statute book and that this should be undertaken by the Statute Law Committee, which was first established in 1868 and whose members are appointed by the Lord Chancellor who is also its chairman. The Committee should be required to report, say, every three years and such reports should be laid before Parliament. This Committee has, however, now been abolished – see p. 45 below. For a description of a committee of this kind in New Zealand see Walter Iles, 'The Responsibilities of the New Zealand Legislative Advisory Committee', 13 *Statute Law Review*, 1992, pp. 11–20. New Zealand also seems to have more effective parliamentary scrutiny of bills than in many countries: see Iles, 'Parliamentary Scrutiny of Legislation', 11 *Statute Law Review* 1991, pp. 165–185.

5.   RESPONSE TO THE CRITICISMS AND PROPOSALS

The proposals made by Sir William Dale, Mr Francis Bennion, the Renton Committee and others have, however, not yet made great impact. Part of the reason is that they have not yet won support where it counts. Even Francis Bennion, himself a sharp critic of the condition of the statute book, was not convinced that Sir William Dale was right to think that the style of continental drafting was preferable to our own. In a review of Sir William's book (*Statute Law Review*, 1980, p. 61), he said:

> Sir William holds that a statute should be drafted so that it can be understood by all affected by it. An author should be able to understand a statute on copyright, a family man a statute on family law, a land owner a statute on land law, and so on. This sounds fine until we look more closely. Copyright law applies to every sort of creator or performer, from the writer of an article in a parish magazine to the man who does lightning sketches on the pier. We are all family men or women, and most of us are at some time landowners or tenants. Thus Sir William might as well have said statute law should be drafted so that it can be understood by all. That only has to be stated for its impracticability to be apparent. Yet the Swedes don't find it impracticable. They draft in layman's language, Sir William tells us. His first extract from a Swedish statute deals with copyright. 'The performance of a work at a place of business for a comparatively large closed group of people shall be considered a public performance.'
>
> It would be interesting to hear laymen discussing whether a public hall hired by a firm for a staff party is a 'place of business', or 43 persons consisting of the firm's staff with a few relatives and friends is a 'comparatively large closed group'. To find the answer the Swedes might go, like most continental users, to the *travaux préparatoires*. For Sir William tells us that 'the legislature has often deliberately left it to the inquirer, whether citizen, lawyer or judge, to go to the legislative material to find out more precisely what was intended.'
>
> What are the essential features of continental drafting? The book does not give a clear answer, perhaps because the concept is not as definite as is sometimes thought. One element is the background presence of a general code: 'Codification, willy-nilly, involves – nay, is – the continental style.' Another element, leading from the first, is the tendency to state a principle.
>
> > 'The continental lawmakers, influenced by their heritage of codes, think out their laws in terms of principle, or at least of broad intention, and express the principle or intention in the legislation. This is the primary duty of the legislator – to make his general will clear. An orderly unfolding of the concepts and rules follows... .'
>
> Sir William castigates the British Copyright Act of 1956, for example, because it nowhere states the principle of what copyright is, but merely lists the acts restricted by the existence of copyright in a work. He overlooks the fact that the pragmatic British are chary of statements of principle. They mistrust them

because they invariably have to be qualified by exceptions and conditions before being fitted for real life. Sir William, quoting the rule in *Leviticus* that when one man strikes another and kills him, he shall be put to death, adds: 'We observe the complete generality, and the utter certainty.' In fact of course, as to some degree he admits later, there is no such certainty. Suppose the striking is accidental, or the striker is insane? Suppose death occurs after a long interval, or the sufferer was already mortally ill? What does 'strikes' mean? Does it include riding a horse at a man, or pulling down his house about his ears? What is the value of a statement of principle that later has to be qualified almost out of existence? In the rare case where statements of principle are possible without suffering this defect they are often made by British draftsmen. Sir William recognises this when he praises the long title to the Consumer Credit Act 1974.

Another feature of continental drafting is willingness to leave more to the courts. Sir William extols this, but it has two undesirable aspects. One is that until a court has had an opportunity of pronouncing on the point the law is uncertain. The other is that too much of the legislative power may thereby pass from Parliament to the judges. Those who hanker for a revival of judge-made law need to remember that the greatness of the common law lay in its defence of the citizen against despotic monarchs. A democratic Parliament cannot sensibly be likened to a despotic monarch. We do not need, nor do most of us desire, to be saved by our judges from the intentions of our Parliament. Sir William records that the French, on the other hand, 'have, under the influence of Gény, allowed the judge to soar from the text into the headier regions of ethics, political science, sociology and the like.' There are those, led by Lord Scarman ... who aim at a similar ascent by the British judiciary.

The value of Sir William's book is that it enables these matters to be debated against an informed background. There is much in the European material reproduced here that is admirably drafted. The French use of the present tense in order to avoid the solecism of giving directions to judges is felicitous. Take this for example, from the divorce law:

'Article 231. The judge examines the application with husband and wife separately, then with both together. He afterwards calls in counsel. If both spouses persist in their intention to divorce, the judge tells them that they are to renew their application after a three months period of reflection.'

The common lawyer might be less happy about such passages as the following, chosen at random from Sir William's texts (the italics are added).

'When copies of a work are produced ... the name of the author shall be stated *to the extent and in the manner required by proper usage.*' (Sweden)

'A work may not be changed in a manner which is prejudicial to the author's literary or artistic reputation, *or to his individuality.*'   (Sweden)

'Copyright shall protect the author with respect to his *intellectual and personal relations* to the work, and also with respect to the utilisation of the work.'   (Germany)

'A published work may be publicly performed at divine services and in connection with education.' (Sweden)

'If the application of a condition in a contract concerning transfer of copyright *obviously is contrary to proper copyright usage or otherwise unfair*, the condition may be *changed or disregarded.*' (Sweden)

'Everyone has the right to *respect for his private life*. The judges may, without prejudice to the making good of damage suffered, order any measure, *such as sequestration, seizure or others*, necessary to prevent or terminate a violation of the intimacy of private life; in cases of urgency the measure may be ordered summarily.' (France)

'For the purposes of the present law, "financial loss" means economic damage which arises without any person having concurrently sustained loss of life, personal injury or loss of or damage to property.' (Sweden)

Sir William does not tell us what practical difficulty drafting of this kind causes continental users, particularly lawyers who wish to advise their clients without forcing them to litigate. He says that the general verdict in Germany is that the drafting of legislation is satisfactory and clear, but cites no research findings in support of this remarkable encomium. Elsewhere he finds that more problems of interpretation have arisen under continental than British copyright law but draws no conclusion from this.

The book gives no proof that we would benefit from going over to the continental system; it could scarcely be expected to. It does show the formidable objections to adoption of that system in Britain. These may be summarised as follows:

It requires the background presence of a code, which we do not have and are not likely to get.

It requires legislation to be prefaced by the statement of principles, which is foreign to British temperament.

It produces a considerable degree of uncertainty.

It does not enable Parliament to assert its will with the particularity British political conditions require.

It gives too much legislative power to non-elected judges.

Also to be considered is the fact that if a change-over were made we would have a dual system for many years while the existing body of statute law was replaced.

Criticism of Sir William Dale's book and its suggestions came also from an Australian parliamentary draftsman:

G. Kolts, 'Observations on the Proposed New Approach to Legislative Drafting in Common Law Countries'. *Statute Law Review*, 1980, p. 144

Dale's book contains much material that is of interest to legislative draftsmen in common law countries, in particular his critical analysis of the formal aspects of certain British statutes and his comparative study of continental statutes dealing with the same topics. However, the present writer would argue that Dale has not put forward a valid case for making radical changes in drafting practices... .

Now Dale's thesis is that the British legal system has resulted in a drafting style that tends to prolixity and obscurity; by way of contrast, he praises the continental system of drafting, which is alleged to result in clarity and simplicity. Nevertheless, the continental system may have imperfections of a different kind; in particular it is open to the objection that it results in greater uncertainty and leaves too much to judicial law-making. Dale attempts to answer this criticism by denying that the continental system does not contain substantial detail. Of the examples of continental statute-drafting given by him, it seems that his denial has substance in the case of the statutes of Germany but is not borne out by the statutes of France and Sweden. However, his claim that certain continental statutes do legislate in some detail seems to undermine his argument because it puts him in a position of appearing to be advocating a change from one system of legislation that involves detailed prescription of rules of conduct to another system that also involves such a detailed prescription. The only difference between the two systems would then appear to be that continental statutes are alleged to be arranged in a more orderly manner with a greater emphasis on general principles. If this is so, it is hard to see the need for radical departures from the system of drafting presently in use in common law countries. In fact, what Dale's book amounts to in essence is a criticism of the organisation and style of some British statutes. It does not follow that the criticism is equally applicable to other British statutes or to the statutes of other common law countries. Indeed, it may be that the widespread adoption in other English-speaking countries of the textual method of amending statutes renders their statutes less open to some of the stylistic objections voiced by Dale... .

Is Legislative Drafting a Specialised Art?
Dale claims that in common law countries legislative drafting is regarded as a specialised art and is endowed with a mystique that it does not possess in civil law countries. He states that in the latter countries it is accepted that competent lawyers are able to take up legislative drafting without difficulty and he concludes that, if the continental system of drafting is adopted in common law countries, the twin problems of the shortage, and the training, of draftsmen will disappear. Would that legislative drafting were as simple as Dale makes out. The writer is not aware of any competent lawyer in Australia who has tried his hand at the discipline and found it easy. Also his own experience, and the experience of all his colleagues and of other legislative draftsmen with whom he has discussed the matter, is that, although the ability to draft improves with experience, an aptitude for the work is essential. What makes a good legislative draftsman is a good basic legal knowledge, a feeling for the proper use of the English language,

a critical ability, lots of imagination and plenty of practice. Experience has shown that general legal ability by itself is not sufficient and that a competent lawyer without practical experience in legislative draftsmanship cannot perform the craft satisfactorily.

Should the Continental Method of Drafting be Adopted?
This is a proposition that commended itself to the Renton Committee. Indeed the impression given to a reader of that Committee's report is that many distinguished English and Scottish judges are champing at the bit to prove that they are better law-makers than the elected legislators. Any factors in their background and experience that would lend credence to this assertion are not readily apparent. Moreover, the frequency of the occasions when judges have by deductive reasoning reached a logical position that does not fit modern social conditions and have had to be extricated from their difficulties by the legislature suggests that, in their belief in their competence as law-makers, they do not recognise their own limitations.

What is often overlooked is that the draftsman is not the policy maker; it is not necessarily the draftsman who decides that legislation should set out in detail how it is to apply in individual cases. He is asked by the proponents of a particular legislative proposal to draft a law that has a particular effect. If the proposed law can be stated as a general principle, the draftsman will so state it. If it is not clear how the stated principle will apply in particular cases, it is the duty of the draftsman to draw this fact to the attention of his instructors. It is really a matter for them to decide the extent to which the legislation is to set out specifically how it is to operate in particular cases. But is it unreasonable for them to want detail in a statute? Surely the requirement of certainty in the application of the law should be the paramount consideration. If this proposition is accepted, the reasons for setting out in a statute the manner of its detailed application are overwhelming. Indeed, according to Dale, the German statutes do just this. However, he has not answered the criticism that, in so far as a continental law deals only in generalities, it must lead to considerable doubt as to the manner of its operation. If ordinary citizens were asked whether they would wish their rights to be clearly set out in the written law or whether they would prefer to leave it to the courts to spell out these rights in the course of legal proceedings, I have no doubt that their answers would be different from those given by the Renton Committee and Sir William Dale. The writer would welcome comments from continental lawyers explaining how they advise their clients of their rights under a statute that is expressed in general terms only.

Should Statutes be Readily Comprehensible to Non-Lawyers?
No doubt the reason behind the recommendations of the Renton Committee and Sir William Dale is that the ordinary citizen should be able to ascertain the law, Dale rightly declares that this is a desirable objective. However, to believe that it can ever be attained in societies as complex as ours is to live in wonderland. Even Dale recognises that complete comprehension of a statute by a layman is not practicable but he says that the ordinary man should be able by reading a statute to obtain a good idea of what the legislator is telling him. In the case of non-technical statutes this proposition is indisputable. In the case of technical statutes it is surely an unattainable objective. For example, the writer would be

greatly surprised if French and Swedish laws designed to counter tax avoidance were comprehensible by the ordinary citizen... .[1]

Dispersion of Draftsmen
Dale suggests that the time has come for the responsibility for the drafting of legislation to be returned to the various Government Departments sponsoring the legislation concerned, provided that a Law Council is established to maintain consistency of the required standards. This proposal is put forward in the context of the British system where, although all English Bills are prepared in the Parliamentary Counsel's Office, most major Departments also have their own legal advisers. The writer is not aware of the position in other Commonwealth countries but the practice in Australia is generally to have a centralised and comprehensive legal service for all Government Departments. If each Department were to be responsible for drafting its own Bills, it would need, as in Britain, to have its own general legal staff and this would no doubt result in competition between Departments for the available lawyers. The Department that succeeded in attracting the best lawyers (and *ipso facto*, according to Dale, the best draftsmen) would succeed in producing its Bills more speedily; and presumably those Bills would be more competently prepared than those of Departments that had less able or less experienced legal staff but nevertheless had a responsibility to produce important and urgent legislation... .

Dale's Proposal for a 'Law Council'
In conjunction with his proposal for the dispersal of draftsmen among the Departments, Dale proposes the setting up of a body (like the *Conseil d'Etat* in France) to examine draft Bills before their introduction into the legislature from the point of view of 'coherent and orderly presentation, clarity, conciseness, soundness of legal principle and suitability for attaining the Government's objective.' It is submitted that this suggestion does not have sufficient regard to the political background in which legislation is drafted and no Government in a country with a British-style Parliamentary system is likely to agree to it unqualifiedly. There would need to be many exceptions because of the need to keep certain draft legislative proposals confidential. Nevertheless, there is a frequent cry for draft legislative proposals to be made public for comment before they enter the legislative process and, in non-confidential matters, there would certainly be great advantages, both to the draftsman and to the public, if this could be done. However, would not an expansion of existing avenues for scrutiny of legislation be more acceptable to the general community than the creation of a new bureaucratic apparatus for this purpose? In Australia, in the case of proposals that do not involve any element of confidentiality, draft Bills are from time to time made available for public scrutiny, for example, draft Bills

1   On this, see also the view of First Parliamentary Draftsman for Scotland: 'It is too often suggested that the intelligibility of a statute to the general public is a prime consideration in drafting. I do not believe that this is so. I am firmly of the opinion that however we draft our statutes, the British public, except perhaps for the remote lunatic fringe, never read the statutes nor are likely to' (Sir William Dale (ed.) *British and French Statutory Drafting*, Institute of Advanced Legal Studies, London, 1986), p. 63, cited in *Statute Law Review*, Summer 1988, p. 80, n. 46 (ed.).

attached to reports of Law Reform Commissions. In such cases the whole community is offered the opportunity of scrutinising the Bills. Sometimes a specialist body such as the Administrative Review Council is asked to comment on draft Bills dealing with matters within its province. In other cases an occasion for scrutiny occurs after introduction of the legislation as non-urgent Bills are usually not proceeded with until a reasonable time has elapsed. The most frequent source of incisive comment on Bills affecting the business community comes from the corporation that will be affected by the proposed legislation (and their legal advisers). Likewise, private bodies such as civil rights organisations and associations of lawyers seek an opportunity to scrutinise proposed legislation and often make constructive criticisms. These pressure groups would certainly not be satisfied merely to have proposed legislation scrutinised by a body such as the proposed Law Council.

Note

Speaking to the Statute Law Society in April 1978, Lord Renton said that little had been done to implement the recommendations of the Renton Committee. The Committee had recommended that statements of purpose should be included in statutes but 'there have been scarcely any statements of purpose occurring in legislation since we published in May 1975'. The Committee had proposed that there be more explanatory material, but although there had been some improvement, there was still 'a long way to go'. For instance in the Wales Bill there were financial clauses running to eight pages – 'by no means easy to understand'. The explanatory memorandum to the bill endeavoured to explain those eight pages 'in about 15 arid lines on half a page'. That was not good enough because the half-page 'tells us nothing about how those new types of clause will work, what the implications are, and exactly what the new machinery will be'.

The Committee had proposed that there be longer intervals between the stages of a bill – to leave some time for reflection. Here the government's record had been deplorable. Between May 1975 and March 1977 no less than 65 bills failed to comply with the suggested intervals – at least two weeks, between publication and second reading, and 14 days between second reading and the start of the committee stage.

But much more important was that the Cabinet had decided not to accept the recommendation that the Statute Law Committee keep 'the structure and language of statutes under continuous review'. No explanation had been given for the decision. (See 'Failure to Implement the Renton Report', speech of Sir David Renton, in *Renton and the Need for Reform* (Sweet & Maxwell, 1979), pp. 2–8.)

It is likely that the failure of the Renton Committee's proposals was due as much as anything to the powerful lobbying of parliamentary counsel's office. If they are against an idea it is difficult for it to come to fruition. Technically they are under the authority of the Prime Minister but in practice they are effectively not accountable to anyone. There is no Minister who has the power or the position to instruct them as to how they should perform their duties. Nor can it be said that they are receptive to comment, criticism or even invitations to engage in dialogue – see for instance F. A. R. Bennion, Letter, *Statute Law Review*, Spring 1987, p. 68. (We now know that in 1964–65 Lord Gardiner, Lord Chancellor in Harold Wilson's Government, proposed that responsibility for Parliamentary Counsel be taken over by the Lord Chancellor. But this proposal 'aroused a storm of protest in Whitehall' and Gardiner dropped the idea.[2])

In June 1991, however, the Lord Chancellor announced that he had decided to replace the Statute Law Committee and the editorial board which supervised the publication of *Statutes in Force* by a new Advisory Committee on Statute Law. This body would advise him 'as and when required on all matters relating to the publication of the statute book, including the availability of up-to-date texts in both printed and electronic form'. It would meet under the chairmanship of the Lord Chancellor or that of the Permanent Secretary. Its membership would comprise the Clerk of the Parliaments, the Clerk of the House of Commons, the Chairman of the Law Commission, the Chairman of the Scottish Law Commission, First Parliamentary Counsel, the Legal Secretary to the Lord Advocate and First Scottish Parliamentary Counsel, First Legislative Counsel for Northern Ireland, the Treasury Solicitor, the Solicitor to the Scottish Office and representatives from Her Majesty's Stationery Office and the Lord Chancellor's Department. In addition it would be able to involve user and consumer groups as necessary – 'either by way of consultation or by invitation to attend meetings'.[3]

The Hansard Society's 1992 *Report on the Legislative Process (Making the Law)* said that it considered but rejected Sir William Dale's proposal for pre-natal scrutiny of bills to consider drafting, constitutional, legal and other non-policy matters. First, it thought it best if the drafting style of statutes should be consistent, which might suffer if such a system were in place. Second, the scrutiny body would not have sufficient expertise to undertake the task since all the experts were in Parliamentary Counsel's Office. Third, the interposition of the scrutiny process would introduce unacceptable additional delay into the process.[4]

However the report said (p. 50) that there was a danger of complacency. It might be a good thing 'for someone to keep an eye on Parliamentary Counsel'. It was not enough to leave responsibility with Ministers in

2   S.Cretney,'The Law Commission: True Dawns and False Dawns', 59 *Modern Law Review*, 1996, pp.631, 636–37.
3   HL Official Reports (5th series) 13 June 1991, WA col. 65.
4   Note 12, p. 7 above, at pp. 49–50.

charge of individual bills – 'neither the Minister or the officials … will have time to read each bill with the care required to test the drafting' (ibid). Also 'maintenance of good drafting standards across the board will not be achieved by having each bill scrutinised in the department that is preparing that bill'. Some central responsibility was required. This function should be performed by the Cabinet's Legislation Committee.

The Hansard Society Report also recommended (p. 51) that the Attorney General rather than the Cabinet Office should be responsible for the establishment and expenses of Parliamentary Counsel, though the most senior appointments should continue to be made by the Prime Minister. The Attorney General should have ministerial responsibility for the work of Parliamentary Counsel 'and particularly for oversight of the drafting methods employed and scrutiny of the drafting of all Government Bills' (p. 51). First Parliamentary Counsel would be accountable to the Attorney General for the day-to-day work of the Office but he would remain responsible to the Chairman of the Legislation Committee for the delivery of drafted bills.

In regard to the style of drafting, the Hansard Report did not agree with Sir William Dale and the Renton Committee that statements of general principle in statutes would help. It shared the view expressed by Sir Patrick Mayhew who said 'I confess to great difficulty in seeing how a general statement of principle or purpose could enable the law to be developed by the judges, and thereby affect the public's rights, in a way foreseeable with sufficient accuracy by that public.[5] It did think however that the courts would be assisted by Notes on Sections to explain the purpose and effect of each section. These should be prepared by government departments with the assistance of Parliamentary Counsel.

A new style of drafting statutes – Martin Cutts' Timeshare Bill

Mr Martin Cutts has worked in the plain language field since 1975. In 1979 he co-founded the Plain English Campaign. In the early 1980s he had meetings with two successive First Parliamentary Counsel to discuss the prospects for plain language in English statutes. They did not encourage him to think that they were persuaded by his suggestion that the statute book could benefit from radical changes in drafting style. But they challenged him to try to produce his own draft of an actual statute.

Some years later Mr Cutts responded to this challenge. In 1993 he circulated *Unspeakable Acts?*[6] as a discussion paper based on his

---

5   Sir Patrick Mayhew, 'Can Legislation Ever be Simple, Clear, and Certain?' 11 *Statute Law Review*, Summer 1990, p. 7.

6   Available from the author, 69 Bings Road, Whaley Bridge, Stockport, Cheshire SK12 7ND. Tel. (01663) 732957.

attempted redraft of the Timeshare Act 1992. (His version, somewhat cheekily, was entitled 'The Clearer Timeshare Act 1993'.) In the light of comments (including eleven and a half pages of comments from the draftsman of the original act – see p. 48 below), Mr Cutts produced a revised text.

The Cutts version had a great variety of changes in regard to structure, typography, lay-out and, above all, drafting. For example:

Defined terms are listed on each page so that the reader can see at a glance whether anything on the page is defined in the definition section.

Definitions are all collected in one section at the end instead of being scattered in more than one section as before.

Sections are grouped with a group heading.

Headings are used more than in ordinary statutes. They are also more informative.

Section numbers are in the form 1.1, 1.2 etc. Further subdivisions however use the present form – thus 1.1(a)(ii).

Section headings are in bold type.

Footnotes are used to indicate cross-references to other Acts and regulations.

Spacing between sections and subsections is more generous than in ordinary statutes.

Typeface is changed to improve appearance.

Type size is somewhat larger. The Schedule is in the same size type as the main part of the act, instead of smaller as is the present style.

Running heads at the top of each page indicate the sections dealt with on that page.

Simpler language is used throughout. Thus, for illustration, section 2 of the Act states:

2.(1) A person must not in the course of a business enter into a timeshare agreement to which this Act applies as offeror unless the offeree has received, together with a document setting out the terms of the agreement or the substance of those terms, notice of his right to cancel the agreement.

(2) A notice under this section must state—
(a)   that the offeree is entitled to give notice of cancellation of the agreement to the offeror at any time on or before the date specified in the notice, being a day falling not less than fourteen days after the day on which the agreement is entered into, and
(b)   that if the offeree gives such a notice to the offeror on or before that date he will have no further rights or obligations under the agreement, but will have the right to recover any sums paid under or in contemplation of the agreement.

The equivalent section in the Cutts' version states:

2 Seller's duty to give information about a timeshare agreement

2.1 Before a seller enters into a timeshare agreement, the seller must give the customer a right-to-cancel notice and a document setting out the terms of the agreement or the substance of its terms.

2.2 The right-to-cancel notice must show that:

(a)   the customer may cancel the agreement by giving the seller a notice of cancellation on or before the date specified in the right-to-cancel notice, which must be at least fourteen days after the agreement is entered into; and
(b)   the customer who cancels has no further rights or duties under the agreement, except to get back any money paid to the seller under the agreement or while considering entering into it.

The commentary on Martin Cutts' first draft by parliamentary counsel who drafted the Timeshare Act has now been published – see Euan Sutherland, 'Clear Drafting and the Timeshare Act 1992: A Response from Parliamentary Counsel to Mr Cutts', 14 *Statute Law Review*, 1993, pp. 163–170. See also to like effect J. Stark, 'Should the Main Goal of Statutory Drafting be Accuracy or Clarity?', 15 *Statute Law Review*, 1994, pp. 207–13. Martin Cutts, who had amended his draft in response to criticisms, replied in 'Plain English in the Law', 17 *Statute Law Review*, 1996, pp. 50–61. He reported that when his version was tested against the real Act by 91 students on placement with leading law firms, the great majority thought that his was the clearer. When answering questions on the Act, the students using his revision performed better on nine out of twelve questions. He concluded that statute law would be clarified markedly without significant loss of accuracy. He returned the challenge originally put to him by First Parliamentary Counsel by asking his successor to say whether if he were an MP, a judge or an ordinary citizen he would prefer to use the real Act or Martin Cutt's version.

The Tax Rewrite

Signs that the Plain English campaign had made some real progress came with the announcement of a major project to simplify the tax law. The project, known as the Tax Law Rewrite, had its origins in the mid-1990s. The Finance Act 1995, s.160 required the Inland Revenue to prepare and present to Treasury Ministers a report on tax simplification. In November 1995, the then Chancellor of the Exchequer Mr Kenneth Clarke MP, in the course of his Budget statement, announced that the plan was that 'the Revenue tax code is rewritten in plain English – a major task' (267 *Hansard*, HC Debates, 1995–96, col. 1066). 'The project', he said, 'is as ambitious as translating the whole of "War and Peace" into lucid Swahili. In fact it is more ambitious. I am told that "War and Peace" is only 1,500 pages long. Inland Revenue law is 6,000 pages long and was not written by a Tolstoy.' (Budget Statement, November 1996).

The Inland Revenue's report 'The Path to Tax Simplification' together with a background report 'The Path to Tax Simplication – a Background Paper' was published in December 1995. It set out the perceived criticisms of tax legislation – complicated syntax, long sentences, archaic or ambiguous language, obscurity of meaning, the spread of relevant provisions among different statutes, the principles underlying the rules not being apparent, excessive detail, especially in primary legislation. The techniques envisaged included the use of plain language, rationalisation of definitions, reordering and renumbering, omitting outdated or unnecessary material and better design and layout. The Inland Revenue would lead but there would be full consultation with experts and with users.

In July 1996 the Revenue published 'The Tax Law Rewrite – The Way Forward'. This stated that arrangements had been made for a novel, formalised pre-parliamentary consultative process. This involved the creation of three distinct bodies: the Project team, the Consultative Committee and the Steering Committee. The task of devising and carrying out the programme of work, including setting of priorities, was for the Project Team. The Consultative Committee's job was to secure maximum consultation. The Steering Committee under the chairmanship of Lord Howe of Aberavon supervises the whole operation.

In late 1998 it was stated that it was hoped to have the first Rewrite Bill ready for introduction early in 2000. The Inland Revenue estimated that the Rewrite would be even longer than the 6,000 pages of statutory material it was replacing. It would take place over some four to five years. Because of the unusual nature of these Rewrite Bills a special procedure had been approved by the House of Commons Select Committee on Procedure under which such Bills would be introduced in the Commons and would then be referred to a Joint Committee of both Houses.

See further D. Salter, 'Towards a Parliamentary Procedure for the Tax Law Rewrite', 19 *Statute Law Review*, 1998, pp. 65–79 and the Rewrite Project Team's website: http://www.open.gov.uk/inrev/rewrite.htm.

For further reading on drafting, see especially Reed Dickerson, *The Fundamentals of Legal Drafting* (1965); G. C. Thornton, *Legislative Drafting* (1970); Sir William Dale, *Legislative Drafting: a New Approach* (1977). The various meanings of statutory intelligibility and of the problems posed are addressed in David Miers, 'Legislation, Linguistic Adequacy and Public Policy', *Statute Law Review*, Summer 1986, pp. 90–113. See also the papers of the Commonwealth Law Conference in September 1986 published in the *Statute Law Review*, Summer 1987, pp. 71–103. See also I. Turnbull, 'Legislative Drafting in Plain Language and Statements of General Principle', 18 *Statute Law Review*, 1997, pp. 21–31.

CHAPTER 2

Legislation — the Westminster stage

1. THE LEGISLATIVE PROCESS

(a) Procedure in both Houses of Parliament

The sequence of events in the legislative process from the introduction of a bill to Royal Assent has been described by a senior member of the office of Clerk to the House of Commons,[1] most kindly written for the second edition of this book:

> A bill must be given 'three readings' in each House before it can be submitted for the Royal Assent. The first reading is purely formal when the Clerk of the House reads the title from a dummy bill and a day is named for second reading. For government bills, the day named is 'tomorrow'. Although the bill will appear amongst the remaining orders of the day for the next sitting, the government will not move the second reading until a later date, which is announced in advance in the weekly business statement and which will be a sufficient time after presentation to give members an opportunity to consider the text.
>
> The debate on second reading is the main consideration of the general principles of a bill, at the end of which a vote [though it need not] be taken on the bill as a whole. Although a bill can be lost at many stages in its career, the second reading is undoubtedly the most important, and the vast majority of bills which get a second reading and proceed into committee also get on to the statute book. For government bills, the Minister in charge of the department concerned usually opens the debate, and one of his junior Ministers replies at the end. Front-bench opposition speakers follow the ministerial opening, and precede the winding-up.
>
> Unless a member moves that the bill be sent to a committee of the whole House (or to a Select Committee if a detailed examination with witnesses is

---

1   To my regret he insisted on remaining anonymous (ed.).

required or to a Special Standing Committee (see p 55 below) which combines both Select Committee and Standing Committee procedure) all bills after second reading (with the exception of certain financial measures) are automatically sent upstairs to a Standing Committee.[2] These committees consist of from sixteen to fifty members and in a session over 500 members are called upon to serve on them. Appointments to Standing Committees are made by a Select Committee, called the Committee of Selection, which is charged with having regard to the 'qualifications of those members nominated and to the composition of the House'. The government thus keeps its majority, but the opposition and minority parties so far as possible are fully represented. The chair is taken by a member selected by the Speaker from a panel of chairmen, who maintains the same standard of impartiality in Committee as the Speaker does in the House. The task of the Committee is to go through the bill and amend it where desirable, bearing in mind that the general principle of the bill has been approved by the House.

A bill in Committee is considered clause by clause and the question that the clause 'stand part of the bill' is put on each one. Before the question is put on a clause, however, amendments may be moved – provided that they are relevant, not 'wrecking', and conform to various technical requirements, such as the limitation imposed by any accompanying financial resolution passed by the House. Members of most Standing Committees are showered with suggestions for amendments from interested bodies – to add to any ideas of their own for amendment of the bill. The government's amendments are drafted by the Parliamentary Counsel who prepare their bills; the private member usually seeks the advice of the Public Bill Office. The office, which is staffed by clerks in the service of the House (the counterpart in parliamentary terms of the administration group in the civil service), has charge of a bill throughout its passage; checks that the text is in accordance with the title and otherwise in order; provides the clerk for the Standing Committee; and supervises the bill through its remaining stages. The Committee clerk not only helps members with their amendments, but advises the chairman on their orderliness and assists him in the exercise of his power to select which amendments shall be debated. He then attends the meetings of the Committee to keep the minutes and advise the chair and members of the Committee, without distinction of party, on any matter of order that may arise. He keeps the authoritative copy of the bill and enters any amendments as they are made.

A bill which has been considered by a committee of the whole House and emerges unamended goes straight on to third reading. Any other bill must have a consideration or 'Report' stage, when further amendments may be moved, and attempts made either to restore parts lost in Committee or to remove parts added. The government frequently use the Report stage to introduce, in a form acceptable to them, amendments the principle of which they have accepted in

2   The word 'Standing' is misleading. It derives from former times when bills were committed to large permanent committees which examined all bills sent to them. In modern times Standing Committees are chosen afresh for each bill. Commonly there are several Standing Committees functioning at a time. On Standing Committees, see further J. A. G. Griffith and M. Ryle, *Parliament*, (Sweet & Maxwell 1989), pp 231–35, 275–77, 314–18 (ed.).

Committee. The members who have been through the Committee stage together very often dominate the debates on Report stage. This is partly because many of the points at issue were postponed in the Committee at the request of the government, and partly because these members are by now (if they were not before) specialists in the subject, which may make it difficult for an 'outsider' to break in. The Report stage is a useful safeguard, however, against a small Committee amending a bill against the wishes of the House, and a necessary opportunity for second thoughts. The Speaker takes account of the time spent on amendments in Committee when selecting what is to be discussed. A large bill may take two or even three days on report, amounting to ten hours' consideration or more.[3]

There remains third reading; and here, unlike second reading, when a bill may be reviewed in the context of the subject to which it relates, debate must be confined to the contents of the bill. Generally by this stage the battle is recognised to be over, and apart from a few set-piece occasions when a formalised debate precedes a vote, a few minutes only are spent reviewing the victories and defeats of the campaign, and in paying compliments to the opponents. Since 1967, the third reading may be taken without debate unless at least six members table a motion, 'that the Question be not put forthwith'. Although a vote may be called on a bill at this stage it would amount almost to a parliamentary accident for a bill which had been given a second reading to fall at this final stage.[4]

Safely read the third time, a bill is endorsed *soit baille aux Seigneurs* and tied up in a green ribbon together with a message asking the Lords' concurrence. The Clerk of the House proceeds to the 'other place' and hands in the bill at the bar of the House.

Since the House of Lords is not weighed down with as great a burden of business as the Commons, and is not to the same extent a political battleground, it does not have the same highly developed procedural rules which control the way in which proceedings are conducted. Their lordships use their own discretion as to what they will say, and are prepared, for example, to make amendments on the third reading of a bill, if it will improve it, in a way quite breathtaking to newly ennobled former members of the Commons. Basically, however, the legislative process of the two Houses is the same, and the greatest practical difference in the field of legislation is that there are no Standing Committees in the House of Lords. This means that on a subject of general interest all members are able to put down amendments, and on a highly controversial measure, such as the Telecommunications Bill in 1983–4, this can result in a very protracted Committee stage. Bills get a formal first reading, a second reading, consideration in Committee and on Report and then a third reading. They must also survive finally a formal motion, 'That this bill do now pass'. Although bills may generally get a smoother passage in the Lords than through the Commons, the Lords have increased their work-load in recent years. Perhaps because many peers are former members of the House of

---

3   On the Report Stage see further Griffith and Ryle, op. cit., n. 2 p.52 above, pp. 235–37, 318–19. (Ed.)

4   Ibid.

Commons, proceedings have taken on a more similar character to those in the Commons.

After a Commons bill has been through the Lords, it is returned with the Lords Amendments to it, which then must be considered in the House. On any bill, the two Houses must finally reach agreement on the amendments made by each other if the bill is not to fall during that Session. Under the Parliament Acts 1911 and 1949, disagreement between the two Houses can delay a bill only for a year if the Commons persist with it;[5] and in the case of a money bill, a bill passed by the Commons can go for Royal Assent after only one month's delay. Where one House cannot agree to the other's amendments, it sends a message to that effect giving reasons. A bill can go back and forth several times but it is only rarely that a bill has had to be reintroduced in a second Session in order to become law, because of the failure of the two Houses to agree, the last occasion being the [War Crimes Bill 1990–91 and the European Parliamentary Elections Bill 1998–99. (ed)].[6]

The final stage in the enacting process is Royal Assent. Under the Royal Assent Act 1961, Royal Assent is given by notification, by which the short title of the bills which have received Royal Assent is read out in each House together with a formula signifying the fact of assent.[7]

Apart from the usual course charted by a bill in the Commons, there are a number of other procedures, introduced since 1964 primarily to save the time of the House, through which a bill may pass. Under Standing Order No. 69, a bill may be referred to a Standing Committee called a Second Reading Committee for its second reading debate, after which the question on second reading is put without debate in the House. This procedure is used a few times each session for largely uncontroversial bills. A similar procedure is sometimes applied to bills relating to Scotland, the less controversial and important of which may have second reading debates in the Scottish Grand Committee.

From this account of the customary procedures for the passage of a bill, it will be seen that, if proper consideration is given at each stage to a substantial measure, whether or not it is opposed in principle, its passage takes a considerable time. In fact major bills will take six months or more to pass. On the other hand a small bill can, if urgency requires it, pass through both Houses in a day.[8] The government business managers have to fit in an average of about sixty government bills, including between ten and twenty substantial bills, each Session, almost all of which will get through to receive the Royal Assent. This contrasts with the ten or so private Members' bills enacted out of the more than 80 such bills which are presented each Session. The key to the productivity of parliament lies in control of the timetable of the House of Commons by the government and the willingness of the House to entrust the Chair with discretion to select amendments for debate, and to accept or reject motions for the closure of debate.

---

5   See S. M. McMurtie, 'The Constitutionality of the War Crimes Act' 13 *Statute Law Review*, 1992, pp. 128–36. (Ed.)
6   See further Griffith and Ryle, op. cit., n. 2 p. 52 above, at pp 238–42, 503–06. (Ed.)
7   See further, p. 73 below. (Ed.)
8   Not only 'small bills'! – see below (ed.)

Special Public Bill ('Jellicoe') Committees

In 1980 the House of Commons approved a new procedure for a Standing Committee to take evidence from outside experts before the usual clause-by-clause examination of a Bill. The procedure allowed for up to four morning sittings at three of which evidence could be given. Five bills passed into law under this procedure but after 1984 it fell into disuse. It proved unpopular with government departments which disliked the delay it involved. In the 1990s a similar device was tried in the House of Lords and for a while seemed to be more successful. It was proposed by a Select Committee chaired by Lord Jellicoe.[9] The Committee recommended that bills put to this new procedure (known in the Lords as a Special Standing Committee) should be 'of a technical nature and largely devoid of party political controversy'. Law Commission Bills would be especially suitable. In the 1993–94 session one measure, the Law of Property (Miscellaneous Provisions) Bill, went to a Special Standing Committee. The minutes of the committee's proceedings contain 62 pages of written and oral evidence, followed by the committee's clause by clause consideration of the Bill. The committee made a number of amendments and the Bill completed all its remaining stages in both Houses in little more than half an hour.

This experiment was initially regarded as a success and in the 1994–95 session several Bills went to Special Standing Committees. One, the Private International Law (Miscellaneous Provisions) Bill involved 68 pages of written evidence from 43 contributors and 886 pages of oral evidence. After that the Bill completed all its stages in the Lords in less than 90 minutes without a division. The Family Homes and Domestic Violence Bill produced a similar volume of evidence (87 pages of written evidence from 48 contributors and 89 pages of oral evidence occupying six evidence sessions). Writing of the experiment, Mr Justice Brooke, Chairman of the Law Commission, said: 'This new procedure enables Parliament itself to hear direct from very knowledgeable people in the course of its own law-making function. The auspices are very encouraging for the future quality of the statutes that are submitted to this process.'[10]

But this optimism proved misplaced. The procedure has not been used in the past few sessions. The main reason it seems is that the procedure involves a considerable burden of extra work both for the Committee members and for officials in the Lord Chancellor's Department.

Second Reading Committees (House of Commons)

The House of Commons for a period used a procedure known as the Second Reading Committee mainly for technical or uncontroversial Bills

---

9   *Report from the House of Lords Select Committee on the Committee Work of the House* (1991–92).
10 'Special Public Bill Committees', *Public Law*, 1995, pp. 351, 356.

such as those based on Law Commission reports. Under this procedure the Bill is referred for its Second Reading to a special committee of something between 16 and 50 MPs. They observe the normal rules that apply to Second Readings – one of which is that no Member may speak more than once without leave of the Committee. After they recommend that the Bill be read a second time, the vote on that question is taken by the full House without any debate. The procedure was initiated in 1965 at the time of the setting up of the Law Commission. Between 1965 and 1993, 139 Bills were put through this procedure of which 105 were Bills started in the Lords and 19 were Law Commission Bills. In the past few sessions, however, the procedure has not been used.

Departmental Select Committees

There are also committees called Departmental Select Committees. The functions of such committees are quite different from the role of the committees already considered. They owe their existence to the report of a Select Committee on Procedure in 1978 which criticised the House of Commons for its inadequate system of scrutinising the activities of the executive. Against the instincts of frontbenchers on both sides, backbench Members of Parliament forced the acceptance of the new concept of select committees to have responsibility for scrutinising the executive within its field. MPs voted for the new system in June 1979. Fourteen such committees were set up and in 1980 a liaison select committee was added consisting of the chairman of the individual select committees. They determine their own agenda, elect their own chairman, call and examine witnesses and appoint specialist advisers. They consist entirely of backbenchers though party strength in the House determines the numbers of each party on the committee. They do not have the adversarial system of the House or of ordinary committees of the House. They try to produce unanimous reports.[11]

In 1990 the House of Commons Procedure Committee considered the suggestion that these departmentally-related select committees could play a legislative role if they took the Committee stage of bills.[12] It thought there was some validity in the argument that 'the questioning approach of select committees could lead to better thought out, and ultimately more workable, legislation'. But there were a number of problems. One was that it would distract them from their inquiries into policy, administration and expenditure. Another was that Ministers were not members of these Select Committees. Even more serious was that it would change the consensual

11 See D. Englefield, *Select Committees: Catalysts for Progress?* (1984) and Griffiths and Ryle, op. cit, n. 2, p. 52 above at pp. 415–33.
12 Second Report of the Select Committee on Procedure of 1989–90 (HC 19–1).

way in which the select committees worked. The Procedure Committee therefore did not favour them having any legislative function.

Note: legislation in haste

Sometimes the legislature moves with amazing, some would say indecent, haste. The second reading of the Commonwealth Immigrants Bill was moved at 4 pm on 27 February 1968 in the House of Commons and the bill passed all stages in the Commons and the Lords on the same day. Notification of the Royal Assent was received in the Lords at 9.45 am on 1 March 1968. The Northern Ireland Bill had its second reading in the House of Commons at 10 pm on 23 February 1972 and the Royal Assent only hours later, on 24 February at 2.11 am. The Prevention of Terrorism (Temporary Provisions) Act 1974, passed in the wake of the Birmingham pub bombings, went through all its stages in both Houses of Parliament in 17 hours. The Imprisonment (Temporary Provisions) Act 1980 passed through all its stages in 13 hours, 20 minutes. It was introduced on a Tuesday afternoon and completed its parliamentary stages by 5.10 am the following morning.

The Official Secrets Bill passed all its stages in one day in August 1911. The junior minister responsible for piloting it through the House of Commons described the event nearly twenty years later:[13]

> I got up and proposed that the Bill be read a second time, explaining, in two sentences only, that it was considered desirable in the public interest that the measure should be passed. Hardly a word was said and the Bill was read a second time; the Speaker left the Chair. I then moved the Bill in Committee. This was the first critical moment; two men got up to speak, but both were forcibly pulled down by their neighbours after they had uttered a few sentences, and the committee stage was passed. The Speaker walked back to his chair and said: 'The question is, that I report this Bill without amendment to the House.' Again two or three people stood up; again they were pulled down by their neighbours, and the report stage was through. The Speaker turned to me and said: 'The third reading, what day?' 'Now, sir,' I replied. My heart beat fast as the Speaker said: 'The question is that this Bill be read a third time.' It was open to anyone of all the members in the House of Commons to get up and say that no bill had ever yet passed through all its stages in one day without a word of explanation from the minister in charge… But to the eternal honour of those members, to whom I now offer, on behalf of that and all succeeding governments, my most grateful thanks, not one man seriously opposed, and in a little more time than it has taken to write these words that formidable piece of legislation was passed.

13   J. E. B. Seely, *Adventure* (1930), p. 145 – cited by D. G. T. Williams in 'Statute Law and Administrative Law', *Statute Law Review*, 1984, p. 166.

(b) Interaction between interested parties during the legislative process

A description of the interaction between ministers, civil servants, MPs and outside interests in the legislative process emerged from an account of the background to the Criminal Justice Act 1972 in a BBC documentary broadcast on 16 September 1972. The presenter was Professor Anthony King of Essex University, who discussed what happened with the Conservative Minister of State at the Home Office, Mr Mark Carlisle, with his opposite number in the Labour Opposition, Sir Elwyn Jones, with one of the senior civil servants involved, Mr Michael Moriarty of the Home Office, and with a backbench MP, Mr Edmund Dell. (By a coincidence the Act in question was also the subject of the extract at p. 4 above from Mr Moriarty's paper.) The transcript is taken from *Westminster and Beyond*, ed. A. King and A. Sloman (1973), chapter 12.

MORIARTY: I'm in charge of the small division which has general responsibility for legislation on the powers of the courts and is also the division that looks after the Advisory Council on the Penal System. So it fell to me and to my staff to report to ministers about the two reports of the Advisory Council on reparation and alternatives to imprisonment, and suggest what might be done about them. And this involved, in fact, putting a memorandum together, collecting the views of various other parts of the Office and, indeed, of other governmental departments that were concerned.

KING: It's not generally realised that civil servants brief their ministers not just behind the scenes but while actual debates are going on on the floor or in committee. Michael Moriarty was present during the second reading debate and I asked him, since he's not allowed to sit next to ministers on the front bench, how he went about communicating with them.

MORIARTY: On the whole by rapidly scribbled notes, some of them things that we ourselves realise the minister is going to need from what we hear someone else saying or what we hear him saying, sometimes things that he asks us to produce. The channel of communication is the parliamentary private secretary. These are, on the whole, fairly young MPs, perhaps with a ministerial career before them, who – as it were – learn the trade, and I think you get to know a great deal about what the functions of government ministers are about by understudying in that sort of way.

KING: You do actually sit there, in effect, in the chamber itself? Not technically but in fact?

MORIARTY: That's right, yes. On the right of the Speaker and behind him under the Gallery there is a box, and officials sit there and listen with their papers, scribble their notes, and there's a certain amount of scope for interchange.

KING: Once a Bill's been read a second time – approved in principle that is – it's sent to a committee where amendments can be moved and the various clauses considered in much more detail. In the case of very important pieces of legislation, like the European Communities Bill, the committee may actually consist of the whole House of Commons operating under a somewhat different procedure. But most Bills, including the Criminal Justice Bill, are sent upstairs, as they say, to one of the standing committees. These committees have about two dozen members each and are, in effect, miniature Houses of Commons. The majority party in the whole House also has a majority on the committee and, as in the whole House, there are ministers and Opposition front-bench spokesmen. Standing committees are not specialised: they consider whatever Bills are sent to them and not just ones on particular topics. But, of course, if an MP is interested in a particular Bill, he can usually see to it that he is included on the appropriate standing committee – or at least he can try.

Everyone agrees that the atmosphere of a standing committee is quite different from that on the floor of the House.

CARLISLE: It's usually considerably more intimate. It's more, I think one can say, constructive. It depends a lot on the Bill. For example, on this Bill the atmosphere throughout was that people were wanting to get down and do a careful revision of the details of the Bill in a constructive manner.

KING: Michael Moriarty describes the contrast in more detail.

MORIARTY: It's a good deal easier and less formal. A committee room is I suppose not much larger than a large school classroom. The MPs, of whom in our case there were about twenty in all, sit at desks facing one another, so to that extent it's a sort of mini-chamber. In place of the Speaker we have a Chairman of the committee, that is an MP, who is on a low dais. On his left he has the House officials and the Hansard people. On the right of the Chairman there is Parliamentary Counsel and then the officials like myself who are there to give advice to the minister on the contents of the Bill.

KING: Let's suppose an MP raises a point and the minister isn't quite sure how he's going to reply: will he in standing committee, actually there and then, turn to you and mutter something to you in order to get some help?

MORIARTY: Yes, because of the geography, which it's slightly difficult to describe. We are, in fact, only a few feet away from the minister, so it's perfectly easy for a minister just to get up from his seat and and take a couple of paces so that he can talk quietly to us, or he can even stage whisper from where he's sitting, or he can ask his parliamentary private secretary, sitting just behind him, to turn round and have a word with us. It is all a good deal easier; there's no need for anyone to move to and fro. And, indeed, one occasionally gets a situation where someone from the Opposition or a Government backbencher asks the minister a question and then does a bit of ad-libbing while it's perfectly clear that the minister is getting the answer.

KING: One major advantage a minister has in piloting a Bill through the House of Commons is sheer numbers: despite occasional near-embarrassments, he can normally count on having enough votes to get his Bill carried. But he also has another major advantage: the detailed information and advice supplied by civil servants. Part of the job of civil servants working on a bill is to take all the amendments – on jury service, suspended sentences, and so on and brief the minister on them, as Michael Moriarty explained:

MORIARTY: This is the main task of officials during the committee stage. Each morning the Order Paper is brought down from the Parliamentary Section as early as they can, and one then drops everything else and sets to work looking at the amendments, trying to work out exactly what an MP is getting at – sometimes, of course, it's quite a job – and this may be because he is approaching something in a confused way or because he's just a lot cleverer than we are on a particular matter. And then one goes through the processes of deciding how far the objective is compatible with the objectives of the Government in the Bill, and how far it's a sensible way of achieving it.

KING: How far is it part of the job of a civil servant to warn a minister of unforeseen consequences of an amendment which he might perhaps be about to accept?

MORIARTY: Oh, I think that is really part of the bread-and-butter of briefing on amendments. Of course, this question, I think, raises in turn the question where the initiative lies, and I suppose this is different on different occasions. In our case, the initiative I think lay with us in the first instance. We would usually tender some briefing and advice on an amendment and, if necessary, Mr Carlisle would discuss these with us, tell us if he saw it differently, and so on. But on the whole he let us get on with working out a brief before telling us what his own thoughts were. But one can certainly see if it worked the other way round: that, if it began with the Minister saying what he thought, it would certainly be the task of the civil servant to say: 'Well, but have you considered A, B, and C?'

KING: Backbenchers and Opposition MPs, however, lack that sort of professional assistance. Where do they get help from? How did Edmund Dell inform himself for purposes of taking part in the Committee proceedings?

DELL: Well, here, of course, I have the great good fortune of having a wife who is very deeply acquainted with this whole area and who was therefore able to draw my attention to all the necessary material on every point on which I wanted to speak. So she was of enormous assistance.

KING: So it was then a question of simply going to the library and reading the stuff up?

DELL: It was a matter of going to the library, reading the stuff up, preparing the speech, and putting the available information before the minister and the Committee and saying: 'This is information which has obviously not been considered in preparing this Bill.'

KING: And in addition to what an MP can do on his own, there are also organisations willing to help him, as well as to press their views on him. I asked Sir Elwyn Jones where he and his colleagues got their information from.

JONES: Well, you will remember that there were the reports of committees, which were the foundation of the clauses in the Bill, which we were able to call upon. But then in the background there are a large number of bodies, fortunately, in this country – this is one of our strengths as a democracy – like Justice, the British Section of the International Commission of Jurists, like the National Council for Civil Liberties, like the Howard League. There are half a dozen bodies at least who have worked on this sort of problem and whose reports and recommendations are available to us.

The time taken by parliamentary debates

Professor John Griffith studied the time taken by debates on government bills in three sessions of Parliament – 1967–8, 1968–9 and 1970–1. In the first session there were 60 bills which took an average of 23 hours each; in the second, 50 bills averaged 20 hours' debate; in the third, 73 bills averaged 16 hours. The overall average was 19 hours 54 minutes. These figures cover the aggregate of time devoted to debates in *both* Houses.[14]

But out of the total of 183 bills no fewer than 74 (40 per cent) were dealt with in less than 5 hours. At the other end of the spectrum, in each of the three sessions there were 7 bills that absorbed over half of the total amount of time. These 21 bills averaged 96 hours of debating time (ibid).

The average distribution of time over the three sessions was:

2nd reading	15%
Committee stage	65%
Report stage	15%
3rd reading	2%
Lords' amendments in Commons	3%
Total	100%

(*Source*: ibid., Table 1.2, p. 17.)

In a later study conducted by Professor Griffith with Mr Michael Ryle, Clerk of Committees in the House of Commons, it was found[15] that there were three main categories of bills. The first was the category of major policy bills of which there might be about ten per session. They are debated on Second Reading on the floor of the House of Commons on one day for six hours, or sometimes over two days for 12 hours. A few are then taken in committee of the full House but most are sent to Standing Committee where they are debated for 50 or more hours. Most are then further debated on Report, Third Reading and consideration of Lords' Amendments.

The second group consists of some 20 or so policy bills which take up somewhat less time – say 30 or more hours in committee.

The third group consists of a further 20 or so bills which for one reason or another go through very quickly. Some are consolidation bills (see p. 63). Some small uncontentious bills are debated in Second Reading Committees off the floor of the House under Standing Order No. 90. The debates average some 30 minutes, a few going through virtually 'on the nod'. Most of these bills are introduced in the Lords. Some of the bills in the group are Consolidated Fund and Appropriation bills the function of which is to 'raise supply' (i.e. moneys). Under Standing Order 54 these are not debated at all.

14   J. A. G. Griffith, *Parliamentary Scrutiny of Government Bills* (1974), pp. 15–16.
15   Griffith and Ryle, *Parliament* (1989), pp. 310–13.

Thus in the two sessions 1984–85, 1985–86 there were a total of 107 government bills. Of these, 20 per cent were not debated on the floor of the House of Commons at all; 19 per cent were debated for under an hour; 11 per cent were debated for between 1 and 5 hours; 29 per cent were debated for between 5 and 13 hours, 10 per cent for between 13 and 20 hours, and 11 per cent for more than 20 hours.

Law Commission Bills generally take only a small amount of Parliamentary time. In the 10 years from 1984/85, 15 uncontroversial Law Commission Bills took an average of three hours altogether. The Law Reform (Year and Day Rule) Act 1996 took 13 minutes in the House of Lords and one minute in the Commons. The Theft (Amendment) Act 1996 took 65 minutes in the Lords and again one minute in the Commons. On the other hand, some Law Commission Bills take a great deal of time – the Public Order Act 1986 took 47 hours, 21 minutes; the Children Act 1989 took 90 hours, 44 minutes.

Note: some further relevant facts

A study by Ivor Burton and Gavin Drewry, *Legislation and Public Policy* (1981), of the years 1970–4, when Mr Edward Heath was Prime Minister, showed the following further facts that bore on the questions of parliamentary procedure:

(1) Of a total of 185 Government bills, 137 (73 per cent) were introduced in the House of Commons and 48 (27 per cent) were introduced in the House of Lords. (Table 4.2, p. 112.)

(2) The bills were categorised by the authors into seven categories: Policy (those intended to change public policy); Administration (providing running repairs to the machinery without changing the policy); Minor Policy (dealing with a small area of public policy); Administrative Reform (designed to achieve substantial reorganisation of the administrative machinery and procedures); Mixed Purpose; Finance; and Other, not classified in the foregoing categories. Of the total of 185 Government bills in the period covered by the study, 71 (38 per cent) were Policy; 62 (33 per cent) were Administration; 22 (12 per cent) were Minor Policy; 19 (10 per cent) were Administrative Reform; 5 were Mixed Purpose; 3 were Finance and 3 were not otherwise classified. (Table 4.1, p. 112.)

(3) In 23 of the 185 bills (12 per cent), the Second Reading in the House of Commons took under one hour. In the House of Lords the equivalent figure was 94 (or 51 per cent). (Tables 4.3 and 4.4, p. 114).

(4) No less than 30 per cent of government bills were sent to a committee of the whole House of Commons rather than one of the Standing Committees. (Table 4.6, p. 115.)

(5) Standing Committees usually consisted of fewer than 20 Members, 16 being the standard size, but a few more important bills were sent to larger Standing Committees with up to 30 members. (See p. 116).

(6) In a high proportion of cases, bills were dealt with by the committee at one sitting. Where the committee was of the whole House, the number that had more than one sitting was 6 out of 52 (11 per cent). Where the committee was a Standing Committee, 36 per cent were disposed of in one sitting. (Tables 4.8 and 4.9, pp. 118–19.)

(7) In a high proportion of cases at the Second Reading the Opposition did not oppose the Government's bills. There was bipartisan support for 90 out of 185 (49 per cent). In another 35 (19 per cent) the Opposition were neutral or critical without however calling any division. In a further 22 (12 per cent) there was either no debate on the floor of the House, or the Second Reading was not reached. In only 38 cases out of 185 (20 per cent) was there any division on the Second Reading. (Table 4.15, p. 123.)

(c)   Consolidation and statute law revision or repeal

Forms of legislation which take very little parliamentary time are consolidation (putting into one statute what was previously to be found in several) and statute law revision or repeal (the repeal of obsolete statutes). Both are dealt with by a special expedited procedure described in the extract that follows:

William Wilson, 'The Consolidation of Statutes', *Law Society's Gazette*, 30 January 1980, p. 84

> Every other Wednesday, when Parliament is in session, at 4.30 in the afternoon in committee room no. 4 in the House of Lords there sits a committee which is both the driest and the most useful committee in the Palace of Westminster. In the 14 years I have served on this committee, only once did a journalist appear – he stayed all of five minutes – never to be seen again. Until recently no member of the public had ever listened to the proceedings of the committee. However, towards the end of last year, when the Palace of Westminster was very full of visitors, half a dozen members of the public who presumably could find nowhere else to go listened to the committee proceedings. They sat glassy-eyed and uncomprehending as the committee deliberated. This committee is the Joint Select Committee on Consolidation Bills.
>
> Many politicians boast of the legislation to which they gave birth. The members of the Joint Select Committee on Consolidation Bills have a truly greater claim to fame. They reduce the size of the statute book. This statutory reduction is achieved by consolidation statutes, correcting minor errors and ambiguities in statutes and taking from the statute book altogether legislation which has become obsolete or spent.
>
> *Origins of Consolidation*
> Consolidation and revision of statutes has been part of the English legal scene for centuries but only comparatively recently has a regular basis of consolidation, revision and repeal of statutes existed.

Sir Francis Bacon when Attorney-General became the first law officer to embark upon a scheme of statutory revision and consolidation, but all to no avail. Thomas Carlisle, writing in 1850 regarding the efforts of the Rump Parliament to tidy up the statute book, complained that the committee of that Parliament saw the spring violets become June roses whilst they were still discussing, without resolving, the meaning of 'incumbrances'. Indeed, he went on to add that the committee are 'Perhaps debating it, if so doomed, in some twilight foggy section of Dante's Nether World, to all eternity, at this hour.'

Even at the end of last century, when in a desultory fashion consolidating statutes had been passed for many years, the issue was successfully raised that consolidation could only be effected if the actual words of the consolidated statutes were not changed. It was this theory and the First World War that stopped consolidation of statutes for nearly 25 years. Today, the Joint Select Committee on Bills has 24 members. Twelve each come from the Lords and the Commons. The chairman is usually a member of the House of Lords. Most members are lawyers.

Consolidation with Corrections

In 1949 the Consolidation of Enactments (Procedure) Act was passed. This act allowed 'corrections and minor improvements' to be made and this ended the argument that consolidation could only be effected if it was pure and unadulterated consolidation. S.2 of the 1949 Act defines corrections and minor improvements as 'resolving ambiguities, removing doubts, bringing obsolete provisions into conformity with modern practice, or removing unnecessary provisions or anomalies…'.

The 1949 Act enabled consolidation and amendment of Acts to take place on a much greater scale but the preparation of the consolidating bill was left to a rather 'hit or miss' process of whether there was a parliamentary draftsman available with the knowledge and time to prepare the consolidating Bill. The establishment of the Law Commission in 1965 gave an entirely new impetus and opportunity for consolidation and repeal. Before 1965, where corrections and minor improvements were involved, the originating process was a recommendation by the Lord Chancellor. The Law Commission has power enabling it to make recommendations involving consolidation where more than pure consolidation is involved. More important, the Law Commission is concerned with statute law repeal. To this revision of statute law the Law Commission brings a new criterion when deciding its recommendations to repeal. This new criterion is that of 'practical utility'. This criterion widens considerably the previous criterion which was that of 'obsolete, spent, unnecessary or superseded'.

Procedure

For a Bill to come before this Joint Consolidation Committee it will have originated in the House of Lords who remit the Bill to the committee for consideration. When the draft Bill comes to the committee members it has with it the comments of the draftsman explaining where the Bill is not pure consolidation and also giving a general outline of the Bill's provisions. Where applicable, recommendations of the Law Commission are also provided for the committee members. The draftsman of the Bill (and he may be accompanied by government departmental officers where their particular department is involved) appears before the committee to give oral explanations on the proposed enactment and to answer questions from the committee members. The Bill is taken clause by clause and the draftsman is obliged to satisfy the committee that it is a Bill that has been consolidated in accordance with the law. If the Bill deals with statute repeal then the draftsman has to satisfy the committee that the repealed legislation is truly spent and obsolete and those departments or organisations which may be affected by the repeal do not raise any objections.

The Joint Select Committee on Consolidation Bills, after having considered the Bill and heard and questioned the draftsman and any other witnesses, reports to the Lords and the Commons that either the Bill is pure consolidation or, that corrections or amendments have been made to the previous legislation in accordance with the procedures laid down.

On a Bill dealing with statute law repeal the committee reports to the Lords and the Commons that only Acts which were obsolete, spent or unnecessary are involved.

The Bills when reported to the Houses are passed through the Houses in a few minutes. There is no debate upon the merits of the particular legislation and only points concerned with the actual alterations that have been made can be raised. In practice this very rarely happens. Any member of the committee soon acquires a profound admiration for the skill and knowledge of Parliamentary draftsmen, but in the consolidation work the members do come to know that even Parliamentary draftsmen make mistakes. Recently the Army Reserve Act 1950 was being consolidated. In a section of that Act it was discovered there was reference to 'Non-commissioned officers and warrant officers'. This is the only time in our statutes that non-commissioned officers have been placed before warrant officers. The Joint Consolidation Committee was solemnly asked to pass an amendment to make 'non-commissioned officers and warrant officers' read 'warrant officers and non-commissioned officers'. The drafting error was corrected and due precedence afforded to warrant officers!

A Report of a Working Party on Consolidation of Statutes set up by the Statute Law Society urged in 1984 that the Law Commission should be somewhat bolder in proposing amendments to consolidation acts. ('Certainly nobody would question that a Bill making use of the streamlined consolidation procedure is not the right vehicle for major or controversial changes. But ... we believe that it should be possible to develop a broader and more liberal approach to the problem without destroying Parliament's confidence in the Joint Committee and its assurance that the consolidation procedure will not be abused', *Statute Law Review*, 1984, para. 112, p. 174.)

See further Lord Simon of Glaisdale and J. V. D. Webb, 'Consolidation and Statute Law Revision', *Public Law*, 1975, p. 285; and J. A. Vallance White, 'Consolidation and Statute Law Revision: A Comment on Recent Developments', ibid., 1976, p. 299. See also D. R. Miers and A. C. Page, *Legislation* (1982), pp. 36–47.

Special procedure for the Tax Rewrite

A special procedure has been agreed for the massive project known as the Tax Rewrite (see p. 49 above) involving the preparation of thousands of pages of primary legislation to replace existing tax laws. It was not possible to use the normal procedure for consolidation because of the substantial changes of language and format involved. On the other hand, it would not practicable or sensible to apply the ordinary Public Bill procedure as this would involve a prohibitively large commitment of parliamentary time. Also that would permit reopening of policy issues that had previously been enacted and established. Also here there would be an elaborate pre-parliamentary process to prepare the way.

The procedure envisaged by the Select Committee on Procedure (Second Report, 30 January 1997 (1996–97) HC 126) is that the House of Commons will be given an opportunity to give its substantive approval to the principles underlying the Rewrite before any Rewrite Bills are introduced. Rewrite Bills are to be introduced in the House of Commons. The Second Reading would not be on the floor of the House but would instead be in a Second Reading Committee (see p. 55 above). The Committee Stage would be by a Joint Committee of both Houses. This would permit evidence to be given by Parliamentary Counsel, by Inland Revenue officials, the chairmen of the Steering Committee or the Consultative Committee of the Tax Rewrite project and by others. The Joint Committee would have a House of Commons majority from whom the chairman would be drawn. It would determine its own procedure but this was envisaged as having three stages: (1) determination of what evidence was needed and taking such evidence; (2) deliberation by the Joint Committee in private with Ministers present; and (3) clause-by-clause examination of the Bill, possibly involving hearing further evidence.

After the Committee Stage it is anticipated that Rewrite Bills would go through the Commons with little, if any, further debate and that the procedure in the House of Lords would be suitably modified to permit maximum expedition. Just as for normal consolidation Bills the House of Lords plays the dominant role, so here it would be accepted that the dominant role would be played by the House of Commons.

On 20 March 1997, the House of Commons adopted the proposed procedure by Standing Order No. 60 for Tax Simplification Bills.

For further description see D. Salter, 'Towards a Parliamentary Procedure for the Tax Law Rewrite', 19 *Statute Law Review* 1998, pp. 65–7.

Note: alternatives to consolidation

Sometimes there is a need for consolidation before an actual consolidation is prepared. If one statute amends another it may be exceedingly awkward for the citizen and his professional advisers to use the two together. There are three techniques that are sometimes used in this situation. One is to postpone the operation of the amending statute until the consolidation is ready. This is obviously unlikely unless the consolidation is well on the way when the amending statute receives Royal Assent. A second is to include in the amending statute a Schedule (known as a Keeling Schedule) which gives the text of the law as amended showing typographically the amending passages. (For an example see the Criminal Evidence (Amendment) Act 1997 which amended the Police and Criminal Evidence Act 1984 provisions on DNA sampling.) This is hardly convenient if the amended statute is very bulky. Nor can it be used when the previous statute has previously been amended. The third technique is to arrange with the editor of the *Statutes in Force* for publication immediately after Royal Assent of the principal Act as amended. This lacks the full authority of statute but at least it gives members of the public and their advisers the text of an intelligible document. (See Lord Simon of Glaisdale, 'Statute Consolidation: Interim Techniques', *Public Law*, 1985, p. 352.)

(d)   Private Members' bills

Most bills are introduced by government Ministers. But each year some time is reserved for the introduction of bills by private Members of Parliament who are not Ministers.

There are three different ways in which Private Members can introduce bills: through the ballot, under Standing Order No. 39 and under the Ten-Minute Rule.

Balloted bills A ballot is held each session among backbench MPs (those who hold no form of government job). Twenty names are drawn. Those who draw high positions in the ballot have a particularly good chance of getting a bill on to the statute book providing they choose their subject with care. But even those who do not draw high positions may succeed, providing they have government support for their bills.

Under Standing Order No. 39 After the twenty balloted bills have been presented, any MP can present a bill to the House. All that is required is at least one day's notice, and its presentation to the Clerk of the table. The major difference between these bills and balloted bills is that the latter will normally absorb virtually all the time available for debates on Private Members' bills. The bill cannot make progress if it is opposed. The objection of only one Member is sufficient to put an end to the bill.

Ten-Minute Rule bills Standing Order No. 13 allows any MP to make a speech of up to ten minutes in support of the introduction of some piece of legislation. Two such speeches can be made in any week. A single speech may be given in opposition. If there is opposition, a vote is taken as to whether the bill should be read a first time. If there is none, a date is given for the Second Reading but this is an empty formality since there is never any time for a Second Reading debate on a Ten-Minute Rule bill. The only possibility for such a bill to proceed is if it gets an unopposed second reading without a debate.[16]

The time available for Private Members' bills is severely limited. Normally there are ten Fridays in each session made available for Private Members' bills. The first six of these are given over to Second Reading debates. The first six Members in the ballot for places should therefore at least get a second reading for their bills. But if any of these bills is opposed, the opponents commonly prolong the debate on the previous bills so as to prevent any consideration of the contentious measure. Even when it is debated, the sponsoring MP has to make sure that he has enough supporters to defeat the closure motion. Private Members' business ends at 2.30 pm. If the bill's opponents are still speaking just before 2.30 pm, the sponsor moves 'that the Question now be put'. The bill will then be talked out unless there are at least one hundred MPs (plus two tellers) present to vote in favour of the motion.

If the bill survives these various procedural hazards it still faces the risk of still-birth through government opposition. If the government is actively against a bill, its chances of success are virtually nil. Conversely a bill that is favoured by the government will normally succeed in reaching the statute book. If there is any prospect of the bill becoming law the government ensures that its drafting is reviewed by parliamentary counsel. But this is often only at a late stage. Until then the promoters of Private Members' bills have to rely on their own resources in the form of legal advice from fellow Members, the help of sponsoring lobbying organisations or the guidance of the clerks in the Public Bill Office. (The House of Commons resolved in 1971 that MPs who drew positions in the first twenty in the annual ballot for Private Members' bills should receive up to £200 towards the cost of drafting assistance for such bills. A comment in 1986 said that the current value of the £200 allowance was then £43.35! In the previous four parliamentary sessions there had been only five applications. Colin T. Reid, *Statute Law Review*, Spring 1986, p. 45.)

MPs who draw high positions in the ballot usually find themselves inundated by suggestions from interest groups hoping to persuade them to adopt their pet schemes for law reform. But in fact, contrary to conventional wisdom, only a minority of successful Private Members' bills are due to private initiative. The great majority these days are in

---

16 An example of a Ten-Minute Rule Bill becoming law is the Bail (Amendment) Act 1993 giving the prosecution a right of appeal against a grant of bail.

reality either government bills or bills to enact the recommendations of some official law reform committee or body such as the Law Commission.

The figures are very striking. They are based on research conducted by David Marsh and Melvyn Read, two political scientists from Essex University, who investigated all Private Members' bills from 1948–9 to 1985–6.[17] They found, first, that in recent years balloted bills had by far the best prospects of success. In the decade from 1970–1 for instance, the total number of successful Private Members' bills was 93, of which 65 (70 per cent) were balloted bills, 24 (26 per cent) were under Standing Order No. 39, and 4 (4 per cent) were Ten-Minute Rule bills. In the period from 1980–1 to 1984–5, there were 57 successful Private Members' bills. Of these, 42 (74 per cent) were balloted bills, 11 (19 per cent) were under Standing Order No. 39 and 4 (7 per cent) were Ten-Minute Rule bills. (Ibid., Table 1.4, p. 23.)

In regard to balloted bills, a high position in the ballot guarantees a Second Reading debate. But Marsh and Read show that it does not by any means guarantee ultimate success. Between 1948 and 1985 there were 259 successful balloted bills. In 95 (37 per cent) the MP introducing the measure drew a position in the first six, in 73 (28 per cent) the MP's position in the ballot was between seventh and twelfth, and in 91 (35 per cent) it was thirteenth to twentieth. (Ibid., Table 2.4, p. 39.)

The major role played by government in the subject-matter of Private Members' legislation emerged from figures presented by Marsh and Read on the origins of successful balloted bills. In the fifteen-year period from 1970 there was a total of 140 such bills. Of these, 35 (25 per cent) were bills suggested to the MP by the government and drafted by parliamentary counsel; 40 (29 per cent) were based on the recommendations of an official law reform committee; a further 12 (9 per cent) were based on Law Commission reports (though 8 of the 12 were passed in the years from 1970 to 1974); a mere 15 (11 per cent) were the result of suggestions from interest groups. In 33 cases (23 per cent) the researchers did not discover the origins of the bill. (Ibid., Table 3.4, p. 48.)

The role of the government is even greater than appears from the above figures since it is directly or indirectly involved not only in the bills which actually emanate from government departments but also in those which derive from official reports and the Law Commission. So, during the Thatcher years from 1979 to 1985, a third of successful Private Members bills came directly from government departments and a further 31 per cent had their origins in official reports. The role of the government is also crucial in making time available for any controversial measure.

During the period 1964 to 1970 Private Members' legislation was used to achieve major legislative changes because the Labour Government of

17 *Private Members' Bills* (Cambridge, 1988.).

Harold Wilson with Mr Roy Jenkins as Home Secretary chose to give such measures its support. Such measures included the Abortion Act 1967 liberalising the abortion laws, the Sexual Offences Act 1967 abolishing criminal penalties for homosexual acts between consenting adults, the Theatres Act 1968 reforming the censorship laws and the Divorce Reform Act 1969 introducing the modern concept of 'no fault' divorce. But since those years very few statutes of such major significance have been Private Members' bills. Most of those that have such potential are defeated. Those that pass tend to be relatively technical and narrow.

It has been calculated that in the twenty-five years from 1950 to 1975, as many as 26 per cent of all Private Members' bills that were introduced received the Royal Assent – compared with 93 per cent of government bills.[18]

It has also been calculated that in two recent sessions, 1983–4 and 1984–5, Private Members' bills constituted no less than 13 out of 73 Public General Acts (18 per cent), and 21 out of 75 (28 per cent) respectively.[19] On average, Private Members' Acts are one-third of the length of government legislation. [20] See also Sir Henry de Waal, 'There Ought to be a Law: A Look at Private Members' Bills', 11 *Statute Law Review*, 1990, pp. 18–22; Griffith and Ryle, *Parliament*, 1989, pp. 385–400, 487–88.

For a vivid account of one such bill by its proposer see Austin Mitchell, 'A House Buyer's Bill: How Not to Pass a Private Members' Bill'. 39 *Parliamentary Affairs*, 1986, p. 1.

(e) Private bill procedure

The discussion so far has been of public bills, but Parliament passes substantial numbers of so-called private bills as well. This difference between public and private bills is not easy to describe. The original conception of a private bill is one that altered the general law in relation to a particular locality, institution or individual. An example drawn from earlier times is the act which granted a divorce before there was any general law of divorce. But today private bills tend to deal with nationalised industries, local authorities, universities, commercial undertakings and other institutions. Personal bills are now rare.

The procedure for private bills is quite different from that for public bills. The main purpose of the rules is to provide proper opportunity for

---

18 H. Beynon, *Independent Advice on Legislation*, unpublished Ph.D., Oxford University, 1982, p. 335.

19 G. Drewry, 'The Legislative Implementation of Law Reform Proposals', *Statute Law Review*, Autumn 1986, p. 165).

20 I. F. Burton and G. Drewry, *Legislation and Public Policy* (1981), p. 207.

those affected by the legislation to prepare and voice their objections. The procedure was described in a recent special study:

The Study of Parliament Group, 'Private Bill Procedure: A Case for Reform', *Public Law*, 1981, p. 206

A second reading of a public bill indicates approval of the principles of the bill: the second reading of a private bill approves the principles, subject to the need for the bill being proved at the committee stage. Also at the second reading stage a motion may be passed giving certain instructions to the committee nominated to look into the details of the bill.

The committee stage is the most complex and most critical part of the procedure. Composition of the committees varies but there is a common feature: no Ministers are present. The procedure depends upon whether a bill is opposed or unopposed. To take the simplest case first: if a bill arouses no objection the promoters have still to demonstrate at least formal proof of the expediency of the proposed measure. They will be represented by their Parliamentary Agents before the Committee on Unopposed Bills. In the Commons this body in practice normally consists of a Deputy Chairman of Ways and Means together with four backbenchers; in the Lords it comprises the Lord Chairman of Committees and, should he see fit, 'such Lords as he may select from the panel of Deputy Chairmen appointed each Session'.

An opposed bill goes to an ad hoc committee consisting in the Commons of four backbenchers and in the Lords of five peers. There is not the same continuity of knowledge and experience on these ad hoc bodies as on the committees on unopposed bills.

Arguably, where such experience is most needed, it is not available. At an opposed bill committee, promoters and opponents will normally be represented by counsel. A long contentious hearing can be very expensive for a local authority. The cost, combined with the lack of certainty of success, has in the past deterred smaller local authorities from bringing forward their own bills.

Opponents of a bill may present a petition of objection. However, promoters may claim that an objector has insufficient *locus standi* and force a preliminary inquiry into whether the petitioners should be heard. In the Lords the decision is made by the committee due to review the bill: in the Commons the issue is referred to the Court of Referees on Private Bills which consists of the Chairman and Deputy Chairmen of Ways and Means, the counsel to the Speaker and eight backbench MPs.[1]

The committee stage of an opposed private bill has something of a judicial flavour. The conflicting cases are normally presented by counsel; witnesses are examined and cross-examined. The promoters of the bill must first prove their preamble – that is, demonstrate the need for the powers requested – and then

---

1   In 1968, Standing Orders were altered to admit petitions by bodies such as amenity societies 'alleging that the interests which they represent will be adversely affected to a material extent by the provisions complained in the bill'. Before then the plaints of petitioners had to be linked to property rights.

follows a clause-by-clause examination. Arguments are not conducted simply on the basis of whether an idea has merit or how far the interests of X will be damaged. The judicial element in the proceedings has become so strong that counsel will quote previous decisions of private bill committees, a type of 'case-law', in order to strengthen their client's case.

A third method of dealing with private bills is used when a bill, although unopposed, is thought to be so important or controversial that it should be treated on the lines of an opposed bill. On such occasions the bill is sent to an Opposed Bill Committee in either or both Houses. The promoters will have to engage counsel and will be expected to provide strong evidence of need for their proposals. The decision to invoke this form of procedure is within the discretion of the Chairman of Ways and Means and the Lord Chairman of Committees.

After the committee stage in the Lords, the bill is sent forward for a third reading. In the Commons there is a report stage unless the bill has not been amended in committee. Third readings are normally a formality. The crux is the committee stage. The fact that a bill has to pass through both Houses *seriatim* involves the possibility of a second lengthy and expensive committee hearing. For any proposal with a semblance of novelty, the outcome is unpredictable. A final opportunity for conflict could arise if the two Houses fail to agree. However, if one House disallows a clause in a private bill, the other House does not reinstate it.

A very high percentage of private bills have involved railways, canals, tramways and the like. Critics of the system argued that it took up too much of the time of Members of Parliament and congested the parliamentary time-table. There was also concern that the procedure did not allow for cooption of expert assessors who could help with the evaluation of technical evidence – such as whether to build a barrage across Cardiff Bay or whether to have a new underground railway in London.

A Joint Committee of both Houses recommended that private bill procedure should no longer be used for such legislation.[2]

Following this process of consultation, the government put forward the Transport and Works Bill which became an Act in 1992. This established a new procedure under which proposals for light railway, tramway, underground railway schemes, those affecting inland waterways, diversions of rivers, canals and the like can no longer be the subject of a Private Act of Parliament. Instead they have to be authorised by Ministerial Order after procedures involving the opportunity for objectors to make representations and in some cases the holding of a public inquiry. See further Griffith and Ryle, op. cit., n. 2, p. 52 above, pp. 270, 411–12, 469–90.

2   See *Report on Private Bill Procedure*, HC 625; HL Paper 97, 1988. The government followed this by a consultation paper – *Private Bills and New Procedures: A Consultation Document*, 1990.

(f)   Hybrid bills

Some bills have features of both public and private bills. These are known as hybrid bills. A House of Commons Speaker defined hybrid bills as 'a public bill which affects a particular private interest in a manner different from the private interests of other persons or bodies of the same category or class'. Thus bills which propose works of national importance but in a local area are generally hybrid. The British Museum Bill 1962–63 and the Channel Tunnel Bill 1986–87 were examples.

Hybrid bills can be introduced by Private Members as well as by government.

The Second Reading for a hybrid bill is taken as usual for a public bill. After Second Reading however it is committed to a Select Committee made up partly of members chosen by the House and of others chosen by the Committee of Selection.

If no petitions opposing the bill are received, the bill goes to a Standing Committee which considers it like any other public bill.

If petitions opposing the bill are received, the Select Committee meets to consider the bill in much the same way as for private bills by hearing submissions and witnesses. There are however some differences. One is that the promoters do not need to establish the need for the preamble since this has already been established by the Second Reading.

Once reported by the Select Committee it goes to a Standing Committee, Report and Third Reading as for normal public bills.

A hybrid bill, like a private bill, can be put forward to be continued from one session to the next if the House of Commons agrees.

(g)   Royal Assent

Under the Royal Assent Act 1967 a new procedure of Royal Assent by Notification was introduced by which the short title of the bills which have received Royal Assent is read out in each House, together with a formula signifying the fact of assent. This is the procedure normally followed now.

For a detailed description of the process of granting Royal Assent see F. A. R. Bennion, 'Modern Royal Assent Procedure at Westminster', *Statute Law Review*, 1981, p. 133. One of the most remarkable features of the procedure is that Her Majesty does not have the texts of the bills to which she signifies her assent. She only has the short title! (ibid., p. 139.) And for a fascinating dissection of the formalities of enactment see Bernard S. Jackson,' Who Enacts Statutes?', 18 *Statute Law Review*, 1997, pp. 177–207.

2. THE IMPACT ON BILLS OF THE PARLIAMENTARY PROCESS

It is commonly assumed that the process of debate in parliament is not merely the visible manifestation of democracy but a significant part of the business of law-making through legislation. But Professor Griffith's study (op. cit., p. 61 above) shows that this is less true than is often supposed, at least if impact is measured by what happens to amendments moved to government bills.

Taking the Committee stage in the House of Commons, one-fifth of amendments were moved by Ministers, 10 per cent by government backbenchers and 70 per cent by Opposition Members (Table 3.6, p. 87). But the number of amendments agreed to in the three categories was:

Ministers	906 out of 907 (100%)
Government backbenchers	40 out of 436 (9%)
Opposition Members	131 out of 3,074 (4%)
Total	1,077 out of 4,417 (24%)

(*Source*: ibid., Table 3.8, p. 93)

Thirty-one of the 40 amendments moved by government backbenchers and agreed to, and 118 of the 131 moved by Opposition Members and agreed to, were agreed without a division. Most were classifiable as drafting, clarificatory or of very minor significance (pp. 93–119).

On Report stage, 56 per cent of amendments were moved by Ministers, 6 per cent by government backbenchers and 39 per cent by Opposition Members (Table 4.1, p. 146). The number agreed to in each category was:

Ministers	864 out of 865 (100%)
Government backbenchers	10 out of 89 (11%)
Opposition Members	29 out of 599 (5%)
Total	903 out of 1,553 (58%)

(*Source:* ibid., Table 4.3, p. 159)

Nine of the ten amendments moved successfully by government backbenchers, and 28 of the 29 moved successfully by Opposition Members, were agreed to without a division (ibid.).

In the entire three sessions there were only 26 substantive matters on which the government was defeated in Committee. On Report the government accepted the defeat in nine of these 26 cases. In the other cases the defeat was reversed (pp. 182–4).

In other words, almost all of the amendments that were moved successfully in the House of Commons were moved by Ministers – 94 per cent of those moved successfully in Committee and 96 per cent of those moved successfully on Report. According to Professor Griffith, they are not commonly the result of arguments advanced by Members. 'Usually they reflect later developments in the thinking of civil servants in the department, often reflecting pressures from interest groups' (p. 197). Of the amendments moved by government backbench and Opposition Members that were agreed to, 'only a very few can be said to be of any real substance' (p. 202). However there was a larger number of occasions when government amendments were the result of something said by Members. Professor Griffith concluded (pp. 206–7):

> Though the direct impact of the House on Government proposals for legislation was unimpressive, the indirect impact shown by the positive response of Government to points made in committee was certainly deeper. On my estimate there were 365 occasions during these three sessions when Government amendments moved on report were traceable to committee points made by Government backbenchers and Opposition Members. And of these, I have classed one-third (125 in all) as important in varying degrees. This is not an inconsiderable number.
>
> More significant than the counting of amendments is their weight and their effect on bills. Eleven bills, all of importance, were markedly affected by their passage through the House of Commons. In 1967–8 the Medicines Bill, the Race Relations Bill, and the Gaming Bill were changed in several important particulars; the Town and Country Planning Bill was reshaped and improved; and the Civil Aviation Bill emerged as a better and more coherent measure. In 1968–9 the Finance Bill was considerably amended in one important group of provisions, as were the Housing Bill and the Children and Young Persons Bill. In 1970–71, the widest range of amendments was to the Highways Bill while important limited amendments were made to the Finance Bill and to the Immigration Bill.
>
> Against these achievements, must be set the long debates, the hundreds of aborted attempts at amendment, the scores of bills, including some of the greatest importance, which remained effectively unchanged despite the efforts of Opposition Members and, to a lesser extent, of Government backbenchers. But even when Members totally fail to persuade the Government to amend its proposals, other purposes of debate may be fulfilled.
>
> When we add the achievements of non-Ministerial Members in committee to those on Report we are left with some sense of great effort making for little result and yet with a sense also that some slipshod thinking by Ministers, civil servants and draftsmen has been removed or clarified and that some bills look much better on third reading than they did on second, and that a few famous victories have been won. Whether this great effort is justified by those improvements is another matter; as is the question of the ways in which the effort might be made more effective.

In the House of Lords the success rate of amendments moved by government backbenchers and Opposition Members was somewhat higher than in the Commons. (Their combined success rate in Committee in the

Commons was 6 per cent, compared with 12 per cent in the House of Lords. The success rate on Report was 5 per cent in the Commons, compared with 19 per cent in the Lords.) Professor Griffith said (p. 231):

> When all allowance has been made for the dangers of using such statistics, the difference is not only considerable but also confirms the impression given by reading the debates in the Lords: that Ministers in the Lords are more willing to accept amendments than they are in the Commons. Partly this may be because the details of a House of Commons Bill are much more settled and firm by the time it arrives in committee in the Lords so that the effect of amendments can be more clearly seen. But partly it may be because the less contentious, less partisan, atmosphere in the Lords makes amendments moved by those who are not Ministers more likely to be accepted... .
>
> A case can always be made out for a second, third or fourth look at any proposal, whether legislative or other. And it is no part of my present task to argue the case for unicameral or bicameral legislatures. What is clear is that, with pressures as they are and with the House of Commons and Government Departments functioning as they do, legislation sometimes leaves the Commons in a state unfit to be let loose on the public. Some kind of reviewing is necessary. And the House of Lords is presently the best reviewing body we have.

But the reality is that even when the House of Lords does play a revising role it rarely controls the text of what goes into the legislation because the text of the crucial amendments is probably drafted by parliamentary counsel at the instance of the government. This was the finding of an examination of the origins of the House of Lords amendments to the British Nationality Act 1981. The original amendments were drafted by their sponsors. But once the debate had persuaded the government of the principle behind an amendment, either the amendment was redrafted by parliamentary counsel or the government brought forward its own text at a later stage.[3]

The author proposed that the House of Lords should be adapted to play a real role in improving the drafting of statutes. It might for instance be possible to imagine a House of Lords Select Committee on Drafting with specialist sub-committees similar to the Select Committee on the European Communities with its specialist subcommittees. Or possibly individuals might be appointed to a Drafting Committee for their special qualifications in the same way that some are made peers as Lords of Appeal.

Such ideas could be thought to be fanciful, the author admits, but 'present-day British legislation is often so obscure and difficult, the texts so hard to find, and it creates so much needless work for the user that one is repeatedly prompted to look for some means of improving it' (pp. 82–3).

3   T. Millett, 'The House of Lords as a Re-Writing Chamber', *Statute Law Review*, Summer 1988, pp. 70, 74.

The view that parliament provides a somewhat ineffectual form of scrutiny of government Ministers was expressed by the late Mr Richard Crossman in his diaries.

R. H. S. Crossman, *The Diaries of a Cabinet Minister* (1975), vol. I, pp. 628–9

I turn finally to the biggest question of all – the relationship of a departmental Minister to Parliament. How effectively does Parliament control him? How careful must he be in his dealings with Parliament? The answer quite simply is that there is no effective parliamentary control. All this time I never felt in any way alarmed by a parliamentary threat, even when we had a majority of only three ...

What about legislation? On the Rating Bill and the Local Government Bill there was virtually no parliamentary control. These were specialist Bills and the Opposition got nothing out of them. On the large Rent Bill there was rather more genuine discussion. As a result of Opposition pressure I was able to make a number of improvements in the Bill which I wanted and which I had been told by the Department or the parliamentary draftsmen were quite impossible. Nevertheless, I agree with those who say that the Committee Stage as managed at present is an intolerable waste of time. The Opposition only have a limited number of objections to make and they pour them all out on the early clauses, and then they get tired and give in on the later clauses and schedules which, though they may be very important, are rushed through without any proper attention.

Of course, I was spoilt by having Jim MacColl.[4] As a result of his presence I never bothered to read any of the Bills I got through. I glanced at them and I read the briefs about them and I also knew the policies from the White Papers and therefore I knew exactly how the briefs and the White Papers corresponded with the clauses of the Bills. But I never bothered to understand the actual clauses, nor did many Members, not even the spokesman for the Opposition. Both sides worked off written briefs to an astonishing extent.

I wonder whether the whole procedure of Standing Committee isn't too formalised today, with Government and Opposition facing each other and debating line by line on amendments. Wouldn't it be possible for the Minister to sit down informally and put the major principles of the Bill for the Committee to discuss? There must be a whole number of Bills on which you ought to be able to get a pooling of minds, which doesn't occur with the Standing Committee procedure in Parliament. I tried to help the Government Members by having a meeting once a week of my own back-benchers to discuss the Bill; it worked very well on the Rent Act but not on the others. I suppose the objection is that you can't do this if the Opposition are really to oppose. But quite frankly, Standing Committee is also intolerable for the Government Members – it is a terrible chore to sit there and listen to the eternal prosying of an Opposition that is usually so badly briefed that it is unable to sustain any long or detailed

---

4   Joint Parliamentary Secretary, Ministry of Housing and Local Government, 1964–9.

criticism of a Bill, and even if the Government Members know something about it they have to sit there saying nothing because discussion prolongs the time and the Government's only concern is getting things through as fast as possible.

Question

Could it be reasonably argued that civil servants play as great, and often a greater, role in legislation than MPs and even Ministers? If so, is this an inevitable feature of the process, or is it something that should be changed?

Improving the legislative process

There have been two recent reports on improving the process of legislation – one by the Commission on the Legislative Process set up by the Hansard Society (*Making the Law*, 1992), the other in 1997 by the Select Committee on the Modernisation of the House of Commons. They are dealt with here *seriatim*. (It has to be said that, so far at least, they have not produced much change.)

Hansard Society's Report The Report[5] looked in detail at what could be done to strengthen Parliament's role in legislation. Broadly it thought that if parliamentary scrutiny was to be effective there was a need for the House of Commons 'to move away from the largely party-political confrontation, substantially orchestrated by the front-benches and Whips on both sides, that at present characterises debate on bills' and to move rather 'towards a more considered approach whereby Members, from all parts of the House, could be enabled better to inform themselves and to look collectively, in a more systematic way, at the Government's legislation proposals' (para. 315, p. 79). The Society's proposals affected all stages of the process.

Pre-legislation proceedings

Departmentally-related Select Committees might helpfully examine Green and White Papers and other consultative documents issued by government and make reports which would assist in the preparatory work on legislation.

Where time allowed and a fuller inquiry into aspects of proposed legislation warranted it, Select Committees should be appointed to carry out pre-legislative inquiries. This might sometimes be done by Joint Committees of the two Houses.

5   For membership see note 12, p. 7 above.

Scrutiny of bills

The Hansard Society's Report (para. 325, p. 81) said it was 'time for a fundamental re-appraisal of these processes, with more radical solutions than hitherto proposed'. It recognised however that radical proposals for reform would be unlikely to be adopted unless they were combined with new measures through timetabling of bills to ensure that there were not worse delays in getting legislation through – on which see p. 84 below.

The Report's recommendations were addressed both to Government and to Parliament – including the Opposition. Parliament had a collective responsibility 'to ensure the quality of the legislation it enacts, and therefore to give full and effective scrutiny to the practicalities involved' (para. 327, p. 81). The Opposition had a key role: 'The Opposition is largely in command of the way bills are examined, and of how debating time is used; it has a heavy responsibility to ensure that these opportunities are not wasted and that legislation is properly scrutinised' (ibid.). Oppositions of all parties had too often failed to live up to these responsibilities: 'Much time has been wasted in standing committees, especially on long filibusters on the early clauses of contentious bills. And too much time has been spent on repetitive debates of policy aspects which should have been settled – and accepted as settled – at Second Reading.' (para. 328, p. 81). The emphasis in committee should be 'on improving the bill and not just on discrediting the policy and the Government (although those are legitimate Opposition objectives).' (para. 329, pp. 81–2).

The Report suggested that there should be two stages for the examination of bills. The first stage would be when members 'should be able to brief themselves about the purpose, meaning, and intended application of the bill' (para. 331, p. 82). At this stage there should also be an opportunity for outside bodies and people to give the House their views and information on the proposed legislation. This stage would be conducted by a Select Committee appointed specifically for the bill with power to take evidence from civil servants, experts, affected parties and the wider public. This should normally take place (as in New Zealand) before the Second Reading – indeed they should be known as First Reading Committees. Ministers and Opposition shadow-Ministers would not be on the Select Committee. The committee, which would have some 12–16 members, would have a staff whose task would include sifting and analysing written submissions made to the committee.

The Select Committee's report could 'draw attention to ambiguities in purpose or meaning, apparent problems in the application or implementation of the legislation, possible consequences of the proposed policies and other practical, technical or drafting points' (para. 337, p. 83). The committee could recommend improvements but would have no power to amend the bill.

This procedure would not be suitable for bills required in a hurry or for simple bills. Its main role would be for complex bills. The advantages would be:

> It would stem the headlong legislative rush which troubled many of those who gave evidence to us. It would make the House of Commons the ultimate focus of the widespread and growing desire to be heard and thus enhance Parliament's standing. It would give Opposition Members a much more constructive and interesting legislative role than the frustrating and negative job of seeking to obstruct proceedings in standing committees. It would enable Government back-benchers to play a more positive part in the scrutiny of bills. And it would be of value to the Government by drawing attention at the first parliamentary stage to practical problems in the application of its proposals that may have been overlooked, by helping to avoid mistakes in statute law, and finally by making legislation more acceptable to those to whom it will apply. In general, improved parliamentary scrutiny should lead to improved quality of statute law. (para. 41, p. 84).

The second stage would be the 'decision-taking stage' starting with the Second Reading. The Hansard Society Report suggested that more use might be made of Second Reading Committees where no division was expected.

The Committee stage absorbed a great deal of time. (In 1989–90, 27 government bills were considered at their Committee stage at 437 meetings – an average of 16 two and a half hour meetings per bill. Some bills had more than 30 meetings.) It was essential to try to ensure that all this time and effort was used effectively (para. 345, p. 85). The 1990 Procedure Committee (para. 312) had said 'there is widespread dissatisfaction with the way the standing committee system operates'. Many members found committee work on bills to be largely a waste of time. Government backbenchers were discouraged by their own Whips from making a contribution; the Opposition felt frustrated because they could make so little impact on the bill.

Much of the problem lay in the procedures used in Standing Committees. One defect was that the committee could not take evidence – as was possible in both the Canadian House of Commons and the Australian Senate. If Special Standing Committees (see p. 55 above) were used more for complex bills this would get over that problem. The committee should consist of the First Reading Committee, if there was one, plus Ministers and shadow-Ministers, Whips and members of the departmentally-related Select Committee. After evidence had been taken the clauses of the bill would be debated as usual. If there had already been evidence called by a First Reading Committee there might be little or no need for such evidence at this second stage. But this should be for the committee itself to decide. Evidence should not be limited, as now, to four sittings.

Circulation to Standing Committee members of Notes on Clauses and Notes on Government Amendments had become fairly general in recent years. It should now become the standard practice (para. 353, p. 87). There would also be value if, where the bill is complex or technical, Ministers and their civil servants could do a pre-committee informal factual briefing for all Members (para. 354, p. 87).

If there were many detailed points to be debated at Report stage, the bill should be re-committed to the Special Standing Committee. This would save time on the floor of the House. The same should apply on Commons consideration of detailed Lords' amendments. (paras. 355, 357, p. 87).

Procedure Committees had suggested that there should be not less than two weekends between First and Second Reading, ten days between Second Reading and the start of the Committee stage, and ten days between the end of the Committee stage and Report. But these proposed minimum time intervals were frequently broken. Sometimes the time to consider new matter was intolerably short. (Thus on the 1986 Finance Bill, 156 government amendments were tabled between 30 June and 4 July. On the 1990 Broadcasting Bill the government tabled 46 pages of technical amendments on Friday 20 July which were due to be considered on Tuesday 24 July.)

The Hansard Society's Report said this problem would be eased by systematic timetabling of all bills (see below) but that in any event minimum time-intervals between stages should be increased and longer notice should be required for amendments on Report.

The Hansard Society's Report also endorsed a recommendation of the Jellicoe Committee[6] in regard to the procedure of the House of Lords where at present all bills are examined on the floor of the House. There is no equivalent of the Standing Committee system employed in the Commons. The Jellicoe Committee recommended that in some instances a bill should be sent to a Special Standing Select Committee.

Post-legislative review

The Hansard Society's Report (para. 393, p. 95) recommended that the operation of every major Act (other than Finance Acts) and its accompanying delegated legislation should be reviewed some two to three years after it came into force by the appropriate departmentally-related select committee. If it did not have the time, a special select committee could be appointed to undertake this.

The Select Committee Report on Modernisation of the House of Commons: The Legislation Process (1997–98, HC 190) The Select

---

6   *Report of the Select Committee on the Committee Work of the House of Lords,* HL Papers 35–1, 1991–92.

Committee was charged with making proposals as to ways in which the procedure for examining legislative proposals could be improved. The proposals included:

- *Publishing Bills in draft* As many Bills as possible should be published in draft. (The Labour Government had announced that this would be done with seven bills in the coming session.) Draft bills might be considered by existing Departmentally-related Select Committees (see p. 56 above) though they tended to have full agendas and might not be able to adjust to the required tight timetable. Or the House might set up permanent legislative committees to do this but there might be a danger of overlap and confusion with departmental select committees as well as a problem of manning such committees. Another option would be ad hoc Select Committees for particular Bills which would allow selection of MPs with an interest in the subject matter. Some Bills, especially ones that were technical, would benefit from having a joint Committee with the House of Lords.

- *First Reading Committees* Some Bills should be referred for examination before Second Reading, as proposed by the Hansard Society Report. This should be done for Bills that could not be published in draft. Ministers might be more receptive to suggested improvements at that stage. The Committee could take the form of any of the four possible models applicable to pre-publication scrutiny.

- *Explanatory material* Notes on Clauses prepared by his officials for the Minister in charge of the Bill were nowadays often made available to all Members taking part in the Committee Stage. They could equally be made available for the House as a whole. This would promote a more informed Second Reading. There would also be value in having the Government Department publish a guide to the legislation, though consideration would need to be given to its status in the courts.

- *Second Reading Committees* These had not been much used. They should be used more often for uncontroversial Bills. But the rules should be changed to permit any MP to attend and to speak rather than confining the debate to the Committee members. That might encourage greater use of the device.

- *The Committee Stage* The procedure of debating amendments first and then the general principle of the clause might be reversed. Amendments might then more often be genuine attempts to improve the Bill. Also the Committee procedure should allow for circulation of written submissions.

- *Lords amendments* They take up quite a bit of time. It might be better if technical amendments were considered by the Commons Standing Committee that had originally dealt with the Bill.

- *Post-legislative scrutiny* There should be some way of Parliament monitoring the effect of legislation. It could be undertaken by Departmentally-related Select Committees and in fact that did sometimes happen. Or ad hoc Select Committees could be set up for the purpose.

- *Programming of Bills* There should be an experiment with programming of some Bills including ones that are politically controversial. On the basis of discussions between 'the usual channels', the Government should move an amendable 'programme motion' after the Second Reading which could include the date by which the Committee Stage should be completed. The Committee would then itself decide how to allocate that time. The motion would also state the amount of time proposed for Report Stage and Third Reading.
- Some Bills should be capable of being carried over from one session to the next.

The recommendations of the Select Committee were debated in the House of Commons on 13 November 1997 and had a generally favourable reception.

Pre-legislative scrutiny of human rights legislation- the requirement of a Ministerial statement of compatibility

The Human Rights Act 1998 received the Royal Assent in November 1998. It is due to be implemented sometime in the year 2000. The chief effect of the Act is to make it possible to bring proceedings in the UK courts regarding alleged breaches by 'public authorities' of the European Convention on Human Rights (ECHR). Previously such proceedings could be brought only in Strasbourg. In the years leading up to the introduction of this Act there were various suggestions for pre-legislative scrutiny of legislation to see whether it complied with the terms of the ECHR. Thus Liberty (formerly the National Council for Civil Liberties) proposed the appointment of a joint committee of both Houses of Parliament charged with the examination of all new legislation to assess its compatibility with the Bill of Rights.[7] The Hansard Society (paras.412–13) suggested that the task be done in the House of Lords by the Select Committee on the Scrutiny of Delegated Legislation. Mr Michael Ryle, former Clerk of Committees in the House of Commons, proposed that there should be two joint committees of both Houses – one for primary legislation and one for delegated legislation.[8]

The Human Rights Act 1998, s.19 requires that the Minister in charge of a Bill make a written statement regarding compatibility before the Second

---

7   F.Klug and J.Wadham, 'The democratic entrenchment of a Bill of Rights: Liberty's proposals'(1993) *Public Law*, p. 579.
8   *Public Law*, 1994, pp. 192–97.

Reading debate. Such a statement would say either that the provisions of the Bill were compatible with the ECHR or that, although no such statement could be made, the Government wished to proceed with the Bill. This will therefore require each proposed piece of Government legislation to be 'Convention proofed' prior to its introduction. Section 19 was brought into force on Royal Assent.

3. THE LEGISLATIVE PROGRAMME AND TIMETABLING

Two-year programming

Governments, as has been seen, work on the basis of a one-year-plus cycle for bills. They are approved in principle by the Future Legislation Committee by the spring, drafted during the spring and summer, introduced sometime from the autumn onwards and have to become law by the following autumn. For ordinary bills this may be enough time. But often it is not – and as a result bills are commonly introduced in a half-baked form.

The Hansard Society's Report proposed (para. 485, p. 116) that governments should move toward the adoption of a two-year cycle. Thus the Future Legislation Committee should decide on the broad shape of the legislative programme for the next two years. In particular, it should identify the larger more complex bills that required preparation over two years.

It also recommended (para. 490, p. 117) that there should be the possibility of carrying bills over from one session to another. This had been rejected by the Procedure Committee in 1984–85 (HC 49-I of 1984–85, para. 24) but the Hansard Society Report said this was based on purely parliamentary considerations. It was able to take a broader view. Carrying a bill on from one session to the next would be especially useful where a bill passed the Commons late in a session. Better to carry it over to the next session than rush it through the Lords or drop it and have to start afresh.

Timetabling of bills

Timetabling of legislation is a problem in the House of Commons. The Hansard Society Report said 'It is essentially a problem for the Commons; in the Lords informal agreements appear to work well and we have received no evidence in favour of change'. In the Commons, it continued, 'timetabling of debates on bills ranges from none at all, through a considerable measure of voluntary timetabling by agreement between the parties, through the use of the closure (a declining practice) to the imposition of a formal guillotine imposed after lengthy time-wasting debate (a growing practice).' (Para. 505, p. 120.)

The closure is a procedure (under Standing Order No. 35) whereby any Member may at any time move 'That the question be now put'. The closure motion is then put forthwith unless the Speaker decides that the motion is an 'abuse of the rules of the House' or 'an infringement of the rights of the minority.' But there must be at least 100 Members in the majority. If the closure is agreed, the question on the motion being closured must then also be put forthwith.[9]

The guillotine[10] is a method of compulsorily timetabling debate on a bill. The guillotine resolution has to be moved in the House of Commons. Once granted, subsequent debate follows the terms of the timetable as laid down in the resolution. It is used when the government finds progress on a bill frustrated by Opposition filibustering – usually during the Committee stage. It normally generates considerable protest from the Opposition and governments do not like using it.

The Commons Select Committee on Procedure in 1984–85 recommended that there should be a Legislative Business Committee of 13 senior Members of the House, having a government majority but acting independently in the interests of back-benchers. If they considered that a government bill was likely to require more than 25 hours in committee, it would recommend that the bill should be reported after a stated maximum number of hours. The details would then be worked out by a business sub-committee drawn from the membership of the standing committee dealing with the bill. The Procedure Committee's proposal when considered by the Commons was however defeated.[11] In 1985–86 the Procedure Committee somewhat modified its proposal to having a timetable worked out by a sub-committee of the standing committee. But the Government took no action. In 1990 the Select Committee on Sittings of the House (the Jopling Committee[12]) recommended timetabling for all bills committed to a standing sub-committee and that the timetable should be worked out as proposed by the Procedure Committee (paras. 63–69). However the government still took no action.

The Hansard Society Report in November 1992 agreed that timetabling was vital if proper scrutiny of legislation was to be achieved. In particular it would be impossible to get Ministers to agree to First Reading Committees or fuller scrutiny by special Standing Committees (p. 55 above) unless they were satisfied that they could get bills through. This meant extensive timetabling.

The most frequently voiced objection was that timetabling would reduce the power of the Opposition but on this the Hansard Society's Report said:

9   See further Griffith and Ryle, *Parliament*, pp. 222–27, 301–07, and G. Ganz, 'Recent Developments in the use of Guillotine Motions'; *Public Law*, Winter 1990, pp. 497–506.
10   See further Griffith and Ryle, *Parliament*, pp. 302–07.
11   92 Official Report (HC), col. 1083–1130 (27 February 1986).
12   HC 20–1 of 1990–91.

We do not believe that this would result in any real loss of influence for the Opposition as research indicates that in very few cases, if any, has the so-called time weapon actually succeeded in making a government change its mind. All that the weapon has usually achieved is long, boring, time-wasting filibusters on the early clauses of controversial bills, followed by guillotines that normally result in many of the provisions of the bill escaping all scrutiny or debate. [Para. 513, p. 122.]

4.   WHEN DOES A STATUTE COME INTO FORCE?

But even when a statute has received the Royal Assent it does not necessarily become law. This is because sometimes the statute specifies that it, or parts of it, shall come into force on a date to be fixed by the Minister. It is then often a matter of some difficulty to discover whether any particular part of the Act has or has not come into force. This problem was the burden of a *cri de coeur* from an academic contributor to *The Magistrate*:

Alec Samuels, 'Is It in Force or Isn't It?', *The Magistrate*, November 1979, pp. 173–4

Parliament has a nasty habit of passing new laws and then either not bringing them into force, or bringing them into force only after inordinate delay, or bringing them into force piece-meal, often in a sudden and haphazard manner. A new Act may look good on paper, and in political terms, but resources are not made available for implementation, and the thing just lies fatuously and uselessly on the statute book.

The law to be applied in magistrates' courts ought to be simple, straightforward, and readily accessible, and it should be possible easily and immediately to ascertain whether or not it is in force. Although the justices' clerk is probably aware of the true position, the relatively young and inexperienced court clerk in court No. 5 may not be so well informed. This is unfair. The court clerk cannot repeatedly leave his court in order to consult the justices' clerk himself.

The Criminal Law Act 1977 is a good example of how not to do things, The Act was really three Acts contained in one Act, namely conspiracy, squatting and magistrates' courts procedure. There were five different commencement dates. Statutory instruments brought different bits of the Act into force on different dates. Bits of sections, bits of subsections and bits of paragraphs were brought into force, at different times. There was no progressive or cumulative table of commencement orders. The section providing for the prosecution to disclose statements to the defence before the trial (s. 48) is still not in force, nor is the power to impose a partly suspended sentence (s. 47).

The power to impose a suspended sentence supervision order for a sentence of more than six months is so far applicable only in the Crown Court (Powers of Criminal Courts Act 1973, s. 26, deriving from the Criminal Justice Act

1972), although for two or more imprisonable offences magistrates frequently have the power to sentence to up to twelve months' imprisonment. The Bail Act 1976 took seventeen months to come into operation, because of the complicated rules and forms.

Several parts of the Children and Young Persons Act 1969 have not been brought into force, and it may be that they never will.

The new adoption law (Adoption Act 1976, deriving from the Children Act 1975) is not yet in force, although the freeing for adoption procedure, i.e. freeing the child before the adoption order itself comes to be made, would be very useful. A custodianship order, i.e. to give greater legal powers to foster parents, is still not available to the court (Children Act 1975, Part II). Provisions for legal representation and legal aid for children are only partly in force (Children Act 1975, s. 65). The Domestic Proceedings and Magistrates' Courts Act 1978, providing for completely new law and procedure in domestic cases, is not yet in force, apart from a few minor bits, and the starting date is still unknown.

The annual Administration of Justice Act and similar miscellaneous provisions legislation constantly amend and tinker about with existing statutes, which gradually become a terrible mess, making for terrible difficulties, for example, the Magistrates' Courts Act 1952 and the Guardianship of Minors Acts 1971 and 1973. They are not reprinted or consolidated in one clean copy.

Pleas to parliament

1. Do not pass a new statute unless and until it can be brought into force promptly.

2. Do not put two or more statutes into one statute.

3. Bring the whole of the statute into force at one time.

4. Bring the statute into force on a sensible date, e.g. 2 January or 1 September or 1 October, i.e. following a national holiday or other break during which the lawyers can study it.

5. Give sufficient advance notice of the commencement date.

6. Draft the statute in such a way that if it really has to be brought into force on different dates this can be simply done, e.g. Part I, Part II, Part III, each part entire and self-contained.

7. If the statute really has to be brought into force in stages, then supply a cumulative table of commencement orders.

8. Remember that the convenience of the users, magistrates, their clerks, advocates, public officials, and ultimately the public at large, is of more importance than the transient convenience of Parliament.

A partial solution to the problem posed by Mr Samuels is to include in the principal Act a Schedule of commencement dates, transitional provisions and repeals. This Schedule would be amended each time the principal Act was amended, so that the text of the Act with amendments would at all times be up to date – through noting up or reprinting.

A report on the problem by the Statute Law Society stated that 64 of the 105 Acts passed between January 1978 and April 1979 postponed commencement in whole or in part and the commencement provisions were of thirteen different kinds. In 34 instances, commencement was on different dates for different sections; in 32 cases, commencement dates were left wholly or partly to be fixed by statutory instrument; and in 28 cases both of these features were present. ('Statute Law Society Working Party on Commencement of Acts of Parliament', *Statute Law Review,* 1980, pp. 40, 41.)

One practical disadvantage of commencement taking place on the day of Royal Assent is that the Act has not been published then and is therefore not available to be purchased at the Stationery Office. Sometimes printing takes several weeks. The Committee proposed (ibid., p. 44) that, unless otherwise stated, all Acts should come into force on a date six weeks after Royal Assent.

In other cases, if commencement was to take place within three months or so of Royal Assent the date should be specified in the Act itself (p. 45). Where different dates were fixed by different statutory instruments, the Committee suggested that the latest such order should always state the full cumulative situation, including the provisions brought into force and their commencement date and a list of provisions not yet in force (p. 48). The government should provide a telephone information service to answer queries about commencement dates.

In regard to statutory instruments, there was a provision (Statutory Instruments Act 1946, s. 3) that in any proceedings for the contravention of such an instrument it should normally be a defence that, at the date of the offence, it had not been published. 'There should be equivalent provisions regarding statutes' (p. 51). In fact such provisions should go further, to provide that no statute should be applied so as to affect anyone's rights adversely unless either it had been published or reasonable steps had been taken to bring the purport of the Act and its commencement provisions to the attention of those likely to be affected (p. 52).

Guidance was issued to government departments in November 1980 that, where there was more than one commencement order, the second and subsequent ones should list earlier orders and the provisions that had already been brought into force.[13]

In 1981 the Law Commission adopted a practice of providing in its bills that they should come into force three months after Royal Assent unless there were specific provisions to the contrary. This has now been adopted.

In 1982 the government announced new guidance to government departments regarding commencement. This stated that where there is no provision for commencement to be appointed by a commencement order, the Act should provide for it to come into force on a day not less than two months from Royal Assent. This would assist both practitioners and the public. Also Parliamentary Counsel had agreed normally to group all

13 See *Statute Law Review,* 1981, pp. 174, 179.

commencement provisions together in statutes (rather than having them scattered throughout the text). Where possible the commencement date would be specified in the Act itself. (See *Law Society's Gazette*, 21 April 1982, p. 427; 28 July 1982, p. 968. See also Francis Bennion, 'Bringing Acts into Force', *New Law Journal*, 2 April 1981, p. 356; J. R. Spencer, 'When is a Law not a Law?', *New Law Journal*, 18 June 1981, p. 644; and *Statute Law Review*, 1982, p. 169, and 1983, p. 42.)

In 1985 Butterworths produced a new solution to the problem in a publication entitled *Is It in Force?* It was intended that this should be an annual publication. It relates to statutes passed since 1960. It gives repeals. For Acts that are still extant it sets out the date of Royal Assent, commencement provisions and indications of provisions not yet in force. Statutes are listed alphabetically under each of the years covered. But obviously it does not cover statutes that have only just been passed, nor those passed before 1960.

The best way of discovering whether the statutory provision in question is in force is through the computerized system called Lexis (p. 253 below), but this only applies to statutes passed since 1980.

Note

Some further 'commencement' horror stories were instanced in Sweet & Maxwell's *Current Sentencing Practice News*, Issue 1, 29 October 1991:

- ss. 108–115 of the Criminal Justice Act 1988 putting the Criminal Injuries Compensation Board onto a statutory basis had not been brought into force. [In the end the sections were never implemented but new legislation was introduced in 1995.]
- The Criminal Justice Act 1988 had two fixed commencement dates in the Act itself and a total of 12 commencement orders to date, some bringing provisions into effect for limited purposes only. Three different sets of provisions were brought into force on different dates within a 14-day-period, others came into effect before related provisions without which they were meaningless.

A different kind of problem was posed by provisions in the Criminal Justice Act 1993 radically amending controversial sentencing provisions in the Criminal Justice Act 1991. The 1993 Act received the Royal Assent on 27 July 1993. The new provisions regarding sentencing came into force less than three weeks later on 16 August. On 9 August *The Guardian* reported that probation officers had been given two days to respond to a draft Home Office circular explaining how the new sentencing rules would work. It was sent out on Wednesday and asked for responses by Friday lunchtime. The 1993 Act involved a major change in the role of probation officers in sentencing in that it required them for the first time to advise courts on the 'seriousness' of an offence. Probation officers were said to fear that without proper training the complex new provisions would 'be open to widely conflicting interpretations and lead to even greater chaos in sentencing'.

But the Government cannot simply ignore a statute and decide to implement the policy by a completely different prerogative system. The House of Lords held that the Home Secretary could not set up a Criminal Injuries Compensation Scheme by prerogative order when the Criminal Justice Act 1988 set one up under statute – *R v Secretary of State for the Home Department, ex p. Fire Brigades Union* [1995] 2 WLR 1, [1995] 2 All ER 244. For comment see A. Samuels, 'Is it in Force?', Must it be Brought into Force?' 17 *Statute Law Review*, 1996, pp. 62–65.

5. STATUTES ON COMPUTERISED DATABASE

The Hansard Society 1992 Report[14] said:

> At present the accessibility of statute law to users and the wider public is slow, inconvenient, complicated and subject to several impediments. To put it bluntly, it is often very difficult to find out what the text of the law is – let alone what it means. Something must be done. [Para. 452, p. 108.]

One problem was that sometimes Acts came into force days or even weeks before they were available at the Stationery Office for sale. The Hansard Society recommended that Acts should not be brought into force until they are published.

One of the main difficulties for users of statutory materials is keeping abreast of amendments in later legislation and statutory instruments.

Since 1991 the Lord Chancellor's Department has been engaged in a new project to put all public Acts currently contained in *Statutes in Force* together with all amendments made since the base date of 1991 onto a computerised database.[15] Amendments would be applied to the database so that the text would always show the latest version of the Act as amended. The Statute Law Database (SLD) project is also to include selected statutory instruments published after the base date. The SLD will therefore hold all the primary legislation and selected delegated legislation current in February 1991 and the full text of all legislation after that date. Where post-1991 legislation is amended the earlier text will therefore be retained as an historical record.

---

14 Note 12, p. 7 above.
15 The contract was awarded to a private concern – Secure Information Systems Ltd based in Fleet, Hampshire.

The project is intended initially for the use of parliamentary counsel and government departments. But when it has been tested within the public service it is intended to make it available to legal practitioners and other users in the private sector – as well as in public libraries, Citizens' Advice Bureaux and the like.

The Hansard Society said that some bodies using the new database would be unable to meet high charges. There would be a need for some government subsidy to keep the cost down. There was equally a need for a subsidy for all legislative materials.

6. THE REACH OF LEGISLATION

Most public Acts apply to the whole of Great Britain: that is to say, England, Scotland and Wales. The Scottish legal system differs in some respects from that of England and Wales. Some Acts apply only to Scotland; some apply only to England and Wales. Between 1921 and 1972 domestic legislation for Northern Ireland was the responsibility of Stormont – the provincial Parliament. Stormont was suspended in 1972 and direct rule was substituted. Most Northern Ireland legislation was proposed in the form of Orders in Council passed like statutory instruments (see below).

But law-making for Scotland, Wales and Northern Ireland will be transformed by the three devolution Acts: The Scotland Act 1998, the Government of Wales Act 1998 and the Northern Ireland Act 1998 passed to give effect to the Good Friday Agreement of Easter 1998. Each provides different machinery for legislation. Scotland will have the most devolved power. The first Scottish and Welsh Assemblies under the 1998 Acts were elected on 6 May 1999. (For analysis of current devolution issues, see for instance, *Constitutional Futures: A History of the Next Ten Years*, ed. R. Hazell, The Constitution Unit, OUP, 1999.)

7. DELEGATED LEGISLATION

Each year over 2,000 sets of rules and regulations are made by Ministers or the Crown in Council[16] or other central rule-making authorities – by comparison with less than a hundred public Acts of Parliament. This form of legislation is under the authority of powers delegated by Parliament. (The residual power to legislate under royal prerogative is no longer of much importance.) The reason is usually to avoid having too much detail

---

16 For the procedure used for Orders in Council, see Cyril E. S. Horsford, 'The Order in Council', *Solicitors' Journal*, 10 April 1987, p. 462.

in the main Act and thereby to waste the time of parliamentarians in minutiae. The delegated power to make regulations also enables the responsible Minister to respond to new circumstances by amplifying the original rules without troubling Parliament with matters of detail that are within principles dealt with in the original legislation. Sometimes, however, Parliament leaves to Ministers power to issue regulations on matters of principle.

The most sweeping grant of delegated legislative power to the Executive is undoubtedly that in s. 2(2) of the European Communities Act 1972, which permits Orders in Council and regulations by designated Ministers and government departments to be made to give effect to Community instruments and provisions of the Treaties which do not have direct effect (see p. 377 below). The Act provides that such delegated powers are to have the effect of Acts of Parliament and can include any provision that could have been included in an Act of Parliament except that they may not impose or increase taxation; have retroactive effect; sub-delegate legislative powers; or create new criminal offences punishable with more than two years' imprisonment or fines of over £400.

For another example of delegated legislation see the Hallmarking Act 1973, s. 7(a) of which gives the Secretary of State, 'after consulting the Council and such other persons as he thinks fit', authority to 'make regulations wholly or partly varying, supplementing or replacing the provisions of the section'. The International Transport Conventions Act 1983, ss. 8 and 9, allows that statute to be amended by delegated legislation; so does the Transport Act 1985, s. 46. The Courts and Legal Services Act 1990, s. 125(4) gives the Lord Chancellor the power by order to 'make such amendments or repeals in relevant enactments as appear to him to be necessary or expedient in consequence of any provision made by Part II with respect to advocacy, litigation, conveyancing or probate services'. Such provisions giving Ministers the power to amend and even to repeal statutory provisions by statutory instruments are known as 'Henry VIII clauses'. (Henry VIII clauses were denounced by Lord Oliver of Aylmerton in an address to the Statute Law Society in 1992): 'Even more reprehensible is the increasingly common use of the so-called "Henry VIII clause", enabling a Secretary of State, which means, in practice, some unelected civil servant, to amend, and even sometimes to repeal, primary legislation.'[17]

Most delegated legislation is issued in the form of statutory instruments which are available from the Stationery Office. Their drafting is usually left to the legal advisers in departments – though in cases of particular importance or difficulty Parliamentary Counsel will be brought in. The process of outside consultation is usually fuller than is the case with legislation proper. The need for secrecy is less, since the principles of the

17 *Statute Law Review*, 1993, p.1,3.

new law have already been laid down and the department is therefore less reluctant to take advice on matters of implementation. Sometimes regulations are published in draft for comment. See for instance *Law Society's Gazette*, 29 October 1986, 3238. In some cases consultation is even mandatory. Thus procedural regulations for tribunals and inquiries must be submitted in draft to the Council on Tribunals (Tribunals and Inquiries Act 1971, ss. 10, 11). Under the Deregulation and Contracting Out Act 1994, s. 3, before making a deregulation order the Minister is obliged to consult organisations representative of the interests substantially affected by his proposals and such other persons as he considers appropriate. If as a result of those consultations he decides to vary his proposals he must consult further on the variations.

Parliamentary scrutiny of delegated legislation is usually slight. Some statutory instruments, whose subject matter is not felt to be of importance, are simply laid before Parliament. There is no actual procedure for them to be discussed, though any MP who wishes can ask the responsible Minister about it or can seek to raise the matter in debate. But more often the enabling Act states that instruments must be laid before Parliament and shall become law unless within a period of a few days a resolution is passed to annul it. This is known as the 'negative resolution' procedure. The period is usually forty days. (The Deregulation and Contracting Out Act 1994, s. 4 provides for an additional sixty days for parliamentary scrutiny before a final order is laid for formal debate and approval. As will be seen below, the Human Rights Act 1998 provides for 120 days.)

But even if a group of Members decide to challenge such an instrument (by what is called a 'prayer') there is no guarantee that the government will provide time for a debate or the opportunity of a vote. The Opposition can use one of their own precious 'Supply Dates' for the debate. A debate is only guaranteed for the minority of statutory instruments which have to be passed by an affirmative resolution[18] (as opposed to the normal 'negative resolution' procedure). But even then the statutory instrument cannot be amended in the course of the debate. It can only be approved, annulled or withdrawn. During the Committee stage of the Courts and Legal Services Bill 1990 Lord Mackay, the Lord Chancellor, said that in future he would see that the affirmative resolution procedure would be used for all statutory instruments giving effect to 'Henry VIII clauses'. The Deregulation and Contracting Out Act 1994 has an unusual procedure. Section 3 of the Act requires the Minister to lay before Parliament an explanatory memorandum with a draft of the order and the reasons for the measure, its specific benefits, the consultation which has been undertaken and the changes, if any, which the Minister has made as a result of those consultations. Such a memorandum has to be considered by a special

18 See further Griffith and Ryle, *Parliament*, pp. 331–37, 343–50.

Deregulation Committee of 16 Members with the power to call evidence. If, in the event, the Committee reports unanimously that an order should be approved without amendment, the matter is determined without debate. If it recommends approval by a majority, the debate is limited to one and a half hours. If the Committee is against approval it can only be approved if the House so decides after a three-hour debate.

Fast track procedure by Order in Council for 'remedial orders' under the Human Rights Act 1998

The Human Rights Act 1998 permits proceedings on the basis that a public authority has acted in a way that is inconsistent with the European Convention on Human Rights (ECHR). If it arises in the form of primary legislation, the courts will not be able to strike it down. Instead, providing the court is of appropriate authority, it will have the power to make a declaration of incompatibility, i.e. that the legislation is incompatible with the ECHR (s.4 (2)). Courts that will have the power to make a declaration of incompatibility are the House of Lords, the Court of Appeal, the Divisional Court and the High Court (s. 4(5)). If the inconsistency (or 'unlawful act') is in the form of subordinate rather than primary legislation the court *can* strike it down or refuse to apply it unless the subordinate legislation is directly required by the parent Act.

A declaration of incompatibility does not invalidate the statutory provision. It simply alerts the Government to the problem. The Government then has to decide whether to change the law to bring it into line with the Convention or whether to wait for the aggrieved litigant to bring proceedings in Strasbourg. But, provided the Minister considers that there are 'compelling reasons' for speedy action, amendment of the primary legislation does not require legislation. Instead it can be done 'by Order in Council – which means by subordinate legislation (s.10 (2)). A remedial order can 'contain such incidental, supplemental, consequential or transitional provision as the person making it considers appropriate' (Sched.2, 1(1)(a)). This phrase, which is typically used in such cases, has been criticised by Lord Oliver of Aylmerton as 'thoroughly objectionable constitutionally': 'It is unfair to the citizen, who is entitled in a democratic society to have the rules by which his life is to be regulated properly debated and scrutinised by his elected representatives'.[19]

The Order in Council has to be approved by affirmative resolution of both Houses of Parliament. But instead of the usual 40 days period of being 'laid before Parliament', such 'remedial orders' are subject to a special procedure (see Schedule 2) by which the proposed Order in Council would have to wait normally for 120 days after first being published (60 days in draft plus another 60 days) before being approved by resolution in both

19 *Statute Law Review*, 1993, pp.1,3.

Houses. (If the matter is urgent it can be done in less time.) If while the Order is in draft, representations are made, the Minister must accompany the re-laying of the draft order after the first 60 days with a statement summarising the representations received and, if they have resulted in changes, giving details of the changes. In urgent cases this information must be given after the Order has been made and a replacement Order must be made to give effect to any changes. This fast track procedure for remedial orders in response to declarations of incompatibility. It has been severely criticised by some as an unwarranted new manifestation of Henry VIII clause.

Joint Select Committee on Statutory Instruments

Since 1973 there has been a Joint Select Committee on Statutory Instruments of both Houses to consider, inter alia, statutory instruments of a general character and those subject to the negative and affirmative resolution procedure. Its function is to review statutory instruments from a technical and not from a policy point of view. Its chairman, to emphasise this point, is a member of the Opposition rather than of the government.

The function of the Committee is to determine whether the special attention of each House should be drawn to an instrument on any of nine grounds:

(i)   that it imposes a tax or a charge;
(ii)   that it is made under primary legislation which expressly excludes the instrument from challenge in the courts;
(iii)   that it purports to have retrospective effect where the enabling Act does not expressly provide for such effect;
(iv)   that there appears to have been unjustifiable delay in the publication of the instrument or in laying it;
(v)   that the instrument has come into operation before being laid and there appears to have been unjustifiable delay in sending notification of this as required by the Statutory Instruments Act 1946, s. 4(1);
(vi)   that it appears doubtful whether the instrument is intra vires the enabling statute, or the instrument appears to make some unusual or unexpected use of the powers in the enabling legislation;
(vii)   that for any special reason the form or purport of the instrument calls for elucidation;
(viii) that the drafting of the legislation appears to be defective;
(ix)   any other ground which does not impinge on the merits of the instrument or on the policy behind it.

In determining these matters the Committee has the assistance of Counsel to the Speaker and Counsel to the Lord Chairman of Committees and, of course, takes written and oral evidence from the departments responsible for making the regulations.

As has been seen, the Committee does not, however, consider the merits of statutory instruments or of the policies behind them. That is done either on the floor of the House or in the case of the House of Commons, in one of the standing committees on statutory instruments. These procedures are also defective. The debates on the floor of the House usually take place late at night and are poorly attended. Debates in standing committees are for up to one and half hours.[20]

See further J. D. Hayhurst and P. Wallington, 'The Parliamentary Scrutiny of Delegated Legislation', *Public Law*, Winter 1988, pp. 547–76. The authors argue that the use of delegated legislation has changed significantly especially in the previous decade or so. 'It is no longer the technical implementation of detail in a legislative mosaic, although undoubtedly the majority of statutory instruments are in this category. More of the policy of a legislative proposal is likely to be delegated, the legislation being enabling not just at a specific but at the broadest level.' (P. 573.) They instanced the recasting of the supplementary benefit system done principally by regulations under the Social Security Act 1986. Other examples were the Legal Aid Act 1988 and the Education Reform Act 1988. The last named Act was an example of the 'increasingly common practice' of conferring power to amend the Act itself and 'of the astonishingly detailed rule-making powers that may be given to a minister' (p. 574). They conclude: 'Delegated legislation, in other words, matters, and matters increasingly, and its scrutiny, whether by parliament or the courts, is not just a tedious corner of the constitutional edifice' (ibid.).

They were pessimistic about the prospects but they did find that the Joint Committee was working well. Its mere presence was helpful quite apart from the content of its reports.

They made a variety of procedural proposals to improve scrutiny of delegated legislation (pp. 575–76).

The Hansard Society's 1992 Report on the Legislative Process *(Making the Law)* said: 'We consider the whole of the approach of Parliament to delegated legislation to be highly unsatisfactory. The House of Commons in particular should give its procedures for scrutiny of statutory instruments a thorough review' (para. 366, p. 90).

One proposal it made was that departmentally-related Select Committees might review statutory instruments in their field when they are laid before Parliament and report on those that raise matters of public importance.

The Report expressed concern that sometimes criticisms made by the Joint Committee on Statutory Instruments were ignored by Ministers. The Committee it said did valuable work. 'However some of its critical findings appear to be ignored by Ministers. We heard from the Chairman of the

20   T. St John Bates, 'Parliament, Policy and Delegated Legislation', *Statute Law Review*, Summer 1986, p. 117.

Committee that some instruments on which his Committee had reported adversely had not been debated. We also understand that debates on affirmative resolutions, approving instruments, are quite often held before the Committee has had time to report' (para. 370, p. 90). The Hansard Society Report said: 'We find this very unsatisfactory. If the Joint Committee is to be effective, its reports must be heeded and Ministers should be required to answer its criticisms in debate' (para. 371, p. 91). It recommended (ibid.) that no statutory instrument should be debated until the Joint Committee had reported. Where the Joint Committee reports that it finds an instrument to be defective a motion to approve the instrument should not be made without a resolution to set aside the Committee's findings. (This in effect is what happened in Australia.)

On the question of how statutory instruments are debated, the Hansard Society Report said (para. 372, p. 91): 'We see little merit in short debates late at night on the floor of the House with few Members taking part, as often happens now'. The Report agreed with the report of the House of Commons Select Committee on Sittings of the House ('the Jopling Report')[1] that it was desirable to free the time of the House itself by sending most delegated legislation to Standing Committees for debate. It recommended that all statutory instruments requiring affirmative resolutions and all 'prayers' for the annulment of a statutory instrument should automatically be referred to Standing Committees for debate. Longer or more complicated statutory instruments which did not have to be approved in a hurry could sometimes be sent to a special Standing Committee which could hear evidence (para. 373, p. 91). A prime objective, it suggested, was to make it possible for Members to play a constructive part in the work of Standing Committees on statutory instruments so that they would find it worthwhile to spend time on them. It made a number of other detailed recommendations:

- Before a committee started debating a statutory instrument, it should be able to question Ministers on the purpose, meaning and effect of the instrument. This would follow the procedure established for European Community documents in Standing Committees which had proved helpful (para. 375, p. 91).
- There should be a substantive motion to enable the committee to approve or reject it or otherwise express an opinion – as opposed to merely stating that it had considered the instrument (para. 376, p. 92).
- Although the Report did not recommend that the House or its committees should be given the power to amend statutory instruments, it should be possible for Members to move and vote on amendments without amending the instrument. This could be achieved if there

1   HC 20–I of 1991–92, paras. 72–73.

were a motion to approve an instrument subject to specified amendments being made. If this passed, the Minister could withdraw the instrument, amend it and bring it back for reconsideration (para. 379, p. 92).

- Subject to general timetabling there should no longer be an arbitrary time-limit on debates on statutory instruments in Standing Committees (para. 380, p. 93).
- Although not all 'prayers' against statutory instruments could be debated, at least those that are serious should be. (In 1985–86, 69 per cent were not debated; in 1990–91, 78 per cent were not debated.) The failure to debate 'prayers' was 'a major erosion of Parliament's rights and a potential weakening of the scrutiny of delegated legislation' (para. 387, p. 94).

In 1993 the government established in the House of Lords a Delegated Powers Scrutiny Committee – following a recommendation of the Jellicoe Committee (the Select Committee of the House of Lords on the Committee Work of the House[2]). The Committee was first established on an experimental basis for one session, but in November 1994 the House of Lords agreed to give the committee permanent status. The purpose of the Committee is to consider 'whether the provisions of any bill inappropriately delegate legislative power, or whether they subject the exercise of legislative power to an inappropriate degree of parliamentary scrutiny'. The Scrutiny Committee has no power to amend bills but simply reports its findings before the Committee stage.

When it started work the Committee had a memorandum from Government which stated an intention that together with each Bill the relevant Government Department should produce a memorandum for the Committee identifying any provisions for delegated legislation, briefly stating their purpose and why the matter had been left to delegated legislation and explaining why the affirmative or negative procedure was being used. The Committee's first report (HL Paper 90, 1993–94) said that these memoranda substantially reduced the occasions when the Committee recommended that a power be considered by the House. The Committee said that it had in every case managed to make its views known on bills before Committee Stage.[3]

See further Alan Beith, 'Prayers Unanswered: A Jaundiced View of the Parliamentary Scrutiny of Statutory Instruments', *Parliamentary Affairs*, 1981, p. 165; P. Byrne, 'Parliamentary Control of Delegated Legislation', *Parliamentary Affairs*, 1976, p. 366; J. D. Hayhurst and P. Wallington, 'The

2   HL 35–1 of 1991–92, para. 306.
3   For the history of the setting up of the Committee and a first assessment see C.M.G.Himsworth, 'The delegated powers scrutiny committee', *Public Law*, 1995, pp. 34–44.

Parliamentary Scrutiny of Delegated Legislation', *Public Law*, 1988, p. 547. On the Deregulation and Contracting Out Act 1994 see Michael Ryle, 15 *Statute Law Review*, 1994, pp. 170–81.

Judicial scrutiny of ordinary legislation is of course not possible under the constitution. The courts must accept a statute as law. But delegated legislation can be challenged both directly and indirectly before the courts. (For a dramatic recent example see *R* v. *Lord Chancellor, ex p. Witham* [1997] 2 All ER 779 in which the Divisional Court ruled that the Lord Chancellor had acted unlawfully in making new regulations regarding court fees for civil cases which did not preserve the traditional special dispensation for poor litigants.) The subject is a large one and is not dealt with here. (See especially on this topic Stanley de Smith, *Constitutional Law and Administrative Practice* (eds H. Street and R. Brazier, 6th edn, 1989), and de Smith, Woolf and Jowell, *Judicial Review of Administrative Action* (5th edn, 1997). For further reading on legislation see generally Miers and Page, *Legislation*.

See also pp. 400–03 below on Codes of Practice, guidelines, circulars, etc.

According to Hayhurst and Wallington, op. cit., p. 98 above, there were 15 cases in which statutory instruments were challenged successfully in the courts between 1914–86. See also A. W. Bradley, 'Judicial Enforcement of Ultra Vires Byelaws: The Proper Scope of Severance', *Public Law*, Autumn 1990, p. 293 and D. J. Whelan, 'Scrutiny of Delegated Legislation by the Australian Senate', 12 *Statute Law Review*, 1991, pp. 87–100.

Delegated legislation – some Anglo-American comparisons

One strange fact is the difference in the interest in delegated legislation in England and the United States. This was the subject of a fascinating comparative study by Professor Michael Asimow of the University of California.[4] His point of departure was the observation that 'In the USA the substance of regulations and the procedure by which they are made, present issues which generate enormous controversy in political, judicial and academic circles. In Britain, nearly everyone seems satisfied with (and hardly anyone seems interested in) procedural and substantive aspects of delegated legislation' (ibid., p. 253).

In the USA, delegated legislation is the field of rule-making by regulatory agencies created by Congress to regulate a great variety of fields – airlines, trucking, roads, railways, radio and television, corporate securities, labour relations, energy pricing, business practices, financial institutions, etc.

---

4   'Delegated Legislation in the United States and United Kingdom', 3 *Oxford Journal of Legal Studies*, 1983, p. 253.

The agencies, in Asimow's phrase, 'generated a huge number of highly controversial regulations which attracted attention to the subject in legal and economic literature as well as in the popular press. A vast number of court decisions have focused on procedural requirements for making rules and clarification of the scope of the court's power to review the rules' (p. 254).

In the first part of his study Asimow drew a picture of the system in the US and in Britain. In the second half he offered some reflections on possible reasons why the subject was of such intense interest and controversy in the one country and so uncontroversial and almost uninteresting in the other.

He looked in turn at a number of possible explanations:

(1) Laying before Parliament It might be argued that since delegated legislation generally had to be laid before Parliament that might explain the British feeling that it was under control. But the explanation foundered in face of the fact that it was widely and indeed generally felt that parliamentary control of delegated legislation was superficial in the extreme and in practice virtually non-existent.

(2) The consultation process In so far as government departments consulted with interest groups it might be said that this defused potential controversy about the rules being made. But in practice such consultation was not very elaborate and often it hardly took place at all. Moreover, it usually only involved those already known to the department and took place behind closed doors. In the US by contrast, a proposed rule had to be published in the Federal Register and often this triggered 'an outpouring of responses'. The courts had laid down a rule that agencies had to respond to the material objections made by commentators in the statement of purpose which accompanied the eventual rule. In addition there were often oral hearings conducted by agencies to enable interested parties to articulate their criticisms of proposed rules. The American system 'thus enriches the quantity and quality of inputs available to decision-makers and is universally considered to enhance democratic values of public participation in the making of crucial decisions as well as to improve the acceptability of those decisions to persons affected by them' (p. 268).

(3) The written constitution and judicial activism Asimow considered whether the difference could lie in the different constitutional systems. He concluded that, although in the narrow sense this cannot be the explanation, there is an important point in the role of the American judiciary as compared with that in Britain. The intense involvement of the federal judiciary with rulemaking had 'catalysed American attitudes toward the subject' (p. 268). 'If the courts had been indifferent to claims that rule-

making procedures were inadequate and deferential to agency contentions that rules were reasonable, much of the legal and political controversy surrounding the subject would probably never have arisen' (p. 268). The willingness of the American judges to involve themselves in highly political and visible confrontations with the executive branch on rule-making questions had its roots in constitutional matters.

> The long tradition of judicial review of the constitutionality of statutes has fostered a peculiar attitude of reliance on courts to solve political controversies where a legislative response is perceived to be inadequate. Every day, American courts issue constitutional rulings on political issues, such as the right to abortion, reforming electoral districts, choice of school library books, or prison reform, which would be reserved to legislative bodies in Britain. Consequently, American litigants displeased with particular regulations look naturally to courts for non-constitutional relief. They did so at a time when popular distrust of government and academic criticism of the regulatory process made judicial interventionism politically feasible. Consequently, the courts responded by rebuilding rule-making procedure along quasi-adversary lines and conducting intensive substantive scrutiny of rules.
>
> Britain seems much less oriented toward using litigation to settle disputes, particularly those in which official discretion is questioned or in which political overtones are present. Instead, it seems that such disputes are usually settled quietly through compromise rather than courtroom confrontations or resolved through conventional political processes. While British judges undoubtedly feel less restrained in second-guessing discretionary decisions, especially those made by local government officials, than in years past,[5] and while the wave of American judicial interventionism has certainly receded from its crest,[6] the difference in attitude and custom remains enormous.

(4)   Importance of delegated legislation Britain has far fewer rules made through delegated legislation and on the whole they are less important than those in the US. Why then did Britain rely so relatively little on this technique? Both countries had to grapple with similar problems of 'controlling technology, ensuring environmental and industrial safety, regulating land use, providing telecommunication and public utility services, administering a welfare state, operating complex schemes of taxation, and so on' (p. 269).

Americans tended to seek solutions in regulation in the broad sense of governmental control of private sector economic behaviour which generally

---

5   See *Bromley London Borough Council* v. *Greater London Council* [1982] 2 W.L.R. 62 (H.L.); *Secretary of State for Educ. & Science* v. *Tameside Metropolitan Borough* [1977] A.C. 1014; *Laker Airways Ltd* v. *Dept of Trade* [1977] Q.B. 643; *Congreve* v. *Home Office* [1976] Q.B. 629; *R.* v. *Sec'y of State for the Environment, ex parte Brent London Borough Council* [1982] Q.B. 593, 640–7.

6   See *F.C.C.* v. *W.N.C.N. Listeners Guild* 450 U.S. 582 (1981); *American Textile Mfrs Inst.* v. *Donovan* 452 U.S. 490 (1981).

entailed regulation in the narrow sense of subordinate legislation. In the US the party battles in the Congress and the inability of the administration to have its way in the primary legislation meant that many issues were left to be resolved through subordinate legislation. In Britain by contrast the executive could get its policy enacted in the primary statute and therefore had less need to leave important details to the regulatory process. Also in Britain alternative methods were commonly used. One was nationalisation of an industry which meant that it would be controlled through managerial or contractual techniques and informal political pressures rather than through formal rules. In America communications, gas and electricity, transport and basic industries like steel remained in private hands and as a result 'a regulatory structure must be created to compel these enterprises to operate in the public interest'.

Another British technique was that of using courts to administer the system – as in licensing – or to supervise it – as in trade descriptions, food quality or housing conditions. Many matters regulated by agencies in America were dealt with in Britain by voluntary codes of practice (see further on this pp. 400–03 below). Another British technique was the local public inquiry into major planning issues where those who would be affected by a Ministerial decision could seek to challenge or at least influence it. But the most important British technique for controlling the private sector was through heavy reliance on official discretion to make individualised orders. Parliament would legislate, giving officials broad discretionary powers. Often the powers were loosely circumscribed by guidelines prepared by the government department concerned. So in the planning field property owners had to ask for planning permission to develop their property. In the US the same problem would be dealt with more by zoning laws. In Britain, regulation of certain forms of pollution was the task of the alkali inspectorate or regional water authorities who had considerable power to compromise disputes. In the US, rules regulated permissible levels of air and water pollution and the scope for discretion was less.

Both systems had their strengths and weaknesses. The British negotiated approach avoided the adversary, confrontational style so characteristic of the American environmental regulation. It produced results more quickly and avoided costly litigation.

But in America distrust of public officials was much greater and there was therefore less willingness to leave them with discretionary powers. More faith was placed in rules, precedents and guidelines, in the belief that executive, legislative and judicial control over agency discretion was inevitably sporadic and often ineffective in preventing maladministration. In Britain the feeling was rather that discretion should not be fettered through the adoption of binding rules, policies or precedents. Agencies could work out presumptive policies but they must be willing to entertain applications to depart from policy or precedent in particular cases. Judicial review of discretionary action occurred but was relatively rare. In general the civil service, at least to an American observer, enjoyed a high level of confidence in the eyes of both the public and the courts.

Professor Asimow's conclusion is that the difference between the approach of the two systems has its roots in deep cultural differences turning in essence on attitudes to public officials, adversary procedures and judicial interventionism. In America there were many more rules and much more dissatisfaction with both the procedural and the substantive results. But each system could learn from the other:

> American rule-making procedures have improved the quality of rules and furnished a sense of participation very satisfying to the persons who must live with the rules. Similarly, British inquiry procedures, for all their defects, have brought the people closer to government decisions having critical effects on their lives. Neither country will, or should, abandon these procedures, though they must be pruned from time to time, lest the desire to make procedures acceptable to those affected overwhelms competing values of efficiency and accuracy. Both countries should begin the process of judicious sampling of the other's fumbling attempts to involve the public in critical administrative decisions. [P. 276.]

8. SUMMARY OF DEFECTS IN STATUTES

A sharply critical article on the defects in legislation by a practising Q.C. was published by the Bar's journal *Counsel*:

James Goudie Q.C., 'The Paper Chase', *Counsel*, June 1991, p. 8

> The inaccessibility of statutory law to the public at large and even to legal practitioners, especially legal practitioners outside major urban centres, has increased, is increasing and ought to be diminished. Statutory law is inaccessible in two major respects: it is hard to find and once found, it is hard to understand.

> *Hard to find*
> A combination of factors make statutory law (which is increasingly bulky and prolix) hard to find to a scandalous extent. These include the following:

> • A major new statute may have been enacted but be unavailable for some weeks thereafter at HMSO. Example: the Local Government and Housing Act 1989. Meanwhile one has to make do with the Bill. The latest print will not, however, include the latest amendments; and clause numbers and section members will not correspond.
> • No sooner has a statute been enacted than it may be subject to massive amendment, as in the case of the Criminal Justice Act 1987 by the Criminal

Justice Act 1988. The former is then misleading without the latter; and the latter is incomprehensible without the former.

- Even when legislation is consolidated this may then be subject to immediate change. Example: the consolidating Town and Country Planning Act 1990 is already being followed by the biggest changes in planning law for twenty years in the Planning and Compensation Bill.
- Primary legislation may be changed by statutory instrument made under other primary legislation: the so-called Henry VIII clause, of which there has been a flurry in recent years.
- Legislation almost never now comes in to force on a single date. Different sections, and even subsections, are brought into effect (by a succession of commencement orders) on a series of different dates over a period that may run to years; and some provisions may never be brought into effect at all. An example is the Consumer Credit Act 1974, in respect of which the final commencement order was made in 1989, and a table included in a textbook as an outline guide to the commencement situation occupies 11 pages.
- Notwithstanding that we are in the age of word processing, and despite experience elsewhere – Canada, for example – how a statute currently stands can be discovered only by an elaborate and time consuming paperchase or by resort (in some areas) to the encyclopaedias or LEXIS.
- Although the legislation itself is rarely skeletal, a mass of flesh is often added by statutory instruments, subject in practice to a minimum of parliamentary scrutiny, with the negative resolution procedure being preferred to the more effective affirmative procedure. Moreover, statutes and statutory instruments thereunder are drafted in different offices.
- Many areas of the law which could now readily be codified are still to be found only from cases decided over many years and scattered across a number of different series of reports.

Hard to understand
If searchers after enlightenment have not already been defeated in the quest to discover what statutes and statutory instruments currently in force say, they are then confronted with the task of divining what they mean.

Bewildering complexity is by no means confined to revenue statutes. Although, as the Renton Committee on the Preparation of Legislation suggested, if there is scope for mathematical formulae, those in Sch 1 to the Child Support Bill (calculation of child support maintenance) are a glaring case of misuse of such formulae. Is it not time for a return to the style of, say, the Sale of Goods Act 1893?

Very often the vices identified above are found in combination. For example, the draft Commonhold Bill is very long, very involved and very complicated, and yet every important provision is to be left to regulations.

Moreover, often three (or more) sets of provisions have to be considered: old law which has been repealed but is still relevant for some purposes; new law which is not yet fully effective; and extremely complex transitional provisions, which will remain part of the statute long after they have ceased to be applicable.

Among the suggestions proposed by James Goudie were:

- The arrangement of statutes (as with Statutes in Force) should be on the basis of subject.
- Statutory instruments enacted under a statute should be appended to any republication of the statute.
- New provisions relating to a subject covered by an existing Act should be incorporated by textual amendment in the existing Act rather than forming a separate statute.
- Publication of new and amending legislation should be in a form that allows quick and easy updating.
- Detail should be in Schedules. Only details of a changing or technical character should be in delegated legislation.
- More use should be made of consolidation (pp. 63–5 above) and codification (pp. 428–49 below).

9. HOW TO DO IT PROPERLY

Occasionally, however, a statute is highly praised. The Arbitration Act 1996 is such a case. In a glowing tribute,[7] Alec Samuels described its many virtues. These included:

- An opening statement of object or purpose
- Use of simple and succinct modern language
- The avoidance of long sentences and subordinate clauses
- The extensive use of subsections and sub-subsections
- An alphabetical index of defined expressions with an indication of the section in the statute where a definition is to be found
- Cross-references in brackets to other relevant sections

The statute was the outcome of long but full and effective effort, pressure and consultation: solicitors in the private sector briefed counsel to produce an early draft; the project was taken in hand by the Department of Trade and Industry Advisory Committee; seminars were held; there was consultation at every stage; there was consultation with interested bodies overseas; the project was strongly supported by the commercial Bar and all those involved in commercial arbitration; parliamentary counsel worked with the Advisory Committee as the work progressed and the drafts emerged. The Departmental Advisory Committee had asked that the Bill should be set out in a logical order, and expressed in language sufficiently clear and free from technicalities to be readily comprehensible to the layman.(pp. 58–59).

---

7   'How to do it properly', *Statute Law Review*, 1997, pp. 58–64.

CHAPTER 3

Statutory interpretation

I. INTERPRETATION IS AN INEVITABLE ASPECT OF COMMUNICATION

Statutory interpretation is a particular form of a general problem – the understanding of meaning or, more broadly still, communication. Like M. Jourdain in Molière's *Le Bourgeois Gentilhomme*, who did not know that he was talking prose, most people are probably unaware of the extent to which the use of language necessarily involves interpretation. Even the simplest statement usually relies on an understanding of habits, knowledge, values and purposes shared between the author and the recipient of the communication. The point was made in a homely example a hundred years ago.

Suppose a housekeeper says to a domestic: 'fetch some soup-meat' accompanying the act with giving some money to the latter; he will be unable to execute the order without interpretation, however easy and, consequently, rapid the performance of the process may be. Common sense and good faith tell the domestic, that the housekeeper's meaning was this: 1. He should go immediately, or as soon as his other occupations are finished; or, if he be directed to do so in the evening, that he should go the next day at the usual hour; 2. that the money handed him by the housekeeper is intended to pay for the meat thus ordered, and not as a present to him; 3. that he should buy such meat and of such parts of the animal, as, to his knowledge, has commonly been used in the house he stays at, for making soup; 4. that he buy the best meat he can obtain, for a fair price; 5. that he go to that butcher who usually provides the family, with whom the domestic resides, with meat, or to some convenient stall, and not to any unnecessarily distant place; 6. that he return the rest of the money; 7. that he bring home the meat in good faith, neither adding anything disagreeable nor injurious; 8. that he fetch the meat for the use of the family and not for himself. Suppose, on the other hand, the housekeeper, afraid of being misunderstood, had mentioned these eight specifications, she would not have obtained her object, if it were to exclude all *possibility* of misunderstanding. For, the various specifications would have required new ones. Where would be the end? We are constrained then, always, to leave a considerable part of our meaning to be found out by interpretation, which, in many cases, must necessarily cause greater or less obscurity with regard to the exact meaning, which our words were intended to convey.[1]

Interpretation, in other words, is not something that happens only in cases of doubt or difficulty; it happens whenever anyone tries to understand language used by another person. Usually the process of understanding is instinctive and immediate. It requires no conscious thought and is therefore not even noticed. For the most part we manage in ordinary life without too many difficulties created by misunderstandings. On the other hand, even in family life where the members of the household share broadly common values and common objectives and have a great deal of knowledge about each other's use of language, misunderstandings are far from rare. Interpretation therefore occurs inevitably wherever there is communication; the *problem* of interpretation occurs only when something goes wrong.

Lord Hailsham has said that probably as many as nine out of ten cases heard on appeal by the Court of Appeal and the House of Lords turn upon or involve the meaning of words contained in statutes or secondary legislation.[2] It is hardly surprising that in legal affairs there are plenty of ways in which things may go wrong. For one thing, legal documents – whether statutes, contracts, leases, mortgages, wills, bills of exchange – tend to be complex. Their subject-matter is difficult. They use a mixture of ordinary language and technical jargon. They are apt to be long-winded. They are frequently the result of drafting by several hands or at least of consultation with a variety of people. The final draft may reflect a compromise between different points of view. Each of these factors militates against simplicity and clarity of expression.

Secondly, a legal document speaks not only to the present but is usually intended to cope with the future. That indeed is normally its chief function. But the draftsman's capacity to anticipate the future is necessarily limited. Even if he provides for thirteen possible contingencies, he may overlook the possibility of the fourteenth which happens to be the one that actually occurs. The late Professor Lon Fuller of Harvard posed the example of a statute that provides 'It shall be an offence punishable by a fine of five dollars to sleep in any railway station.' Does the offence cover the case of a passenger waiting for a delayed train who was found at 3 a.m. on a station bench, sitting upright but asleep and even snoring? Equally, does

1   F. Leiber, *Legal and Political Hermeneutics* (3rd edn, 1880), p. 18.
2   *Hamlyn Revisited: The British Legal System Today* (1983), p. 65.

it cover the case of the tramp who was stopped on his way into the station carrying a bed-roll and heading for a bench, apparently with a view to settling down for the night? Neither case is adequately dealt with in the statute. No draftsman, however fertile his imagination, can think of everything.

Moreover, space will not permit him to put down everything that he does think of. In order to avoid the danger of misconstruction of the simple request 'fetch some meat for soup', the careful draftsman/communicator would be best advised to specify that he means – from the shop at the bottom of the road; before lunch; at the customary price; meat of the kind normally eaten by the family; that the change be returned, etc. In ordinary life, time and patience do not permit such tedious prolixity. Much is left to common sense. But precisely the same is true of legal documents. However pedantic the draftsman, there will be much that he will have to leave to common sense. If everything had to be defined, there would be no end to the document. The draftsman must perforce select what he thinks are the most important matters to be set down. Moreover, there are some things that he cannot foresee simply because later developments are not within the knowledge of anyone at the time. The draftsman who uses the word 'vehicle' in the days of horse-drawn carriages cannot be blamed for any uncertainty as to whether the word applies to motorcars or aeroplanes.

The third and most important reason for the singular tendency of legal documents to give rise to difficulties is that they commonly reflect attempted solutions to problems affecting different and conflicting interests. A will is the sharing out of property amongst individuals each of whom might prefer to have more than their allotted share; a contract is an agreement between, say, a buyer and a seller who have contrary points of view on the deal; a lease is an allocation of rights and responsibilities between landlord and tenant whose interests diverge at many points. A statute commonly prescribes a new way of dealing with a particular range of problems as between the different groups affected. The problem of drafting language so as to avoid ambiguity and uncertainty is great enough where the relevant parties have broadly the same point of view. It is infinitely greater where they have an incentive to find different meanings in the words used. The English language is richly endowed with words that bear multiple meanings and there is almost no limit to the number of ambiguities that can be found in the ordinary legal document once ingenious and motivated lawyers start picking it over. It is not necessarily a matter of the lawyers being 'bloody-minded'. They may simply be doing their job by looking for ways in which the document can be construed to serve the best interests of their client. Ambiguity here is not the fault of the draftsman nor is it a reflection of the shortcomings of the language; it is simply the result of the obvious fact that where people look at a text from different points of view they are apt to find different meanings in the language used.

If problems of interpretation do occur, they may be resolved in a variety of ways. The opposing parties may come to some accommodation of their dispute without ever calling on their lawyers. Or the lawyers may agree on some formula that is acceptable to the clients. But if the disagreement cannot be solved by negotiation and agreement, the only way to secure an authoritative decision is to take it to the courts. This book is concerned with law-making on a national scale and the remainder of this chapter deals with the way in which the courts approach problems of statutory interpretation. But much of what is said here applies as much to the attitude of the courts to the interpretation of instruments drafted by practising lawyers whether they be contracts, leases, mortgages or any other legal document.

2. THE THREE BASIC SO-CALLED 'RULES' OF STATUTORY INTERPRETATION

It is often said that there are three basic rules of statutory interpretation – the literal rule, the golden rule and the mischief rule. As will be seen, it would be better to describe these more as tendencies or approaches than as rules. It is also important to appreciate that this classification is a considerable over-simplification of the process of statutory interpretation.

But we commence by establishing what the so-called rules mean and then proceed to an examination of each in turn.

(a) The literal rule

According to the literal rule it is the task of the court to give the words to be construed their literal meaning regardless of whether the result is sensible or not. Lord Esher put the proposition succinctly in 1892:

> If the words of an Act are clear, you must follow them, even though they lead to a manifest absurdity. The Court has nothing to do with the question whether the Legislature has committed an absurdity.[3]

In another of the innumerable judicial formulations of the same rule, Lord Bramwell in 1884 similarly reflected the idea that the court should not be concerned whether the construction it gives to a statute is absurd:

> I should like to have a good definition of what is such an absurdity that you are to disregard the plain words of an Act of Parliament. It is to be remembered that what seems absurd to one man does not seem absurd to another.... I think it is infinitely better, although an absurdity or an injustice or other objectionable result may be evolved as the consequence of your construction, to adhere to

3   R. v. *Judge of the City of London Court* [1892] 1 Q.B. 273 at 290.

the words of an Act of Parliament and leave the legislature to set it right than to alter those words according to one's notion of an absurdity.[4]

(b) The golden rule

The so-called 'golden rule' was attributed to Lord Wensleydale by Lord Blackburn in *River Wear Commissioners* v. *Adamson*, in which he said:

> I believe that it is not disputed that what Lord Wensleydale used to call the golden rule is right, viz., that we are to take the whole statute together, and construe it all together, giving the words their ordinary signification, unless when so applied they produce an inconsistency, or an absurdity or inconvenience so great as to convince the Court that the intention could not have been to use them in their ordinary signification, and to justify the Court in putting on them some other signification, which, though less proper, is one which the Court thinks the words will bear.[5]

But the first recorded use of the phrase 'golden rule' seems in fact to have been by Jervis C.J. in *Mattison* v. *Hart* (1854) 14 C.B. 357 at 385 ('We must, therefore, in this case have recourse to what is called the golden rule of construction, as applied to acts of parliament, viz. to give the words used by the legislature their plain and natural meaning unless it is manifest from the general scope and intention of the statute injustice and absurdity would result').

In *Grey* v. *Pearson*, Parke B. said:

> I have been long and deeply impressed with the wisdom of the rule now, I believe, universally adopted, at least in the courts of law in Westminster Hall, that in construing wills and indeed, statutes, and all written instruments, the grammatical and ordinary sense of the words is to be adhered to, unless that would lead to some absurdity, or some repugnance or inconsistency with the rest of the instrument, in which case the grammatical and ordinary sense of the words may be modified, so as to avoid the absurdity and inconsistency, but no farther.[6]

According to the golden rule, therefore, the court is supposed to follow the literal approach unless it produces absurdity (and perhaps inconvenience and inconsistency), in which case it should find some other meaning.

---

4   *Hill* v. *East and West India Dock Co.* (1884) 9 App. Cas. 448 at 464–5.
5   (1877) 2 App. Cas. 743 at 764–5.
6   (1857) 6 H. L. Cas. 61 at 106.

(c)   The mischief rule

The classic statement of the mischief rule is that given by the Barons of the Court of Exchequer in *Heydon's* case (1584) 3 Co. Rep. 7a:

> And it was resolved by them, that for the sure and true interpretation of all statutes in general (be they penal or beneficial, restrictive or enlarging of the Common Law), four things are to be discerned and considered:
> 1st. What was the Common Law before the making of the Act.
> 2nd. What was the mischief and defect for which the Common Law did not provide.
> 3rd. What remedy the Parliament hath resolved and appointed to cure the disease of the commonwealth.
> And, 4th. The true reason of the remedy; and then the office of all the Judges is always to make such construction as shall suppress the mischief, and advance the remedy and to suppress subtle inventions and evasions for continuance of the mischief, and *pro privato commodo*, and to add force and life to the cure and remedy, according to the true intent of the makers of the Act, *pro bono publico*.

Coke himself later referred to the same approach in his *Institutes*:

> Equity is a construction made by the judges, that cases out of the letter of a statute, yet being within the same mischief, or cause of the making of the same, shall be within the same remedy that the statute provideth; and the reason hereof is, for that the law-makers could not possibly set down all cases in express terms. [I *Inst.* 24b.]

3.   THE THREE BASIC RULES CONSIDERED

(a)   The dominant rule has been the literal rule

There seems to be little dispute that for most of the past hundred years or more the literal rule has been the dominant one. *Maxwell on Interpretation of Statutes* (12th edn, 1969) stated that the literal rule was the primary one – the golden and the mischief rules were merely 'other main principles of interpretation'. The literal rule developed in the early nineteenth century. The first sustained judicial support for it appears to have come from Lord Tenterden in cases decided in the 1820s. According to one authority,[7] the golden rule and the literal rule contended for the allegiance of the judges for the next thirty years but by the latter part of the century the literal approach had clearly triumphed. The most rigorous expression of it was

---

7   J. A. Corry, 'Administrative Law: Interpretation of Statutes', *University of Toronto Law Journal*, 1935, p. 286 at pp. 299–300.

Lord Halsbury's statement in *Hilder* v. *Dexter* [1902] A.C. 474 that the draftsman of a statute was the worst person in the world to interpret a statute because he was unconsciously influenced by what he meant rather than by what he had said. He had himself drafted the statute in that case and refused to give judgment on the ground that he might not fully appreciate the literal, objective meaning of the words he had used. One of the chief reasons for this approach was said to be the length of legislation by comparison with former times. In 1840 Lord Brougham said:

> If we depart from the plain and obvious meaning on account of such views, we in truth do not construe the Act but alter it … are really making the law and not interpreting it. This becomes peculiarly improper in dealing with a modern statute because the extreme conciseness of ancient statutes was the only ground for the sort of legislative interpretation frequently put upon their words; and the prolixity of modern statutes is still more remarkable than the shortness of the old.[8]

A hundred years later Lord Evershed was echoing the same point: 'The length and detail of modern legislation has undoubtedly reinforced the claim of literal construction as the only safe rule.' If the statute was long, this suggested that Parliament had expressed its full meaning and that there was no need or scope to imply any additional meanings. Anything omitted was a *casus omissus* which the judge could not supply because that would amount to legislation. But the literal approach was used equally for wills, contracts, and other legal documents, so that the philosophy was by no means based exclusively on the constitutional relationship between courts and Parliament nor on the growing length of statutes.

A clear demonstration of the literal approach in operation is the sequence of events in *Magor and St. Mellons* v. *Newport Corporation*:

Magor and St. Mellons v. *Newport Corpn* [1950] 2 All E.R. 1226 (Court of Appeal) and [1951] 2 All E.R. 839 (House of Lords)

The Newport Corporation had expanded its boundaries by taking in large parts of two neighbouring rural districts. The parts taken in were mainly the richer parts whose ratepayers paid the highest rates. The Local Government Act 1933, ss. 151 and 152, provided for reasonable compensation to the two District Councils by the one that had become enriched through the alteration in the boundaries. But the Minister made an Order amalgamating the two District Councils into one. The Newport Corporation used this fact to argue that the new council could claim no compensation at all. The statute, it said, provided for compensation only to a surviving council, whereas here the two old councils had been abolished and the claim was therefore invalid.

8   *Gwynne* v. *Burnell* (1840) 6 Bing. N.C. 453 at 561.

The trial judge Parker J. and the Court of Appeal (Cohen and Somervell L.JJ.) agreed with the Corporation. Lord Denning, however, dissented. In his view the intention of Parliament and of the Minister was obvious. The order dissolving the old councils was not their death but their marriage.

LORD DENNING: The burdens which each set of ratepayers had previously borne separately became a combined burden to be borne by them all together. So, also, the rights to which the two councils would have been entitled for each set of ratepayers separately became a combined right to which the combined council was entitled for them all together. This was so obviously the intention of the Minister's order that I have no patience with an ultra-legalistic interpretation which would deprive them of their rights altogether ... We do not sit here to pull the language of Parliament and of Ministers to pieces and make nonsense of it. That is an easy thing to do, and it is a thing to which lawyers are too often prone. We sit here to find out the intention of Parliament and of Ministers and carry it out, and we do this better by filling in the gaps and making sense of the enactment than by opening it up to destructive analysis.

It may be said that these heroics are out of place, and I agree they are, because I think that Parliament has really made its intention plain enough. The Act which conferred the title to compensation conferred it on each of the district councils, not in its own right, but in right of its ratepayers: (see s. 152(1)(*b*) of the Act of 1933). The district council was the hand to receive the compensation, but it only received it so that it might give relief to the ratepayers for the increased burden which the change of boundaries cast on them. The amalgamation changed the legal identity of the two district councils, but it did not change the ratepayers at all, nor did it relieve them of their burdens: and there is no reason whatever why the amalgamated council should not claim the compensation due to the ratepayers.

The House of Lords upheld the trial judge and the Court of Appeal. The first judgment was given by Lord Simonds, who said he agreed with the judgment to be given by Lord Morton of Henryton but that he wished to add his reaction to the philosophy expressed by Lord Denning:

LORD SIMONDS: My Lords, the criticism which I venture to make of the judgment of the learned lord justice is not directed at the conclusion that he reached. It is after all a trite saying that on questions of construction different minds may come to different conclusions and I am content to say that I agree with my noble and learned friend. But it is on the approach of the lord justice to what is a question of construction and nothing else that I think it desirable to make some comment, for at a time when so large a proportion of the cases that are brought before the courts depend on the construction of modern statutes it would not be right for this House to pass unnoticed the propositions which the learned lord justice lays down for the guidance of himself and, presumably, of others. He said ([1950] 2 All E.R. 1236):

'We sit here to find out the intention of Parliament and of Ministers and carry it out, and we do this better by filling in the gaps and making sense of the enactment than by opening it up to destructive analysis.'

The first part of this passage appears to be an echo of what was said in *Heydon's* Case three hundred years ago, and so regarded, is not objectionable. But the way in which the learned lord justice summarises the broad rules laid down by SIR EDWARD COKE in that case may well induce grave misconception of the function of the court. The part which is played in the judicial interpretation of a statute by reference to the circumstances of its passing is too well known to need re-statement. It is sufficient to say that the general proposition that it is the duty of the court to find out the intention of Parliament – and not only of Parliament but of Ministers also – cannot by any means be supported. The duty of the court is to interpret the words that the legislature has used. Those words may be ambiguous, but, even if they are, the power and duty of the court to travel outside them on a voyage of discovery are strictly limited: see, for instance, *Assam Railways & Trading Co. Ltd* v. *Inland Revenue Comrs.* and, particularly, the observations of LORD WRIGHT ([1935] A.C. 445, 458).

The second part of the passage that I have cited from the judgment of the learned lord justice is, no doubt, the logical sequence of the first. The court, having discovered the intention of Parliament and of Ministers too, must proceed to fill in the gaps. What the legislature has not written, the court must write. This proposition, which re-states in a new form the view expressed by the lord justice in the earlier case of *Seaford Court Estates Ltd.* v. *Asher* [1950] A.C. 508 (to which the lord justice himself refers), cannot be supported. It appears to me to be a naked usurpation of the legislative function under the thin disguise of interpretation and it is the less justifiable when it is guesswork with what material the legislature would, if it had discovered the gap, have filled it in. If a gap is disclosed, the remedy lies in an amending Act. For the reasons to be given by my noble and learned friend I am of opinion that this appeal should be dismissed with costs.

Lord Morton said that s. 151 of the 1933 Act made it clear that the only bodies which could claim a financial adjustment were public bodies affected by an alteration of boundaries. The new amalgamated district council was not such a body since it was not in existence when the boundary change took place.

The present case is one in which each of two local authorities loses a wealthy portion of its area and is abolished immediately after the loss occurs. It may be that, if the legislature had contemplated such a state of affairs, some special provisions would have been inserted in the Act of 1933. What these provisions would have been can only be a matter of guesswork.[9]

He clearly agreed with Lord Simonds' view of Lord Denning's approach. Lord Morton (with whom Lords Simonds and Goddard agreed) said:

In so far as the intention of Parliament or of Ministers is revealed in Acts of Parliament or orders, either by the language used or by necessary implication,

9   [1951] 2 All E.R. 839, 845.

the court should, of course, carry these intentions out, but it is not the function of any judge to fill in what he conceives to be the gaps in an Act of Parliament. If he does so, he is usurping the function of the legislature [at 846].

Lord Tucker similarly found himself unpersuaded by Lord Denning's approach:

> I think it is clear that the situation which has arisen in the present case was never present to the minds of those responsible for the Local Government Act 1933, and that the language is quite inappropriate to meet it. In these circumstances your Lordships would be acting in a legislative rather than a judicial capacity if the view put forward by DENNING L.J. in his dissenting judgment were to prevail.

But Lord Radcliffe, without referring to him or to his approach, nevertheless found a way to reach the same result as Lord Denning:

> My Lords, I differ very little from the views expressed by my noble and learned friend, LORD MORTON OF HENRYTON, but that small difference has led me to come to an opposite conclusion as to what should be the fate of this appeal... .

He thought that s. 151 of the 1933 Act was not so narrow as to require that the courts give a result which was unjust to the ratepayers of the new amalgamated district council. The sum to which the ratepayers were entitled was not known when the old councils were abolished, but the right to have the sum ascertained was in existence at the moment that the boundary changes were made.

> Supposing that it has been the right to an ascertained sum, say £1,000 per annum, there would not have been any dispute that the appellants would have been entitled to receive it. Does it make an essential difference that the sum, though its basis was determined, remained to be ascertained by agreement or arbitration? To me the difference appears as one of form, not of substance.

A similar clash between the strict or literal constructionists and a more liberal school occurred in a will case, *Re Rowland*, again featuring Lord Denning as one of the protagonists:

Re Rowland [1963] Ch. 1 (Court of Appeal)

Before going to the Far East a doctor and his wife made identical wills on printed will forms which provided that each left his property to the other, but in the event of the other's death 'preceding or coinciding' with that of the testator, the property was to go to selected alternative relatives. In the case of the husband, his property would in that event go to his brother and nephew. Both husband and wife were aboard a small ship which disappeared in the South Pacific. The circumstances of the disaster were never discovered. The question for the Court of Appeal was whether the property should go to the wife's relations or to those of the husband. The leading judgment for the majority was given by Lord Justice Russell:

> What has the testator said? It is in my judgment quite plain that 'coinciding' in the context of 'preceding' means coinciding in point of time; its natural and normal meaning in that context is not coincidence in any other respect such as type or cause of death, though coincidence in time would normally require coincidence in type or cause. The process of dying may take even an unconscionable time: but the event of death, to which the testator referred, is the matter of a moment, the moment when life is gone for ever. I see no room, therefore, for 'coinciding', in its normal and natural meaning, to involve some broad conception of overlapping or of occurring within a particular period. In my judgment the normal and natural meaning of 'coinciding with' in relation to deaths occurring is the same as 'simultaneous' – namely, as referring to circumstances in which the ordinary man would say that the two deaths were coincident in point of time or simultaneous.
>
> In the light of these considerations did the wife's death on the facts of this case precede the testator's death or coincide in point of time with it? There is certainly no evidence to show that her death preceded his: this is not suggested. Do the facts lead on balance of probabilities to the conclusion that the ordinary man would consider that their deaths coincided in point of time? Or to put, as I think, the same question in different terms, would he, without regard to metaphysical problems of the infinite divisibility of time, consider on the evidence that they died simultaneously? The answer must I think clearly be: No. The evidence is wholly insufficient to warrant the conclusion.... . If the evidence was that the testator and his wife were below decks in their cabin and the vessel plunged abruptly to the bottom of the sea, the view might be taken that their deaths were, metaphysics apart, coincident in point of time. But we simply do not know what happened to them. Counsel for the appellants could not suggest, in the case of either spouse, whether the correct inference was death by drowning, trapped in the ship, or death by drowning, sucked down by the sinking ship after going overboard, or death by shark or similar fish, or by thirst, or by drowning after swimming about or floating for a greater or less period with or without a life belt. This makes it plain that there is no evidence at all that the deaths were coincident in point of time (in the natural sense of simultaneous) in the mind of the ordinary man.
>
> It was argued that the words 'coinciding with' were not used by this testator in what I have described as their natural meaning. The suggestion is that this testator (in his particular armchair) meant something wider – something which during the hearing was described as 'on the same occasion and by the same cause'. It was pointed out that the wills of the spouses were made at a time when they knew they were going in 1956 to employment in the Pacific which would involve such perils or risks as may be inherent in (inter alia) travel between islands and atolls in small ships. Therefore, it was said, this testator should be considered as having had in mind just this kind of episode, and accordingly this phrase in this will should be construed as embracing this

event. This appears to me to be a wholly erroneous approach to the problem of construction. One may hazard the guess that if he could now be asked to whom in the events which happened he would wish his property to go, he would say that he would wish it to go to his selected alternates. That would not mean, however, that he has expressed that wish by his will: his answer would be consistent with his having selected language which failed to appreciate all the possible circumstances which would make that outcome desirable. It is an unsound approach to the construction of the will to ask oneself what the testator, if he had thought of an event not covered by the natural and normal meaning of his language, would have wished had he directed his mind to the event. The question is what events does his language cover? To ask more is to desert the source from which his intention is to be gathered, his will as proved.

Moreover, what is really meant by the suggestion that 'coinciding with' should be taken as meaning 'on the same occasion and by the same cause'? Presumably 'on the same occasion' is intended to contain a time element and to indicate deaths roughly about the same time. But how roughly? This seems quite uncertain. In any event it is implicit in this proposition that the alternative beneficiaries would have taken even if the evidence had demonstrated clearly that the wife survived the testator, and by survival had become entitled to his estate under the first part of the will. The suggested construction would thus involve a divesting of a vested interest, a process which is generally recognized as one which requires a clear expression of intention. I cannot for my part see that the testator's language can be stretched to produce such a result.

In the last analysis the appellants really are asking the court to hold (a) that the testator was intending to cover any situation in which it was uncertain whether his wife had survived him – a private solution to the problem which s. 184 of the Law of Property Act, 1925,[10] was designed to solve: and also, I think, (b) that he was intending to cover any situation in which the wife survived him by so short a time that the disposition in her favour would be of no use to her. The testator's language, however, is not such as reveals either of these intentions. As I have indicated, the key to his expressed intention is the context of the words 'preceding or', which demonstrate that 'coinciding with' means 'coinciding in point of time with'. This cannot be equated with 'if we shall die together' in the sense in which people are referred to as commorientes. For these reasons I am clearly of the opinion that the testator's language does not fit the facts of the case, so far as they are known. To hold otherwise would not in my judgment be to construe the will at all: it would be the result of inserting in the will a phrase which the testator never used by guessing at what a man in his position would have wished had he directed his mind and pen to the facts as they now confront us. There is no jurisdiction in this court to achieve a sensible result by such means.

Lord Justice Harman agreed:

It is for those claiming under the gift over to prove their case that the deaths of the testator and his wife were coincident. This word in the context in which it

---

10 The effect of s. 184 is explained below in the dissenting judgment of Lord Denning (ed.).

appears can in my judgment only be a reference to the time and not the occasion of death. In other words, 'coincident' is equivalent to 'simultaneous'. That was the only event which the testator on the language he used could have contemplated. He had already made the gift to his wife if she survived him and to the defendants if she did not. Can these deaths on the evidence be held to have been simultaneous.... I am satisfied that it cannot. Not enough is known. It is not even known at what date, within a week, the ship went down, nor is the whereabouts of either the testator or his wife at that time certain. One or other of them may easily have survived the going down of the ship and the event is too uncertain to infer a simultaneous death, as was possible for COHEN J., in the case of two persons killed in close proximity to each other by the same bomb.

If this meaning of the word be out of the question, it is argued that 'coincident' is a little looser and can mean in this will 'at about the same time and as a result of the same catastrophe'. This in my opinion is an impossible view. 'The will has provided for both possibilities of survivor-ship and there is no warrant for introducing a reference to something other than time, namely, the same catastrophe. I am, therefore, of the same opinion as the learned judge and would dismiss this appeal.

But Lord Denning M.R. dissented:

The question now is: what is to happen to the estate of Dr Rowland? It has been sworn at £2,798 2s. 6d. Is it to go to his brother and his nephew? Or is it to go to his wife's niece? This all depends on whether her death 'coincided with' his death. If it did, then under his will his property goes to his own relatives. If her death did not 'coincide with' his, then under s. 184 of the Law of Property Act, 1925, she, being younger than her husband, is deemed to have survived him, and his property will go under his will to his wife, and thence under her will to her niece. So the critical question is: what does the word 'coincide' mean in this will? And this seems to me to raise a point of some importance in the interpretation of wills.

One way of approach, which was much favoured in the nineteenth century, is to ask simply: what is the ordinary and grammatical meaning of the word 'coincide' as used in the English language? On that approach, the answer, it is said, is plain: it means 'coincident in point of time', and that means, so it is said, the same as 'simultaneous' or 'at the same point of time'. So, instead of interpreting the word 'coincide', you turn to interpreting the word 'simultaneous'. At that point you run into a difficulty, because, strictly speaking, no two people ever die at exactly the same point of time; or, at any rate, you can never prove that they do. LORD SIMONDS said in *Hickman* v. *Peacey*[11] that 'proof of simultaneous death is impossible'. If, therefore, the word 'coincide' is given its ordinary and grammatical meaning, it would lead to an absurdity, for it would mean that the testator was providing in his will for an impossible event.

11 [1945] 2 All E.R. at 235; [1945] A.C. at 345.

In order to avoid the absurdity, you must do, it is said, what COHEN J. did in *Re Pringle, Baker* v. *Matheson*,[12] you must interpret the word 'coincide' to mean death in such circumstances that the ordinary man would infer that death was simultaneous. So the argument proceeds to ask: when would an ordinary man say death was simultaneous?, and the answer is given: he would say so when two people are both blown to pieces at the same moment, such as by a bomb falling on the room in which they are sitting, or by an aircraft in which they are travelling exploding in mid-air. In short, where there is instantaneous death at the same instant of time. Thus a little latitude is allowed to the word 'coincide'. It covers death so close together that there is no measurable period of time between them. But no further latitude is allowed. According to this argument, if the deaths are separated by any measurable interval, even by so much as a few seconds, they do not 'coincide'... .

I must confess that, if ever there were an absurdity, I should have thought we have one here... . It seems to me that the fallacy in that argument is that it starts from the wrong place. It proceeds on the assumption that, in construing a will, 'It is not what the testator meant, but what is the meaning of his words' that matters. That may have been the nineteenth-century view; but I believe it to be wrong and to have been the cause of many mistakes. I have myself known a judge to say: 'I believe this to be contrary to the true intention of the testator, but nevertheless it is the result of the words he has used'. When a judge goes so far as to say that, the chances are that he has misconstrued the will. For in point of principle the whole object of construing a will is to find out the testator's intentions, so as to see that his property is disposed of in the way he wished. True it is that you must discover his intention from the words that he has used; but you must put on his words the meaning which they bore to him. If his words are capable of more than one meaning, or of a wide meaning and a narrow meaning, as they often are, then you must put on them the meaning which he intended them to convey, and not the meaning which a philologist would put on them. In order to discover the meaning which he intended, you will not get much help from a dictionary. It is very unlikely that he used a dictionary, and even less likely that he used the same one as you. What you should do is place yourself as far as possible in his position, taking note of the facts and circumstances known to him at the time, and then say what he meant by his words... . I decline, therefore, to ask myself: what do the words mean to a grammarian? I prefer to ask: What did Dr Rowland and his wife mean by the word 'coincide' in their wills? When they came to make their wills it is not difficult to piece together the thoughts that ran through their minds. The doctor might well say: 'We are going off for three years to these far-off places and in case anything happens to either of us we ought to make our wills. If I die before you, I would like everything to go to you, but if you die before me, I should like it to go to my brother and his boy.' She might reply: 'Yes, but what if we both die together? After all, one of those little ships might run on the rocks or something and we might both be drowned: or we might both be killed in an aeroplane crash'. 'To meet that,' he would say, 'I will put in that if your death coincides with mine, it is to go to my brother and his boy just the same'. He

12 [1946] 1 All E.R. at 93; [1946] Ch. at 131.

would use the words 'coinciding with', not in the narrow meaning of 'simultaneous', but in the wider meaning of which they are equally capable, especially in this context, as denoting death on the same occasion by the same cause. It would not cross Dr Rowland's mind that anyone would think of such niceties as counsel for the first defendant has presented to us. I decline to introduce such fine points into the construction of; this will. I would hold that Dr Rowland, when he made his will, intended by these words 'coinciding with' to cover he and his wife dying together in just such a calamity as in fact happened: and that we should give his words the meaning which he plainly intended they should bear. I would allow the appeal accordingly.

Question

Consider the strengths and weaknesses of the approach of the judges for the majority and of Lord Denning's dissenting views in both the previous cases.

The virtues of the literal approach were outlined in an article in the *Canadian Bar Review* in 1937:

E. R. Hopkins, 'The Literal Canon and the Golden Rule', 15 *Canadian Bar Review*, 1937, p. 689

Literal interpretation means nothing if plain words may be qualified according to common sense and justice as conceived judicially. If the absurdity clause were given free rein, the judicial inquiry would be 'what ought the Act to mean', rather than 'what does the Act mean': the former process has been variously impugned as 'juristic chemistry', 'spurious, interpretation', and 'evasion'.

Then, should the literal canon be dislodged from, or relegated to the position of a presumption in a modern theory of interpretation? ... It is submitted that the formal approach is within its province most consonant with the judicial function. In our constitutional theory, the function of innovation rests primarily with legislative bodies. It is true that the final word in law-making must rest with the courts and that the exercise of any conscious mental process involves an element of discretion: yet, if the assignment of legislative power to parliament is to be otherwise than fictional, the process of interpretation must be divorced so far as may be from that of legislation. What must be sought for by the courts are criteria of meaning as objectivised and impersonal as can be found, so that the initial discretion inherent in legislation will be impaired as little as possible by a supervening discretion in interpretation. From this point of approach, the present attitude of the courts toward the literal canon, namely, that words are to be assigned their plain literal meaning in their context, merits more sympathy than it is currently accorded. Recognizing the defects of any theory of statutory construction and without finding in literalness the quality of eternal verity, the judges have proceeded on the basis that the literal canon is founded on truths approximately accurate and criteria sufficiently objectivised for a workaday world and a busy court. The patent meaning is treated as the surest guide to the latent meaning of the statute, and the field of discretion which trenches upon the field of legislation while not eliminated is at any rate reduced to a minimum. If individual hardship, or a socially undesirable result, follows, legislative machinery provides the appropriate corrective, and if, as has been suggested, the literal canon has sometimes been inexpertly applied it must be remembered that to indict a workman is not necessarily to criticize his tools. While it will undoubtedly be necessary where the statutory meaning is obscure to make extensive and important demands upon judicial discretion, hope may be expressed that an improved draftmanship and a more studious regard to the boundaries of literal theory may result in at once an extension of the province and an improvement in the process of formal construction.

But the literal rule has also been subjected to severe criticism:

(1) The most fundamental objection to the rule is that it is based on a false premise, namely that words have plain, ordinary meanings apart from their context. Professor H. L. A. Hart of Oxford argued that a word has a core meaning 'or standard instance in which no doubts are felt about its application' even though at the edges there is margin of uncertainty.[13] But Professor Lon Fuller has contested this by urging that meaning attaches not to individual words but to sentences and paragraphs, and that 'surely a paragraph does not have a "standard instance" that remains constant whatever the context in which it appears'.[14] If a statute seems to have a core meaning, 'this is because we can see that, however one might formulate the precise objective of the statute, *this* case would still come within it'.[15]

(2) Those who apply the literal approach often talk of using the 'dictionary meaning' of the words in question, but dictionaries normally provide a number of alternative meanings.

(3) The plain-meaning approach cannot be used for general words, which are obviously capable of bearing several meanings.

(4) Not infrequently the courts say that the meaning of the words is 'plain' but then disagree as to their interpretation.[16]

---

13 H. Hart, 'Positivism and the Separation of Law and Morals', 71 *Harvard Law Review*, 1958, p. 593 at p. 607.
14 L. Fuller, 'Positivism and Fidelity to Law – a Reply to Professor Hart', 71 *Harvard Law Review*, 1958, p. 630 at p. 663.
15 Ibid.
16 See, for instance, *London and N.E. Railway Co.* v. *Berriman* [1946] A.C. 278. In *Ellerman Lines* v. *Murray* [1931] A.C. 126, all the judges agreed that the meaning was 'plain' but there were at least three different views as to what the plain meaning was. See similarly *Nothman* v. *Barnet London Borough Council* [1979] 1 W.L.R. 67, in which the House of Lords divided three to two; and *Newbury District Council* v. *Secretary of State for the Environment* [1980] 2 W.L.R. 379, where the five judges in the House of Lords unanimously gave a different meaning to the word 'repository' from that given to it by the Secretary of State and the six judges below, including the Lord Chief Justice and the Master of the Rolls. The six thought it clear their way. The five thought it clear the other way.

(5) The plain-meaning theory may be acceptable outside the court room, since it could be true that a high proportion of statutory materials and other legal documents can in fact be interpreted without recourse to any mischief or golden rule. But in the court room there are by definition two parties, usually represented by counsel, arguing over the meaning of the relevant passage. It makes little sense to dispose of the issue between them by reference to the plain meaning when there are two meanings in issue. As Professor Glanville Williams has pointed out, often one party is contending for an 'obvious' meaning of the words while the other argues for a secondary meaning of the words. The choice cannot then be made sensibly without regard to the context.[17]

The most common retort from those who favour the literal approach is that, in spite of some problems, it promotes the certainty which is one of the chief objectives of any legal system. But does it?

If all judges *always* followed the policy of literalism, it may be that there would be some gain in certainty. But in practice they do not. Even the most die-hard advocates of the literal approach sometimes lapse into some alternative method. One commentator has written:[18] '[T]he doctrine of literalness can never be applied successfully to general words. For they always include something more than the scope and object of the statute required and so it leads to ridiculous results'. Judges were torn between a feeling of obligation to adhere to the doctrine and a feeling of revolt against what they regarded as an absurdity and injustice. So if literalness seemed too ridiculous or threatened things which the judge regarded as fundamental, he exerted himself to escape its conclusions. Even those judges who insisted strongly upon the principle of literal adherence to the words, deserted it in such circumstances. 'Lord Tenterden, who fathered the doctrine, sometimes found that literal meanings could not have been intended.[19] And Lord Bramwell, who affirmed the doctrine with his usual vigour and challenged anyone to show him an absurdity so great as to entitle him to depart from the plain meaning, had some interesting lapses.[20]

... Lord Halsbury stated the doctrine of literalness as uncompromisingly as anyone.

But in a case before the House of Lords in 1890 he deserted it and appealed to the "equity of the statute".'[1]

---

17 Glanville Williams, 'The Meaning of Literal Interpretation', *New Law Journal*, 1981, pp. 1128, 1149.
18 J. A. Corry, 'Administrative Law: Interpretation of Statutes', *University of Toronto Law Journal*, 1935, p. 286 at pp. 301–3.
19 *Margate Pier Co.* v. *Hannam* (1819) 3 B. & Ald. 266; *Edwards* v. *Dick* (1821) 4 B. & Ald. 212; *Bennett* v. *Daniel* (1830) 10 B. & C. 500.
20 E.g. *Twycross* v. *Grant* (1877) 46 L.J.Q.B. 636; *Ex parte Walton* (1881) 17 Ch.D. 746; *Hill* v. *East and West India Dock Co.* (1884) 9 App. Cas, 448.
1 *Cox* v. *Hakes* (1890) 15 App. Cas. 506.

The result of the inevitable inconsistency as to the application of the literal approach is that it loses much of its claim to be the basis of greater certainty. Lord Justices Russell and Harman in *Re Rowland* may justify their decision on the ground that it will assist in the future by reducing litigation if lawyers can predict that the court will adopt the literal approach. But a lawyer advising Dr Rowland's brother and nephew is bound to tell them that there is at least some chance of persuading the court to take a reasonable line. The testator plainly intended to leave his property to the brother and nephew if he and his wife died in the same accident. (Lord Justice Russell himself recognised this when he said 'One may hazard the guess that if he could now be asked to whom in the events which happened he would wish his property to go, he would say that he would wish it go to his selected alternates. That would not mean, however, that he had expressed that wish by his will'.[2]) The chance of succeeding in such a case is good enough to justify litigation. A lawyer would properly tell the client that there are many judges who insist on applying the literal approach but that equally there are others who prefer a more liberal approach and even the literalists can sometimes be persuaded to adopt a more relaxed approach. It is only if judges uniformly applied the literal approach that the lawyer would have to advise that the chances of success were negligible.

If the literal approach does not therefore reduce litigation, does it promote better and more precise draftsmanship? There can be no doubt that the draftsman in the *Rowland* case used the word 'coinciding' inappropriately. Had he thought more carefully about the problem he might have used a phrase such as 'if we die in or as the result of the same accident' or, better still, he might have said, 'if my wife does not survive me by thirty days'. Will draftsmen be frightened into using language more accurately by dreadful warnings such as the *Rowland* case? To imagine that this is likely to be the result of such decisions strains credulity. First, it has to be assumed that the potential draftsmen even become aware of the Court of Appeal's ruling in the *Rowland* case. Most legal drafting is done by solicitors who are extremely busy and have little time to pore over the law reports. Some will notice the case; many will not. Some drafting, especially of wills, is done by laymen. It is obvious that they are highly unlikely to come to hear of the decision. If the case concerns a statutory provision, it is more likely that at least some of the small number of parliamentary draftsmen will see the report and note its significance.

But even assuming that the draftsman sees the decision, what difference will it make in practice to the quality of his work in his office? He does not need the Court of Appeal to tell him that he has to take care in drafting to select the right formula and the appropriate words. It is part of the nature

2   [1963] Ch. 1, 17.

of the activity. He has had it dinned into him ever since he came to the office as a trainee, pupil barrister or other junior. It is impossible to draft the simplest document without being all too conscious of the problem of finding the right phrase to express one's meaning. If he reads of the fate of some unfortunate draftsman's phrase in a report such as the *Rowland* case, it is improbable that he will do his work better that day as a result. He is already doing his work as well as he can according to his lights. There are far more effective pressures on him to draft well than the remote possibility that his labours will one day fall foul of the High Court or Court of Appeal. His superiors and colleagues in the office will be reading his work and making suggestions in any event. (As has been seen, parliamentary draftsmen work in pairs in order to improve the quality of their work.) The probable benefits of the literal approach in terms of improved draftsmanship are at best therefore highly speculative. When set against the manifest disadvantage of deciding an actual case in a sense contrary to what the judges believe to be the reasonable result for those parties, they appear unimpressive.

The literalist approach makes too little allowance for the natural ambiguities of language, for the frailties of even the most skilled of draftsmen and for the impossibility of foreseeing future events. In its 1969 report, *The Interpretation of Statutes*, the Law Commission said:

> To place undue emphasis on the literal meaning of the words of a provision is to assume an unattainable perfection in draftsmanship; it presupposes that the draftsmen can always choose words to describe the situations intended to be covered by the provision which will leave no room for a difference of opinion as to their meaning. Such an approach ignores the limitations of language, which is not infrequently demonstrated even at the level of the House of Lords when Law Lords differ as to the so-called 'plain meaning' of words. [para. 30.]

The literal approach is based on a narrow concentration on the actual words used, to the exclusion of the surrounding circumstances that might explain what the words were actually intended to mean. It is very closely connected with the traditional common law rule that excludes evidence as to the meaning of written documents. Llewellyn Davies wrote of this:

> A very marked feature of the common law rules for the construction of written instruments has been the rigidity with which they excluded all extrinsic evidence, and their insistence that the meaning of a document must be ascertained from its words as they stood. This attitude may well have originated in what Pollock and Maitland call the 'mystical awe' with which the early Common Law regarded the written instrument, and there can be no doubt but that the particular solemnity attributed to the instrument under seal has exercised a great influence on the attitude of the courts towards the written law.[3]

3   D. J. Llewellyn Davies, 'The Interpretation of Statutes in the Light of their Policy', 35 *Columbia Law Review*, 1935, p. 519 at p. 522.

It is a characteristic of some primitive legal systems that they attach excessive weight to the importance of words so that, for instance, the plaintiff who makes a slip in stating his claim is nonsuited. The literal approach to language by lawyers may be a form of this tradition. The draftsman is in effect punished for failing to do his job properly (except that it is his client, or in the case of statutes, the wider community, that bears the cost). The punitive or disciplinarian school of judicial interpretation remains a powerful element in the operation of the English legal system. ('If the draftsman has not got it right, let him try again and do better next time.')

At first sight the literal approach to statutory interpretation could be said to be based on a sense of the court's deference to the sovereignty of Parliament. ('It is not for the court to put words into parliament's mouth – we are simply the humble servants who will faithfully implement Parliament's will providing only that we are told clearly what Parliament desires.') But this humble posture is misleading. It conceals an ancient tradition amongst the judges that the common law is a superior form of creation to statutes. The judges have for instance often applied the presumption that Parliament does not intend to alter the common law unless it plainly states its intention to do so. (According to *Maxwell* 'few principles of statutory interpretation are applied as frequently'.)[4] The literal approach is part of the same philosophy. ('We cannot be expected to move unless we are given clear marching orders. If we do not consider the marching orders to be clear enough we will refuse to budge and the fault will be parliament's not ours.') This is hardly the attitude of the interpreter that is likely to produce the best results.

A final criticism of the literal approach to interpretation is that it is defeatist and lazy. The judge gives up the attempt to understand the document at the first attempt. Instead of struggling to discover what it means, he simply adopts the most straightforward interpretation of the words in question – without regard to whether this interpretation makes sense in the particular context. It is not that the literal approach necessarily gives the wrong result but rather that the result is purely accidental. It is the intellectual equivalent of deciding the case by tossing a coin. The literal *interpretation* in a particular case may in fact be the best and wisest of the various alternatives, but the literal *approach* is always wrong because it amounts to an abdication of responsibility by the judge. Instead of decisions being based on reason and principle, the literalist bases his decision on one meaning arbitrarily preferred. The limitations of this approach may be seen in a case decided a hundred years ago.

---

4 *Maxwell on the Interpretation of Statutes* (12th edn, 1969), p. 116.

Whiteley v. *Chappell* (1868–9) 4 L.R.Q.B. 147

A statute made it an offence for anyone in an election of guardians of the poor 'wilfully, fraudulently and with intent to affect the result of such election … to personate any person entitled to vote at such election'. The defendant was charged with personating someone who was deceased. The full text of the judgments delivered in the case is as follows:

> LUSH J.: I do not think we can, without straining them, bring the case within the words of the enactment. The legislature has not used words wide enough to make the personation of a dead person an offence. The words 'a person entitled to vote' can only mean, without a forced construction, a person who is entitled to vote at the time at which the personation takes place; in the present case, therefore, I feel bound to say the offence has not been committed. In the cases of *Rex* v. *Martin*, and *Rex* v. *Cramp* (Russ. & Ry. 324, 327) the judges gave no reasons for their decision; they probably held that 'supposed to be entitled' meant supposed by the person personating.
>
> HANNEN J.: I regret that we are obliged to come to the conclusion that the offence charged was not proved; but it would be wrong to strain words to meet the justice of the present case, because it might make a precedent, and lead to dangerous consequences in other cases.
>
> HAYES J. concurred.

If the court applied the literal approach, its refusal to discuss the problem was perfectly correct. It gave no attention to the question whether the statute was designed to protect the integrity of the election by preventing voting in the name of *anyone* else or whether it was aimed rather at the protection of the votes of living voters. In another statute it had been made an offence to personate 'a person entitled or supposed to be entitled to any prize money'. In *Rex* v. *Martin* and *Rex* v. *Cramp*, cited by Lush J., the court had held that 'supposed to be entitled' could include the case where the personation was of someone known to be dead. Counsel for the prosecution argued that these cases were in point and that they reflected the policy of trying to stop personation by anyone. 'The gist of the offence', he argued, 'is the fraudulently voting under another's name; the mischief is the same, whether the supposed voter be alive or dead.' Counsel for the defence, on the other hand, drew the court's attention to the Parliamentary Registration Act, s. 83 of which made it an offence to personate 'any person whose name appears on the register of voters, whether such person be he alive or dead'. Under the statute being considered by the court there was no express reference to the dead voter – 'the person must be entitled, that is could have voted himself'.

But the court did not do counsel the courtesy of paying any attention to their arguments. The judges looked at the words of the statute and nothing else. A dead person plainly was not entitled to vote. Ergo, the prosecution failed. Similarly, in the *Rowland* case, according to the dictionary or the plain meaning, 'coinciding' means two things occurring at the same moment. There being no evidence that Dr and Mrs Rowland died at the same moment, the will was inoperative and the property passed under the provisions of the Law of Property Act. The approach is mechanical, divorced both from the realities of the use of language and from the expectations and aspirations of the human beings concerned and, in that sense, it is irresponsible.

As will be seen (see especially cases cited on p. 175 below), the courts are increasingly moving away from the literal-mindedness seen in cases such as *Rowland* or *Whiteley* v. *Chappell* towards what is nowadays called a 'purposive approach'. But there are unfortunately still plenty of examples of the literal approach. See for instance *Shah* v. *Barnet L.B.C.* [1983] 1 All E.R. 226, in which the House of Lords said that overseas students who had been in this country for the purposes of schooling were 'ordinarily resident' in the country and were therefore entitled to mandatory local authority grants for university study. The Law Lords reached this view by analysing the meaning of the words without regard to their context or legislative intent. The decision was immediately cancelled by the government.

In *Griffith* v. *Secretary of State for the Environment* [1983] 2 W.L.R. 172, the plaintiff had to appeal against the Secretary of State's refusal of planning permission within six weeks from the date on which the Secretary of State took action. The House of Lords held by a majority that action was taken when an official put the date stamp on the decision letter even though the letter was never posted and the plaintiff therefore never received it.

In *Reynolds* [1981] 3 All E.R. 849, the Court of Appeal, Criminal Division unanimously quashed a conviction where the jury foreman had announced that the conviction was agreed to by ten of the jury but failed to state that two had dissented! (The Juries Act 1974, s. 17(3), required that the number voting both for conviction and against should be stated. The House of Lords later overruled the decision in *Pigg* [1983] 1 All E.R. 56.)

In *Lees* v. *Secretary of State for Social Services* [1985] 2 All E.R. 203, the House of Lords held that a blind person who could only go out with a human guide did not qualify for a mobility allowance because his physical disablement did not come within the phrase of being 'unable to walk or virtually unable to do so'.

The *Shah, Griffith, Reynolds* and *Lees* cases showed that the literal approach is still alive and flourishing.

For a bizarre application of the literal approach and the rejection of the 'purposive' approach of interpretation, see also *R.* v. *Broadcast Complaints Commission, ex parte Owen* [1985] 2 All E.R. 522. Dr David Owen on behalf of the Alliance parties complained to the Broadcast Complaints Commission regarding the allocation of time for party political broadcasts. The statutory terms of reference of the Commission on a literal interpretation covered that type of complaint. But the Divisional

Court held that it was clearly Parliament's intention that the Commission's terms of reference be limited to complaints affecting the reputation of individuals. In spite of this it was prepared to hold that the Commission did have jurisdiction to deal with the matter. Although it was legitimate for a court to adopt a purposive approach to hold that a statutory provision applied when it was clearly intended to do so, even though it would not apply under a strict or literal interpretation, the converse was not true. Therefore it was not legitimate, the court held, to adopt a purposive interpretation which precluded the application of a statute which would apply if the literal approach were adopted. (For comment see *Statute Law Review*, Summer 1985, p. 116.)

See further on literal interpretation Glanville Williams, 'The Meaning of Literal Interpretation', *New Law Journal*, 5 and 12 November 1981, pp. 1128 and 1149. Professor Williams argued that the question whether words are plain and unambiguous must always be considered in context. It is futile to ask first 'Are the words plain?' and secondly, 'Can we give effect to the probable interpretation of Parliament?' A court that decides that words are unambiguous is really deciding that the other interpretation suggested is impossible on the wording.

(b)   What of the golden rule?

If the literal rule is unacceptable, is the golden rule any better? The answer must be that it is not – for the golden rule is based on the literal rule. It tells the judge to follow the literal approach unless that results in absurdity, in which case he should find some other solution. Admittedly, the golden rule does at least have the saving grace that it may protect the court from egregious foolishness. But it does so only in the rare case where the judge is prepared to hold that the result is so absurd or unreasonable as virtually to require that he find some other construction. It is better to have such a rule than not to have it but it provides an answer to very few cases. Most statutory interpretation problems that come before the courts do not present such easy answers. There is usually a difficult choice to be made between two fairly plausible arguments. (If the matter were clear-cut one would assume that the lawyers would so advise their clients and the case would normally not reach the court.) The golden rule therefore only rescues the court in a tiny number of instances.

Moreover, there is no way of predicting what will strike a court as an absurdity sufficiently clear to justify this exceptional response. The point was made by John Willis in a famous article:

> What is an 'absurdity'? When is the result of a particular interpretation so 'absurd' that a court will feel justified in departing from a 'plain meaning'? There is the difficulty. 'Absurdity' is a concept no less vague and indefinite

than 'plain meaning': you cannot reconcile the cases upon it.[5] It is infinitely more a matter of personal opinion and infinitely more susceptible to the influence of personal prejudice. The result is that in ultimate analysis the 'golden rule' does allow a court to make quite openly exceptions which are based not on the social policy behind the Act, not even on the total effect of the words used by the legislature, but purely on the social and political views of the men who happen to be sitting on the case... .

What use do the courts make of the 'golden rule' today? Again the answer is the same – they use it as a device to achieve a desired result, in this case as a very last resort and only after all less blatant methods have failed. In those rare cases where the words in question are (a) narrow and precise, and (b) too 'plain' to be judicially held not plain, and yet to hold them applicable would shock the court's sense of justice, the court will, if it wishes to depart from their plain meaning, declare that to apply them literally to the facts of this case would result in an 'absurdity' of which the legislature could not be held guilty, and, invoking the 'golden rule', will work out an implied exception.[6]

One serious objection to the golden rule is therefore that it is erratic. One can never know whether a particular conclusion will be so offensive to the particular judge to qualify as an absurdity and, if so, whether the court will feel moved to apply the golden rather than the literal rule. There are plenty of decisions in which the courts have preferred to follow the literal approach notwithstanding the fact that it led to absurdity. But a further and equally strong objection is that the rule is silent as to how the court should proceed if it does find an unacceptable absurdity. It must find an answer to the problem, but the rule gives the court no guidance as to how it should set about the task. The golden rule is therefore little more than an unpredictable safety-valve to permit the courts to escape from some of the more unpalatable effects of the literal rule. It cannot be regarded as a sound basis for judicial decision-making.

(c)   Is the mischief rule any better?

The mischief rule (nowadays called the 'purposive' approach, see p. 175 below) is a very great improvement on the other two, in that it at least

---

5   Contrast *Vacher* v. *London Society of Compositors* [1913] A.C. 107, 117, 118 and *Washington* v. *Grand Trunk Railway*, 28 S.C.R. 184, where the court refused to find an absurdity, with *Ex parte Walton* (1881) 17 Ch.D. 746 and *The Ruahepu* [1927] P. 47, where the court did find an absurdity. See also *The Altrincham Electric Supply Co. Ltd* v. *Sale U.D.C.* (1936) 154 L.T.R. 379, in which the arbitrator, the trial judge and a majority of the House of Lords applied the literal interpretation, and the Court of Appeal and a minority of the House of Lords applied the mischief rule.

6   John Willis, 'Statute Interpretation in a Nutshell', 16 *Canadian Bar Review*, 1938, pp. 13–14.

encourages the court to have regard to the context in which the doubtful words appear. It is therefore entirely different from the literal and the golden rules which direct attention instead purely at the words themselves. Language cannot be properly understood without some knowledge of the context. ('Teach the children a game' is not likely to be intended to include strip poker.) It is therefore obviously sensible to permit and even encourage the court to go beyond the narrow confines of the disputed phrase itself. The mischief rule is designed to get the court to consider why the Act was passed and then to apply that knowledge in giving the words under consideration whatever meaning will best accord with the social purpose of the legislation.

But a crucial issue is where the court may look to discover 'the mischief'. As Lord Diplock explained in *Black-Clawson* [1975] A.C. 591 at 638, when the mischief rule was first propounded, the judges were not supposed to look further than the statute itself:

> LORD DIPLOCK: Statutes in the sixteenth century and for long thereafter in addition to the enacting words contained lengthy preambles reciting the particular mischief or defect in the common law that the enacting words were designed to remedy. So, when it was laid down, the 'mischief' rule did not require the court to travel beyond the actual words of the statute itself to identify 'the mischief and defect for which the common law did not provide', for this would have been stated in the preamble. It was a rule of construction of the actual words appearing in the statute and nothing else. In construing modern statutes which contain no preambles to serve as aids to the construction of enacting words, the 'mischief' rule must be used with caution to justify any reference to extraneous documents for this purpose.

The right to inquire into the background to, and reasons for, legislation has therefore been restricted. What then is permitted?

4. UNDERSTANDING THE CONTEXT – STATUTES AND JUDICIAL DECISIONS

(a) The court can read the whole statute

There is no doubt, first of all, that a court may read the whole of the statute that has produced the problem. It may also read both *the long and the short title*. Until well into the nineteenth century, the long title could not be considered in construing a statute – on the ground that it was not regarded as part of the statute. But the modern view, which emerged during the nineteenth century, is that the title of the statute may be consulted for the purpose of ascertaining its meaning.[7]

---

7   For examples see *Fisher* v. *Raven* [1964] A.C. 210; *Brown* v. *Brown* [1967] P. 105 at 110; *Haines* v. *Herbert* [1963] 1 W.L.R. 1401 at 1404.

It may also read *the preamble*. Old statutes commonly had lengthy preambles setting out the purposes of legislation; today they are rare. But the House of Lords ruled decisively in 1957 that the courts could have regard to the preamble when construing a statute.

The case was *Attorney General* v. *Prince Ernest Augustus of Hanover* [1957] A.C. 436, in which the courts had to consider an application by the Prince to be recognised as a British subject under a statute which granted British nationality to 'all persons lineally descended from the Electoress Sophia of Hanover'. Lord Normand said (at 467, 468):

> When there is a preamble it is generally in its recitals that the mischief to be remedied and the scope of the Act are described. It is therefore clearly permissible to have recourse to it as an aid to construing the enacting provisions.... The courts are concerned with the practical business of deciding a *lis* [a piece of litigation], and when the plaintiff puts forward one construction of an enactment and the defendant another, it is the court's business in any case of some difficulty, after informing itself of what I have called the legal and factual context including the preamble, to consider in the light of this knowledge whether the enacting words admit of both the rival constructions put forward. If they admit of only one construction, that construction will receive effect even if it is inconsistent with the preamble, but if the enacting words are capable of either of the constructions offered by the parties, the construction which fits the preamble may be preferred.

In *Prince Ernest's* case it was found that the enacting words were clear and they could not therefore be affected by contrary indications in a rather vague preamble.

Marginal notes printed at the side of sections in an Act which purport to summarise their effect have sometimes been used as an aid to construction. The weight of the authorities is to the effect that they are not part of the statute and should not be considered, for they are 'inserted not by Parliament nor under the authority of Parliament but by irresponsible persons'.[8] For a learned article of over 40 pages on marginal notes see G. Stewart, 'Legislative Drafting and the Marginal Note', 16 *Statute Law Review*, 1995, pp. 21–67.

The *headings* prefixed to sections or sets of sections in some statutes are regarded as preambles to those sections. They may explain ambiguous words. But clear words in the statute cannot be affected by contrary indications in the heading (*R.* v. *Surrey (N.E. Area) Assessment Committee* [1948] 1 K.B. 28 at 32, 33).[9]

Schedules to a statute are treated as fully part of the statute and may be used in construing the Act.

---

8   *Re Woking Urban Council (Basingstoke Canal) Act 1911* [1914] 1 Ch. 300 per Phillimore L.J. at 322.
9   See also *DPP* v. *Schildkamp* [1971] A.C. 1, 10, 20, 28.

According to some authorities *punctuation* is supposed to be disregarded in the construction of statutes since there was normally no punctuation in ancient statutes. Before 1850 there was no punctuation and there was no authority for the printers to insert any thereafter. In a modern tax case Lord Reid said 'even if punctuation in more modern Acts can be looked at (which is very doubtful), I do not think that one can have any regard to punctuation in older Acts' (*I.R.C.* v. *Hinchy* [1960] A.C 748 at 765).[10] The effect of this principle is that existing punctuation in a statute can be ignored or, if the court chooses, it can re-punctuate the words in a way different from that in the text. This view is, however, controversial and some (including three great experts, Thornton, Dreidger and Bennion), hold that punctuation *is* to be regarded as part of the statute.[11]

An Act is to be read as a whole, so the court can and indeed should read all of a statute in order to understand any particular part of it. So, in *Gibson* v. *Ryan* [1968] 1 Q.B. 250 the question for the court was whether an inflatable rubber dinghy and a fish basket found on the appellant were within the meaning of the word 'instrument' in s. 7(1) of the Salmon and Freshwater Fisheries Protection (Scotland) Act 1951. The Divisional Court said they were not. Diplock L.J. referred to s. 10 of the Act which drew a distinction between instruments on the one hand, boats on the other hand and baskets on the third hand.

But sometimes the court may find that a word used in part of a statute is not to be given the same meaning as the same word in a different part of the same statute. Everything depends on the particular context.

(b)   The court can read earlier statutes

Sometimes, by tracing the history of a particular phrase back through earlier Acts one can throw light on its meaning. If the language changes between one statute and another, inferences can be drawn from the fact; alternatively, sometimes understanding of meaning can be based on a similarity of language in the present Act and some earlier statute when the historical position was different. In *Armah* v. *Government of Ghana* [1968] A.C. 192 the court had to interpret s. 5 of the Fugitive Offenders Act 1891 which required that evidence should raise 'a strong or probable presumption that the fugitive committed the offence'. Lord Reid showed that nineteenth-century Acts drew a distinction between two kinds of evidence – that which raised a strong presumption of guilt and that which

---

10   See also *DPP* v *Schildkamp*, at 10; and *Hanlon* v. *The Law Society* [1980] 2 W.L.R. 756 at 815, per Lord Lowry.
11   See V.C.R.A.C. Crabbe, 'Punctuation in Legislation', *Statute Law Review*, Summer 1988, p. 87.

simply gave reason to inquire into guilt. The distinction, he said, must have been known to those who framed the 1891 Act and indicated that the disputed words must refer to the first kind of evidence. It was therefore not sufficient for the magistrate to be satisfied that there was enough evidence against the fugitive on which a jury might properly convict.

A phrase used in one Act can be construed by reference to the same or a similar phrase used in earlier Acts – at least if the Acts deal with the same subject-matter. But the qualification about the similarity of the subject-matter is not always made. The Betting and Gaming Act 1960, for instance, required an applicant for a betting shop to insert a notice 'in a newspaper circulating in the authority's area'. It was held that an advertisement in *Sporting Life* was sufficient and that the Act did not require an advertisement either in a local paper or in a national paper circulating in the area. The court drew a distinction between the 1960 Act and s. 12 of the Highways Act 1959 which specifically referred to 'a local newspaper circulating in the area' (*R.* v. *Westminster Betting Licensing Committee, ex parte Peabody Donation Fund* [1963] 2 Q.B. 750).

The last case cited is an example of the court inferring that the draftsman of one piece of legislation is aware of the use of similar phrases in earlier Acts and that a difference in wording between one Act and another is conscious and intentional. This theory, based on the omniscience of Parliamentary draftsmen, is often carried to improbable lengths. It may be that the draftsman of, say, the latest Rent Act will be aware of the use of language in previous Rent Acts – though given the extreme length and complexity of such legislation even that may be assuming a good deal too much. But it is hardly reasonable to assume that the draftsman has in mind the language used in a mass of other prior statutes which have no direct connection with the one he is presently engaged in drafting.

An example of the court being influenced by the assumption that Parliament must be deemed to have been aware of earlier legislation and non-usage (regarding the meaning of the words 'immoral conduct') was *Crook* v. *Edmondson*. Consider whether the majority's view in this regard was reasonable:

Crook v. *Edmondson* [1966] 1 All E.R. 833 (Divisional Court, Q.B.D.)

E., a male, was charged with persistently soliciting for immoral purposes through 'kerb-crawling' in a public place contrary to s. 32 of the Sexual Offences Act 1956. The Act was a consolidation measure. Its preamble said it was to 'consolidate ... the statute law of England and Wales relating to sexual crimes, to the abduction, procuration and prostitution of women and to kindred offences'. The statute repealed, inter alia, the Vagrancy Act 1898, s. 1(1) of which made it an offence for a male person persistently to solicit or importune for immoral purposes in any public place. The justices dismissed the case on the ground that although the conduct of the accused was immoral it was not within the meaning of 'immoral purposes' in the 1956 Act. The prosecution appealed. The Divisional Court was divided.

WINN L.J.: In my judgment the words 'immoral purposes' in their ordinary meaning connote in a wide and general sense all purposes involving conduct which has the property of being wrong rather than right in the judgment of the majority of contemporary fellow citizens. In that sense, as the justices appreciated, the words are, at least arguably, apt to cover the conduct alleged against the respondent in the present case.

However I am convinced at least of this. That Parliament cannot be supposed to have used those words in their general sense, as comprising all wrong conduct, in a statute relating solely to sexual offences; soliciting persons to commit non-sexual crime is dealt with by the law relating to accessories before the fact or specifically by statute, e.g., in respect of mutiny, breach of security or Post Office offences. It seems to me to follow that the 'immoral purposes' here in question must be immoral in respect of sexual conduct. If, then, some limitation is properly to be put on the words the problem is to define their meaning in less general terms. There is a presumption in construing a consolidating statute that it is not intended to alter the law enacted by any statute which it repeals and a further, perhaps less persuasive, presumption that words or phrases which have obtained, at the time when any enactment is passed, an accepted meaning by force of decisions or usage of courts or even of the public, have been used by Parliament to convey the like meaning and effect. The court has not been informed by affirmative evidence, nor were the justices, that in 1898 sexual intercourse or intimacy between a man and a female prostitute was 'immoral', in the sense of the definition which I have adopted (scilicet without reference to any matrimonial implication). What is known, by concession of counsel for the appellant, is that there is no reported case in which any court so treated, or it seems was invited so to treat, such conduct. Parliament must be taken, I think, to have been aware of what may be perhaps termed 'this non-usage', extending over a period of over fifty years before 1956, no less than of the usage which had by then become general of relying on the Act of 1898 in charging males with inviting homosexual intimacies whether or not for reward. If s. 32 of the Act of 1956 is to be given the meaning contended for by the prosecution it effected a marked change not shown to be intended by any other provision of the Act of 1956. In their context in the Act of 1898 the words 'solicits ... for immoral purposes' may well, it seems to me, have been intended to relate not merely to soliciting for homosexual intimacies but also to the soliciting of customers for prostitutes, sometimes called 'pimping', as well as conceivably, to persuasion of girls to become prostitutes. In my judgment such a context and the context of subject-matter of trading in or exploiting prostitution even more plainly displayed by s. 22 to s. 31 and s. 33 to s. 36 of the Sexual Offences Act 1956, must, apart altogether from any considerations derived from the history and application of the relevant legislation and practice, produce a controlling effect on the construction of s. 32 of the Act of 1956. A possible view of that effect might be that it is equivalent to expanding the phrase in the section into: such immoral purposes as are referred to in this part of the Act of

1956. That was the view of the justices and I concur in it solely for the purposes of the present appeal and to the extent which they require: I am not prepared, however, to attempt any definition of the section. It is enough to say that in my view the conduct alleged was not an offence under the section.

It is noteworthy, I think, as the justices thought, when considering how special is the s. 32 offence, that the penalty is six months' imprisonment on summary trial, or on an indictment two years; that any person may arrest, without a warrant, any person found committing it; that a person accused under the section has no right to claim to be tried on indictment under s. 25 of the Magistrates' Courts Act, 1952; that women cannot be charged with the offence. For the reasons which I have endeavoured to state, whilst I recognise that the prosecution had in this case the good motive of protecting virtuous women from annoyance, I think that they have sought to put on the relevant words a meaning which is not only new but unwarranted. I would dismiss this appeal.[12]

LORD PARKER C.J.: I have had the advantage of reading the judgment which has just been delivered by WINN L.J.; I entirely agree and have nothing to add.

SACHS J. read the following judgment: The essence of the case of the prosecution was that the respondent spoke in succession to two known common prostitutes in a street which they frequent in order to solicit for prostitution: there was no evidence of the respondent having approached anyone other than a common prostitute. It is thus an inference that can and probably should be drawn that at the material time each woman was herself soliciting – offering herself for payment. On giving the matter further consideration it now seems to me that there arose a serious issue whether the prosecution had on those facts established a prima facie case that the respondent had solicited or importuned anyone. Do the words 'solicit or importune' when properly construed apply to a man who has done no more than approach a common prostitute who has in fact already offered herself to him for money?

This issue, however, was one which was not canvassed before this court, … nor was it part of the question raised for the consideration of this court, i.e.,

'The question for the opinion of the High Court is whether the persistent importuning by a man of a woman for the purpose of having sexual intercourse with him, is an offence under s. 32 of the Sexual Offences Act, 1956.'

It would in these circumstances not be proper for me to express an opinion on this issue, although had it been raised it might have enabled a decision to be reached in this case without having to deal with the above question.

On that question itself I have the considerable misfortune to differ, with natural diffidence, from the views of the majority of this court. I agree that

12 In the debates on the Street Offences Act 1959, however, the Lord Chancellor had said that s. 32 of the 1956 Sexual Offences Act covered pestering of women by men and that there was therefore no need for an amendment to cover such solicitation (House of Lords, *Hansard*, vol. 216, col. 806). (Ed.)

'immoral purposes' in s. 32 of the Act of 1956 must relate to sexual purposes. I also consider (in agreement, I think, with what has been said by WINN L.J.), that one cannot insert the words 'another man' after the word 'importune' (so as to make it read 'solicit or importune another man for immoral purposes') either in s. 32 of the Act of 1956 or in the earlier Vagrancy Act, 1898. I am, however, unable to agree that in s. 32 one can in effect substitute for the broad words 'immoral purposes' some such words as 'purposes which by other provisions of this Act are declared to be offences': and a fortiori would be unable to agree to such a substitution in the Act of 1898. As in other matters which took the field of public morals (cf. per the speeches of VISCOUNT SIMONDS, LORD MORRIS OF BORTH-Y-GEST and LORD HODSON in *Shaw* v. *Director of Public Prosecutions* [1962] A.C. 220, 268, 292, 293), it seems to my mind appropriate that the decision as to what is an 'immoral purpose' should be the responsibility of the jury of the day or of whoever is entrusted with that decision in lieu of a jury. I would, incidentally, be averse to that decision being fettered by the result of any preliminary inquiry into either what were the prevalent sexual vices at the end of the last century or what were then the prevalent views on some aspect of sexual immorality. If on the basis just expressed it were found that the now unfortunately prevalent conduct known as kerb crawling (i.e. a man from a slowly driven car importuning ordinary young women to accompany him for sexual intercourse) fell within the ambit of s. 32, that would not seem to me inherently wrong. Accordingly, I would have preferred to reserve the position as to what is the answer to the exact question posed in the Case Stated: whilst on the particular facts of this case not regretting the failure of this prosecution as proposed by my lords.

But *Farrell* v. *Alexander* [1977] A.C. 59 shows that the assumption that the draftsman knew of the existing statutory precedents or even case law should not *necessarily* be made. The House of Lords was interpreting the meaning of the words 'any person' in the Rent Act 1968, a consolidation measure. In 1972 the Court of Appeal had held that the words in that context meant 'the landlord' and did not include tenants, agents and other middlemen. In its 1972 decision the Court of Appeal had placed emphasis on the fact that in 1921 the Court of Appeal had construed the words 'any person' in a similar provision of an earlier Act in such a way as to limit its meaning to landlords. In 1949 and 1965 there had been further legislation on the same topic and Parliament had used the same phrase. It was contended that this showed that Parliament intended the phrase to mean only landlords. Lord Wilberforce disagreed:

LORD WILBERFORCE (at 74): My Lords, I have never been attracted by the doctrine of parliamentary endorsement of decided cases: it seems to me to be based upon a theory of legislative formation which is possibly fictional. But if there are cases in which this doctrine may be applied, and I must respect the opinions of those judges who have so held, any case must be a clear one.... This case is certainly not such a case. It really cannot be said if our reasoning is to have any contact with reality that the draftsman of the Act of 1949 (a) must have had in mind a decision of 1921 [*Remmington* v. *Larchin* [1921] 3 K.B. 404], whose reported headnote opens with the words 'that section 8(1) was reasonably capable of two constructions' and all of the judgments which underlined the ambiguity and obscurity of the enactment, (b) decided to perpetuate this ambiguity while removing one of the grounds of the decision, (c) should have committed Parliament to the continued existence of a lacuna or loophole which had no merits to commend it.

To impute such a process of thought to the architect of the new section and to those who voted it into existence really strains credibility.

Lord Simon of Glaisdale likewise thought the doctrine was sometimes carried too far:

It is a fact that a parliamentary draftsman (like any draftsman) does acquaint himself thoroughly with the existing law (statutory and judge-made) before starting to draft. Any draftsman of a rent restriction Act after 1921 may be presumed (nor is it an idle presumption) to have had *Remmington* v. *Larchin* in mind. When, then, he used language which had been interpreted in *Remmington* v. *Larchin* he presumptively used it in the sense in which it had there been interpreted. If therefore the object of statutory interpretation were to ascertain what Parliament meant to say, the *Barras* doctrine would indeed be potent and primary. But the object of statutory interpretation is rather to ascertain the meaning of what Parliament has said. On this approach the previous judicial interpretation is merely one of the facts within the knowledge of the draftsman in the light of which he will draft... . If Parliament wishes to endorse the previous interpretation it can do so in terms... . The sovereignty of Parliament is fundamental constitutional law; but courts of law have their own constitutional duties, important amongst which is to declare the meaning of a statutory enactment. To pre-empt a court of construction from performing independently its own constitutional duty of examining the validity of a previous interpretation, the intention of Parliament to endorse the previous judicial decision would have to be expressed or clearly implied. Mere repetition of language which has been the subject of previous judicial interpretation is entirely neutral in this respect – or at most implies merely the truism that the language has been the subject of judicial interpretation, for whatever (and it may be much or little) that is worth. [At p. 107.]

In this particular case the House of Lords decided to extend the meaning of 'any person' to include a wider range of persons and it was therefore seeking for ways around the argument that Parliament must have been assumed to have meant the same by the phrase as in the cases decided in 1949 and 1965 and 1968. The 1968 Act was a consolidation Act and three of the Lords (Lords Wilberforce, Simon and Edmund-Davies) said that if the words of a consolidation measure were clear there was no need to refer to the legislative antecedents. Again this is a way for a court to disembarrass itself of the awkward fact that the legislative history suggests a different answer to the problem from the one it had in mind. Given the difference of judicial opinion over the meaning of the words 'any person', it was somewhat disingenuous to argue that they were so clear as not to require elucidation, inter alia, from the previous legislation on the subject.

5.   UNDERSTANDING THE CONTEXT – EVIDENCE BEYOND STATUTES AND JUDICIAL DECISIONS

In *Attorney-General* v. *Prince Ernest Augustus* [1957] A.C. 436, Lord Simonds, normally a strict constructionist, stated that in interpreting a statute 'I conceive it to be my right and duty to examine every word of a statute in its context, and I use "context" in its widest sense, which I have already indicated as including not only other enacting provisions of the same statute, but its preamble, the existing state of the law, other statutes *in pari materia*, and the mischief which I can by those *and other legitimate means* discern the statute was intended to remedy' (at 461, emphasis supplied).

By this phrase 'and other legitimate means' Lord Simonds suggested that the search for the context might properly go beyond the statute itself, other statutes and the precedents. In 1938 John Willis, in his article 'Statute Interpretation in a Nutshell', argued that the mischief rule was 'without doubt unworkable' because of the narrow way in which the courts interpreted the nature of the materials that might be consulted: 'You cannot interpret an Act in the light of its policy without knowing what that policy is: that you cannot discover without referring to all the events which led up to the legislation: but a well-settled rule of law forbids reference to any matters extrinsic to the written words of the Act as printed.'[13] But since that time there has been considerable development of the law.

(a)   International conventions or treaties as a source

The English courts took a more relaxed attitude to the use of an international treaty where it forms the basis for internal legislation – at least if the legislation is ambiguous. In *Salomon* v. *Commissioners of Customs and Excise* [1967] 2 Q.B. 116, the Court of Appeal said it was entitled to resolve ambiguities or obscurities to look at a 1950 international convention, although the 1952 Act did not refer to it, because English law ought to be interpreted in such a way as to be consistent with international law. The terms of the statute and of the convention being virtually identical, the inference was irresistible that the statute was intended to embody the convention. Lord Denning and Lords Justices Diplock and Russell all agreed on this.

13   *Canadian Bar Review*, 1938, p. 15.

In *James Buchanan & Co. Ltd* v. *Babco Forwarding and Shipping (UK) Ltd* [1977] 3 All E.R. 1048, the House of Lords held that the correct approach in construing a UK statute which incorporates and gives effect to a European convention is to interpret the English text by the special rules applicable to the interpretation of international conventions unconstrained by technical rules of English law but on broad principles. Where the convention is printed in the statute in both French and English it was legitimate to look at the French text – providing that the English text was ambiguous.

In *Warwick Film Productions Ltd* v. *Eisinger* [1969] 1 Ch. 508, by contrast, the Chancery Division refused to permit reference to an international convention on the ground that there was no ambiguity in the English Act. See also *Fothergill* v. *Monarch Airlines* [1980] 3 W. L.R. 209 where the House of Lords preferred the French text of the Convention to the English. The case is also authority for the proposition that English judges interpreting an international convention forming part of English law may take account of the preparatory materials leading up to the convention (the *travaux préparatoires*). The Law Lords were influenced in reaching this conclusion by the fact that in most other countries preparatory materials were admissible in evidence even on the interpretation of internal legislation. It seemed right, therefore, that in this country they should be admissible at least on the interpretation of international agreements – not least because of the desirability of the courts in different countries achieving uniformity in their approach to the same issues.

The special case of international conventions even permitted the court to look at Hansard. In *Pickstone and Others* v. *Freemans p.l.c.* [1988] 2 All E.R. 803, the courts had to interpret the Equal Pay Act 1970 which implemented obligations taken on by the UK under article 119 of the EEC Treaty and a European Community Council Directive. Three of the judges in the House of Lords referred to the speech of the Secretary of State given in introducing regulations which were made part of the 1970 Act, as a guide to the intention of Parliament. Lord Templeman seemed to place emphasis on the fact that the regulations were not subject to any process of amendment by Parliament. 'In these circumstances the explanations of the government and the criticisms voiced by MPs in the debates which led to approval of the draft regulations provide some indications of the intentions of Parliament' (at 814). The other two (Lords Keith and Oliver) made no reference to this aspect of the case.

(b) General historical background

The courts have always been willing to hear counsel state what he understands the general historical setting of legislation to have been, where this is relevant. Counsel may certainly cite earlier cases for this purpose and may also probably refer to legal textbooks. Often the court will refer to such surrounding circumstances in the course of its judgment. But this is not to say that the court would welcome citation by counsel of historical works by learned non-lawyer authors. If this were attempted by counsel, it would be likely to be resisted by the court.

(c) Government publications

There are two categories of relevant official publication. One is the report of a commission or committee – Royal Commission, departmental committee, Law Commission, etc. – which precedes and leads to the statute in question. The second is other material. The rule in regard to the latter was supposed to be clear – the courts could not look at any such document either for the purposes of understanding the mischief or of construing the words in question. The courts were not, for instance, permitted to look at the explanatory memorandum attached to all bills before Parliament. (See *Escoigne Properties Ltd* v. *I.R.C.* [1958] A.C. 549). In *Katikiro of Buganda* v. *Attorney-General* [1961] 1 W.L.R. 119, a White Paper containing the recommendations of a constitutional conference held in Uganda was held inadmissible as an aid to the construction of the Buganda Agreement 1955 (Order in Council, 1955).

On official reports that lead to legislation the *locus classicus* was the *Black-Clawson* case.[14] The Law Lords divided as to whether such reports could be consulted in the construction of the disputed words under consideration. Two (Lords Reid and Wilberforce) thought that they could not, even where the legislation corresponded exactly with the draft bill in the report; two (Lords Dilhorne and Simon of Glaisdale) disagreed. Lord Diplock thought they could be used to understand the context, including the construction of an ambiguous phrase, so as to give effect to Parliament's aim. But all five held that the reports were admissible for the purpose of understanding the mischief with which the legislation was intended to deal. Lord Reid said (p. 613):

> The mischief which this Act was intended to remedy may have been common knowledge 40 years ago. I do not think that it is today. But it so happens that a committee including many eminent and highly skilled members made a full investigation of the matter and reported some months before the Act was passed: Foreign Judgments (Reciprocal Enforcement) Committee 1932 (Cmd. 213).

14 *Black-Clawson International Ltd.* v. *Papierwerke Waldhof-Aschaffenburg A.G.* [1975] A.C. 591.

I think that we can take this report as accurately stating the 'mischief' and the law as it was then understood to be, and therefore we are fully entitled to look at those parts of the report which deal with those matters.

But the report contains a great deal more than that. It contains recommendations, a draft Bill and other instruments intended to embody those recommendations, and comments on what the committee thought the Bill achieved. The draft Bill corresponds in all material respects with the Act so it is clear that Parliament adopted the recommendations of the committee. But nevertheless I do not think that we are entitled to take any of this into account in construing the Act.

Construction of the provisions of an Act is for the court and for no one else. This may seem technical but it is good sense. Occasionally we can find clear evidence of what was intended; more often any such evidence, if there is any, is vague and uncertain. If we are to take into account evidence of Parliament's intention the first thing we must do is to reverse our present practice with regard to consulting Hansard... . [on which see below].

If we are to refrain from considering expressions of intention in Parliament it appears to me that a fortiori we should disregard expressions of intention by committees or royal commissions which reported before the Bill was introduced. I may add that we did in fact examine the whole of this report – it would have been difficult to avoid that – but I am left in some doubt as to how the committee would have answered some of the questions which we have now to answer, because I do not think that they were ever considered by the committee.

LORD WILBERFORCE (at 629–30): My Lords, we are entitled, in my opinion, to approach the interpretation of this subsection, and of the Act of 1933 as a whole, from the background of the law as it stood, or was thought to stand, in 1933 and of the legislative intentions. As to these matters the report to which my noble and learned friend, Lord Reid, has referred is of assistance. He has set out in his opinion the basis upon which the courts may consult such documents. I agree with his reasoning and I only desire to add an observation of my own on one point. In my opinion it is not proper or desirable to make use of such a document as a committee or commission report, or for that matter of anything reported as said in Parliament, or any official notes on clauses, for a direct statement of what a proposed enactment is to mean or of what the committee or commission thought it means – on this point I am in agreement with my noble and learned friend Lord Diplock. To be concrete, in a case where a committee prepared a draft Bill and accompanies that by a clause by clause commentary, it ought not to be permissible, even if the proposed Bill is enacted without variation, to take the meaning of the Bill from the commentary. There are, to my mind, two kinds of reason for this. The first is the practical one, that if this process were allowed the courts would merely have to interpret, as in arguments we were invited to interpret, two documents instead of one – the Bill and the commentary on it, in particular annex V, paragraph 13. The second is one of constitutional principle. Legislation in England is passed by Parliament, and put in the form of written words. This legislation is given legal effect upon subjects by virtue of judicial decision, and it is the function of the courts to say what the application of the words used to particular cases or individuals is to be. This power which has been devolved by the judges from the earliest times is an essential part of the constitutional process by which subjects are brought under the rule of law – as distinct from the rule of the King or the rule of Parliament; and it would be a degradation of that process if the courts were to be merely a reflecting mirror of what some other interpretation agency might say.[15]

The rule laid down by the House of Lords in *Black-Clawson* was clear but it was never certain whether it could be applied. If the judges read a text for the purpose of understanding the mischief how can they exclude from their minds what they have read when it comes to interpreting the statutory provision in question?

(d) Parliamentary debates

The rule as to the admissibility of parliamentary debates was clear. Until very recently it was accepted by all that for the purposes of interpretation of a statutory provision it was not permissible to look at the parliamentary debates. (Indeed, until 1980 it was technically not permissible to cite in a court anything said in the House of Commons without prior consent of the House. This rule (which was not always observed) dated back to 1818 but it was abolished in 1980 – see Patricia M. Leopold, *Public Law* (1981), pp. 316–21; 15 *Legal Studies*, 1995, pp. 204–18; and David Miers, 'Citing Hansard as an Aid to Interpretation', *Statute Law Review*, 1983, pp. 98–102.)

The rule that judges should not consult parliamentary debates was first challenged by Lord Denning, the former Master of the Rolls. In the course of the Court of Appeal's decision in *Davis* v. *Johnson*, Lord Denning confessed that he had been aided in reaching his view by what had been said in parliament:

Davis v. *Johnson* [1979] A.C. 264 (Court of Appeal)

The case concerned the provisions of the Domestic Violence and Matrimonial Proceedings Act 1976 and in particular whether the Act provided protection for cohabitees as well as wives.

LORD DENNING M.R. (at 276–7): Some may say, and indeed have said, that judges should not pay any attention to what is said in Parliament. They should grope about in the dark for the meaning of an Act without switching on the light. I do not accede to this view. In some cases Parliament is assured in the most explicit terms what the effect of a statute will be. It is on that footing that members assent to the clause being agreed to. It is on that understanding that an

15 But see p. 160 below. (Ed.)

amendment is not pressed. In such cases I think the court should be able to look at the proceedings. And, as I read the observations of Lord Simon of Glaisdale in *Dockers' Labour Club and Institute Ltd.* v. *Race Relations Board*,[16] he thought so too. I would give an instance. In the debate on the Race Relations Act 1968 there was, I believe, a ministerial assurance given in Parliament about its application to clubs; and I have a feeling that some of their Lordships looked at it privately and were influenced by it: see *Charter* v. *Race Relations Board*.[17] I could wish that, in those club cases, we had been referred to it. It might have saved us from the errors which the House afterwards held we had fallen into. And it is obvious that there is nothing to prevent a judge looking at these debates himself privately and getting some guidance from them. Although it may shock the purists, I may as well confess that I have sometimes done it. I have done it in this very case. It has thrown a flood of light on the position. The statements made in committee disposed completely of counsel for the respondent's argument before us.

On appeal, the House of Lords [1979] A.C. 317 did not, however, look kindly on Lord Denning's approach. All five Lords said expressly that he was wrong. Lord Kilbrandon and Lord Salmon did not elaborate but the other three added some reasons and further thoughts.

LORD DILHORNE (at 337): There is one other matter to which I must refer. It is a well and long-established rule that counsel cannot refer to Hansard as an aid to the construction of a statute. What is said by a Minister or by a member sponsoring a bill is not a legitimate aid to the interpretation of an Act. [As Lord Reid said in *Beswick* v. *Beswick* [1968] A.C. 58 at 73–4]

'In construing any Act of Parliament we are seeking the intention of Parliament, and it is quite true that we must deduce that intention from the words of the Act ... For purely practical reasons we do not permit debates in either House to be cited: it would add greatly to the time and expense involved in preparing cases involving the construction of a statute if counsel were expected to read all the debates in Hansard, and it would often be impracticable for counsel to get access to at least the older reports of debates in select committees of the House of Commons; moreover, in a very large proportion of cases such a search, even if practicable, would throw no light on the question before the court ...'

If it was permissible to refer to Hansard, in every case concerning the construction of a statute counsel might regard it as necessary to search through the Hansards of all the proceedings in each House to see if in the course of them anything relevant to the construction had been said. If it was thought that a particular Hansard had anything relevant in it and the attention of the court was drawn to it, the court might also think it desirable to look at the other Hansards. The result might be that attention was devoted to the interpretation of ministerial and other statements in Parliament at the expense

16 [1974] 3 All E.R. 592 at 600, 60; [1976] AC 285 at 299.
17 [1973] 1 All E.R. 512 at 526, 527; [1973] A.C. 868 at 899–901.

of consideration of the language in which Parliament had thought to express its intention. While, of course, anyone can look at Hansard, I venture to think that it would be improper for a judge to do so before arriving at his decision and before this case I have never known that done. It cannot be right that a judicial decision should be affected by matter which a judge has seen but to which counsel could not refer and on which counsel had no opportunity to comment.

LORD SCARMAN (at 349–50): There are two good reasons why the courts should refuse to have regard to what is said in Parliament or by Ministers as aids to the interpretations of a statute. First, such material is an unreliable guide to the meaning of what is enacted. It promotes confusion, not clarity. The cut and thrust of debate and the pressures of executive responsibility, essential features of open and responsible government, are not always conducive to a clear and unbiased explanation of the meaning of statutory language. And the volume of parliamentary and ministerial utterances can confuse by its very size. Secondly, counsel are not permitted to refer to Hansard in argument. So long as this rule is maintained by Parliament (it is not the creation of the judges), it must be wrong for the judge to make any judicial use of proceedings in Parliament for the purpose of interpreting statutes.[18]

Lord Diplock (at 329) drew a distinction between consulting parliamentary debates and continental courts or the European Court of Justice looking at *travaux préparatoires*:

I have had the advantage of reading what my noble and learned friends, Viscount Dilhorne and Lord Scarman, have to say about the use of Hansard as an aid to the construction of a statute. I agree with them entirely and would add a word of warning against drawing too facile an analogy between proceedings in the Parliament of the United Kingdom and those travaux préparatoires which may be looked at by the courts of some of our fellow member states of the European Economic Community to resolve doubts as to the interpretation of national legislation or by the European Court of Justice, and consequently by English courts themselves, to resolve doubts as to the interpretation of community legislation. Community legislation, viz. regulations and directives, are required by the EEC Treaty to state reasons on which they are based, and when submitted to the EEC Council in the form of a proposal by the EEC Commission the practice is for them to be accompanied by an explanatory memorandum by the commission expanding the reasons which appear in more summary form in the draft regulation or directive itself. The explanatory memoranda are published in the Official Journal together with the proposed regulations or directives to which they relate. These are true travaux préparatoires: they are of a very different character from what is said in the passion or lethargy of Parliamentary debate; yet a survey of the judgments of the European Court of Justice will show how rarely that court refers even to these explanatory memoranda for the purpose of interpreting community legislation.

18 As has been seen (p. 142 above), this rule was abrogated in October 1980. (Ed.)

The House of Lords ruling in *Davis* v. *Johnson* seemed to have settled the question of courts looking at Hansard.[19] But only 13 years later in November 1992 the House of Lords changed its mind.

(e) *Pepper v. Hart*

In *Pepper* v. *Hart* [1993] A.C.593, [1993] 1 All E.R. 42 heard by seven Law Lords (Lords Mackay, Keith, Bridge, Griffiths, Ackner, Oliver and Browne-Wilkinson),[20] the House of Lords, the Lord Chancellor dissenting, held that judges could consult Hansard. The decision is widely regarded as an important development in the English system.

The case, as so often in appeals to the House of Lords, was a tax case. It concerned nine schoolmasters at a well-known public school, Malvern College, who were assessed to tax by the Inland Revenue in respect of the benefit they enjoyed because their sons were educated at the school for one fifth of the ordinary fees. The schoolmasters lost in the Court of Appeal but they won in the House of Lords after the Law Lords took notice of a statement in Parliament that the purpose of the relevant statutory provision was to tax concessionary education for teachers' children on the marginal cost to the employer and not on the average cost of the benefit.

The leading judgment was given by Lord Browne-Wilkinson. He said that the rule forbidding access to Hansard had already been broken in regard to a statutory instrument – see *Pickstone* v. *Freeman plc* [1988] 2 All E.R. 803 and 807 where the House of Lords had had regard to what was said by the Minister in initiating a debate on the regulations.

He set out the reasons for the traditional rule (at p. 63):

> Thus the reasons put forward for the present rule are, first, that it preserves the constitutional proprieties, leaving Parliament to legislate in words and the courts (not parliamentary speakers) to construe the meaning of the words finally enacted, second, the practical difficulty of the expense of researching

---

19 See however *R* v. *Acton Justices, ex parte McMullen* (1990) 92 Cr. App. R. 98 in which the Court of Appeal Criminal Division looked at proceedings in the House of Commons Standing Committee on the Bill [1991] *Criminal Law Review*, 352–53.

20 The appeal was first heard by five Law Lords as is usual. But at the conclusion of the hearing it was relisted for argument before seven judges after it was realised that there had been a statement relevant to the matter in Parliament and the appellants wanted to challenge the rule that judges could not consult Hansard. (The page numbers given here are those to the All England Report of the case.)

parliamentary material which would arise if the material could be looked at, third, the need for the citizen to have access to a known defined text which regulates his legal rights and, fourth, the improbability of finding helpful guidance from Hansard.

He then put the arguments of opposing counsel (at pp. 63–64):

Mr Lester submitted that the time has come to relax the rule to the extent which I have mentioned. He points out that the courts have departed from the old literal approach of statutory construction and now adopt a purposive approach, seeking to discover the parliamentary intention lying behind the words used and construing the legislation so as to give effect to, rather than thwart, the intentions of Parliament. Where the words used by Parliament are obscure or ambiguous, the parliamentary material may throw considerable light not only on the mischief which the Act was designed to remedy but also on the purpose of the legislation and its anticipated effect. If there are statements by the minister or other promoter of the Bill, these may throw as much light on the 'mischief' which the Bill seeks to remedy as do the white papers, reports of official committees and Law Commission reports to which the courts already have regard for that purpose. If a minister clearly states the effect of a provision and there is no subsequent relevant amendment to the Bill or withdrawal of the statement it is reasonable to assume that Parliament passed the Bill on the basis that the provision would have the effect stated. There is no logical distinction between the use of ministerial statements introducing subordinate legislation (to which recourse was had in *Pickstone's* case [1988] 2 All E.R. 803, [1989] A.C. 66) and such statements made in relation to other statutory provisions which are not in fact subsequently amended. Other common law jurisdictions have abandoned the rule without adverse consequences. Although the practical reasons for the rule (difficulty in getting access to parliamentary materials and the cost and delay in researching it) are not without substance, they can be greatly exaggerated: experience in Commonwealth countries which have abandoned the rule does not suggest that the drawbacks are substantial, provided that the court keeps a tight control on the circumstances in which references to parliamentary material are allowed.

On the other side, the Attorney-General submitted that the existing rule had a sound constitutional and practical basis. If statements by ministers as to the intent or effect of an Act were allowed to prevail, this would contravene the constitutional rule that Parliament is 'sovereign only in respect of what it expresses by the words used in the legislation it has passed' (see the *Black-Clawson* case [1975] 1 All E.R. 810 at 836, [1975] A.C. 591 at 638 per Lord Diplock). It is for the courts alone to construe such legislation. It may be unwise to attach importance to ministerial explanations which are made to satisfy the political requirements of persuasion and debate, often under pressure of time and business. Moreover, in order to establish the significance to be attached to any particular statement, it is necessary both to consider and to understand the context in which it was made. For the courts to have regard to parliamentary material might necessitate changes in parliamentary procedures to ensure that ministerial statements are sufficiently detailed to be taken into account. In addition, there are all the practical difficulties as to the accessibility of parliamentary material, the cost of researching it and the use of court time in analysing it, which are good reasons for maintaining the rule. Finally, to use what is said in Parliament for the purpose of construing legislation would be a breach of s 1, art 9 of the Bill of Rights as being an impeachment or questioning of the freedom of speech in debates in proceedings in Parliament.

He concluded:

My Lords, I have come to the conclusion that, as a matter of law, there are sound reasons for making a limited modification to the existing rule (subject to strict safeguards) unless there are constitutional or practical reasons which outweigh them. In my judgment, subject to the questions of the privileges of the House of Commons, reference to parliamentary material should be permitted as an aid to the construction of legislation which is ambiguous or obscure or the literal meaning of which leads to an absurdity. Even in such cases references in court to parliamentary material should only be permitted where such material clearly discloses the mischief aimed at or the legislative intention lying behind the ambiguous or obscure words. In the case of statements made in Parliament, as at present advised I cannot foresee that any statement other than the statement of the minister or other promoter of the Bill is likely to meet these criteria.

I accept Mr Lester's submissions, but my main reason for reaching this conclusion is based on principle. Statute law consists of the words that Parliament has enacted. It is for the courts to construe those words and it is the court's duty in so doing to give effect to the intention of Parliament in using those words. It is an inescapable fact that, despite all the care taken in passing legislation, some statutory provisions when applied to the circumstances under consideration in any specific case are found to be ambiguous. One of the reasons for such ambiguity is that the members of the legislature in enacting the statutory provision may have been told what result those words are intended to achieve. Faced with a given set of words which are capable of conveying that meaning it is not surprising if the words are accepted as having that meaning. Parliament never intends to enact an ambiguity. Contrast with that the position of the courts. The courts are faced simply with a set of words which are in fact capable of bearing two meanings. The courts are ignorant of the underlying parliamentary purpose. Unless something in other parts of the legislation discloses such purpose, the courts are forced to adopt one of the two possible meanings using highly technical rules of construction. In many, I suspect most, cases references to parliamentary materials will not throw any light on the matter. But in a few cases it may emerge that the very question was considered by Parliament in passing the legislation. Why in such a case should the courts blind themselves to a clear indication of what Parliament intended in using those words? The court cannot attach a meaning to words which they cannot bear, but if the words are capable of bearing more than one meaning why should not Parliament's true intention be enforced rather than thwarted?

Lord Browne-Wilkinson said that under *Black-Clawson* the courts were already allowed to look at White Papers and official reports for the purposes of finding the 'mischief – though not at the draft clauses or proposals for remedying the mischief'. There was not much difference between such materials and a ministerial statement in Parliament. Moreover, the distinction between looking at reports to identify the mischief but not to find Parliament's intention was 'highly artificial'. It was also now legitimate to look at a draft bill to see that a provision in the draft was not included in the legislation.[1] 'Given the purposive approach to construction now adopted by the courts in order to give effect to the true intentions of the legislature, the fine distinctions between looking for the mischief and looking for the intention in using words to provide the remedy are technical and inappropriate. Clear and unambiguous statements made by ministers in Parliament are as much the background to the enactment of legislation as White Papers and parliamentary reports.'

He then dealt with the Attorney-General's objections. One was the practical difficulties:

It is said that parliamentary materials are not readily available to, and understandable by, the citizen and his lawyers, who should be entitled to rely on the words of Parliament alone to discover his position. It is undoubtedly true that Hansard and particularly records of committee debates are not widely held by libraries outside London and that the lack of satisfactory indexing of committee stages makes it difficult to trace the passage of a clause after it is redrafted or renumbered. But such practical difficulties can easily be overstated. It is possible to obtain parliamentary materials and it is possible to trace the history. The problem is one of expense and effort in doing so, not the availability of the material. In considering the right of the individual to know the law by simply looking at legislation, it is a fallacy to start from the position that all legislation is available in a readily understandable form in any event: the very large number of statutory instruments made every year are not available in an indexed form for well over a year after they have been passed. Yet, the practitioner manages to deal with the problem, albeit at considerable expense. Moreover, experience in New Zealand and Australia (where the strict rule has been relaxed for some years) has not shown that the non-availability of materials has raised these practical problems.

Next, it is said that lawyers and judges are not familiar with parliamentary procedures and will therefore have difficulty in giving proper weight to the parliamentary materials. Although, of course, lawyers do not have the same experience of these matters as members of the legislature, they are not wholly ignorant of them. If, as I think, significance should only be attached to the clear statements made by a minister or other promoter of the Bill, the difficulty of knowing what weight to attach to such statements is not overwhelming. In the present case, there were numerous statements of view by members in the course of the debate which plainly do not throw any light on the true construction of s. 63. What is persuasive in this case is a consistent series of answers given by the minister, after opportunities for taking advice from his officials, all of which point the same way and which were not withdrawn or varied prior to the enactment of the Bill.

1   *Factortame* v. *Secretary of State for Transport* [1989] 2 All E.R. 692, [1990] 2 A.C. 85.

Then it is said that court time will be taken up by considering a mass of parliamentary material and long arguments about its significance, thereby increasing the expense of litigation. In my judgment, though the introduction of further admissible material will inevitably involve some increase in the use of time, this will not be significant as long as courts insist that parliamentary material should only be introduced in the limited cases I have mentioned and where such material contains a clear indication from the minister of the mischief aimed at, or the nature of the cure intended, by the legislation. Attempts to introduce material which does not satisfy those tests should be met by orders for costs made against those who have improperly introduced the material. Experience in the United States of America, where legislative history has for many years been much more generally admissible than I am now suggesting, shows how important it is to maintain strict control over the use of such material. That position is to be contrasted with what has happened in New Zealand and Australia (which have relaxed the rule to approximately the extent that I favour): there is no evidence of any complaints of this nature coming from those countries.

There is one further practical objection which, in my view, has real substance. If the rule is relaxed legal advisers faced with an ambiguous statutory provision may feel that they have to research the materials to see whether they yield the crock of gold i.e. a clear indication of Parliament's intentions. In very many cases the crock of gold will not be discovered and the expenditure on the research wasted. This is a real objection to changing the rule. However, again it is easy to overestimate the cost of such research: if a reading of Hansard shows that there is nothing of significance said by the minister in relation to the clause in question, further research will become pointless.

In sum, I do not think that the practical difficulties arising from a limited relaxation of the rule are sufficient to outweigh the basic need for the courts to give effect to the words enacted by Parliament in the sense that they were intended by Parliament to bear. Courts are frequently criticised for their failure to do that. This failure is due not to cussedness but to ignorance of what Parliament intended by the obscure words of the legislation. The courts should not deny themselves the light which parliamentary materials may shed on the meaning of the words Parliament has used and thereby risk subjecting the individual to a law which Parliament never intended to enact... .

I therefore reach the conclusion, subject to any question of parliamentary privilege, that the exclusionary rule should be relaxed so as to permit reference to parliamentary materials where: (a) legislation is ambiguous or obscure, or leads to an absurdity; (b) the material relied on consists of one or more statements by a minister or other promoter of the Bill together if necessary with such other parliamentary material as is necessary to understand such statements and their effect; (c) the statements relied on are clear. Further than this, I would not at present go.

The Lord Chancellor's dissent was based wholly on his concern about the practical aspects – the concern that it would lead to research in parliamentary materials being undertaken by lawyers at significant cost in a high proportion of cases and often to no purpose:

The principal difficulty I have on this aspect of the case is that in Mr Lester's submission reference to parliamentary material as an aid to interpretation of a statutory provision should be allowed only with leave of the court and where the court is satisfied that such a reference is justifiable (a) to confirm the meaning of a provision as conveyed by the text, its object and purpose, (b) to determine a meaning where the provision is ambiguous or obscure or (c) to determine the meaning where the ordinary meaning is manifestly absurd or unreasonable.

I believe that practically every question of statutory construction that comes before the courts will involve an argument that the case falls under one or more of these three heads. It follows that the parties' legal advisers will require to study Hansard in practically every such case to see whether or not there is any help to be gained from it. I believe this is an objection of real substance. It is a practical objection, not one of principle. The submission which Mr Lester makes is not restricted by reference to the type of statute and indeed the only way in which it could be discovered whether help was to be given is by considering Hansard itself. Such an approach appears to me to involve the possibility at least of an immense increase in the cost of litigation in which statutory construction is involved. It is of course easy to overestimate such cost but it is I fear equally easy to underestimate it. Your Lordships have no machinery from which any estimate of such cost could be derived. Two inquiries with such machinery available to them, namely that of the Law Commission and the Scottish Law Commission, in their joint report on *Interpretation of Statutes* (Law Com no 21; Scot Law Com no 11 (1969)), and the Renton Committee report on *Preparation of Legislation* (Cmnd 6053 (1975)) advised against a relaxation on the practical grounds to which I have referred. I consider that nothing has been laid before your Lordships to justify the view that their advice based on this objection was incorrect.

In his very helpful and full submissions Mr Lester has pointed out that there is no evidence of practical difficulties in the jurisdictions where relaxations of this kind have already been allowed, but I do not consider that, full as these researches have been, they justify the view that no substantial increase resulted in the cost of litigation as a result of these relaxations, and, in any event, the parliamentary processes in these jurisdictions are different in quite material respects from those in the United Kingdom.

Your Lordships are well aware that the costs of litigation are a subject of general public concern and I personally would not wish to be a party to changing a well-established rule which could have a substantial effect in increasing these costs against the advice of the Law Commissions and the Renton Committee unless and until a new inquiry demonstrated that that advice was no longer valid.

It is worth noting that, as the Lord Chancellor stated, his concerns were shared by the English and Scottish Law Commissions in their 1969 Report *The Interpretation of Statutes*. They urged adoption of the 'mischief' or 'purposive' approach to statutory interpretation but they did not favour recourse to parliamentary debates. One reason was the lack of clarity of such debates. But another was the fact that practitioners did not have easy access to collections of *Hansards*. On balance, the Law Commissions thought, the value to be derived from parliamentary debates was likely to be outweighed by the burden of consulting them. The Renton Committee in 1975 took the same view. So too did the Hansard Society in its *Report on the Legislative Process* (note 12, p. 7 above). Its scepticism was based more on the scope parliamentary debates would give to fresh argument. ('The possibilities for confusion – and for time-wasting argument and counter-argument in the court – are endless' (para. 243, pp. 61–2).)

(f) The significance of *Pepper v. Hart*

There are various questions arising from the House of Lords' decision in *Pepper* v. *Hart*.

1. What does it mean?

Lord Browne-Wilkinson was at pains to indicate that the relaxation of the rule was intended to be a narrow one applying only where the legislation is ambiguous or obscure or leads to an absurdity and a clear ministerial statement made in Parliament would resolve the ambiguity. Lord Oliver expressly agreed with the speech of Lord Browne-Wilkinson, endorsing his narrow conditions. Lords Ackner, Bridge, Griffiths and Keith also said they agreed with the whole of the speech. But will the courts in practice hold to a narrow interpretation of *Pepper* v. *Hart*? Early indications suggested that they will not.

Thus in *Warwickshire County Council* v. *Johnson* [1993] 1 All E.R. 299 the House of Lords referred to Hansard even though there did not seem to be any ambiguity about the statutory language. Recourse to *Hansard*, Lord Roskill said, merely confirmed the view he had reached independently. Lord Roskill made no reference to the Minister's statement having resolved an ambiguity, clarified an obscurity or prevented an absurdity. As one commentator suggested, 'the House seems to have authorised recourse to Hansard wherever there is a clear ministerial statement relating directly to the construction of the legislation'.[2]

In several other cases the House of Lords has referred to Hansard to confirm interpretations that would have been adopted anyway.[3]

Lord Browne-Wilkinson's original formulation was restricted to ministerial statements that *positively* resolved an ambiguity. But sometimes

---

2 C. Scott, 'Consumer Sales and Credit Transactions', *Jrnl. Business Law*, 1993, p. 491.
3 See *Stubbings* v. *Webb* [1993] 2 W.L.R 120 at 128; *ex p. Johnson* [1993] 2 W.L.R. 1 at 7, 8; *Chief Adjudication Officer* v. *Foster* [1993] 2 W.L.R. 292 at 306.

one might wish to produce the parliamentary record to advance an interpretation *negatively* by demonstrating that nothing was said to a particular effect. A Scottish Court allowed such a submission in *Hamilton* v. *Fife Health Board* (Lexis).

Lord Browne-Wilkinson's original formulation was restricted, in terms, to ministerial statements. But what of the statement of a Member who successfully moves an amendment or a new clause? In *Chief Adjudication Officer* v. *Foster*, above, reference was made to the observations of the mover of a successful amendment in the House of Lords.

By contrast, in *Doncaster Borough Council* v. *Secretary of State for the Environment* (1993, unreported) statements made by a Minister were excluded, partly for lack of clarity, but partly because they were 'final remarks [which] were necessarily *extempore* responses to various points raised during the debate'. But even *extempore* remarks by a Minister would probably have been made after seeking advice from his advisers.

In *Melluish* v. *BMI (No.3) Ltd* [1995] 4 All E.R. 453 the House of Lords refused to refer to parliamentary material which the Crown sought to introduce because it was not directed to the specific provisions under consideration.

In *Three Rivers District Council* v. *Bank of England (No.2)* [1996] 2 All E.R. 363 the Commercial Court judge held that where the court was seeking to construe a statute purposively and consistently with any relevant European legislation, or where the purpose of the legislation was to introduce into English law the provisions of an international convention or European directive, the court could adopt a more flexible approach to the admissibility of parliamentary materials than where the court was construing purely domestic legislation.

There is also the question what material will be allowed in as 'contextual material' under the heading of Lord Browne-Wilkinson's category of 'such other parliamentary material as is necessary to understand' the ministerial statements and their effect. In *Pepper* v. *Hart* itself Lord Browne-Wilkinson referred to a press statement issued at the same time as a ministerial parliamentary statement. In *Doncaster Borough Council* v. *Secretary of State for the Environment* (above) the Court of Appeal heard submissions on what the Minister of Housing and Local Government meant in Parliament by 'multi-occupation' and 'multiple dwelling house' by reference to the debate as a whole.[4]

---

4   I am indebted to T. St John Bates, 'Judicial Application of *Pepper* v. *Hart*', *Journal of Law Society Scotland*, July 1993, p. 251 for some of the foregoing. See also the same author's 'Parliamentary Material and Statutory Construction: Aspects of the Practical Application of *Pepper* v. *Hart*', 14 *Statute Law Review*, 1993, pp. 46–55 and to his very valuable 'The Contemporary Use of Legislative History in the United Kingdom', 54 *Cambridge Law Journal*, 1995, pp. 127-52.

In *Pepper* v. *Hart* Lord Browne-Wilkinson referred to the fact that it was permissible to consult White Papers and official reports to find the mischief. He continued (at p.65): 'Given the purposive approach to construction now adopted by the courts in order to give effect to the true intentions of the legislature, the fine distinctions between looking for the mischief and looking for the intention in using words to provide the remedy are technical and inappropriate. Clear and unambiguous statements made by ministers in Parliament are as much the background to the enactment as White Papers and parliamentary reports.'

2. How often will it cause costs for litigants?

There is no way of assessing how often litigants now have to pay new costs for the research done by lawyers amongst the parliamentary materials. For the future the cost will be reduced for those with access to the Internet since Hansard for the proceedings in both Houses of Parliament became available on the worldwide web from 1996 onwards. (Address: House of Commons http://www.parliament.the-stationery-office.co.uk/pa/cm/cmhansrd.htm; House of Lords – the same but ending pa/ld/ldhansrd.htm). The House of Commons Committee Stage has also been available on the web since 1997 (address http://www.parliament.the-stationery-office.co.uk/pa/cm/cmpubns.html). Failure to conduct the necessary research might found an action for negligence so lawyers will feel as much obliged to check Hansard as to check the law in statute and case law. As has been seen above, the courts are already showing every sign of taking a broad rather than a narrow view of the implications of the decision. The broader the licence to use parliamentary materials, the greater the costs to litigants. In some cases, admittedly, access to the parliamentary record could have the effect of stopping litigation that would otherwise have taken place – as both sides accept that a categorical ministerial statement regarding the meaning of the provision in question would dispose of the dispute.

In a lecture in June 1998 Lightman J. said that it could be questioned whether use of *Hansard* achieved anything worthwhile.[5] The cost was substantial and beyond the means of many litigants, creating disparities between litigants who could and could not afford such researches. ('I have yet to hear a case where the exercise [of consulting *Hansard*] proved the slightest bit helpful but many when it proved time consuming and wasteful' (*ibid*).)

---

5 'Civil Litigation in the 21st Century', 17 *Civil Justice Quarterly,*1998, 373, 383.

3.   How often will recourse to Hansard reveal the legislative intent?

There is no substantial empirical study which shows how often recourse to Hansard would throw useful light on the statutory interpretation problem before the court. A small-scale study conducted by Vera Sacks before *Pepper* v. *Hart* was decided suggested that it might not be often. The study took 34 cases on employment law, land law, family law, criminal law and housing law. There was some positive benefit from looking at Hansard. In some cases it threw light on the general legislative purpose. But reference to Hansard would very rarely have solved the problem before the court: 'In every case studied the disputed clause was either undebated or received obscure and confusing replies from the Minister'.[6]

In preparing this section of the fifth edition of this work, the writer–with the help of an LSE law student, Miss Katie Pritchard–undertook a small follow-up study. I first did a Lexis search of all mentions of *Pepper* v. *Hart* in the six years from the date of the House of Lords decision in November 1992 to October 1998. This produced a total of 232 cases. We started by looking at the reported cases in the first 100 in the Lexis print-out (excluding those reported only in newspaper law reports)–beginning with the most recent. There were 60 such cases. What we found was so consistent that it seemed pointless to continue the exercise beyond the first 100 listed cases. The results strikingly confirmed the results of the survey carried out pre-*Pepper* v. *Hart* by Vera Sacks.

In every case, by definition, *Pepper* v. *Hart* had been cited by counsel in argument as the basis for introducing Parliamentary material. But looking for a case in which Parliamentary material appears to have made any difference to the result was like looking for a needle in a haystack. Often the judgment(s) did not even mention *Pepper* v. *Hart* or Parliamentary material. Presumably, in the great majority of those cases the court did not permit the material to be introduced. When *Pepper* v. *Hart* argument and/ or material were mentioned in the judgment(s), the mention was usually a variation on one or more of the following themes: a) The rules laid down in *Pepper* v *Hart* as to the preconditions for admissibility were not fulfilled. Either there was no ambiguity in the statutory text or the Parliamentary materials sought to be introduced were not directed to the specific statutory provision under consideration.[7] 'Judges should be astute to check such

---

6   Vera Sacks, 'Toward Discovering Parliamentary Intent', *Statute Law Review*, 1982, pp. 143, 157. The article did not disclose how the 34 cases were selected and there is therefore no way of knowing to what extent the study was representative of statutory interpretation cases in the law reports, let alone of statutory interpretation cases that come before the courts.

7   The House of Lords, in the person of Lord Browne-Wilkinson himself, gave courts a sharp warning against relaxing this rule in *Melluish (Inspector of Taxes)* v. *BMI (No.3)Ltd* [1995] 4 All E.R.453,468. The Crown had unsuccessfully tried to persuade the Law Lords to consider Ministerial statements on another provision

misuse of the new rule by making appropriate orders as to costs wasted.'
b) We did look at the *Pepper* v. *Hart* material – either because there was
ambiguity in the statute, or because we were persuaded to do so *de bene
esse* – but it was of no assistance in that it threw no clear light on the
matter. c) We looked at the *Pepper* v. *Hart* material, there was a clear
statement by the Minister which was to the point but it only confirmed the
court in the view it had already taken of the matter anyway. Sometimes the
court used b) in combination with a). (We looked at the material even
though there was no ambiguity but it did not advance matters.) There
were virtually no cases in which the court appears actually to have been
influenced by reading the Parliamentary material.[8] The fact that the court
fails to acknowledge that it was influenced by parliamentary material does
not prove that it was not. But one suspects that in most cases the failure
to acknowledge it reflects the reality.

Thus even in cases where the court agrees to look at *Pepper* v. *Hart*
material, it appears to be exceedingly rare that the material affects the
outcome. When considering the balance of advantage flowing from the
decision one also has to put into the scale not only the considerable
number of cases where the court refuses even to look at the material, but
the presumably much greater number of cases where *Hansard* has been
scoured by the lawyers in vain. The research turns up nothing in the
parliamentary debates which could even arguably be made the subject of
a *Pepper* v. *Hart* submission to the court.

In short, it seems that the Lord Chancellor, Lord Mackay, who, as has
been seen, dissented in *Pepper* v. *Hart* mainly out of concern that the
costs of the reform would outweigh the likely benefits, was probably right.

4. Some other implications of Pepper v. Hart

The courts have not yet decided whether previous statutory interpretation
decisions given in ignorance of the contents of Hansard can now be
regarded as given *per incuriam* (in ignorance – see below pp. 220–23) and
therefore not be binding.

It also remains to be seen what effect the decision will have on the use
that can be made of other materials that might elucidate the meaning of a
statute, such in particular as the official report that was the basis for the
statute. In both *Stubbings* v. *Webb* [1993] 2 W.L.R. 120 and *Westdeutsche
Landesbank Girozentrale* v. *Islington Borough Council* [1996] AC 669)

---

and another problem and to argue from those statements by analogy. Lord
Browne-Wilkinson said that such 'interpretation' (what one might call 'reading
across') of Ministerial statements was an improper use of the relaxed rule introduced
by *Pepper* v. *Hart* and added, for good measure:

8   *Thomas Witter Ltd* v. *TBP Industries Ltd* [1996] 2 All E.R. 573 may have been
     such a case – see p.590 at *d* to *j*.

parliamentary material showed that the statute was based on the report of an official committee (in the former case the Report of the Tucker Committee on the Limitation of Actions, in the latter an Interim Report of the Law Reform Committee). In both cases the court then looked at the report to confirm parliament's intention.

Pepper v. *Hart* will certainly create problems for lawyers who will have to master new research skills.[9]

One effect may be more time having to be spent by Parliamentary Counsel vetting papers prepared by Departments for Ministers. This point was made by Mr Christopher Jenkins, then Second Parliamentary Counsel, speaking at a conference in October 1993 on the effects of *Pepper* v. *Hart* organised by the Statute Law Society:[10]

> Departments sponsoring legislation prepare various briefings for their Ministers. In future the draftsman may have to take a more active part in vetting this material. This could be very time-consuming. It means looking at notes on clauses, notes on amendments and Ministers' Speaking Notes to check that they accurately and comprehensively explain the provisions of the Bill, and that they include any supplementary material which it is not felt necessary to put in the Bill but which may have to be put on the record in response to questions raised in debate.
>
> In addition the draftsman may in future have to look at other material produced by the Department in connection with the Bill to check its accuracy, in case it is regarded by the courts as 'other parliamentary material ... necessary to understand such statements'. I do not know how wide this will go; but in *Pepper* v. *Hart*, Lord Browne-Wilkinson looked at a press release produced by the Inland Revenue.
>
> The draftsmen and the civil servants in the departments will also have to check what was actually said in the House or in Standing Committee to ensure that no additional statements or corrections are needed.

Mr Jenkins said that at present if a Minister gave information during a debate which he later realised was incomplete or inaccurate he would often write to the member who had requested the information. Now he might feel it necessary also to make the correction on the record. By the same token M.P.s might be more inclined to ask questions with a view to having explanations on the record for the benefit of later potential judicial interpretation. It had been said that in the US 'much debate on the floor of Congress takes the form of elaborate, prearranged colloquies in which possible supporters of a particular programme obtain detailed and very

9 For a detailed guide to the mechanics of research in parliamentary materials see Victor Tunkel, 'Research after *Pepper* v. *Hart*', *Law Society's Gazette*, 12 May 1993, p. 17.

10 J.C. Jenkins, *Pepper* v. *Hart*: A Draftsman's Perspective', 15 *Statute Law Review,*1994, pp. 23,25.

technical assurances from its sponsors as to its effects'. The same issue of the *Statute Law Review* published papers on *Pepper* v. *Hart* by the two opposing counsel in the case–the Attorney-General Sir Nicholas Lyell (pp.1–9) and Lord Lester QC (pp.10–22). See also D.Oliver, '*Pepper v Hart* – a suitable case for reference to *Hansard*?' [1993] *Public Law* 2; G. B. Born, 'Making Law with Hansard' 90 *Law Society's Gazette*, 1993, p. 2; David Miers, 'Taxing Perks and Interpreting Statutes:*Pepper* v. *Hart*, 56 *Modern Law Review* 695, 701; F. A. R. Bennion, 'Hansard – A Help or Hindrance', 14 *Statute Law Review*, 1993, pp. 149–62.)

For the view that *Pepper* v. *Hart* represents a powerful tool for conservative interpretation of statutes see David Robertson, *Judicial Discretion in the House of Lords* (OUP, 1998). Robertson devotes a whole chapter of his book to *Pepper* v. *Hart*. He argues that if the words used in Parliament have to be treated as serious evidence of the meaning of the statute the judges lose their capacity to give the law a sensible interpretation in light of changing times. 'The problem is, essentially, that reference to *Hansard* necessarily sets an interpretation within the immediate contemporary understanding of the government of the day.'(P.171.) It risks imposing a literalism in interpretation rather than an interpretation in keeping with the spirit of the law. (P.172.)

(g) Other extrinsic aids

In their 1969 Report *The Interpretation of Statutes*, the Law Commissions urged the use of a *new type of explanatory memorandum* to assist the courts in the search for the context in which statutory provisions should be read. It would be a mixture of three existing documents:

(a) the preamble that used to be a feature of statutes;
(b) the explanatory memorandum attached to a bill, published for the benefit principally of members of the two Houses, giving a brief summary of its provisions;
(c) notes on clauses prepared by civil servants as a detailed brief to the Minister responsible for piloting the legislation through each House.[11]

The Law Commissions' proposed new explanatory memorandum would be drafted by the promoters of the bill and the bill to which it related would specifically authorise its use as an aid to interpretation. Ideally the document would be amended as the bill itself was amended and would receive ultimate parliamentary approval. Its status would be like that of a

---

11 It is increasingly the practice for Ministers to make their notes on clauses available to members of the Committee for the Committee stage on a bill.

preamble under present law and practice. If this took up too much parliamentary time, an alternative would be to give the power to amend and approve to officials. Or officials might be required to submit it for parliamentary approval on Third Reading or perhaps by laying it before the House like an Order in Council. But the document would not bind the courts:

> [E]ven if the explanatory statement were amended during the course of the Bill's passage and given some measure of Parliamentary approval, it would be no more binding on the courts than much other contextual material (e.g., other provisions of the statute, earlier legislation dealing with the same subject matter and non statutory material dealing with the mischief) of which under the existing law the courts are entitled to take account. It might however give assistance to the courts in making more explicit the contextual assumptions which at present have to be gleaned, sometimes with great difficulty, from a number of sources of varying reliability. No interpretative device can relieve the courts of their ultimate responsibility for considering the different contexts in which the words of a provision might be read, and in making a choice between the different meanings which emerge from that consideration. The existence of an explanatory statement would not prevent a court from regarding the meaning of the words in an enacting provision in the light of other relevant contexts as so compelling that it must be preferred to a meaning suggested by the statement. As we have already pointed out, even Continental courts, which have a much wider freedom than our courts to consider contextual material outside the statute itself, are not bound by that material. [Para. 70.]

In order to test the viability of the idea, it might be used first for selected topics – for instance bills implementing Law Commission reports. 'The usefulness of an explanatory memorandum might be especially great for the kind of codification measures that the Law Commissions were to bring forward:

> The degree of particularity in which the applications of these principles to specific situations are stated in the code may vary, but, even where detailed application is lacking, a court is expected to discover in the code the principles from which the answer to a particular problem can be worked out. In such a situation we think that an explanatory and illustrative commentary on the code could provide authoritative, but not compelling guidance on the interpretation of the code, which would be particularly valuable in the early years of the operation of the code.

The Renton Committee did not think that explanatory materials prepared for the benefit of legislators should be admissible for the purposes of judicial interpretation. To do so, it thought, would risk having a 'split level statute' of which only the primary stage would have been debated in Parliament.[12]

---

12 *The Preparation of Legislation*, 1975, Cmnd 6053, para. 19.24.

The 1992 Hansard Society's Report on the Legislative Process (see note 12, p. 7 above) said: 'We are impressed by the wide desire for more explanation of the meaning and implications of legislation. The practitioners and users need it. The wider public may need it even more.' It thought that efforts to provide a better explanation might be even more productive than attempts to simplify drafting (p. 112). Notes on sections (based on the Minister's notes on clauses) should be made for every Act of Parliament. The notes on sections would be prepared by government departments with the assistance of parliamentary counsel. These notes on sections should be approved by Ministers and laid before Parliament but should not require formal Parliamentary approval. They should be published at the same time as the Act. There should similarly be explanatory notes on statutory instruments to explain their purpose and effect (para. 250, p. 63). The courts should be allowed to use the notes on sections and the explanatory notes on statutory instruments as an aid to interpretation (para. 254, pp. 63–4).

As has been seen (p.82 above) the First Report of the Select Committee on Modernisation of the House of Commons recommended greater use of explanatory material to accompany the publication of a Bill. The Committee invited Parliamentary Counsel to explore ways in which this might be done.

In December 1997, in its Second Report (1997–98, HC 190) the Select Committee said that it had now received the report from First Parliamentary Counsel. He proposed that the existing Explanatory Memorandum and Notes on Clauses should be replaced by a single document entitled 'Explanatory Notes'. The Notes would be revised twice, once to accompany the first print of the Bill in the Second House and again on Royal Assent. They should be available on the Internet alongside the Bill and then the Act. The Select Committee said 'we wholeheartedly welcome the proposals as the House of Lords Procedure Committee has done in its Second Report, and recommend that the Government implement them as soon as possible' and that it endorsed the proposal made. They are now being produced.

As to the status of the Notes, Parliamentary Counsel's report, appended to the Select Committee's report, said:

> The notes will have the same status as the present explanatory memorandum. They are not intended to make law, and so it is not proposed that they should be amendable in either House. Their purpose is to help the reader to get his bearings and to ease the task of assimilating the new law. If the notes are successful in the purpose of helping the reader, they will of course be read by judges as well as by others. However they are not designed to resolve ambiguities in the legislative text – if ambiguities are identified as the Bill progresses, they should be removed by amendment. Occasionally, it may be that the notes are referred to in litigation in the same way that Hansard is, under the rule in *Pepper v Hart*. So it will be important for those producing the notes to achieve

a high degree of accuracy, and also to restrict the notes so that they do not seem to take the law further than the Bill or the Act does. (Paras.17–18.)

The New Zealand Law Commission, in a report entitled *The Format of Legislation* in 1993, pp.10–12, proposed:

> Cross-references to other Acts, to cases, or to reports of law reform or other relevant bodies on which legislation is based … might all be useful. And sometimes material from the explanatory notes which usually accompany Bills might usefully be included in notes to the Act.

Francis Bennion, for many years a member of Parliamentary Counsel's Office, commenting on the New Zealand recommendations[13] argued that the prospect of such innovation was 'nightmarish'.

> What if the 'other Acts' are later amended? What if 'the cases' are overruled? How are explanatory notes prepared (as they mostly are) after the bill has been introduced to be got into the text of the Bill without unduly prolonging debate? Suppose amendments to the notes are put down by MPs or they seek to insert additional notes? What if the MP claims that a note does not accurately reflect what is in the bill?
>
> The danger of lengthening the time needed for drafting and debate is obvious, Where is this time to come from? Where are the extra skilled draftsmen to be found? How will the extra cost be raised? How will law be made more simple when there are risks of discrepancy between what the text says and what the note says it says?
>
> These are obvious questions, but there is something more fundamental at stake. The difference between the legislative text itself and any comments made on it in notes is one of kind. Only the former should constitute the law. Let the comments be added by other hands, in other ways. Then there is no risk of conflict within the body of the Act, and it is plain where law ends and comment begins.

(h)   Recent developments in other common law countries[14]

Australia

Traditionally the Australian courts followed the English strict exclusionary rule, refusing to look at proceedings in Parliament as an aid to construction.

---

13 'If it's not broke don't fix it', 15 *Statute Law Review*, 1994, 164 at 169.
14 This note is based on material presented by Anthony Lester Q.C. appearing for the appellant in *Pepper* v. *Hart* in the House of Lords. The material has been deposited in the Manuscripts Library at University College, London.

But this rule began to break down in the early 1980s – see *TCN Channel Nine Property Ltd* v. *Australian Mutual Provident Society* (1982) 42 ALR 496, at 507–8 Federal Court; and *Sentry Life Assurance Ltd* v. *Life Insurance Commissioner* (1983) 49 ALR 292 Federal Court.

In 1983 there was an important symposium on statutory interpretation. Senior members of the judiciary questioned the traditional exclusionary rules. (Lord Wilberforce, who had been one of the majority in *Black-Clawson*, said at the meeting that he had changed his mind. He now thought the decision was wrong and his own reasoning 'specious'.)

In 1984 Australia enacted legislation. The Commonwealth Statute Acts Interpretation Amendment Act 1984 states that extrinsic material may be consulted in order either to confirm that the meaning of the provision 'is the ordinary meaning conveyed by the text of the provision taking into account its context in the Act and the purpose or object underlying the Act; or to determine the meaning of the provision when (i) the provision is ambiguous or obscure; or (ii) the ordinary meaning conveyed by the text of the provision taking into account its context in the Act and the purpose or object underlying the Act leads to a result that is manifestly absurd or is unreasonable'.

The Act then states eight items that can be referred to: anything in the Queen's Printer's text of an Act; reports of Royal Commissions, Law Reform Commissions and committees of enquiry; reports of committees of Parliament; treaties or other agreements referred to in the Act in question; an explanatory memorandum laid before Parliament; a Minister's Second Reading speech; any document which the Act under interpretation declares to be 'a relevant document'; and lastly, any relevant material in the Senate Journals, the House Votes and Proceedings and the official debates of either House of Parliament.

Several similar statutory provisions have been enacted in New South Wales, Western Australia and the Australian Capital Territory. The State of Victoria has adopted a version which permits the use of extrinsic materials, but there are no guidelines as to the circumstances in which they can be used. The matter is left to the court's discretion. (See the Interpretation of Legislation Act 1984, s. 35.) As has been seen, the Commonwealth legislation by contrast only allows reference to parliamentary records for the purpose of departing from the ordinary meaning of the text if the provision to be construed is ambiguous or the ordinary meaning leads to a result which is manifestly absurd or is unreasonable.

A review of the Australian legislation in 1988 by the Secretary of the Commonwealth Attorney-General's Department suggested that it had been a success. 'The worst apprehensions that the ability to rely on extrinsic materials might cause substantially longer proceedings as well as significantly longer preparation of cases, leading to significantly greater costs, seem not to have been realised.'[15]

New Zealand

In the early 1980s, the New Zealand courts abandoned the distinction between consulting extrinsic material for the purpose of understanding the mischief and for the purpose of discovering the legislative intent. More recently, without any assistance from the legislature, they have adopted a full-blown rule permitting access to extrinsic aids. Thus in *Marac Life Assurance Ltd* v. *Cmnr. of Inland Revenue* [1986] 1 NZLR 694 four judges of the Court of Appeal referred to the budget speech of the Minister of Finance to assist interpretation of the statutory provision – see pp. 701–2, 713, 716, 718. The use of parliamentary materials has been affirmed in many cases by the Court of Appeal and the High Court.

In *Brown* v. *Langwoods Photo Stores Ltd* [1991] 1 NZLR 173 the Court of Appeal *per* Cooke P. allowed reference to extrinsic aids (in that case a report of a Law Reform Committee) even though the statutory provision seemed clear as to its meaning. ('Not to be willing even to look at [the reports] would be unacceptably pedantic. Although they could not of course override the Act, which must govern in the end, if they did suggest a different intention it would be necessary to reconsider whether the Act is really clear on the point, but no such query arises', at 176.)

Canada

Canadian courts have recently liberalised the exclusionary rule at least to permit references to parliamentary materials for the purpose of studying the mischief addressed by the legislation. (See in particular *Reference re Anti-Inflation Act* [1976] 2 S.C.R. 373; *Lyons* v. *The Queen* [1984] 2 S.C.R. 633, 688–84.) An academic com·mentator has suggested that in time this will lead to total abandonment of the exclusionary rule (P. A. Cote, *The Interpretation of Legislation in Canada* (2nd edn., 1991) at 366).

Ireland

The Irish courts too have recently made reference to legislative materials to explain the legislative intent. (See for instance *Wavin Pipes Ltd* v. *Hepworth Iron Co. Ltd.* [1982] FSR 32, High Court at 38 per Costello J. and

---

15 P. Brazil, 'Reform of Statutory Interpretation – the Australian Experience of Use of Extrinsic Materials: With a Postscript on Simpler Drafting', 32 *Australian Law Jrnl.*, 1988, 503 at 512. See also M. J. Bryson, 'Statutory Interpretation: an Australian Judicial Perspective', 13 *Statute Law Review*, 1992, pp. 187–208, 209–15.

The People (Director of Public Prosecutions) v. *Quilligan* [1986] IR 495
Supreme Court, at 509–10 per Walsh J.)

For a warning based on US experience about the dangers of using
legislative history, see Reed Dickerson, 'Statutory Interpretation in America:
Dipping into Legislative History', *Statute Law Review*, 1984, pp. 76 and
141.

6. INTERPRETING CONSTITUTIONAL PROVISIONS AND BILLS OF RIGHTS – PROSPECTS FOR THE HUMAN RIGHTS ACT 1998

One of the characteristic features of constitutional provisions and Bills of
Rights is that they are couched in broad, open-textured phrases. The
European Convention of Human Rights is a good example. The Convention
guarantees such rights as the right to liberty, the right to a fair trial, the
right to respect for private life, the right to freedom of expression, freedom
of peaceful assembly and freedom of association etc. Since 1966, persons
complaining of breaches of the Convention by the United Kingdom have
had the right to complain to the Convention machinery in Strasbourg. The
Human Rights Act 1998, in the phrase coined by Labour, 'brings the
Convention home' by making it possible for such proceedings to be
brought in the courts of this country. The effect in terms of an increase in
the number of cases raising Convention points could be considerable.

But how will the judges deal with such broad phrases? This question
was addressed in a recent lecture by the Chairman of the Law Commission,
Dame Mary Arden. She suggested that decisions given by the Privy Council
on appeals in constitutional and human rights cases indicated that in such
cases the courts were prepared to give a broad interpretation to statutory
provisions:

Dame Mary Arden, 'Modernising Legislation', *Public Law*, 1998, 65, 74–
76

The Commonwealth consitution cases show that the courts may take a vigorous
approach to the construction of provisions conferring human rights. In *Ministry
of Home Affairs* v. *Fisher*[16] the Privy Council had to decide whether the word
'child' as used in the Constitution of Bermuda included an illegitimate child, so
that the child would be entitled to Bermuda status. It was argued on the basis
of a long line of reported cases that it was a principle of statutory interpretation
that 'child' meant legitimate child. The Privy Council expressed the view that
it had two routes to reach the conclusion that illegitimate children were included.
It could either accept that the correct starting point was to say that there was
a presumption that 'child' in a statute meant legitimate child, and then to

16 [1980] A.C. 319.

conclude that there was no room for applying the presumption with less rigidity where one was dealing with a constitution, as opposed to, say, a statute dealing with property or succession. The other route was the bolder course of treating the Constitution as sui generis, calling for principles of interpretation of its own, suitable for the fact that the purpose of the consitution was to protect fundamental rights and freedoms. This would mean that not all the presumptions applicable to other legislation dealing with private law would be relevant. Lord Wilberforce giving the judgment of the Privy Council said:

> It is possible that as regards the question now for decision, either method would lead to the same result. But their Lordships prefer the second. This is in no way to say that there are no rules of law which should apply to the interpretation of a Consitution. A Constitution is a legal instrument giving rise, among other things, to individual rights capable of enforcement in a court of law. Respect must be paid to the language which has been used and to the traditions and usages which have given meaning to that language. It is quite consistant with this, and with the recognition that rules of interpretation may apply, to take as a point of departure for the process of interpretation a recognition of the character and origin of the instrument, and to be guided by the principle of giving full recognition and effect to those fundamental rights and freedoms with a statement of which the Constitution commences. In their Lordship's opinion this must mean approaching the question what is meant by 'child' with an open mind.

The Privy Council found that the Constitution recognised the unity of the family group and acceptance that young children should not be separated from a group which as a whole belong to Bermuda. In the instant case the illegitimate children of a Jamaican woman who had married a Bermudan were 'children' for the purpose of the Bermudan Consitution and therefore had the right to stay in Bermuda with their mother and their stepfather, who had accepted them into the family.

This approach to interpretation was endorsed by a later judgment of the Privy Council in *Attorney-General of the Gambia* v. *Jobe*[17] in which Lord Diplock delivering the judgement of the Privy Council said that:

> A constitution, and in particular that part of it which protects and entrenches fundamental rights and freedoms to which all persons in the state are to be entitled, is to be given a generous and purposive construction.

In another Privy Council case, *Maharaj* v. *Attorney-General of Trinidad and Tobago (No 2)*,[18] the question arose as to whether there was a right of redress for a breach of human rights. The breach occurred when the claimant, a barrister, was committed to prison for seven days without being told the grounds on which the court considered that he had been guilty of contempt, before being sentenced, so that he could offer an explanation or apology, and

17   [1984] A.C. 689 at 700H.
18   [1979] A.C. 385.

thus in breach of the rules of natural justice. The finding of contempt was set aside on appeal, but the claimant wanted compensation under provisions of the constitution of Trinidad and Tobago entitling persons to redress if there was a breach of human rights. It was held that this provision enabled the court to grant damages in public law for the infringement. The claim was against the state, which was directly liable for the acts of the judge, not on the basis of vicarious liability.

These cases are already in our jurisprudence and they will be pressed into service when the Courts are asked to apply a bold and innovative approach to the application of the Convention.

The *Maharaj* case was applied in *Simpson* v. *Attorney-General (Baigent's case)*,[19] a decision of the Court of Appeal of New Zealand. In that case the question at issue was whether a claim for compensation could be made against the New Zealand government under the New Zealand Bill of Rights Act even though there was no provision for this in the Bill of Rights Act itself. The Court of Appeal of New Zealand held by a majority that such a claim could be made. Cooke P. noted that one of the purposes of the legislation was to affirm New Zealand's committment to the International Covenant on Civil and Political Rights. This imposes an obligation on states which are parties to ensure an effective remedy for violation. Cooke P. said:

...we would fail in our duty if we did not give an effective remedy to a person whose legitimately affirmed rights have been infringed.

Another case which shows that a different and more liberal approach to interpretation may apply to cases where the statute lays down fundamental or consititutional rights is the decision of the Western Samoan Court of Appeal in *Attorney-General* v. *Sapa'ai Olomalu.*[20] There the question was whether the constitution guaranteed suffrage only to certain members of the population or whether it conferred universal suffrage. This very question had been considered by the convention which led to the Consitution, and universal suffrage had been rejected. The Court held that it would be artificial to ignore this material. However, they had already reached the same conclusion without reference to it. This case indicates that in interpreting constitutional rights the courts may be able to go beyond the terms of the Constitution or legislation in question to determine its meaning.

7. PRESUMPTIONS AND SUBORDINATE PRINCIPLES OF INTERPRETATION AS AN AID TO CONSTRUCTION

There are a number of presumptions that have been applied by the courts to assist in the construction of statutes. They are set out at length with a

---

19 [1994] 3 L.R.C. 202.
20 26 August 1982; see *Symposium on Statutory Interpretation,* Australian Government Publishing Service 1983, App. 3.

wealth of examples in *Maxwell*. It is not necessary here to do more than give a brief mention of the best known.

(1) Penal statutes should be construed strictly in favour of the citizen.[1]
(2) It is to be presumed that a statutory provision was not intended to change the common law.
(3) Normally, statutes creating criminal offences require a blameworthy state of mind (*mens rea*) in the defendant.
(4) It is presumed that Parliament did not intend to oust the jurisdiction of the courts.
(5) It is presumed that a statute does not have retrospective effect.
(6) Words take meaning from the context: *Noscitur a sociis*. (Thus in the Refreshment Houses Act 1860 dealing with houses 'for public refreshment, resort and entertainment', the last word was held not to cover theatrical or musical entertainment but to refer rather to refreshment rooms and the reception and accommodation of the public – *Muir* v. *Keay* (1875) L.R. 10 Q.B. 594 at 597–8.) *Expressio unius exclusio alterius* – the express mention of one member of a class by implication excludes other members of the same class. (The word 'land' would normally include mines but a reference to 'lands, houses and coalmines' may mean that no other mines are included in the word 'land'.) *Ejusdem generis* – general words at the end of a list of more particular words take their meaning from the foregoing list. (So the statement in the Sunday Observance Act 1677 that 'no tradesman, artificer, workman, labourer or other person whatsoever' shall work on a Sunday was held not to apply to a coach proprietor, farmer, barber or estate agent. The words 'other person whatsoever' were held to be confined to persons in similar occupations to those more specifically defined in the list.)
(7) It is presumed that municipal law is to be interpreted to be in conformity with international law.[2]

Note: The Human Rights Act 1998 – a new presumption of interpretation

There is a presumption that where primary legislation is ambiguous it is to be interpreted in a manner which is consistent with the UK's treaty

1 For an example where the presumption gave a remarkable result, see *R.* v. *Cuthbertson* [1980] 3 W.L.R. 89, in which the House of Lords held that the Misuse of Drugs Act 1971 did not permit forfeiture of assets in a bank account obtained by the defendants through trafficking in illegal drugs. The Act allowed forfeiture of 'anything shown to the satisfaction of the court to relate to the offence'. But the House of Lords said this did not cover conspiracy to commit the offence, since this was not specifically mentioned.
2 See further p. 138, above.

obligations. But, if the primary legislation is clear this presumption does not apply to ambiguous subordinate legislation nor to executive action taken under the primary legislation.[3]

Under the Human Rights Act 1998, s. 3 the courts will be required to disapply or quash subordinate legislation that is inconsistent with the European Convention on Human Rights unless the inconsistency arises from primary legislation. As has been seen above (p. 94), if the higher courts find such inconsistency they are empowered to make a declaration of incompatibility (s. 4).

The Human Rights Act 1998 does not incorporate the European Convention on Human Rights into UK law. Instead, it states: 'So far as it is possible to do so, primary legislation and subordinate legislation must be read and given effect in a way which is compatible with the Convention rights' (s. 3(1)). This presumption of interpretation is said to apply both to primary and to subordinate legislation 'whenever enacted'. (s. 3(2)(a)). The crucial difference between this and the previous law is that it will no longer be necessary to find an ambiguity. In fact it may be that the courts will hold that a strained interpretation which is consistent with the Convention should be preferred to a more natural interpretation which is inconsistent with the Convention. This was the approach of the House of Lords in *Litster* v. *Forth Dry Dock and Forth Estuary Engineering* [1990] 1 A.C. 546 in applying European Community law. The issue there was whether statutory protection extended to employees unfairly dismissed shortly before a transfer of an undertaking. The applicants had clearly not been employed in the business immediately before the transfer as these words would normally be interpreted. Nor were the words in the Transfer of Undertaking Regulations ambiguous. Yet the House of Lords interpreted the provisions of the Regulations by implying the additional words 'or would have been so employed if they had not been unfairly dismissed' – in order to accord with the European Court's interpretation of the relevant law. The Lord Chancellor Lord Irvine, in a lecture on the Human Rights Bill, said that this approach would apply under the Act. 'This implication of appropriate language into an apparently ambiguous provision is the sort of tool which could have led to a different result in a case like *Brind*. It shows the strong interpretative techniques that can be expected in Convention cases'.[4]

3 *R* v. *Secretary of State, ex p. Brind* [1990] 1 All E.R. 469 which upheld the Home Secretary's ban on broadcasting by the I.R.A.

4 Lord Irvine, 'The Development of Human Rights in Britain', *Public Law*, 1998, pp. 221, 228.

8.　ARE THE RULES, PRINCIPLES, PRESUMPTIONS AND OTHER GUIDES TO INTERPRETATION BINDING ON THE COURTS?

The main principles of statutory interpretation – the literal rule, the golden rule and the mischief rule – are all called rules, but this is plainly a misnomer. They are not rules in any ordinary sense of the word since they all point to different solutions to the same problem. Nor is there any indication, either in the so-called rules or elsewhere, as to which to apply in any given situation. Each of them may be applied but need not be. The same is true of every one of the principles, presumptions or other guides to interpretation that fill the 350 or so pages of *Maxwell on the Interpretation of Statutes*. In other words, for most problems of interpretation there is nothing in that book (nor in any other book) which tells one how to solve the difficulty that has arisen. For every proposition, there is one or more counter-principle. Each side in litigation will always find support in the authorities for whatever principle of interpretation it wishes to advance. The rules and principles of interpretation therefore do little or nothing to solve problems. They simply justify solutions usually reached on other grounds.

　　Professors Hart and Sacks give a helpful example. The bear trainer who comes to the station with his bear sees a notice, 'No dogs allowed on the trains'. By applying the maxim *expressio unius exclusio alterius,* he would claim to be entitled to board the train with the bear. (The express mention of dogs not being allowed may be used to argue that other animals, including bears, are allowed.) The competing argument is that if dogs are not allowed on, a fortiori, or by analogy, bears are not either. The solution to the problem does not depend on the deployment of maxims but on some notion as to what the rule is intended to achieve and the application of whatever interpretation best suits this objective.[5] It is the judge and not the rule or principle that determines the outcome. The principles may suggest an answer but there will usually be a counter-principle to suggest the opposite result. Justice Frankfurter of the United States Supreme Court said of statutory interpretation 'Though my business throughout most of my professional life has been with statutes, I come to you empty-handed. I bring no answers. I suspect the answers to the problems of an art are in its exercise'.[6] Sir Carleton Allen summarised his lengthy discussion of the problems of statutory interpretation with the words 'we are driven in the end to the unsatisfying conclusion that the whole matter ultimately turns on impalpable and indefinable elements of judicial spirit or attitude'.[7]

5　H. Hart and A. Sacks, *The Legal Process* (1958, unpublished), p. 1409.
6　*The Record of the Association of the Bar of the City of New York* (1947), p. 213 at pp. 216–17.
7　C. K. Allen, *Law in the Making* (7th edn, 1964), pp. 526, 529.

9. WOULD LEGISLATION TO STATE THE RULES OF STATUTORY INTERPRETATION HELP?

In most countries there is some form of Interpretation Act for the assistance of draftsmen, defining common terms or stating that, for instance, the male shall include the female unless the context indicates otherwise. In England there has been such an Act since 1889. A modern version was enacted in 1978.[8] As has been seen, pp. 000–00 above, there is also legislation in some countries on what extrinsic aids to interpretation are permitted.

But some countries have gone beyond guidance on such matters to attempt to guide the judges on the main problems of interpretation. Thus for instance the New Zealand Interpretation Act 1888 provided that 'Every Act, and every provision or enactment thereof, shall be deemed remedial, whether its immediate purport is to direct the doing of anything Parliament deems to be for the public good, or to prevent or punish the doing of anything it deems contrary to the public good, and shall accordingly receive such fair, large, and liberal construction and interpretation as will best ensure the attainment of the object of the Act and of such provision or enactment according to its true intent, meaning, and spirit.' (The provision is now to be found in the Acts Interpretation Act 1924, s. 5(*j*).)[9] Obviously the purpose behind the provision was to deter the judges from applying a narrow, literal approach to interpretation. It was a modern restatement of the mischief rule in *Heydon's* case – cast in mandatory form. The provision has been part of the law of New Zealand for some ninety years. How has it worked? The answer was given by Mr Denzil Ward who for twenty-four years had been a parliamentary draftsman in New Zealand. The Act, he said, had been invoked occasionally but for every case in which it had been applied there were many others in which it had been ignored. The courts in fact had continued to apply the 'heterogeneous collection of canons of construction developed by the English courts over a period of several hundred years':

---

8 See W. A. Leitch, 'Interpretation and the Interpretation Act 1978', *Statute Law Review*, 1980, p. 5.

9 A similar provision was inserted in 1981 into the Australian Acts Interpretation Act 1901:

'15AA.(1) In the interpretation of a provision of an Act, a construction that would promote the purpose or object underlying the Act (whether that purpose or object is expressly stated in the Act or not) shall be preferred to a construction that would not promote that purpose or object.'

Section 11 of the Canadian Interpretation Act 1967–8 states that 'every enactment shall be deemed remedial, and shall be given such fair, large and liberal construction and interpretation as best ensures the attainment of those objects.'

D. A. S. Ward, 'A Criticism of the Interpretation of Statutes in the New Zealand Courts', *New Zealand Law Journal,* 1963, p. 293

Sometimes it is difficult to discover just which approach has been favoured by the court. Usually no reason is given for preferring one approach to any other. The most that can be said is that some judges at some periods have been fairly consistent in using the approach that they prefer.

Thus we occasionally find a court applying the 'mischief rule' laid down in *Heydon's* case ...

Sometimes it is clear that the court, by its concentration on the actual words it is construing, is applying the 'literal rule' which in the nineteenth century dominated the judicial approach to a spate of legislation in general terms.

Sometimes ... it applies one of the presumptions (such as the presumption that a statute is not intended to alter the common law or the presumption of *mens rea*) which developed mainly during the eighteenth century when the courts regarded themselves more as standing between parliament and the people than as interpreters of authoritative texts. Alternatively a presumption may be brought into play to reinforce one of the other rules.

There are other cases where a court applies one of the maxims (such as the '*ejusdem generis* rule') which are really no more than condensed statements of the ordinary use of English; or decides the case on any one of a number of subsidiary and technical 'rules' secreted in the judgments of the past.

These 'rules' and presumptions and maxims are inconsistent, and often flatly contradict each other, but they are treated in the textbooks and in judgments as having equal validity today, regardless of the differing social, political, and constitutional conditions in which they arose. The 'literal rule' cannot be reconciled with the 'mischief rule'. Many of the presumptions have become unreal in these days when legislation invades so many aspects of life with its administrative machinery for the Welfare State, its taxes, its controls, and its innumerable minor offences. Some of them cannot be reconciled with the statement in s. 5(*j*) that every enactment shall be deemed remedial.

The result is chaos. It is impossible to predict what approach any court will make to any case. The field of statutory interpretation has become a judicial jungle. It is only fair to say that the jungle has been inherited; but our courts have been so busy cultivating the trees that they have lost sight of the pathway provided by parliament in the Acts Interpretation Act.

It is obvious from this account that a statutory enactment of the mischief rule has not been successful in New Zealand. It is predictable that the result would be much the same if it were tried in the United Kingdom. The Law Commission in their 1969 report on statutory interpretation were surely right in offering the possible explanation of the New Zealand history that 'exhortations to the courts to adopt "large and liberal" interpretations beg the question as to what is the real intention of the legislature, which may require in the circumstances either a broad or a narrow construction of language' (para. 33).[10] But the Law Commission did nevertheless propose

10　The Canadian provision requiring a 'fair, large and liberal' construction of every enactment was held in 1981 not to override the principle that penal statutes must

that it should be provided by statute that among the principles to be applied in the interpretation of statutes was that 'a construction which would promote the general legislative purpose underlying the provision in question is to be preferred to a construction which would not'. The Renton Committee supported this proposal (see *The Preparation of Legislation*, 1975, Cmnd 6053, para. 19.28). But when Lord Scarman attempted to introduce legislation to achieve the same result he failed. (See p.173 below.)

Note — codification of criminal law

During the work done for the Law Commission leading to the production of a Draft Criminal Code (p. 448 below) the code drafting team was asked to draft a code and 'rules which should govern its interpretation'. In its report to the Law Commission in 1985 the drafting team included a clause dealing with interpretation. The draft code was then sent out for comment. Comments on the interpretation clause were mixed and included so many adverse comments that the Law Commission decided to drop it altogether from the next draft, seemingly on the ground that there was no need for such a clause since the general rules of interpretation would apply. See A. Ashworth, 'Interpreting Criminal Statutes: A Crisis of Legality', 107 *Law Qtrly. Rev.*, 1991, pp. 419, 425–26. Professor Ashworth suggests that there may be a constitutional principle that statutory interpretation is for the courts rather than for Parliament.

10. WOULD STATEMENTS OF GENERAL PRINCIPLE ASSIST?

One of the recommendations of the Renton Committee was that the use in statutes of statements of principle should be encouraged (*The Preparation of Legislation*, Cmnd 6053, 1975, para. 10.13).

Mr I. M. L. Turnbull, First Parliamentary Counsel in Canberra, commented on this suggestion, and similar suggestions, at a conference in 1983:

I. M. L. Turnbull, 'Problems of Legislative Drafting', *Statute Law Review,* Summer 1986, pp. 72–3

> Although it sounds like a good idea in theory, it is very different in practice. If the clause is to cover the scope of the whole Bill, it must necessarily be drafted in very general terms. Yet its very generality will render it redundant and it will be little more than what Professor Reed Dickerson, the American draftsman and author, has described as a 'pious incantation'. The general purpose of a Bill

---

be given a narrow construction – *R.* v. *Philips Electronics Ltd* (1981) 116 D.L.R. (3d) 298, reported in *Statute Law Review*, 1981, p. 111.

will be apparent on the reading of its clauses: the problems of interpretation do not arise from the main body of cases that fall within the scope of a Bill, but from the cases that are on the borderline, requiring a consideration of the details of the legislation.

For example, section 2 of the Conciliation and Arbitration Act 1904 sets forth the chief objects of the Act as being:

'(*a*) to promote goodwill in industry;
(*b*) to encourage, and provide means for, conciliation with a view to amicable agreement, thereby preventing and settling industrial disputes;
(*c*) to provide means for preventing and settling industrial disputes not resolved by amicable agreement, including threatened, impending and probable industrial disputes, with the maximum of expedition and the minimum of legal form and technicality;
(*d*) to provide for the observance and enforcement of agreements and awards made for the prevention or settlement of industrial disputes;
(*e*) to encourage the organisation of representative bodies of employers and employees and their registration under this Act; and
(*f*) to encourage the democratic control of organisations so registered and the full participation by members of such an organisation in the affairs of the organisation.'

I suggest, first, that there is nothing in section 2 that is not apparent on the reading of the 200 sections of the Act, and secondly, that section 2 is of very little assistance, if at all, in the interpretation of the details of those sections. It is interesting to note that, notwithstanding the hundreds of amendments that have been made to different provisions of the Act since it was first enacted, section 2 has been remade once and amended twice. If the terms of the section have been wide enough to encompass so many alterations made by the legislature, they are wide enough to encompass an equal number of different interpretations made by the judiciary.

The Renton Committee (para. 11.B) recognised the problem of the generality of such clauses:

'a distinction should, however, be drawn between a statement of purpose which is designed to delimit and illuminate the legal effects of the Bill and a statement of purpose which is a mere manifesto. Statements of purpose of the latter kind should in our view be firmly discouraged.'

Yet it is difficult to conceive of an objects clause that can 'delimit and illuminate' the legal effects of the Bill with sufficient accuracy to be of any use unless it is comparable in length with the clauses of the Bill.

The Hansard Society's 1992 Report on The Legislative Process (*Making the Law*), as has been seen, also said it disagreed with the Renton Committee's suggestion that there should generally be a statement of principle and purpose: 'We firmly believe that certainty in the law must be the paramount aim in the drafting of statutes, and we do not believe that the automatic inclusion of statements of principle or purpose in the body of the Act would help to that end' (para. 239, pp. 60–1). ' In the first place, statements of principle or purpose would still have to be interpreted by the courts, even if other detail remained in the Act, and their very generality would leave open the possibility of differing interpretations' (para. 240, p. 61). Second, 'we see considerable problems in including in an Act two different formulations of what must be intended to be the same law on a single point – one in the form of a statement of principle or purpose (in some cases perhaps both) and the other in the form of detailed provisions' (para. 241, p. 61). That would be a recipe for confusion. Generally therefore it thought it would not be helpful to have statements of principle or purpose in statutes.

Note: Lord Scarman's Interpretation of Legislation Bill

In February 1980 Lord Scarman, formerly chairman of the Law Commission, introduced a bill to implement some of the recommendations of the Law Commission in the 1969 Report on Statutory Interpretation. Its purpose was to make available to the courts a wider range of aids to construction. It would have permitted reference to the reports of any Royal Commission, committee or other body moved or laid before Parliament or any document declared by the Act to be relevant. It also specified that among the principles to be applied in the interpretation of statutes was that a construction 'which would promote the general legislative purpose underlying the provision in question is to be preferred to a construction which would not'. But the Law Lords gave the bill an extremely frosty reception and it was withdrawn.[11]

Nothing daunted, Lord Scarman returned to the subject a year later and introduced another, slightly amended, version of the original bill. This time it received a rather warmer welcome, and in fact went through all its stages in the House of Lords.[12] But the bill went no further and was not even debated in the House of Commons.

For a commentary on the history of this abortive attempt to reform statutory interpretation see Francis Bennion, 'Another Reverse for the Law Commission's Interpretation Bill', *New Law Journal*, 13 August 1981, p. 840.

11 See House of Lords, *Hansard*, 13 February 1980, cols 276–306.
12 See House of Lords, *Hansard*, 9 March 1981, cols 64–83, and 26 March 1981, cols 1341–7.

11.   WHAT IS THE COURT'S PROPER FUNCTION IN INTERPRETING A STATUTE?

(a)   To seek out the intention or purpose of Parliament?

There are innumerable statements in judicial decisions that the chief duty of a court faced with a problem of statutory interpretation is to discover the intention of Parliament. But this approach has also been severely criticised. Thus it has been pointed out[13] that it is a fiction to speak of the intent of the legislature, which is an abstraction that can have no intention. In most cases only a few people drafted the statute, only a few spoke in the debates, many voted against it and many more had little notion of what they were voting about when they voted in favour. Whose intention represents that of the legislature? Frequently it is manifest that the draftsmen did not anticipate the problem that has occurred or, in other cases, that the statute did not provide any clear solution. For these reasons the concept of legislative intention is today somewhat discredited.

But these points can be met.[14] An amorphous group can have an intention even though it cannot be linked to any particular individuals. Those who voted against it obviously did not share the intent – but under the ordinary principles of democracy the majority prevails and the minority can for this purpose be disregarded. Those who voted without fully understanding the subject are deemed to have accepted the intention that emerges from the document. Those who were actively involved in formulating and promoting the statute could be said to be those who had a subjective intent which may or may not have been reflected in the ultimate language of the document. Matters that were not anticipated could still be said to be covered by the legislative intent in the sense that the statute may show how such problems should be solved. The authors of the statute may not have foreseen the particular problem, but they may nevertheless have had an intention which covers the situation that occurs – through reasoned elaboration of their text or by way of analogy.

Of course, the fact that there is some generalised intent implicit in a statute does not mean that there will have been something approaching a specific intent in regard to the problem under consideration. If the concept of intention is required to mean detailed answers to the problem in hand, it must be conceded that in many cases no such intention can be said to

13   See, for instance, M. Radin, 'Statutory Interpretation', 43 *Harvard Law Review*, 1930, p. 863; Douglas Payne, 'The Intention of the Legislature in the Interpretation of Statutes', *Current Legal Problems*, 1956, p. 96.
14   This discussion is based largely on Reed Dickerson, *The Interpretation and Application of Statutes* (1975), pp. 67–86. See also S. Vogenauer, 'What is the proper role of legislative intention in judicial interpretation?', *Statute Law Review*, 1997, p.235-43.

have existed. But if the concept of intention is defined in a broader and more realistic way, it does have genuine application to the situation. Certainly in the layman's sense the legislators had an intention and the layman's common-sense approach seems sufficiently close to the real situation to make the word 'intention' not as inappropriate as has often been suggested.

Those who have objected to the phrase 'legislative intention' have tended to prefer the seemingly more objective phrase 'legislative purpose'. This phrase, it is said, avoids most of the difficulties associated with the word 'intention'. It has already been argued that some of these objections have been exaggerated, but perhaps the more telling argument is that, on analysis, 'legislative purpose' is really only a different way of stating the same concept as 'legislative intent'. Both are ways of stating that the function of the interpreter is to give the words, to the best of his ability, a meaning that reflects the objectives of those responsible for the statute, insofar as this has been expressed in the language used.

There have been many recent statements by courts to the effect that the task of the court in interpreting a statute is to seek to give effect to the legislative purpose. The most weighty perhaps was the statement to that effect in *Pepper* v. *Hart* [1993] 1 All E.R. 42 already quoted above. Thus Lord Browne-Wilkinson giving the leading judgment said (at p. 64): 'The courts are faced simply with a set of words which are in fact capable of bearing two meanings. The courts are ignorant of the underlying parliamentary purpose ... [I]n a few cases it may emerge that the very question was considered by Parliament in passing the legislation. Why in such a case should the courts blind themselves to a clear indication of what Parliament intended in using those words?' Lord Griffiths in his separate but concurring speech said (at p. 50): 'The days have long passed when the courts adopted a strict constructionist view of interpretation which required them to adopt the literal meaning of the language. The courts now adopt a purposive approach which seeks to give effect to the true purpose of legislation and are prepared to look at much extraneous material that bears on the background against which the legislation was enacted.'

For other instances of the courts applying the purposive approach see for instance, *Kammins Ballroom Co. Ltd* v. *Zenith Investments Ltd* [1970] 2 All E.R. 871; *Johnson* v. *Moreton* [1978] 3 All E.R. 37; *Suffolk County Council* v. *Mason* [1979] A.C. 705; *Stock* v. *Frank Jones (Tipton)* [1978] 1 W.L.R. 231; *Attorney-General's Reference (No. 1 of 1988)* (1989) 89 Cr. App. R. 60. In *Fothergill* v. *Monarch Airlines Ltd* [1980] 3 W.L.R. 209 Lord Diplock said (at 222):

The audience to whom the language that [the draftsman] chooses is addressed is the judiciary, whose constitutional function is to resolve any doubts as to what written laws mean; and the resulting Act of Parliament will be couched in language that accords with the traditional, and widely criticised, style of legislative draftsmanship which has become familiar to English judges during the present century and for which their own narrowly semantic approach to statutory construction, until the last decade or so, may have been largely to blame. That approach for which parliamentary draftsmen had to cater can hardly be better illustrated than by the words of Lord Simonds in *Inland Revenue Commissioners* v. *Ayrshire Employers Mutual Insurance Association Ltd* [1946] 1 All E.R. 637, 641:

'The section ..., section 31 of the Finance Act 1933, is clearly a remedial section, ... It is at least clear what is the gap that is intended to be filled and hardly less clear how it is intended to fill that gap. Yet I can come to no other conclusion than that the language of the section fails to achieve its apparent purpose and I must decline to insert words or phrases which might succeed where the draftsman failed.'

The unhappy legacy of this judicial attitude, although it is now being replaced by an increasing willingness to give a purposive construction to the Act, is the current English style of legislative draftsmanship.

For another example see *IRC v McGuckian* [1997] 1 W.L.R. 991 in which Lord Steyn said: 'During the last 30 years there has been a shift away from the literalist approach to purposive methods of construction. When there is no obvious meaning to a statutory provision the modern emphasis is on a contextual approach designed to identify the purpose of a statute and to give effect to it'.

Note, however, *Page v Lowther* (1983) 57 T.C. 199 in which the Court of Appeal held that if there is a clash between a provision in a statute indicating its purpose and an operative provision, the latter should prevail.

For several recent highly unsatisfactory criminal law cases of statutory interpretation see A. Ashworth, 'Interpreting Criminal Statutes', 107 *Law Qrtly. Rev.*, 1991, pp. 419, 433–35.

On problems of the purposive approach, see Lord Oliver, 'A Judicial View of Modern Legislation', 14 *Statute Law Review*, 1993, pp. 5–11. Lord Oliver illustrated his point with the case of *R v Central Criminal Court, ex p.Francis & Francis* [1988] 3 All E.R. 775 where the House of Lords had to decide when legal professional privilege was lost by reason of a criminal purpose under the Police and Criminal Evidence Act 1994, s.10(2). The majority gave the statutory words an interpretation which both ignored the literal reading of the text and which conflicted with a statement by the Minister in *Hansard* as to the purpose of the provision.

For a sharp critique of the Court of Appeal for applying the purposive approach when a literal reading of the statutory provision was indicated see F.Bennion, 'Last Orders at *La Pentola*', *New Law Journal*, 1998, pp.953,986.

(b) To give effect to what parliament has said, rather than what it meant to say?

The school of thought which insists on focusing prime attention on the words used regardless of context has a fundamental point of great importance. If the words and meaning of the statute *are* clear, then the fact that there is strong evidence to suggest that some other meaning was intended cannot prevail. The intellectual integrity of the process demands that there be some limitation to the process of 'interpretation'. Humpty Dumpty was wrong in suggesting that you can make words mean whatever you want. The point may be made by reference to the will in the *Rowland* case (p. 115 above) . If the evidence had shown that Dr Rowland survived his wife by, say, forty-eight hours by clinging on to a raft which eventually sank, it would be straining the meaning of words to have held that their deaths coincided. On the other hand, if it had appeared that they died within half an hour of each other – he in New York, she in Melbourne – it would surely have been within the legitimate elaboration of the word 'coinciding' in the context to have held that it covered the event. In both cases it would have been obvious that the testator would have wished his property to go to his own relatives rather than to his wife's, but in the one case it would have been reasonable and in the other case unreasonable to have given effect to his intention.

The literalists are therefore not wrong to focus attention on the text. Their error is rather to focus exclusive attention on the text, and to deny the importance of seeing and comprehending at least some of the context. Clearly there must be some limit to the amount of context that the court has the time and the inclination to consider. But to apply the literal approach is unnecessarily to put on blinkers.

Sometimes the courts have even been prepared to insert missing words into the statute. A striking instance was *D.P.P.* v. *Hester* [1973] A.C. 296 where the House of Lords inserted words into a criminal enactment to the prejudice of the defendant. (See further F. A. R. Bennion, *Statutory Interpretation*, (2nd edn. 1992, pp. 334–43).)

However, often the question whether there is an ambiguity can only be answered when at least some context has been considered. It may seem that the words are clear but when seen in the light of the background they may take on a quite different shading. The court should therefore be willing to receive sufficient material to establish the nature of the issue raised between the parties – so that it can give an informed decision.

When deciding whether to give a text a narrow ('literal') or a broader ('liberal' or 'strained') interpretation the court needs to take into account all relevant factors. But if the court is unable to discover the purpose of the enactment and has no other material to guide it as to the likely meaning it will usually have no basis for departing from the literal meaning.

An illustration is *Attorney-General's Reference (No. 1 of 1988)* [1989] 2 All E.R. 1 (HL) concerning insider trading. The question was whether the accused had 'obtained' information in breach of the rules against insider trading when the information had been given to him unsolicited. The accused argued that he should have the benefit of the normal presumption that any ambiguity in a penal statute should be construed narrowly in favour of the citizen. But Lord Lowry giving the leading judgment for the House of Lords said that their first task was to ascertain what meaning Parliament intended to give the word 'obtained'. The White Paper which preceded the legislation showed that the mischief was dealing with securities while in possession of insider information. Lord Lowry said that, having weighed all the arguments, he was satisfied that the wider rather than the narrower meaning was the meaning which Parliament must have intended. Therefore there was no ambiguity to which they could apply the presumption in penal statutes.

It would be more accurate to say that the word 'obtained' was still ambiguous but that the Law Lords thought the presumption of narrow interpretation of penal statutes was displaced on balance by Parliament's intention.

(c) Should interpretation reflect changing times?

It is a familiar principle of statutory interpretation that 'the words of an Act will generally be understood in the sense they bore when it was passed'.[15] The statute should be construed, it has been said, 'as if we had read it the day after it was passed'.[16] But it is also a familiar fact, notwithstanding this principle, that interpretation does change with the times. (See on this subject especially D. J. Hurst, 'The Problem of the Elderly Statute', *Legal Studies*, 1983, vol. 3, no. 1, p. 21, from which some of the examples that follow are drawn.) An obvious instance is when the statutory words are later interpreted to apply to some concept which was unknown at the time when the statute was passed. Thus in *Barker* v. *Wilson* [1980] 1 W.L.R. 884, Caulfield J. said he had no doubt that the Bankers' Books Evidence Act 1879, s. 9, could be interpreted so as to include microfilm in the definition of bankers' books as 'ledgers, day books, cash books, account books and all other books used in the ordinary business of the bank'. Some phrases have been held by the courts to be mobile – changing in content as society changes. This is true of words like 'insulting' in section 5 of the Public Order Act 1936, or 'obscene' in the Obscene Publications Act 1959.[17]

15 *Maxwell on Interpretation of Statutes* (12th edn, 1969), p. 85.
16 *Sharpe* v. *Wakefield* (1888) 22 Q.B.D. 239.
17 See *Brutus* v. *Cozens* [1973] A.C. 854 at 861; *D.P.P.* v. *Jordan* [1977] A.C. 699 at 719.

In *Dyson Holdings Ltd* v. *Fox* [1976] Q.B. 503 the Court of Appeal had to decide whether a Miss Fox could succeed as a statutory tenant to a rent-protected house after the death of the tenant, Mr Wright, with whom she had been living for twenty-one years. In order to qualify she had to be a member of his family. In 1950 in *Gammans* v. *Ekins* [1950] 2 K.B. 328 the Court of Appeal had held that the phrase member of the tenant's family could not extend to a man who had been living for some years with a lady who was not his wife – though she had taken his name. Lord Evershed said there that it 'was indeed difficult to imagine any context in which by the proper use of the English language a man living in such a relationship with her could be described as of the tenant's family'.

But in the case of Miss Fox a different view prevailed. Lord Justice James, commenting on the changed circumstances since the 1950 decision, said (at 511):

> Between 1950 and 1975 there have been many changes in the law effected by statute and decisions of the courts. Many changes have their foundations in the changed needs and views of society. Such changes have occurred in the field of family law and equitable interests in property. The popular meaning given to the word 'family' is not fixed once and for all time. I have no doubt that with the passage of years it has changed. The popular meaning of 'family' in 1975 would, according to the answer of the ordinary man, include the defendant as a member of Mr Wright's family. It is not so easy to decide whether in 1961 [the date when Mr Wright had died] the ordinary man would have regarded the defendant as a member of Mr Wright's family. The changes of attitude which have taken place cannot be ascribed to any particular year. Had we to consider the position as at 1955 I would not be satisfied that the attitude reflected in the words of Asquith LJ in *Gammans* v. *Ekins* [1950] 2 KB 328, 331 had changed. I am confident that by 1970 the changes had taken place. There is no magic date in 1961. I think that, having regard to the radical change which has by 1975 taken place, it would be a harsh and somewhat ossified approach to the present case to hold that in 1961 the defendant was not in the popular sense a member of the family

Lord Justice Bridge went even further (at 513):

> … if language can change its meaning to accord with changing social attitudes, then a decision on the meaning of a word in a statute before such a change should not continue to bind thereafter, at all events in a case when the courts have consistently affirmed that the word is to be understood in its ordinary accepted meaning…. When the modern meaning is plain, we should, I think, be prepared to apply it retrospectively to any date, unless plainly satisfied that, at that date, the modern meaning would have been unacceptable.

This approach has not, however, been greeted with enthusiasm by later judges. In *Helby* v. *Rafferty* [1979] 1 W.L.R. 13, Lord Justice Cumming Bruce said that *Dyson* 'gave rise to many difficult problems'. He continued (at 25):

... Where a word is used in a succession of Acts of Parliament ... and ... is an ordinary English word ... I have the greatest difficulty in following how the meaning of that word ... changes over a period of 25 years. I still find it difficult to see how the change in social habit, to which James and Bridge LJJ referred in the *Dyson* case, has the effect of changing the meaning of the word enacted and re-enacted in successive Acts of Parliament – the word being an ordinary word – and, to my mind, the judges in the majority judgments in the *Dyson* case formulated a canon of construction which is novel to me and for which I know no previous authority.

Albie Sachs and Joan Hoff Wilson have shown how in the nineteenth century the courts in both England and America consistently interpreted the statutory words 'any person' in such a way as to deprive women of the right to participate in public life – by voting, being elected to office or becoming a member of a profession. Finally, in 1929 the Privy Council in an appeal from Canada[18] held that women were persons. 'The exclusion of women from all public offices is a relic of days more barbarous than ours ...' Lord Sankey swept away nearly fifty years of judicial history with the brief statement 'The word "person" may include members of both sexes, and to those who ask why the word should include females, the obvious answer is why not. In these circumstances the burden is upon those who deny that the word includes women to make out their case' (at 138). What had changed was not the statutory formula but the approach of the judges. The climate of the times had altered and what was unthinkable in the latter part of the nineteenth century had become tolerable and indeed unexceptionable in the late 1920s.[19]

An equally clear if less dramatic example was the change between 1876 and 1928 in judicial attitudes to the problem of liability without fault. In 1876 the House of Lords decided *River Wear Comrs* v. *Adamson* (1876) 1 Q.B.D. 546 (Ct of App.); (1877) 2 App. Cas. 742 (H.L.). Under the Harbour Clauses Act 1847, the owner of every vessel 'shall be answerable to the undertakers [the harbour authority] for any damage done by such vessel or by any person employed about the same to the harbour dock ...' A ship which had been abandoned was blown by a gale into a harbour and crashed into the dock causing considerable damage. In spite of the clear words of the statute, both the Court of Appeal and the House of Lords (though for different reasons) held that the shipowner was not liable. The notion of liability without fault was clearly so offensive to the judges that they found that Parliament could not have intended such a result. Almost fifty years later in 1928 the House of Lords took the exactly opposite view of

18 *Edwards* v. *Attorney-General, Canada* [1930] A.C. 124.
19 See generally Albie Sachs and Joan Hoff Wilson, *Sexism and the Law* (1978), pp. 4–66.

the same section on similar facts. (*The Mostyn* [1927] P. 25.) What had changed was the judges' attitude to allocation of losses in the light of insurance – Lord Haldane actually referred to the fact. It is inevitable and proper that the courts should reflect changing attitudes in their approach to statutes.

D. J. Hurst shows in his 1983 article (op. cit. p. 178 above at pp. 39–40) how the same kind of development took place in the judicial attitude to the word 'cruelty' used in matrimonial legislation. Conduct that would never have been recognised as within the concept in the mid-nineteenth century was accepted as being cruelty in the mid-twentieth century. But more, the word which for decades was treated by the judges as having a technical legal sense, was reinterpreted in modern times on the basis that it should be read in an ordinary and popular sense. He suggests that the same is true of the phrase 'actual occupation' as used in dozens of statutes before the 1925 Land Registration Act and in the 1925 Act itself. Until the decision of *Williams and Glyn's Bank Ltd* v. *Boland* [1981] A.C. 487, the phrase was a term of art. In that case the House of Lords held that a popular meaning for the phrase was to be preferred. 'As a result', Hurst says (at p. 41), 'a substantial part of both land law textbooks and building society mortgage deeds [was] having to be rewritten.'

Hurst (pp. 41–2) suggests that this is basically a dishonest way of proceeding. The judges felt a pressure, notably from politicians and the press, to state the law in a modern way. But a much better way was to have a modern statute: '[J]udge-made novelty ... which by a fiction declares the new rule always to have existed at a stroke revokes or nullifies established and well-founded interests. It is a crude and harsh weapon. But the most sinister effect of the rewriting of statutes by judges is that it wholly unsettles the law; nowhere is any principle in any judgment reliable if it derives from more than a few decades ago.'

In other words if the process of pouring contemporary attitudes into old statutes is carried too far, the judges will be exceeding their proper role. Here again they must find the right balance between adherence to precedent and continuity on the one hand, and a necessary flexibility and creativity on the other.

As noted above, (p.157) David Robertson in his book *Judicial Discretion in the House of Lords* (OUP,1998) has argued that the effect of the decision in *Pepper* v. *Hart* will be to freeze interpretation of statutes in the meaning that was given contemporaneously. In his discussion of the problem of interpreting 'elderly statutes' he says (p.170) that in Code Law countries the legislative history is 'simply disregarded' where legislation is too old for it to be apposite. In the United States the problem was a serious one–'sticking to the original intent of the framers of the constitution, as evidenced by the history of the constitutional convention, has become a prime methodological tool for ideologically conservative judges' (p.171).

Two contrasting cases that illustrate the way the courts have dealt with the problem of trying to reconcile statutory words with changing times are *ex parte Adedigba* and *Re Bravda*, both decided by the Court of Appeal in February 1968 and both of which required interpretation of statutory provisions that were more than a hundred years old and that had been interpreted judicially on many occasions.

R. v. Bow Road Domestic Proceedings Court, ex parte Adedigba [1968] 2 All E.R. 89 (Court of Appeal)

An unmarried Nigerian woman applied for maintenance against the putative father of her two children both of whom were born abroad. The court considered the effect of *R. v. Blane* (1849) 13 Q.B. 769, which had held that no maintenance could be awarded under the statute to a woman whose children were born abroad and which had been applied many times.

LORD DENNING M.R. (at 92): None of those cases is binding on this court: and I think that the time has come when we should say that *R. v. Blane* in 1849 was wrongly decided and also the two cases which followed it. It seems plain to me that if the mother and father are both here and the child is here, the words of the statute are satisfied. I can see no possible reason for denying the court's jurisdiction to order maintenance; and every reason for giving them jurisdiction. The father ought to be made to pay for the child …

I know that since *R. v. Blane* the statutory provisions have been reenacted in virtually the same words; but that does not trouble me. I venture to quote some words that I used in *Royal Crown Derby Porcelain Co. Ltd* v. *Russell* [1949] 2 K.B. 417, 429:

'I do not believe that whenever Parliament re-enacts a provision of a statute it thereby gives statutory authority to every erroneous interpretation which has been put on it. The true view is that the court will be slow to overrule a previous decision on the interpretation of a statute when it has long been acted on, and it will be more than usually slow to do so when Parliament has, since the decision, re-enacted the statute in the same terms, but if a decision is, in fact, shown to be erroneous, there is no rule of law which prevents it being overruled.'

Nor am I troubled by the fact that *R. v. Blane* has stood for 118 years. It is not a property or commercial case. It has not formed the basis of titles or commercial dealings. It is the sort of precedent which we can and should overrule when it is seen to be wrong. Only yesterday in *Conway* v. *Rimmer* [1968] 1 All E.R. 874 LORD MORRIS OF BORTH-Y-GEST used words appropriate to the situation:

'Though precedent is an indispensable foundation on which to decide what is the law, there may be times when a departure from precedent is in the interests of justice and the proper development of the law.'

If we were to affirm today *R.* v. *Blane* as being the law of this land, the only consequence would be a reference to the Law Commission; then a report by them, and eventually a Bill before Parliament. It would be quite a long time before the law could be set right. Even then the law would only be set right for future cases. Nothing could be done to set right this present case. The mother here would not get maintenance for the child which she needs now. So I would overrule *R.* v. *Blane* now. In the days of 1849 the question may not have been of any particular social significance; but now there are many illegitimate children here in England who were born abroad. It is only right and just that the mothers of those children should be able to take out proceedings against the fathers, and that the fathers should be ordered to pay reasonable maintenance for their own children. Otherwise what is the position? The children will be left to the care of the State. The national assistance fund will have to pay – the father will get out of his just responsibilities. That would be a most undesirable state of affairs.

SALMON L.J. (at 94): It is only if one goes back to the Statute of Elizabeth in 1576 that there is any warrant for the view that Parliament was legislating only for illegitimate children born in this country. The aphorism that time marches on and the law marches with it was just as valid in 1849 when *R.* v. *Blane* was decided as it is today, but its validity was then perhaps not so generally recognised. In 1849 time had indeed marched on since the reign of Elizabeth, and today it has marched on still further. There is no reason to suppose that Parliament intended then or now that the law should be the same as it was in 1576.

It is said that however wrong the decision in *R.* v. *Blane* may have been, it was made 118 years ago. Moreover, it has been followed ever since, as it had to be followed, by the courts on which it was binding; and accordingly the principle of stare decisis should apply. Certainly we do not readily interfere with the decisions which have stood for 118 years, or, indeed, for any lengthy period of time. This is particularly true of decisions in fields in which it might be said that the community has arranged its affairs in accordance with what has been regarded as the law for many years past. It is, for example, very true of decisions relating to the law of contract; but even in that field, the courts reverse a very old decision when they are completely satisfied that it was wrong. For example, recently this court[20] overruled *The Parana*[1] which had stood for nearly ninety years and had been generally accepted as stating the law relating to the measure of damage for breach of contract for the carriage of goods by sea; and the House of Lords[2] upheld the decision of this court.

In the present case none of these considerations underlying the principle of stare decisis apply. I do not suppose that the incidence of illegitimate children being conceived and born abroad has been affected in the slightest by the decision in *R.* v. *Blane*. I think it unlikely that any woman in Nigeria, or indeed anywhere else, would forbear to conceive and give birth to an illegitimate child abroad because she might contemplate that if she and the child came to this country with the putative father, she would not, according to the law as laid down in *R.* v. *Blane*, ever have a chance of recovering any sum from him by way

20 *The Heron* [1966] 2 Q.B. 695.
1   (1867) 2 P.D. 118.
2   [1967] 3 All E.R. 686.

of maintenance for the child. Nor do I think that putative fathers have arranged their affairs on the basis that *R.* v. *Blane* was correctly decided; and if they had, I should have no qualms about upsetting it.

The only matter that has given me any pause is that there has been a great deal of legislation concerning this subject in the last 118 years, and Parliament has never taken the opportunity of correcting *R.* v. *Blane*. The father has contended that since Parliament has not corrected *R.* v. *Blane* it must be taken to have approved and endorsed the decision. It is quite true that it is a principle of construction that the courts may presume that when there has been a decision on the meaning of a statute, and the statute is reenacted in much the same terms, it was the intention of Parliament to endorse the decision; but this is merely a rule of construction for the guidance of the courts. It is not a presumption that the courts are bound to make (see *Royal Crown Derby Porcelain Co. Ltd* v. *Russell* [1949] 2 K.B. 417). It is always possible that Parliament, however vigilant, may overlook a decision. I think that *R.* v. *Blane* has been overlooked by the legislature. I am certainly not satisfied that it was the intention of Parliament to endorse it. Indeed, if that decision had been considered by Parliament at any time when the intervening legislation was passed, I have little doubt but that it would have been corrected for it manifestly works gross injustice.

[Lord Justice Edmund Davies delivered a concurring judgement.]

In the second case the court was again unanimous but its decision went the other way. (Lord Justice Salmon was a member of the court on both occasions.)

In the Estate of Bravda [1968] 2 All E.R. 217 (Court of Appeal)

A testator made a will on one side of a piece of notepaper. Evidence showed that two independent witnesses signed first but that his two daughters, who were the chief beneficiaries under the will, then signed above them 'to make it stronger'. The gift to the daughters was challenged on the ground that under s. 15 of the Wills Act 1837 a beneficiary who signed the will as attesting witnesses could not take a gift. (The Wills Act, s. 15 stated that 'if any person shall attest the execution of any will ... to whom ... any beneficial devise ... shall be given, such device ... shall so far only as concerns such person ... be utterly null and void'.) All three judges refused to adjust the traditional interpretation of s. 15:

WILMER L.J. (at 221): The suggestion is made that s. 15 of the Wills Act, 1837, was never intended to apply in a case where there was already a valid execution by two unimpeachable witnesses. It has been suggested that the object of the section was merely to ensure that a will would not fail altogether if one or both of the two witnesses required were named as beneficiaries, as had been the case earlier. In other words, what is said is that the object of the section was merely to ensure that both those witnesses would be 'credible' witnesses. That result was achieved by requiring that they should forgo any benefits they would otherwise derive, but that the will would be left unimpaired. That is a point which does not appear to have been argued in the court below. It is not, of course, raised in the notice of appeal. There has been no cross-notice on behalf of the plaintiffs; and I do not think, in those circumstances, that the point is strictly open in this court. If it were open, I should merely say that, in my judgment, it is a point of no substance, for two reasons. One is that I think the words of the section are much too plain to admit of this rather tortuous construction. Secondly, I think that, after 130 years, it is now much too late to endeavour to put this entirely new construction on the well-known words of this section.

RUSSELL L.J. (at 224): It was debated in argument (the point originating from the Bench) whether s. 15 could be construed so as not to destroy a benefit given to an attesting witness if, without that witness, there were not less than two other witnesses to whom no benefit was given. This suggestion was made by analogy from the old law. A will of realty, for example, before the Wills Act 1752, required three credible witnesses for validity, a beneficiary not being a credible witness; but, as I understand it, provided there were three credible witnesses, the will was valid and a fourth witness, being a beneficiary, could take his benefit. The Act of 1752 first introduced the system found in s. 15 of the Wills Act 1837, by which all witnesses were in effect made credible by avoiding any benefit given. I would have thought it a very reasonable system of law that benefits to witnesses are not avoided if there are two independent witnesses; but the other view has been generally accepted in the authorities for a very long time indeed, and the language of s. 15 of the Act of 1837 is, I think, too forthright to be overcome by the analogy suggested. I have not myself looked at the language of the Act of 1752.

I would welcome a change in the law in this regard. I would expect most people to regard the outcome of this case as monstrously unfair to the testator and to his daughters. I do myself; but every time a beneficiary is an attesting witness, s. 15 of the Wills Act 1837 deprives him of his benefit and defeats the testator's intention. This is considered necessary to ensure reliable unbiased witnesses of due execution; but why it was thought necessary to interfere in cases where there are the requisite number of unbiased witnesses, I cannot imagine. I regretfully agree that the appeal succeeds.

SALMON L.J. (at 224): With very great regret, I also agree that this appeal succeeds. I was at an early stage struck by the force of the argument on the part of the defendant. I confess that I tried very hard to find some way round it – some ground on which in conscience I could find in favour of the plaintiffs; but I have failed. The words of s. 15 of the Wills Act 1837, are too plain, and the evidence filed on behalf of the plaintiffs is wholly inadequate. Section 15 makes it clear that, if any person attests the execution of any will to whom or to whose wife or husband any benefit is given under the will, then that part of the will which gives the benefit shall be null and void, but such person shall be a competent witness to prove the validity or invalidity of the will.

That statutory provision makes it impossible for the intentions of the testator to be carried out in the case of a beneficiary signing the will as a witness. That is the very object of the statutory provision. So, when the court is faced with the kind of problem which arises in this case, it is not open to the beneficiary to urge that the intention of the testator must not be defeated.

Parliament has clearly laid down that, when the testator intends to benefit a person who signs the will as a witness, the testator's intention shall be defeated. I wholly agree with RUSSELL L.J., for the reasons which he gives, that it is high time that this provision of the Wills Act 1837, should be amended, so that, when there are two independent credible witnesses, the mere fact that a beneficiary has also signed as a witness should not operate (as it now does) to defeat the intention of the testator.

Question

Why was the court prepared to move in *Adedigba* but not in *R.* v. *Blane*? One of the chief reasons given for the decision in *Adedigba* was that no one could reasonably be said to have arranged his affairs in reliance on the decision in *R.* v. *Blane*. But would the reasonable expectations of testators have been upset if the court had interpreted s. 15 of the 1837 Wills Act in such a way as to discount the signatures of beneficiaries if there were already two independent witnesses?[3]

Note

In this particular instance Parliament intervened with remarkable speed to correct the defect in the law revealed by *Re Bravda*. The Court of Appeal's decision was handed down on 2 February 1968. On 14 February a Private Member's bill was introduced to deal with the problem. It was reintroduced under a new title (the Wills Bill) on 21 February. It received the Royal Assent in May, only three months after the Court of Appeal had asked for legislative action!

Such speed is of course very rare. Another example was the County Court (Penalties for Contempt) Act which received the Royal Assent on 13 May 1983, only two months after the House of Lords held, in *Peart* v. *Stewart* [1983] 1 All E.R. 859, that a county court's power to punish for contempt of court was limited to one month's imprisonment.

(d)   Is membership of the European Community changing the principles of statutory interpretation?

There are dicta in some recent cases suggesting that belonging to the European Community (on which see further p. 374 below) may in the long

---

3   Cf. *Beswick* v. *Beswick* [1966] Ch. 538 (C.A.), [1968] A.C. 58 (H.L.), in which the Court of Appeal gave a statutory provision a startling interpretation in order to reform the law but the House of Lords reversed the decision on this point.

run have an impact on the approach of English courts to questions of statutory interpretation. Lord Denning, here as in so much else, was the leader. In *Bulmer* v. *Bollinger* he described the differences between the English and the European approach to statutory interpretation:

H. P. Bulmer Ltd v. *J. Bollinger S. A.* [1974] Ch. 401 at 425 (Court of Appeal)

Action was brought over use of the word 'champagne' in champagne cider and champagne perry. There was a request for the case to be transferred to the European Court for a ruling as to whether such use infringed Community regulations. The court refused to make a reference and this point was then appealed. In the course of refusing the appeal, Lord Denning spoke of the nature of Community Law.

LORD DENNING M.R.:

10. The principles of interpretation
It is apparent that in very many cases the English courts will interpret the Treaty themselves. They will not refer the question to the European Court at Luxembourg. What then are the principles of interpretation to be applied? Beyond doubt the English courts must follow the same principles as the European Court. Otherwise there would be differences between the countries of the nine. That would never do. All the courts of all nine countries should interpret the Treaty in the same way. They should all apply the same principles. It is enjoined on the English courts by section 3 of the European Communities Act 1972, which I have read.

What a task is thus set before us! The Treaty is quite unlike any of the enactments to which we have become accustomed. The draftsmen of our statutes have striven to express themselves with the utmost exactness. They have tried to foresee all possible circumstances that may arise and to provide for them. They have sacrificed style and simplicity. They have forgone brevity. They have become long and involved. In consequence, the judges have followed suit. They interpret a statute as applying only to the circumstances covered by the very words. They give them a literal interpretation. If the words of the statute do not cover a new situation which was not foreseen – the judges hold that they have no power to fill the gap. To do so would be a 'naked usurpation of the legislative function': see *Magor and St Mellons Rural District Council* v. *Newport Corporation* [1952] A.C. 189, 191. The gap must remain open until Parliament finds time to fill it.

How different is this Treaty! It lays down general principles. It expresses its aims and purposes. All in sentences of moderate length and commendable style. But it lacks precision. It uses words and phrases without defining what they mean. An English lawyer would look for an interpretation clause, but he would look in vain. There is none. All the way through the Treaty there are gaps and lacunae. These have to be filled in by the judges, or by Regulations or Directives. It is the European way. That appears from the decision of the Hamburg court in *In re Tax on Imported Lemons* [1968] C.M.L.R. 1.

Likewise the Regulations and Directives. They are enacted by the Council sitting in Brussels for everyone to obey. They are quite unlike our statutory instruments. They have to give the reasons on which they are based: article 190. So they start off with pages of preambles, 'whereas' and 'whereas' and 'whereas'. These show the purpose and intent of the Regulations and Directives. Then follow the provisions which are to be obeyed. Here again words and phrases are used without defining their import … In case of difficulty, recourse is had to the preambles. These are useful to show the purpose and intent behind it all. But much is left to the judges. The enactments give only an outline plan. The details are to be filled in by the judges.

Seeing these differences, what are the English courts to do when they are faced with a problem of interpretation? They must follow the European pattern. No longer must they examine the words in meticulous detail. No longer must they argue about the precise grammatical sense. They must look to the purpose or intent. To quote the words of the European court in the *Da Costa* case [1963] C.M.L.R. 224, 237, they must deduce 'from the wording and the spirit of the Treaty the meaning of the community rules.' They must not confine themselves to the English text. They must consider, if need be, all the authentic texts, of which there are now six: see *Bestuur der Sociale Verzekeringsbank* v. *Van der Vecht* [1968] C.M.L.R. 151 . They must divine the spirit of the Treaty and gain inspiration from it. If they find a gap, they must fill it as best they can. They must do what the framers of the instrument would have done if they had thought about it. So we must do the same. Those are the principles, as I understand it, on which the European Court acts.

Lord Denning returned to the theme in 1977:

Buchanan and Co. Ltd v. Babco Forwarding and Shipping (UK) Ltd [1977] 2 W.L.R. 107 (Court of Appeal)

Defendants agreed to carry 1,000 cases of the plaintiffs' whisky to Iran. The contract was subject to the terms and conditions of the Convention on the Contract for the International Carriage of Goods by Road, set out in the Schedule to the Carriage of Goods by Road Act 1965. The whisky was stolen from the defendants. The plaintiffs had to pay the excise duty and claimed this sum from the defendants. Judgment was given for the plaintiffs and the Court of Appeal dismissed the appeal. In the course of giving judgment, attention was given to the interpretation of an international convention scheduled to a UK statute:

LORD DENNING: This article 23, paragraph 4, is an agreed clause in an international convention. As such it should be given the same interpretation in all the countries who were parties to the convention. It would be absurd that the courts of England should interpret it differently from the courts of France, or Holland, or Germany. Compensation for loss should be assessed on the same basis, no matter in which country the claim is brought. We must, therefore, put on one side our traditional rules of interpretation. We have for years tended to stick too closely to the letter – to the literal interpretation of the words. We ought, in interpreting this convention, to adopt the European method. I tried to describe it in *H. P. Bulmer Ltd* v. *J. Bollinger S.A.* [1974] Ch. 401, 425–6. Some of us recently spent a couple of days in Luxembourg discussing it with the members of the European Court, and our colleagues in the other countries of the nine.

We had a valuable paper on it by the President of the court (Judge H. Kutscher) which is well worth study: 'Methods of interpretation as seen by a judge at the Court of Justice, Luxembourg 1976.' They adopt a method which they call in English by strange words – at any rate they were strange to me – the 'schematic and teleological' method of interpretation. It is not really so alarming as it sounds. All it means is that the judges do not go by the literal meaning of the words or by the grammatical structure of the sentence. They go by the design or purpose which lies behind it. When they come upon a situation which is to their minds within the spirit – but not the letter – of the legislation, they solve the problem by looking at the design and purpose of the legislature – at the effect which it was sought to achieve. They then interpret the legislation so as to produce the desired effect. This means that they fill in gaps, quite unashamedly, without hesitation. They ask simply: what is the sensible way of dealing with this situation so as to give effect to the presumed purpose of the legislation? They lay down the law accordingly. If you study the decisions of the European Court, you will see that they do it every day. To our eyes – shortsighted by tradition – it is legislation, pure and simple. But, to their eyes, it is fulfilling the true role of the courts. They are giving effect to what the legislature intended, or may be presumed to have intended. I see nothing wrong in this. Quite the contrary. It is a method of interpretation which I advocated long ago in *Seaford Court Estates Ltd* v. *Asher* [1949] 2 K.B. 481, 498–9. It did not gain acceptance at that time. It was condemned by Lord Simonds in the House of Lords in *Magor and St. Mellons Rural District Council* v. *Newport Corporation* [1952] A.C. 189, 191, as a 'naked usurpation of the legislative power'. But the time has now come when we should think again. In interpreting the Treaty of Rome (which is part of our law) we must certainly adopt the new approach. Just as in Rome you should do as Rome does, so in the European Community, you should do as the European Court does.

LORD JUSTICE ROSKILL agreed: I would like to support what Lord Denning M.R. has said and what Lawton L.J. will say regarding the need to alter the traditional English method of approach to questions of construction of statutes such as the Act of 1965 which give effect on a matter of municipal law to international conventions. Some such conventions are drafted in languages other than English. The English language, though used, may in other cases not be the predominant language of the convention, or in yet other cases may at the most be only of equal force with one or more other European languages. Now that this country has joined the European Community our courts are likely to be increasingly concerned with the interpretation of legislation of one kind or another of which English is not the original or the dominant language. Such legislation is likely also to fall for interpretation in the courts of other members of the community. It would be disastrous if our courts were to adopt constructions of such legislation different from those of other courts whose method of approach is different and far less narrow than ours merely because of over-rigid adherence to traditional –

some might call them chauvinist – English methods. Conflict would arise between courts in different jurisdictions within the European Community with the untoward consequences to which Lord Denning M.R. and Lawton L.J. refer and if it became known that if a party sued in one country one result would follow, but if in another country another – a state of affairs which has arisen in other branches of the law between, for example, this country and the United States – what is sometimes known as forum-shopping would be encouraged, whereas within the community it should be discouraged. I think in the future our courts should be far more ready, in cases where international conventions, especially those affecting the members of the European Community, are under judicial consideration, to assimilate their approach to questions of the construction of our legislation giving effect to those conventions to that which the courts of other members of the Community are likely to adopt. The doctrine once proclaimed in the phrase 'Athanasius contra mundum' caused much trouble many centuries ago. That attitude of mind has no place in our courts in the latter part of the 20th century.

See further Vera Sacks and Carol Harlow, 'Interpretation European Style', 40 *Modern Law Review*, 1977, p. 578. See also Shael Herman, 'Quot judices tot sententiae: A Study of the English Reaction to Continental Interpretative Techniques', 1 *Legal Studies*, 1981, p. 165, Lord Slynn, 'Looking at European Community Texts', 14 *Statute Law Review*, 1993, pp. 12–27, T. Millett, 'Rules of Interpretation of EEC Legislation', 10 *Statute Law Review*, 1989, pp. 163–82; T. Rensen, 'British Statutory Interpretation in the Light of Community and other International Obligations, 14 *Statute Law Review*, 1993, pp. 186–203; and Tracey Reeves, 'Opposites attract: plain English with a European interpretation', *New Law Journal*, 18 April 1997, p. 576.

(e)   What is the proper limit to the creative function of the interpreter?

There are few today who deny that the interpreter of legislation exercises some creative role. In recent years this has even become conventional wisdom amongst the judges themselves. In 1965, for instance, Lord Diplock told his audience at Birmingham University:

Lord Diplock, 'The Courts as Legislators', Holdsworth Club Lecture, 1965, pp 5–6

> … there are also cases – many more than one would expect – where there is room for dispute as to what the rule of conduct really is. This is so as much with rules laid down by Act of Parliament as with those which have evolved at common law… .

... [E]very revenue appeal that comes before the court – generally after any dispute of fact there may have been has already been decided by the Commissioners – involves a dispute as to whether a particular kind of gain is taxable, whether a particular kind of document attracts stamp duty. Whenever the Court decides that kind of dispute it legislates about taxation. It makes a law taxing all gains of the same kind or all documents of the same kind. Do not let us deceive ourselves with the legal fiction that the court is only ascertaining and giving effect to what Parliament meant. Anyone who has decided tax appeals knows that most of them concern transactions which Members of Parliament and the draftsman of the Act had not anticipated, about which they had never thought at all. Some of the transactions are of a kind which had never taken place before the Act was passed: they were devised as a result of it. The court may describe what it is doing in tax appeals as interpretation. So did the priestess of the Delphic oracle. But whoever has final authority to explain what Parliament meant by the words that it used makes law as much as if the explanation it has given were contained in a new Act of Parliament. It will need a new Act of Parliament to reverse it.

See, to similar effect, Lord Radcliffe, p. 293 below; Justice Cardozo, p. 296 below; Lord Devlin, pp. 308–311 below; Lord Edmund-Davies, p. 347 below; Lord Pearson, p. 347 below. See also Michael J.Beloff, 'Wednesbury, Padfield and All That Jazz: A Public Lawyer's View of Statute Law Reform', *Statute Law Review*, 1994, pp.147–63.

But how can one describe the extent of judicial creativity in statutory interpretation? One helpful image is that used by Reed Dickerson in his book, *The Interpretation and Application of Statutes* (1975). Dickerson uses the simile of the restorer of an ancient vase. Everything depends on how much of the original vase is available to him. Sometimes he is simply making a substitute for a small piece missing from the body of the vase. 'Here he is guided by the adjacent contours, and, if he is skilful, the result blends well enough to attract little or no attention ... His job is harder if the vase has been decorated, but the difficulty is small if the decoration follows a discernible pattern' (p. 26). In this activity there is some creativity but it is of the lowest order. It still falls within the general heading of 'ascertainment of meaning' in the sense of discovering something that is in a real sense latent in the material.

But the position is plainly very different if the craftsman has only a single piece and the decoration is free and non-recurring. Here by imaginative speculation he must attempt to produce something 'in the general style' of the original without being able to pretend that his effort will necessarily approximate to it very closely. Here the element of creativity is very considerable. The greater the range of choice open to the judge, the greater his law-making as opposed to his law-finding function. If the statute is a Bill of Rights with broad, open-textured provisions, the scope for judicial legislation will be vast compared with the opportunities offered by the tight provisions of, say, an income tax Act. There is, however, no general way that the proper limit of the creative function of judges in statutory interpretation can usefully be defined. The judge should be open and sensitive to the subtleties and complexity of language, to the fallibility of draftsmen and to the variety of interests that may be reflected in legal documents. On the other hand he must respect the limits of language and not place on the disputed words a meaning they will not fairly bear. The judges must not threaten to compete with the legislature, but they should recognise that intelligent interpretation necessarily involves a creative function.

For an example of the judge refusing to accept an imaginative argument as to the meaning of words, see *Bourne (Inspector of Taxes)* v. *Norwich Crematorium* [1967] 2 All E.R. 576, in which the question was whether the activities of a crematorium could be said to be within the statutory phrase 'the subjection of goods or materials to any process'. He declined to accept the suggestion (at 578):

> I can only say that, although the human body is no doubt material in the same sense that all things visible are material, there is in my judgment something in the word 'materials', in the plural, which forbids the construction of the phrase 'goods and materials' that is urged on me. In my judgment it would be a distortion of the English language to describe the living or the dead as goods or materials...
>
> [H]aving given the matter the best attention that I can, I conclude that the consumption by fire of the mortal remains of homo sapiens is not the subjection of goods or materials to a process within the definition of 'industrial building or structure' contained in s. 271 (1) (c) of the Income Tax Act 1952.

In a recent case the House of Lords said that 'it might be perfectly proper to adopt a strained construction to enable the object and purpose of legislation to be fulfilled, but it could not be taken to the length of applying unnatural meanings to familiar words or of so stretching the language that its former shape was transformed into something which was not only significantly different but had a name of its own'. The House of Lords refused to define the word 'road' to include a car park in the context of an action against an uninsured driver (*Clarke* v. *Kato, Cutter* v. *Eagle Star Insurance Co Ltd* [1998] 4 All ER 417.)

On statutory interpretation generally, see especially: Reed Dickerson, *The Interpretation and Application of Statutes* (1975); Rupert Cross, *Statutory Interpretation* (3rd edn, ed. John Bell and Sir George Engle, 1995); *Maxwell on the Interpretation of Statutes* (12th edn, 1969); Felix Frankfurter, 'Some Reflections on the Reading of Statutes', 47 *Columbia Law Review*, 1947, p. 527. See also F. A. R. Bennion, *Statutory Interpretation* (3rd edn. 1997), a *tour de force* in which Mr Bennion has single-handedly produced a 900-page code of statutory interpretation with an extended commentary and a wealth of examples. On the view of a German lawyer see R.Zimmermann, 'Statuta Sunt Stricte Interpretenda'? Statutes and the Common Law: A Continental Perspective', 56 Cambridge Law Journal, 1997, pp. 315–28.

CHAPTER 4

Binding precedent – the doctrine of *stare decisis*

It is difficult to conceive of a legal system in which precedent plays no part at all. One of the fundamental characteristics of law is the objective that like cases should be treated alike. It is therefore natural that other things being equal one court should follow the decision of another where the facts appear to be similar. But in the common law systems precedents have a greater potency than simply as models for imitation. The rules *require* that in certain circumstances a decision be followed whether the second court approves of the precedent or not. Thus in *Re Schweppes Ltd's Agreement* [1965] 1 All E.R. 195, the Court of Appeal, with Willmer L.J. dissenting, ordered discovery of documents in a case involving restrictive trade practices. On the same day the same three judges gave judgment in a second case involving the same point – *Re Automatic Telephone and Electric Co. Ltd's Agreement* [1965] 1 All E.R. 206. Judgment in the second case was delivered by Lord Justice Willmer who simply said: 'If the matter were res integra, I should have been disposed to dismiss the appeal in this case for the same reasons as those which I gave in my judgment in the previous case. It seems to me, however, that I am now bound by the decision of the majority in the previous case. In these circumstances, I have no alternative but to concur in saying that the appeal in the present case should be allowed.' The second decision was therefore unanimous. The example illustrates not only the impact of binding precedent but also the fact that under the English system the effect is instantaneous. In civil law countries based on Roman law, by contrast, precedents may be followed and commonly are, but there is no rule requiring that they be followed.(Note however, that under the Human Rights Act 1998, the operation of the doctrine of precedent may be set aside. Courts which would normally be bound by the decisions of higher courts may be free not to follow them – on which see further p.232 below.)

The doctrine of binding precedent is called *stare decisis* (more precisely *stare rationibus decidendis*, keep to the decisions of past cases). It must be distinguished from the very different doctrine of *res judicata*. *Res judicata* signifies that the parties to a litigated dispute cannot reopen it after the normal period for an appeal has lapsed or after they have exhausted their right to appeal. There is an exception in criminal cases, permitting the later reopening of a case *on the facts* if it appears that there may have been a miscarriage of justice.[1] But, subject to that, the parties are bound by the result of the case once it is finally concluded. *Stare decisis* is a doctrine that affects not the parties but everyone else – it concerns the impact of the decision for the future on others in the community and especially on later courts.

The first essential ingredient of the doctrine of binding precedent is a hierarchy of courts and rules that indicate the inter-relationship of the different courts.

1. THE HIERARCHY OF COURTS AND THE DOCTRINE OF BINDING PRECEDENT

(a) The House of Lords

The decisions of the House of Lords are binding on all lower courts. For virtually all this century they were also binding on the House of Lords itself. The House of Lords ruled in *London Tramways* v. *London County Council* [1898] A.C. 375 that it was bound by its own decisions. In fact this rule was virtually settled nearly forty years earlier in *Beamish* v. *Beamish* (1861) 9 H.L.C. 274, but the *London Tramways* case finally decided the matter. Lord Halsbury delivered the only speech, of which the crucial passage (at 380) was perhaps:

> Of course I do not deny that cases of individual hardship may arise, and there may be a current of opinion in the profession that such and such a judgment was erroneous; but what is that occasional interference with what is perhaps abstract justice, as compared with the inconvenience – the disastrous inconvenience – of having each question subject to being reargued and the dealings of mankind rendered doubtful by reason of different decisions, so that in truth and in fact there would be no real final court of appeal. My lords, 'interest rei publicae' is that there should be 'finis litium' sometime and there can be no 'finis litium' if it were possible to suggest in each case that it might be reargued because it is 'not an ordinary case' whatever that may mean.

---

1 In a criminal case it is also possible to petition the Criminal Cases Review Commission (formerly the Home Secretary) to have the case referred back to the Court of Appeal on the ground that the law has changed. In civil cases there are exceptional circumstances where the courts have allowed a point of law to be reopened – see for instance *Arnold* v. *National Westminster Bank plc* [1988] 3 All E.R. 977.

In the decades that followed, the doctrine that the House of Lords was bound by its own decisions seemed solidly established even though it was criticised from time to time – see especially Lord Wright's famous article, 'Precedent', *Cambridge Law Journal*, 1944, p. 118. On 26 July 1966, however, Lord Gardiner, the Lord Chancellor, read a statement on behalf of himself and all the other Lords of Appeal in Ordinary announcing that the House of Lords would in future regard itself as free to depart from its own previous decisions:[2]

Practice Statement (Judicial Precedent) [1966] 1 W.L.R. 1234

Their Lordships regard the use of precedent as an indispensable foundation upon which to decide what is the law and its application to individual cases. It provides at least some degree of certainty upon which individuals can rely in the conduct of their affairs, as well as a basis for orderly development of legal rules.

Their Lordships nevertheless recognise that too rigid adherence to precedent may lead to injustice in a particular case and also unduly restrict the proper development of the law. They propose therefore to modify their present practice and, while treating former decisions of this House as normally binding, to depart from a decision when it appears right to do so.

In this connection they will bear in mind the danger of disturbing retrospectively the basis on which contracts, settlements of property and fiscal arrangements have been entered into and also the especial need for certainty as to the criminal law.

This announcement is not intended to affect the use of precedent elsewhere than in this House.

The above is the statement that appears in the law reports. However, it was issued to the press with the following additional explanatory note:

Since the House of Lords decided the English case of *London Street Tramways* [sic] v. *London County Council* in 1898, the House have considered themselves bound to follow their own decisions, except where a decision has been given per incuriam in disregard of a statutory provision or another decision binding on them.

The statement made is one of great importance, although it should not be supposed that there will frequently be cases in which the House thinks it right not to follow their own precedent. An example of a case in which the House might think it right to depart from a precedent is where they consider that the earlier decision was influenced by the existence of conditions which no longer prevail, and that in modern conditions the law ought to be different.

One consequence of this change is of major importance. The relaxation of the rule of judicial precedent will enable the House of Lords to pay greater

2   For an insight into the background that led to the Practice Statement, see A. Paterson, *The Law Lords* (1982), pp. 146–51.

attention to judicial decisions reached in the superior courts of the Commonwealth, where they differ from earlier decisions of the House of Lords. That could be of great help in the development of our own law. The superior courts of many other countries are not rigidly bound by their own decisions and the change in the practice of the House of Lords will bring us more into line with them.

The House of Lords' Practice Statement was hailed as an event of great consequence,[3] but in the three decades and more that have passed since 1966 it has become apparent that the new freedom to depart from previous decisions is used extremely sparingly. The point came up in *Jones* v. *Secretary of State for Social Services* [1972] A.C. 944 which was heard specially by seven Law Lords. (Normally the House of Lords sits with five.) The case required interpretation of a statutory provision regarding injury benefit in the light of the House of Lords' own prior decision in *Re Dowling* [1967] 1 A.C. 725. Four Lords (Wilberforce, Dilhorne, Diplock and Simon) were clear that the House's 1967 decision in *Dowling* was wrong and, of these, three thought that it should be departed from under the 1966 Practice Statement but one (Lord Simon) thought it should not. The other three Lords (Reid, Morris and Pearson) thought the *Dowling* decision was right but they also addressed themselves to the question of what they would have thought if they had shared the view that *Dowling* was wrong. They all took the view that they would not have been prepared to depart from it. All the Law Lords seemed to be agreed that the mere finding that an earlier decision is wrong would not in itself be enough to justify the House from departing from the decision. More was required. The following statements give some clues as to the kind of circumstances in which the House might consider it appropriate to depart from one of its own prior decisions:

LORD REID (at 966): I would not seek to categorise cases in which it [the Practice Statement] should or cases in which it should not be used. As time passes experience will provide some guide. But I would venture the opinion that the typical case for reconsidering an old decision is where some broad issue is involved, and that it should only be in rare cases that we should reconsider questions of construction of statute or other documents… . Holding these views, I am firmly of opinion that *Dowling's* case ought not to be reconsidered. No broad issue of justice or public policy is involved nor is any question of legal principle. The issue is simply the proper construction of complicated provisions in a statute.

LORD WILBERFORCE (at 995): On a question of construction of an Act of Parliament, as to which this House has the last word until Parliament itself

---

3 Though at least one commentator doubted whether the Practice Statement was sound in law – see F. A. Mann, 'Reflections on English Civil Justice and the Rule of Law', *Civil Justice Quarterly*, 1983, pp. 320, 330–2.

intervenes, there are strong objections against a change of course by this House. Unless the cases, first and subsequent, wholly coincide, there may be a doubt which decision of the House … prevails, and litigants may be encouraged in future disputes … to take the chance of an appeal here, in the hope of procuring a departure.

LORD PEARSON (at 996): … in my opinion the decision in *Dowling's* case ought to be followed for several reasons. First, there is the principle of stare decisis. A decision of this House has had the distinctive advantage of being final both in the sense that it put an end to the litigation between the parties and in the sense that it established the principle embodied in the ratio decidendi. Consequently it provided a firm foundation on which commercial, financial and fiscal arrangements could be based.[4] Also it marked a definite step in the development of the law, irreversible except by Act of Parliament. This distinctive advantage of finality should not be thrown away by too ready use of the recently declared liberty to depart from previous decisions. [Lord Pearson also drew attention to the fact that the decision in *Dowling*, counting the judges at all three levels, had only been by six to five. A majority of six to five was not very strong but it showed that the view that prevailed was a tenable view.] That seems to me to be a sufficient reason for not overruling the decision in *Dowling's* case. If a tenable view taken by a majority in the first appeal could be overruled by a majority preferring another tenable view in a second appeal, then the original tenable view could be restored by a majority preferring it in a third appeal. Finality of decision would be utterly lost.

LORD DIPLOCK (at 1014–15): It [*Dowling's* case] is a recent decision, but I see no greater reason for perpetuating recent error than for leaving ancient error uncorrected. [The decision could be reversed by Parliament but] it would be unrealistic to suppose that this could be done quickly. [In the meanwhile harmful practical consequences would follow for victims of accidents so that Lord Diplock would have overruled *Dowling's* case notwithstanding that it was] a decision on the construction of a statute which after some delay could be put right by Parliamentary action.]

LORD SIMON OF GLAISDALE (at 1023–6): I am clearly of the opinion that it would be wrong now to seek to depart from that decision [in *Dowling*] for the following reasons: (1) The declaration of 26 July 1966 itself implies that the power to depart from a previous decision of your Lordships' House is one to be most sparingly exercised. (2) A variation of view on a matter of statutory construction … would, I should have thought, rarely provide a suitable occasion… (3) Your Lordships will, I apprehend, be reluctant to encourage frequent litigants like the Secretary of State for Social Services in this type of case or the Commissioners of Inland Revenue in revenue cases to reopen arguments once concluded against them… (4) On the instant issue there is obviously much to be said for each side… (5)… despite dire prophecy the decision in *Dowling's* case has not rendered the statutory scheme unworkable… (6) If *Dowling's* case really causes inconvenience, it seems to me that the remedy lies far more appropriately with the legislature than in your Lordships'

---

4   It is not apparent how commercial, financial or fiscal arrangements could be based on the decision in *Dowling*, which ruled that a decision by statutory authorities that an injury arose from an accident was final (ed.).

House sitting judicially. Parliament has facilities for advice (both from the executive and from industry) as to all possible repercussions, which your Lordships do not have... (9) I am left uncertain what would be the effect of overruling *Dowling's* case on decisions thereafter come to on the basis that it was correctly decided. Before departing from a previous decision your Lordships, I surmise, would require to be positively satisfied that such a course would not involve unacceptably the re-opening of issues long concluded or the risk of individual hardship in cases intermediately decided.

The same broadly negative view about the chances of getting the House of Lords to change its mind was given in *Fitzleet Estates* v. *Cherry* [1977] 1 W.L.R. 1345. The House of Lords has also held that it will not reopen one of its own decisions – even if it feels in principle inclined to do so – where to do so would be academic on the facts of the actual case: see *Food Corpn. of India* v. *Antclizo Shipping Corpn. The Antclizo* [1988] 2 All E.R. 513 where reopening the previous decision would not have affected the outcome of the appeal. There have, however, been at least a few cases in which the House of Lords has gone back on its own previous decisions. In *Miliangos* [1976] A.C. 443, it changed the rule that a damages award in an English court had to be expressed in sterling. The decision (which is considered further below, p. 206) was based largely on the changed position of sterling in the modern world. In *British Railways Board* v. *Herrington* [1972] A.C. 877, the House softened its 1929 ruling that an occupier owed virtually no duty of care to a trespasser even when he was a child. The reason appears to have been a change in the climate of opinion as to the acceptable distribution of risks between occupiers and those injured on their premises. (Lord Pearson, for instance, said that the previous decision's 'formulation of the duty of occupier to trespasser is plainly inadequate for modern conditions' (at 930). Lord Diplock said he explained the decision as reflecting 'the general development of legal concepts since 1929 as to the source of one man's duty to take steps for the duty of another' (at 935).) In the *Johanna Oldendorff* [1974] A.C. 479 the Law Lords departed from the decision in *The Aello* [1961] A.C. 135 as to when a ship became 'an arrived ship'. See generally G. Maher, 'Statutory Interpretation and Overruling in the House of Lords', *Statute Law Review*, 1981, p. 85.

In *Murphy* v. *Brentwood District Council* [1991] 1 A.C. 398 the House of Lords, with seven judges sitting, expressly overruled its decision in *Anns* v. *Merton London Borough* [1978] A.C. 728 on the important question of the extent of the duty of care owed by local authorities in respect of defects in buildings arising out of their function of supervising compliance with building regulations.

The first decision involving the criminal law in which the House of Lords agreed to depart from one of its own rulings was *Shivpuri* [1986] 2 All E.R. 334. Within ten months, however, in *Howe* [1987] 1 All E.R. 771 it did so again.

The first opportunity for the Law Lords to exercise the new power in regard to a criminal law case had been *Knuller* v. *D.P.P.* [1973] A.C. 435, where the House was invited to overrule its highly controversial decision in *Shaw* v. *D.P.P.* (the Ladies Directory case) [1962] A.C. 220. It refused. Even Lord Reid, who had dissented in *Shaw*, thought it would be wrong to use the Practice Statement to upset the decision; 'however wrong or anomalous a decision may be it must stand ... unless or until it is altered by Parliament' (at 455).

In *Shivpuri* [1986] 1 All E.R. 334 the House of Lords overruled *Anderton* v. *Ryan* [1985] 2 All E.R. 355 on the interpretation of the Criminal Attempts Act 1981. Although the precedent was so recent and although it related to a matter of statutory interpretation, Lord Bridge said that if a serious error had distorted the law, the sooner it was corrected the better. Criticism of *Anderton* v. *Ryan* showed correctly that it had virtually emasculated the Act. Moreover, it was improbable that anyone would be able to say that he had been unfairly treated because he had innocently relied on the decision in *Anderton* v. *Ryan*. He therefore held that the earlier decision, in which he himself had played a leading part, was wrong.

A commentator congratulated the House of Lords – and contrasted this decision favourably with that of *Moloney* [1985] A.C. 905, in which the House impliedly overruled two of its earlier decisions on murder without admitting that the previous decisions were wrong.[5] The difference of approach, he said, was 'both refreshing and reassuring' (at p. 492).

In *Howe* the House of Lords departed from its own decision on whether it was open to someone to plead duress to a charge of murder. It had held in *D.P.P. for N. Ireland* v. *Lynch* [1975] A.C. 653 by 3–2 that it was; it held in *Howe* unanimously that it was not. The Law Lords gave three reasons. One was that *Lynch* had been judicial legislation. But this reason had been rejected in *Knuller* as a ground for departing from *Shaw*. Secondly, the legislature had failed to implement a recommendation of the Law Commission in 1977 that the defence of duress should extend to all offences. This, the House said, showed that Parliament did not want the defence to exist at all – a singularly unpersuasive *non sequitur*. Thirdly, the reasoning that applied in *Shivpuri* applied here. But, as the above-mentioned commentator pointed out,[6] this argument too was unpersuasive. In *Anderton* v. *Ryan* the House had plainly gone wrong. But in *Lynch* its decision was at most controversial and many thought it was right. The result is that there is now a good deal of uncertainty as to when the House will or will not depart from a decision in criminal law.

5   See E. M. Clare Canton, 'The House of Lords and Precedent: A New Departure', *New Law Journal*, 29 May 1987, pp. 491–2.
6   Ibid.

For a strongly worded view that the House of Lords should be prepared to reconsider its own decisions in the criminal law field because of its deplorable record in this field, see Conor Gearty, 'Precedent in the House of Lords in Criminal Cases', *New Law Journal*, 31 July 1987, p. 707. Professor Gearty suggested that 'honest fallibility is to be preferred to confused invulnerability'.

According to Professor Alan Paterson, the most influential judge in formulating the principles on which the House ought to exercise its discretion under the Practice Statement was Lord Reid:

Alan Paterson, *The Law Lords* (1982), pp. 156–7

In a series of cases between 1966 and 1975 Lord Reid articulated at least seven criteria relating to the use of the new freedom. They were:

1. The freedom granted by the 1966 Practice Statement ought to be exercised sparingly (the 'use sparingly' criterion).[7]

2. A decision ought not to be overruled if to do so would upset the legitimate expectations of people who have entered into contracts or settlements or otherwise regulated their affairs in reliance on the validity of that decision (the 'legitimate expectations' criterion).[8]

3. A decision concerning questions of construction of statutes or other documents ought not to be overruled except in rare and exceptional cases (the 'construction' criterion).[9]

4. (a) A decision ought not to be overruled if it would be impracticable for the Lords to foresee the consequences of departing from it (the 'unforeseeable consequences' criterion).[10] (b) A decision ought not to be overruled if to do so would involve a change that ought to be part of a comprehensive reform of the law. Such changes are best done 'by legislation following on a wide survey of the whole field' (the 'need for comprehensive reform' criterion).[11]

5. In the interest of certainty, a decision ought not to be overruled merely because the Law Lords consider that it was wrongly decided. There must be some additional reasons to justify such a step (the 'precedent merely wrong' criterion).[12]

6. A decision ought to be overruled if it causes such great uncertainty in practice that the parties' advisers are unable to give any clear indication as to what the courts will hold the law to be (the 'rectification of uncertainty' criterion).[13]

7 *Jones* v. *Secretary of State for Social Services* [1972] A.C. at 966.
8 *Ross-Smith* v. *Ross-Smith* [1963] 1 A.C. 280, 303; *Indyka* v. *Indyka* [1969] 1 A.C. 33, 69.
9 *Jones*, op. cit., at 966.
10 *Steadman* v. *Steadman* [1976] A.C. 536, 542.
11 *Myers* v. *DPP* [1965] A.C. 1001, 1022; *Cassell* v. *Broome* [1972] A.C. 1027, 1086; *Haughton* v. *Smith* [1975] A.C. 476, 500.
12 *Knuller* v. *DPP* [1973] A.C. 435, 455.
13 *Jones*, op. cit., at 966; *Oldendorff & Co.* v. *Tradex Export S.A.* [1974] A.C. 479, 533, 535.

7. A decision ought to be overruled if in relation to some broad issue or principle it is not considered just or in keeping with contemporary social conditions or modern conceptions of public policy (the 'unjust or outmoded' criterion).[14]

Alan Paterson found that in the years 1966 to 1980 there were 29 cases in which the House of Lords was invited to overrule one of its own precedents (or in which the question was raised by the Law Lords themselves without any prompting from counsel). The success rate was 28 per cent (8 out of the 29) but in a further 10 cases at least one of the Law Lords was willing to overrule the previous House of Lords precedent. But Paterson also argues that in a considerable number of other cases the Law Lords seemed to have a preference for getting round earlier decisions by distinguishing them (see p. 270 below) rather than directly overruling them. The Practice Statement, he thought, had even greater impact thereby than was suggested by the number of House of Lords cases that had been overruled.

Note – Numbers of judges sitting

Technically, the effect of a decision of the House of Lords is the same whether there are the normal five Law Lords sitting or whether, as happens occasionally, there are seven. But seven are empanelled for cases that are of particular importance. One such case, as has been seen was *Jones* v. *Secretary of State for Social Services* (p. 197 above) in which the House of Lords considered its approach to the new freedom to depart from its own previous decisions. Another was *Pepper* v. *Hart*, (p. 151 above), in which the issue was whether Hansard could be used by the courts as an aid to statutory interpretation. See also *Murphy* v. *Brentwood District Council* [1990] 2 All E.R. 908 in which the House of Lords overruled *Anns* v. *Merton London Borough Council*.[15]

For a suggestion that the House of Lords should sit with its full complement of judges, like the Supreme Court of the United States and the European Court of Justice in Luxemburg, see A. Samuels, 'The House of Lords in Banc', 10 *Civil Justice Quarterly*, (1991), p. 6.

Questions

1.   What appear to be the grounds on which the House of Lords will and will not reconsider one of its own previous decisions?

---

14   *Jones*, op. cit., at 966; *Conway* v. *Rimmer* [1968] A.C. 910, 938.
15   See to like effect in relation to a two-judge Court of Appeal *Langley* v. *North West Water Authority* [1991] 3 All E.R. 610 (C.A.).

2.   Is there any reason why the House should be less ready to reconsider
     a decision involving a point of statutory construction than a common
     law point?
3.   Should the fact that the earlier decision is a relatively recent one be
     influential?
4.   If the House of Lords departs from its earlier decision, could it later
     return to it? In other words is the effect of departing from its decision
     the same as overruling it?
5.   Would one expect any final appeal court to reconsider its own
     decisions readily?

(b)   The Court of Appeal, Civil Division

There are two main issues to be explored. One is the relationship between
the Court of Appeal and the House of Lords, and the other is the
relationship of the Court of Appeal towards its own previous decisions.

(i)   Is the Court of Appeal bound by the decisions of the House of Lords?

Until the 1970s there had never been any doubt about the fact that the
Court of Appeal was bound by the decisions of the House of Lords. But in
Broome v. *Cassell* [1971] 2 Q.B. 354 the Court of Appeal had the temerity
to hold (unanimously) that the House of Lords had been wrong in its view
in *Rookes* v. *Barnard* [1964] A.C. 1129, at 1221–31, per Lord Devlin, on the
circumstances in which exemplary damages could be awarded. In *Rookes*
v. *Barnard* Lord Devlin, with the unanimous approval of his brethren, had
laid down that exemplary damages could only be awarded in three types of
circumstances. The trial judge in *Cassell* v. *Broome* regarded himself as
bound by this ruling. But the Court of Appeal (Lord Denning M.R., Salmon
and Phillimore L.JJ.) held that the House of Lords' decision on this was not
binding because it ignored two other House of Lords cases, *Hulton* v.
Jones decided in 1910 and *Ley* v. *Hamilton* decided in 1935. They therefore
invoked the doctrine that the House of Lords in *Rookes* v. *Barnard* had
acted per incuriam (on what see p. 220 below). The suggestion was not
well received. When the case went on appeal to the House of Lords, Lord
Hailsham delivered a magisterial rebuke to Lord Denning and his
colleagues.

> I am driven to the conclusion that when the Court of Appeal described the
> decision in *Rookes* v. *Barnard* as decided 'per incuriam' or 'unworkable' they
> really only meant that they did not agree with it. But, in my view, even if this
> were not so, it is not open to the Court of Appeal to give gratuitous advice to
> judges of first instance to ignore decisions of the House of Lords in this
> way… . The fact is, and I hope it will never be necessary to say so again, that,

in the hierarchical system of courts which exists in this country, it is necessary for each lower tier, including the Court of Appeal, to accept loyally the decisions of the higher tiers. [[1972] A.C. 1027 at 1054.]

Lords Reid, Wilberforce, Diplock and Kilbrandon all agreed with Lord Hailsham that it was not open to the Court of Appeal to advise judges to ignore decisions of the House of Lords on the ground that they were decided per incuriam, or were unworkable.

Nevertheless the issue came up again only two years later. In *Schorsch Meir GmbH* v. *Hennin* [1975] Q.B. 416 the Court of Appeal held by two to one (Lord Denning and Foster J., Lawton LJ. dissenting) that judgment in an English court could be given in a currency other than sterling notwithstanding a clear decision to the contrary by the House of Lords in 1961 in the *Havana Railways* case. Lord Denning based his view on the maxim *cessante ratione cessat ipsa lex* (when the reason for the rule goes the rule lapses):

LORD DENNING (at 424–5): Why have we in England insisted on a judgment in sterling and nothing else? It is, I think, because of our faith in sterling. It was a stable currency which had no equal. Things are different now. Sterling floats in the wind. It changes like a weathercock with every gust that blows. So do other currencies. This change compels us to think again about our rules. I ask myself: Why do we say that an English court can only pronounce judgment in sterling? Lord Reid thought that it was 'primarily procedural': see the *Havana* case [1961] A.C. 1007, 1052. I think so too. It arises from the form in which we used to give judgment for money. From time immemorial the courts of common law used to give judgment in these words: 'It is adjudged that the plaintiff *do recover* against the defendant £x' in sterling. On getting such a judgment the plaintiff could at once issue out a writ of execution for £x. If it was not in sterling, the sheriff would not be able to execute it. It was therefore essential that the judgment should be for a sum of money in sterling: for otherwise it could not be enforced.

There was no other judgment available to a plaintiff who wanted payment. It was no good his going to a Chancery Court. He could not ask the Lord Chancellor or the Master of the Rolls for an order for specific performance. He could not ask for an order that the defendant do pay the sum due in the foreign currency. For the Chancery Court would never make an order for specific performance of a contract to pay money. They would not make it for a sterling debt... .

Those reasons for the rule have now ceased to exist. In the first place, the form of judgment has been altered. In 1966 the common law words 'do recover' were dropped. They were replaced by a simple order that the defendant 'do' the specified act. A judgment for money now simply says that: 'It is [this day] adjudged that the defendant do pay the plaintiff' the sum specified: see the notes to R.S.C. Ord. 42, r. 1 and the appendices [in the *Supreme Court Practice*, vol. II]. That form can be used quite appropriately for a sum in foreign currency as for a sum in sterling. It is perfectly legitimate to order the defendant to pay the German debt in Deutschmarks. He can satisfy the judgment by paying the Deutschmarks: or, if he prefers, he can satisfy it by paying the equivalent sum in sterling, that is, the equivalent at the time of payment.

In the second place, it is now open to a court to order specific performance of a contract to pay money. In *Beswick* v. *Beswick* [1966] Ch. 538; [1968] A.C. 58, this court and the House of Lords held that specific performance could be ordered of a contract to pay money, not only to the other party, but also to a third party. Since that decision, I am of opinion that an English court has power, not only to order specific performance of a contract to pay in sterling, but also of a contract to pay in dollars or Deutschmarks or any other currency.

Seeing that the reasons no longer exist, we are at liberty to discard the rule itself. Cessante ratione legis cessat ipsa lex. The rule has no support amongst the juridical writers. It has been criticised by many. Dicey[16] says:

> 'Such an encroachment of the law of procedure upon substantive rights is difficult to justify from the point of view of justice, convenience or logic.'

Only last year we refused to apply the rule to arbitrations. We held that English arbitrators have jurisdiction to make their awards in a foreign currency, when that currency is the currency of the contract: see *Jugoslavenska Oceanska Plovidba* v. *Castle Investment Co. Inc.* [1974] Q.B. 292. The time has now come when we should say that when the currency of a contract is a foreign currency – that is to say, when the money of account and the money of payment is a foreign currency – the English courts have power to give judgment in that foreign currency.

Foster J. simply said he agreed with the judgment of Lord Denning and with his reasons. But Lord Justice Lawton did not agree. He was, he said, a timorous member of the court. 'I stand in awe of the House of Lords.' He regarded himself bound by the *Havana Railways* decisions. It was disturbing to find that a rule which did injustice to a foreign trader was based, as he thought it was, on archaic legalistic nonsense. 'It is however my duty to apply the law, not to reform it' (at 430).

The case did not go to the House of Lords, but the issue did, only a year later, in *Miliangos* v. *George Frank (Textiles) Ltd* [1976] A.C. 443 which, as has already been seen, raised precisely the same problem. In *Miliangos* the trial judge, Bristow J., had to choose between the 1961 House of Lords' decision in the *Havana Railways* case that judgment could only be given in sterling and the Court of Appeal's decision in *Schorsch Meier* holding that this was no longer the case. He chose the House of Lords' decision on the ground that it was still binding on him – Parliament had not altered it nor had the House of Lords itself. It represented the view of the law held in this country for some 350 years – [1975] 1 Q.B. 487 at 492. On appeal to the Court of Appeal, Lord Denning, Stephenson

---

16 Dicey & Morris, *The Conflict of Laws* (9th edn, 1973), p. 883.

and Geoffrey Lane L.JJ. held unanimously that they were bound by the Court of Appeal's decision in *Schorsch Meier* [1975] Q.B. 416. But the House of Lords held that the Court of Appeal had been wrong – though it agreed with the Court of Appeal that the rule regarding the currency of judgments should be changed.

Miliangos v. *George Frank (Textiles) Ltd* [1976] A.C. 443

LORD SIMON OF GLAISDALE (at 472): Since the Court of Appeal is absolutely bound by a decision of the House of Lords and (at least on its civil side) by a previous decision of the Court of Appeal itself, it would be surprising if the meaning and application of the maxim 'cessante ratione' were really that accepted by the majority of the Court of Appeal in *Schorsch Meier* and again by the learned Master of the Rolls in the instant case. For as such it would enable any court in the land to disclaim any authority of any higher court on the ground that the reason which had led to such higher court's formulation of the rule of law was no longer relevant. A rule rooted in history could be reversed because history is the bunk of the past. Indeed, taken literally, there is no ground for limiting 'lex' to judge-made law. Coke, apparently the originator of the tag (Co. Litt. 70b), was quite prepared to say that a statute which conflicted with reason could be declared invalid by the courts (*Dr Bonham's Case* (1610) 8 C.Rep. 107a, 118a).... . It would be easy to compile a bulky anthology of authoritative citations to show that those courts of law which are bound by the rule of precedent are not free to disregard an established rule of law because they conceive that another of their own devising might be more reasonable.... .

To sum up on this part of the case: (1) the maxim in the form 'cessante ratione cessat ipsa lex' reflects one of the considerations which your Lordships will weigh in deciding whether to overrule, by virtue of the 1966 declaration, a previous decision of your Lordships' House; (2) in relation to courts bound by the rule of precedent the maxim 'cessante ratione cessat ipsa lex,' in its literal and widest sense, is misleading and erroneous; (3) specifically, courts which are bound by the rule of precedent are not free to disregard an otherwise binding precedent on the ground that the reason which led to the formulation of the rule embodied in such precedent seems to the court to have lost cogency; (4) the maxim in reality reflects the process of legal reasoning whereby a previous authority is judicially distinguished or an exception is made to a principal legal rule; (5) an otherwise binding precedent or rule may, on proper analysis, be held to have been impliedly overruled by a subsequent decision of a higher court or impliedly abrogated by an Act of Parliament; but this doctrine is not accurately reflected by citation of the maxim 'cessante ratione cessat ipsa lex.'

Lord Simon dissented on the question whether the rule should now be changed; Lords Wilberforce and Fraser expressly agreed with Lord Simon on the maxim *cessante ratione*. Lord Cross went even further and thought that although normally the Court of Appeal was bound to follow its previous decisions, it should not have done so in *Miliangos* – since the Court of

Appeal's decision in *Schorsch Meier* was wrong in departing from the *Havana* decision of the House of Lords:

> LORD CROSS (at 495–6): It will be apparent from what I have said that I do not view the decision of this House in the *Havana* case with any enthusiasm. Indeed, to speak bluntly, I think it was wrong on both points. But as Lord Reid said in *Reg.* v. *Knuller (Publishing, Printing and Promotions) Ltd* [1973] A.C. 435, 455, the fact that we no longer regard previous decisions of this House as absolutely binding does not mean that whenever we think that a previous decision was wrong we should reverse it. In the general interest of certainty in the law we must be sure that there is some very good reason before we so act. In the *Schorsch Meier* case [1975] Q.B. 416, 425, Lord Denning M.R., with the concurrence of Foster J., took it on himself to say that the decision in the *Havana* case that our courts cannot give judgment for payment of a sum of foreign currency – though right in 1961 – ought not to be followed in 1974 because the 'reasons for the rule have now ceased to exist'. I agree with my noble and learned friend, Lord Wilberforce, that the Master of the Rolls was not entitled to take such a course. It is not for any inferior court – be it a county court or a division of the Court of Appeal presided over by Lord Denning – to review decisions of this House. Such a review can only be undertaken by this House itself under the declaration of 1966. Moreover, although one cannot but feel sympathy for Stephenson and Geoffrey Lane L.JJ. in the embarrassing position in which they found themselves, I think that it was wrong for the Court of Appeal in this case to follow the *Schorsch Meier* decision. It is no doubt true that the decision was not given 'per incuriam' but I do not think that Lord Greene M.R., when he said in *Young* v. *Bristol Aeroplane Co. Ltd* [1944] K.B. 718, 729 that the '*only*' exceptions to the rule that the Court of Appeal is bound to follow previous decisions of its own were those which he set out, can fairly be blamed for not foreseeing that one of his successors might deal with a decision of the House of Lords in the way in which Lord Denning dealt with the *Havana* case.

The Court of Appeal seems now to have accepted the very strong indications from the House of Lords, first in *Broome* v. *Cassell* and then in *Miliangos*, that the Court of Appeal *is* absolutely bound by the decisions of the House of Lords – whatever it may think of them. But in his autobiographical book *The Discipline of Law* (1979), Lord Denning made it clear (p. 308) that *he* did not regard the Court of Appeal's *lèse-majesté* in *Schorsch Meier* as having been necessarily wrong:

> If in the *Schorsch Gmb.H.* v. *Henning* case we had held ourselves bound by the *Havana* case, we would have given judgment in sterling. In that event, in the *Miliangos* case the Swiss firm [the plaintiffs] would automatically have taken judgment in sterling also.... The Swiss firm would not have appealed. The House of Lords would never have had the opportunity of overruling the *Havana* case. The law would still have been that an English court could only give judgment in sterling. That would have been a disaster for our trade with countries overseas.

Note

A surprising echo of Lord Denning's approach emerged in a unanimous decision of the Court of Appeal in 1989 in which it was held that a decision of the House of Lords should not be followed because it had become obsolete![17] The House of Lords held in *Smith* v. *Baker* in 1891 that an appeal could not be brought from the county court to the Court of Appeal on a point of law not raised below. The Court of Appeal in 1989 held that the 1891 decision was not binding:

> For these reasons we hold that the rule in *Smith* v. *Baker & Sons* ought no longer to be applied. We are conscious that it may seem a strong thing for this court to hold thus of a rule established by the House of Lords, albeit one enfeebled by exceptions, the statutory support which gave it life at last turned off. But, where it can see that the decision of the higher court has become obsolete, the lower court, if it is not to deny justice to the parties in the suit, is bound to say so and to act accordingly.

Moreover the Court of Appeal refused the losing party leave to appeal to the House of Lords.

See further, on this issue, C. E. F. Rickett, 'Precedent in the Court of Appeal', 43 *Modern Law Review*, 1980, pp. 136–43.

Questions

1. Is a court ever justified in knowingly breaking the rules of precedent in order to precipitate an appeal so as to get a more authoritative ruling on the matter?
2. Do you think the House of Lords is right to insist that the Court of Appeal should loyally follow its decisions, no matter what?

(ii) Is the Court of Appeal bound by its own decisions?

The classic modern statement of the rule of *stare decisis* for the Court of Appeal (Civil Division) is that in *Young* v. *Bristol Aeroplane Co. Ltd*:[18]

Young v. *Bristol Aeroplane Company Ltd* [1944] K.B. 718 (Court of Appeal)

Plaintiff claimed damages for injuries at work. The defendant argued that his claim was bad since according to a Court of Appeal decision, *Perkins*

17 See *Pittalis* v. *Grant* [1989] 2 All E.R. 622, per Slade, Nourse and Stuart-Smith L.JJ.
18 The rule that the Court of Appeal is bound by its own decisions in fact appears to date back to its origins – see D. Pugsley, 'Precedent in the Court of Appeal', *Civil Justice Quarterly*, 1983, pp. 48, 54–7.

v. *Hugh Stevenson & Sons, Ltd* [1940] 1 K.B. 56, a claim for common law damages was barred where the injured workman had received compensation under the Workmen's Compensation Acts. The plaintiff appealed.

Lord Greene M.R., in the course of giving judgment for a full court of six judges, said (at 723, 725):

> The question thus raised as to the jurisdiction of this court to refuse to follow decisions of its own was obviously one of great general importance and directions were given for the appeal to be argued before the full court. It is surprising that so fundamental a matter should at this date still remain in doubt. To anyone unacquainted with the rare cases in which it has been suggested or asserted that this court is not bound to follow its own decisions or those of a court of co-ordinate jurisdiction the question would, we think, appear to be beyond controversy. Cases in which this court has expressed its regret at finding itself bound by previous decisions of its own and has stated in the clearest terms that the only remedy of the unsuccessful party is to appeal to the House of Lords are within the recollection of all of us and numerous examples are to be found in the reports. When in such cases the matter has been carried to the House of Lords it has never, so far as we know, been suggested by the House that this view was wrong and that this court could itself have done justice by declining to follow a previous decision of its own which it considered to be erroneous. On the contrary, the House has, so far as we are aware, invariably assumed and in many cases expressly stated that this court was bound by its own previous decision to act as it did.
>
> ... The Court of Appeal is a creature of statute and its powers are statutory. It is one court though it usually sits in two or three divisions. Each division has co-ordinate jurisdiction, but the full court has no greater powers or jurisdiction than any division of the court. Its jurisdiction is mainly appellate, but it has some original jurisdiction... . Neither in the statute itself nor (save in two cases mentioned hereafter) in decided cases is there any suggestion that the powers of the Court of Appeal sitting with six or nine or more members are greater than those which it possesses when sitting as a division with three members. In this respect, although we are unable to agree with certain views expressed by Greer L.J.[19] as will presently appear, we think that he was right in saying that what can be done by a full court can equally well be done by a division of the court. The corollary of this is, we think, clearly true, namely, that what cannot be done by a division of the court cannot be done by the full court... .
>
> On a careful examination of the whole matter we have come to the clear conclusion that this court is bound to follow previous decisions of its own as well as those of courts of co-ordinate jurisdiction. The only exceptions to this rule (two of them apparent only) are those already mentioned which for convenience we here summarise: (1) The court is entitled and bound to decide which of two conflicting decisions of its own it will follow. (2) The court is bound to refuse to follow a decision of its own which, though not expressly overruled, cannot, in its opinion, stand with a decision of the House of Lords.

19 *In re Shoesmith* [1938] 2 K.B. 637, 644.

(3) The court is not bound to follow a decision of its own if it is satisfied that the decision was given per incuriam.

Two main issues have arisen since the decision in *Young's* case in 1944. One is whether the House of Lords' Practice Statement in July 1966 could in any way be invoked by the Court of Appeal to release it from the rule that it was generally bound by its own decisions and, secondly, if not, what is the extent of the exceptions to the rule in *Young's* case.

Is the Court of Appeal bound to follow Young v. Bristol Aeroplane?

For many years after 1966 Lord Denning led a campaign to establish the principle that the House of Lords' Practice Statement should apply to the Court of Appeal as well. (In view of this campaign, there was some irony in the categorical assertion by Lord Denning in *Miliangos* (p. 206 above) that the Court of Appeal had to follow its own decision in *Schorsch Meier* because it was bound to do so.) The culmination of this campaign came in *Davis* v. *Johnson:*

Davis v. Johnson [1979] A.C. 264

The appellant and the respondent were cohabiting as man and wife in a council flat. The respondent was the father of the applicant's daughter. After much violence the applicant fled to a refuge for battered women. She applied under the Domestic Violence and Matrimonial Proceedings Act 1976 for an injunction to restrain him from using violence and ordering him to vacate the flat. At the hearing the respondent argued that the Court of Appeal was bound to follow its own two previous and very recent decisions given on the interpretation of the 1976 Act – which had ruled that a person with a proprietary interest in property could not be excluded by an injunction granted under the 1976 Act. The case was heard by five judges. Three (Lord Denning, Sir George Baker P., and Shaw L.J.) held that the Court of Appeal was free to depart from its previous decisions. Two (Goff and Cumming-Bruce L.JJ.) disagreed:

LORD DENNING M.R. (at 278–83):

Departure from previous decisions
    I turn to the second important point: can we depart from those two cases? Although convinced that they are wrong, are we at liberty to depart from them? What is the correct practice for this court to follow?
    On principle, it seems to me that, whilst this court should regard itself as normally bound by a previous decision of the court, nevertheless it should be at liberty to depart from it if it is convinced that the previous decision was wrong. What is the argument to the contrary? It is said that, if an error has been

made, this court has no option but to continue the error and leave it to be corrected by the House of Lords. The answer is this: the House of Lords may never have an opportunity to correct the error; and thus it may be perpetuated indefinitely, perhaps for ever. That often happened in the old days when there was no legal aid. A poor person had to accept the decision of this court because he had not the means to take it to the House of Lords. It took 60 years before the erroneous decision in *Carlisle and Cumberland Banking Co.* v. *Bragg*[20] was overruled by the House of Lords in *Gallie* v. *Lee* ([1971] A.C. 1004). Even today a person of moderate means may be outside the legal aid scheme, and not be able to take his case higher, especially with the risk of failure attaching to it. That looked as if it would have been the fate of Mrs Farrell when the case was decided in this court,[1] but she afterwards did manage to collect enough money together, and by means of it to get the decision of this court reversed by the House of Lords. Apart from monetary considerations, there have been many instances where cases have been settled pending an appeal to the House of Lords; or, for one reason or another, not taken there, especially with claims against insurance companies or big employers. When such a body has obtained a decision of this court in its favour, it will buy off an appeal to the House of Lords by paying ample compensation to the appellant. By so doing, it will have a legal precedent on its side which it can use with effect in later cases. I fancy that such may have happened in cases following *Oliver* v. *Ashman*. By such means an erroneous decision on a point of law can again be perpetuated forever. Even if all those objections are put on one side and there is an appeal to the House of Lords, it usually takes 12 months or more for the House to reach its decision. What then is the position of the lower courts meanwhile? They are in a dilemma. Either they have to apply the erroneous decision of the Court of Appeal, or they have to adjourn all fresh cases or await the decision of the House of Lords. That has often happened. So justice is delayed, and often denied, by the lapse of time before the error is corrected. The present case is a crying instance. If it took the ordinary course of appeals to the House, it would take some months before it was decided. Meanwhile many women would be denied the protection which Parliament intended they should have. They would be subjected to violence without redress; because the county court judges would have to say to them: 'We are sorry but the Court of Appeal says we have no jurisdiction to help you.' We were told that, in this very case, because of the urgency, the House might take special measures to hear it before Christmas. But, even so, I doubt whether they would be able to give their decision until well on in the New Year. In order to avoid all the delay, and the injustice consequent on it, it seems to me that this court, being convinced that the two previous decisions were wrong, should have the power to correct them and give these women the protection which Parliament intended they should have. It was suggested that, if we did this, the county court judges would be in a dilemma. They would not know whether to follow the two previous decisions or the later decision of this court. There would be no such dilemma. They should follow this later decision. Such a position always arises whenever the

20   [1911] 1 K.B. 489.
1   *Farrell* v. *Alexander* [1976] Q.B. 345 at 359.

House of Lords corrects an error made by a previous decision. The lower courts, of course, follow the latest decision. The general rule is that, where there are conflicting decisions of courts of co-ordinate jurisdiction, the later decision is to be preferred, if it is reached after full consideration of the earlier decision: see *Minister of Pensions* v. *Higham* ([1948] 2 K.B. 153, 155).

So much for principle. But what about our precedents? What about *Young* v. *Bristol Aeroplane Co. Ltd*?

The position before 1944
I will first state the position as it was before the year 1944. The Court of Appeal in its present form was established in 1873. It was then the final court of appeal. Appeals to the House of Lords were abolished by that Act and only restored a year or two later. The Court of Appeal inherited the jurisdiction of the previous courts of appeal such as the Court of Exchequer Chamber and the Court of Appeal in Chancery. Those earlier courts had always had power to reconsider and renew the law as laid down in previous decisions; and, if that law was found to be wrong, to correct it; but without disturbing the actual decision. I take this from the statements of eminent judges of those days who knew the position. In particular in 1852 Lord St Leonards L.C. in *Bright* v. *Hutton, Hutton* v. *Bright*[2] said in the House of Lords:

> '… you are not bound by any rule of law which you may lay down, if upon a subsequent occasion, you should find reason to differ from that rule; that is, that this House, *like every Court of Justice*, possesses an inherent power to correct an error into which it may have fallen…'

Young v. *Bristol Aeroplane Co. Ltd*[3]
The change came about in 1944. In *Young* v. *Bristol Aeroplane Co. Ltd* the court overruled the practice of a century. Lord Greene M.R.,[4] sitting with a court of five, laid down that this court is bound to follow its previous decision as well as those of co-ordinate jurisdiction, subject to only three exceptions: (i) where there are two conflicting decisions, (ii) where a previous decision cannot stand with a decision of the House of Lords, (iii) if a previous decision was given per incuriam.

It is to be noticed that the court laid down that proposition as a rule of law. That was quite the contrary of what Brett M. R. had declared in *The Vera Cruz (No 2)*[5] in 1884. He said it arose only as a matter of judicial comity. Events have proved that in this respect that Brett M.R. was right and Lord Greene M.R. was wrong. I say this because the House of Lords in 1898 had held itself bound by its own previous decisions as a rule of law: see *London Street Tramways Co. Ltd* v. *London County Council.*[6] But yet in 1966 it discarded that rule. In a statement it was said:[7]

2 (1852) 3 H.L. Cas. 341 at 388.
3 [1944] K.B. 718.
4 [1944] K.B. 718 at 729, 730.
5 (1884) 9 P.D. 96 at 98.
6 [1898] A.C. 375.
7 [1966] 1 W.L.R. 1234.

'Their Lordships nevertheless recognise that too rigid adherence to precedent may lead to injustice in a particular case and also unduly restrict the proper development of the law. They propose, therefore, to modify their present practice, and while treating former decisions of this House as normally binding, to depart from a previous decision when it appears right to do so.'

That shows conclusively that a rule as to precedent (which any court lays down for itself) is not a rule of law at all. It is simply a practice or usage laid down by the court itself for its own guidance; and, as such, the successors of that court can alter that practice or amend it or set up other guidelines, just as the House of Lords did in 1966. Even as the judges in *Young* v. *Bristol Aeroplane Co. Ltd* thought fit to discard the practice of a century and declare a new practice or usage, so we in 1977 can discard the guidelines of 1944 and set up new guidelines of our own or revert to the old practice laid down by Brett M.R. Nothing said in the House of Lords, before or since, can stop us from doing so. Anything said about it there must needs be obiter dicta. This was emphasised by Salmon LJ. in this court in *Gallie* v. *Lee.*[8]

'The point about the authority of this court has never been decided by the House of Lords. In the nature of things it is not a point that could ever come before the House for decision. Nor does it depend on any statutory or common law rule. This practice of ours apparently rests solely on a concept of judicial comity laid down many years ago and automatically followed ever since… . Surely today judicial comity would be amply satisfied if we were to adopt the same principle in relation to our own decisions as the House of Lords has recently laid down for itself by pronouncement of the whole House.'

The new guidelines
So I suggest that we are entitled to lay down new guidelines. To my mind, this court should apply similar guidelines to those adopted by the House of Lords in 1966. Whenever it appears to this court that a previous decision was wrong, we should be at liberty to depart from it if we think it right to do so. Normally, in nearly every case of course, we would adhere to it. But in an exceptional case we are at liberty to depart from it.

Alternatively, in my opinion, we should extend the exceptions in *Young* v. *Bristol Aeroplane Co. Ltd*[9] when it appears to be a proper case to do so. I realise that this comes virtually to the same thing, but such new exceptions have been created since *Young* v. *Bristol Aeroplane Co. Ltd*. For instance, this court can depart from a previous decision of its own when sitting on a criminal cause or matter: see the recent cases of *R.* v. *Gould*[10] and *R.* v. *Newsome, R.* v. *Brown*.[11] Likewise by analogy it can depart from a previous decision in regard to contempt of court. Similarly in the numerous cases when this court is sitting

8   [1969] 2 Ch. 17 at 49.
9   [1944] K.B. 718.
10 [1968] 2 Q.B. 65.
11 [1970] 2 Q.B. 711.

as a court of last resort. There are many statutes which make this court the final court of appeal. In every jurisdiction throughout the world a court of last resort has, and always has had, jurisdiction to correct the errors of a previous decision: see *Webster* v. *Ashton-under-Lyne Overseers, Hadfield's Case*.[12] In the recent case of *Tiverton Estates Ltd* v. *Wearwell Ltd*,[13] we extended the exceptions by holding that we could depart from a previous decision where there were conflicting principles as distinct from conflicting decisions, of this court: likewise we extended the notion of per incuriam in *Industrial Properties (Barton Hill) Ltd* v. *Associated Electrical Industries Ltd*.[14] In the more recent cases of *Re K (minors) (wardship: care and control)*,[15] and *Re S (BD)* v. *S (DI) (infants: care and control)*,[16] this court in its jurisdiction over children did not follow the earlier decision of *Re L (infants)*.[17] I would also add that when the words of the statute are plain, then it is not open to any decision of any court to contradict the statute; because the statute is the final authority on what the law is. No court can depart from the plain words of a statute. On this ground may be rested the decisions in *W and J B Eastwood Ltd* v. *Herrod (Valuation Officer)*,[18] and *Hanning* v. *Maitland (No. 2)*,[19] where this court departed from previous interpretations of a statute. In *Schorsch Meier GmbH* v. *Henning*,[20] we introduced another exception on the principle 'cessante ratione legis cessat ipsa lex'. This step of ours was criticised by the House of Lords in *Miliangos* v. *George Frank (Textiles) Ltd*;[1] but I venture to suggest that, unless we had done so, the House of Lords would never have had the opportunity to reform the law. Every court would have held that judgments could only be given in sterling. No one would have taken the point to the House of Lords, believing that it was covered by *Re United Railways of the Havana and Regla Warehouses*.[2] In this present case the applicant, Miss Davis, was at first refused legal aid for an appeal, because the point was covered by the two previous decisions. She was only granted it afterwards when it was realised by the legal aid committee that this court of five had been specially convened to reconsider and review those decisions. So, except for this action of ours, the law would have been regarded as settled by *B* v. *B* and *Cantliff* v. *Jenkins*; and the House of Lords would not have had the opportunity of pronouncing on it. So instead of rebuking us, the House of Lords should be grateful to us for giving them the opportunity of considering these decisions.

The truth is that the list of exceptions from *Young* v. *Bristol Aeroplane Co. Ltd* is now getting so large that they are in process of eating up the rule itself; and we would do well simply to follow the same practice as the House of Lords.

12 [1873] L.R. 8 C.P. 306.
13 [1975] Ch. 146.
14 [1977] Q.B. 580.
15 [1977] Fam. 179.
16 [1977] Fam. 109.
17 [1962] 1 W.L.R. 886.
18 [1968] 2 Q.B. 923.
19 [1970] 1 Q.B. 580.
20 [1975] Q.B. 416 at 425.
1   [1976] A.C. 443.
2   [1961] A.C. 1007.

Sir George Baker P. agreed, but he put his principle rather differently (at 290–1):

I listened with care to counsel for the applicant's careful argument that *Young's* case does not bind this court. I cannot agree with that, but I am prepared to accept that there should be, and must be, a further carefully limited exception which is in part founded on an extension of, or gloss on, the second exception in *Young's* case that the court is bound to refuse to follow a decision of its own which though not expressly overruled cannot in its opinion stand with a decision of the House of Lords.

I would attempt to define the exception thus: 'The court is not bound to follow a previous decision of its own if satisfied that that decision was clearly wrong and cannot stand in the face of the will and intention of Parliament expressed in simple language in a recent Act passed to remedy a serious mischief or abuse, and further adherence to the previous decision must lead to injustice in the particular case and unduly restrict proper development of the law with injustice to others.' My reasons, briefly, are (1) the practice statement in the House of Lords which recognises the danger of injustice, (2) that there is a conflict between a statutory provision and a decision which has completely misinterpreted the recent statute and failed to understand its purpose, (3) and to me the most compelling, by his judicial oath a judge binds himself to do 'right to all manner of people after the laws and usages of this Realm'. Here, by refusing the injunction, I would be doing a great wrong to the applicant, her child, and many others by following a decision which I firmly believe is not the law. The statute is the law, the final authority.

It is said that the proper course for this court is to be bound by the precedent of *B* v. *B*, whatever we may think of it, give leave to appeal and grant an injunction until the hearing which can be expedited. If one learns anything in the Family Division it is that the unexpected always happens in family affairs. There is no certainty that this case will ever reach the House of Lords. The respondent may end his tenancy. The applicant may decide to go and stay elsewhere. There are many possibilities which could lead to the withdrawal of legal aid which is not normally given in order that an important point of law may be decided where the decision will not benefit the immediate parties.

For the rest, I agree with the judgment of Lord Denning M.R.

Shaw L.J. put his exception to *Young's* case even more narrowly (at 308):

For my part I venture to think that if in 1944 a situation like the present had been in contemplation a further exception might have found a place in the judgment in *Young* v. *Bristol Aeroplane Co. Ltd.* It would be in some such terms as that the principle of stare decisis should be relaxed where its application would have the effect of depriving actual and potential victims of violence of a vital protection which an Act of Parliament was plainly designed to afford to them, especially where, as in the context of domestic violence, that deprivation must inevitably give rise to an irremediable detriment to such victims and create in regard to them an injustice irreversible by a later decision of the House of Lords.

Neither of the other two judges, however, would go along with the majority:

> GOFF L.J. (at 292): In my judgment, with the greatest respect to those who think otherwise, this court when exercising its civil jurisdiction is bound by the general rule in *Young's* case, save possibly where it is the final court of appeal, and further the class of exceptions is closed. My reasons for this conclusion are the necessity for preserving certainty in our law, which has great value in enabling persons to obtain definite advice on which they can order their affairs, the care which should always be taken to see that hard cases do not make bad law and the oft repeated occasions on which *Young's* case has been approved on the highest authority... .
>
> CUMMING-BRUCE L.J. (at 311) agreed: It seems to me that in any system of law the undoubted public advantages of certainty in civil proceedings must be purchased at the price of the risk of injustice in difficult individual situations. I would think that the present practice holds the balance just about right. The temptation to depart from it would be much less seductive if there could be readier access to the House of Lords. The highest tribunal is within the reach of those whose modest means enable them to qualify for legal aid, and of the extremely rich. Its doors are closed, for practical purposes, to everyone else. The injustice which today is liable to flow from the fact that unsatisfactory old cases are so seldom capable of review in the House of Lords would be mitigated or removed if Parliament decided to give this court and the House of Lords power to order that costs in the House of Lords should be paid by the Exchequer in those cases in which this court or the House of Lords on an application for leave to appeal certified that an appeal to the House of Lords was desirable in order to enable that House to review a decision regarded as mistaken but binding on the Court of Appeal. The expense to the public and any resulting inconvenience would be infinitely less than that which would flow from a relaxation of the present practice in respect of stare decisis as declared in *Young's* case. I consider that we are bound to act in accordance with the practice as stated in *Young's* case and the *Morelle Ltd* case.[3] This is because I consider that the constitutional functions of their Lordships sitting in their judicial capacity include the function of declaring with authority the extent to which the Court of Appeal is bound by its previous decisions, and the function of defining with authority the exceptional situations in which it is open to this court to depart from a previous decision. So I hold that this court is bound by the declaration made by Viscount Dilhorne, Lord Simon of Glaisdale and Lord Russell of Killowen in *Farrell* v. *Alexander*,[4] that this court is bound by precedent exactly as stated by Scarman L.J.[5] in his judgment in the Court of Appeal in that case affirming the declaration made by Lord Hailsham of St Marylebone L.C. in *Cassell & Co. Ltd* v. *Broome*,[6] a declaration again which commanded the express assent of a majority of their Lordships' House.

3   [1955] 2 Q.B. 379.
4   [1977] A.C. 59.
5   [1976] Q.B. 345 at 371.
6   [1972] A.C. 1027 at 1055.

On appeal the House of Lords [1979] A.C. 317 rejected the view of the majority and admonished the Court of Appeal to abide by its own previous decisions save to the extent allowed by *Young's* case:

LORD DIPLOCK (at 326, 328): In an appellate court of last resort a balance must be struck between the need on the one side for the legal certainty resulting from the binding effect of previous decisions and on the other side the avoidance of undue restriction on the proper development of the law. In the case of an intermediate court, however, the second desideratum can be taken care of by appeal to a superior appellate court, if reasonable means of access to it are available; while the risk to the first desideratum, legal certainty, if the court is not bound by its own previous decisions grows ever greater with increasing membership and the number of three-judge divisions in which it sits, as the arithmetic which I have earlier mentioned shows. So the balance does not lie in the same place as in the case of a court of last resort. That is why Lord Gardiner L.C.'s announcement about the future attitude towards precedent of the House of Lords in its judicial capacity concluded with the words: 'This announcement is not intended to affect the use of precedent elsewhere than in this House.'...
In my opinion, this House should take this occasion to re-affirm expressly, unequivocally and unanimously that the rule laid down in the *Bristol Aeroplane* case as to stare decisis is still binding on the Court of Appeal.

LORD SALMON (at 344): I am afraid that I disagree with Lord Denning M.R. when he says that the Court of Appeal is not absolutely bound by its own decisions and may depart from them just as your Lordships may depart from yours. As my noble and learned friend, Lord Diplock, has pointed out, the announcement made in 1966 by Lord Gardiner L.C. about the future attitude of this House towards precedent ended with the words: 'This announcement is not intended to affect the use of precedents elsewhere than in this House.' I would also point out that that announcement was made with the unanimous approval of all the Law Lords, and that, by contrast, the overwhelming majority of the present Lords Justices have expressed the view that the principle of stare decisis still prevails and should continue to prevail in the Court of Appeal. I do not understand how, in these circumstances, it is even arguable that it does not. I sympathise with the views expressed on this topic by Lord Denning M.R., but until such time, if ever, as all his colleagues in the Court of Appeal agree with those views, stare decisis must still hold the field. I think that this may be no bad thing. There are now as many as 17 Lords Justices in the Court of Appeal, and I fear that if stare decisis disappears from that court there is a real risk that there might be a plethora of conflicting decisions which would create a state of irremediable confusion and uncertainty in the law. This would do far more harm than the occasional unjust result which stare decisis sometimes produces but which can be remedied by an appeal to your Lordships' House. I recognise, as Cumming-Bruce L.J. points out, that only those who qualify for legal aid or the very rich can afford to bring such an appeal. This difficulty could however be surmounted if when the Court of Appeal gave leave to appeal from a decision it has felt bound to make by an authority with which it disagreed, it had a power conferred on it by Parliament to order the appellants' and/or the respondents' costs of the appeal to be paid out of public funds. This would be a very rare occurrence and the consequent expenditure of public funds would be minimal.

Lord Dilhorne (at 336), Lord Kilbrandon (at 340) and Lord Scarman (at 349) all expressly agreed. There can therefore be no doubt that in the view of the House of Lords the Court of Appeal is bound by its own decisions – subject to the exceptions admitted in *Young's* case. Lord Denning, writing in *The Discipline of Law* (1979), p. 300, described the House of Lords' decision as a 'crushing rebuff.' 'My arguments were rejected by the House of Lords. So my plea failed.' But he remained unrepentant:

> I am consoled to find that there are many intermediate Courts of Appeal in the Commonwealth which adopt the course which I have advocated. So this has made my dissent worthwhile. There are the Courts of Appeal in New South Wales, Victoria, South Australia and New Zealand. In particular, in *Bennett* v. *Orange City Council* [1967] 1 N.S.W. 502 Wallace P. said: 'Giving full credit to the desirability of certainty in the law (which occasionally appears to be a pious aspiration) I consider that even an intermediate Court of Appeal may, on special occasions and in the absence of higher authority on the subject in hand, play its part in the development of the law and in ensuring that it keeps pace with modern conditions and modern thought, and accordingly, in an appropriate case, I do not think that an earlier decision of the Court (including this Court) should be allowed to stand when justice seems to require otherwise'.

Lord Denning said that these words from New Zealand prompted the question whether the Court of Appeal should always simply cut short parties who wished to reargue points already settled by the Court of Appeal. Should they apply the leap-frog procedure under the Administration of Justice Act 1969, s. 12, for sending cases direct to the House of Lords? In either case the House of Lords would then not have the benefit of the views of the Court of Appeal.

Questions

1. Do you prefer the view of the House of Lords or of Lord Denning as to whether the Court of Appeal should be bound to follow its own prior decisions?
2. Could Lord Salmon's concern about the Court of Appeal sitting in so many divisions be met by requiring that the overruling of any previous decision could only be done by a full court of five or even seven?
3. Is the Court of Appeal bound to follow the views on this matter expressed by the House of Lords? (See, on this, further p. 262 below.)

If *Young's* case is binding on the Court of Appeal, what is the extent of the exceptions?

Lord Greene in *Young's* case (p. 209 above) stated three exceptions to the general rule that the Court of Appeal was bound by its own decisions:

Prior conflicting decisions The first was where there were two conflicting prior decisions and it had to decide between them. This could happen in two possible ways. One is where the two conflicting decisions were both reached before *Young's* case in 1944 established that the Court was bound by its own decisions. The second possibility is that the Court discovers a conflict where previously it had thought that none existed. This happened in a series of cases relating to annulment of marriage. In *Casey* v. *Casey* [1949] P. 420, the Court of Appeal held that English courts had no jurisdiction to hear a petition for nullity when the marriage was voidable and the only links with this country were that the marriage was celebrated in England and the petitioner resided in England. In *Ramsay Fairfax* v. *Ramsay Fairfax* [1956] P. 115, this case was distinguished by the Court of Appeal, which held that English courts did have jurisdiction to annul a marriage wherever it had been celebrated and whether or not it was voidable, provided both parties were resident in England. In *Ross-Smith* v. *Ross-Smith* [1961] P. 39, the Court of Appeal treated the two cases as irreconcilable and chose to follow the former. Presumably once the Court of Appeal has decided which of two conflicting decisions to follow, the other is then regarded as overruled and the Court cannot therefore in a fourth case later change its mind and return to the discarded decision.

Inconsistent House of Lords' decision The second exception was where a Court of Appeal decision, though not expressly overruled, could not stand with a decision of the House of Lords. Where the House of Lords' decision is subsequent to that of the Court of Appeal this exception creates no problem. This is simply a case of implied overruling. But does the doctrine also cover the case of inconsistency with a *prior* decision of the House of Lords? This would happen where the Court of Appeal held that one of its decisions had been wrongly decided because it had ignored a then-existing House of Lords' decision. This is precisely what did happen in *Fitzsimmons* v. *Ford Motor Co. Ltd* [1946] 1 All E.R. 429, where the Court of Appeal refused to follow two earlier decisions of its own because they were inconsistent with a previous decision of the House of Lords. This was in spite of the fact that in both cases the Court of Appeal had actually discussed the House of Lords' decision.

In *Miliangos* (p. 206 above) two Law Lords disagreed as to whether the Court of Appeal could disregard one of its own decisions because it conflicted with a prior decision of the House of Lords. It will be recalled that the Court of Appeal in *Schorsch Meier* (p. 204 above) had refused to follow the earlier House of Lords' decision in the *Havana Railways* case. Lord Denning in *Miliangos* said that Lord Greene's second exception did not permit it to reopen the question. It had simply to follow its own decision in *Schorsch Meier* since the House of Lords' decision had been prior to and not after *Schorsch Meier* ([1975] Q.B. at 502). Lord Simon in the House of Lords agreed ([1976] A.C. at 479); whilst Lord Cross thought, to the contrary, that the Court of Appeal in *Miliangos* should have followed the *Havana Railways* case and not its own erroneous decision in *Schorsch Meier* ([1976] A.C. at 496). In *McGoldrick & Co.* v. *CPS* [1990] 2 Q.B. 261, the Lord Chief Justice on behalf of a unanimous Court of Appeal, Criminal Division, said that it was not bound to follow its own previous decision in which a previous House of Lords' decision had been wrongly distinguished. The report states that 'His Lordship inclined to the view that the court's duty was to follow the law as it believed it to have been laid down in the previous decision of the House of Lords'. (The case concerned the circumstances when solicitors can be made liable for costs as a result of serious dereliction of duty. The question was whether the Court of Appeal had to follow the previous decision of the Civil Division of the Court of Appeal in *Sinclair-Jones* v. *Kay* [1989] 1 W.L.R. 114 which had distinguished the House of Lords' decision of *Myers* v. *Elman* [1940] A.C. 282.)

A variant of the second exception is where the first case decided by the Court of Appeal goes on appeal to the House of Lords which rules that the point decided by the Court of Appeal did not arise for decision. If the issue then comes up again, the Court of Appeal is not bound by its own previous decision – see *R* v. *Secretary of State for the Home Department, ex p. Al-Mehdavi* [1989] 1 All E.R. 777.

Per incuriam The third and most difficult exception is where the earlier decision was given per incuriam (in ignorance). In *Miliangos* [1975] Q.B. 487 (at 503) Lord Denning gave some guidance as to the meaning of the phrase 'per incuriam':

> Another exception is where a previous decision has been given per incuriam. 'Such cases,' said Lord Greene M.R. in *Young* v. *Bristol Aeroplane Co. Ltd* [1944] K.B. 718, 729 – 'would obviously be of the rarest occurrence and must be dealt with in accordance with their special facts.' So it has been held that a decision is not given per incuriam because the argument was not 'fully or carefully formulated': see *Morelle Ltd* v. *Wakeling* [1955] 2 Q.B. 379, 399, or was 'only weakly or inexpertly put forward': *Joscelyne* v. *Nissen* [1970] 2 Q.B. 86, 99; nor that the reasoning was faulty: *Barrington* v. *Lee* [1972] 1 Q.B. 326, 345 by Stephenson L.J. To these I would add that a case is not decided per incuriam because counsel have not cited all the relevant authorities or referred to this or that rule of court or statutory provision. The court does its own researches itself and consults authorities; and these may never receive mention in the judgments. Likewise a case is not decided per incuriam because it is argued on one side only and the other side does not appear. The duty of

counsel, in those circumstances, as we all know, is to put the case on both sides to the best of his ability: and the court itself always examines it with the utmost care, to protect the interests of the one who is not represented. That was done in the *Schorsch Meier* case itself.

The cases in which we have interfered are limited. One outstanding case recently is *Tiverton Estates Ltd* v. *Wearwell Ltd* [1975] Ch. 146, where this court in effect overruled *Law* v. *Jones* [1974] Ch. 112, on the ground that a material line of authority was not before the court and that the point called for immediate remedy.

But the leading statement of the principle of per incuriam is by Lord Evershed in *Morelle* v. *Wakeling*:

Morelle v. *Wakeling* [1955] 2 Q.B. 379 (Court of Appeal)

The Court of Appeal had to decide whether to follow its own previous decision given the same year. It was contended that the previous decision was given per incuriam, in that the arguments were brief (counsel for one side having only been instructed the afternoon before the hearing) and the law was highly specialised.

The Court of Appeal sat with five judges. Lord Evershed M.R. gave the judgment of the Court (at 406):

As a general rule the only cases in which decisions should be held to have been given per incuriam are those of decisions given in ignorance or forgetfulness of some inconsistent statutory provision or of some authority binding on the court concerned: so that in such cases some part of the decision or some step in the reasoning on which it is based is found, on that account, to be demonstrably wrong. This definition is not necessarily exhaustive, but cases not strictly within it which can properly be held to have been decided per incuriam must, in our judgment, consistently with the stare decisis rule which is an essential feature of our law, be, in the language of Lord Greene M.R., of the rarest occurrence. In the present case it is not shown that any statutory provision or binding authority was overlooked, and while not excluding the possibility that in rare and exceptional cases a decision may properly be held to have been per incuriam on other grounds, we cannot regard this as such a case. As we have already said, it is, in our judgment, impossible to fasten upon any part of the decision under consideration or upon any step in the reasoning upon which the judgments were based and to say of it: 'Here was a manifest slip or error'. In our judgment, acceptance of the Attorney-General's argument would necessarily involve the proposition that it is open to this court to disregard an earlier decision of its own or of a court of co-ordinate jurisdiction (at least in any case of significance or complexity) whenever it is made to appear that the court had not upon the earlier occasion had the benefit of the best argument that the researches and industry of counsel could provide. Such a proposition would, as it seems to us, open the way to numerous and costly attempts to re-open questions now held to be authoritatively decided. Although as was pointed out in *Young* v. *Bristol Aeroplane Co. Ltd*, a 'full court' of five judges of the Court of Appeal has no greater jurisdiction or higher authority than a normal division of the court consisting of three judges, we cannot help thinking that, if the Attorney-General's argument were accepted, there would be a strong tendency in cases of public interest and importance, to invite a 'full court' in effect to usurp the function of the House of Lords and to reverse a previous decision of the Court of Appeal. Such a result would plainly be inconsistent with the maintenance of the principle of stare decisis in our courts.

The Court of Appeal applied the per incuriam rule in *Williams* v. *Fawcett* [1985] 1 All E.R. 787. It discarded four previous Court of Appeal decisions on the formalities necessary for a notice to commit someone to prison for contempt on the ground that they were based on error. Sir John Donaldson said there were special features that justified this extension of the per incuriam doctrine. One was the 'clearness with which the growth of the error can be detected if the decisions are read consecutively'. Second, the cases concerned the liberty of the subject (committal for contempt of court). Third, the cases were very unlikely to go on appeal to the House of Lords.

But in *Duke* v. *Reliance Systems Ltd* [1987] 2 All E.R. 858 the Court of Appeal refused to apply the per incuriam doctrine to avoid one of its own decisions which it accepted was probably wrong in the light of an EEC Directive. Sir John Donaldson M.R. said that per incuriam only applied where another division of the Court of Appeal had 'reached a decision in the absence of knowledge of a decision binding on it or a statute, and that in either case it has to be shown that, had the court had this material, it must have reached a contrary decision. That is per incuriam. I do not understand the doctrine to extend to a case where, if different arguments had been placed before it or if different material had been placed before it, it *might* have reached a different conclusion' (at 860).

In *Rickards* v. *Rickards* [1989] 3 All E.R. 193, Lord Donaldson said previous decisions 'show that this court is justified in refusing to follow one of its own previous decisions not only where that decision is given in ignorance or forgetfulness of some inconsistent statutory provision or some authority binding upon it, but also, in rare and exceptional cases, if it is satisfied that the decision involved a manifest slip or error' (at p. 199). Usually it would be preferable to refuse the appeal and grant leave to appeal to the House of Lords. Certainty in relation to substantive law was usually to be preferred to correctness since that allowed the public to order their affairs with confidence. But in questions of procedure a change from established procedure affected only the parties and was therefore less objectionable.

In *Rakhit* v. *Carty* [1990] 2 All E.R. 202 which concerned the fixing of rent in premises covered by the Rent Acts, the Court of Appeal applied *Rickards* v. *Rickards* in holding that it was not bound to follow a previous decision which was based solely on the authority of an earlier Court of Appeal decision which was itself given per incuriam in that the court had not been referred to a crucial statutory provision.

It is not clear whether a court is permitted to apply the *per incuriam* doctrine to decisions of higher courts – whether the Court of Appeal can refuse on the ground of the *per incuriam* rule to regard itself bound by the decision of the House of Lords or the Divisional Court or a High Court judge can refuse to apply a decision of the Court of Appeal. It happened recently in *Hughes* v. *Kingston Upon Hull City Council*[7], where the Divisional Court declined to follow the Court of Appeal's decision in *Thai Trading Co* v. *Taylor* [1998] 3 All E.R. 65 on the ground that the Court of Appeal had not been asked to consider the House of Lords, decision in *Swain* v. *Law Society* [1982] 2 All E.R. 827. The propriety of this has not been considered by the Court of Appeal or the House of Lords.

Other exceptions to stare decisis in the Court of Appeal

Although only three exceptions were mentioned in *Young's* case and although the House of Lords in *Miliangos* urged the Court of Appeal to follow its own decisions unless one of the three exceptions mentioned in *Young* applied, a considerable number of other exceptions appear in fact to have been created. Lord Denning set out a long list in the section of his judgment in *Davis* v. *Johnson* headed 'The new guidelines' (p. 213 above). He could have added two more. In *Boys* v. *Chaplin* [1968] 2 Q.B. 1, all three members of the Court of Appeal held that three judges in the Court of Appeal are not bound by an earlier decision of two judges on an interlocutory appeal – i.e. an appeal on a preliminary point. In *Worcester Works Finance Ltd* v. *Cooden Engineering Co. Ltd* [1972] 1 Q.B. at 217 Lord Denning himself said that 'although decisions of the Privy Council are not binding on this Court, nevertheless when the Privy Council disapproves of a previous decision of this Court or casts doubt upon it, we are at liberty to depart from the previous decision'. There are other examples of the Court of Appeal preferring a later decision of the Privy Council to its own prior decision – see, for instance, *Doughty* v. *Turner Manufacturing Co. Ltd* [1964] 1 Q.B. 518 in which the Court of Appeal followed the Privy Council's decision in the *Wagon Mound, No. 1* [1961] A.C. 388 rather than its own decision in *Re Polemis* [1921] 3 K.B. 560. See generally C. E. F. Rickett, 'Precedent in the Court of Appeal', *Modern Law Review*, 1980, p. 136; and Peter Aldridge, 'Precedent in the Court of Appeal – Another View', *Modern Law Review*, 1984, p. 187.

---

7   [1999] 2 All E.R. 49. For comment see J. Levin, 'No win, no fee, no costs', *New Law Journal*, 19 January 1999, p. 48–50.

(c)   The Court of Appeal, Criminal Division

The Court of Appeal (Criminal Division) is the successor of the Court of Criminal Appeal which was set up in 1907 and which existed until it became one of the divisions of the Court of Appeal in 1966. The Court of Criminal Appeal had in turn been the successor of the old Court of Crown Cases Reserved.

In principle, in all three stages of its existence – as Court of Crown Cases Reserved, Court of Criminal Appeal and Court of Appeal (Criminal Division) – the basic rule has been that *stare decisis* applied. But it has always been true that the doctrine has not been rigidly endorsed and there are not a few examples where the court has refused to follow an earlier decision.[8] The greater flexibility on the criminal side was formally recognised in *R*. v. *Taylor* in 1950:

R. v. *Taylor* [1950] 2 K.B. 368 (Court of Criminal Appeal)

The appellant had pleaded guilty to a charge of bigamy. He had been advised to do so because the facts of the case were virtually identical to those of *R*. v. *Treanor*, a previous decision given by three judges of the Court of Criminal Appeal. Judgment was given by Lord Goddard C.J. on behalf of himself and the other six members of the court:

> I desire to say a word about the reconsideration of a case by this court. The Court of Appeal in civil matters usually considers itself bound by its own decisions or by decisions of a court of co-ordinate jurisdiction. For instance, it considers itself bound by its own decisions and by those of the Exchequer Chamber; and, as is well known, the House of Lords also always considers itself bound by its own decisions.[9] In civil matters this is essential in order to preserve the rule of stare decisis.
>
> This court, however, has to deal with questions involving the liberty of the subject, and if it finds, on reconsideration, that, in the opinion of a full court assembled for that purpose, the law has been either misapplied or misunderstood in a decision which it has previously given, and that, on the strength of that decision, an accused person has been sentenced and imprisoned it is the bounden duty of the court to reconsider the earlier decision with a view to seeing whether that person had been properly convicted. The exceptions which apply in civil cases ought not to be the only ones applied in such a case as the present, and in this particular instance the full court of seven judges is unanimously of opinion that the decision in *Rex* v. *Treanor* was wrong.

---

8   See, for instance, *Ring* (1892) 61 L.J.M.C. 116; *Power* [1919] 1 K.B. 572; *Norman* [1924] 2 K.B. 315; and *Newsome and Browne* [1970] 2 Q.B. 711.

9   This was of course before the House of Lords Practice Statement of July 1966.

See to the same effect *Gould* [1968] 2 Q.B. 65, 68–9, per Diplock L.J. But the true scope of *Taylor* is unclear. It is not clear, for instance, whether a full court must sit to depart from a previous decision. In *Newland* (1953) 37 Cr. App. Rep. 154, 167, for example, Lord Goddard doubted the wisdom of the Court of Criminal Appeal's decision in the 1933 case of *Manley*. But instead of indicating that the Court would decline to follow it, he hoped instead that *Manley* might some day be considered by the House of Lords. Professor Graham Zellick has suggested that *Newland* should be regarded as an aberration to be ignored ('Precedent in the Court of Appeal Criminal Division', *Criminal Law Review*, 1974, pp. 222, 224).

But it has also been argued that recent decisions show that the Court of Appeal, Criminal Division is bound by its own decisions in the same way as the Civil Division (and subject to the same exceptions). See Rosemary Pattenden, 'The Power of the Criminal Division of the Court of Appeal to Depart from its Own Precedents', *Criminal Law Review*, 1984, p. 592. Pattenden relies in particular on *Sheppard* (1980) 70 Cr. App. R. 210; *Pigg* (1982) 74 Cr. App. R. 352; and *Terry* [1983] R.T.R. 321.

In the Court of Appeal, Civil Division (and in the Divisional Court) a full court has no more authority than a court of three. The late Professor Glanville Williams objected that there was no basis for taking a different view in regard to the Court of Appeal, Criminal Division (*Salmond on Jurisprudence* (11th edn, 1957), pp. 193–14, quoted by Zellick in his 1974 *Criminal Law Review* article at p. 226). But Professor Zellick argues that the case of *Newsome and Browne* [1970] Q.B. 711 establishes that a full court of five of the Criminal Division can depart from an earlier decision on grounds not covered by the exceptions in *Young* v. *Bristol Aeroplane* where the law has been 'misapplied or misunderstood'. Zellick contends that the difference between the Civil and the Criminal Divisions of the Court of Appeal can be justified by the rarity of appeals in criminal cases to the House of Lords and the consequential greater importance of appeals at the Court of Appeal level.

In Professor Zellick's view, when the exceptions in *Bristol Aeroplane* apply the Criminal Division should follow the same approach as the Civil Division of the Court of Appeal. But this view has not been supported by the court itself. In *Jenkins* [1983] *Criminal Law Review*, p. 386, the court was faced with conflicting decisions of its own. The court dealt with this by preferring the decision which favoured the defendant: 'We may depart from the decision in *Carpenter* [1979] 76 Cr. App. Rep. 320n as to do so would be in favour of the applicants, but we may not depart from the decision in *Wilson* [1983] 1 All E.R. 993 for the contrary reason.' In *Spencer* [1985] 1 All E.R. 673, the Criminal Division said that there was no difference between it and the Civil Division in regard to precedent save that when the liberty of the subject was at stake it might decline to follow one of its own decisions.

(d) Divisional Courts

The leading authority on whether a Divisional Court is bound by its own decisions is that of *Police Authority for Huddersfield* v. *Watson*, in which Lord Goddard C.J. made it clear that the rule was the same as that applied in *Young* v. *Bristol Aeroplane Co. Ltd* to the Court of Appeal (Civil Division):

Police Authority for Huddersfield v. *Watson* [1947] K.B. 842 (Divisional Court, Q.B.D.)

The Divisional Court had to consider whether it was bound by its own prior decision in *Garvin* v. *Police Authority for City of London* [1944] K.B. 358.

LORD GODDARD C.J. (at 846–8): Mr Streatfield has argued that it is open to us to depart from *Garvin's* case if we think it was wrongly decided. As we have not heard his full argument, I prefer only to say this: Nothing that I have heard in this case, as far as the argument has gone, satisfies me that Garvin's case was wrongly decided; but whether it was rightly decided or not I am clearly of opinion that we ought to follow it. This court is made a final court of appeal in these matters, and I can imagine nothing more disastrous than that where the court has given a decision upon the construction or application of this Act another court should give a decision contrary to the decision already given, because there then would be two conflicting cases. You might get a court consisting perhaps of different judges choosing one of those decisions, and another court choosing the other decision, and there would be no finality in the matter at all. For myself, I think we ought to hold that we are bound by this decision. [Lord Goddard referred to the rule laid down in *Young* v. *Bristol Aeroplane Co. Ltd* for the guidance of the Court of Appeal.]

If that is the rule which is applicable in the Court of Appeal – it is to be remembered that Court of Appeal judgments are reviewable in the House of Lords, at any rate by leave – and the Master of the Rolls pointed out in the course of his judgment that in some cases Court of Appeal judgments are final, as in bankruptcy, and in others are reviewable by the House of Lords and yet he draws no distinction – and if, therefore, in a court most of whose decisions are reviewable, although it may be only by leave, in the House of Lords, those decisions are binding on the court, how much more important is it that this court, which is a final court, should follow its own decisions and consider that it ought to give full force and effect to them. Otherwise, as I have said, a great deal of uncertainty would be introduced into the law.

I know that in the writings of various eminent people the doctrine of stare decisis has been canvassed from time to time. In my opinion, if one thing is certain it is that stare decisis is part of the law of England, and in a system of law such as ours, where the common law, and equity largely, are based on decisions, it seems to me it would be very unfortunate if a court of final appeal has given a decision and has laid down a definite principle and it cannot be said the court has been misled in any way by not being referred to authorities, statutory or judicial, which bear on the question, that it should then be said that that decision was not to be a binding authority. [Atkinson and Lewis JJ. agreed.]

This meant that the exceptions recognised in *Young's* case were equally accepted as exceptions in the Divisional Court but that the basic rule was that the Divisional Court was bound by its own decisions. See also *Nicholas* v. *Penny* [1950] 2 K.B. 466. Now, however, a recent decision has thrown some doubt on this proposition. In May 1984 the Divisional Court decided that, although it would normally follow one of its own decisions, it could depart from it if it was convinced that the previous decision was wrong (*R.* v. *Greater Manchester Coroner, ex p. Tal* [1984] 3 All E.R. 240). The court distinguished the *Huddersfield Police Authority* case on the ground that the foundation of that decision was that the Divisional Court was sitting as a final court of appeal – because at that time there was no appeal to the House of Lords in criminal cases. This had become possible since 1960 just as it was from the Court of Appeal, Criminal Division. Robert Goff L.J. for the court said that the position of the Divisional Court in criminal cases was the same as that of the Court of Appeal, Criminal Division under *R.* v. *Taylor* and *R.* v. *Gould* (above). But the case before the court was not an appeal but a case of judicial review in which the court was exercising a first instance jurisdiction. It would only be in a rare case that a Divisional Court would depart from a decision of another Divisional Court but it could do so if convinced that the decision was wrong.

The judges in *Tal's* case did not have before them the decisions mentioned above which suggest that the Court of Appeal, Criminal Division may in fact be bound to follow its own decisions. Since the reasoning of part of the judgment was based on the analogy with *Taylor* this somewhat undermined the authority of the pronouncement on this point.

The *Tal* case was considered in *Hornigold* v. *Chief Constable of Lancashire* [1985] *Criminal Law Review* 792, where the appellant had sought to reargue a point regarding the admissibility of evidence of excess alcohol in a driving case which had been decided by the Divisional Court earlier the same year. Lords Justices Goff and Beldam held that, although the decision in *Tal* was right in stating that the Divisional Court was not absolutely bound by a previous decision of a previous Divisional Court, it was plain from what was said in *Tal* that there would be a departure from a previous decision only where the court was convinced that the earlier decision was wrong. The case could not be used as the basis for having a point reargued simply because the later court might reach a different conclusion.

But in so far as the decision in the actual case was based on the fact that it was a first-instance procedure rather than an appeal, the reasoning may not be affected by the comparison with the Court of Appeal, Criminal Division.

In *R* v. *Stafford Justices, ex p. Customs and Excise Commissioners* [1991] 2 All E.R. 201 the Divisional Court declined to follow its own previous decision in *R* v. *Ealing Magistrates' Court, ex parte Dixon* [1989] 2 All E.R. 1050 because it was persuaded that the previous decision was 'wrongly decided'. The case concerned the question as to whether the customs and excise could conduct criminal proceedings. One ground of justification for not following the earlier decision was that the court in *Dixon's* case had not had before it 'the wide-ranging arguments which have been urged upon us'.

In the earlier case of *Re Osman* [1988] *Criminal Law Review* 611 the Divisional Court declined to follow its own decision in *Tomsett* because the prosecution in that case had declined to argue the point. (Lloyd L.J. said 'The law of England cannot be made or unmade by the willingness of counsel to argue a point. The ratio of *Tomsett* stands. It was not per incuriam. But the present point was left undecided.') Commenting on the decision (ibid., p. 614), Professor Sir John Smith agreed this could not be an application of the per incuriam rule.

In *Shaw* v. *DPP* (1992) *Times*, 23 November, 142 *New Law Journal* 1683 the Divisional Court declined to follow its own decision in *DPP* v. *Corcoran* [1992] RTR 289, [1993] *Criminal Law Review* 139 on the ground that it had been reached per incuriam, or if not per incuriam, was simply wrong. Professor Sir John Smith's commentary in the *Criminal Law Review* argued that this left the law in the unsatisfactory state of two conflicting decisions of the Divisional Court.

A Divisional Court exercising civil jurisdiction is bound by the decisions not only of the House of Lords but also of the Court of Appeal, Civil Division – see *Read* v. *Joannou* (1890) 25 Q.B.D. 300 at 302–3. Equally a Divisional Court exercising criminal jurisdiction is bound by decisions of the Court of Criminal Appeal and is now bound by its successor, the Court of Appeal, Criminal Division – see *Ruse* v. *Read* [1949] 1 K.B. 377 at 384. See also *Carr* v. *Mercantile Products Ltd* [1949] 2 K.B. 601 at 605 per Goddard C.J., holding that a Divisional Court exercising criminal jurisdiction was bound by a decision of the civil Court of Appeal. In *R.* v. *Northumberland Compensation Appeal Tribunal* [1951] 1 K.B. 711 the Divisional Court, per Goddard C.J., refused to follow one of its own decisions on the ground that it was inconsistent with an earlier decision of the House of Lords. But this was implicitly disapproved of by the House of Lords in *Cassell* v. *Broome* [1972] A.C. 1027, when the Lords held that the Court of Appeal had been wrong to treat one of the House of Lords' earlier decisions (*Rookes* v. *Barnard*) as mistaken. By the same token presumably the Divisional Court should follow its own decisions rather than an earlier decision of the House of Lords, even if it concludes that the earlier House of Lords' decision is inconsistent with its own later decision.

(e)   Trial courts

The decisions of trial courts are not binding on that court. Thus the decisions of the High Court are not binding on any High Court judge, and the decisions of the county court and of magistrates' courts are not binding on those courts. But magistrates' courts and county courts are bound by the decisions of the High Court and of all the appellate courts.

But it has also been held that when a decision of the High Court has been fully considered and not followed, the second decision should be regarded as having settled the issue and in a later case the High Court judge should therefore follow the second of the two conflicting decisions:

Colchester Estates (Cardiff) v. *Carlton Industries plc* [1984] 2 All E.R. 601, 604–5

> NOURSE J.: Both counsel for the plaintiff and counsel for the defendant submitted that the existence of two conflicting decisions of judges of coordinate jurisdiction meant that I was entirely free to choose between them and should not start with any preference for one over the other. While I readily accepted that that would be the position where the second decision was given, for example, in ignorance of the first, I was troubled at the suggestion that it would necessarily be the same where the second was given after a full consideration of the first. Since this is a question on which the court has an interest of its own, I thought it right to make an independent research. That led me to the decision of Denning J. in *Minister of Pensions* v. *Higham* [1948] 1 All E.R. 863, [1948] 2 K.B. 153. I put that case to counsel during the course of argument yesterday afternoon and I hope and believe that they both had an opportunity of saying what they wanted to say about it.
>
> *Minister of Pensions* v. *Higham* was a case where Denning J., who was then the judge nominated to hear appeals from the pensions appeal tribunals in England, was faced with a conflict between a dictum in an earlier case of his own and a decision of the Court of Session on an appeal from one of the pensions appeal tribunals in Scotland. In the later case the Court of Session, having considered the dictum in the earlier one and having no doubt considered it fully, said that it was unable to agree with it. Denning J., having stated the special position in which he was there placed, said ([1948] 1 All E.R. 863 at 865, [1948] 2 K.B. 153 at 155):
>
>> 'I lay down for myself, therefore, the rule that, where the Court of Session have felt compelled to depart from a previous decision of this court, that is a strong reason for my reconsidering the matter, and if, on reconsideration, I am left in doubt of the correctness of my own decision, then I shall be prepared to follow the decision of the Court of Session, at any rate in those cases when it is in favour of the claimant because he should be given the benefit of the doubt.'
>
> Had the judge stopped there, I might well have agreed with counsel that the case could not, by reason of its special features, be treated as being of any general value. However, he went on to say this:

'In this respect I follow the general rule that where there are conflicting decisions of courts of co-ordinate jurisdiction, the later decision is to be preferred if it is reached after full consideration of the earlier decisions.'

That unqualified statement of a general rule comes from a source to which the greatest possible respect is due. It is fortuitous that my own instinct should have coincided with it. However diffident I might have been in relying on instinct alone, the coincidence encourages me to suggest a reason for the rule. It is that it is desirable that the law, at whatever level it is declared, should generally be certain. If a decision of this court, reached after full consideration of an earlier one which went the other way, is normally to be open to review on a third occasion when the same point arises for decision at the same level, there will be no end of it. Why not in a fourth, fifth or sixth case as well? Counsel for the defendant had to face that prospect with equanimity or, perhaps to be fairer to him, with resignation. I decline to join him, especially in times when the cost of litigation and the pressure of work on the courts are so great. There must come a time when a point is normally to be treated as having been settled at first instance. I think that that should be when the earlier decision has been fully considered, but not followed, in a later one. Consistently with the modern approach of the judges of this court to an earlier decision of one of their number (see e.g. *Huddersfield Police Authority* v. *Watson* [1947] 2 All E.R. 193 at 196, [1947] KB 842 at 848 per Lord Goddard C.J.), I would make an exception only in the case, which must be rare, where the third judge is convinced that the second was wrong in not following the first. An obvious example is where some binding or persuasive authority has not been cited in either of the first two cases. If that is the rule then, unless the party interested seriously intends to submit that it falls within the exception, the hearing at first instance in the third case will, so far as the point in question is concerned, be a formality, with any argument on it reserved to the Court of Appeal.

Applying the rule to the present case, first, I am satisfied that the decision of Vinelott J. was reached after full consideration of the decision of McNeill J. Second, I am not convinced that Vinelott J. was wrong in not following McNeill J. I have heard full and careful arguments on both sides, each of which was almost certainly fuller than the argument on the same side in either of the earlier cases. I think it inappropriate either that I should examine those arguments or express any further view of my own. That implies no disrespect or ingratitude to counsel. Indeed, the contrary is the case. Whatever may be thought appropriate on any other occasion, this is a question on which it is in my judgment inappropriate that there should be any further debate or expression of judicial view below the level of the Court of Appeal. In the circumstances I need say only that I propose to follow and apply the decision of Vinelott J. in *Hamilton* v. *Martell Securities Ltd.*

The High Court is bound by the decisions of higher courts, but a problem arises where these conflict. Should the High Court judge, for instance, follow the Court of Appeal or an inconsistent House of Lords' decision? As has been seen (p. 205 above), this dilemma faced Bristow J. in *Miliangos* v. *George Frank (Textiles) Ltd* [1975] Q.B. 487 and he chose to follow the House of Lords' decision in *Havana Railways* (holding that damages had to be awarded in sterling), rather than the Court of Appeal's decision in *Schorsch Meier* (holding that this ancient rule had lapsed). But when the case went to the House of Lords, one of the Law Lords criticised the trial judge:

> LORD SIMON OF GLAISDALE (at 477, 478): Greatly as I sympathise with Bristow J. in his predicament, I feel bound to say, with all respect, that I think he was wrong.... It is the duty of a subordinate court to give credence and effect to the decision of the immediately higher court, notwithstanding that it may appear to conflict with the decision of a still higher court. The decision of the still higher court must be assumed to have been correctly distinguished (or otherwise interpreted) in the decision of the immediately higher court. For example, in the instant case, in my respectful opinion, Bristow J. should have assumed that the Court of Appeal in *Schorsch Meier* had correctly interpreted and applied the maxim 'cessante ratione ...' and had in consequence correctly held that it was not bound to apply the *Havana* decision [1961] A.C. 1007 to the facts judicially ascertained in *Schorsch Meier*. Any other course is not only an invitation to legal chaos but in effect involves a subordinate court sitting in judgment on a decision of its superior court. That is contrary to law. Moreover, in this respect, as so often, the law is a distillation of practical experience, even though all knowledge of the experience may be lost. Here, however, the experience is recoverable. If a subordinate court fails to abide loyally by the judgment of its superior court, the decision of the subordinate court is likely to be appealed to the superior court, which is in turn likely to vindicate its previous decision.

Lords Wilberforce and Cross both said simply that no one except the House of Lords could review decisions of the House of Lords. They did not however express any views on whether a trial judge faced with the dilemma of Bristow J. should do as he did.

In *Amanuel* v. *Alexandros Shipping Co., The Alexandros P* [1986] 1 All E.R. 278, Webster J. had to consider whether he was bound by an ex parte Court of Appeal decision. He held that a High Court judge was bound by a Court of Appeal decision whether ex parte or inter partes unless that decision had been overruled by a subsequent decision of the House of Lords or there was a subsequent inconsistent decision of the Court of Appeal or the decision was per incuriam.

The case of crown courts is different in that the judge does not decide the case in the same way that he does in the High Court, or as the county court or the magistrates decide it. The judge in the crown court sums up the law for the jury and he may give rulings on points of law that come up during the trial. Very occasionally the summing-up or the gist of a ruling may be reported (for instance in the *Criminal Law Review*). For an argument that a crown court ruling does not bind another crown court or even a magistrates' court, see *Criminal Law Review* [1980] 402.

(f)   Precedents that are not binding

The decisions of lower courts are never binding. Thus the House of Lords cannot be bound by a decision of the Court of Appeal nor the Court of Appeal by a decision of the High Court. The decisions of the Judicial Committee of the Privy Council are not binding on any of the courts in the United Kingdom except in devolution cases – see p. 239 below.

A non-binding precedent may of course be of very great persuasive power. The precise extent of its persuasive power will depend on all the circumstances. Precedents, as will be seen, are minutely weighed and measured for their proper impact and effect. But a precedent that does not bind the court considering it cannot by some mysterious process create law that is in some way binding. If a decision is not binding on the court it means that the court is ultimately free to accept or reject the rule for which the case stands. The nature of this process will be explored in the next chapter.

(g)   The effect of the Human Rights Act 1998 on precedent

The Human Rights Act 1998 marks a major and completely novel development in regard to precedent. Implementation of the Act (due on a date in 2000) will give all the courts considerable freedom to ignore precedent when deciding points of law under the European Convention on Human Rights (ECHR).

The Act makes it unlawful for a public authority 'to act in a way which is incompatible with a Convention right' (s. 6(1)). The section states that a public authority includes a court or tribunal. (s. 6(3)). A 'Convention right' under the Act is defined to mean a right set out in the provisions of the ECHR which are set out in Schedule 2 to the Act (s. 1(1)). So a court acts unlawfully if it gives a decision that is inconsistent with the ECHR. Section 2 provides that in determining any question concerning a Convention right a court 'must take into account' the full range of judgments, decisions and opinions of the relevant organs of the ECHR – namely, the European Court of Human Rights, the Commission and the Committee of Ministers. All Strasbourg jurisprudence thereby becomes available as a source for legal argument by anyone arguing in a UK court about the meaning or application of the ECHR. The UK court is not bound by any Strasbourg case cited as authority but it must 'take it into account' – whatever that means. If the UK court concludes that an otherwise binding decision of a higher court is inconsistent with Convention law as expressed by, say, a decision of the Strasbourg Court it is required by s. 6(1) to give effect to its understanding of the inconsistent ECHR rule rather than to the otherwise binding decision of the higher court. That represents a revolution in the

UK system. It will potentially affect the courts at all levels, though one imagines that the lower courts will tread very warily in using this new freedom. It will probably be several years before one will be able to assess the impact of this new development.

However, this new freedom to ignore binding precedent will not apply to decisions of higher courts given *after* implementation of the 1998 Act. So, the Court of Appeal would be free to hold in 2001 that a 1980 House of Lords decision was inconsistent with the Convention and should therefore not be followed. But if the House of Lords in 2001 were to decide that its 1980 decision was correct, the Court of Appeal in 2002 would be obliged to follow the 2001 decision.

2.   A COMPARISON WITH SOME OTHER COUNTRIES

The English doctrine of precedent is unlike that followed in civil law countries and is not even identical to that operating in other common law jurisdictions. The late Professor Sir Rupert Cross, in his book *Precedent in English Law*, has described some of the differences between our system and others:

Rupert Cross and J.W. Harris, *Precedent in English Law* (4th edn, 1991), pp. 10–23.

COMPARISON WITH FRANCE[10]
Although there are important differences between them, the French legal system may be taken as typical of those of western Europe for the purposes of the present discussion.

From the standpoint of strict legal theory, French law is not based on case-law (*la jurisprudence*) at all. The Civil and Penal Codes are theoretically complete in the sense that they (and other statutory provisions) are supposed to cover every situation with which the ordinary courts are concerned. It can still be argued that, strictly speaking, case-law is not a source of law in France because a judge is not obliged to consider it when coming to a decision. Art. 5 of the Civil Code forbids his laying down general rules when stating a decision, and it would be possible for a French appellate court to set aside a ruling founded exclusively on a past decision on the ground that the ruling lacked an adequate legal basis.[11] None the less, there is a substantial body of case-law dealing with the construction of the Codes and the solution of problems on which they are in fact silent. Moreover, there is no code governing the *droit*

---

10 For precedent in International Law see *Trendtex Trading Corporation* v. *Central Bank of Nigeria* [1977] 1 All E.R. 881.
11 David and De Vrees, *The French Legal System*, p. 115.

administratif of the Conseil d'Etat, which is not numbered among the ordinary courts, and it is mainly based on case-law.

From the practical point of view one of the most significant differences between English and French case-law lies in the fact that the French judge does not regard himself as absolutely bound by the decision of any court in a single previous instance. He endeavours to ascertain the trend of recent decisions on a particular point. To quote a distinguished French legal writer: 'The practice of the courts does not become a source of law until it is definitely fixed by the repetition of precedents which are in agreement on a single point.'[12]

Three of the principal reasons for the difference between the French and English approaches to the doctrine of precedent are that the need for certainty in the law was formerly felt more keenly by the English judge than most of the judges on the Continent; the highly centralized nature of the hierarchy of the English courts; and the difference in the position of the judges in the two countries.

The need for certainty

The first point has been stressed by Dr Goodhart. The continental judge has no doubt always wanted the law to be certain as much as the English judge, but he has felt the need less keenly because of the background of rules provided first by Roman law and codified custom, and later by the codes of the Napoleonic era. These resulted in a large measure of certainty in European law. Roman law was never 'received' in England, and we have never had a code in the sense of a written statement of the entirety of the law. 'English justice, if it were not to remain fluid and unstable, required a strong cement. This was found in the common-law doctrine of precedent with its essential and peculiar emphasis on rigidity and certainty.[13]

The hierarchy of the courts

The French judicial system is based on the division of the country into districts. So far as civil cases are concerned, each district has a court of first instance and a court of appeal. The district courts of first instance are not bound by their own previous decisions or those of any other district court of first instance, nor are such courts of first instance bound by the previous decisions of their own appellate courts or that of any other district. The district appellate courts are not bound by their own past decisions or those of any other district court of appeal. There is a right of appeal on points of law from the district appellate court to the *Cour de cassation* in Paris. In theory, this body is not bound by

---

12 Lambert, 'Case-method in Canada', 39 *Yale L.J.* 1 at p. 14. A helpful account of the operation of precedent in France together with examples of the judgments of French courts is given by F. H. Lawson, *Negligence in Civil Law*, (Clarendon, Oxford, 1950) pp. 231–5. See also O. Kahn-Freund, C. Lévy and B. Rudden, *A Sourcebook on French Law*, pp. 98–140. In Spain it seems that two decisions of the Supreme Court constitute a 'doctrina' binding on inferior courts, though the Supreme Court may later alter the 'doctrina' (Neville Brown, 'The Sources of Spanish Law', 5 *Int. Comp. L.Q.* 367 (1956)).

13 Goodhart, 'Precedent in English and Continental Law', 50 *L.Q.R.* 40 at p. 62 (1934).

any previous decision of its own, and the district courts are not bound to follow an individual decision of the *Cour de Cassation* in a previous case. So far as the actual litigation under consideration by the *Cour de Cassation* is concerned, that court may remit it for re-hearing by an appellate court of a district near to that from which the appeal came. If the case should be brought before the *Cour de Cassation* again, it is only since 1967 that the Court has had power finally to dispose of the case instead of remitting it to yet another district court of appeal with a binding direction concerning the manner in which it was to be decided.

The more serious criminal cases are tried by a district assize court from which there is no appeal apart from the possibility of an application to the *Cour de Cassation* on a question of law which may result in an order for a new trial.

With a system of courts as decentralized as that which has just been sketched, it would have been difficult for France to have evolved a doctrine of precedent as rigid in every respect as our own. Even if the *Cour de Cassation* had come to treat itself and the district courts as absolutely bound by each of its past decisions, there would almost inevitably have been considerable flexibility at the level of the district courts of appeal. It would have been too much to expect anything approximating to the uniformity of decision demanded of the English judges. French law owes its uniformity to the various codes in which it is declared and to *la doctrine* – the opinions of jurists – rather than to *la jurisprudence*.

The different position of the judges

The French judge occupies a very different position from that of his English counterpart. In the first place, there are fewer judges of our superior courts than there are members of the French judiciary. Secondly, the French judiciary is not, like ours, recruited from the Bar but from the civil service, and thirdly, many French judges are relatively young and inexperienced men. They go into the Ministry of Justice with the intention of taking up a judicial career and become junior judges in small district courts after what is little more than a period of training. The result is that the judiciary tends to be considered as less important in France than in England, and, although it is difficult to assess the significance of these matters, it is generally, and probably rightly, assumed that they help to explain the greater regard which is paid to case-law in this country than that which is paid to it on the Continent. Still more important is the fact that the judges have been the architects of English law.

> 'The common law is a monument to the judicial activity of the common law judge. He, not the legislator or the scholar, created the common law. He still enjoys the prestige of that accomplishment.'[14]

Further reasons for the difference

Allowance must also be made for the difference in the structure of the judgments of English and French courts and for the vast number of cases decided by the

Cour de Cassation. A rule that a single precedent should be binding would be unlikely to develop when it was difficult to discover a precise *ratio decidendi* and it is not always easy to extract a precise *ratio* from a French judgment. A rule that one single decision of an appellate court should suffice to constitute a binding precedent is hardly likely to develop in a jurisdiction in which there are numerous appeals. The House of Lords only hears some 30 appeals from the English courts each year, but some 10,000 cases are dealt with annually by the different chambers of the *Cour de Cassation.*

Notwithstanding the great theoretical difference between the English and French approaches to case-law, and the total absence of rules of precedent in France, the two systems have more in common than might be supposed. In the first place, French judges and writers pay the greatest respect to the past decisions of the *Cour de Cassation.*

Secondly, the manner in which the English judges interpret the *ratio decidendi* of a case tends to assimilate their attitude towards a legal problem to that of their French counterparts... . It would be wrong to say that, in deciding case D, an English High Court judge of first instance considers cases A and B, decided by the Court of Appeal, together with case C, decided by another High Court judge of first instance, in order to see whether the law has become 'definitely fixed by the repetition of precedents which are in agreement on a single point'. However, his attitude towards the *ratio decidendi* of Case A might be profoundly affected by the observations of the judges in cases B and C. English case-law is not the same as *la jurisprudence*, but it is a mistake to suppose that our judges permanently inhabit a wilderness of single instances... .

CONTRAST WITH U.S.A.

Although the North American practice of giving judgment in the form of elaborate discussions of previous cases is more like the English than the continental, the United States Supreme Court and the appellate courts in the different states do not regard themselves as absolutely bound by their past decisions. There are many instances, some American lawyers would say too many, in which the Supreme Court has overruled a previous decision.

Thanks to the change of practice in the House of Lords, the English rules of precedent may come to approximate more closely to the North American, but two reasons why the North American rules should remain more lax suggest themselves. These are the number of separate State jurisdictions in the former country and the comparative frequency with which the North American courts have to deal with momentous constitutional issues.

Numerous jurisdictions

A multiplicity of jurisdictions produces a multiplicity of law reports which has, in its turn, influenced the teaching of law and led to the production of 'restatements' on various topics. The 'case method' of instruction which, in one form or another, prevails in most North American law schools, aims at finding the best solution of a problem on the footing of examples from many jurisdictions, and few schools confine their instruction to the law of any one State. The restatements are concise formulations and illustrations of legal principles based on the case-law of the entire United States and, from time to time, model codes and sets of uniform rules relating to various branches of the law are produced in a form fit for immediate adoption by the legislature. Judges who have been trained by the case method and who are familiar with the restatement and kindred documents will tend to concentrate on recent trends after the fashion of the French courts.

Constitutional issues

When a court is construing a written constitution the terms of that document are the governing factor and the case-law on the meaning of those terms is only a secondary consideration. This point was put very clearly by Frankfurter J. when he was giving judgment in the Supreme Court. He said:

'The ultimate touchstone of constitutionality is the Constitution itself, and not what we do about it.'[15]

A further reason why North American courts in general, and the United States' Supreme Court in particular, should not apply our rule of the absolute binding effect of a single decision to constitutional matters is provided by the momentous nature of the issues involved in such cases. To quote Lord Wright:

'It seems clear that, generally speaking, a rigid method of precedent is inappropriate to the construction of a constitution which has to be applied to changing conditions of national life and public policy. An application of words which might be reasonable and just at some time, might be wrong and mischievous at another time.'[16]

When the difficulty of amending the Constitution of the United States is borne in mind, it is scarcely surprising that the Supreme Court has become less and less rigorous in its adherence to the principle of *stare decisis*.

CONTRAST WITH SCOTLAND

The following remarks made by a Scottish court as recently as 1950 certainly suggest that the Scottish doctrine of precedent is less strict than our own.

'If it is manifest that the *ratio decidendi* upon which a previous decision has rested has been superseded and invalidated by subsequent legislation or from other like cause, that *ratio decidendi* ceases to be binding.'[17]

No doubt it would be quite incorrect to represent the English judiciary as a body which pays no attention to the maxim *cessante ratione cessat ipsa lex*, but the House of Lords considers that it should be treated as a ground for creating an exception to a binding rule when that is possible, not as a ground for disregarding it. The maxim also indicates a fact to be taken into account by an English court when deciding whether to overrule a case which it has power to overrule... .[18]

---

15 *Graves* v. *New York*, 306 U.S. 466 at p. 491 (1939). The importance of the fact that the United States' Supreme Court is frequently concerned with constitutional problems is stressed by Goodhart in 'Case Law in England and America' in *Essays in Jurisprudence and the Common Law*. See also Goodhart, 'Some American Interpretations of Law', in *Modern Theories of Law*, p. 1.

16 'Precedents', 8 *C.L.J.* 118 at p. 135.

17 *Beith's Trustees* v. *Beith* 1950 S.C. 66 at p. 70; see also *Douglas-Hamilton* v. *Duke and Duchess of Hamilton's ante-nuptial marriage contract trustees* 1961 S.L.T. 305 at p. 309.

18 *Miliangos* v. *George Frank (Textiles) Ltd* [1976] A.C. 443 at pp. 472–6.

CONTRAST WITH PARTS OF THE COMMONWEALTH

The Judicial Committee of the Privy Council used to be the final court of appeal for all Commonwealth countries outside the United Kingdom. The Judicial Committee has never considered itself to be absolutely bound by its own previous decisions on any appeal. The form in which the decisions are expressed is often said to militate against the adoption of a rigid rule of precedent, for the judgment of the Committee consists of advice tendered to the Sovereign together with the reasons upon which such advice is based... .

The Judicial Committee is, however, strongly disposed to adhere to its previous decisions.[19] The decisions of the Privy Council are only of strong persuasive authority in the English courts.

The right of appeal to the Privy Council has been abolished in some Commonwealth countries, including Canada, and Australia. In the days when there was still an appeal to the Privy Council, the Supreme Court of Canada regarded itself as bound by its own past decisions although there was a saving clause relating to 'exceptional circumstances'.[20] Since the abolition of the right of appeal to the Privy Council, the Supreme Court of Canada has claimed the power of declining to follow its own past decisions as it is the successor to the final appellate jurisdiction of the Privy Council which is not bound by its own past decisions.[1]

The High Court of Australia has never regarded itself as absolutely bound by its own past decisions.[2] As long ago as 1879 it was said to be of the utmost importance that in all parts of the Empire where English law prevails, the interpretation of that law by the courts should be as nearly as possible the same.[3] It is for this reason that, in the absence of some special local consideration to justify a deviation, the Australian and Canadian courts would be loath to differ from decisions of the House of Lords, but there does not appear to be any question of the decisions of the House being binding in either country. The High Court of Australia in fact stated that a leading decision on the English criminal law (since largely overruled by an English statute) was to be treated as no authority in Australia,[4] and the Judicial Committee of the Privy Council has held in a civil case that the Australian High Court was right not to follow a decision of the House of Lords on exemplary damages.[5]

On the history of the doctrine of precedent, see T. Ellis Lewis, 'The History of Judicial Precedent', *Law Quarterly Review*, vol. 46 (1930), pp. 207, 341; vol. 47 (1931), p. 411; vol. 48 (1932), p. 230. See also T. B. Smith, *The Doctrines of Judicial Precedent in Scots Law* (1952) and André Tunc, 'The not so common law of England and the United States, or precedent in

---

19   *Fatuma Binti Mohamed Bin Salim* v. *Mohamed Bin Salim* [1952] A.C. 1.
20   *Stuart* v. *Bank of Montreal* (1909), 41 S.C.R. 516 at p. 535. See '*Stare Decisis* in the Supreme Court of Canada', by Andrew Joanes, 36 *Canadian Bar Review* 174 (1958).
1   *Re Farm Products, Marketing Act* (1957), 7 D.L.R (2nd) 257 at p. 271.
2   *A.-G. for N.S.W.* v. *Perpetual Trustees Co.* (1952), 85 C.L.R 189.
3   *Trimble* v. *Hill* (1879) 5 App. Cas. 342 at p. 345.
4   *Parker* v. *R.* [1963] A.L.R. 524.
5   *Australian Consolidated Press, Ltd* v. *Uren* [1967] 3 All E.R. 523.

England and in the United States, a field study by an outsider', *Modern Law Review*, 1984, pp. 151, 169.

On the differences between common law and civil law techniques of law-making, see Joseph Dainow, 'The Civil and the Common Law: Some Points of Comparison', 15 *American Journal of Comparative Law*, 1967, p. 419; and B.Markesinis, 'A Matter of Style', 110 *Law Quarterly Review*, 1994, pp. 607–28.

For an assessment of the role of the Judicial Committee of the Privy Council in common law jurisdictions generally see J.W. Harris, 'The Privy Council and the Common Law', 106 *Law Quarterly Review*, 1990, pp. 574–600.

The Privy Council in devolution issues Under the 1998 devolution legislation for Scotland, Wales and Northern Ireland, the Judicial Committee of the Privy Council will play a new and crucial role as the final court of appeal whose decisions will be binding on all courts in the United Kingdom – though not on the Privy Council itself.[6] The Privy Council rather than the House of Lords was made the final court of appeal for devolution issues because it was felt inappropriate that a part of the Westminster Parliament should be the arbiter of devolution matters, including decisions as to the competence of the devolved assemblies.

Under the three devolution Acts the Privy Council may take references on devolution issues arising in the course of litigation, it may hear appeals against determination of a devolution issue from the High Court, the Court of Appeal, the Inner House of the Court of Session in Scotland, or the Court of Appeal in Northern Ireland.[7] The House of Lords may refer devolution issues to the Judicial Committee though each of the three Act states that it may also decide the matter itself if it considers it more appropriate'.[8]

The Judicial Committee includes the present and retired Law Lords, past and present Lord Chancellors, and past and retired Lords Justices of Appeal. If the Lord Chancellor sits, he presides, though the composition of the Judicial Committee is by convention a matter for the senior Law Lord. The devolution Acts, however, contain provisions specifically excluding Commonwealth judges from hearing such cases.[9]

---

6   See Scotland Act 1998 s 103, Government of Wales Act 1998, Sched. 8, para.32 and the Northern Ireland Act 1998, s.82.
7   Scotland Act, ss, 32, 33, 98 and Sched.6; Government of Wales Act 1998, s. 109 and Sched.8; Northern Ireland Act 1998, ss 11, 79 and 82 and Sched. 10.
8   Scotland Act 1998, Sched.6, para.32; Government of Wales Act 1998, Sched 8, para. 29; Northern Ireland Act 1998, Sched.10, para.32.
9   Scotland Act 1998, s. 103(2); Government of Wales Act 1998, Sched 8, para.33; Northern Ireland Act 1998, s 82(2).

CHAPTER 5

Law reporting

One of the essential elements in a system based on precedent is some tolerably efficient method for making the precedents available to those wishing to discover the law. An unreported decision is technically of precisely the same authority as one that is reported, but decisions that are unreported have at least until very recently been more or less inaccessible to all but scholars.[1] It is through law reporting that the common law is available to the profession and anyone else wishing to know the law. Law reporting in England goes back to the earliest days of the system but even today it has not yet become fully official nor is it organised in a systematic way.

1. THE HISTORY OF LAW REPORTING

There have been three distinct periods in the history of law reporting. The first, dating from 1282 to 1537, was the period of the Year Books. They are not law reports in the full modern sense, since they appear to have been designed more as guides to pleadings and procedure for advocates than as accounts of the decisions of the courts. They were written originally in Norman French and later in law French – a mixture of Norman French, English and Latin. In modern times they have been published in two editions – the Rolls Series (R.S.) and the Selden Society Series (S.S.). They are mainly of historical and antiquarian interest. Practitioners virtually never have occasion to consult or cite the Year Books.

The second period was that from 1537 to 1863. When the Year Books ceased around 1537, private sets of reports started to appear. They began

---

1   Unreported Court of Appeal decisions are, however, briefly summarised in *Current Law*.

to include summaries of counsel's argument and of the judge's decisions. The citation of reports in court became more common as the reports improved in quality. Some were excellent – the best is probably Coke, whose reports were published between 1600 and 1658. Coke was also a judge, as was Dyer (Chief Justice of the Common Pleas) and Saunders (Chief Justice of the King's Bench). But contemporaneous reports were rare until the end of the eighteenth century. The private reports are now collected in one great series – the English Reports. These are occasionally cited in the courts.

The third period is that dating from 1865, when the profession was responsible for establishing the Incorporated Council of Law Reporting for England and Wales. The Council produces a series called The Law Reports and, although they are not an official publication, they are regarded as the most authoritative reports. (Until 1990 any law report to be regarded as worthy of the name had to be prepared by a barrister – but see now p. 258 below.) The reporter must have been present in court when the judgment was delivered. In addition to The Law Reports there are of course a great variety of other series – the Weekly Law Reports, the All England Law Reports, Lloyd's Law Reports, Criminal Appeal Reports, etc.

An official committee inquired into the whole system of law reporting in 1940. Its report is of value partly for the historical background it presented of the system:

Report of the Law Reporting Committee (HMSO, 1940)

4. It is a commonplace to lawyers at least that the law of this country consists substantially of legislative enactments and judicial decisions. The former are made known to the public in the most solemn form, printed at the public expense and preserved under conditions which ensure that they shall be permanently and authentically recorded. With the latter it always has been and still is far otherwise. Yet the importance of accurate and permanent reports of judicial decisions is and always has been obvious. We need not discuss at what stage in our legal history the theory of the binding force of precedent first appeared. In its present form it would have received little favour from the judges of the 14th and 15th centuries but already it was plain, as the pages of the Year Books testify, that uniformity and certainty of the law, the essentials of its just administration, cannot be attained without some measure of judicial consistency. As late as the latter half of the 18th century, on the one hand, Blackstone wrote 'For it is an established rule to abide by former precedents, where the same points come again in litigation; as well to keep the scale of justice even and steady, and not liable to waver with every new judge's opinion; as also because the law in that case being solemnly declared and determined, what before was uncertain, and perhaps indifferent, is now become a permanent rule, which it is not in the breast of any subsequent judge to alter or vary from, according to his private sentiments: he being sworn to determine, not according to his own private judgments, but according to the known laws and customs of

the land; not delegated to pronounce a new law, but to maintain and expound the old one'.[2] On the other hand Lord Mansfield took a more elastic view of the relation of precedent to principle. 'The law of England', he said, 'would be a strange science indeed if it were decided upon precedents only. Precedents serve to illustrate principles, and to give them a fixed certainty. But the law of England, which is exclusive of positive law, enacted by statute, depends upon principles; and these principles run through all the cases according as the particular circumstances of each have been found to fall within the one or other of them'.[3] To-day, whatever the reasons may be, the theory of the binding force of precedents is firmly established, if not unreservedly, at least only with some such reservation as that a decision need not be followed if it appears to have been given *per incuriam* e.g. by reason of a relevant statute not having been called to the attention of the court.

6.... . It may seem strange but it is true that, except for a brief interlude in the reign of King James I, the State has taken no part in, and made no financial contribution to, the publication of law reports.... . Apart from this single instance of State aid or interference the task of law reporting has been, as it still is, left wholly to private enterprise. Nor do we find any record of supervision by the State of an enterprise so vitally affecting the common welfare except that by a Statute of Charles II in 1662 (14 Car. II C. 33. S.2) it was enacted that 'All Books concerning the Common Lawes of this Realm shall be printed by the special allowance of the Lord Chancellor or Lord Keeper of the Great Seal of England for the time being the Lords Chiefe Justices and Lord Chiefe Baron for the time being or one or more of them or by theire or one or more of theire appointments'.... .

It was left, as we have said, to private enterprise to preserve in law reports that part of our law which consists of judicial decisions. How was this task performed? It is at this stage necessary to recall that at an early date in our legal history the right was established to cite as an authority before any tribunal a law report which had annexed to it the name of a barrister. It is probable that this right arose from a still earlier privilege of a member of the Bar as amicus curiae to inform the court of a relevant decision of which he was aware. It was his right and perhaps his duty to give oral evidence of the law by stating that such and such a decision had been given. Thence followed the right to cite his written report of decisions which he personally vouched as a member of the Bar. Nor must it be forgotten that if it was the privilege of a barrister to write reports that might be cited to the courts, it was his privilege alone except so far as His Majesty's Judges from time to time might for the public benefit and perhaps their private profit devote a part of their leisure to the compilation of reports.

Here then was a field for private enterprise, for profit and for abuse. In earlier times, as now, the barrister must rely both on reason and authority, and if he must choose between them, would choose the latter. To the law-reporter the opportunity was given and he took advantage of it. It had been calculated that in the period between 1535 (when the Year Books ceased) and 1765 (when Burrow's Reports began to appear) more than one hundred persons were

2   Comm. 69.
3   *Jones* v. *Randall* (1774) Cowper 37, 39.

responsible for volumes of reports. Great names are among them – Dyer, Plowden, Coke, Saunders – and their reports have at all times been of high authority. But there are many others to whom perhaps a higher degree of authority is likely to-day to be given than was by their contemporaries. Some indeed were of such ill repute that, rule or no rule, privilege or no privilege, the judges would not listen to quotations from them. Of them Sir Harbottle Grimson wrote in 1657: 'A multitude of flying reports (whose authors are as uncertain as the times when taken …) have of late surreptitiously crept forth … we have been entertained with barren and unwanted products; which not only tend to the depraving the first grounds and reason of our students at the common law, and the young practitioners thereof, who by such false lights are misled; but also to the contempt of our common law itself, and of divers our former grave and learned justices and professors thereof; whose honoured and revered names have, in some of the said books, been abused and invocated to patronise the indigested crudities of these plagiaries.'

The last third of the eighteenth century saw an improvement which the first half of the nineteenth century maintained. Douglas, who in the Preface to his report showed the high purpose that he meant to serve, Burrows with his introduction of headnote and scientific division of his report, Durnford and East with their Term Reports, which for the first time aimed at a timely and regular publication – these and other reporters at least set a standard which had not been reached in earlier times. Moreover, at some date which we cannot discover, but which the late Sir Frederick Pollock put as at least later than 1782, the Judges or some of them were willing to revise reports of their judgment or even to supply written copies of them to the reporter, and a custom grew up whereby as a matter of professional etiquette some one reporter in each Court was supposed to have a monopoly of this assistance from the Judge. This reporter was thus in a sense 'authorised' and his reports were known as 'authorised' or 'regular' reports as distinguished from other reports, which were 'irregular' or 'unauthorised'. This did not, however, prevent all reports, whether regular or irregular, from being cited if they satisfied the single condition of being vouched by the name of a barrister. And so the flood of reports did not subside but, on the contrary, was increased by a new kind of publication which, anonymous in title and originally disclaiming any intention of competing with the regular reports, became in due course a serious rival and by its merits and in particular by its speedier publication commanded a larger sale than any of the regular reports. Such was the Law Journal first published in 1822 as a weekly and in 1830 as a monthly series. It was natural that its immediate success should provoke competition and it was in due course followed by the Jurist, established in 1837, the Law Times in 1843, the Weekly Reporter, established in 1852 and united in 1858 with the already established Solicitors Journal… .

7. This was the condition of affairs when in 1863 certain members of the Bar inspired and led by the late W. T. S. Daniel, Q.C., commenced the agitation which led to the establishment of the series of reports known to us all as 'The Law Reports'… . The objective which Mr Daniel had from the outset was to establish a series of reports under the control of the profession. It was still to be private enterprise in the sense that it received no State aid and was subject to no State interference. But it was not to be profit-making except so far as was

necessary to render it self-supporting. No other purpose was to be served than to produce the best possible reports at the lowest possible price for the benefit of the profession and of the public at large. Inaugurated with such aims and under such auspices such a series, it was confidently hoped, would drive all competitors from the field and thus there would be established a single series of reports, accurate and scientific, reporting all cases that ought to be reported and none that ought not to be reported.

11. In the face of no little difficulty Mr Daniel and his friends carried the day. A council representative of the profession was established consisting of two *ex officio* members, the Attorney-General and the Solicitor-General for the time being, eight barristers, two of whom were chosen by each of the four Inns of Court, two serjeants chosen by Serjeants' Inn and two solicitors chosen by the Incorporated Law Society. This council, whose constitution remains substantially unchanged except that Serjeants' Inn has ceased to exist and therefore is not represented, was in 1870 incorporated under the Companies' Acts with the title 'The Incorporated Council of Law Reporting for England and Wales.' Its first object as stated in its Memorandum of Association was 'the preparation and publication in a convenient form, at a moderate price, and under gratuitous professional control of Reports of Judicial Decisions of the Superior & Appellate Courts of England.'

12. With the issue of the 'Law Reports' the old authorised Reports disappeared except that Best and Smith and Beavan and a few others for a very short time continued their publications. In 1867 the Jurist, one of the Reports, also ceased. The other Reports, the Law Journal, the Law Times, the Weekly Reporter and Solicitors Journal, continued and still continue, the last-named series under the name of the Solicitors' Journal, and to them there have been added two more publications, the 'Times Law Reports' first published in 1884 and the 'All England Reports' first published in 1936.

2.   CRITICISMS OF THE PRESENT SYSTEM

The 1940 report then referred to a number of criticisms made of the system – cost, repetition of the same case in different sets of reports and the problem of tracing cases.

14(e) The next criticism is of a far-reaching and very different character. Its substance really is not so much that the Reports are numerous, as that, being numerous, they are what they are. The 'Law Reports' are recognised as accurate: against them the criticism is made that they are incomplete in that they omit to report cases which ought to be reported, not merely cases of a special character which are properly relegated to special Reports, but cases in which light is thrown upon general legal principles or the construction of Acts of Parliament. Against other general Reports it is said that, while they may to some extent make good the deficiencies of the Law Reports by reporting cases not reported there, yet their accuracy is not beyond challenge and it is a grave matter if, as has more than once happened in recent years, the profession and the public are misled by an inaccurate Report. In our opinion it is impossible to emphasise too strongly the seriousness of this criticism. Further it is said that even the number of Reports does not ensure safety, but on the contrary decisions of importance may be unreported and at some future date be disinterred from their grave in forgotten shorthand notes. The complaint is echoed of an old editor of a text-book well known in its day, 'Watkins' Principles of Conveyancing': 'Is the law of England to depend upon the private notes of an individual and to which an individual only can have access? ... Is a paper evidencing the law of England to be buttoned up in the side pocket of a judge or to serve for a mouse to sit upon in the dusty corner of a private library? If the Law of England is to be deducted from adjudged cases, let the reports of those adjudged cases be certain, known and authenticated.'

(f) Finally, the criticism is heard that far too many cases are reported. It is said that the hearing of suits is protracted and the time of the court wasted by the citation of authorities of doubtful relevance, and that, if counsel is not darkened, at least first principles are apt to be obscured by the introduction of exceptions and refinements which had better be forgotten.

The Committee considered but rejected the idea that there should be any form of monopoly for a single official set of reports:

To such a proposal or anything like it we are unanimously opposed. It ignores, as we think, the fundamental fact that the law of England is what it is not because it has been so reported but because it has been so decided. Thus, as we have said before in this report, it is the privilege, if not the duty, of a member of the Bar to inform the court, whether as counsel engaged in the case as *amicus curiae*, of a relevant decision whether it had been reported or not. So it is the duty of a Judge to follow the decision of a competent court whether reported or not: it may well be that there has not been time to report it. The basis of the rule of precedent is the need for certainty and uniformity – suppose that a decision has been given on a question of (say) banking or insurance law or some other topic of professional interest which is likely to be quickly disseminated amongst a large circle of interested persons, and suppose that it be reported by a barrister in a Journal, whether devoted exclusively to law reports or not, is a judge to approach that question of law unaware of the previous decision, unless it has been reported in the Law Reports or other official Reports? Is a lawyer to advise his client: 'This is the law according to Mr Justice A, but his decision has not been reported in the Law Reports: if then your case comes, not before him, but before Mr Justice B, the latter may come to a different decision, for he may not be told what Mr Justice A has decided?' And what of a text-book writer? Is he to ignore decisions except those reported in the Law Reports? It appears to us that it is only necessary to ask these questions to show that a monopoly of citation would run counter to the spirit in which English law has been administered these many centuries.

Nor would it be right if some reporters were specially licensed – to put a check on the multiplicity of reports:

In our view such proposals are fundamentally wrong. They strike, as we think, at the base of a principle which is one of the pillars of freedom, that the administration of justice must be public. The decision of the court must be open for publication, discussion and criticism. It is not consistent with this principle that a licence to report should be given to one man and withheld from another. If a case is once reported, then, as we have already pointed out, it is proper that it should be cited in order that the law may be interpreted and administered in the same way for all men. Nor can a Judge by any means deny the right to publish as laws that which he has decided to be law. Technical competence of the reporter there ought to be, and it exists to some extent in the requirements that a report should be vouched by a barrister-at-law; but that is a very different thing from monopolistic reporting... .

19. We repeat, and it cannot be said too often, that the first essential of a Report is accuracy. In that lies its value as a precedent. In this respect the Law Reports maintain a remarkably high standard and they are assisted by the fact that judges themselves read and approve the reports of their decisions before they are published. We have been told that the same privilege is sometimes given to the Reports of patents, etc., cases, and to the Law Journal Reports, but to no other Reports. For this reason it has been generally but not universally the custom in the courts to demand that, if a case is reported in the Law Reports, it should be cited from those Reports and no other. We venture to hope that this practice may except in very special circumstances be rigidly enforced. We were indeed told that by some persons other reports were preferred for the very reason that it was supposed that they contained judgments as actually delivered and not as the judges, on second thoughts, would like to have delivered them. We need perhaps say no more about this point of view than that it appears to us a somewhat unscientific way of regarding an exposition of law.

The Committee considered whether it should recommend that a shorthand writer take down the exact text of every judgment, that this should be sent to the judge for correction and that a copy should be filed with the office of the Records of the Court. This would avoid the occasional instance of faulty reporting. It would also ensure a full record of all decisions. The Committee said the proposal would obviously cost money and it would impose an additional burden on the judges. It thought on the whole that most decisions that ought to be reported, were. ('What remains is less likely to be a treasure house than a rubbish heap in which a jewel will rarely, if ever, be discovered,' p. 20). On the whole it did not think there was a need to record all judgments.

A strong dissenting report from Professor A. L. Goodhart dealt with the fact that large numbers of reports were uncorrected by the judges and many more were not reported at all. An unreported decision was nevertheless authoritative law.

He dealt in turn with the three problems mentioned by the Committee. The cost of having each judgment recorded he thought would not be great. The burden on the judges revising them would equally, he thought, not be serious. Nor need it add greatly to delays in getting publication. The advantage would be to reduce inaccurate reports. Judges would be able to delete phrases which did not accord with their considered opinions. He hoped that shorthand writers would be attached to each court and that judgments would be placed after revision in an official library.

This proposal was however not implemented. The only reports that are lodged officially anywhere are those of the Court of Appeal, Civil Division. From 1951 the Lord Chancellor's Department required that they all be placed in the Bar Library in the Royal Courts of Justice in the Strand. Access to the Bar Library was open principally to barristers and, with permission, to solicitors and others. Since 1978 these reports have all been moved to the Supreme Court Library in the Royal Courts to which lawyers and members of the public alike have free access. Case-name and subject indexes are maintained on a cumulative basis.

In 1986 the Lord Chancellor's Department made 13,613 Court of Appeal decisions more widely available in microfiche form published by HMSO. They represent 30 years' worth of decisions.[4]

Unreported judgments of the House of Lords are kept in the Record Office of the House of Lords, where they can be consulted by the public. But there is no subject index and there is therefore no way of tracing a decision on a particular point unless one happens to know its name beforehand.

Judgments of other courts are not officially filed anywhere. However, there are now shorthand writers who attend the proceedings of all the courts save county courts and magistrates' courts. They take down the evidence, legal arguments and judgments in civil cases or the judge's summing-up in crown courts. If anyone wants to have copies of the judge's summing-up or his judgment, they can order it from the shorthand writers. In some courts, especially in London, the process of taking down the proceedings is done by tape-recording equipment – but the work of transcription is still mostly done by the shorthand writers.

What finds its way into the pages of the law reports is, however, to an extent a matter of happenstance. It has been estimated that only about a quarter of the decisions of the Civil Division of the Court of Appeal appear in the officially sanctioned *Weekly Law Reports*. This is now almost certainly an over-estimate. Curiously it seems that the number of reported decisions has remained relatively constant in spite of an increase in recent years in the numbers of decisions. In 1980 the Court of Appeal produced 976 transcripts of judgments of which only 223 (or 23 per cent) were reported.[5] Probably only about 70 per cent of those of the House of Lords and the Privy Council appear in the law reports and about 10 per cent of those of

4   See Victor Tunkel, 'Available at Last: The Court Of Appeal Transcripts', *New Law Journal*, 31 October 1986, p. 1045.
5   See V. Tunkel, op. cit. above, p. 1046, Table A.

the Court of Appeal, Criminal Division. The body of case law as reflected in the *Weekly Law Reports* grows at the rate of three volumes per year.

The question whether it is satisfactory to leave the decision as to the reporting of cases to the decisions of law reporters[6] was addressed by the late Dr Olive Stone, then of the London School of Economics:

Olive Stone, 'Knowing the Law', 24 *Modern Law Review*, 1961, p. 475 at pp. 476–7

> Even if proper reports or transcripts were available of all cases, it seems very doubtful if the final decision on whether a case is reportable should lie with an editor responsible to no one but those who employ him. Surely this is pre-eminently a decision to be taken by a committee, which should have the fullest information about all cases decided, and should not be drawn exclusively from practising members of the Bar. Solicitors, law teachers and magistrates should obviously be represented, and in the field of family law (which suffers greatly from meagre reporting), there is also a case for representation of the social services to counterbalance the excessive stress on the types of litigation most profitable to the legal profession.

A more recent evaluation of some of the problems in the field of law reporting was published in 1978:

R. J. C. Munday, 'New Dimensions of Precedent', *Journal of the Society of Public Teachers of Law*, 1978, p. 201

> Three recent developments in the field of precedent have added considerably to the volume of authorities upon which the legal profession has a tendency to draw... .
>
> A NEW GENERATION OF LAW REPORTS
> Complaints concerning the bulk of English case-law are perennial. No one recently has troubled to calculate just how many reported cases our system possesses. But in 1951 it was estimated that in common law and equity there existed more than 312,000 reported decisions. Such statistics on their own mean little. However, the clear trend today is for an increasing number of cases to be reported, either in complete or abbreviated form, in an expanding range of law reports... .
>
> In themselves, new series of law reports may be quite innocuous, if not desirable additions to the lawyer's armoury. Even if they do add appreciably to the volume of reported cases, there exist digests which compile and list all the decided authorities and these are perfectly capable of coping with any fresh

6   See further Burton M. Atkins, (Communication of Appellate Decisions: A Multivariate Model for Understanding the Selection of Cases for Publication), 24 *Law & Society Rev.*, 1990, 1171.

additions. The bulk of case-law is tolerated by the common lawyer as an occupational hazard. Our rules of practice of course conspire to this result in as much as counsel are under a duty to the court to cite all relevant authorities, and an authority is probably still taken to mean an account of a case, whether written or oral, attested to by a member of the Bar present at the decision. The existence of a published report of a case does at least ensure that there is a permanent and reliable record of the judgment. However, the proliferation of series of reports raises a number of serious practical problems which were diagnosed by the Law Reporting Committee in 1940: namely, those of expense and accommodation, not to mention needless duplication, the difficulty of tracing authorities, the danger of textual variants and inaccuracies, and the fact that important cases can still be over-looked.

But problems of another kind are also posed by the type of case currently reported in some of the new volumes. Several series now devote their pages to judgments of tribunals. One point of practice which Devlin, L.J. in 1962 insisted that tribunals at large observe was that they should not consider themselves bound by an over-rigid doctrine of precedent nor should they pursue consistency at the expense of the merits of individual cases.[7] Although it is possible to exaggerate the effect of this prohibition, it is permitted to wonder whether the reams of tribunal reports accumulating on the shelves may not encourage abandonment of a practice, considered by some to constitute one of the great procedural differences between courts and tribunals. There must be a danger, wherever lawyers are in the offing, that available legal materials will come to be used in an orthodox, lawyer-like manner. Such decisions are already from time to time being cited as authorities before the law courts. It is conceivable that this mounting body of reported tribunal law will contribute to a more rigid adherence to a system of precedent similar to that which binds English courts.

CITATION OF OVERSEAS AUTHORITIES

... English judges with increasing frequency, are prepared to have recourse to overseas authorities in order to lend support to their judgments, either where the English law may be in doubt or where a new judicial approach is being advocated ... and sometimes, one suspects, simply for the pleasure of citing them. In 1962 Megarry V.-C. already detected that citation of overseas authorities was beginning to find favour with the English Bench and felt that it was to be encouraged: '(l)et authors and editors be more industrious, let the Bar be more comprehensive, and let the Bench be more uniformly receptive: all three contributions must be made', he declared.[8] These exhortations to greater endeavour have elicited a stern rebuke from certain quarters, but are clearly being heeded by a substantial portion of the judiciary. The practice has revealed itself to be capable of abuse... .

The question of the rôle of the courts in matters of law reform is much to the forefront of legal minds at present. The balance between what is coming to

---

7   *Merchandise Transport Ltd* v. *B.T.C.* [1962] 2 Q.B. 173, 193.
8   *Lawyer and Litigant in England* (1962), p. 163.

be termed 'judicial activism' and 'strict constructionism' is delicate to maintain,[9] particularly in light of the greater freedom permitted to the House of Lords following its Practice Statement of 1966.[10] The position of the Court of Appeal in this process is vexed and the members of that Court are sometimes openly divided on how they perceive their function. As *Farrell* v. *Alexander* shows,[11] the Master of the Rolls felt that in order to spare parties unnecessary expense and to do justice in that particular case the Court of Appeal should be free to depart from binding rules which it now felt to be wrong. Scarman L.J., in contrast, took a broader view of the Court's responsibilities and expressed serious reservations:

'… I have immense sympathy with the approach of Lord Denning M.R. I decline to accept his lead only because I think it damaging to the law in the long term – though it would undoubtedly do justice in the present case. To some it will appear that justice is being denied by a timid, conservative adherence to judicial precedent. They would be wrong. Consistency is necessary to certainty – one of the great objectives of law. The Court of Appeal – at the very centre of our legal system – is responsible for its stability, its consistency, and its predictability… . The talk of law reform, which calls for wide ranging techniques of consultation and discussion that cannot be compressed into the forensic medium, is for others.'[12]

Although the extent to which the courts should be entitled to take the initiative in reforming the law is a highly contentious issue today, suffice it to say that the tempo of judicial lawmaking is quickening perceptibly[13] and one strong fillip to such law reform is provided by the lessons we can derive from overseas jurisdictions.

Whilst recognising the desirability of the legal mind remaining receptive to other countries' solutions to legal problems, a number of observations deserve to be made on this developing interchange of ideas. The question of how far the court is entitled to go in modifying accepted doctrines of English law in light of them and the broader and more delicate problem of demarcating the respective bounds of Parliament's and the judiciary's preserves have already been adverted to. Scarman L.J.'s reservations in *Farrell* v. *Alexander* are not simply the technical quibbles of a narrow-minded magistrate. On the contrary, they accurately reflect the *malaise* within the profession over the uncertainty which is coming to infect our law. These problems are far from resolving themselves

9 The expression 'judicial activism' gained some currency in England through the publication of Jaffé, *English and American Judges as Lawmakers* (1969). See Lord Edmund-Davies, 'Judicial Activism' [1973] *Current Legal Problems* 1.

10 [1966] 1 W.L.R 1234. [See p. 196 above. (Ed.)]

11 [1976] Q.B. 345.

12 Ibid. at p. 371. See also *Ulster-Swift Ltd and Pigs Marketing Board (Northern Ireland)* v. *Taunton Meat Haulage Ltd and Fransen Transport NV* [1977] 1 Lloyd's Rep. 346, 351, *per* Megaw L.J.

13 Diplock, *The Courts as Legislators*, 1965 (Holdsworth Club Presidential Address); Hailsham, *The Problems of a Lord Chancellor*, 1972 (Holdsworth Club Presidential Address). [And see pp. 311-44 below. (Ed.)]

at present and our increasing willingness to examine and adopt overseas solutions contributes further to the dilemma.

But on a more practical plane, recurrent references to overseas case-law – as also references to what one might term the new generation of law reports – inevitably put pressure on libraries, both professional and scholastic, to subscribe to the series of reports in question. Whilst encouraging the profession to avail themselves of foreign materials, Megarry V.-C. also urged that the Law Courts equip themselves with sets of Commonwealth law reports. Apart from the financial difficulties facing many libraries, the very problem of finding shelf-space to accommodate such acquisitions provides a source of anxiety. In addition, given libraries equipped with the volumes in question, the new receptivity to overseas solutions, in particular, can contribute substantially to the time spent by lawyers and students in researching any given problem. These factors ineluctably figure amongst the penalties which must be paid for the open-mindedness which is coming to possess the profession. But, if used intelligently and with a proper sense of discretion, the comparative lawyer can but approve the developing willingness on the part of Bench to look with favour upon overseas jurisdictions' solutions to problems akin to our own.

UNREPORTED CASES

Before turning to consider broader questions of policy affecting our methods of law reporting, it remains to examine one further development in the realm of precedent: namely, the rise to prominence of the unreported case. That the citation of unreported cases is on the increase scarcely requires a statistical proof. Such a trend was to be expected from the moment that the Bar Library made available all transcripts in civil cases delivered in the Court of Appeal. In the absence of an indexing system the new facilities were little used at first. But the more recent practice of the English edition of *Current Law*, which produces monthly lists of all such unreported cases along with brief summaries of their contents, and the *New Law Journal*, which periodically notes select unreported Court of Appeal decisions, has doubtless contributed to the popularity of such transcripts as a source of authorities, merely by rendering them more readily accessible.... .

Although, as has been indicated already, there is no novelty in the citation of unreported cases, it is becoming increasingly widespread and we are fast approaching the point where serious thought must needs be given to a practice which gives rise to a number of significant problems. Not the least disturbing is that the unreported case renders the practitioner's search after precedent considerably more arduous. Given the quickening geographical fragmentation of the Bar, even Court of Appeal transcripts are not immediately available to barristers practising in the provinces. Similarly, academics and law students will often be in no position to study the unreported judgments referred to by judges. This all serves to add to the inaccessibility of the law not only to the layman – who has presumably grown accustomed to such a state of affairs – but, paradoxically, even to the lawyer.[14]

14 'Such is the ingratitude of man that the resultant headaches for practitioners, teachers and reporters have led some to sigh again for the old days when the obscurity surrounding the unreported was usually impenetrable'. Megarry, *Miscellany-at-Law*.

[Dr Munday considered a number of possible solutions to the problems he had identified. One was to prohibit the citation of unreported decisions. Another, at the opposite end of the spectrum, would be to put all decisions on computerised systems which could be retrieved at will – on which see further, p 253 below. A third approach was that adopted by Professor A. L. Goodhart in his minority report to the Law Reporting Committee Report in 1940:] He considered that in order to reduce the possibility of important cases being omitted from the reports through inadvertence, to avoid textual variants and to ensure that some reliable record of High Court judgments be retained, a shorthand note of all judgments should be made and a transcript prepared. This transcript would then be sent to the judge to be corrected and subsequently returned by the judge and filed at a Central Office at the Law Courts. There would thus be extant a corrected copy of every judgment delivered in the High Court which law reporters, in particular, could consult. Professor Goodhart repudiated the suggestion that such a scheme would be too expensive or that it would involve undue waste of time and effort for the judges. Such an arrangement, he argued, would bring us into alignment with most Commonwealth jurisdictions which retain copies of their High Court judgments. It would also reduce the risk of vital cases being overlooked by the reports and would ensure that there existed a single authoritative text of any given judgment, rather than a number of sometimes significant textual variants, as at present. If anything, the arguments in favour of such a scheme, which found favour with Sir William Holdsworth, are stronger today than ever they were in 1940 when the recommendation was made. However, this modest proposal, which would not lead to an inevitable increase in the volume of reported case-law, has largely been ignored.

Dr Munday ended with a reflection on the curious state of the art of law reporting in England:

To the outsider it must appear paradoxical that a legal system which traditionally relies upon its reported precedent to as great an extent as our own should have paid such casual regard to its methods of law reporting. The common lawyer in the past has tended to accept the vagaries of his system unreflectingly. But with the deluge of case-law being reported today and the widening scope of authorities to which persistent reference is being made, a more critical stance may be expected of him and it is permitted to wonder whether the day is not far off when intervention of some kind becomes inevitable. The lawyer is torn by two competing sentiments. On the one hand, counsel's right to cite all relevant authorities is an established privilege which he associates with common law method and upon which he is by upbringing reluctant to impose trammels. On the other hand, the volume of reported precedent is beginning to reach disturbing proportions and, even though the ancients may not have taken our precise meaning, exhortations to the profession to make wider and concerted use of foreign materials and the availability of transcripts is but to heap Pelion upon Ossa.

3.   COMPUTER RETRIEVAL SYSTEMS

In 1978 when Dr Munday wrote his comments he was able to say that a computerised system of data retrieval for law reports would be 'totally undesirable' since it would result in the availability of far too much material. A few years later, however, this revolution had already taken place.

In 1980 Butterworths introduced into the English market the American system known as Lexis, and at about the same time a competitive system known as Eurolex also became available. Subsequently Lexis swallowed up Eurolex. Its database includes the full text of cases and practice directions published since 1945 in all the main reports and many specialist series of reports and transcripts of unreported decisions since 1980. (It also has all public general Acts currently in force in their amended form and all statutory rules, regulations and orders in force published in the statutory instruments series.)

The latest development is the increasing availability of judgments on the Internet. Thus, for instance, judgments of the House of Lords are available on the UK Parliament Home Page on http://www.parliament.uk from 4pm on the day of delivery of judgment at 2pm.

Another development has been law reports on CD-ROMs. The official Law Reports, comprising some 750 volumes, 480,000 pages, occupying 180 feet of shelf space are available from Context Electronic Publishing Co. on two CD-ROMs.[15]

4.   THE IMPACT OF COMPUTER RETRIEVAL ON THE CITATION OF UNREPORTED DECISIONS

Lexis records all Court of Appeal transcripts and some other unreported cases – a total, including reported decisions, of some 3,000 decisions a year. Of these only about one-third are reported. This means that vast quantities of unreported decisions are now easily available to lawyers preparing their legal arguments, and, not surprisingly, the citation of unreported decisions has risen very significantly.

In 1983 the House of Lords responded to this development by laying down a new rule as to the circumstances in which it would be prepared to allow unreported decisions to be cited:

15   In 1999 the cost was £5,000–or £10,000 for a commercial organisation–compared with £18,000 for the complete set of volumes. The six-monthly updates were £500 for individuals or £1,000 for commercial organisations.

Roberts Petroleum Ltd v. *Bernard Kenny Ltd* [1983] 2 A.C. 192, at 200

LORD DIPLOCK: I do desire, however, to comment upon the use sought to be made both in this House and in the Court of Appeal of previous judgments of that court which do not appear in any series of published law reports. This is a growing practice and one which, in my view, ought to be discouraged.

Transcripts of the shorthand notes of oral judgments delivered since April 1951 by members of the Court of Appeal, nearly all extempore, have been preserved at the Royal Courts of Justice, formerly in the Bar Library but since 1978 in the Supreme Court library. For much of this period, this course has been followed as respects all judgments of the civil division of the Court of Appeal, though recently some degree of selectivity has been adopted as to judgments to be indexed and incorporated in the bound volumes. Unreported judgments which have been delivered since the beginning of 1980 are now also included in the computerised data base known as Lexis and this has facilitated reference to them. Two such transcripts are referred to in the judgment of the Court of Appeal in the instant case. One of these was a case, *Hudson's Concrete Products Ltd* v. *D.B. Evans (Bilston) Ltd* to which my noble and learned friend refers, which had been the subject of a note in the *Solicitors' Journal*. The other had not been noted in any professional journal, nor had either of the two additional transcripts to which your Lordships were referred at the hearing in this House. For my part, I gained no assistance from perusal of any of these transcripts. None of them laid down a relevant principle of law that was not to be found in reported cases; the only result of referring to the transcripts was that the length of the hearing was extended unnecessarily.

This is not surprising. In a judgment, particularly one that has not been reduced into writing before delivery, a judge, whether at first instance or upon appeal, has his mind concentrated upon the particular facts of the case before him and the course which the oral argument has taken. This may have involved agreement or concessions, tacit or explicit, as to the applicable law, made by counsel for the litigating parties in what they conceived to be the interests of their respective clients in obtaining a favourable outcome of the particular case.

The primary duty of the Court of Appeal on an appeal in any case is to determine the matter actually in dispute between the parties. Such propositions of the law as members of the court find necessary to state and previous authorities to which they find it convenient to refer in order to justify the disposition of the actual proceedings before them will be tailored to the facts of the particular case. Accordingly propositions of law may well be stated in terms either more general or more specific than would have been used if he who gave the judgment had had in mind somewhat different facts, or had heard a legal argument more expansive than had been necessary in order to determine the particular appeal. Even when making successive revisions of drafts of my own written speeches for delivery upon appeals to this House, which usually involve principles of law of wider application than the particular case under appeal, I often find it necessary to continue to introduce subordinate clauses supplementing or qualifying the simpler, and a stylistically preferable, wording in which statements of law have been expressed in earlier drafts.

There are two classes of printed law reports: the two weekly series of general law reports (a) the Weekly Law Reports of the Incorporated Council of

Law Reporting, of which the more important, contained in Parts 2 and 3, are later reproduced in the Law Reports proper, together with a summary of the arguments of counsel, and (b) the All England Law Reports which report much the same cases as the former series; these do not err on the side of overselectivity. Then there are the various series of specialised law reports which seem to have proliferated in the course of the last few decades; these may be useful in helping lawyers practising in specialised fields to predict the likely outcome of the particular case in which they are advising or instituting proceedings, by seeing how previous cases in which the facts were in various respects analogous were actually decided; but these specialised reports contain only a small minority of leading judgments in which some new principle of law of general application in the specialised field of law is authoritatively propounded, as distinct from some previously accepted principle being applied to the facts of a particular case. If a civil judgment of the Court of Appeal (which has a heavy case load and sits concurrently in several civil divisions) has not found its way into the generalised series of law reports or even into one of the specialised series, it is most unlikely to be of any assistance to your Lordships on an appeal which is sufficiently important to reach this House.

My Lords, in my opinion, the time has come when your Lordships should adopt the practice of declining to allow transcripts of unreported judgments of the civil division of the Court of Appeal to be cited upon the hearing of appeals to this House unless leave is given to do so; and that such leave should only be granted upon counsel's giving an assurance that the transcript contains a statement of some principle of law, relevant to an issue in the appeal to this House, that is binding upon the Court of Appeal and of which the substance, as distinct from the mere choice of phraseology, is not to be found in any judgment of that court that has appeared in one of the generalised or specialised series of reports.

[The four other members of the House of Lords sitting on the appeal expressly agreed with Lord Diplock's pronouncement.]

Lord Diplock had in fact referred to the problem of excessive citation of authorities in previous cases – see *de Lasala* v. *de Lasala* [1979] 2 All E.R. 1146, and *Lambert* v. *Lewis* [1982] A.C. 225 at 274–5. In *Lambert* v. *Lewis* all the other Law Lords again agreed with Lord Diplock that there were dangers in counsel citing a plethora of authorities for propositions that no one would dispute. It wasted judicial time and the parties' money and could lead to the court being unable to separate the wood of legal principle from the trees of paraphrase.

The Court of Appeal Civil Division has laid down a rule that 'leave to cite unreported cases will not usually be granted unless counsel are able to assure the court that the transcript in question contains a relevant statement of legal principle not found in reported authority' (*Practice Note* [1996] 3 All E.R. 382).

The House of Lords' edict in *Roberts Petroleum* aroused strong critical comment. See, in particular, G. W. Bartholomew, 'Unreported Judgments in the House of Lords', *New Law Journal*, 2 September 1983, p. 781. Mr

Bartholomew made a number of points. First, there was no need to ban unreported decisions. If counsel was citing an authority which was not useful, the remedy was to stop counsel. They did this with reported decisions and could presumably do so just as much with unreported cases. Secondly, most of the points made by Lord Diplock as to the shortcomings of unreported judgments applied equally to those that were reported. Both were dependent on the facts of the case in question, both were liable to include statements of principle that might be wider or narrower than the facts required. He continued:

> It is surely still true that it is the judges who make the law (to the extent that they do so) and not the editors of either the generalised or specialised law reports. If that remains true then the publication of a judgment should have little or nothing to do with its citability... .
>
> For transcripts of unreported judgments of the Civil Division of the Court of Appeal to be citable in the House of Lords then, in Lord Diplock's view, two conditions must be satisfied. First, the principle of law for which the transcript is being cited must (*a*) be binding on the Court of Appeal, and (*b*) not be found in any reported judgment of that court. Second, counsel must give an assurance that both limbs of the first condition are satisfied. Now the first limb of the first condition is part and parcel of the traditional doctrine of precedent, and needs no further comment in this context. It is the second law of the first condition, with its implicit distinction between principles of law on the one hand, and the circumstances of their application and the form in which they are stated, on the other, which will surely prove difficult to apply.
>
> The somewhat amoeboid principles of the common law grow or are restrained by their application, re-application or non-application to varying fact situations. They are re-phrased, re-stated and re-iterated over and over again, and what eventually emerges is often startlingly different from that from which one started. The great principle of the common law in this context is that 'great oaks from little acorns grow' – this is the *leitmotif* of the judicial process. It is of the essence of the common law system that freedom, and all other principles of law, broaden down from precedent to precedent.
>
> The fact that a so-called principle of law applies in this situation rather than that, is in fact part and parcel of the principle itself. The fact that a so-called principle is phrased in one way rather than another – something which Lord Diplock tended to dismiss as a 'mere choice of phraseology' – is not separable from the principle itself. To paraphrase Wittgenstein: the principle is its statement. Counsel must surely be allowed to mount their arguments not only in terms of what the so-called principles of law are, but also in terms of the circumstances in which they have been applied, and the way in which they have been phrased, and this must surely be so whether the judgment to which reference is made was reported or not.

Similar objections were made in 1998 to the extension of the restrictive approach to unreported decisions to the Court of Appeal – see F. A. R. Bennion, 'Citation of unreported cases- a challenge', *New Law*

Journal, 16 October 1998, p. 1520. Mr Bennion stated that in the 1997 edition of his textbook there are no fewer than 1,463 citations of unreported decisions. He argues that the courts have no right to abridge the citizen's basic right to conduct legal proceedings as they see fit – subject to the court's power to control repetitious, irrelevant or improper argument.

Other problems identified by commentators in response to the House of Lords' ruling in *Roberts Petroleum* include the following:

(1) Decisions of the courts are the law in the sense that they may contain the articulation of a legal rule and must in any event amount to the application of a rule.[16]
(2) In an adversary system, counsel should be left to make his case as best he can. Lexis provides full-text access to decisions and is therefore to be preferred to the many forms of edited reports.[17]
(3) Lord Diplock described the role of the Court of Appeal in terms that were more suitable to that of a trial court in a provincial town. He seemed to discount its vital role in the law-making process.[18]
(4) Lord Diplock seemed to downgrade the role of courts generally by complaining that facts constrained him to qualify the principles of law. But law is about facts – the facts define the categories of situations that are covered by the rule. The function of the court is to generalise from the facts.[19]
(5) The effect of Lord Diplock's ruling is to make the law reporters, rather than the judges, the arbiters of what is the law.[20]
(6) In some areas the law suffered from under-reporting of decisions, not over-reporting. This was true, for instance, in the company law field.[1]

A different but very powerful attack on the House of Lords ruling in *Roberts Petroleum* was announced by Nicolas Harrison, Managing Director of Butterworths (Telepublishing) Ltd – the company that markets Lexis. His main point was that in reality there was little evidence of a great upsurge of irrelevant unreported decisions being cited. In *Roberts Petroleum* itself although Lord Diplock said that three out of four transcripts cited were unreported, in fact all four had been referred to in traditional legal sources. None was to be found in any computer database! Moreover, he argued, the House of Lords ruling was based on an unworthy view that counsel could not be relied on to do their duty efficiently.[2]

16 Colin Tapper, *Law Society's Gazette*, 29 June 1983, p. 1636.
17 Ibid.
18 Francis Bennion, *New Law Journal*, 30 September 1983, p. 874.
19 Ibid.
20 W. H. Goodhart, *New Law Journal*, 1 April 1983, p. 296.
1   Ibid.
2   See N. Harrison, 'Unreported Cases: Myth and Reality', *Law Society's Gazette*, 1 February 1984, p. 257. See also Bennion, ibid., 29 June 1983, p. 1635.

In the view of Dr Munday, the time has never been riper for the establishment of a fresh committee to review the entire system of reporting, citation and storage of English case law.[3]

For a comment on the differing results of the American and the English approach to copyright in law reports see Paul von Nessen, 'Law Reporting: Another Case for Deregulation', *Modern Law Review*, 1985, p. 412.

Note–Availability of judgments handed down

In former times, reserved judgments were read aloud in open court. Nowadays the court hands down reserved judgments in written form. The parties' legal representatives normally receive the judgment 36 hours in advance of the hearing – in the hope that they will communicate any errors to the court in time for them to be corrected.[4] Sometimes the judgment is made available on the Internet's Worldwide Web.

Note – Citation of authorities

When a case is reported in the official Law Reports published by the Incorporated Council of Law Reporting for England and Wales that is the report that should be cited as authority. If a case is not, or is not yet, reported in the Law Reports, a report in the Weekly Law Reports or the All England Law Reports should be cited. Failing that a report in any of the specialist series of reports may be cited.[5]

Note – Law Reporters

The Courts and Legal Services Act 1990, s. 115 provided that a law report by a person who is a solicitor or who has a 'Supreme Court qualification' within the meaning of s. 71 of the Act has the same authority as a report by a member of the bar. (A Supreme Court qualification is having a right of audience in relation to all proceedings in the Supreme Court.)

---

3   *Law Society's Gazette*, 25 May 1983, p. 1339. See also N. H. Andrews, 'Reporting Case Law: Unreported Cases, the Definition of a *Ratio* and the Criteria for Reporting Decisions', *Legal Studies*, 1985, p. 205.
4   See *Practice Statement* [1998] 2 All E.R. 667.
5   *Practice Statement* [1998] 2 All E.R. 667.

CHAPTER 6

How precedent works

Precedents are the raw material from which lawyers and judges distil rules of law. Anyone wishing to state the law on a matter not governed by statute – whether he be a judge, a practitioner, an academic or a student – must look at the decided cases. But how does he use the raw material?

The first principle is that anything relevant may be grist to the mill. If there is a clear decision of the House of Lords which is precisely in point, one need usually search no further. If in that case all five Law Lords agreed that the rule of law is X, then for all practical purposes one may assume that it is X. One may still argue that Y would be a better rule and, if one is advising a client prepared to litigate all the way up to the House of Lords, one may consider with him the practical prospects of persuading the Lords to change the rule. But, subject to that rather remote possibility, lawyers are likely to agree that the rule on that point is X.

At the opposite extreme, search for relevant precedents may reveal nothing more than a decision on the point by a county court judge reported briefly only in the *Solicitors' Journal,* and a remark to the same effect made in the course of giving judgment on a related point in a decision of the High Court of Australia. Anyone wishing to propound the rule in England would be likely to say that there was virtually no authority on the matter. He would cite the county court decision and the remark of the Australian court and would then speculate as to whether the rule on which they appeared to agree would be likely to commend itself to a court somewhat higher in the hierarchy than the county court. Little confidence could be placed in the precedents as giving authoritative guidance as to the prevailing role, but for what they are worth they are the best available. In other words, even the slenderest of authorities are some evidence of the law.

Usually, the relevant precedents will be a mixed bag of decisions of different levels of court, different degrees of relevance to the facts under consideration, coming from different periods and, often, appearing to state conflicting rules. The lawyer's task then is to organise the available material in the most coherent fashion depending on his purpose. A lawyer advising a client will start with the bias that he wishes, if possible, to provide advice that the client will find constructive and encouraging. He will therefore seek to marshal the material in such a way as to enable him to tell the client that he can do what he wishes to do – subject however to the important caveat that he will not want to lose the client through incompetence. The better he is as a lawyer the more likely it is that he will draw his client's attention to the weaknesses and doubts about his analysis of the state of the law.

If he is preparing a legal argument to be presented on behalf of his client in court, he will try to present the precedents in the most attractive form with as few concessions to his opponent as possible. It is a rule of professional etiquette that counsel must cite to a court all the relevant precedents whether they help his client's case or not. But this is only common sense. Far better to draw the court's attention to an awkward precedent and so have the first opportunity of dealing with it oneself – by showing that it can be explained away – than to have it produced as a trump card by one's opponent.

If the person in question is a scholar writing a book, he will present his material as objectively as he can. But he too may have a bias in the sense that he favours one approach to the problem under consideration rather than another, and may be seeking to persuade the reader that his approach is justified by the state of the authorities. In the case of the practitioner who is paid to represent the interests of a client, everyone understands and forgives a little stretching of the argument to favour the client's point of view. If the authorities do not quite go all the way for his client, he is permitted to push them to their utmost limits and then a little further in the hope of persuading the court to adopt his argument. Providing the arguments are not far-fetched, the lawyer's reputation will not suffer from such imaginative exegesis of the precedents. The case of the scholar, however, is different. When presenting an analysis of what the law is, he is expected to remain severely within the limits of straightforward analysis. As will be seen, this may still offer a good deal of scope but it will not normally give as much licence for 'interpretation' as is available to the practitioner.

The case of the judge is different again. In a sense his position is somewhere between that of the practitioner and of the scholar. He will normally have heard argument from opposing counsel each seeking to persuade the judge to adopt his view of the precedents and to reject that offered by his learned friend. Having made up his mind as to which argument he prefers he will present it in his judgment as representing the law. He will wish to be 'right' in the sense of not being the subject of a successful appeal by the disappointed loser. Judges, until they become members of the highest court, are accustomed to the minor irritation of being told by a superior court that their view of the law was wrong. It is simply an occupational hazard. (They may still on occasion harbour the distinct feeling that it was the appeal court rather than themselves that got the law wrong but such feelings are normally veiled in decent silence. Only Lord Denning permitted himself the luxury of sometimes informing the world that he preferred his own solution to the problem to that offered by his 'superiors' in the House of Lords.) But, however case-hardened or thick-skinned he may be, a judge would normally prefer to be upheld than reversed on appeal and he will therefore have some concern for the likely opinion of other judges when formulating his decision. He will also wish if possible to avoid merited criticism from writers in the professional and scholarly journals. The more unpredictable his decision, the more likely that he will be subjected to waspish attack by some indignant academic expert. Also his sense of the dignity of his office will tend to incline the judge to construct his decision in such a way as to conform with professional expectations.

On the other hand, a judge is not a machine. Some attention will be given later in this book to the vexed question of whether judges do, or should, allow their personal views to obtrude into their decision-making, but it is obvious that where two arguments are presented by counsel there will frequently be enough merit in both to make a decision either way a practicable possibility. If one side is so weak as to make its success highly improbable, the client will normally accept the advice of his lawyers and withdraw or settle the dispute. Litigated cases, whether they raise issues of law or of fact, almost by definition can often be decided respectably either way. Much may then depend on the particular way the judge sees the question. His view of the precedents may be affected by some feeling about the respective merits of the two parties before him or by some sense that the law on the point 'ought to be' X rather than Y. In a marginal case such impressions can have an effect.

In fact, the person most likely to bring a dispassionate and 'objective' approach to the process of reading the precedents may be the law student. He has no client; the facts of the problem with which he is dealing are usually stated in so arid a way as to denude it of emotional impact; and he will probably lack the self-confidence to have any strong opinion as to what the law on the point ought to be. He will be likely to come to the question of what the law on that point is with the belief that there is a 'right' answer which he wants to discover. The judge, the practitioner and the scholar all know that there are no right answers – there are only better or worse answers, answers that are more or less likely to find acceptance in the courts or in the eyes of the client, the profession or the community. There are answers that will solve the particular problem and stand the test of time, and others that will not. But whatever the particular vantage point or perspective of the person concerned, the raw material with which he is dealing will be the same precedents and the methods he uses will be the same professional techniques.

I.   PROFESSIONAL TECHNIQUES FOR USING PRECEDENTS

(a)   Ratio, dictum or obiter dictum

The first thing a lawyer wants to know when inspecting a precedent is whether the proposition of law in which he is interested forms the ratio decidendi of the case, or whether it is only something said which is dictum or obiter dictum.

The ratio (pronounced rayshio) of a case is its central core of meaning, its sharpest cutting edge. It is the ratio and only the ratio that is capable of being binding. Whether it *is* binding will depend on the position in the hierarchy of the court that decided the case and of the court that is now considering it. Thus, as has been seen, the ratio of a decision of the House of Lords binds all lower courts; the ratio of a High Court decision binds only the county courts; the ratio of a county court decision binds no one; the ratio of a Court of Appeal case binds the Court of Appeal and all lower courts but does not bind the House of Lords.

If the proposition of law does not form part of the ratio it is by definition either dictum or obiter dictum. (Dicta or judicial dicta is the term used when they relate to a matter in issue in the case; obiter dicta are dicta that are more peripheral. Obiter dicta is however also commonly used to cover both meanings.)

Dicta may be of very great persuasive weight but they cannot under any circumstances be binding on anyone. The most carefully considered and deliberate statement of law by all five Law Lords which is dictum cannot bind even the lowliest judge in the land. Technically he is free to go his own way. In practice, of course, weighty obiter pronouncements from higher courts are likely to be followed and will certainly be given the greatest attention, but in strictest theory they are not binding. (For an example of a weighty dictum, see *Hedley Byrne* v. *Heller Bros.*, p. 353 below) This is the reason that technically the Court of Appeal is not bound by statements in the House of Lords that the Court of Appeal should follow its own decisions. Such a statement cannot form part of the ratio of the House of Lords decision, since a case in the House of Lords does not require a decision as to the handling of precedents by the Court of Appeal and therefore anything said on the subject is necessarily obiter.[1]

Being bound, therefore, is a function of three different elements – the precedents must have been pronounced by a court that stands in the hierarchy in a position to bind the present court, the proposition of the law must have formed the ratio of that decision and, thirdly, it must be relevant to the facts of the present case. (The issue of relevance is considered below.) An obiter dictum does not qualify, since it fails to meet the second test.

But, other things being equal, a statement of law that is the ratio of the case even if it is not binding ranks higher than the same statement of law that is only an obiter dictum. Thus if the House of Lords, for instance, is evaluating a proposition of law emanating from the Court of Appeal, it will regard it as weightier if it proves to be the ratio of the case than if it turns out to have been said obiter. So the distinction between ratio and obiter dicta is of importance whether or not the case is capable of being binding in the particular situation.

There have been many definitions of the ratio decidendi. My own is – a proposition of law which decides the case, in the light or in the context of the material facts. If there appear to be more than one proposition of law which decide the case, it has more than one ratio and both are binding – see *Jacobs* v. *L.C.C.* [1950] A.C. at 369. Any statement of law, however carefully considered, which was not the basis of the decision is obiter.

The crucial problem in ascertaining the ratio of a case is usually to determine how widely or narrowly the principle of law should be stated. Another way of putting this is, at what level of abstraction should the facts be stated? The law report will state a mass of facts, some of which will be properly part of the ratio and others of which will be ignored. The judge in the concluding part of his judgment may indicate what he conceives the ratio to be – but normally judges do not do this explicitly. They know that, in any event whatever they say, later courts have the right to interpret and re-interpret the ratio of their case. The ratio of each case must take into account the facts of that particular case and then generalise from those facts as far as the statement of the court and the circumstances indicate is desirable.

Thus the case may have concerned an action brought by a blind purchaser of a defective car. The fact that the purchaser was blind would not be part of the ratio of the case unless the fact of blindness was relevant to the rule of law. This would only be the case if the rule formulated by the

1   For differing views on this issue see P. J. Evans, 'The Status of Rules of Precedent' 1982, 41 *Cambridge Law Journal*, 162; L. Goldstein, 'Some Problems About Precedent', 1984, 43 *Cambridge Law Journal*, 88; P. J. Evans, 'A Brief Reply', ibid., p. 108.

court depended in some way on the purchaser's capacity to inspect the car visually. The rule might then be different for a purchaser who was blind. But if the defect in the car would have been equally obvious to or equally hidden from a sighted and a blind purchaser, then the rule for both situations would be framed without reference to the fact of blindness. Equally, the fact of blindness would not be part of the ratio if the rule were framed without regard to the purchaser's ability or otherwise to inspect the car. The greater the number of facts in the ratio, the narrower its scope; conversely, the fewer, or the higher the level of abstraction, the broader the reach of the ratio – the more fact situations it covers.

Karl Llewellyn's famous book *The Bramble Bush*, based on lectures first given at Columbia Law School, has a passage which helps to elucidate the meaning of the ratio decidendi:

K. N. Llewellyn, *The Bramble Bush* (1930, Oceana edition 1975), pp. 42, 43

… 3) The court can decide the particular dispute only according to a general rule which covers a whole class of like disputes. Our legal theory does not admit of single decisions standing on their own… . But how wide, or how narrow, is the general rule in this particular case? … That is a troublesome matter. The practice of our case-law, however, is I think fairly stated thus: it pays to be suspicious of general rules which look too wide; it pays to go slow in feeling *certain* that a wide rule has been laid down at all, or that, if seemingly laid down, it will be followed. For there is a fourth accepted canon:

4) *Everything, everything, everything, big or small, a judge may say in an opinion, is to be read with primary reference to the particular dispute, the particular question before him.* You are not to think that the words mean what they might if they stood alone. You are to have your eye on the case in hand, and to learn how to interpret all that has been said *merely* as a reason for deciding *that* case *that* way.

… I do believe, gentlemen, that here we have as fine a deposit of slow-growing wisdom as ever has been laid down through the centuries by the unthinking social sea. Here, hardened into institutions, carved out and given line by rationale. What is this wisdom? Look to your own discussion, look to any argument. You know where you would go. You reach, at random if hurried, more carefully if not, for a foundation, for a major premise. But never for itself. Its interest lies in leading to the conclusion you are headed for. You shape its words, its content, to an end decreed. More, with your mind upon your object you use words, you bring in illustrations, you deploy and advance and concentrate again. When you have done, you have said much you did not mean. You did not mean, that is, *except* in reference to your point. You have brought generalisation after generalisation up, and discharged it at your goal; all, in the heat of argument, were over-stated. None would you stand to, if your opponent should urge them to *another* issue.

So with the judge. Nay, more so with the judge. He is not merely human, as are you. He is, as well, a lawyer; which you, yet, are not. A lawyer, and as such skilled in manipulating the resources of persuasion at his hand. A lawyer, and as such prone without thought to twist analogies, and rules, and instances, to his conclusion. A lawyer, and as such peculiarly prone to disregard the implications which do not bear directly on his case.

More, as a practiced campaigner in the art of exposition, he has learned that one must prepare the way for argument. You set the mood, the tone, you lay the intellectual foundation – all with the case in mind, with the conclusion – all, because those who hear you also have the case in mind, without the niggling criticism which may later follow. You wind up, as a baseball pitcher will wind up – and as in the pitcher's case, the wind-up often is superfluous. As in the pitcher's case, it has been known to be intentionally misleading.

With this it should be clear, then, why our canons thunder. Why we create a class of dicta, of unnecessary words, which later readers, their minds now on quite other cases, can mark off as not quite essential to the argument. Why we create a class of *obiter dicta,* the wilder failings of the pitcher's arms, the wilder motions of his gum-ruminant jaws. Why we set about, as our job, to crack the kernel from the nut, to find the true rule the case in fact decides: the *rule of the case.*

Now for a while I am going to risk confusion for the sake of talking simply. I am going to treat as the rule of the case the *ratio decidendi,* the rule *the court tells you* is the rule of the case, the ground, as the phrase goes, upon which the court itself has rested its decision. For there is where you must begin, and such refinements as are needed may come after.

The court, I will assume, has talked for five pages, only one of which portrayed the facts assumed. The rest has been discussion. And judgment has been given for the party who won below: judgment affirmed. We seek the rule… .

Perhaps in this, as in judging how far to trust a broadly stated rule, we may find guidance in the facts the court assumes. Surely this much is certain: the actual dispute before the court is limited as straitly by the facts as by the form which the procedural issue has assumed. What is not in the facts cannot be present for decision. Rules which proceed an inch beyond the facts must be suspect.

But how far does that help us out? What are *the* facts? The plaintiff's name is Atkinson and the defendant's Walpole. The defendant, despite his name, is an Italian by extraction, but the plaintiff's ancestors came over with the Pilgrims. The defendant has a schnauzer-dog named Walter, red hair, and $30,000 worth of life insurance. All these are facts. The case, however, does not deal with life insurance. It is about an auto accident. The defendant's auto was a Buick painted pale magenta. He is married. His wife was in the back seat, an irritable, somewhat faded blonde. She was attempting back-seat driving when the accident occurred. He had turned around to make objection. In the process the car swerved and hit the plaintiff. The sun was shining; there was a rather lovely dappled sky low to the West. The time was late October on a Tuesday. The road was smooth, concrete. It had been put in by the McCarthy Road Works Company. How many of these facts are important to the decision? How many of these facts are, as we say, legally relevant? Is it relevant that the road was in the country or the city; that it was concrete or tarmac or of dirt; that it was a private or a public way? Is it relevant that the defendant was driving a Buick, or a motor car, or a vehicle? Is it important that he looked around as the car swerved? Is it crucial? Would it have been the same if he had been drunk, or had swerved for fun, to see how close he could run by the plaintiff, but had missed his guess?

Is it not obvious that as soon as you pick up this statement of the facts to find its legal bearings you must discard some as of no interest whatsoever, discard others as dramatic but as legal nothings? and is it not clear, further, that when you pick up the facts which are left and which do seem relevant, you suddenly cease to deal with them in the concrete and deal with them instead in *categories* which you, for one reason or another, deem significant? It is not the road between Pottsville and Arlington; it is 'a highway'. It is not a particular pale magenta Buick eight, by number 732507, but 'a motor car', and perhaps even 'a vehicle'. It is not a turning around to look at Adorée Walpole, but a lapse from the supposedly proper procedure of careful drivers, with which you are concerned. Each concrete fact of the case arranges itself, I say, as the *representative* of a much wider abstract *category* of facts, and it is not in itself but as a member of the category that you attribute significance to it. But what is to tell you whether to make your category 'Buicks' or 'motor cars' or 'vehicles'? What is to tell you to make your category 'road' or 'public highway'? The court may tell you. But the precise point that you have up for study is how far it is safe to trust what the court says. The precise issue which you are attempting to solve is whether the court's language can be taken as it stands, or must be amplified, or must be whittled down.

This brings us at last to the case system. For the truth of the matter is a truth so obvious and trite that it is somewhat regularly overlooked by students. *That no case can have a meaning by itself!* Standing alone it gives you no guidance. It can give you no guidance as to how far it carries, as to how much of its language will hold water later. What counts, what gives you leads, what gives you sureness, *that is the background of the other cases* in relation to which you must read the one. They colour the language, the technical terms used in the opinion. But above all they give you the wherewithal to find which of the facts are significant, and in what aspect they are significant, and how far the rules laid down are to be trusted.

Here, I say, is the foundation of the case system. For what, in a case class, do we do? We have set before you, at either the editor's selection or our own, a *series* of opinions which in some manner are related. They may or may not be exactly alike in their outcome. They are always supposedly somewhat similar on their legally relevant facts. Indeed, it is *the aspects in which their facts are similar* which give you your first guidance as to what *classes* of fact will be found legally relevant, that is, will be found *to operate alike,* or to operate *at all,* upon the court. On the other hand, the states of fact are rarely, if ever, quite alike. And one of the most striking problems before you is: when you find two cases side by side which show a difference in result, then to determine *what* difference in their facts, or *what* difference in the procedural set-up, has produced that difference in result.

This, then, is the case system game, the game of matching cases. We proceed by a rough application of the logical method of comparison and difference.

And here there are three things that need saying. The first is that by this matching of facts and issues in the different cases we get, to come back to where we started, some indication of when the court in a given case has over-generalised; of when, on the other hand, it has meant all the ratio decidendi that it said. 'The Supreme Court of the United States,' remarks the sage Professor T. R. Powell, 'are by no means such fools as they talk, or as the people are who think them so.' We go into the matter expecting a certain amount of inconsistency in the broader language of the cases. We go into the matter set in advance to find distinctions by means of which we can reconcile and harmonise the outcomes of the cases, even though the rules that the courts seem to lay down in their deciding may be inconsistent. We are prepared to whittle down the categories of the facts, to limit the rule of one case to its new whittled narrow category, to limit the rule of the other to its new other narrow category – and thus to make two cases stand together. The first case involves a man who makes an offer and gets in his revocation before his offer is accepted. The court decides that he cannot be sued upon his promise, and says that no contract can be made unless the minds of both parties are at one at once. The second case involves a man who has made a similar offer and has mailed a revocation, but to whom a letter of acceptance has been sent before his revocation was received. The court holds that he can be sued upon his promise, and says that his offer was being repeated every moment from the time that it arrived until the letter of acceptance was duly mailed. Here are two rules which are a little difficult to put together, and to square with sense, and which are, too, a little hard to square with the two holdings in the cases. We set to work to seek a way out which will do justice to the holdings. We arrive perhaps at this, that it is not necessary for the two minds to be at one at once, if the person who has received an offer thinks, and thinks reasonably, as he takes the last step of acceptance, that the offeror is standing by the offer. And to test the rule laid down in either case, as also to test our tentative formulation which we have built to cover both, we do two things. First and easiest is to play variations on the facts, making the case gradually more and more extreme until we find the place beyond which it does not seem sense to go. Suppose, for example, our man does think the offeror still stands to his offer, and thinks it reasonably, on all his information; but yet a revocation has arrived, which his own clerk has failed to bring to his attention? We may find the stopping-place much sooner than we had expected, and thus be forced to recast and narrow the generalisation we have made, or to recast it even on wholly different lines. The second and more difficult way of testing is to go to the books and find further cases in which variations on the facts occur, and in which the importance of such variations has been put to the proof. The first way is the intuitional correction of hypothesis; the second way is the experimental test of whether an hypothesis is sound. Both are needed. The first to save time. The second, to make sure... . Not the least important feature in the cases you are comparing will be their dates. For you must assume that the law, like any other human institution, has undergone, still undergoes development, clarification, change, as time goes on, as experience accumulates, as conditions vary. The earlier cases in a series, therefore, while they *may* stand unchanged today, are yet more likely to be forerunners, to be indications of the first gropings with a problem, rather than to present its final solution even in the state from which they come. That holds particularly for cases prior to 1800. It holds in many fields of law for cases of much more recent date. But in any event you will be concerned to place the case in time as well as in space, if putting it together with the others makes for difficulty.

The third thing that needs saying as you set to matching cases, is that on your materials, often indeed on all the materials that there are, a perfect working out of comparison and difference cannot be had. In the first case you have facts *a* and *b* and *c*, procedural set-up *m*, and outcome *x*. In the second case you have, *if* you are lucky, procedural set-up *m* again, but this time with facts *a* and *b* and *d*, and outcome *y*. How, now, are you to know with any certainty whether the changed result is due in the second instance to the absence of fact *c* or to the presence of the new fact *d*? The court may tell you. But I repeat: your object is to *test* the telling of the court. You turn to your third case. Here once more is the outcome *x*, and the facts are *b* and *c* and *e*, but fact *a* is missing, and the procedural set-up this time is not *m* but *n*. This stengthens somewhat your suspicion that fact *c* is the lad who works the changed result. But an experimentum crucis still is lacking. Cases in life are not made to our hand. A scientific *approach* to prediction we may have, and we may use it as far as our materials will permit. An exact science *in result* we have not now. Carry this in your minds: a scientific approach, no more. Onto the green, with luck, your science takes you. But when it comes to putting you will work by art and hunch... .

But if you arrive at the conclusion that a given court did not mean all it said in the express ratio decidendi it laid down, that the case must really be confined to facts narrower than the court itself assumed to be its measure, then you are ready for the distinction that I hinted at earlier in this lecture, the distinction between the ratio decidendi, the court's own version of the rule of the case, and the *true* rule of the case, to wit, what *it will be made to stand for by another later court*. For one of the vital elements of our doctrine of precedent is this: that any later court can always re-examine a prior case, and under the principle that the court could decide only what was before it, and that the older case must now be read with that in view, can arrive at the conclusion that the dispute before the earlier court was much narrower than that court thought it was, called therefore for the application of a much narrower rule. Indeed, the argument goes further. It goes on to state that no broader rule *could* have been laid down ex-cathedra, because to do that would have transcended the powers of the earlier court.

You have seen further that out of the matching of a number of related cases it is your job to formulate a rule that covers them all in harmony, if that can be done, and to test your formulation against possible variants on the facts. Finally, to test it, if there is time, against what writers on the subject have to say, and against other cases.

The ratio is therefore something that can be ascertained tentatively as soon as the case has been decided. The law reporter in preparing his account of the case will attempt a formulation of the ratio which he will state in his headnote. He will base this partly on the facts of the case, partly on what the judge has said in his judgment and partly on his sense of the proper limits of the doctrine formulated in the case. Thereafter the ratio may be widened in later cases (by reducing the facts stated in it thus raising the level of abstraction), or, conversely, it may be narrowed by the opposite process. The ratio is therefore not fixed but a formula that is capable of adjustment according to the force of later developments.

The process has been described in another classic American book:

Benjamin N. Cardozo, *The Nature of the Judicial Process* (1921), pp. 48–9

The implications of a decision may in the beginning be equivocal. New cases by commentary and exposition extract the essence. At last there emerges a rule or principle which becomes a datum, a point of departure, from which new lines will be run, from which new courses will be measured. Sometimes the rule or principle is found to have been formulated too narrowly or too broadly and has to be reframed. Sometimes it is accepted as a postulate of later reasoning, its origins are forgotten, it becomes a new stock of descent, its issue unite with other strains, and persisting permeate the law. You may call the process one of analogy or of logic of philosophy as you please. Its essence in any event is the derivation of a consequence from a rule or principle or a precedent which, accepted as a datum, contains implicitly within itself the germ of the conclusion. In all this, I do not use the word philosophy in any strict or formal sense. The method tapers down from the syllogism at one end to mere analogy at the other. Sometimes the extension of a precedent goes to the limit of its logic. Sometimes it does not go so far. Sometimes by a process of analogy it is carried even farther. That is a tool which no system of jurisprudence has been able to discard. A rule which has worked well in one field, or which, in any event, is there whether its workings have been revealed or not, is carried over into another. Instances of such a process I group under the same heading as those where the nexus of logic is closer and more binding. At bottom and in their underlying motives, they are phases of the same method. They are inspired by the same yearning for consistency, for certainty, for uniformity of plan and structure. They have their roots in the constant striving of the mind for larger and more inclusive unity, in which differences will be reconciled, and abnormalities will vanish.

Questions

1. Who formulates the ratio of a case?[2]
2. How does one discover the right level of abstraction at which to state the ratio?
3. What determines whether a proposition of law is ratio or obiter? Can it move from one category to the other?

---

2   On the nature and definition of the ratio, see further N. H. Andrews, 'Reporting Case Law: Unreported Cases, the Definition of a *Ratio* and the Criteria for Reporting Decisions', *Legal Studies,* 1985, pp. 205, 209–24.

(b)   Is the precedent distinguishable?

Having assigned the statement of law to one or other of the two categories
of ratio or dictum, the lawyer will wish to determine its relevance to the
facts in issue. If one side can marshal a precedent that is binding and in
point, that will conclude the debate. The only way for the opponent to
avoid losing the case is by showing that the case is *distinguishable*. The
process of distinguishing is important, however, not simply as the only
means of avoiding a threatening precedent that is binding but equally as
a means of avoiding one that is merely of persuasive authority. Very
commonly the lawyers on one side of an argument will produce one or
more precedents that they claim are in point and which their opponents
claim are distinguishable, whilst in turn their opponents rely on a different
line of authorities which the first side maintain have no relevance.
Distinguishing between factual situations and applying the appropriate
rule of law is one of the lawyer's and judge's most crucial functions. It is
the business of drawing lines, or seeing how far to take a particular rule
and of expanding or contracting the scope of rules to meet new
circumstances. The question is always the same – are there any material
differences between the facts of the present case and the facts of the
precedents to warrant the rule being different?

Sometimes the court distinguishes the indistinguishable – as the only
way to escape from the clutches of an unwelcome precedent which would
otherwise be binding. This process brings the law into disrepute, for it
abuses the integrity of the process and cheapens the intellectual tools of
the trade. This cannot be said, however, of the two cases that follow
because, although they give opposite answers to virtually identical facts,
they were decided by the same judges on the same day:

Whitton v. *Garner* [1965] 1 All E.R. 70 (Divisional Court, Q.B.D.)

BRABIN J. delivered the first judgment at the invitation of LORD PARKER
C.J.
This is an appeal by way of Case Stated from a decision by the justices for the
county of Lancaster sitting at Bolton. They heard a summons under the
Affiliation Proceedings Act, 1957, by the respondent, who maintained that the
appellant was the putative father of her child. The respondent is, and at all
material times was, a married woman, and the point that arises is whether a
married woman can be a single woman within the meaning of s. 1 of the
Affiliation Proceedings Act, 1957 [which provided for claims for maintenance
to be made by a single woman against the putative father of her child]. That is
a matter which has been decided many times in the affirmative. In this particular
case, at the time when the summons was taken out the respondent was living
in the same house as her husband. She gave evidence before the Justices, and
the justices found as a fact on that evidence, that for four years she had

occupied a separate bedroom in the house in which both parties lived and that she and her husband had lived separate and apart during the whole of that time. The respondent gave further evidence, and a finding of fact was made by the justices in respect of it, that the child had been registered by the respondent's husband as his child, but that such registration was made without the respondent's consent, approval or knowledge.

It is submitted on behalf of the appellant that the justices could not come to the finding that the respondent was a single woman within the meaning of s. 1, because she and her husband were both living in the same house. It is urged further that there is a rule of law that the magistrates cannot, in such circumstances, act on the evidence of the respondent complainant unless that part of her evidence is corroborated. I know of no such rule of law. The rule of law in respect of corroboration is by statute laid down in s. 4(2) of the Act of 1957. There is no rule of law specifically relating to s. 1 of the Act. Clearly, when a husband and wife are living in the same house, it is much more difficult for a wife in those circumstances to establish that she is a single woman within the meaning of s. 1 of the Act of 1957. This matter was dealt with by this court in *Watson* v. *Tuckwell* (1947) 63 T.L.R. at p. 635, when LORD GODDARD C.J. said:

> 'I agree that if a husband and wife are found living under the same roof, it is prima facie evidence that the parties are living together; but it is no more than prima facie evidence. It is evidence that can be rebutted, and if the justices are satisfied that it has been rebutted they are justified in finding that there was a de facto separation. It is clearly a question of fact, and, in my opinion, there is evidence upon which they could find that fact.'

Applying that direction to this particular appeal, the evidence of the respondent that she lived separate and apart from her husband over this period of four years and that, during that time, there had been no access to her by her husband, was evidence which the justices could accept or reject. The justices accepted that evidence, and it appears from the Case Stated that, on these material matters in the respondent's evidence, no cross-examination was addressed to the respondent in respect of them. The prima facie presumption that exists when husband and wife are living in the same house was rebutted in this case to the satisfaction of the justices and, in my judgment, the justices were right in holding that, on the evidence called before them, the respondent was a single woman within the meaning of s. 1 of the Act of 1957. I, therefore, consider that this appeal should be dismissed.

ASHWORTH J.: I agree.

LORD PARKER C.J.: I also agree.

Giltrow v. *Day* [1965] 1 All E.R. 73 (Divisional Court, Q.B.D.)

Case Stated.

This was a Case Stated by justices of the county of Middlesex Quarter Sessions in respect of their adjudication on an appeal sitting at The Guildhall, Westminster, London, on 20 March 1964. On that day the respondent, Ivor Day, appeared before the justices of the county of Middlesex Quarter Sessions as appellant against an order made by the magistrates' court sitting at Ealing on 6 February 1964, whereby the respondent was adjudged to be the putative father of a male child born to the appellant, Maureen Margaret Giltrow, on 8 May 1963, and the magistrates' court ordered that he pay to the appellant the weekly sum of £1 5s. towards the maintenance of the child until he reached the age of sixteen years. The general grounds of the appeal were stated to be that the order was made against the weight of evidence in that the respondent, on the evidence, could not have been held to be the putative father of the child, and that the order was wrong in law in that the appellant was not a single woman within the meaning of the Affiliation Proceedings Act, 1957. At the hearing of the appeal the first ground was not proceeded with, and the appeal was heard only on the preliminary issue of law before the justices, who allowed the appeal.

BRABIN J.: The justices who heard this appeal have carefully set out the facts as they find them in the case as stated. It is quite clear from their findings that the appellant and her husband had ceased to have sexual intercourse together or to occupy the same bedroom since August, 1961, and that, from that date, the appellant had not visited her husband's bedroom. The husband and wife lived together in a flat, and the flat was occupied by reason of an arrangement by which the appellant supplied services in respect of, no doubt, the main building. There were two children of the marriage, one who slept with the father and one who slept with the mother, and, when the mother became pregnant, the child who slept with her then moved into the husband's bedroom. The finances of the household were provided by the husband, as they had always been, and the appellant bought the food and cooked the meal which the husband ate daily in the house. The husband always prepared his own breakfast, and his mid-day meal was eaten away from home. These arrangements existed before, and were continued after, the parties occupied separate bedrooms. There is no doubt that the appellant and her husband were not living in amity; they each went their separate ways. The one manifestation of that after August, 1961, when the marriage in the normal circumstances might be said to have broken down, was that the appellant ceased to do the mending of the husband's clothes or to clean his bedroom, but a cleaner was provided who did the latter. There was further evidence as found by the justices that, on one occasion and one only at Christmas, 1963, when the appellant was entertaining some friends, the husband unexpectedly insinuated himself into the party and dispensed the drinks. This method of living, which continued after August, 1961, was found to have so continued because both parties acquiesced in it.... . On the facts found by the justices, I consider that the justices hearing the appeal were wholly justified in finding that the presumption existing in these circumstances [that a husband and wife living under the same roof are living together] was not rebutted, and that, therefore, the appellant was not a single woman within the meaning of the Affiliation Proceedings Act, 1957.

Question

What appear to have been the critical differences between this and the previous case which explain the different result arrived at? Were they sufficient in your view to justify the distinction drawn?

(c) What weight should be given to the precedent?

Having determined the status of the precedent as ratio or dictum and whether, and if so to what extent, it is in point, the lawyer will now wish to scrutinise the precedent minutely for its true worth. The process is similar to that of assaying precious metals. He will take into account a number of different considerations:

(1) Which court decided the case?

Other things being equal, the higher the court in the hierarchy the greater its authority.

(2) Which judges were involved?

All judges are equal but some are a little more equal than others. Not much can be made of this point, however, unless the judge(s) who decided the case were in the rare category regarded by the profession as being of special eminence – Lord Atkin, Lord Justice Scrutton, Lord Reid are three examples. Apart from the few luminaries, counsel is usually wise to avoid making invidious distinctions between the reputations of former judges.

(3) Was there a dissent?

The existence of any dissenting opinions would affect the weight of a decision, especially, of course, if the dissenting judge(s) were of particular eminence.

(4) When was the case decided?

If the precedent is old, one side no doubt will argue that it reflects well-settled law whilst the other will contend that it is no longer apt for modern conditions. Something may then turn on whether or not it has been challenged in previous cases. Every time that a precedent is put to the test of argument and emerges unscathed it develops new roots and accordingly to that extent becomes harder to dislodge. If, on the other hand, it has stood unchallenged, one side will suggest that this shows that its roots are shallow and flimsy whilst the other will argue that the fact of no challenge over a long period demonstrates the strength of the rule – it was so clear and so deeply rooted that no one even thought to contest the point.[3]

---

3   For discussion of relevant authorities see 'The Aged Precedent', *Scottish Law Times*, 1965, p. 53.

(5)   How does the precedent fit with the surrounding law?

Sometimes it can be argued that the precedent is based on faulty reasoning, or illogically drawn analogies, or that it is at odds with other, better established principles.

(6)   How has the decision been dealt with in later cases?

There are various possibilities:

(a) It may have been *overruled* by the decision of a higher court that it was wrongly decided. Overruling can be explicit or implicit. The former is clear and has the effect of removing the precedent entirely from the field of play – subject only to the possibility of being brought back into the game if a still higher court decides that it was, after all, rightly decided. Implied overruling occurs where it is arguable that the decision cannot stand with a later decision of a higher court. But this contention often meets determined counter-argument.

(b) The precedent, whilst not being overruled, may nevertheless have been undermined either by direct aspersions cast upon it by judges in later cases or because it was not applied to factual situations that appeared to be well within the scope of the principle for which it stands (*not following* or *restrictive distinguishing*).

(c) On the other hand, it may have been approved and followed in later cases and expanded by being applied to new factual situations not apparently within the contemplation or the scope of the principle as first framed.

(7)   What reputation does the precedent enjoy generally?

Any published comment on the case or the principle of law for which it stands could be significant in either strengthening or weakening its authority. The case may have been the subject of discussion in some scholarly writings. It may have given rise to problems in the community of which the courts could be made aware. Suggestions may have been made for the reform of the rule by law-reform bodies. Any such indications may create a climate of opinion about a precedent which can be turned to advantage by one or other side in litigation.

An academic study attempted to assess the influences that are likely to weigh most heavily with the judges in the House of Lords. Interviews with the Law Lords themselves suggested that the source of critical evaluations which were most influential were the views of other Law Lords, very much more than either those of academic writers or those expressed by counsel.[4]

4   Alan Paterson, *The Law Lords* (1982), p. 33.

(d)   Inconvenience and injustice

Counsel arguing a case is permitted to assert that a precedent has had unhappy consequences or, alternatively, that such consequences would ensue if the court adopted the rule proposed by his opponent. But counsel is not normally permitted to offer *evidence* as to the consequences of any existing or proposed formulation of law. He may not even cite official reports, statistics, or other economic or social data on the matter. The only exception is foreign law. Expert witnesses, normally practitioners in the foreign system, are permitted to testify on oath as to the prevailing state of the law on the matter in contention in the foreign country concerned. Foreign law, therefore, is treated as matter of fact to be proved by evidence. English law by contrast is something of which the court takes judicial notice.

The 'Brandeis brief'

In the United States, for most of this century, the courts have taken a more expansive attitude to the problem of providing information to courts about the present or likely future effects of rules of law. This technique of argument is called the 'Brandeis brief' – after the later Supreme Court justice, Louis Brandeis, who first introduced it:

Alpheus Thomas Mason, *Brandeis* (1956), pp. 248–51

> ... in 1907, Mrs Florence Kelly and Miss Josephine Goldmark learned that the Oregon ten-hour law for Women was to be contested before the United States Supreme Court. To defend the law, these women wanted the most competent legal talent in the land... . The next day they asked Brandeis, who accepted at once ...
>
> The invitation was gladly extended. Brandeis then outlined the material needed for his brief. The legal part he would himself cover in a few pages. For the economic and social data showing the evil of long hours and the possible benefits from legislative limitation, he would look to his sister-in-law. It was on these materials, not on the legal argument, that he would base his case.
>
> This was a bold innovation... . Many years earlier he had recorded in his *Index Rerum*: 'A judge is presumed to know the elements of law, but there is no presumption that he knows the facts.' In this spirit he drew up his revolutionary social and economic brief... .
>
> Brandeis's brief-making enormously extended the bounds of common knowledge and compelled the court to 'take judicial notice' of this extension. In the Muller brief only two scant pages were given to conventional legal arguments. Over one hundred pages were devoted to the new kind of evidence drawn from hundreds of reports, both domestic and foreign, of committees, statistical bureaux, commissioners of hygiene, and factory inspectors – all proving that, long hours are *as a matter of fact* dangerous to women's health, safety and

morals, that short hours result in social and economic benefits.

Brandeis appeared in oral argument in January 1908, before a court dominated by superannuated legalists, including Chief Justice Fuller, Justices Peckham, Brewer, and Day. The 'dry bones of legalism rattled' as opposing counsel argued that women were endowed, equally with men, with the fundamental right of free contract, that woman's 'freedom' to bargain with employers must not be impaired. This time, however, the court could not be screened from all knowledge of the living world… .

The Oregon ten-hour law was upheld, and the court, speaking through Justice Brewer, approved Brandeis's technique and, most unusually, mentioned him by name. The court's spokesman, Justice Brewer, said:

> 'In the brief filed by Mr Louis D. Brandeis … is a very copious collection of all these matters… .
>
> 'The legislation and opinions referred to in the margin may not be, technically speaking, authorities, and in them is little or no discussion of the constitutional question presented to us for determination, yet they are significant of a widespread belief that woman's physical structure, and the functions she performs in consequence thereof, justify special legislation restricting or qualifying the conditions under which she should be permitted to toil.'

Here for the first time the Supreme Court was recognising the need for facts to establish the reasonableness or unreasonableness of social legislation. For the time being the court had rejected its own freedom-of-contract fiction as regards working women. Brandeis followed up this advantage immediately. After the Muller case he appeared for oral argument in defence of other labour laws and sent briefs to some fourteen different courts.

The value of the Brandeis brief approach to legal argument can be seen in one of the rare English cases in which the court admitted, and appeared to have been decisively influenced by, evidence on a matter of law derived from statistics. In *Nowotnik* v. *Nowotnik* [1967] P. 83 the Court of Appeal had given an extremely narrow interpretation to a provision in the Legal Aid Act 1964 designed to compensate the successful defendant who had the misfortune to be sued by a legally aided plaintiff. The section provided that such a person could ask to have his costs paid out of the legal aid fund if he could show that he would otherwise suffer 'severe financial hardship'. N., the husband, was the successful respondent in divorce proceedings. He claimed under the Act. His costs had been £345. His capital was £5 17s 9d; he earned £24 a week as a manual labourer; he had a car and had had two holidays in Germany. The court (Lord Denning and four other lords justices) held that there was insufficient evidence of severe financial hardship. The husband's capital admittedly was low but he had not had to restrict his activities. They rejected his claim.

Three years later precisely the same issue came up in *Hanning* v. *Maitland (No. 2)* [1970] 1 Q.B. 580. The successful defendant had an earned income of £18 or £19 gross, and savings of between £2,500 and

£3,000. The costs he was claiming from the fund were £325. Lord Denning, delivering judgment as he had in *Nowotnik*, said that the court had been given some figures by counsel for the Law Society who appeared as *amicus curiae* (friend of the court – see p. 358 below). These showed the sums set aside each year in the legal aid accounts, for payments expected to be made out of the fund under the 1964 Act. In the first three years the Law Society had estimated the expected payments and the government had paid into the fund the sum of £40,000 a year against this liability. The payments out in the three years were £74, £838 and £243 respectively (*Nowotnik* was decided in the middle of the second year.) Lord Denning (at 587) said, 'Those figures show one of two things: either that the Act itself was badly worded so that it did not give effect to the intention of the makers of it; or the courts have interpreted it wrongly so as to defeat the intention of Parliament. I am afraid that it is the second. We can and should learn by experience. In the light of it, I must confess that this court in *Nowotnik* v. *Nowotnik* interpreted the Act wrongly.' The court gave the defendant his costs, and so changed the interpretation of the phrase 'severe financial hardship' that in 1972 an insurance company was able to claim successfully under the Act – see *General Accident Fire and Life Assurance Ltd* v. *Foster* [1972] 3 All E.R. 877. (The case is also another example of the Court of Appeal unanimously declining to follow one of its own previous decisions despite the clear indications of *Young* v. *Bristol Aeroplane Ltd.* Lord Denning referred specifically to the point by saying that the Court of Appeal was *not* bound by its own decisions; Lord Justice Salmon did not allude to the problem; Lord Justice Edmund Davies, somewhat disingenuously, said he was not 'conscious of departing substantially from the test of "severe financial hardship" laid down in *Nowotnik*'!)

A different example of the court being influenced by statistics in formulating a legal principle was *Haley* v. *London Electricity Board* [1964] 3 All E.R. 185 involving the duty of care owed to a blind person. The House of Lords referred to evidence that one in five hundred persons in London were blind in support of the proposition that it was reasonably foreseeable that a blind person would be affected by an obstacle in the street.

In *R* v. *Preston Supplementary Benefits Appeal Tribunal, ex p. Moore* [1975] 1 W.L.R. 624 information concerning the working of the supplementary benefit system was presented to the Court of Appeal. In *R* v. *Lord Chancellor, ex p. Witham* [1997] 2 All E.R. 779 the Public Law Project was permitted to submit a supporting affidavit which read 'more like a Brandeis brief than evidence in support of the individual application'[5].

5   Rosalind English, 'Wrongfooting the Lord Chancellor: Access to Justice in the High Court' [1998] 61 M.L.R. 245, 251.

Since *Pepper* v. *Hart* one can also use Parliamentary debates to inform courts of legislative facts. This may become of particular importance when the Human Rights Act 1998 is implemented.[6] In *R* v. *Ministry of Defence, ex p. Smith* [1996] 1 All E.R. 257 Lord Justice Henry said (at 272): '[I]f the [European Human Rights] convention were to be made... part of our domestic law, then in the exercise of the primary jurisdiction, the court in, for it, a relatively novel constitutional position, might well ask for more material than the adversarial system normally provides, such as a 'Brandeis brief'.

Questions

Is there any valid reason for excluding evidence in the form of factual information about the background to disputed legal rules? If it were permitted, how could it be controlled so as to prevent the court being swamped? Should it be confined to written material or should it include oral evidence? (See further, p. 357 below for consideration of the American practice of having *amicus* briefs from non-parties to litigation, and p. 360 for the American practice of having written briefs to supplement oral argument.

2. PREPARATION AND DELIVERY OF JUDGMENTS

(a) Extempore judgments

One of the peculiar features of English judicial method by comparison with that of most other countries is the high proportion of cases in which the judges deliver their judgments 'off-the-cuff' immediately after the case is over. This is so even in the Court of Appeal. The Bowman *Review of the Court of Appeal (Civil Division)*, 1997, said that the percentage of Court of Appeal judgments that are reserved has fluctuated in recent years between about one quarter and one third. (Para. 47, p. 90.) The House of Lords always reserves judgment.

(When a court reserves judgment this is indicated in the law reports by the phrase *Cur. adv. vult.*) It is rare for counsel to make much of this point as a factor in evaluating the weight of the precedent, but a revealing

---

6   See Andrew Henderson, 'Brandeis briefs and the proof of legislative facts in proceedings under the Human Rights Act 1998', *Public Law*, 1998, 563–71.

lecture by Lord Justice Russell suggests that more attention might well be paid to this point:

Sir Charles Russell, 'Behind the Appellate Curtain', Holdsworth Club Lecture, 1969, pp. 3–8

It is important in considering appellate judgments to differentiate between reserved judgments and unreserved judgments. The quality of the former is, or should be, better than that of the latter. Many may think that in the Court of Appeal judgment should be more often reserved, since in I suppose 95% of cases it is in fact a judgment of the court of final decision. I would not dissent from that view. Some appellate judges have a great ability for stating the relevant facts without significant omission or error, and I think those with a background of summing up to juries in criminal cases have an advantage in this respect. Others – among whom I number myself – find some difficulty in giving judgment off the cuff, and would prefer reservation of judgments more frequently. But it must be recognised that the pressure of civil appellate business discourages the practice of reservation of judgments.

Accordingly I take, first, academic consideration by academic lawyers and others of reserved judgments of the Court of Appeal. The production of these may involve different combinations of events. Suppose that in general terms all three judges are at the end in agreement on the outcome. Away they go and write their judgments in draft and circulate them. Here sometimes is the crunch. Lord Justice Frog does not altogether approve of a particular ratiocination of Lord Justice Toad. What does he do? This is apt to depend upon the state of Frog, L.J.'s work. If he is busy – and he may now be sitting in a different division of the C.A. with its own problems – he may be content to leave his judgment to stand without arguing the toss or trying to persuade Toad, L.J. to amend his judgment. Or he may add to his judgment words of doubt of the proposition of Toad, L.J. Now what happens? In the latter case lawyers – and not only academic lawyers – hasten to point out that Frog, L.J. took the opposite view. But in fact Frog, L.J. in his mind has done no more than *suspect* the proposition. He has not had the time to discuss the proposition with Toad, L.J. – one or other has had a committee meeting at 4.30 p.m. every evening for a fortnight, and Frog, L.J. lives in West Sussex. In effect the apparent dissent of Frog, L.J. should not be regarded as anything except an undigested reservation that has no persuasive value in the formation of legal principles. It should do no more than encourage a critical approach to the views of Toad, L.J. If he leaves it alone, this should not be taken as wholehearted agreement. Take another case of reserved judgments. There may be a full scale battle behind the scenes between Frog, L.J. and Toad, L.J. on some matter of principle, with Slug, L.J. a trifle out of his depth and relatively disinterested, but on the whole prepared to march with Toad, L.J. in the decision. Now in such a case Frog and Toad read each other's drafts. Frog observes in Toad what he considers to be gross heresy and amends his draft in a manner calculated to expose it as such, hoping that thus he will bring Toad to his senses. Undeterred, Toad fortifies his draft by analogy with other branches of the law. Frog is drawn unwillingly into this new field, and by postponing his first gin and catching the late train to West Sussex works hard at it for his third draft. Toad, L.J. – who lives in London and never touches gin – produces an amendment digging into ancient authorities including a resounding declaration about the turn of the century that has in fact (unknown to him because this tangential approach to the problem was never discussed by counsel) been later roundly disapproved. Frog, L.J. reads the amended judgment of Toad and is too busy to trouble further. What happens? Slug, L.J. agrees in general terms with Toad, L.J. Frog, L.J. has not objected to the reliance on the turn of the century declaration. And, lo and behold! it has apparently been reinstated as the law. This is an example that should warn us all that when in search of the law as authoritatively propounded by an appellate court (1) it is important to stick to what was necessarily said for the decision of the particular case, and (2) silence does not necessarily mean consent.

The latter point is even more relevant in the case of *unreserved judgments* in the Court of Appeal, and most particular caution is to be recommended in such cases. It must be realised that when the shorthand writer circulates transcripts of such judgments for correction he sends only the individual transcript to the individual Lord Justice. It is true that reported cases are entire: but speaking for myself I only check my own judgments in proof, being sufficiently hard put to remember what I had said.

Envisage, please, the production of unreserved judgments in the C.A. Ordinarily the first judgment is delivered by the presiding Lord Justice. Of course in many cases the way the minds are working on the bench has been to a greater or lesser extent displayed in the course of exchanges during the argument. If there has been an adjournment during the case no doubt the members of the Court have discussed the progress of the case and have exchanged tentative views on the points emerging. But in the end the moment arrives when judgment is to be given. Often a short huddle is to be observed in the face of the public. Sometimes – and I think with more dignity – the Court adjourns for a few minutes. But, whatever the discussion, in many cases Frog, L.J. is never quite sure how Toad, L.J. will express himself; and Slug, L.J. is unsure about both, however much they may all be agreed on dismissing or allowing the appeal. Toad, L.J. leads off. Slug, L.J. as the junior has decided to say nothing of his own. Frog, L.J. has decided to say a little piece of his own. Consider the situation of Frog, L.J. who prefers to jot down his thoughts. With his right hand and most of his brain he is doing this. With his left ear and the rest of his brain he is at the same time trying to follow what Toad, L.J. is saying – not really an easy exercise. All too often Frog, L.J. is rash enough to start his judgment with the words 'I agree'. Really he means by this that he agrees with the order proposed and that he has not been able to detect in what he has grasped of the judgment of Toad, L.J. any errors, or any error that he is able at such short notice to denounce as such or refute. But what happens? Other lawyers – and I do not confine them to the writers of text books or articles or the teachers of youth – pick upon those two introductory words and claim for some proposition the weighty authority of not only Toad, L.J. but also Frog, L.J. Whereas in truth Toad, L.J. had a brilliant notion half way through a sentence, a notion that he much later rather regretted, and Frog, L.J. never heard the notion, or having heard assumed that he had misheard or was unwilling to produce an undigested disclaimer. Moreover, even if Frog, L.J. follows the cautious practice – one that I approve myself – of never starting with 'I agree', but if anything at all with the phrase 'I agree that this appeal fails/succeeds', what happens? It is said by others that Frog, L.J. did not dissent from or disagree with what was said by Toad, L.J., therefore he must be taken to have agreed. And what of Slug, L.J. who had decided to say nothing original? He was as a result able to listen to everything that was said by the other two. But suppose that he heard from them or one of them something with which he was not altogether happy? Poor Slug is in rather a fix. Is he to recite his objections, which anyway he finds it difficult to formulate at short notice, and add 'otherwise I agree'? Or suppose he prefers the way in which Frog, L.J. has put it to that of Toad, L.J.? Does he say that for the reasons given by Frog, L.J. he agrees with the order proposed by Toad, L.J.? Even more delicate is his position if he happens to be Slug, L.J. standing in for Grub, L.J. who has been taken away from his proper task in order to conduct an enquiry on a subject on which he has no expertise, because the government is anxious not to carry the burden of decision? In the end Slug, L.J. or J. contents himself with saying tersely 'I agree' – though he may, frequently with every justification, continue 'and there is nothing I can usefully add', an addendum that denies its own function... .

Now what is the moral of all this? For my address, so far, though based upon the principle that a light touch sometimes illuminates, is intended to seek a moral. As I see it it is one not only for the teacher and text book writer but also for the practitioner. In particular in the case of unreserved judgments weight should be attributed only to pronouncements that in express terms approve of other pronouncements, and with particularity rather than generality. All else should be suspect in point of value... .

(b) Judgments in the House of Lords

Little has been known in this country about the processes that take place behind the scenes in the preparation of reserved judgments by the Law Lords. But some knowledge of the matter is now available from Professor Alan Paterson's book *The Law Lords* (1982). According to his account (pp. 92–121), the Law Lords generally have a first conference about the case immediately it has finished. If the argument finishes before one of the times when the judges adjourn – e.g. before 1 p.m. or 4 p.m. – they will normally meet in the same committee room where the argument was heard. The presiding Law Lord asks each of his brethren (starting with the most junior) to state their preliminary views. It is rare for these to be a surprise to their colleagues because usually their views have become plain during the course of the oral argument – either in the court room itself or in the corridors or robing rooms where the judges commonly chat about cases as they develop.

If they are not unanimous the presiding judge asks whether anyone wishes to change his mind, and debate often ensues. There is then discussion as to who should write a speech (as judgments in the House of Lords are called). Sometimes it is agreed that one speech should be written on behalf of all – though agreement to this effect does not then prevent any judge from changing his mind and writing a separate speech. The decision as to who should write the single or the leading opinion emerges from discussion. It is not the tradition according to Paterson (p. 92) that the presiding judge should allocate the task – though obviously, depending on his personality, he may have considerable influence on the outcome of this decision.

Obviously, a judge can only write an opinion which will be concurred in by his brethren if they agree with his reasons. If they agree with the result but for different reasons they will normally write their own speeches and if they disagree with the result they will write a dissent. Sometimes judges write their own speeches even when they wholly or mainly agree with both the result and reasons.

Paterson says (p. 93) that the first conference tends to last about half an hour, 'though some may be over in ten minutes, while others … may go on for up to two hours'. There is then the drafting stage which tends to last about six weeks (in the Supreme Court of the United States it commonly takes many months). When ready, the speeches are circulated to the others who took part in the case – never to anyone else. Sometimes one judge (or more) who has written an opinion decides that what he wanted to say has been said better by someone else and withdraws his own speech. Sometimes, on the contrary, a judge who thought that he would not need to write a separate opinion decides that after all he should do so.

The speeches are eventually printed in order of seniority of the judges but this does not necessarily mean that the order in which they were produced is the same.

The judges interviewed by Professor Paterson were divided as to whether it was good or not to have multiple opinions. But a large majority favoured having several speeches in common law hard cases while there was considerable support for a norm of single speeches in criminal appeals – especially those based on points of statutory construction (p. 98).

Judges varied as to whether or not to make public a dissent. Sometimes they did not do so in the belief that it was better that the court should speak with one voice. The dissent was written with the objective of persuading the other judges; that having failed, the dissenting judge gave up the struggle. About half of the sample of Law Lords interviewed by Paterson agreed at least to some extent with the view that judges should exercise a measure of self-restraint in publishing their dissents – that resorting too frequently to the right to dissent created uncertainty in the law. Even Lord Denning said, 'I don't think any of us would want to dissent unless we felt strongly about it… . I don't dissent unless I feel sufficiently strongly in a sense' (p. 102).

Lord Radcliffe thought that attitudes had changed somewhat. When he first went to the Lords in 1949, 'there was a bit of an olde-worlde feeling, you know, that we all ought to hang together and you oughtn't to expose the differences in the House of Lords because it weakened its authority' (p. 103). But by the time he retired in 1964 that view no longer prevailed. Many of the judges agreed that the right to individual expression was more important than any pressure to present a united front.

The role of the presiding judge in the Supreme Court has often been described as being of critical importance. Commentators speak of 'the Warren court' or 'the Burger court'. There has never been any equivalent in the House of Lords. The senior judge presides every time he sits but he plays no equivalent role to that in the US Supreme Court. He does not provide intellectual leadership; he does not seek to impose his views; he does not regard it as his responsibility to reconcile differences between the judges or to achieve any particular result. Occasionally, of course, any of these things may occur, but it is not a normal part of the business of being the senior judge. Paterson concludes: '[T]he prevailing ethos on these matters in the House of Lords is that of laissez faire. By and large it is up to the individual Law Lord whether he writes or not, and whether he dissents or not. Except in a small minority of appeals the support for unity in the court is only tentative; there is little resistance to dissents on the ground that they are detrimental to the authority of the court and attempts to reconcile differences in the court are the exception rather than the rule' (pp. 108–9).

Bargaining between the justices of the US Supreme Court is common (for a vivid description of the process see B. Woodward and S. Armstrong, *The Brethren* (1979)). They bargain (sometimes passionately) over their votes and the content of their judgments. In the House of Lords each judge tends much more to go his own way.

For a similar verdict on decision-making by the Law Lords see David Robertson, *Judicial Discretion in the House of Lords* (Clarendon, Oxford, 1998). Robertson says that it is rare for there to be a second meeting after the initial discussion at the close of the oral argument for reconsideration or discussion of drafts. Opinions, he suggests, are circulated 'for information, not for discussion'. It is rare for draft opinions to be altered. 'To an extent vastly greater than seems to be the case in equivalent courts, the Law Lords make their law as individuals' (pp. 15–16). 'In a real sense the Lords seldom argue, because they do not address each other's points. Only relatively rarely will a dissenting opinion actually take on the logic of the majority and try to rebuff it.' (P. 77.)

Robertson's book also raises important issues on the delicate question as to which particular judges sit in the House of Lords and the process by which they are selected for the actual case. This issue surfaced dramatically in December 1998 in the context of the appeal over the extradition to Spain of the former Chilean dictator General Pinochet. The first decision of the House of Lords (*R* v. *Bow Street Metropolitan Stipendiary Magistrate, ex p. Pinochet Ugarte* [1998] 4 All E.R. 897) had to be set aside by the House of Lords and a new hearing ordered when it emerged that Lord Hoffmann had failed to reveal his involvement with Amnesty International which was an intervenor in the case. (Lord Hoffmann was a Director and Chairman of Amnesty International Charity Limited, an Amnesty fund-raising company.) Since the first decision that General Pinochet did not have immunity from extradition as a former Head of State had been by a bare majority of three to two the case threw into high relief the significance of the identity of individual judges in a case.

Virtually nothing is known about the process that leads to the selection of the judges for a particular case. (In the first Pinochet hearing in the House of Lords it seems that the five judges were chosen simply because they were already scheduled to hear another case due to begin on that day which was postponed on account of the urgency of the Pinochet case. It is safe to assume that for the second hearing when seven judges sat the senior and presiding judge, Lord Browne-Wilkinson, had a considerable influence on the selection.)

The significance of the selection of the individual judge for the case was confirmed in David Robertson's book, the main purpose of which was to develop the thesis that the judges in the House of Lords have almost unlimited freedom in their decision-making. Basing himself on a statistical analysis of decisions by 15 judges in the years from 1986 to 1995 he demonstrates that it is predictable which way a case will be decided by reference simply to what combination of judges is sitting on the appeal. So the selection of the judges really matters – though the degree of predictability varied somewhat from subject area to subject area. (It was highest in constitutional cases.)

3. ARE PRECEDENTS LAW OR ONLY EVIDENCE OF THE LAW?

There is an important jurisprudential debate as to whether judges make law or whether they simply declare the law, and whether precedents are law or only evidence of the law. The two issues are closely related.

In the eighteenth century, Blackstone said: 'the decisions of courts of justice are the evidence of what is common law'.[7] In 1892 Lord Esher stated: 'There is in fact no such thing as judge-made law, for the judges do not make the law though they frequently have to apply existing law to circumstances as to which it has not previously been authoritatively laid down that such law is applicable'.[8] According to the late Professor Cross these views are mistaken. A rule stated in a precedent, he argued, 'is law

7   *Commentaries* (13th edn) vol. i, pp. 88–9.
8   *Willis* v. *Baddeley* [1892] 2 Q.B. 324 at 326.

properly so called and law because it was made by the judges, not because it originated in common usage, or the judge's idea of justice and public convenience.'[9] So far as Lord Esher's statement was concerned, the application of existing law to new circumstances could never clearly be distinguished from the creation of a new rule of law. If there were no such thing as judge-made law, it would be impossible to account for the evolution of much legal doctrine which had been formulated by the judges and no one but the judges.[10]

> 'If a previous decision were only evidence of what the law is, no judge could ever be absolutely bound to follow it, and it could never be effectively overruled because a subsequent judge might always treat it as having some evidential value.'[11]

But this is not entirely convincing. Of course there cannot be any cavil with Cross's statement that 'the fact that our judges can and do make law is now universally recognised by writers on the British Constitution.'[12] As Lord Radcliffe said: '... there was never a more sterile controversy than that upon the question whether a judge makes law. Of course he does. How can he help it?'[13] But this leaves open the question whether there is not also merit in the declaratory theory of law and in the theory that precedents are evidence of law rather than law itself.

When a judge decides a point of law, he is declaring what he finds the law on that point to be. He is not saying what he thinks it ought to be but what he believes it is. In giving voice to his opinion as to what the law is, he may have added something new to the existing corpus of the law. In fact, unless he has simply restated an existing principle or applied it in a totally predictable way to new facts, he *will* have done so. Many decisions on points of law add something new in this sense and can therefore be said to be 'making law'. From the judge's point of view, his function is to declare the law; from the point of view of the observer, he may in declaring it have added something new or even changed the law. The 'declaratory theory' and the 'judges-do-make-law theory' therefore appear both to be right.

But there is a further dimension. It is possible that the judge, having stated what he thinks the law to be, proves to be in error. He may be reversed almost immediately on appeal or his ratio may be overruled in a later case by a higher court. This shows that inspection of a precedent at the time when it is handed down does not necessarily reveal whether the

9   Cross, *Precedent in English Law* (3rd edn, 1977), p. 27.
10   Ibid.
11   Ibid., p. 28.
12   Ibid., p. 29.
13   Radcliffe, *Not in Feather Beds* (1968), p. 215.

precedent reflects 'good law'. This will only emerge later when, with the advantage of hindsight, one will be able to say that the judge in 1976 stated what judges in the succeeding two or three decades agreed was the law on that point. Even then, fifty years later a different view may prevail.

The theory that precedents are no more than evidence of the law has the advantage that it seems to fit the facts. It explains one of the most fundamental and important aspects of the doctrine of precedent – that every principle that emerges from a judicial decision is capable of being changed. However well settled a principle of law may appear to be, it can be challenged and changed at any time. Even if the House of Lords itself has enunciated the rule, it can now be altered by the House of Lords. In other words, it is possible to look at the rule of law that seems to emerge from a precedent and say 'That cannot be right and to prove it I shall litigate the point up to a higher court to get the rule changed.'

Moreover, whenever a rule of law is enunciated by a court, its effect is retrospective. The rule is now the law and in theory always has been. Any different previous formulations of the rule were mistaken. The retrospective effect of the new rule is of course fiction – but it has the practical result that a person may bring an action based on an injury suffered before the new rule and claim the benefit of the new formulation. The only exceptions are where the case has already been litigated (in which case the doctrine of *res judicata* prevents the issue being reopened), and where the Statute of Limitations operates to bar the action through the lapse of time. (An action for personal injuries, for instance, cannot normally be brought more than three years after the injury has been suffered). However, the theory that precedents are only evidence of the law is consistent with the reality that what is thought to be the law at one time may turn out to be wrong.

Professor Cross objected that if a previous decision were only evidence of what the law is, no judge could be bound to follow it and it could never be effectively overruled – because some other judge might always treat it as having some evidential value. But the doctrine of precedent can be said to operate something like the best-evidence rule in the law of evidence – that the court wishes always to have the best evidence on any issue. The doctrine of precedent lays down rules as to how the courts should approach precedents. A decision of the House of Lords, other things being equal, is better evidence than one of the Court of Appeal, etc. Moreover, so far as the Court of Appeal is concerned, a decision of the House of Lords is not only the best evidence of what the law is, but creates an irrebuttable presumption that it is correct. On the other hand, the House of Lords reviewing its own prior decision will treat the precedent as the best extant evidence of the rule, but the presumption that it is right is rebuttable since the House of Lords is free to depart from its own prior decisions. Equally there is no difficulty with the problem of overruling. Again, the doctrine of precedent acts, in effect, to prohibit a court from receiving as evidence a decision that has been overruled. The exclusion of otherwise admissible evidence is a familiar principle of the law of evidence.

The view that precedents are evidence of the law and not the law itself is not only consistent with the innate flexibility and fluidity of the common law system, but also reflects the actual practice of the courts. Argument in a court as to what the law is, is based on marshalling by each side of its proofs – counsel comes armed with his precedents or his reinterpretation of his opponent's precedents and submits that his view of the law is the correct one. Having heard each side, the judge decides between them. To say that the precedents *are* the law is the equivalent of saying that the witnesses to a question of fact are the truth. Whether the precedents reflect the law cannot emerge authoritatively until after the judge has spoken and even then only in the partial and qualified sense that at most the decision reflects the best evidence available at that moment as to what the law is.

There is a somewhat similar dispute as to whether the rules of precedent are themselves 'law' or 'rules of practice'. See on this issue, for instance, L. Goldstein, 'Four Alleged Paradoxes in Legal Reasoning', *Cambridge Law Journal,* 1979, p. 373; P. J. Evans, 'The Status of Rules of Precedent', *Cambridge Law Journal,* 1982, p. 162; C. E. F. Rickett, 'Precedent in the Court of Appeal', *Modern Law Review,* 1980, p. 136; P. Aldridge, 'Precedent in the Court of Appeal – Another View', *Modern Law Review,* 1984, p. 187.

It is a nice question whether our doctrine of precedent promotes law-making in too rapid a way by over-emphasising the importance of individual decisions. Whilst it is true that the ultimate shape of a rule cannot be fully discerned until it has had time to mature, there is nevertheless a tendency to dramatise the significance of the latest case. Lord Radcliffe has reflected on the dangers of this tendency:

Lord Radcliffe, *Not in Feather Beds* (1968), pp. 216–17

I cannot help thinking that there is a tendency today to give too much importance to particular decisions, and by so doing to discover leading cases before they have proved that they have in them the quality to lead. There is too much forcing of unripe growth. Seen from the inside hardly any decision comes out ready made as of general authority; nor, I believe, do those who participate in it think of it in that way. One learns the vast difficulty of generalising on any matter of principle, just because, short of genius, there are very few minds that have the imaginative grasp to see the full implications of a generalisation and to pass in review its effect upon the interconnected strands of our body of law. It is not a question of playing safe: it is rather that a sensitive, not a blinkered, concentration upon the direct issue that has to be resolved makes for sounder construction of that legal body. And, perhaps, only their successors who have to work upon them appreciate how flashy have been the gnomic utterances of some of our best known judicial sages.

I do not regret this counsel of reticence. It accords well with the methodology of our law-making. Just as under our system a court decision is formed out of the work of those who prepare a case, those who argue it before the court and those who ultimately explain and record their view, so a decision of even a final court, when pronounced, has only begun its life as a constituent of the full corpus of the law. It is a mistake, just because it is final, to think that the matter is then closed. On the contrary, it has been handed over to the care of the profession. It will be chewed over by barristers and solicitors, commented on in law journals, made the subject of moots and law lectures, reviewed by the writers of the legal text books. It will be read in the light of previous decisions, upon which it is itself a commentary: and it will be read in the light of later decisions, to which itself it forms a text. In the end, but only in the end, general legal opinion will come to assign to it a more or less determined place in the whole compendium of law, important or unimportant, formative or a dead end, malleable or rigid. Until a decision has been subjected to a process of this kind, in the course of which indeed it may come out wearing a very different air from that with which it entered and serving a purpose hardly intended by its authors, I should be reluctant to class it as a leading authority. We must not declare a vintage before it is made.

If you happen to share the rather sober view I am putting forward you may share too my strong feeling that contemporary comment tends to attach far too much weight to particular phrases or passages in the body of a decision. Analysis of this order is almost morbid in its intensity, and it can, so often, be only sterile skill and ingenuity. A man must work according to his material. The English language is peculiarly ill-adapted to such elaborate analysis, being, as we know, though copious and expressive, a pliable and shifting medium, in which even key words and phrases take shape and colour from their context and have no rigid internal structure of fixed meaning. The difficulty becomes that much the greater when the decision of a final court is conveyed not by a single pronouncement but in the separate deliveries of several judges. Then indeed a baffling task awaits the reader. Is one deliverance more leading than another, and, if so, how do you identify it? In course of time, no doubt, there will be selection through the operation of the kind of winnowing process that I have been describing. We all know how one particular speech or judgment comes to be regarded as the critical one, the one which is turned to as the core of the decisions. But time is needed for that. Again, does a particular passage in one of the judgments represent the hinge of the author's conclusion, and, if it serves as such for him, ought one to think that it so serves for others just because they agree with his general conclusion?

4. THE VALUES PROMOTED BY THE SYSTEM OF PRECEDENT

A catalogue of the values promoted by the common law system of precedent was drawn up by Professors Hart and Sacks of the Harvard Law School in their widely known but unpublished set of materials on the legal process:

Henry Hart and Albert M. Sacks, *The Legal Process* (Tentative edition, 1958, mimeographed), pp. 587–8

In furtherance of private ordering

(a) The desirability of enabling people to plan their affairs at the stage of primary private activity with the maximum attainable confidence that if they comply with the law as it has theretofore been announced, or can fairly be expected to be announced thereafter, they will not become entangled in litigation.

(b) The desirability of providing private counsel so far as possible with stable bases of reasoning. Think about this factor, in particular, from the point of view of efficient social engineering. The potential contribution of the legal profession in the avoidance of social friction is very large, is it not? A lawyer must have tools with which to work if he is to make this contribution.

(c) The desirability of encouraging the remedial processes of private settlement by minimising the incentives of the parties to try to secure from a different judge a different decision than has been given by the same or other judges in the past.

In furtherance of fair and efficient adjudication

(a) The desirability, from the point of view of the litigants, of expediting litigation and minimising its costs by sparing them the necessity of relitigating every relevant proposition in every case.

(b) The need, from the point of view of the judicial system, of facilitating the dispatch of business – indeed, the sheer impossibility of re-examining *de novo* every relevant proposition in every case.

(c) The need of discouraging a rush of litigation wherever there is a change of personnel on the bench.

(d) The desirability, from the point of view of fairness to the litigants, of securing a reasonable uniformity of decision throughout the judicial system, both at any given time and from one time to another.

(e) The desirability of promoting genuine impersonality of decision by minimising the elements of personal discretion, and of facilitating the operation of the check of professional criticism.

(f) The propriety of according respect to the conclusions of predecessor judges.

(g) The injustice of disappointing expectations fairly generated at the stage of primary private activity.

In furtherance of public confidence in the judiciary

(a) The desirability of maximising the acceptability of decisions, and the importance to this end of popular and professional confidence in (1) the impersonality of decisions and (2) their reasoned foundation, as manifested both by the respect accorded to them by successor judges and by their staying power.

(b) The necessity, considering the amorphous nature of the limits upon judicial power and the usual absence of an effective political check at the ballot box, that judges be subject to the discipline and the restraint of an obligation to build upon the prior law in a fashion which can withstand the test of professional criticism.

There are, however, various problems associated with law-making by judges and the doctrine of precedent, which have to be set against the positive aspects of the system:

(1) It over-emphasises the importance of individual decisions (see p. 287 above).
(2) It creates law which may upset expectations with no advance notice to those likely to be affected.
(3) The system depends on the accidents of litigation. A bad decision may stand for many years.
(4) It tends to be backward-looking and conservative, and therefore to be slow to respond to changing needs.
(5) Once a point has been decided at the level of the Court of Appeal or the House of Lords, it tends to remain the law whether or not it is apt for the situation.
(6) There are often technical problems associated with the fact that the judges give separate decisions so that it is difficult to ascertain what is the ratio. Or a judge may give several reasons for his decision so that again the ratio is obscure. Also the proliferation of precedents makes it difficult for lawyers to discover what the law is.
(7) The doctrine of precedent focuses attention on minute differences of fact between cases at the expense of consideration of principle and policy.

5. FLEXIBILITY AND STABILITY IN THE COMMON LAW SYSTEM

It is not the system but the judges that create the balance between flexibility and stability. Whether it is a good balance is for judgment in each country where the common law system operates. (More discussion of the problems posed by this question is presented in the next chapter.) But the system itself does permit both flexibility and stability. Inevitably with a system of precedent there is a strong tendency to follow the precedents whether they are binding or not and whether or not the precedent seems a wise one. A doctrine of precedent that progressed on the basis that precedents would only be followed when the court agreed with the decision reached in the earlier case, would be a weak doctrine. Equally it would dissipate much of the benefit of stability to which the system of precedent aspires. Professor Julius Stone expressed this tendency of the common law in memorable form in an article in 1959:

J. Stone, 'The Ratio of the Ratio Decidendi', 22 *Modern Law Review,* 1959, pp. 597–8

> The doctrine *of stare decisis,* in addition to whatever it may enjoin upon the intellect, certainly evokes an atmosphere and a mood to abide by ancient decisions, to follow the old ways, and conform to existing precedents. It suggests a condition of rest, even of stasis, a system of law whose content is more or less settled, the past content by past decisions, and the present and future content because they too are controlled by those past decisions. It implies the stability of the legal system along the stream of time, that despite all the vast social, economic and technological changes of the last eight or nine hundred years, society remains nevertheless in some meaningful sense under the governance of the same system of law.

On the other hand, there is no doubt that the doctrine does lead to the perpetuation, sometimes for long periods, of bad decisions. Not infrequently they are even widely recognised to be bad decisions, and yet the courts somehow lack the energy to change them.

However, the doctrine of precedent has many gaps to permit judges wishing to avail themselves of the opportunity to refuse to be crabbed by it:

(a) The House of Lords is not bound by its own decisions, nor is the High Court, and the Court of Appeal (Criminal Division) is only lightly bound.

(b) There appears to be a long list of exceptions to the rule that the Court of Appeal is bound by its own decisions (see pp. 213–14 above).

(c) The Judicial Committee of the Privy Council is not bound by its own decisions and the English courts sometimes prefer to follow its decisions in preference to inconsistent decisions from within the system by which they are technically bound.

(d) An unwelcome precedent can in the last resort be distinguished and thus be avoided.

(e) The appeal system allows *any* principle of common law to be challenged and thus changed by a court high enough in the hierarchy.

(f) If a decision is not binding it *need* not be followed.

Obviously, individual judges vary in their instincts – some are keener on stability, others prefer to emphasise the objective of keeping the law abreast of changing times. But each type of judge usually can find the means to achieve his purpose within the common law system.

A quite different source of flexibility in the system is that judges can manipulate precedents, logic, social policy and all the other bases of arguments presented to them by counsel in any way they please. This is not something that is usually acknowledged. But it emerged with great force from an important article by two (then) lecturers at the London School of Economics in 1981–2, based on close textual analysis of speeches by House of Lords judges in all the 58 cases decided by the Law Lords in the twelve months from October 1979. Their paper demonstrated that frequently the judges dealt with precedent by simply asserting that it was or was not relevant, with no explanation or reasoning to justify the assertion. Case law was sometimes described and discussed at length and at other times was simply rejected as being 'unhelpful' without discussion. In general the quality of reasoning in their lordships' judgments proved to be less impressive than one would have expected. If this is true of judgments in the House of Lords, how much more is it likely to be true of judgments in lower courts?[14]

For further reading on precedent, see especially: Cross and Harris *Precedent in English Law* (4th edn, 1991); C. K. Allen, *Law in the Making* (7th edn, 1964); Benjamin Cardozo, *The Nature of the Judicial Process* (1925); Karl Llewellyn, *The Bramble Bush* (1930); Jerome Frank, *Law and the Modern Mind* (1930). There is also much of value on precedent in Peter Goodrich, *Reading the Law* (1986). For further, advanced, reading see R. A. Wasserstrom, *The Judicial Decision* (1961); and L.J. Goldstein (cd.), *Precedent in Law* (1987).

---

14 See W. T. Murphy and R. W. Rawlings, 'After the ancien regime: the writing of judgments in the House of Lords 1979/80', *Modern Law Review*, 1981, p. 617; 1982, p. 34.

CHAPTER 7

The nature of the judicial role in law-making

A great deal has been written about the judicial role and no attempt can be made here to cover all aspects of this topic. The issues addressed are only some of those that affect the law-making process but they are perhaps some of the most important. The first is what role is played by the judge himself in the process.

1. THE PERSONAL ELEMENT IN JUDICIAL LAW-MAKING

The first extract is from the writings of one of Britain's most distinguished post-war judges.

Lord Radcliffe, *Not in Feather Beds* (1968), pp. 212–16

> More and more I am impressed by the inescapable personal element in the judicial decision. We are fond of saying, approvingly, that a judge should be objective, but is it perhaps the wrong metaphor, an idea borrowed, like so much else that obscures our thinking on general topics, from an analogy between the physical sciences and things incommensurable with them? Say indeed that a judge must be fair, or that he must be impartial: that is essential. He must strip himself of all prejudices, certainly; except, I ought to add, those prejudices which on consideration he is prepared to stand by as his sincere convictions. You see how quickly, just because he is not a machine, one begins to tie oneself in words and qualifications of words. He has no right to be biased; but then no human mind is constructed with perfect balance. He must give an honest hearing to all points of view and to arguments that do not even introduce themselves to him as plausible; but it is unreal to think of a judge of experience as if he were a mere hearing aid. It was said of the late Lord Bryce that to him all facts were born free and equal. That may be all right for facts, before the work of evaluation begins, but a judge is a mature man, of long and professional experience, with prepared approaches and formed attitudes of mind, and it

would be, I think, almost hypocritical to speak of him as if each case presented itself to his eye in the light of the first dawn of creation. To me fairness of mind cannot involve such innocence as that.

The trust is, I believe, that the law must not be mistaken for a scientific pursuit. Much contemporary analysis and criticism seem to be based on this false analogy. Let me put the contrasting points of view. At the back of your mind you may think of the law on some particular questions as being a given fact, an absolute, which it is the judge's duty to discover. It is all there already, hidden in the ground and needing only excavation, or shrouded in a veil which requires no more than to be drawn apart. To excavate or to unveil, neatly and accurately, calls for the exercise of no minor talents, and to do the work well there should be a solid apparatus of equipment, a detailed knowledge of the formulae of law (statutes, authorities and commentaries) and an ability to use the reasoning power with strict regard to its own inherent rules. The legal answer, you may say, is written out in close print or even in archaic language on some distant tablet. To read it off, you should choose for your judge the man with unusual length of sight or one who has had the skill to construct a powerful telescope or, for that matter, one who has made a study of the ancient tongues. Then he will read it off and announce to you what is there.

I would not deny that, in a legal system such as that which we operate in this country, a great deal of a judge's work involves no more than the practice of this science or skill of 'reading off'. But the essence of that curious activity, the judicial decision, does not consist in that. The law has to be interpreted before it can be applied, and interpretation is a creative activity. The law was not there until that particular decision was given. Once it has been given, the whole enormous component, which is the body of the law, has changed its composition by the addition of a new element, significant or insignificant, which in some degree modifies the whole.

There are two things that have impressed themselves on me when I have thought in this way. One is that, if the judge is not a machine, however ingeniously constructed, that is to work a mechanical system, it does very much matter what personal quality he brings to his work, because it is not going to be only his command of the reasoning process or his knowledge and learning that will determine his interpretation, but, in the end, his experience of life and the structure of thought and belief that he has built upon it. Most questions are debatable, just as most arguments can be made plausible: but what will incline him to one side or the other is what I called his whole structure of thought. I hope that you do not think that I am putting forward the judge as a sort of prophet or seer, making his pronouncements by some uncriticisable right of divination. Perhaps a few of the great ones have been something of that order, and for better or worse, sometimes for the worse, we take them as such. I do not see them that way at all, but I do think that it is of some importance in the society of today that the judge's function should not be confused with that of a reading clerk and that it should be realised that judicial decisions, no matter who gives them, must always be related to certain basic beliefs about the nature and purpose of a human being which are held by another human being. In that sense he may not be 'objective'; but he can be honest and fair. Of the two it is much the more valuable achievement.

It has been a pity, I think, that so much of judicial opinion in this country has been conveyed by the method of logical deduction. It was natural enough that this should be the preferred route, since the deductive method based on the syllogism was the favoured weapon of Western Europe thinkers in the Middle Ages, and the judges probably inherited its use from them. But, as we know, syllogistic reasoning is only conclusive if you first import your chosen meaning into the words of the premise you start with. It is only a demonstration of a truth if you have already been converted to the truth. In our history of judgment-making too many decisions have begun by insisting that particular words have one particular meaning and then deducing that, if they have, certain consequences must necessarily follow. That is to put the icing on the cake, not to bake it. I am afraid that what I am saying is that the making of law is not a subject which is capable of anything like scientific demonstration, and there are some disadvantages in dressing it up to look as if it were. It is the unexpressed assumptions, which are nevertheless very much present, that are often the real hinges of decision. After all, what a judgment seeks to do is to persuade or convince, and there are sometimes cogent considerations that achieve this without having any resort to deductive reasoning. Arrangement, by which an illuminating spark is generated from the skilful combination of certain facts and considerations, is one of them. Anyone who makes a careful study of the judgments of a great master of exposition, such as was Lord Macnaghten, for instance, will see how much conviction he can bring from nothing more than his skill of arrangement.

In this context there was never a more sterile controversy than that upon the question whether a judge makes law. Of course he does. How can he help it? The legislature and the judicial process respectively are two complementary sources of law-making, and in a well ordered state each has to understand its respective functions and limitations. Judicial law is always a reinterpretation of principles in the light of new combinations of facts, of which very relevant ones, unprovable by evidence, are the current beliefs of the society in which those facts occur. True, judges do not reverse principles, once well established, but they do modify them, extend them, restrict them or even deny their applicability to the combination in hand. But does Parliament do anything very different in its law-making, except in some revolutionary context to which no ordinary rule can be referred? I doubt it. It is not that the well known phrase, 'That is not for us, it is for the legislature' does not carry plenty of significant meaning. What it means is, I think, that, while it is an illusion to suppose that the legislature is attending or can possibly attend all the time to all aspects of the law, there are certain areas of public interest which at any one time can be seen to be a matter of its current concern. It has recently legislated on that subject according to certain principles (if they can be detected) or it regularly legislates on the whole field covered by that subject (as, for instance, the law of taxation). In those areas I think that the judge needs to be particularly circumspect in the use of his power to declare the law, not because the principles adopted by Parliament are more satisfactory or more enlightened than those which would commend themselves to his mind, but because it is unacceptable constitutionally that there should be two independent sources of law-making at work at the same time.

The next extracts are from the pen of one of America's greatest judges:

Benjamin N. Cardozo, *The Nature of the Judicial Process* (1921), pp. 12–13, 111–15, 129, 141, 167–8

There is in each of us a stream of tendency, whether you choose to call it philosophy or not, which gives coherence and direction to thought and action. Judges cannot escape that current any more than other mortals. All their lives, forces which they do not recognise and cannot name, have been tugging at them – inherited instincts, traditional beliefs, acquired convictions; and the result is an outlook on life, a conception of social needs, a sense in James's phrase of 'the total push and pressure of the cosmos,' which, when reasons are nicely balanced, must determine where choice shall fall. In this mental background every problem finds its setting. We may try to see things as objectively as we please. None the less, we can never see them with any eyes except our own. To that test they are all brought – a form of pleading or an act of parliament, the wrongs of paupers or the rights of princes, a village ordinance or a nation's charter.... .

I have spoken of the forces of which judges avowedly avail to shape the form and content of their judgments. Even these forces are seldom fully in consciousness. They lie so near the surface, however, that their existence and influence are not likely to be disclaimed. But the subject is not exhausted with the recognition of their power. Deep below consciousness are other forces, the likes and dislikes, the predilections and the prejudices, the complex of instincts and emotions and habits and convictions, which make the man, whether he be litigant or judge.... . There has been a certain lack of candor in much of the discussion of the theme, or rather perhaps in the refusal to discuss it, as if judges must lose respect and confidence by the reminder that they are subject to human limitations. I do not doubt the grandeur of the conception which lifts them into the realm of pure reason, above and beyond the sweep of perturbing and deflecting forces. None the less, if there is anything of reality in my analysis of the judicial process, they do not stand aloof on these chill and distant heights; and we shall not help the cause of truth by acting and speaking as if they do. The great tides and currents which engulf the rest of men do not turn aside in their course and pass the judges by.... .

My analysis of the judicial process comes then to this, and little more: logic, and history, and custom, and utility, and the accepted standards of right conduct, are the forces which singly or in combination shape the progress of the law. Which of these forces shall dominate in any case must depend largely upon the comparative importance or value of the social interests that will be thereby promoted. One of the most fundamental social interests is that law shall be uniform and impartial. There must be nothing in its action that savors of prejudice or favor or even arbitrary whim or fitfulness. Therefore in the main there shall be adherence to precedent. There shall be symmetrical development, consistently with history or custom when history or custom has been the motive force, or the chief one, in giving shape to existing rules, and with logic or philosophy when the motive power has been theirs. But symmetrical development may be bought at too high a price. Uniformity ceases to be a good when it becomes uniformity of oppression. The social interests served by symmetry or certainty must then be balanced against the social interest served by equity and fairness or other elements of social welfare. These may enjoin upon the judge the duty of drawing the line at another angle, of staking the path along new courses, of marking a new point of departure from which others who come after him will set out upon their journey. If you ask how he is to know when one interest outweighs another, I can only answer that he must get his knowledge just as the legislator gets it, from experience and study and reflection; in brief, from life itself. Here, indeed, is the point of contact between the legislators' work and his. The choice of methods, the appraisement of values, must in the end be guided by like considerations for the one as for the other. Each indeed is legislating within the limits of his competence. No doubt the limits for the judge are narrower. He legislates only between gaps. He fills the open spaces in the law. How far he may go without travelling beyond the walls of the interstices cannot be staked out for him upon a chart. He must learn it for himself as he gains the sense of fitness and proportion that comes with years of habitude in the practice of an art. Even within the gaps, restrictions not easy to define, but felt, however impalpable they may be, by every judge and lawyer, hedge and circumscribe his action. They are established by the traditions of the centuries, by the example of other judges, his predecessors and his colleagues, by the collective judgment of the profession, and by the duty of adherence to the pervading spirit of the law… . Nonetheless, within the confines of these open spaces and those of precedent and tradition, choice moves with a freedom which stamps its action as creative.

For the view that the personal element in judicial decision-making is crucial, see further, in particular, Jerome Frank, *Law and the Modern Mind*.

The question was addressed also in a major recent article by an Australian jurist:

H. K. Lücke, 'The Common Law: Judicial Impartiality and Judge-Made Law', 98 *Law Quarterly Review*, 1982, pp. 29, 60–61, 74–6, 88

'[T]he common law possesses a great deal of historical and contemporary colour: it is lively, realistic and, incidentally, eminently teachable.' The student of the common law rubs shoulders with Indian princes, fishwives, conjurors, shopkeepers and sea-captains of the East India Company. Translated into statutory language, only the pale shadows of this colourful assembly would remain, they would become plaintiffs, traffic accident witnesses, promisors of rewards, hire-purchasers and applicants for public office. The common law is a storehouse for worm tubs, ornamental broughams, snails in ginger beer bottles and fancy waistcoats, all of which would long since have turned to rust and rubbish had the cases which brought them into prominence been governed by some statute.

This element of colour may be thought a trivial advantage in itself, but it helps to create and keep alive a keen sense of reality and respect for the special circumstances of each case. The facts of precedents are always vividly remembered as the background against which all proposed general formulae must be understood. Facts are like safe, dry ground: when judges venture on to the sea of abstraction, they try at least to remain within sight of the coast. This primacy of the facts, this preference for the concrete, this reluctance to use general concepts and abstract legal ideas is one of the main characteristics of the common law. Without a full understanding of the reasons for this stylistic element and of its consequences no critical evaluation of the common law can be worthwhile.

Proximity breeds engagement. Being so close to the conflict, to the interests and aspirations, needs and fears which have given rise to it, will engage the judge's direct sympathetic (or antipathetic) understanding of the parties' roles in the situation which he is called upon to judge. Although he has no personal stake in the case, he will nevertheless find his feelings invoked vicariously, on behalf of the various *dramatis personae*. He will experience sentiments ranging from approval to disapproval, from warm appreciation to indignation. What is at work here is a kind of emphatic 'sense of touch' to which any case involving real conflict must be exposed before it can be fully understood. A feeling human being is needed for such understanding: no computer would ever be able to perform the task.

It might be argued that a judge should act 'purely rationally' and that he can no longer do so once he allows his feelings to play any part in his decision-making. Undeniably, the judge's empathic responses to the case are deeply suspect: they seek to predispose him in favour of one party or the other. If uncontrolled, they would be quite irreconcilable with the necessary attitude of impartiality. However, emotion is not incompatible with justice. If the judge's empathic responses are to work impartially, they must, to adapt Cardozo's famous words, be 'informed by tradition, methodised by analogy, disciplined by system.' So controlled, they are the essence of the judge's sense of justice.

Professor Lücke considered the reaction to a judicial decision on a point of law that might have gone either way:

The most critical of all observers, the losing party, might respond:

'No rule such as the one you have stated was to be found in the law before you chose to announce it. You are a skilful lawyer and master rationaliser: hence it was easy enough for you to formulate such a proposition and to act as if it were a rule of general application. To me it is only window dressing, intended to conceal your real motive: to vent your prejudice against me and people like me. Even if you have tried to be sincere, your attitudes and prejudices have still had a decisive, though perhaps subconscious, impact upon your judgment.'

To such a charge the judge appears to have three answers: his first line of defence is to invoke the great reputation of the judiciary to which he belongs, for independence and impartiality. He may refer to great constitutional battles for the independence of the judiciary, the purpose of which was to gain for judges the freedom to be impartial. He may point to his professional ethos and to his judicial oath. All this is impressive evidence of impartiality; but the more loudly it is invoked, the more suspect it must seem to an already suspicious mind. Even the greatest traditions are sometimes broken, or may, indeed, cease to be a living reality.

The judge's second line of defence lies in the quality, as a 'socio-moral norm', of the ratio he has stated. His credibility will be enhanced if his ratio balances fairly the interests of the disputants in this and in similar disputes, and if it thus seeks to order the affairs of the community in a rational, fair and sensible way. If, on the other hand, it appears forced, unjust or obscure it will be less likely to quell suspicion that the judge's real motives had nothing to do with his alleged ratio and were incompatible with impartiality. However, the 'socio-moral' quality of the ratio, without more, will not overcome the argument that the ratio is just 'window-dressing', used ad hoc to camouflage the judge's bias and likely soon to be discarded.

To rebut this charge of 'window-dressing', the judge's third and final argument will be to show the strength of his commitment to his ratio. He will reply to his critics as follows:

> 'Don't see the ratio I have provided solely in the context of the present dispute. Under the rule of precedent, the law offers you the following assurance. Should your and your adversary's roles ever be reversed in a future, but otherwise identical dispute, I (or any other judge) will give judgment for you and against the other side, acting in accordance with the very same rule which I have just formulated and applied against you. The rule will also be applied to all other substantially identical future disputes, whoever the parties may be, for the legal system places confidence in the ratio I have stated and regards it as a strongly persuasive or even (depending upon my place in the judicial hierarchy) as a binding rule. If the law accepts it, why should you not accept it also?'

The rule of precedent is an essential chain in the argument which establishes the judge's impartiality, and is therefore an instrument of effective and convincing adjudication. To know that his decision will be treated by the law as setting a persuasive, or even a binding, standard adds to the burden of responsibility felt by the judge. It is a powerful reminder that the judge's duty is to base his decisions upon rules fit for general application rather than upon factors which may raise doubts as to his impartiality. The rule of precedent offers reassurance to the parties and to the public that judges will continue to act in a principled and impartial way. If the rule of precedent is seen in this light, judicial impartiality no longer depends upon adherence to declaratory theories.

If *rationes decidendi* are to play their role effectively as instruments of adjudication, they must be formulated in concrete and specific terms.... In fact, this has been the practice among common law judges for so long that it is rightly seen as one of the most characteristic style elements of the common law. Only when *rationes decidendi* are stated in this way can the 'reversal test' be applied with complete confidence: broad and abstract premises do not dictate results in the same way as specific premises do.... .

The judge's task is to reconcile and, if necessary, to adjust conflicting interests. Before he can do so fairly and with true understanding, he must strain his powers of empathic identification with both parties so as to gain a full appreciation of their personalities, their interests and positions in the particular dispute. His exposure to the detailed facts gives him a unique advantage as he seeks to gain such understanding. As he 'identifies' with each party in turn, he must maintain an attitude of impartiality. That is a deeply problematic commitment, for it is contrary to man's innate tendency which is (if not to take flight) to adopt a partisan role in any conflict to which he is exposed at close quarters. A studied attitude which combines continuing involvement in the conflict with continuing impartiality seems a highly civilised, if not an artificial form of conduct. There is no such thing as a basic human urge or instinct to remain impartial in the face of conflict. This may explain why the reality of impartiality is denied by many critics of the legal system and why its value as an element of government is so often grossly underrated.

The role of discretion available to the judge in deciding cases may vary according to the level of court. This is one of the points made in the extract that follows:

Brian Abel-Smith and Robert Stevens, *In Search of Justice* (1968), pp. 167–73

Among the middle classes (and particularly among those members who have had little contact with the courts) the English judges are held in awe not only as the embodiment of 'all that is good and excellent', but also as the epitome of impartiality and objectivity. Politicians are not reticent about making use of this reputation. Embarrassing political situations may be resolved by setting up a tribunal chaired by a judge... .By importing a judge to head some Commission or Committee, the most embarrassing political matter can suddenly be taken out of politics... .

The non-political position of the judges has been enhanced by their withdrawal (or in some cases expulsion) from some of the more politically contentious areas of decision-making. During this century few new powers have been given to the courts. In exercising the powers which have remained in their hands, the judges have tended to stress that their task is merely to apply pre-existing doctrines of the common law to new fact situations and to apply the 'ordinary meaning' of words to the interpretation of statutes. They have thus assiduously cultivated the notion that the judicial process is a mechanical one which leaves virtually no room for discretion or the introduction of inarticulate premises or value judgments into their decisions.

In so far as the judicial role can be purely declaratory this has clear advantages for the lay public (and we do not for a moment deny that the very definition of law demands an element of predictability which in turn involves an element of the mechanical). In a way unknown in many other countries, the belief in 'the law' as something which has an existence and internal logic of its own enables counsel and judges to advise or hold on certain matters – that the law would or would not allow certain acts – with an assurance which lawyers abroad might well envy. Indeed counsel's opinion in some situations is accorded a quasi-judicial reverence.

Every legal system, of course, involves the existence of a body of principles which are thought of as binding, at least in some situations, but in England it sometimes seems to be assumed, even by leading lawyers, that the 'legal' answer to virtually any problem may be discovered by the appropriate use of legal logic and analogies. Moreover the predictability of most legal issues is thought to be so obvious that there is no need to resort to litigation. The English businessman expects to be given a clear answer about whether something is legal or whether an arrangement is binding or not. While from an academic point of view this may be intellectually unsatisfactory, the belief in such predictability coupled with the analytic refinements of English legal thinking, if it leaves something to be desired because of its inflexibility and formality, does provide effectively for the settlement of a wide range of disputes outside the court room.

The coherence and predictability of the common law are made much easier to preserve not only because relatively few politically sensitive decisions are now left to the courts, but also because the number of judges at the higher level is sufficiently small for them to have close contact with one another... .The appeal courts sit exclusively in London and the High Court is very much based in London. The extensive use of arbitration by businessmen and the establishment of administrative tribunals for certain purposes have all helped to limit the work and thus the size of the High Court bench. As the Permanent Secretary to the Lord Chancellor put it to the Franks Committee in 1957, the tribunal system has 'positively contributed to the preservation of our judicial system'. The fact that most administrative 'law' operates outside the courts of law, that most criminals are tried and sentenced by laymen, and that permanent civil courts of general jurisdiction for important cases are not available outside London are the price England pays for an élite corps of judges of the higher courts. In turn, the fact that there need be so few of them makes it easier to ensure that all those appointed will uphold the tradition of the judiciary for integrity and independence; and this in turn makes it possible to hand on the traditional beliefs in the certainty of legal doctrines and the predictability of legal reasoning. Predictability can, however, be sought at too high a price. In particular we would challenge the English assumption that certainty of doctrine and formality of approach necessarily produce predictability. If courts really operated like slot machines, it would rightly be asked why it was necessary to staff them with persons of such high intellectual calibre and pay such staff such large salaries, or why appeal courts were necessary. Moreover, the more predictable the law attempts to become the less it can be adjusted to changing circumstances... .

The practical tasks of a judge trying either a civil or a criminal case are those of evaluating the creditability of witnesses and applying the relevant legal doctrine or doctrines. In most cases this consists of deciding, for instance, whether the defendant was negligent in his behaviour, or whether the activities of the accused amounted to larceny. In this sense, the judicial process is not a particularly creative one. It is true that the decision about whether some behaviour is negligent or dishonest, in so far as it is performed by the judge rather than the jury, may require some element of value judgment. But with the exception of those few cases where there is a disputed point of law or where some novel point of law has to be interpreted, this aspect of the trial judge's work is essentially a mechanical one – involving considerable skill in evaluating evidence, but not of necessity making the view of the judge of any major importance.

From the point of view of discretion, however, the power of trial judges comes into its own when, after the decision or verdict has been reached, the judge is required to assess damages, pass sentence or exercise any other form of discretion. In all these cases there will be some semblance of rules to guide him. There are principles for assessing damages, there has been growing agreement on sentencing policy, and even the exercise of discretion in favour of a petitioner in a divorce case has certain guidelines. But none of these principles or guidelines comes close to the apparently binding and objective nature of the rule of law as traditionally understood in England. In such areas as these, then, the judge is forced to exercise a genuine discretion and, as with other types of persons, the exercise of such discretion will, to some extent, reflect the social and political outlook of the judge. His legal training will instil a measure of rationality into such operation, but it can, by no means, obviate the personal value judgment.

As a case proceeds farther up the judicial hierarchy, such social and political views are likely to become steadily more important. In the Court of Appeal the judges are primarily concerned to see that the judge of first instance applied the 'right' doctrine, or applied this doctrine correctly. They are also to some extent concerned with the proper interpretation of fact. But also to a greater extent than at the trial level, courts of appeal are concerned to develop doctrines, by deciding whether some particular principle should embrace the fact situation with which they are faced; or alternatively they are required to decide within which of two competing legal principles some fact situation falls. This creative role of the judges becomes more important still in the final court of appeal – the House of Lords. Here, although the judges work within the framework of legal principles, they are enabled to perform an essentially creative function by extending (or for that matter refusing to extend) some particular legal doctrine, or by interpreting some particular statute or section of a statute in a broad or a narrow way.

In his recent book, *Judicial Discretion in the House of Lords* (Clarendon, Oxford, 1998) David Robertson, an Oxford political scientist, argues that, at least in the House of Lords, the personal views of the judges dominate decision making. His thesis is radical: that 'law in almost any case that comes before the Lords turns out to be whatever their Lordships feel it ought to be' (p. 108). Robertson presents statistical evidence to establish the proposition that 'a good prediction can be made of case resolution by knowing who is on the panel, which hears the appeal' (p. 70). He also makes his point through analysis of decisions in a variety of fields.

Powerful support for Robertson's view came rather surprisingly in a recent pronouncement by Lord Browne-Wilkinson the current senior Law Lord in a brief chapter he contributed to a series of lectures on the Human

Rights Act.[1] Lord Browne-Wilkinson started his lecture with the following remarkable words:

> When I was first made a judge, a wily old judge advised me–'just remember, Nick, dirty dogs don't win'. That is a principle which lies at the heart of the common law. It is the basis on which the overwhelming majority of cases are decided. The judge looks for what are called 'the merits' and having found them seeks to reach a result, consistent with legal reasoning, whereby the deserving win and the undeserving lose.
>
> Unfortunately, this judicial method is seldom reflected in judicial behaviour or in the reasons given by judges for their decisions.... The outward presentation of the process of adjudication on questions of law is that the blind goddess rules, and that, willy-nilly, the judge is forced to the conclusion which he reaches. When we get to the judgment, we very seldom find any reference to 'the merits'. The articulated reasoning purports to be based on a process of compelling legal argument leading inexorably to the result achieved....
>
> In the case of statutory interpretation, the courts have acted in much the same way.

The features of judicial reasoning, Lord Browne-Wilkinson said, consist of three elements.

> First, the actual decision is primarily based on moral, not legal factors. Second, those moral reasons are not normally articulated in the judgment. Third, the morality applied in any given case is the morality of the individual judge: although this will, to an extent, reflect the values of contemporary society...

The background of judges If the personal element in judicial decision-making is important, it may matter that most judges in most countries and certainly in England are drawn from a relatively narrow social class. It is hardly surprising that English judges are mainly from the class that sends their sons and daughters to public schools and to Oxbridge, for this is true of the Bar generally. (A study in 1977 by the College of Law showed that 84 per cent of its barrister students were from the professional, managerial, executive or administrative class – and the same was true of no less than 77 per cent of the solicitor students.)[2]

The question of the background of the judges was addressed more recently by the House of Commons Home Affairs Select Committee in its report *Judicial Appointments Procedures* (Third Report, HC 52–1, 1995–96). The Committee was unanimous in all but two paragraphs. On those they divided on party lines. The first concerned the educational background of the judges. The Report (para. 113) cited an article in the October 1994

---

1   *The Impact of the Human Rights Bill on English Law* (ed. Basil Markesinis, 1998, OUP, pp. 22–23).
2   Evidence to the Royal Commission on Legal Services of the College of Law, 1977, p. 5.

issue of the journal *Labour Research* which stated that the proportion of those holding higher judicial office who were educated at an independent school had risen from 70 per cent in 1987 to 80 per cent in 1994 and that the proportion educated at Oxford and Cambridge had risen from 80 per cent to 87 per cent. A memorandum supplied to the Committee by the Lord Chancellor's Department showed that 80 per cent of the senior judiciary, 51 per cent of circuit judges and 12 per cent of district judges obtained their first degree from either Oxford or Cambridge. The Select Committee's Report, whilst admitting that it was 'certainly remarkable' that the proportion of Oxbridge graduates in the higher judiciary was so high, did not think that it was evidence of bias. Rather it thought that this reflected the background of those entering the Bar 30 years previously. Nowadays the proportion of Oxbridge entrants from state schools was almost equal to that from public schools. (This is the case. In 1995, 43 per cent of Oxford entrants were from state schools, compared with 46 per cent from public schools. The figures in Cambridge were 45 per cent from both sectors with 9 per cent from Other and Overseas.) The Home Affairs Committee concluded (para. 117) 'we are confident that decisions on judicial appointments are not guided by information on where candidates were educated'.

The Labour minority on the Committee disagreed. ('We find it hard to think of a good reason why four-fifths of the senior judges should come from the same two universities.') It thought this situation was an indictment of the present system of appointments. It suggested that there was a glass ceiling between the middle and the higher judiciary beyond which those of the 'wrong' background or gender found it difficult to progress. Reform of the system was needed. The minority thought that matters would be improved by the setting up of a broadly based judicial appointments commission to advise the Lord Chancellor on appointments. The majority disagreed. ('From the evidence we have taken, we have not been persuaded that the quality of appointees would necessarily improve if a Judicial Appointments Commission were to be established.' (Para. 142.))

Judges are appointed after elaborate consultation. Magistrates, masters, assistant recorders, recorders, district judges and circuit judges are appointed by the Lord Chancellor. High Court judges are appointed by the Queen on the advice of the Lord Chancellor. Lords Justices of Appeal and Law Lords are appointed by the Queen on the advice of the Prime Minister, though no doubt the Lord Chancellor is highly influential in the most senior appointments as well. Since 1994 judicial positions up to the level of Circuit judge have been advertised and in February 1998 this was extended to High Court judicial positions.

Shortly after Labour became the Government in May 1997, the new Lord Chancellor, Lord Irvine, stated that he would look into the question of a Judicial Appointments Commission but a few months later in October 1997 he said that he had shelved the idea. However, after the debacle over the Pinochet case in December 1998 when the House of Lords had to cancel its decision and order a rehearing because Lord Hoffmann had failed to reveal his connection with Amnesty International, Lord Irvine allowed that the subject of a Judicial Appointments Commission was back on the agenda.[3]

It has often been said that the narrow social-class background of English judges influences them, and in particular explains the alleged fact that the judges have shown themselves to be biased against the trade unions. A study of judicial decisions affecting trade unions does not, however, quite bear out the claim that these decisions do show any clear bias.[4] The authors analysed every judicial decision arising out of disputes between groups of workers and employers or between groups of organised or unorganised workers. The cases in the study were those referred to in the three leading textbooks concerned with industrial conflict (Citrine,[5] Grunfeld[6] and Wedderburn[7]). Between 1871 and 1966 there were seventy cases arising out of industrial conflict. Of these, fifty were civil and twenty were criminal. The article showed which side won in these seventy cases.

On the basis of the information in the article, it is possible to present the data in tabular form:[8]

	Determined in favour of workers	Determined against workers
Civil courts:		
House of Lords and Privy Council	5	8
Court of Appeal	17	12
High Court	16	29
Divisional Court	4	1
Total	42	50
Criminal courts:		
Court of Criminal Appeal	1	1
Divisional Court	2	11
First instance	3	17
Total	6	29
Grand total	48	79

3   *The Times*, 22 March 1999.
4   Paul O'Higgins and Martin Partington, 'Industrial Conflict: Judicial Attitudes', 32 *Modern Law Review* (1969), p. 53.
5   N. A. Citrine, *Trade Union Law* (2nd edn, 1960).
6   Cyril Grunfeld, *Modern Trade Union Law* (1966).
7   K. W. Wedderburn, *The Worker and the Law* (1965).
8   Based on the 70 cases decided between 1871 and 1966. The numbers exceed 70 because the article traced the fate of appeals and many cases are therefore counted more than once.

For an analysis of the male prejudices of English and American judges in cases involving sex-equality issues, see Albie Sachs and Joan Hoff Wilson, *Sexism and Judicial Bias* (1978). See also Zsuzsanna Adler, 'Rape – the intention of Parliament and the practice of the courts', 45 *Modern Law Review*, 1982, p. 664. For the suggestion that judges' attitudes to landlord-tenant issues are influenced by conscious or unconscious pro-landlord attitudes, see J. I. Reynolds, 'Statutory Covenants of Fitness and Repair: Social Legislation and the Judges', 37 *Modern Law Review*, 1974, p. 377. See also a reply by M. J. Robinson, 'Social Legislation and the Judges: A note by way of rejoinder', 39 *Modern Law Review*, 1976, p. 43.

On the attitude of the judges to public law issues, see P. McAuslan, 'Administrative Law, Collective Consumption and Judicial Policy', 46 *Modern Law Review*, 1983, p. 1. By far the most substantial study of judicial attitudes and their influence on decision-making is Robert Stevens, *Law and Politics: the House of Lords as a Judicial Body, 1800—1976* (1979). The book is fascinating for instance on the changing judicial attitudes to tax laws – see pp. 170–6, 204–8, 312, 392–6, 411–14, 600–13.

In a provocative book, first published in 1977, Professor John Griffith of the London School of Economics argued that judges generally were biased in their approach to certain issues not so much because of their social background as because of the nature of their function. According to this thesis the judge, by virtue of his office, is mainly concerned to uphold and maintain the status quo and therefore inevitably tends to find himself in conflict with any groups in society whose purpose is to seek change – the more so if they proceed by other than conventional methods:

J. A. G. Griffith, *The Politics of the Judiciary* (Fontana, 4th edn, 1991), pp. 319, 327–29.

My thesis is that judges in the United Kingdom cannot be politically neutral because they are placed in positions where they are required to make political choices which are sometimes presented to them, and often presented by them, as determinations of where the public interest lies; that their interpretation of what is in the public interest and therefore politically desirable is determined by the kind of people they are and the position they hold in our society; that this position is a part of established authority and so is necessarily conservative and illiberal. From all this flows that view of the public interest which is shown in judicial attitudes such as tenderness towards private property and dislike of trade unions, strong adherence to the maintenance of order, distaste for minority opinions, demonstrations and protests, indifference to the promotion of better race relations, support of governmental secrecy, concern for the preservation of the moral and social behaviour to which it is accustomed, and the rest... .

Many regard the values of the bench and bar as wholly admirable and the spirit of the common law (as presently expressed) to be a national adornment. The incorruptibility of the English bench and its independence of the Government are great virtues. All this is not in issue. When I argue that they regard the interests of the State or the public interest as pre-eminent and that they interpret those interests as meaning that, with very few exceptions, established authority must be upheld and that those exceptions are made only when a more conservative position can be adopted, this does not mean that the judges are acting with impropriety. It means that we live in a highly authoritarian society, fortunate only that we do not live in other societies which are even more authoritarian. We must expect judges, as part of that authority, to act in the interests, as they see them, of the social order.

The judges define the public interest, inevitably, from the viewpoint of their own class. And the public interest, so defined, is by a natural, not an artificial, coincidence, the interest of others in authority, whether in government, in the City or in the church. It includes the maintenance of order, the protection of private property, the promotion of certain economic aims, the containment of the trade union movement, and the continuance of governments which conduct their business largely in private and on the advice of other members of what I have called the governing group.

Far more than on the judiciary, our freedoms depend on the willingness of the press, politicians and others to publicise the breach of these freedoms and on the continuing vulnerability of ministers, civil servants, the police, other public officials and powerful private interests to accusations that these freedoms are being infringed. In other words, we depend far more on the political climate and on the vigilance of those members of society who for a variety of reasons, some political and some humanitarian, make it their business to seek to hold public authorities within their proper limits. That those limits are also prescribed by law and that judges may be asked to maintain them is not without significance. But the judges are not, as in a different dispensation and under a different social order they might be, the strong, natural defenders of liberty.

Judges are concerned to preserve and to protect the existing order. This does not mean that no judges are capable of moving with the times, of adjusting to changed circumstances. But their function in our society is to do so belatedly. Law and order, the established distribution of power both public and private, the conventional and agreed view amongst those who exercise political and economic power, the fears and prejudices of the middle and upper classes, these are the forces which the judges are expected to uphold and do uphold.

In the societies of our world today judges do not stand out as protectors of liberty, of the rights of man, of the unprivileged, nor have they insisted that holders of great economic power, private or public, should use it with moderation. Their view of the public interest, when it has gone beyond the interest of the governments, has not been wide enough to embrace the interests of political, ethnic, social or other minorities. Only occasionally has the power of the supreme judiciary been exercised in the positive assertion of fundamental values. In both democratic and totalitarian societies, the judiciary has naturally served the prevailing political and economic forces. Politically, judges are parasitic.

That this is so is not a matter for recrimination. It is idle to criticise institutions for performing the task they were created to perform and have performed for centuries. The principal function of the judiciary is to support the institutions of government as established by law. To expect a judge to advocate radical change is absurd. The confusion arises when it is pretended that judges are somehow neutral in the conflicts between those who challenge existing institutions and those who control those institutions. And cynicism replaces confusion whenever it becomes apparent that the latter are using the judges as open allies in those conflicts.

Thus it is usual for judges in political cases to be able to rely on the rules of law for the legitimacy of their decisions. As we have seen, there are innumerable ways – through the development of the common law, the interpretation of statutes, the refusal to use discretionary powers, the claims to residual jurisdiction and the rest – in which the judges can fulfil their political function and do so in the name of the law.

Professor Griffith's thesis did not pass unchallenged, however. The first edition was critically examined by Lord Devlin in a review article:

Lord Devlin, 'Judges, Government and Politics', 41 *Modern Law Review*, 1978, pp. 505–11

The professor begins with a concise and interesting account of how judges work, what they are paid, their social origins and so on. This covers a good deal more ground than is necessary for his conclusion which is that the judicial political outlook, while not extreme, is right of centre. Judges are 'neither Tories, nor Socialists, nor Liberals' but 'protectors and conservators of what has been, of the relationships and interests on which, *in their view*, our society is founded.'[9] He is talking chiefly of the small group, less than 30, of the senior judges in the House of Lords and the Court of Appeal whose views matter. '*These judges*,' he writes, '*have by their education and training and the pursuit of their profession as barristers, acquired a strikingly homogeneous collection of attitudes, beliefs and principles, which to them represents the public interest.*'[10] Since he is writing of men in their sixties and seventies whose working life has given them a common outlook on many questions, by no means all political, I have very little doubt that he is right. I have very little doubt either that the same might be written of most English institutions, certainly of all those which like the law are not of a nature to attract the crusading or rebellious spirit... .

But the real question posed by the author is on other subjects. Do the judges allow their devotion to law and order to distort their application of the law when they apply it to those who do not think as they do? In exploring the cases to get the answer to this the author is faced with two difficulties. The first is the lack of discipline among the judges; they do not always toe what Professor Griffith declares to be their party line. The law lords are sometimes divided: more frequently they quarrel with the Court of Appeal. The second difficulty is that the scale of the work does not permit any analysis of the cases. Leaving Lord Halsbury to his own generation, it is difficult to get much from the modern cases without looking for the legal errors and examining them to see whether they disclose a pattern of thought. Without such an analysis the reader is left to go by the result: in the trade union cases, for example, the

9   J. A. G. Griffith, *The Politics of the Judiciary* (1977), p. 52.
10   Emphasis supplied.

implication seems to be that a decision against the union cannot be in the public interest... .

It is this section containing the cases which is the core of the book. What matters after all is not whether judges have the political prejudices of their age and upbringing, but whether or to what extent they allow the prejudice to get into their judgments. Most people, including judges, are prejudiced against crime, but judges have to learn to keep that prejudice out of a trial. His purpose is to show that there are certain types of cases that the judges as a body do not decide fairly. I am not sure that in the end he proves much more than that there are cases which he, often in accord with dissenting judges, would have decided differently from the final court... .

To my mind none of the evidence, general or specific, adds much to the inherent probability that men and women of a certain age will be inclined by nature to favour the *status quo*. Is it displeasing to the public at large that the guardians of the law should share this common tendency? The editorial instructions to the author were to identify pressure groups. He does not name any; perhaps there are none. Professor Griffith and those who think like him. But they ought to be satisfied if it is possible to do so. So what ought to be done?

This is the question which the editors assigned to the third part of the book. Their instruction to the author for the first and second parts was to be objective. Professor Griffith has certainly tried to be objective and I think that in general he has been; he puts the other side of the case wherever he sees it and it is nothing to the point that a reviewer sees some of it differently. Now, as he approaches the final question, he ought to be dropping objectivity and becoming polemical and stimulating. Professor Griffith cannot be unstimulating but he can be unpolemical and he is. In reaching his conclusion he is even more objective than before. He answers the question by saying in effect that there is nothing to be done. He thinks that the attitude of the judges is too repressive, too authoritarian, but he writes,

> 'We live in a highly authoritarian society, fortunate only that we do not live in other societies which are even more authoritarian. We must expect judges, as part of that authority, to act in the interests as they see them of the social order.'[11]

It is the same or worse in every country except for the Supreme Court of the United States which Professor Griffith twice praises.

What is wrong with this book is highlighted by this conclusion. It is its editorial setting. It is extravagant to talk of politics of the judiciary as one of the 'major issues of British politics today.' Their politics are hardly more significant than those of the army, navy and the airforce; they are as predictable as those of any institution where maturity is in command. What the book presents is not a major issue but a problem, or rather one facet of the universal problem caused by the fact that in any peaceful and law-abiding democratic society in which the mortality rate is constantly declining, government falls into the

11 Ibid., at p. 213.

hands of the ageing. No doubt power rises upward from the people, who are of all ages, but it becomes effective only when it is channelled, and the controllers of the channels are, as Professor Griffith says, oligarchs. The oligarchs who rise to the top in the democratic society are usually mature, safe and orthodox men. Autocracy sometimes runs risks in selection, democracy hardly ever. So throughout the whole apparatus of the state, in every institution, whether it be the judiciary, the civil service or the political party, the men at the top, especially perhaps the senior judges because of their training, are seen by the young, among whom I count Professor Griffith because age has not wearied him nor the years condemned, as showing too much concern with stability and too little with movement. Of course the silent majority may see this as a very good thing: let the judges protect the laws and customs of the realm and the traditional values and leave movement to others. But assuming that the judges admire stability more than they should, what is the solution?

I half expected Professor Griffith to take the Supreme Court as an institution to be imitated and to revive the paeans of the early Warren days, the thumbs down for the 'look-it-up-in-the-library' types and the exaltation of the 'result-oriented' judgment. The solution would be to make the Law Lords much more like Supreme Court justices, give them a politician like Taft, Hughes or Warren as their leader, make the right attitude to social questions a more important qualification than learning in the law, open the door to professors, and by making direct appointments from the Bar get men at a far younger age than can be got if judicial experience is the prime quality desired. The really essential one of these qualifications is the right attitude to social questions; the others are ways of arriving at this desideratum.

But how do you ensure that they have the right attitude? If only law lords were all appointed by a socialist Prime Minister (not just any socialist, but one who like Professor Griffith is perhaps a little left of centre; Mr Callaghan would not be any good), all would be well. But it would be even more unwise to trust to that than to trust to the immutability of the Supreme Court. As Professor Berger's book reminds us there will come a day when the liquors for the 'empty vessels' are differently brewed and when 'due process' becomes once again, as it used to be, 'the symbol habitually evoked by private right, the barrier that guards the frontier of business against the interference of the state.'[12]

Is there then no solution except the pragmatic one of making the best of what we have got? I do not think that Professor Griffith exhausts the possibilities for this. For the social reformer the English judiciary should have three attractive features. First, it has not got its own source of power; there is no Constitution, no 'empty vessels' for it to fill. Second, if it has a bias, its bias is known and for a known bias allowance can be made. So regarded its homogeneity is a virtue; a gun that is wrongly sighted is less risky than one which is liable to go off in any direction. Third and most important, one of the advantages of even a mildly authoritarian state is that it does not put in command men and women who have not learnt to obey. A new minister with his ideas brought piping hot from the hustings may find his civil servants obstructive but a positive command they will not disobey. Neither will the judges disobey an Act of Parliament. But where novel measures are imposed by a minister or by Parliament, they

12 *The Constitution Reconsidered*, ed. Conyers Reade (1938), p. 167.

must be expressed in language which is emphatic enough and clear enough to penetrate the bias against them of those who are set in their ways; it is no use praying for the rejuvenation of the elderly. A strong minister can be as emphatic as he wants in his own ministry. But when the proposed measures have to be submitted to parliamentary and public criticism, under-emphasis is very seductive. A minister is unlikely, for example, to say bluntly in the House that the Race Relations Act was intended to restrict freedom of speech and should be so interpreted, still less to have the sentiment expressed as a preamble to the Act.

There is the other side of the coin. It must be part of any pragmatic deal that judges should watch out for the perils of maturity. It is as a warning to them that *The Politics of the Judiciary* is most valuable. It is not analytical but it is illustrative. When, for example, the courts are subjecting the proceedings of a domestic tribunal to the test of natural justice, is there a tendency to make the test stiffer for a tribunal that is disciplining a troublesome student? Surely this is a question which is worth asking. The judge who is confident that he has no prejudices at all is almost certain to be a bad judge. Prejudice cannot be exorcised, but like a weakness of the flesh it can be subdued. But it has first to be detected. This is the great value of the book. It presents the judiciary with its portrait as seen by some of its critics. It is a skilful presentation, moderate and friendly, and a pleasure to read. If only on the principle of *audi alteram partem* judges should read it.

See further and generally, John Bell, *Policy Arguments in Judicial Decisions* (1983). and Michael J. Beloff, 'Wednesbury, Padfield, and All that Jazz: A Public Lawyer's View of Statute Law Reform', *Statute Law Review*, 1994, 147–63.

Questions

1. Could it be argued that Professor Griffith and Lord Devlin are really saying much the same thing in different words? Professor Griffith argues that all judges, irrespective of their social class or the country in which they sit, are members of the Establishment who favour the status quo. Lord Devlin contends that judges tend to be 'mature, safe and orthodox men'.

2. Lord Devlin says that judges should 'watch out for the perils of maturity'. Is this a practicable suggestion? What might be done to assist the process?

2.   SHOULD THE JUDGES BE ACTIVIST OR PASSIVE?

If judges are human beings who have private opinions or even prejudices, should their basic stance be activist or passive? Should they seek opportunities creatively to develop or even reform the law, or should they leave law reform to the legislature? Needless to say there are different schools of thought on this issue.

The traditional and dominant posture of the English judiciary on this question has been that the judge's role is broadly passive. The leading exponent of this approach in modern times has undoubtedly been Lord Simonds, who was Lord Chancellor from 1951 to 1954 but who sat in the House of Lords for nearly twenty years from 1944 to 1962. Robert Stevens has written of him that 'during the time that the House was dominated by Simonds, its purpose, intellectually and practically, remained the preservation of the status quo'.[13] In one case, for instance, he rejected Lord Denning's invitation to overrule the ancient rule that a third party cannot sue on a contract with a responding affirmation of the principle of judicial conformity to what has previously been decided:

> To that invitation I readily respond. For to me heterodoxy, or as some might say, heresy, is not the more attractive because it is dignified by the name of reform. Nor will I easily be led by an undiscerning zeal for some abstract kind of justice to ignore our first duty, which is to administer justice according to law, the law which is established for us by an Act of Parliament or the binding authority of precedent. The law is developed by the application of old principles to new circumstances. Therein lies its genius. Its reform by the abrogation of these principles is the task not of the courts of law but of Parliament... .I would cast no doubt upon the doctrine of stare decisis without which law is at hazard. [*Midland Silicones Ltd* v. *Scruttons Ltd* [1962] A.C. 446, 467–9.]

There are countless similar, if less vivid, statements in the law reports.

At the opposite end to the spectrum represented by Lord Simonds stands Lord Denning, who was a judge from 1944 for almost 40 years and Master of the Rolls from 1962 to 1982. For him certainty in the law was an overrated virtue and judges not only did make law but should do so. On innumerable occasions, both on the bench and off, he proclaimed the law-making potential of the judiciary:

> The truth is that the law is uncertain. It does not cover all the situations that may arise. Time and again practitioners are faced with new situations, where the decision may go either way. No one can tell what the law is until the courts decide it. The judges do every day make law, though it is almost heresy to say so. If the truth is recognised then we may hope to escape from the dead hand of the past and consciously mould new principles to meet the needs of the present. ['The Reform of Equity', in C. J. Hamson (ed.), *Law Reform and Law-Making* (1953), p. 31.]

For him the function of the judge was to be active in reforming the law – 'if the law is to develop and not to stagnate, the House must, I think recapture

13 *Law and Politics* (1979), p. 342.

this vital principle – the principle of growth. The House of Lords is more than another court of law… .It acts for the Queen as the fountain of justice in our land.' (*From Precedent to Precedent* (1959), p. 34. This statement was made whilst he was still in the House of Lords and before he returned to the Court of Appeal – the better, as he said, to make a mark on the law.) Lord Denning's stimulating book *The Discipline of Law* (1979), published to mark his eightieth birthday, was a celebration of his reforming zeal – with chapter and verse. Unfortunately, however, neither in his book nor elsewhere has Lord Denning expressed his passion for reform in any coherent philosophy. He never, for instance, formulated principles to guide judges as to the kind of cases in which they should intervene and when they should follow precedent and leave reform to the legislature. Over and over again he chipped away at doctrines that seemed to him to be wrong – on third-party beneficiaries to a contract,[14] sovereign immunity,[15] the doctrine of frustration in contract,[16] fundamental breach,[17] the right of married women to remain in the matrimonial home,[18] the action for negligent misstatement,[19] exclusion clauses in consumer contracts,[20] equitable estoppel[1] and many others.[2] But there was no very clear articulation of the proper relationship between law and justice – beyond the repeated assertion that precedent must not stand in the way of justice. In the final words of his book Lord Denning said only that while precedent was the foundation of our system of case law it must not be applied too rigidly. 'You must cut out the dead wood and trim off the side branches, else you will find yourself lost in thickets and brambles. My plea is simply to keep the path to justice clear of obstructions which would impede it.'[3] But we are not told how the path may be recognised.[4]

Between these two extremes of Lords Simonds and Lord Denning there are a number of other significant voices. One certainly is Lord Devlin, who retired from the bench in 1964 at the early age of fifty-nine after only three years in the House of Lords. His years on the bench coincided with the high-water mark of the Simonds era, and in 1962 Lord Devlin was clearly despondent about the role of the judge. At that time he wrote: 'I doubt if

---

14   *Midlands Silicones Ltd* v. *Scruttons Ltd* [1962] A.C. 446.
15   *Rahimtoola* v. *Nizam of Hyderabad* [1958] A.C. 379.
16   *British Movietonews Ltd* v. *London and District Cinemas Ltd* [1952] A.C. 166.
17   *Karsales (Harrow) Ltd* v. *Wallis* [1956] 1 W.L.R. 936.
18   *National Provincial Bank* v. *Ainsworth* [1964] 1 All E.R. 688.
19   *Candler* v. *Crane Christmas* [1951] 2 K.B. 164.
20   *Adler* v. *Dickson* [1955] 1 Q.B. 158.
1   *Central London Property Trust Ltd* v. *High Trees House Ltd* [1947] K.B. 130.
2   *For an extended survey, see Robert Stevens, Law and Politics* (1979), pp. 488–505.
3   Denning, *Discipline of Law*, p. 314.
4   See generally *Lord Denning: The Judge and the Law* (ed. J. L. Jowell and J. P. W. B. McAuslan, 1984).

judges will now of their own motion contribute much more to the development of the law.'[5] Even if the House of Lords changed the rule that it was bound by its own decisions 'it might do its own lopping and pruning ... and perhaps even a little drafting, instead of leaving all that to the legislature. But it could not greatly alter the shape of the tree.'[6] But by 1978 he had formed a rather different view. Delivering the Chorley Lecture at the London School of Economics, he expressed a conservative but by no means passive philosophy of the judicial role. He was against a judiciary that was dynamically activist, but on the other hand he saw a useful and quite considerable role for judges in shaping the common law:

Patrick Devlin, *The Judge* (1979), pp. 3, 5, 9, 17

What is the function of the judge? Professor Jaffé has a phrase for it – 'the disinterested application of known law.'[7] He would put it perhaps as the minimal function. I should rank it as greater than that. It is at any rate what 90 per cent or more of English judges – and I daresay also of all judges of all nationalities – are engaged in for 90 per cent of their working lives. The social service which the judge renders to the community is the removal of a sense of injustice. To perform this service the essential quality which he needs is impartiality and next after that the appearance of impartiality. I put impartiality before the appearance of it simply because without the reality the appearance would not endure... .

The disinterested application of the law calls for many virtues, such as balance, patience, courtesy and detachment, which leave little room for the ardour of the creative reformer. I do not mean that there should be a demarcation or that judges should down tools whenever they meet a defect in the law. I shall consider later to what extent in such a situation a judge should be activist. But I am quite convinced that there should be no judicial dynamics.

So much for the nature and function of the judge. I return to the lawmaker and consider what, if anything, judges and lawmakers have in common.

The lawmaker takes an idea or a policy and turns it into law. For this he needs the ability to formulate principle, and a judge in common with any other trained lawyer should have that. Is the judge any different in this respect from a professor or a parliamentary draftsman? Yes, because he has experience of the administration of the law. So has the barrister and the solicitor, but it is an advantage to see it working from the Bench. So there is no reason why, given the policy, a judge should not be a good activist lawmaker. The question, to which I shall return, is whether he should be the complete lawmaker or whether he would not do better work in committee, pooling his judicial experience with the social, commercial and administrative experience of others.

Let me repeat the distinction, since it may be one which I have freshly drawn, between activist and dynamic lawmaking. In activist lawmaking the

---

5   *Samples of Lawmaking* (1962), p. 23.
6   Ibid., p. 116.
7   Jaffé, *English and American Judges and Lawmakers* (1969), p. 13.

idea is taken from the consensus and demands at most sympathy from the lawmaker. In dynamic lawmaking the idea is created outside the consensus and, before it is formulated, it has to be propagated. This needs more than sympathy; it needs enthusiasm. Enthusiasm is not and cannot be a judicial virtue. It means taking sides and, if a judge takes sides on such issues as homosexuality and capital punishment, he loses the appearance of impartiality and quite possibly impartiality itself... . It is essential to the stability of society that those whom change hurts should be able to count on evenhanded justice calmly dispensed, not driven forward by the agents of change.

It is this evenhandedness which is the chief characteristic of the British judiciary and it is almost beyond price. If it has to be paid for in impersonality and remoteness, the bargain is still a good one... . The reputation of the judiciary for independence and impartiality is a national asset of such richness that one government after another tries to plunder it. This is a danger about which the judiciary itself has been too easygoing. To break up the asset so as to ease the parturition of judicial creativity, an embryo with a doubtful future would be a calamity. The asset which I would deny to governments I would deny also to social reformers.

I have not made it plain that I am firmly opposed to judicial creativity or dynamism as I have defined it, that is, of judicial operations in advance of the consensus. The limit of the consensus is not a line that is clearly marked, but I can make certain what would otherwise be uncertain by saying that a judge who is in any doubt about the support of the consensus should not advance at all. This however leaves open quite a large field for judicial activity. In determining its extent it is, I think, necessary to distinguish between common law and statute law. This is because the requirement of consensus affects differently the two types of law. The public is not interested in the common law as a whole. When it becomes interested in any particular section of it, it calls for a statute; the rest it leaves to the judges. The consensus is expressed in a general warrant for judicial lawmaking. This warrant is an informal and rather negative one, amounting to a willingness to let the judges get on with their traditional work on two conditions – first, that they do it in the traditional way, i.e. in accordance with precedent, and second, that parliamentary interference should be regarded as unobjectionable. In relation to statute law, by contrast, there can be no general warrant authorising the judges to do anything except interpret and apply.

But although there was scope for judicial activism, there were limits:

In every society there is a division between rulers and ruled. The first mark of a free and orderly society is that the boundaries between the two should be guarded and trespasses from one side or the other independently and impartially determined. The keepers of these boundaries cannot also be among the outriders. The judges are the keepers of the law and the qualities they need for that task are not those of the creative lawmaker. The creative lawmaker is the squire of the social reformer and the quality they both need is enthusiasm. But enthusiasm is rarely consistent with impartiality and never with the appearance of it.

Why is it, I ask in conclusion, that the denunciators of judicial inactivity so rarely pause to throw even a passing curse at the legislators who ought really to be doing the job. They seem so often to swallow without noticing it the quite preposterous excuse that Parliament has no time and to take only a perfunctory interest in an institution such as the Law Commission. Progressives of course are in a hurry to get things done and judges with their plenitude of power could apparently get them done so quickly; there seems to be no limit to what they could do if only they would unshackle themselves from their precedents. It is a great temptation to cast the judiciary as an elite which will bypass the traffic-laden ways of the democratic process. But it would only apparently be a bypass. In truth it would be a road that would never rejoin the highway but would lead inevitably, however long and winding the path, to the totalitarian state.

Question

If, as Lord Devlin suggests, judges are to restrict themselves to development of the common law within the consensus, how are they to know whether there is a consensus on the matter before the court?[8]

For Lord Radcliffe, 'The Law has to be interpreted before it can be applied and interpretation is a creative activity.'[9] But he preferred the judges to work creatively with caution and without alerting the populace to what they were about: '[I]f judges prefer to adopt the formula – for that is what it is – that they merely declare the law and do not make it, they do no more than show themselves wise men in practice. Their analysis may be weak, but their perception of the nature of law is sound. Men's respect for it will be the greater, the more imperceptible its development.'[10] If public opinion might lose respect for creative judges, parliament certainly would: 'I think that the judge needs to be particularly circumspect in the use of his power to declare the law, not because the principles adopted by parliament are more satisfactory or more enlightened than those which would commend themselves to his mind but because it is unacceptable constitutionally that there should be two independent sources of law-making at work at the same time.'[11] He saw (and exercised) a modest creative role for the judges but without advertising the fact.

Possibly the most influential judge of recent years has been Lord Reid, who was a Law Lord from 1948 to 1974 and was senior judge in the House of Lords from 1962. Robert Stevens has admirably captured his views:

8   For an account of Lord Devlin's own notable decisions developing the common law, see R. Stevens, *Law and Politics*, pp. 464–6.
9   *Not in Feather Beds* (1968), p. 213.
10   *Law and Its Compass* (1960), p.39.
11   Ibid., p. 216.

Robert Stevens, *Law and Politics* (1979), pp. 468–88

In the period between 1948 and the end of 1974, and especially after he became the senior Lord of Appeal in 1962, Reid was the most influential judge in the House of Lords. Whether the issue was one of common law or statute, Reid's judgment was almost invariably the most sophisticated treatment and the one that commanded the most respect. As a Scottish lawyer he brought to the common law a sense of principle and breadth generally lacked by those who dominated the House when he arrived, although he was comfortable putting the bulk of his effort into his judicial work rather than into extrajudicial public service, as a former politician he had an innate sense of the relationship of the legislature and the courts – something often denied to more 'courageous or timorous' souls ... With respect to the common law his philosophy was simple:[12]

> 'I suppose that almost every doctrine of the common law was invented by some judge at some period in history, and when he invented it he thought it was plain common sense – and indeed it generally was originally. But, with the passage of time, more technically minded judges have forgotten its origin and developed it in a way that can easily cause injustice. In so far as we appellate judges can get the thing back on the rails let us do so; if it has gone too far we must pin our hopes on Parliament.'[13]

Reid was well aware that the relative functions of the courts and Parliament would have to vary in different areas. 'When we are dealing with property and contract it seems right that we should accept some degree of possible injustice in order to achieve a fairly high degree of certainty.'[14] But he saw no such underlying policy when it came to tort.[15] Criminal law, on the other hand, was not to be extended by the judges, although they might remain guardians of the requirement of *mens rea*. Yet, subject to these reservations, Reid had no doubt that lawyers' law – by which he meant the basic areas of common law delegated to the judiciary – was best developed by the final appeal court. 'If you think in months, want an instant solution for your problems and don't mind that it won't wear well, then go for legislation. If you think in decades, prefer orderly growth and believe in the old proverb more haste less speed, then stick to the common law. But do not seek a middle way by speeding up and streamlining the development of the common law.'[16]

Unlike many appeal judges, Reid, towards the end of his life, clarified his theory of the criteria for judicial development of the law. First, the direction in

12 See, for instance, *Midland Silicones Ltd* v. *Scruttons Ltd* [1962] A.C. 446, 475–7 (1961).

13 James S. C. Reid, 'The Law and the Reasonable Man', 1968, *Proceedings of British Academy*, 193, 194–5.

14 Reid, 'The Law and The Reasonable Man', 197.

15 'A man knows quite well that what he intends to do may injure his neighbour; he may even intend such injury. Would the law be defective if his lawyer could not tell him with the same degree of certainty just how far he can go without having to pay damages?' Ibid.

16 'Judge as Law Maker', *Journal of Society of Public Teachers of Law*, 1972, 28.

which the law should be developed was to be tested by the criterion of common sense, something that was 'not static', but that prevented 'technically minded judges [from pressing] precedents to their logical conclusions'.[17] Common sense appeared to serve Reid as a humanist substitute for the Christian base on which Radcliffe and Denning ultimately purported to rely.[18] Second, the new law had to take into account principle, although not narrow, notions of precedent.[19] 'Rigid adherence to precedent will not do. And paying lip service to precedent while admitting fine distinctions gives us the worst of both worlds. On the other hand, too much flexibility leads to intolerable uncertainty.[20]' Finally, judicial developments in the law had to be tested against public policy. While avoiding those cases where public opinion was sharply divided – to be left in Parliament[1] – Judges should no longer be afraid of public policy. 'So long as the powers that be can see to it that the new race of judges are not mere technicians, but are men of the world as well, we can – indeed, we must – trust them to acquaint themselves with public policy and apply it in a reasonable way to such new problems as will arise from time to time.'[2] Indeed, by the end of his judicial career, Reid was a master of the art of balancing the conflicting policy goals involved in the decisions of the House.[3]

Yet, from the earliest part of his career he refused to be a slave to precedent.[4] He was committed to the idea that '[t]he common law ought never to produce a wholly unreasonable result, nor ought existing authorities to be read so literally as to produce such a result in circumstances never contemplated when they were decided.'[5] The same attitude characterised his approach when he found little authority. 'To my mind the best way of approaching this question is to consider the consequences of a decision in either sense. The circumstances are such that no decision can avoid creating some possible hard cases, but if a

---

17 Ibid., pp. 25–6.
18 See, for instance, his Holmesian position in one of his last decisions. 'I would not, however, decide the matter entirely on logical argument. The life blood of the law has not been logic but common sense.' He went on to reject an argument because '[t]he law may be an ass but it cannot be so asinine as that'; *R* v. *Smith* [1975] A.C. 476, 500.
19 'Judge as Law Maker', note 16, p. 317 above, 26.
20 Ibid.
1   Ibid., p. 23.
2   Ibid., p. 27.
3   See, for instance, *F. Hoffman-La Roche & Co. A. G.* v. *Secretary of State for Trade & Indus.* [1975] A.C. 295 (1973), where Reid articulated the conflicting goals of drug manufacturers and society and then attempted to balance the interests. He concluded that process by deciding that tradition and balancing required that an interim injunction be granted, but without the Crown giving an undertaking on damages, adding, '[I]f I thought that the appellants had a strong case on the merits I would try to stretch a point in their favour to protect them from obvious injustice though I would find difficulty in doing so'; ibid., p. 342.
4   See, for instance, his dissent in *London Graving Dock C.* v. *Horton* [1951] A.C. 737, 786: 'I have come to the conclusion that to hold there was such a duty would infringe no principle and would conflict with no binding or well-recognised authority'.
5   *Cartledge* v. *D. Jopling & Sons* [1963] A.C. 758, 772.

decision in one sense will on the whole lead to much more just and reasonable results, that appears to me to be a strong argument in its favour.'[6] ...

... Reid had no doubt that at a certain point, either because of the strength of the earlier precedent or because of the subject matter of the appeal, radical change was the province of Parliament. Thus, in *Cartledge* v. *E. Jopling and Sons, Limited*, where the plaintiff did not discover he had pneumoconiosis until the limitation period had expired, so that Reid felt obliged to dismiss the appeal, he announced that 'some amendment of the law is urgently necessary'.[7] Parliament obliged almost at once.[8] So too, in holding that car manufacturers' records of cylinder block registration numbers were inadmissible under the hearsay rule in *Myers* v. *Director of Public Prosecutions* Reid announced, '[W]e cannot introduce arbitrary conditions or limitations; that must be left to legislation.'[9] In Reid's view judicial legislation should be limited to 'the development and application of fundamental principles.'[10] While both of these cases were decided before the 1966 Practice Statement, the approach he exhibited in them probably continued to reflect his basic approach.[11]

Certainly Reid had a more developed sense than the other law lords about areas where it was inappropriate for the judiciary to legislate even interstitially. In the *Shaw* case, where Simonds led the attack to reactivate and extend the concept of criminal conspiracy, Reid countered:

> 'Even if there is still a vestigial power of this kind it ought not, in my view, to be used unless there appears to be general agreement that the offence to which it is applied ought to be criminal if committed by an individual. Notoriously, there are wide differences of opinion today as to how far the law ought to punish immoral acts which are not done in the face of the public. Some think the law already goes too far, some that it does not go far enough. Parliament is the proper place, and I am firmly of the opinion the only proper place to settle that. When there is sufficient support from public opinion, Parliament does not hesitate to intervene. Where Parliament fears to tread it is not for the courts to rush in.'[12]

Lord Reid himself expressed his philosophy in a lecture to the Society of Public Teachers of Law entitled 'The Judge as Law Maker':

6 *Starkowski* v. *Attorney-General* [1954] A.C. 155, 170.
7 [1963] A.C. 758, 773.
8 Limitation Act of 1963. On this incident, see Blom-Cooper and Drewry, *Final Appeal* (1972) 361.
9 [1965] A.C. 1001, 1021 (1964). See Blom-Cooper and Drewry, *Final Appeal* 362. Reid's position was attacked by Jaffé, *English and American Judges as Lawmakers* 28–9. In fairness it should be noted that Parliament responded to Reid's plea by passing the Criminal Evidence Act of 1965.
10 *Myers* v. *D.P.P.* [1965] A.C. 1001, 1021–2 (1964).
11 The approach remained a 'balanced' one. See, for instance, his reactions in *Broome* v. *Cassell & Co.* on the issue of penal damages: '[F]ull argument ... has convinced me that I and my colleagues made a mistake in concurring with Lord Devlin's speech in *Rookes* v. *Barnard*'; [1972] A.C. 1027, 1084.
12 *Shaw* v. *D.P.P.* [1962] A.C. 220, 275 (1961).

Lord Reid, *Journal of the Society of Public Teachers of Law*, vol. 12; N.S. 1972, pp. 22, 24–7

The pure doctrine of precedent is quite simple. We want certainty in the law. Ideally elegance is desirable but practically it is unattainable and its value is small. How better can we obtain certainty than by accumulating actual decisions. In time every point will have been decided and then we shall have reached our goal. But then we find that there has to be added to that a farther step. Cases are so various in their facts that if we only regarded actual decisions as binding we should not reach our goal until the Greek Kalends. So we say that not only the decision but also the *ratio decidendi* is binding and expect that that will hasten the achievement of certainty. But fortunately judges are human. If they do not like an existing decision or *ratio* because it will produce an unjust or unreasonable result in the case before them they try to distinguish it. And that is where the trouble starts, and you begin to get an impenetrable maze of distinctions and qualifications which destroy certainty because no one advising on a new case can predict how it will go… .

Of course we must have a general doctrine of precedent – otherwise we can have no certainty. But we must find a middle way which prevents precedent from being our master. That would be necessary even if the law were to remain static: it is still more necessary if the law is to develop as the needs of the time require.

Some years ago we decided in the House of Lords that we would no longer regard previous decisions as binding. It is good constitutional doctrine that Parliament cannot bind its successors. So we saw no reason why a rule set up by our predecessors should not be altered by us. I am glad we did: we now have more freedom of movement. But it was never intended to lead to a legal revolution. We have got rid of one or two real blots like absolute Crown privilege and the paramountcy of domicile in divorce jurisdiction and there may be a few more to come – but not very many.

Even if we do not greatly relax the doctrine of precedent and if we do not encroach on the sphere of Parliament there is still considerable scope for judges to mould the development of the common law. I propose now to say something of the way in which I think we should proceed in a case where we feel we have some freedom to go in one or other direction.

We should, I think, have regard to common sense, legal principle and public policy in that order. We are here to serve the public, the common ordinary reasonable man… .

Sometimes the law has got out of step with common sense. We do not want to have people saying: 'if the law says that the law is an ass'. If they say that about a statute our withers are unwrung. But if they say it about the common law we can usually trace the trouble to one or other of two causes.

Common sense is not static. What passed for common sense three hundred or even one hundred years ago sometimes seems nonsense today. I do not say that modern notions are necessarily better. We may fight against some of them but we can hardly help being influenced. *Communis error facit jus* may seem a paradox but it is a fact. Take for instance the doctrine of common employment – that a master is not liable to his servant for the fault of his fellow servant.

That seems nonsense today. But look at the cases from Chief Justice Shaw in Massachusetts to the House of Lords just over a century ago. They thought it was plain good sense. But then in the 1870s the tide began to turn. But the doctrine was too strongly entrenched and we had to wait for Parliament to abolish it... .

But common sense alone is not enough. The law is or ought to be organised common sense and that brings me to my second guide, legal principle. That is not very easy to define. We have to avoid on the one hand the rock Scylla where sits the austere figure of Austin and on the other the whirlpool Charybdis where some modern theorists for ever go round in circles. But we must get rid of the idea which still seems to animate some of our pedestrian confreres, that law is a congerie of unrelated rules. That results in the dreary argument that the case is similar to *A.* v. *B* and *C* v. *D*, but is distinguishable from *X.* v. *Y.* and *In re Z.* That way lies confusion and uncertainty. We must try to see what was the principle or reason why *A.* v. *B.* should go one way and *X.* v. *Y.* the other.

One often says to oneself when some proposition is put forward: 'That just can't be right' and then one looks to see why it cannot be right. Sometimes it offends against common sense, sometimes against one's sense of justice, but more often it just will not stand with legal principles, though it may seem to be supported by some judicial observations read apart from their context. I would say that in dealing with precedents the most dangerous pitfall is to treat the words of eminent judges as if they were provisions in an Act of Parliament. You infer from the case the sort of circumstances the judge must have had in mind. There what he said is generally quite right. But you must be very careful when the circumstances are entirely different.

People want two inconsistent things; that the law shall be certain, and that it shall be just and shall move with the times. It is our business to keep both objectives in view. Rigid adherence to precedent will not do. And paying lip service to precedent while admitting fine distinctions gives us the worst of both worlds. On the other hand too much flexibility leads to intolerable uncertainty... .

Now I must come to the vexed subject of public policy. Long ago it was said to be an unruly horse and elderly judges did not like unruly horses. That applied particularly to those who have led cloistered lives. But today they are a much smaller proportion than they used to be, thanks partly to most of us having had war service in the field and partly to the fact that economic circumstances prevent most of us from living in a world of our own.

If the law is to keep in step with movements of public opinion then judges must know how ordinary people of all grades of society think and live. You cannot get that from books or courses of study. You must have mixed with all kinds of people and got to know them. If you only listen to those who hit the headlines you get quite the wrong impression. If we are to remain a democratic people those who try to be guided by public opinion must go to the grass roots. That is why it is so valuable for a judge to have given public service of some kind in his early days. I sincerely hope that the 'rat race' of today will not prevent our young men from acquiring the breadth of mind that comes from widespread personal contacts in different strata of society.

See further Alan Paterson, *The Law Lords* (1982), chs 6 and 7, and Paterson 'Lord Reid's Unnoticed Legacy: A Jurisprudence of Overruling', 1 *Oxford Jrnl of Legal Studies*, 1981, p. 375. See also John Griffith, *Judicial Politics Since 1920* (Blackwell, 1993).

The issues under consideration here were the subject of a valuable review by Professor Patrick Atiyah delivering the 1980 Lionel Cohen lecture at the Hebrew University in Jerusalem. In the first part of his lecture he traced the different theories about the judicial role and pointed in particular to the battle between the declaratory theory and the realist theory as to the scope for judicial discretion in law-making. In his view English judges today overwhelmingly subscribe to the realist view that judges must and do legislate at least interstitially but at the same time many believe with Lord Radcliffe that it is not desirable that they should be too open about their law-making role.

In the second half of his lecture he addressed the question whether Lord Radcliffe was right:

Patrick Atiyah, 'Judges and Policy', *Israel Law Review*, 1980, pp. 346, 360–70

I may perhaps begin by suggesting that there is nothing new in this belief of the English judiciary that it is best in the long run if the public does not fully understand the creative powers of the judges. Indeed, it is an old tradition, going back at least to the eighteenth century and perhaps beyond. In the eighteenth century, at any rate, when England was a very free country, compared with most European despotisms, and yet was ruled by a small class of landed aristocrats, one of the principal functions of the judges was to provide an element of majesty and mystique to the law which would help to keep the lower orders in their place. Most probably the law was already replacing the Church as the main weapon in disciplining the minds of the mass of Englishmen, and persuading them to accept their lot. Clearly if the law was to fulfil this role it had to have some superhuman mystique to it. In his stimulating essay on 'Property, Authority and the Criminal Law',[13] Douglas Hay has argued that it was an important part of the process that judges themselves talked and argued as though the law were something above them, controlling their very decisions. Their willingness to bow to the most absurd technicalities, to acquit manifestly guilty men because of some technical legal rule, was, from this perspective, confirmatory evidence that the judges were powerless before the very law itself. Later, to Bentham and other rational reformers, some of these rules seemed absurd and served only to demonstrate the incompetence and conservatism of the judges. 'But it seems likely', says Douglas Hay,

> that the mass of Englishmen drew other conclusions from the practice. The punctilious attention to forms, the dispassionate and legalistic exchanges

13 In *Albion's Fatal Tree* (Hay and others, eds. London, 1975).

between counsel and the judge, argued that those administering and using the laws submitted to its rules. The law thereby became something more than the creature of a ruling class – it became a power with its own claims, higher than those of prosecutor, lawyers and even the great scarlet-robed assize judge himself. To them too, of course, the law was The Law. The fact that they reified it, that they shut their eyes to its daily enactment in Parliament by men of their own class, heightened the illusion. When the ruling class acquitted men on technicalities they helped instil a belief in the disembodied justice of the law in the minds of all who watched. In short, its very inefficiency, its absurd formalism, was part of its strength as ideology.[14]

I myself have also argued elsewhere that the retention of Equity, as a distinct body of law until late in the last century, as well as the use of legal fictions and various other devices, may have served a similar purpose.[15] Equity, as a residuary form of mercy to be applied in hard cases, is always a useful part of the laws of a civilised state. But historically it may have been especially useful when its existence and extent was not widely known among the mass of the people. If equitable rules are applied on a regular and uniform basis so that they come to supplant the legal rules altogether, then the deterrent effect of the legal rules may be greatly weakened. Who will pay his debts punctually if everybody knows that the legal sanction for failing to do so is, as a matter of course, disregarded by Courts of Equity?

Arguments of this nature suggest that there was a strong elitist tradition in English law until relatively recent times. Saying one thing, and doing another, or keeping quiet about powers of mercy or Equity, was an important contribution to the mystique of the law. The process helped to reconcile the relatively free political condition of Englishmen with the fact that they had no political power. So the modern judiciary's belief that it is best not to be too explicit about the true nature of the judicial role has a long historical tradition behind it. But of course this historical explanation immediately raises the question whether the argument continues to be valid in present-day circumstances. Let me first attempt to look a little more closely at why the judiciary appears to retain this belief today. Of necessity, some of the answers here are speculative, but given the necessary time and patience, I suspect that evidence for most of them could be found scattered here and there in the Law Reports. I will identify five separate arguments which I believe may influence the present attitude of the judiciary.

Firstly, there is some evidence that the traditional historical elitism still has weight. Lord Devlin, for instance, has argued that it is useful for the judge to be able to dissociate himself from the law, to hint to the litigant that he would prefer to decide otherwise, but is bound by the law. But if a judge leaves the law and makes his own decisions, 'he loses the protection of the law and sacrifices the appearance of impartiality which is given by adherence to the law. He expresses himself personally to the dissatisfied litigant and exposes himself to criticism.' On the other hand, if the judge is able to lay the responsibility for the

---

14 Ibid., at 55.
15 See my *The Rise and Fall of Freedom of Contract* (Oxford, 1979) 191–3.

decision at the door of the law itself, he saves himself from criticism and the decision 'leaves no sense of individual injustice.'[16] This might be taken for a somewhat shabby attempt to evade responsibility for one's professional duties. If the judge acknowledges his responsibility in creative decision-making, he must of course accept criticism; if on the other hand, he folds his hands and disclaims all creative power, he may console his conscience with the thought that he has no responsibility for the consequences. It is difficult to avoid the conclusion that some judges have sincerely and genuinely believed this to be the case, but I do not believe Lord Devlin's point is as narrow as that. He appears to be arguing that it is desirable in the public interest, and not just in the interest of judges, that litigants should not attribute responsibility for the law to the judges themselves. This, however, is to restate the argument, not to provide a justification for it. We are still left with the question: why is it (if it is) desirable that litigants should not attribute responsibility for the law to the judges?

The second argument is the familiar one that it is somehow undemocratic for judges to make law. Legislation is the function of legislators in the modern democratic state, and legislators should be elected. Unelected judges have therefore no legitimate authority to legislate, and should not do so. This is, of course, an argument (insofar as it is valid at all) for judges not legislating, it is not an argument for legislating but pretending not to do so, or disclaiming that they do so. Nevertheless, it may well be because judges are uneasy about their unelected positions, and undemocratic power, that they fear the reactions of the populace should the truth become known. It is therefore necessary to deal with this argument in two sub-divisions: (a) do the principles of democracy make it undesirable for judges to legislate, and (b) in any event, do they make it undesirable openly to admit that judges legislate? I will consider these in turn.

As to the first, it may of course be argued, that since judges must legislate, come what may, the question is a futile one. However, the answer to that must surely be that if it is truly undemocratic and hence undesirable for judges to legislate, then at least their creative decision-making should be confined within the narrowest possible limits. I do not myself subscribe to this thesis. For a start, I am far from clear that there is anything undemocratic about judicial creativity. It is, of course, undeniable that, as Professor Jaffé puts it, the election of its political leaders is 'the single most significant aspect of a modern democracy',[17] but it is also undeniable that, in nearly all democratic states, the power of elected legislatures and executives has invariably been balanced by the power of unelected judges. An independent and not politically accountable judiciary is surely just as essential to modern democratic government as elected and politically accountable legislatures and executives. A cynic might indeed argue that it is the independence and non-accountability of the judiciary which makes democracy tolerable and workable.

Those who argue that judicial law-making is undemocratic must be prepared to elaborate on their concept of democracy. For it is notorious that democracy

16 *The Judge* (Oxford, 1979) 4.
17 *English and American Judges as Lawmakers* (Oxford, 1969) 32.

is a weasel word which can be made to mean a great many different things. Even if we confine our attention to more or less 'genuine' democracies in which political leaders are elected by free elections the variations in the process are almost infinite. Furthermore slight variations in the electoral process may produce governments or legislatures of quite different complexions, either of which would be regarded as 'democratic'. There are, moreover, many devices for limiting the speed and ease with which changes may be imposed on a society, for example the existence of second chambers, or entrenched constitutional laws which can only be changed in a prescribed manner, not to mention actual bills of rights which are expressly open to judicial interpretation. The fact is that even those who quite literally believe that the purpose of democratic government is to give effect to the will of the people must recognise that there are inherent difficulties in recognising that will and translating it into practical effect. Thus in most if not all democratic states, one of the prime purposes of constitutional laws is to provide rules for the ascertainment of the popular will and the modes of giving effect to that will. Naturally then, it must be one of the prime purposes of the judiciary to see that those rules are observed. A judicial decision which may appear to thwart the immediate will of the legislature or the executive may thus be ultimately more democratic than the legislative or executive decision itself. Indeed, the independence of the judiciary is, it has been well said, a logical corollary of the very concept of enacted law. The enactment of laws in accordance with set procedures is the very process by which the popular will is translated into the views of a majority. This too is a very large theme which I can barely touch on: to demand that enacted law be construed by democratically subservient judges is, as Judge Learned Hand once said, 'In the name of a more loyal fealty to the popular will … to defeat the only means by which that will can become articulate and be made effective.'[18]

Then again, the popular will tends to be highly volatile in many modern democracies. In Britain we have been getting used to the fact that almost every general election brings a change of government; indeed public opinion polls often suggest that most governments would be turned out of office within a year or two of being elected if elections were held more frequently. Do the principles of democracy require that this constantly changing popular will be translated into law? The two major political parties in Britain appear to assume that the answer is 'Yes,' subject to the fact that elections are only held every four or five years. But the resulting social and political upheavals, with the vast changes in the law which they bring every few years, are enormously costly, both economically and in terms of social stability. To assume that this is what 'the people' want, because general election results produce changes of government, is to endow the electorate with a corporate identity which it does not possess. All this, of course, is a very large theme, and one which is perhaps more the province of the political theorist than the lawyer. All I want to do is to stress how facile is the argument that democracy requires judges not to legislate, or to legislate only to the minimum possible degree.

18 'The Contribution of an Independent Judiciary to Civilisation' (1942) reprinted in *Jurisprudence in Action*, Legal Essays selected by the Association of the Bar of New York (N.Y., 1953) 227.

Then there is the yet further question whether democratic principles themselves do not require some limitations to be imposed on the power upon. [*sic*] In countries like the United States where severe constitutional restraints are imposed on the powers of legislative majorities, the judges often appear to be less inhibited about their legislative or constitutional role. In particular, they make no secret of the importance of their function in the protection of minorities. In Britain, on the other hand, it is becoming hard in modern times to argue that such protection is a part of the democratic process. And yet the way in which majorities treat minorities has surely been a mark of the truly democratic society through the ages. The creative role of the judges as protectors of minorities has, unfortunately, received little attention recently in England. Professor Griffith has concluded that the judiciary cannot invoke this ground in defence of a creative legislative role because in fact their record in the protection of minorities in recent years has been very poor. It is, he says, a great myth that English judges are alert to protect individuals against the power of the state; on the contrary, they are almost obsessed with maintaining the structure of constitutional authority.[19] Only in dealing with trade unions are there signs that the judges wish to protect minority groups, and that is why the left are so distrustful of the law and the courts. I do not myself believe that the record of the judiciary is quite so dismal on this issue as Professor Griffith seems to think; but there is undoubtedly cause for concern for anyone who believes that the traditional role of the judges includes the protection of minorities against the wielders of majority power in whatever shape or form it comes. But all this takes me too far afield. My aim is once again the very simple one of reminding lawyers that there are various aspects of the judicial function which do not lack justification even if they may appear contrary to what are today so easily taken for democratic principles.

The second part of the question that I posed was whether, even if judicial creativity is not inherently undemocratic, it may nevertheless be wiser either to conceal or to minimise the extent of that function. The argument essentially is that even if there is nothing objectionable about judicial creativity, those who in fact wield majority power in the state may take a different view. This then leads on to the third identifiable reason which underlies the belief of the English judges that it is best to be discreet about their legislative or creative role. Put bluntly, it comes to this, that Parliament and the people are willing to tolerate the present exercise of legislative power by judges because they do not wield the power too openly. If they did proclaim more loudly what they were at, Parliament might respond by cutting down judicial power. The argument, which is itself an astonishingly political one, is to be found set out quite clearly (though not, of course, *fortissimo*) in Lord Scarman's speech in *Duport Steel Ltd*. v. *Sirs*[20] as follows:

Great judges are in their different ways judicial activists. But the Constitution's separation of powers, or more accurately, functions must be observed if judicial independence is not to be put at risk. For, if people and

19 *The Politics of the Judiciary* (1977) 196–7.
20 [1980] 1 All E.R. 529, at 551.

Parliament come to think that the judicial power is to be confined by nothing other than the judge's sense of what is right (or, as Selden put it, by the length of the Chancellor's foot), confidence in the judicial system will be replaced by fear of it becoming uncertain and arbitrary in its application. Society will then be ready for Parliament to cut the power of the judges. Their power to do justice will become more restricted by law than it need be, or is today.

I am bound to say that this looks much like the elitist argument set forth again, but bolstered this time with predictions of what will happen if 'the people' come to understand or misunderstand what is going on in law courts. The argument is a difficult one to combat on its own terms. For there are undoubtedly signs that the political left in England is increasingly restive with the creative power of the judiciary in sensitive political areas. So Lord Scarman's prediction that, if judges were more open at what they are doing, the response of Parliament might be to cut their powers, appears to me to be quite likely to be fulfilled. And that is a result which I, in common with Lord Scarman, and most lawyers, would find deplorable. But it does not follow that I think this result can or should be avoided by a policy which is ultimately based on the belief that you can fool most of the people most of the time.

It may be that Lord Scarman meant to say no more than that if judges exceed the proper scope of judicial creativity, they must expect their powers to be cut. But the passage suggests to me that in truth his real anxiety is that people will not understand the nature of the judicial function. For surely Lord Scarman himself does not believe that the judicial power is confined by nothing other than the judge's sense of what is right; it seems that what worries him therefore is that people will misunderstand the judicial role if judges are too open about their creative functions.

This does, however, lead me to the fourth factor which I believe underlies the present English judicial attitude on this question. Judges ought to understand the nature of judicial techniques better than anyone else, for they are the only people who actually exercise it, but it is curiously the fact that they often seem to have surprisingly simplistic ideas about it. It often seems to be assumed that the choice facing the judge is either to be strictly subservient to the law, on the one hand, or to cast off all fetters and do what he thinks is right on the other hand. It is possible that Lord Scarman, in the passage I have just cited, was indicating his adherence to this simplistic belief, though I do not think so. But there is no doubt that English judges often do speak as though this were indeed the choice before them. They make frequent references in this context to the hoary old joke about Equity depending on the length of the Chancellor's foot, and they sometimes speak disparagingly of discretionary justice or 'palm-tree' justice, as though that were the only alternative to a strict and slavish adherence to the passive role of pure interpreter.

In fact the legislative or creative role of the judiciary is far more complex than this. For a start, all judicial decisions must be justified by open and publicly stated reasons. These reasons, moreover, must be reasons of a particular type, though it is easier to indicate the kind of reasons which are unacceptable than those which are acceptable. But beyond these broad generalities, there are issues of great complexity even for those who believe in the most extensive use of the creative judicial role. For example, should a judge attempt to do justice in the circumstances of the particular case; or should he attempt to find the most desirable or satisfactory rule or principle? These are by no means the same thing, even though it is an accepted tradition that all decisions must be justified by some rule or principle, unless they can be openly justified by invoking some judicial discretion. It is, for instance, no secret that Lord Denning regards the judicial function as that of doing justice in the particular case: rules and principles must be accommodated to that ultimate goal, with the result of course, that his rules and principles often appear to lack generality or binding force.

Then there are questions about where the judge is to look for his sense of justice or fairness. Does he look, as some have argued, entirely in his own breast, or (as Cardozo argued)[1] does he look to what he conceives to be the community's sense of justice or fairness? That in turn raises obvious difficulties where the community is not a homogeneous body, but one riven into majority and minority factions. Next, there are obvious questions about the breadth of rules or principles to be invoked. Should the judge move inch by inch, laying down the narrowest possible rule which will justify his decision? Or should he go for the broad generalisation, even though that may have to be cut down later? The former technique, which is perhaps more often favoured today, tends in the end, to become indistinguishable from that of doing justice in every individual case; the latter is not appropriate to every case – it need hardly be said – but it is, of course, itself a complex, though not an irrational question, to decide which cases are appropriate for the broad generalisations.

In addition, courts are peculiarly subject to what have been called 'institutional reasons'.[2] Should this judge be bound by that decision? What does the relationship between Parliament and judiciary suggest in this or that situation? To what extent can the judges co-operate with Parliament in this legislative function? These are, it seems to me, complex questions which have been too little studied in England. It is facile to dismiss them by suggesting outrageous and extreme examples and then knocking them over like Aunt Sallies, as has sometimes been done. Lord Devlin, for instance, rejects the idea of a partnership in the legislative process as absurd. Is the judge to ring up the minister and find out what he wants about some controversial legislation?[3] The answer to that is, of course not. But examples of this kind do not eliminate the fact that the courts and the legislature are necessarily involved in some sort of co-operative enterprise, whether they like it or not. Obviously, this does not mean that judges should abandon their primary function of judging, but within the constraints which the different roles of legislator and judge involve, it ought to be possible for some kind of dialogue to take place in appropriate cases. And it ought to be possible, for example, for judges to iron out obvious absurdities and mistakes in legislation, and gaps in the common law, rather more satisfactorily than they sometimes do today.

1   *The Making of the Judicial Process* (Yale, 1921) 107–8.
2   See R. S. Summers, 'Two Types of Substantive Reasons; The Core of a Theory of Common Law Justification' (1968) 63 *Cornell L.R.* 707.
3   *The Judge*, at 17.

Once again, I am trenching on a very large theme. My excuse for doing so is that when judges discuss the desirability of keeping quiet about the creative role of the judiciary they often seem to assume that the nature of that role is a very simple matter. On the contrary, it is a highly complex business. To recognise that the judge has a creative role does not imply that he can create exactly what he pleases… .

I come finally to the fifth argument which underlies present English judicial attitudes. This is the argument, made powerfully by Lord Devlin, that the judge's impartiality may be gravely prejudiced by an active judicial role where there is no community consensus. So long as there is a consensus, activism is all right, presumably because neither party will feel offended if the judge makes law in a way which all people would agree with. But in more controversial areas, activism of this kind is bound to seem like taking sides. And so, impartiality, which is the judge's greatest and most important attribute, is threatened. Undoubtedly this is an argument for judicial restraint, but nobody has ever suggested that judges ought to go chasing after totally new and idiosyncratic ideals of their own, As Professor Jaffé puts it, 'The case for judicial creativity is *not* a challenge to the judiciary to go it alone, to invent completely new principles'.[4] In any event, given that judges must decide unclear cases, and that in the process of deciding almost any case, clear or unclear, ideas of fairness and justice cannot be excluded from consideration, this broad notion of what constitutes partiality must surely be rejected. Does a judge cease to be impartial if he prefers justice to injustice? Fairness to unfairness? Right to wrong?

*

I turn now to explain briefly why I dislike this combination of actual adherence to the realist theory with a publicly acknowledged adherence to the declaratory theory. The simplest argument is that it is unlikely to work. This sort of elitism may have been possible in the eighteenth century. But we have today a literate and educated population in Western democratic societies, even if the mass of the people are still somewhat simple and unsophisticated in their beliefs about complex subjects like the law. Moreover, the practice of law is not confined to a 'priest' class. There are plenty of educated and sophisticated lawyers who understand the nature of the creative judicial role, and dislike it for political reasons. These people cannot be prevented from opening up to public discussion the precise issues which the judiciary would apparently prefer to avoid opening up. The de-mystification of the law has gone too far for this policy to work.

Secondly, the policy rests ultimately on an intellectually dishonest position, and in an open society that is something which is hard to justify. It is, of course, right to say that English judges are probably not conscious of any dishonesty in their position on these questions; and that, even if the accusation is a fair one, the judges have adopted this position for the best of motives. Nevertheless, the fact remains that it is not possible to reconcile a realist theory of the judicial role for the *cognoscenti* while fobbing off the masses with the declaratory theory. For the reconciliation of these two positions would require that we (or the judges) should wish the public to believe things which

4   *Op. cit., supra* n. 17, p. 324 at 73.

we (or they) do not believe. I have referred above to the remarks of Lord Radcliffe who thought that it was better that the public should believe in the law as a constant, safe in the hands of the judges, than as a finely tuned instrument, responding to changing needs and values. But is it better for the public to believe this if it is not true? Similarly, I have referred to Lord Devlin's views on the need to preserve the public confidence in the impartiality of the judges. But is it desirable that the public should think the judges more impartial than they actually are – impartial, in this rather special sense, that is to say.

These are intellectual and moral issues about the sort of society we wish to live in. But there are also serious empirical questions which are not as easily answered as some judges appear to think. Is it true that the public has more confidence in judges who fold their arms and say: 'That is the law, regrettable though it may be; we cannot do anything about it'? Certainly there is *some* evidence that public confidence in the law and in the judges is not improved when out-dated or old-fashioned rules are invoked to justify decisions in this way, even when combined with disclaimers of responsibility by the judges. I do not know myself which of these attitudes is more likely to enhance respect for the law among the public; but at the least it seems dangerous to assume that the arguments are all one way.

Moreover, this difficult intellectual balancing act between realism and the declaratory theory has two very serious practical results. The first is that it makes it even more unlikely that the policy will actually work. Not only will people come to realise that the judges have a wider role than they wish to acknowledge, but it may even come to be felt that the judges have something to hide. Judges who habitually say, in relation to controversial statutes, that their only function is to give effect to the intention of the legislature, will find that they are simply not believed, as Professor Griffith has warned.[5] And that may, in the end, threaten their impartiality, or the belief in their impartiality, more effectively than a complete candidness about their true role.

The second practical argument against the present position is that it makes the creative judicial role much less useful and effective than it could be. If judges continue to deny or minimise the policy nature of the issues which they often have to decide, then counsel are not encouraged to argue cases in policy terms. In some areas of the law this has, I believe, led to curious and quite harmful results. For example, in the development of the law of negligence, so far as it relates to damage to property, judges have, from time to time, openly admitted the policy nature of the issues, as Lord Denning and Lord Diplock both did in the *Dorset Yacht* case.[6] But the fact that the declaratory theory still plays such a large role in judicial practice is attested by the fact that it is not even now customary for cases of this nature to be argued in openly policy terms. Legal arguments in these cases still centre around the familiar old doctrinal issues of duties of care, remoteness of damage, foreseeability of consequences and so on.

It would, however, be wrong of me to conclude this lecture without expressing my anxieties about some of the issues which I believe inhibit the judges from

5   *Op. cit., supra* n. 19, p. 326 at 176.
6   [1970] A.C. 1004. I am in this paragraph using 'policy' in the broadest sense to include what Dworkin would call 'principles'.

too open an adherence to the realist theory. Although I believe we are too committed to the open society for the present policy of concealment to work, I do not have undiluted enthusiasm for the results in this particular context. I believe that we sacrifice the mystique element in law by openly adopting the realist theory, and I am far from convinced that society can do without this element, well-founded or ill-founded though it may be. In a country such as Britain where the constitutional restraints against majority decision-making are so slender, and where the majorities themselves often seem to regard their rights over minorities as absolute, the dangers are particularly grave. At the end of the day, one must take what comfort one can from the first, if not the second part of Judge Learned Hand's remark that 'a society so riven that the spirit of moderation is gone, no court *can* save; ... a society where that spirit flourishes, no court *need* save.[7]

See also Patrick Atiyah's article 'Lawyers and Rules: Some Anglo-American Comparisons', 37 *Southwestern Law Journal*, 1983, p. 545 in which he suggested that English judges are much less adventurous in law-making than American judges. One reason he thought was that 'English judges do generally believe that law is a system of rules, and act on that belief to a greater degree than most American judges, particularly in courts of last resort.' (P. 545):

> A judge's duty, an English judge would say, is primarily to apply the law, and previous judicial decisions in the courts of last resort *are* the law. The judge does, of course, have a secondary, lawmaking function where there are no prior decisions, but these gaps in the law are relatively few and far between. Only in quite exceptional circumstances, therefore, should the judge's secondary, law-making function be permitted to operate where a clear prior decision already determines the rules. These perceptions of law, rules, and gaps in the system are, of course, open to philosophical challenge, but few observers of the English legal scene would dispute that they are held by an overwhelming number of judges, and indeed by most practicing lawyers too. Conversely, equally few observers of the American legal scene would doubt that, though similar perceptions are widely found in American courts, alternative perceptions also may be found. I would hypothesize that many American judges regard rules as having less importance than do English judges; that they see judicial decisions as illustrations of underlying principles (often seen as drawn from morality or natural law) rather than as rules in themselves and of themselves; that they see the law-making function of courts of last resort as more important than English judges do; and that they do not in consequence feel bound by prior decisions to the same degree as English judges.

Professor Atiyah thought that one reason was the different background of English and American judges, with the American judge being more

---

7   But for the argument that the courts may be able to play a useful role in a society where the spirit of moderation does flourish, see Rostow, 'The Democratic Character of Judicial Review' (1952) 66 *Hvd. L.R.* 193.

likely to be and to see himself as part of the political process. English judges rely more on the argument of counsel than American judges who often do their own research. In US courts the role of dissent is quite different. A dissenting judge in an English court will follow the majority view next time the issue comes up. American dissenting judges regard themselves as free to continue their disagreement with fellow judges from one case to the next.

Also in US cases it is much more common for there to be a dissent. Thus in the 1950s, 70 per cent or more of US Supreme Court full opinions had a dissent. In the 1980 term, 69 per cent of full opinions were subject to a dissent. In the House of Lords they varied from year to year from 10 per cent to 46 per cent. Even Lord Denning, a judge known to be a dissenter, dissented in only a small minority of cases – 4.7 per cent of 1,742 cases as compared with Justice William Douglas of the US Supreme Court who dissented in 19.2 per cent of 6,863 cases.

The significance of the greater frequency of dissents, Professor Atiyah suggested, was that it reflected a different perception of the nature of the judicial role and even of the nature of law itself:

> First, judges who are more concerned to impress the public with the idea that law in some sense represents neutral and eternal values of truth and right may be more concerned to present a united front, and suppress their differences of opinion. Hence the infrequency of dissent in a particular jurisdiction may reflect 'acceptance of the notion that unanimity denotes precision and truth and, therefore, is more convincing.' I think English judges are more influenced than most American judges by a desire to promote this goal. By contrast, American judges often appear to have viewed dissent as a way of asserting 'a personal, or individual responsibility ... of a higher order than the institutional responsibility owed by each to the Court, or by the Court to the public.'
>
> Second, as I have already suggested, judges who perceive the law as a system of rules binding on the judges as on everyone else are more likely to arrive at the same conclusion in a given case. For to put it at the lowest level, such a view of the nature of law and the judicial rule narrows the range of choice open to the judge and therefore makes unanimity more likely.

One of the most sophisticated attempts to diagnose when courts should and should not legislate is that of Professor Michael Freeman in a major article in 1973 – 'Standards of Adjudication, Judicial Law Making and Prospective Overruling', 26 *Current Legal Problems*, 1973, p. 166. He listed certain basic differences between courts and legislatures. First, judges were not democratically answerable to the electorate, which made it inappropriate for them to enact their own social policies. Second, courts had to justify their decisions by articulating reasons, whereas legislators were not under this constraint. Third, judges came from a narrow social background and represented only one profession. The information available to a court when it was considering law reform was very limited. Also the range of options available to the courts was much more limited:

> When Parliament decides that something ought to be the law it can consider the different ways of achieving that goal. It might wish to stop policemen extracting confessions from suspects. It could do this in a number of ways. It could make such confessions inadmissible evidence. It could make the extraction of confessions a criminal offence and expose the offending police officer to a long term of imprisonment. It could set up a state board which paid compensation to victims of such police conduct. It could direct that offending police officers be dismissed or demoted. But the judge could only adopt the first of these steps. Or, to take a second example, the development of a 'deserted wife's equity'[8] by the Court of Appeal was an attempt (some would say of dubious propriety) to ground protection for the deserted wife in legal principle. With its collapse in *Ainsworth*,[9] the legislature intervened and passed the Matrimonial Homes Act in 1967. This set up machinery whereby a spouse could gain protection by registering a charge on the other spouse's property. The Court of Appeal had suggested this might be the solution, but with a court's limited powers they were unable to initiate such a scheme.
>
> Judges then do not have available to them the very important instruments of administrative enforcement, licensing or positive rewards. They can use only damages and specific orders, injunctions, specific performance, *certiorari*, *mandamus*, declaratory judgments and so on. And without this institutional machinery the steps they can undertake are limited. [At p. 178.]

Another distinguishing feature had been seen by Lon Fuller in his *Anatomy of the Law* (Pelican, 1971). The rules applied by judges to individual cases must be 'brought into, and maintained in, some systematic interrelationship; they must display some coherent internal structure' (p. 134). Parliament by contrast can take 'leaps into the dark'. If judicial decisions were to be predictable by practitioners and their clients, they must be grounded in principle. ('This means that judges develop the law incrementally' (Freeman, op. cit., p. 179).) Society expected judges to decide disputes in a rational way. There was much room for creativity but the judge did not have a clean slate on which to write.

Freeman then illustrated what he regarded as good and bad examples of judicial activity and inactivity. He distinguished between judicial restraint, judicial cowardice, judicial boldness, and judicial creativity.

Judicial restraint was shown in *Morgans* v. *Launchbury* [1973] A.C. 127 which raised for decision the question whether injured persons could sue a wife whose husband had taken her car with permission and then loaned it to a third person who caused the accident. On accepted principles prevailing at that time there was no doubt that no such action lay, but the

8   In *Bendall* v. *McWhirter* [1952] 2 Q.B. 466 and many other cases until 1965.
9   [1965] A.C. 1175.

House of Lords was urged to introduce a new rule. It refused to do so (the Court of Appeal had held for the plaintiffs): Lord Salmon recognised that:

'it is an important function of this House to develop and adapt the common law to meet the changing needs of time'

but

'[i]n the present case ... the proposed development constitutes such a radical and far-reaching departure from accepted principle that it seems to me to smack of naked legislation.'[10]

There are similar sentiments in the judgments of Lord Cross and Lord Pearson[11]. but it is in Lord Wilberforce's judgment that we get the clearest exposition of the problem.

He was in no doubt that some adaptation of common law rules of agency could be made by the judges. He admitted that traditional concepts of vicarious liability might be proving inadequate. He saw some attractions in being creative. But he spurned any invitation to do so in this case. His reasons deserve careful examination. He said that the assumption was that it was desirable to fix liability in cases of negligent driving on the owner of the car. Such a policy was disputable, though his lordship saw no need to discuss such a question. He rather averted his attention to the different systems that could be introduced. He catalogued four: a system of liability based on the concept of the 'matrimonial' car; one based on the 'family' car; one stating that any owner who permits another to use his car should be liable by the fact of permission; and possibly even a system of strict liability. But as Lord Wilberforce rightly said,

'I do not know on what principle your Lordships acting judicially can prefer one of these systems to the others or on what basis any one can be formulated with sufficient precision or its exceptions defined. The choice is one of social policy; there are arguments for and against each of them.'[12]

... To summarise, *Morgans* v. *Launchbury* shows judicial restraint at its best. It was a polycentric dispute *par excellence*. It involved a policy choice upon which the judges had no information or guidance. Law-making would have involved upturning the rightful expectations of thousands. The effect of a wider test on insurance, on premiums, on organisations like the Motor Insurers' Bureau could only be guessed at; and that is not an adequate basis for law-making. [Freeman, pp. 187–9.]

10 [1973] A.C. 127 at 151.
11 Ibid., at 146 and 142–3.
12 Ibid., at 136.

To illustrate *judicial cowardice* Freeman used the case of *Myers* v. *D.P.P.* [1965] A.C. 1001. The question was whether the House of Lords would stretch the exceptions to the hearsay rule to include records kept in a mechanical way by a business. The prosecution wanted to introduce in evidence the numbers fixed on to cars to show that the defendants had stolen and altered parts of cars in order to conceal their origin. Three Law Lords (Lords Morris, Hodson and Reid) held the evidence was inadmissible.

> Lord Morris stated that it had been decided eighty years earlier that hearsay is not admissible unless authority 'be found to justify its reception within some established … rule.'[13] Lord Hodson took the position that to create a new exception 'would be judicial legislation with a vengeance in an attempt to introduce reform of the law of evidence which if needed can properly be dealt with only by the legislature'.[14] Lord Reid believed that the 'common law must be developed to meet changing economic conditions and habits of thought… . But there are limits… . If we are to extend the law it must be by the development and application of fundamental principles… . If an exception were created here, others should be created, and there would be a series of appeals… . If we are to give a wide interpretation to our judicial functions questions of policy cannot be wholly excluded, and it seems to me to be against public policy to produce uncertainty.'[15] He also advocated legislation.
>
> Lord Pearce and Lord Donovan dissented. Lord Pearce's judgment is particularly persuasive. He showed that the admission of the evidence in question was fully in accordance with the shared principles and expectations of the legal profession. On a technical matter of 'lawyers' law' concerned with the machinery of justice this must be the appropriate audience. He demonstrated that they could admit the evidence in question without violating the substance of the rule purporting to exclude it. Indeed, that there were principles in the law which clamoured for its acceptance. Suppose, he argued, the anonymous workman could be identified. If he was dead, 'the records would be admissible as declarations in the course of duty.'[16]
>
> Legislation was in due course passed,[17] but judicial legislation was feasible and apposite. The laws of evidence are better developed by those who operate them than by Parliament, though radical policy changes even in this area must be left to the legislature. If Lord Pearce's reasoning had been followed it is difficult to see whose reasonable expectations could have been thwarted. [Freeman, pp. 190–92.]

Judicial boldness, Freeman said, was exemplified by *Knuller* v. *D.P.P.* [1973] A.C. 435, which raised the question of extending the criminal law. *Shaw* v. *D.P.P.* [1962] A.C. 220, in which the House of Lords had in effect

---

13   [1965] A.C. 1001 at 1028.
14   Ibid., at 1034.
15   Ibid., at 1021–2.
16   Ibid., at 1036.
17   Criminal Evidence Act 1965.

invented a new offence of conspiracy to corrupt public morals, had met with widespread opprobrium. But in *Knuller* the Law Lords went further and recognized another offence – of conspiracy to outrage public decency. The case was brought against the publisher of *International Times* in respect of small ads by homosexuals.

> The Lords in *Knuller* created new law.… . Lord Diplock's judgment is an exemplary exposure of the illogical, unhistorical and often hypocritical reasoning underlying the judgments in *Shaw's* case and those of his brethren in *Knuller*. But the other four Lords tied themselves into knots in their attempts to rationalise their judgments.… .
>
> *Knuller* had injected uncertainty into criminal law and its administration. It flies in the face of legislative policy[18] and ministerial assurance.[19] If it endorses the values of certain sectional interests it flouts others. In a democratic society consensus demands compromise. Legislation embodies this:*Knuller* rejects it. It exemplifies judicial law-making at its worst. [Ibid., pp. 192–3, 194–5.]

(For extended consideration of the problems of law-making in the field of criminal law, see especially A. T. H. Smith, 'Judicial Law Making in the Criminal Law', 100 *Law Quarterly Review*, 1984, p. 46.)

The final category identified by Freeman, that of *judicial creativity*, he illustrated by *British Railways Board* v. *Herrington* [1972] A.C. 877, in which the House of Lords had to decide whether to overrule its own decision of *Addie* v. *Dumbreck* (1929) on the liability of occupiers towards trespassers. The most interesting judgment, Freeman thought, was that of Lord Wilberforce:

> He made his ideology clear. A law of tort based on fault liability was 'outdated'. '[C]ases such as these could be more satisfactorily dealt with by a modern system of public enterprise liability devised by Parliament.'[20] But such wholesale institutional change could not be devised by judges, even if it were desirable for them to do so. Parliament had, of course, passed in 1957 the Occupiers' Liability Act, and this had preserved the common law ruling on trespassers. This did not mean that 'the House was bound hand and foot by *Addie's* case at its narrowest.'[1]
>
> The common law, his lordship argued, 'always leaves a residue to be completed by common sense.'[2] Common sense dictated that the development of the law would best be served by concentrating on the particular type of case which worries the courts and on which the law has been tested by experience. Most twentieth-century litigation was brought against public utilities. A duty

18   Obscene Publications Act 1959; Theatres Act 1968.
19   House of Commons, *Hansard*, vol. 695, col. 1212, 3 June 1964.
20   [1972] A.C. 877 at 922.
1   Ibid., at 921.
2   Ibid., at 921.

of care arises, he held, 'because of the existence, near to the public, of a dangerous situation.'[3] ...

Law-making such as that perpetrated by Lord Wilberforce is a legitimate activity. It does not create injustice (the argument of 'system') as public utilities and, for example, farmers are not 'alike'. In one sense what is being done is classification of legal concepts on to a more factual basis. It is right for a judge to take the minor step taken by Lord Wilberforce. He knows that other judges now have a framework, that as new problems arise there is something against which to test the formulation. *Herrington* clears a lot of dead wood, and enables judges to focus on unresolved problems. It may be that as they do this, as the *Herrington* ruling is tested and re-tested, that a new principle will emerge. But for the present the common law has been developed to accommodate a social problem: the pre-existing rules have hardly changed yet the seed of public enterprise liability has been sown. [pp. 198–200.]

Robert Stevens' massive study of the House of Lords' judges from 1800 to 1976 traces a succession of stages. (Dr Alan Paterson similarly analyses the attitude of the Law Lords in terms of changes over time in his much more limited period – 1957–62, 1962–6, 1966–73 – see A. Paterson, *The Law Lords* (1982), pp. 132–53.) Stevens traces the gradual shift in the modern era from the period of the rigid and narrow formalism under Lord Simonds to a more open and policy-oriented period under Lords Reid, Wilberforce, Diplock, Salmon and Simon: 'By the mid-seventies it [the House of Lords] was no longer regarded as the restater of accepted doctrines, but rather as the incremental developer of new doctrines... . [W]hile the belief in the predictability of "clear rules" was no doubt still stronger than in any other common law jurisdiction, the belief in the anonymity and irrelevance of the judicial contribution had largely evaporated.'[4] The 1966 Practice Statement advising the world that the House of Lords might depart from its previous decisions added legitimacy to a process that had been going on since the late fifties and was accelerating in the early sixties.[5] The statement seemed to confirm that Parliament had no objection to the judges making law in those areas of society primarily entrusted to dispute settlement in the courts. Thus it is not surprising that, although rarely mentioned, the statement encouraged a greater flexibility of approach and, in particular, an emphasis on principle rather than rule and precedent and a noticeably greater inclination to talk about policy.'[6]

It was true that the traditional view of the role of the courts had by no means disappeared. A substantial element in the profession still preferred to emphasize the role of logic, certainty and predictability, and to play

3 Ibid.
4 R. Stevens, *Law and Politics* (1979), p. 589.
5 Ibid., p. 621.
6 Ibid.

down discretion and creativity. Thus Sir Henry Fisher, formerly a High Court judge, attacked the 1966 Practice Statement arguing that judges 'should refrain from broad statements on principle and from obiter dicta. They should be scrupulous to apply the law as it exists even if they think it to be wrong or unfair or unjust and should resist the temptation to twist the law to conform with their sympathies or theories, as the proper instrument for the reform of the law is Parliament, aided where necessary by the Law Commission, a Law Reform Committee, or Royal or departmental commission.'[7] Professor L. C. B. Gower, a former Law Commissioner, urged the relative unsuitability of the House of Lords as a law-reform agency, and even the Law Commission had criticised the Law Lords' reform of the law on occupier's liability towards trespassers in *Herrington* v. *British Railways Board* [1972] A.C. 877 because it had not produced 'a clear principle applicable to the generality of cases.'[8]

> Yet in spite of all these factors, by the mid-1970s forces were gathering and trends were developing that in the long run were likely to accentuate the creative force of the final appeal court... . By English standards the approach to precedent evidenced rapid changes. After 1966 even the more conventional law lords began to talk the language, if not the litany, of judicial creativity. When overruling, the House talked less about the errors of legal logic made in the prior case and more about the underlying policies that had changed since the earlier decision.
>
> In 1955 ... law-making by judges had been seen in simplistic terms – it either competed with Parliament or it did not, and it was either good or bad. That had been largely abandoned. Various North American influences helped inject into English thinking the American concepts of judicial restraint and judicial activism[9] – that there are shades of desirability of law-making. Rather than the competition between the legislature and judiciary that had so concerned Radcliffe, it was increasingly argued that '[t]he organs of government are partners in the enterprise of lawmaking'. Out of this ... grew a much greater awareness of when judicial legislation was appropriate.[10]

Judicial law-making in the field of criminal law seems to be especially problematic. Dr A. T. H. Smith in discussing the creative powers of the courts listed the main objections to judicial law-making as the usurpation of Parliament's function, the creation of uncertainty and the retrospective effect of judge-made law. ('Judicial law-making in the criminal law' 100*Law Qrtly. Rev.*, 1984, p. 46.) See to like effect Marianne Giles, 'Judicial Law-Making in the Criminal Courts: the Case of Marital Rape', [1992]*Crim. L.R.* 407. The author suggests that waiting for reform of the criminal law through

7   119 *Solicitors' Journal* (1975), p. 854.
8   *Report of the Law Commission on Occupiers' Liability* (Cmnd 6928, 1975).
9   Louis L. Jaffé, *English and American Judges as Lawmakers* (1969), pp. 28–9.
10   Stevens, op. cit., p. 624.

legislation is the lesser evil 'compared with judicial law-making which seems to create at least as many problems as it solves ... and additionally is objectionable in point of principle as a means of law reform'. A recent example is the decision of the House of Lords in *C.* v. *D.P.P.* [1995] 2 All E.R. 43 upholding the presumption that a person between the age of 10 and 14 is deemed not to have the intent to make his act criminal unless it can be positively proved by the prosecution that he knew what he did was seriously wrong. The Divisional Court ([1994] 3 All E.R. 190) had held that the presumption of *doli incapax* was outdated and no longer had any application in the changed conditions of society. The House of Lords agreed that the presumption had been 'subject to weighty criticism over many years by committees, by academic writers and by the courts' (p. 45). Nevertheless it still represented the law. In a 20-page judgment with which the four other law lords agreed, Lord Lowry said that if the rule was to be changed it should be done by Parliament. The invitation was taken up and the rule was changed in the Crime and Disorder Act 1998, s. 34. See further the excellent and informative account of the former and current judicial attitude to law-making by Anthony Lester, 'English Judges as Law-Makers', *Public Law*, Summer 1993, pp. 269–90.

Two examples of the courts dealing more openly with policy issues

Lord Denning was of course never shy of looking at policy issues. Yet he seemed to approach such issues even more squarely in his later years. *Dutton* v. *Bognor Regis U.D.C.* was an example:

Dutton v. *Bognor Regis U.D.C.* [1972] 2 W.L.R. 299 at 313

LORD DENNING M.R.: This case is entirely novel. Never before has a claim been made against a council or its surveyor for negligence in passing a house. The case itself can be brought within the words of Lord Atkin in *Donoghue* v. *Stevenson*; but it is a question whether we should apply them here. In *Dorset Yacht Co. Ltd* v. *Home Office* [1970] A.C. 1004, Lord Reid said, at p. 1023, that the words of Lord Atkin expressed a principle which ought to apply in general 'unless there is some justification or valid explanation for its exclusion.' So did Lord Pearson at p. 1054. But Lord Diplock spoke differently. He said it was a guide but not a principle of universal application (p. 1060). It seems to me that it is a question of policy which we, as judges, have to decide. The time has come when, in cases of new import, we should decide them according to the reason of the thing.

In previous times, when faced with a new problem, the judges have not openly asked themselves the question: what is the best policy for the law to adopt? But the question has always been there in the background. It has been concealed behind such questions as: Was the defendant under any duty to the plaintiff? Was the relationship between them sufficiently proximate? Was the injury direct or indirect? Was it foreseeable, or not? Was it too remote? And so forth.

Nowadays we direct ourselves to considerations of policy. In *Rondel* v. *Worsley* [1969] 1 A.C. 191, we thought that if advocates were liable to be sued for negligence they would be hampered in carrying out their duties. In *Dorset Yacht Co. Ltd* v. *Home Office* [1970] A.C. 1004, we thought that the Home Office ought to pay for damage done by escaping Borstal boys, if the staff was negligent, but we confined it to damage done in the immediate vicinity. In *S.C.M. (United Kingdom) Ltd* v. *W. H. Whittall & Sons Ltd* [1971] 1 Q.B. 337, some of us thought that economic loss ought not to be put on one pair of shoulders, but spread among all the sufferers. In *Launchbury* v. *Morgans* [1971] 2 Q.B. 245, we thought that as the owner of the family car was insured she should bear the loss. In short, we look at the relationship of the parties: and then say, as a matter of policy, on whom the loss should fall.

What are the considerations of policy here? I will take them in order.

First, Mrs Dutton has suffered a grievous loss. The house fell down without any fault of hers. She is in no position herself to bear the loss. Who ought in justice to bear it? I should think those who were responsible. Who are they? In the first place, the builder was responsible. It was he who laid the foundations so badly that the house fell down. In the second place, the council's inspector was responsible. It was his job to examine the foundations to see if they would take the load of the house. He failed to do it properly. In the third place, the council should answer for his failure. They were entrusted by Parliament with the task of seeing that houses were properly built. They received public funds for the purpose. The very object was to protect purchasers and occupiers of houses. Yet they failed to protect them. Their shoulders are broad enough to bear the loss.

Next I ask: is there any reason in point of law why the council should not be held liable? Hitherto many lawyers have thought that a builder (who was also the owner) was not liable. If that were truly the law, I would not have thought it fair to make the council liable when the builder was not liable. But I hold that the builder who builds a house badly is liable, even though he is himself the owner. On this footing, there is nothing unfair in holding the council's surveyor also liable.

Then I ask: If liability were imposed on the council, would it have an adverse effect on the work? Would it mean that the council would not inspect at all, rather than risk liability for inspecting badly? Would it mean that inspectors would be harassed in their work or be subject to baseless charges? Would it mean that they would be extra cautious, and hold up work unnecessarily? Such considerations have influenced cases in the past, as in *Rondel* v. *Worsley* [1969] 1 A.C. 191. But here I see no danger. If liability is imposed on the council, it would tend, I think, to make them do their work better, rather than worse.

Next, I ask: Is there any economic reason why liability should not be imposed on the council? In some cases the law has drawn the line to prevent recovery of damages. It sets a limit to damages for economic loss, or for shock, or theft by escaping convicts. The reason is that if no limit were set there would be no end to the money payable. But I see no such reason here for limiting damages. In nearly every case the builder will be primarily liable. He

will be insured and his insurance company will pay the damages. It will be very
rarely that the council will be sued or found liable. If it is, much the greater
responsibility will fall on the builder and little on the council.

Finally I ask myself: If we permit this new action, are we opening the door
too much? Will it lead to a flood of cases which neither the council nor the
courts will be able to handle? Such considerations have sometimes in the past
led the courts to reject novel claims. But I see no need to reject this claim on this
ground. The injured person will always have his claim against the builder. He
will rarely allege – and still less be able to prove – a case against the council.

All these considerations lead me to the conclusion that the policy of law
should be, and is, that the council should be liable for the negligence of their
surveyor in passing work as good when in truth it is bad.

For Lord Denning to speak so plainly was one thing; for the House of
Lords to do so is something rather different. Yet, as Robert Stevens has
shown, the House of Lords is increasingly willing to follow the Denning
lead. A clear example is *Miliangos* v. *George Frank (Textiles) Ltd* [1976]
A.C. 443, in which, it will be recalled, the House of Lords had to decide
whether to abolish the ancient rule that damages in an English court could
only be awarded in sterling. All the five judges who took part in the decision
addressed themselves principally to the policy problems.

Four of the five Law Lords said that the rule should be changed, one
thought it should not. The reasons advanced by the four who wanted to
change the rule included:

(1)   It was now possible procedurally to order payment of foreign currency
      debts in the foreign currency – this had not been possible before
      (Wilberforce at 462–3; Cross at 497; Edmund-Davies at 499).
(2)   Sterling was no longer so stable a currency as before (Wilberforce at
      463; Cross at 479; Edmund-Davies at 500).
(3)   There were two precedents in the field of arbitrations of awards in
      foreign currencies (Wilberforce at 463–4; Cross at 479; Edmund-Davies
      at 500).
(4)   Changing the rule would 'enable the law to keep in step with commercial
      needs and with the majority of other countries facing similar problems'
      (Wilberforce at 467).
(5)   It was possible to state a better rule (Wilberforce at 467–70).
(6)   The fact that a rule was long established was not necessarily a reason
      to require that it be uprooted; if at all only by legislation:

LORD WILBERFORCE (at 469–70): My Lords, in conclusion I would say
that, difficult as this whole matter undoubtedly is, if once a clear conclusion is
reached as to what the law ought now to be, declaration of it by this House is
appropriate. The law on this topic is judge-made: it has been built up over the
years from case to case. It is entirely within this House's duty, in the course of

administering justice, to give the law a new direction in a particular case where, on principle and in reason, it appears right to do so. I cannot accept the suggestion that because a rule is long established only legislation can change it – that may be so when the rule is so deeply entrenched that it has infected the whole legal system, or the choice of a new rule involves more far-reaching research than courts can carry out. A recent example of the House changing a very old established rule is *West Midland Baptist (Trust) Association (Inc.)* v. *Birmingham Corporation* [1970] A.C. 874. Lord Reid thought that it was proper to re-examine a judge-made rule of law based on an assumption of fact (as to the stability of money) when the rule was formulated but which was no longer true and which in many cases caused serious injustice. So in that case the House selected a new date and did not think it necessary or right to wait for legislation and I would not think it necessary or right here. Indeed, from some experience in the matter, I am led to doubt whether legislative reform, at least prompt and comprehensive reform, in this field of foreign currency obligation, is practicable. Questions as to the recovery of debts or of damages depend so much upon individual mixtures of facts and merits as to make them more suitable for progressive solutions in the courts. I think that we have an opportunity to reach such a solution here.

But even the activist and creative judge feels the discipline of the precedents. This sense of the primacy of the precedents was expressed by Lord Justice Robert Goff (as he then was) in a case concerning the definition of the word 'reckless' in the Criminal Damage Act 1971. The judge said that he agreed with his brother judge most reluctantly:

ROBERT GOFF L.J.: I agree with the conclusion reached by Glidewell J., but I do so simply because I believe myself constrained to do so by authority. I feel moreover that I would be lacking in candour if I were to conceal my unhappiness about the conclusion which I feel compelled to reach. In my opinion, although of course the courts of this country are bound by the doctrine of precedent, sensibly interpreted, nevertheless it would be irresponsible for judges to act as automatons, rigidly applying authorities without regard to consequences. Where therefore it appears at first sight that authority compels a judge to reach a conclusion which he senses to be unjust or inappropriate, he is, I consider, under a positive duty to examine the relevant authorities with scrupulous care to ascertain whether he can, within the limits imposed by the doctrine of precedent (always sensibly interpreted), legitimately interpret or qualify the principle expressed in the authorities to achieve the result which he perceives to be just or appropriate in the particular case. I do not disguise the fact that I have sought to perform this function in the present case. [*Elliott* v. *C.* [1983] 2 All E.R. 1005 at 1010.]

But in spite of careful and anxious consideration of the precedents, he felt himself unable to reinterpret them (and especially the words of Lord Diplock in *Metropolitan Police Comr* v. *Caldwell* [1982] A.C. 341) in such a way as to give the result that he favoured.

Can judges undertake their own researches into the law?

Another aspect of judicial creativity is whether judges can use their own research in the process of hearing or deciding cases. In regard to the process of hearing argument the answer is clearly yes. (For an example see Nourse J., p. 229 above.) There is nothing whatever to prevent a judge from asking counsel to meet a point that has occurred to him as a result of his own reading or study in the library during an adjournment. But when it comes to the judgment itself the position is very different. There have been instances when judges have taken points in their judgments or have referred to precedents which were not discussed by counsel during argument. But this is extremely rare and when it happens it has sometimes been the subject of critical comment by a higher court – see, for instance, *Rahimtoola* v. *Nizam of Hyderabad* [1958] A.C. 379 at 398, where Lord Simonds said that he did not assent to Lord Denning's views on questions and authorities 'in regard to which the House has not had the benefit of the arguments of counsel or of the judgment of the courts below'. Lords Reid, Cohen and Somervell said they entirely agreed with Lord Simonds' observations.[11] Alan Paterson reported that his interviews with judges and counsel showed that amongst the majority 'there was a shared expectation that a Law Lord in giving his reasons for deciding for or against the appeal ought to confine his propositions of law to matters covered by the arguments of counsel.'[12] There were some who doubted the rule. Lord Hailsham, for instance, said that it applied 'usually but not necessarily'. The quality of counsel's arguments varied and it was 'sometimes necessary to break new ground' (ibid., p. 40). Lord Simon said that a court which did its own research 'should proceed with special caution' (ibid.), but he did not rule it out altogether.

The judicial self-denying ordinance applies not only in regard to precedents which might be discovered by the judges but also to propositions of law. In general judges seem to accept the view that in their judgments they should not advance points not put to them by counsel. The best practice in such cases seems to be to restore the case for further argument, and this is sometimes done.[13] Sometimes, however the rule is ignored.[14] Nevertheless, overall, although the position was more fluid than in the past, the expectation still held sway that the judges should not go beyond submissions made by the lawyers in the case.[15] For an argument

11 See also *Hadmor Productions Ltd* v. *Hamilton* [1982] 1 All E.R. 1042.
12 A. Paterson, *The Law Lords* (1982), p. 38.
13 For examples see Paterson, op. cit., p. 42.
14 Paterson (at p. 42) cites as examples: *R.* v. *Hyam* [1975] A.C. 55, per Lords Diplock and Dilhorne; *Miliangos* v. *George Frank (Textiles) Ltd* [1976] A.C. 443, per Lord Simon at 478; and *D.P.P.* v. *Humphreys* [1977] A.C. 1, per Lords Salmon and Edmund-Davies.
15 Paterson, op. cit., p. 43.

that courts should be permitted to require counsel to argue points of law that seem relevant even if counsel does not wish to do so see N. H. Andrews, 'The Passive Court and Legal Argument', 7 *Civil Justice Qrtrly.*, 1988, p. 125. Andrews reviews the case law as to the judge doing his own research into the law.

3.   WHAT THE LAW IS AND WHAT IT OUGHT TO BE

Is there a danger that through focusing more openly on policy issues the courts will come to decide cases on the basis of what the law ought to be rather than what the law is? This question lies at the heart of one of the most vital debates about the nature of the judicial process. It reflects the anxieties of the many judges and lawyers who have deprecated the efforts made in particular by Lord Denning to improve the quality of justice by looking beyond the form to the substance below.

Any young counsel unwise enough to argue in court that his submission represents what the law ought to be will immediately be interrupted by the court – 'Mr Smith,' he will be told, 'we are here to decide what the law is, not what it ought to be.' The statement, in one sense, is absolutely true. The court, in deciding the question of law before it, must decide on the basis of what it thinks the law is. (The only exception is if the court could say – we think the law in the past was X and that is the law we are applying to the present case, but in future we will decide that it is Y. This technique, known as prospective overruling, is discussed below.) But the statement that the court is only interested in what the law is, misrepresents the position. It is based on the false premise that, in determining the issue before it, the court is exercising no choice or discretion. This view is the classic formalistic position actually adopted by countless English judges. An example is the reply given in 1951 by Lord Jowitt, the Lord Chancellor, when he was asked at an Australian conference what the House of Lords would do if there was an appeal in the then recently decided case of *Candler* v. *Crane, Christmas*:

> We should regard it as our duty to expound what we believe the law to be and we should loyally follow the decisions of the House of Lords if we found there was some decision which we thought was in point. It is not really a question of being a bold or a timorous soul; it is a much simpler question than that. You know there was a time when the earth was void and without form, but after these hundreds of years the law of England, the common law, has at any rate got some measure of form to it. We are really no longer in the position of Lord Mansfield who used to consider a problem and expound it ex aequa et bona – what the law ought to be … I do most humbly suggest to some of the speakers today that the problem is not to consider what social and political conditions do today require; that is to confuse the task of the lawyer with the task of the

legislator. It is quite possible that the law has produced a result which does not accord with the requirements of today. If so, put it right by legislation, but do not expect every lawyer, in addition to all his other problems, to act as Lord Mansfield did, and decide what the law ought to be. He is far better employed if he puts himself to the much simpler task of deciding what the law is.[16]

Lord Jowitt's response would accurately reflect the view of generations of English lawyers and judges up to the present day. However, it would be difficult to find many American practitioners or judges who would today accept the proposition in that form. The difference in the two countries is that American legal culture has in the past two or three decades absorbed the insights of the so-called Realist School, which flourished from the 1930s and whose leading exponents were writers such as Jerome Frank in *Law and the Modern Mind*. The chief contribution of the Realists was to expose the role of the judge himself in deciding the outcome of cases raising points of law. Some of the claims of the Realists no doubt go too far (a caricature of their view is that the decision is ultimately determined by, say, the state of the judge's digestion). But their central claim has now become fully accepted by virtually all American lawyers. By contrast, many and possibly even most English lawyers still live in an earlier (flat earth) age of innocence.

The validity of the Realist view seems readily demonstrable. The judge hears argument from two parties, each of whom is normally represented by a professional lawyer. Each side advances argument as to why his position represents the law. The court must decide between them. Sometimes it may be that the question virtually decides itself. There are, let us say, six precedents each of which says that the law on the point is X. The proposition has been unchallenged for 150 years. Every textbook confirms it. X seems a reasonable rule – no one has criticized it. The party that seeks to show that the law on that point is Y obviously has an extremely uphill task. Indeed, few lawyers would undertake it. The great majority would advise the client that the prospects of success were nil and would urge him to spend his money on something more promising. This case is therefore most unlikely ever to reach the courts.

In any case before the courts where both parties are professionally represented (where one can therefore rule out the possibility of cranks and vexatious litigants), the court is almost always required to decide between two arguments that have some substance. One side may come with stronger precedents but the other side will perhaps have greater merits on the facts. Or the strength of the precedents may be fairly evenly matched and the real battle will be to capture the sympathy of the court for

16 Cited by W. K. Fullagar, 25 *Australian Law Journal*, 1951, p. 278, and referred to by Robert Stevens in *Law and Politics*, p. 338.

the client's position. Of course, in some cases the lawyers on both sides will accurately predict the outcome and to that extent it may be that there was little scope for the judge's individual discretion. He was 'forced' by the strength of the precedents and the lack of any solid argument to the contrary to decide in favour of one of the two litigants. But, again, those cases tend not to come to court and when they do the decision is often only predictable after the event – before it is handed down, there appears to be the possibility that it might go the other way. Moreover, after the decision there remains the chance of an appeal. The higher one goes in the appeal system, the greater the chance of getting free of the clutches of the precedents – one climbs above the clouds and can survey the mountain peaks. At the level of the House of Lords the judges are absolutely free to decide either way.

The significance in this context of the House of Lords' Practice Statement has not yet been fully grasped by the English profession. If the House of Lords is free to depart from its own previous decisions, it means *by definition* that they do not necessarily reflect the law. When the House first enunciated the principle it thought the law was X; now it may conclude that the rule is Y. It is impossible for the precedents to reveal this – it must be the result of a conscious decision by the members of the House of Lords. But this is only a particularly clear demonstration of something that occurs each time a court reaches a view of the law which is contrary to the existing precedents – for instance through the ordinary process of overruling. The very possibility that the Court of Appeal can overrule the decisions of the High Court means, again by definition, that it need not follow even the clearest precedents established by the High Court. But precisely the same is true even of the High Court. Since the High Court is not bound by its own decisions, it too can look at the precedents and reject them – in the name of some other better argument. In other words, whenever a court is faced with precedents that are not binding on it, it has the choice of whether to follow them or not. Even if there are ten previous precedents all saying that the law is X, providing none is binding, the court is free to reject them and find the law to be Y. (Where the precedent is binding there is of course also a choice, since ultimately it is the court and not the precedent that decides that the precedent is apposite and not distinguishable.) Needless to say the court will be slow to reject a relevant precedent. It will need to have strong reasons for doing so. In some fields it will be most reluctant to upset settled rules. This is especially true in areas of the law where people can be assumed to have arranged their affairs in reliance on the existing state of the law, such as in commercial, tax or property matters. But in the final analysis, not being bound by a decision means that one can depart from it. Ten non-binding precedents still do not add up to a binding rule – ten times nothing remains nothing. Of course, ten non-binding precedents present more of an obstacle than one, but it remains an obstacle that a determined court can surmount if it can be persuaded that it is worth the effort.

It has become respectable in recent years to recognize that judges make law – even conservative judges affirm as much. Thus Lord Edmund-Davies said in 1975: 'The simple and certain fact is that judges inevitably act as legislators.... The inevitable interim between the discovery of social needs and demands and the provision of legislative remedies to meet them presents judges with the opportunity (indeed, it imposes upon them the *duty*) of filling the need and meeting the demand in accordance with their notions of what is just. Nolens volens they thereby act as law-makers.'[17] Similarly, Lord Pearson, another judge who can hardly be described as a radical, said in *Herrington* v. *British Railways Board* [1972] 2 W.L.R. 537 of *Addie* v. *Dumbreck*, the House of Lords' decision that stood in the plaintiff's way: 'It seems to me that the rule of *Addie's* case has been rendered obsolete by changes in physical and social conditions and has become an incumbrance impeding the proper development of the law ... In my opinion the *Addie* v. *Dumbreck* formulation of the duty of occupiers to trespassers ... has become an anomaly and should be discarded.'

But it has not yet become fully respectable to talk in courts of law of what the law ought to be. One is still constrained to talk there only of what the law is with insufficient recognition of the fact that for the court the question what the law is necessarily *includes* the question what the law ought to be. To discuss what the law ought to be is only another way of defining the proposition that a court is inevitably and properly involved in law-making. As Lord Edmund-Davies put it – *nolens volens* they act as law-makers. But if they are law-makers, perhaps it would be preferable that the judges should not only recognize the fact but permit and indeed encourage debate before them of what law they should make.

(a)   The practical effect of the retrospective impact of common law decisions

When a court delivers a ruling which is perceived to change the law the effect is not only for the future. It also affects the past. This is because of the fiction that when it states the law a court is stating the law as it always has been. To use the familiar metaphor, the law is a seamless web. The jagged edges when the law changes should not be seen. If the judges were thought to be engaged in law making it might generate unease. The best way to cover up the fact of judicial creativity is to pretend that it does not happen. The new rule is the law and always has been.

17 'Judicial Activism', 28 *Current Legal Problems*, 1975, p. 1.

Of course if the case has already been litigated it cannot be reopened. It is subject to the principle expressed in the phrase *res judicata*. Equally, if the time allowed under the Statute of Limitations for bringing proceedings of that kind has expired, no case can now be brought on the basis of the changed rule. But if neither *res judicata* nor the Statute of Limitations applies, an action can be brought based on circumstances that occurred before the new decision.

The effect of this rule was the nub of a disagreement between the law lords in a recent case of great significance. Local authorities had invested millions of pounds in what were called 'interest rate swap transactions'. A district auditor challenged the lawfulness of such investments by a local authority on the grounds that they amounted to speculative trading for profit. In 1991 the House of Lords upheld that view. (*Hazell* v. *Hammersmith and Fulham London Borough Council* [1991] 1 All E.R. 545.) The decision led to much further litigation. In one such action a bank sought to recover moneys paid to local authorities under interest swap agreements. The money had been paid by the bank more than six years previously and action for its recovery would therefore normally have been barred by lapse of time. But the Limitation Act states that where money is paid under a mistake, time should only run when the mistake has been discovered or could with reasonable diligence have been discovered. In the High Court the bank lost on the basis of binding Court of Appeal authority that no action lay for the recovery of money paid under a mistake of law. The case went on appeal directly to the House of Lords.[18]

The House of Lords held that that rule, which had been established for over a century, should no longer form part of English law. It was inconsistent with a modern approach to the principle of unjust enrichment. The law should recognise a general right to recover money paid under a mistake regardless of whether it was a mistake of fact or a mistake of law. The bank could recover its money. Time only started to run when the mistake was discovered which was the date of the new judicial decision. This ruling has remarkable implications. The lengthy leading judgment was given by Lord Goff. In the course of his magisterial review of the subject he accepted that this decision was one of those rare cases where judicial development of the law was of an unusually radical nature.

Lord Browne-Wilkinson, dissenting, said he did not agree that the money should be recoverable since when it was paid the payer was not labouring under a mistake. At the time of the payment the bank thought that local authorities could lawfully enter into swap transactions. The majority's view meant that payments which when made and for years after were irrecoverable would subsequently be recoverable if the courts changed the rule. 'This result would be subversive of the great public interest in the

18 *Kleinwort Ltd* v. *Lincoln City Council* [1998] 4 All E.R. 513.

security of receipts and the closure of transactions. The position is even worse because all your Lordships consider that the claims to recover money paid under a mistake of law are subject to s. 32(1) of the Limitation Act 1980, i.e. that in such a case time will not begin to run until the "mistake" is discovered. A subsequent overruling of a Court of Appeal decision by the House of Lords could occur many decades after payments have been made on the faith of the Court of Appeal decision: in such a case "the mistake" would not be discovered until the later overruling. All payments made pursuant to the Court of Appeal ruling would be recoverable.' (p. 519) He would have urged that instead the law should be changed by Parliament on the advice of the Law Commission and that a satisfactory way be found to limit the impact of the change in the law by regulating the limitation period. Lord Lloyd took the same view. He said that he viewed with alarm the possibility that whenever the House of Lords overruled a Court of Appeal decision it would be open to those who have entered into transactions in reliance on the previous decision to seek to reopen their transaction.

What then of the retrospective effect of changes in the law in criminal cases? Is a person who was convicted and sentenced to a prison term on the basis of one judicial view of the law entitled to be freed from prison if that view of the law is overruled in a later case? Curiously, the answer is not clear.

The first question is whether the Court of Appeal will regard the change in the law as a reason for giving leave to appeal out of time. In *Hawkins* (1977) 1 Cr. App. Rep. Lord Bingham, Lord Chief Justice, cited a dictum from *Mitchell* (1977) 65 Cr. App. Rep. 185 where Lord Lane had said: 'It should be clearly understood... that the fact that there has been an apparent change in the law or, to put it more precisely, that previous misconceptions about the meaning of a statute have been put right, does not afford a proper ground for allowing an extension of time in which to appeal against conviction.'

But in a previous case *Ramsden* [1972] Crim. L.R. 547, CA) Lord Lane had said that in such a situation the court might grant leave to appeal out of time. In the last analysis, he said, 'this must in every case be a matter of discretion'. In *Hawkins* (1977) 1 Cr. App. Rep. Lord Bingham said 'If such convictions were to be readily reopened it would be difficult to know where to draw the line or how far to go back'. The general practice of the Court he said was to set its face against the reopening of convictions in these circumstances, but the Court should 'eschew undue technicality and ask whether any substantial injustice has been done'. Hawkins, the Court found, could have been successfully prosecuted for other criminal acts, so leave to appeal out of time after a change in the relevant principle of law was refused. But in *David Cooke* (2 December 1996, unreported, CA No. 9604988) the decision went the other way. Leave to appeal out of time was granted because the appellant was serving a prison sentence – though, in the event, convictions for different offences were substituted.

What happens when a case is referred back to the Court of Appeal Criminal Division (previously by the Home Secretary and now, under the Criminal Appeal Act 1995, by the Criminal Cases Review Commission)? Often the reference comes years after the original conviction. In such a case the Court is not restricted to consider the law as it stood at the time of the conviction. It can take later developments into account. Thus in the famous case of Judith Ward it was able to overturn the conviction on the basis of non-disclosure by the prosecution to the defence even though at the time of the trial the prosecution's conduct had not been in breach of the rules (*Ward* [1993] 2 All E.R. 577). Similarly in the Carl Bridgwater murder appeal (*Molloy*, 23 July 1997, unreported, CA 96/5131/SI) the Court took into account recent decisions on relevant points of law as a ground contributing to the unsafeness of the conviction.[19]

(b) Prospective overruling as an aid to creative law-making

One sign of a new judicial attitude to law-making has been the reference in one or two recent cases to the American device of prospective overruling, whereby the court announces that it will change the relevant rule – but only for future cases. In *Jones* v. *Secretary of State for Social Services* [1972] A.C. 944, Lord Simon of Glaisdale (at 1026) said:

> I am left with the feeling that, theoretically, in some ways the most satisfactory outcome of these appeals would have been to have allowed them on the basis that they were governed by the decision in *Dowling's* case, but to have overruled that decision prospectively. Such a power – to overrule prospectively a previous decision, but so as not necessarily to affect the parties before the court – is exercisable by the Supreme Court of the United States, which has held it to be based on the common law: see *Linkletter* v. *Walker* (1965) 381 U.S. 618.
>
> In this country it was long considered that judges were not makers of law but merely its discoverers and expounders. The theory was that every case was governed by a relevant rule of law, existing somewhere and discoverable somehow, provided sufficient learning and intellectual rigour were brought to bear. But once such a rule had been discovered, frequently the pretence was tacitly dropped that the rule was pre-existing: for example, cases like *Shelley's Case* (1581) 1 Co. Rep. 93b, *Merryweather* v. *Nizan* (1799) 8 Term Rep. 186 or *Priestley* v. *Fowler* (1837) 3 M. & W. 1 were (rightly) regarded as new departures in the law. Nevertheless, the theory, however unreal, had its value –

---

19 See generally H. Blaxland, 'Developments in the Common Law Since Conviction: the Approach of the Court of Appeal', *Archbold News*, Issue 8, 10 October 1997, p. 6.

in limiting the sphere of lawmaking by the judiciary (inevitably at some disadvantage in assessing the potential repercussions of any decision, and increasingly so in a complex modern industrial society), and thus also in emphasising that central feature of our constitution, the sovereignty of Parliament. But the true, even if limited, nature of judicial lawmaking has been more widely acknowledged of recent years; and the declaration of July 20, 1966, may be partly regarded as of a piece with that process. It might be argued that a further step to invest your Lordships with the ampler and more flexible powers of the Supreme Court of the United States would be no more than a logical extension of present realities and of powers already claimed without evoking objection from other organs of the constitution. But my own view is that, though such extension should be seriously considered, it would preferably be the subject-matter of parliamentary enactment. In the first place, informed professional opinion is probably to the effect that your Lordships have no power to overrule decisions with prospective effect only; such opinion is itself a source of law; and your Lordships, sitting judicially, are bound by any rule of law arising extra-judicially. Secondly, to proceed by Act of Parliament would obviate any suspicion of endeavouring to upset one-sidedly the constitutional balance between executive, legislature and judiciary. Thirdly, concomitant problems could receive consideration – for example, whether other courts supreme within their own jurisdictions should have similar powers as regards the rule of precedent; whether machinery could and should be devised to apprise the courts of the potential repercussions of any particular decision; and whether any court (including an Appellate Committee in your Lordships' House) should sit in banc when invited to review a previous decision.

See, to the same effect, Lord Simon of Glaisdale's statement in *Miliangos v. George Frank (Textiles) Ltd* [1976] A.C. 443 at 490. Lord Diplock has also lent support to the idea. In a lecture several years earlier, he referred to the fact that the retrospective impact of judicial decisions was one of the reasons that judges were reluctant to correct previous errors or to adapt an established rule to changed circumstances. Yet the retrospective effect of judicial decisions was simply a reflection of the legal fiction that the courts merely expounded the law as it always had been. The time had come, he thought, 'to reflect whether we should discard this fiction', and he thought that the development of prospective overruling in appellate courts in the United States deserved consideration.[20]

The problems of prospective overruling are considered in the extract that follows:

Andrew Nicol, 'Prospective Overruling: A New Device for English Courts?', 39 *Modern Law Review*, 1976, p. 542

Prospective overruling is used by several [American] states and by the United States Supreme Court.... The justification most often advanced has been

20 'The Courts as Legislators', Holdsworth Club Lecture, 1965, pp. 17–18.

reliance. Several states, for instance, have been taking a fresh look at various immunities from tort suit.[1] A court may believe that the decision on which a particular immunity was based ought to be overruled, but it may also have to recognise that institutions which benefit from this immunity have not taken out insurance in reliance on it. Prospective overruling of the case granting the immunity has been used to break the *impasse*... . A somewhat different reliance has been claimed by prosecutors and police when faced with a court determined to tighten the procedures which must be followed in a criminal investigation. It is unfair, they say, to penalise the prosecution for failing to observe standards which were not set down until after the investigation has taken place.[2] The United States Supreme Court accepted this argument as one ground for limiting the effect of *Miranda* v. *Arizona*.[3]

Another justification for the use of prospective overruling has been that the desire which impels the court to overrule is the desire to implement a new policy, but a policy which need not be retroactive to be effective. In *Mapp* v. *Ohio*,[4] the United States Supreme Court held that evidence which was discovered in an unlawful search could not be used at trial. In *Linkletter* v. *Walker*,[5] the court held that the *Mapp* rule was to be prospective only. The new rule, the court said, was intended to discourage unlawful searches. It was too late to discourage those searches which had already taken place. Therefore nothing could be gained by giving *Mapp* retroactive effect... .

Objections to prospective overruling
... (3) *It allows a court to make new law without applying it to the case before the court*: There are few lawyers now who would agree with Montesquieu that 'the judges are the mere mouthpieces of the law.'[6] The opportunity for creativity in choosing 'the' relevant statutes or precedents, in favouring one of a pair of antagonistic canons of construction,[7] in distinguishing a case on its facts or following it on principle, is apparent on both sides of the Atlantic.

However, a traditional restraint on this law-making power has been that courts are limited to expounding the law on the facts to dispose of the instant case and then add an unnecessary postscript as to how they will act in the

---

1   Units of government, *Molitor* v. *Kaneland Community School Dist.* No. 32 163 N.E. 2d 89 (1959) Ill.; charities, *Kojis* v. *Doctor's Hospital*, 107 N.W. 2d 131 (1961) Wis.; intra-family, *Goller* v. *White*, 122 N.W. 2d 193 (1963) Wis.; religious institution, *Widell* v. *Holy Trinity Catholic Church*, 121 N.W. 2d 249 (1963) Wis. Plaintiff in this case had tripped over a negligently placed prayer kneeler.
2   *Johnston* v. *New Jersey*, 384 U.S. 719 (1966).
3   384 U.S. 436 (1966). This case required the police to issue a caution before questioning a suspect, on pain of having the statement excluded from the trial. The caution is similar to the English one, except that the accused must also be told, if he is indigent, that he has the right to a free lawyer.
4   367 U.S. 643 (1961).
5   381 U.S. 618 (1965).
6   *Esprit de Lois*, XI 6.
7   See Llewellyn, 'Remarks on the Theory of Appellate Decision and the Rules or Canons of How Statutes are to be Construed', 3 *Vand. L. Rev.* 395, 401 (1950).

future. Another version of the same argument is to say that the new rule is
obiter, and therefore a waste of time.

Yet a similar practice is already used by the courts. In *Hedley Byrne* v.
Heller Partners,[8] the House of Lords stated a new principle of liability for
negligent misrepresentors, but the defendant, who came within the general
description, was not held liable. The court added a rider, absolving from liability
a representor who had expressly excluded his liability at the time he made his
statement. An announcement by the court, as it prospectively overrules, that
it will apply a new and different rule in other situations, is no more *obiter* than
the House of Lords saying that in other cases it would hold negligent
misrepresentors liable. In both situations, the court lays down a principle,
argues that there is an exception, and finds that the parties to the suit come
without the exception. While the principle is not conclusive, it is applied in the
instant case, and it is difficult to see how it can be said to form no central part
of the reasoning of the court.

(4) *The* Hedley Byrne *technique referred to in* (3) *is prospective overruling
in disguise. A naked use of prospective overruling is therefore unnecessary.*[9]
This is not so. In *Hedley Byrne*, the court was able to declare a new rule without
applying it to the party in the instant case, but it achieved this result by
qualifying substantively the new rule. If, the following day, a similar case had
come up for judgment, but where the representor could not bring himself
within the qualification, the representor would have been held liable, even
though the representation may have been made many years previously. On the
other hand, if *Candler* v. *Crane, Christmas*[10] had been prospectively overruled,
the temporal qualification would have protected all persons (not liable under
some other doctrine) who had made negligent misrepresentations before the
date of the overruling. The *Hedley Byrne* technique goes some way, but not far
enough, in protecting those who relied on a prior statement of the law.

(5) *A judge who uses prospective overruling has too much the appearance
of a legislator*: It is argued[11] that however much judges are innovators in
practice, in popular belief they are still the 'finders' of law, not its 'makers'.
This belief, the argument runs, could not be sustained if judicial opinions read:
'this precedent is out-of-date and ought to be changed, but the change will only
be effective from today.'

This writer has serious doubts as to whether the public would have greater
respect for a court that slavishly followed precedent, than for one that tried to
reconcile the competing claims of change and reliance. However, for the sake of
appearances, there is another formula that the court might use: 'the rule that we
announce today is and always was the correct view of the law. However,
recognising the reliance which was placed on the old view, we will not apply
the true view to events happening before today.'

---

8   [1964] A.C. 465.
9   Friedmann, 'Limits of Judicial Law-making and Prospective Overruling (1966)
     29 M.L.R. 593, 605.
10   [1951] 2 K.B. 164, the Court of Appeal decision overruled in *Hedley Byrne*.
11   Devlin, 'Judges and Lawmakers' (1976) 39 M.L.R. 1.

This form was used in *Golak Nath* v. *State of Punjab*,[12] when the Supreme Court of India prospectively overruled the Land Reform Statutes. The court held that these statutes violated fundamental rights, guaranteed by the constitution, but because of the property interests which had been transferred and settled in reliance on them, they should be struck down with prospective effect only... .

(7) *If prospective overruling were available, it would make overruling more common and upset the certainty which results from a strict doctrine of stare decisis*: However, 'for the most part, certainty is an illusion.'[13] The discovery of old cases, the power to distinguish, the uncertainty of which facts will be believed in court[14] mean the outcome of a particular dispute is not necessarily certain, even in a system where overruling is rarely used. It is appreciated that a sense of proportion is necessary. Many disputes are within the 'core application'[15] of a rule. Most rules would be affirmed on challenge, even by a court with the power to overrule prospectively. Nevertheless, one must ask, as Goodhart did,[16] whether, if the rule is unjust, certainty is not bought at too high a price. To add a gloss to Goodhart's comment; if through prospective overruling, we take away the element of individual reliance, then although stability and predictability are important, can it always be said that they will be more important than the removing of injustice or correcting the anomaly.

(8) *Prospective overruling is undesirable because it encourages judicial law reform. The principal thrust of law reform should come from a democratically elected Parliament, rather than an appointed judiciary.* ... In 1953, the Evershed Committee considered a proposal for financing litigation on points of law of general public interest. In its conclusion it stated:[17]

> 'We do not think this method of a law reform committee fully meets the public need. Legislation is slow and cumbersome. Parliamentary time is notoriously limited, and may in future become even more precious. Clarification of the law by judicial decision is a swifter and surer process which can go forward at all times, without regard to parliamentary time and quite independent of the political process.'

Judicially developed law also has the advantage that it can be more cautious and developed according to experience. A judgment need not, indeed it is probably better if it does not, set out the whole ambit of the rule, complete with all qualifications. The courts are bound by the words of a statute, but only

---

12 [1967] 2 S.C.R. (India) 762 and see Pillai, 'Precedent in the House of Lords and the Doctrine of Prospective Overruling in the U.S.A. and India' (1967) 1 *Sup. Ct. Jo.* 79; Rajput, 'The Doctrine of *Stare Decisis* and Prospective Overruling' (1968) II *Sup. Ct. Jo.* 51.
13 Holmes, *The Path of the Law*, p. 465.
14 Jerome Frank, *Courts on Trial, passim.*
15 H. L. A. Hart, *The Concept of Law*, Chap. VII and pp. 120 et seq.
16 'Precedent in English and Continental Law' (1934) 50 L.Q.R. 934.
17 Final Report of the Committee on Supreme Court Practice and Procedure, H.M.S.O. Cmnd. 8878 (1953).

by the *ratio decidendi* of a decision. Statutory law has been scorned in the past for disturbing the growth of the common law. The scorn is often a reflection of the conservatism of the speaker, but it is true that the words of a statute have a rigidity which is not always desirable …

Thus I conclude that judicial law-making is inevitable. Parliament and the courts, in the words of Jaffé, are in the law business together and should be continually at work on the legal fabric of our society.[18] The establishment of the Law Commission has reduced, but not abolished the part which the courts should play in law reform. They will always be the junior partner in the partnership, but even so their methods enjoy some advantages over statute. Prospective overruling gives the courts more scope for reforming judicially developed law, but does not deny the superior weight which must be given to the words of the senior partner.

On the other hand, Lord Devlin has expressed himself unpersuaded by the arguments for prospective overruling:

Lord Devlin, 'Judges and Lawmakers', 39 *Modern Law Review*, 1976, p. 11

Courts in the United States have begun to circumvent retroactivity by the device of deciding the case before them according to the old law while declaring that in future the new law will prevail: or they may determine with what measure of retroactivity a new rule is to be enforced. This device has attracted the cautious attention of the House of Lords. I do not like it. It crosses the Rubicon that divides the judicial and the legislative powers. It turns judges into undisguised legislators. It is facile to think that it is always better to throw off disguises. The need for disguise hampers activity and so restricts the power. Paddling across the Rubicon by individuals in disguise who will be sent back if they proclaim themselves is very different from the bridging of the river by an army in uniform and with bands playing. If judges can make law otherwise than by a decision in the case at Bar, why do they wait for a case? Prevention is better than cure, so why should they not, when they see a troublesome point looming up, meet and decide how best to deal with it? Judicial lawmaking is at present, as Professor Jaffé phrases it,[19] a by-product of an *ad hoc* decision or process.' That this is so is of course in itself one of the objections to judicial lawmaking. Dependent as it is upon the willingness of individuals to litigate, it is casual and spasmodic. But to remove the tie with the *ad hoc* process would be to make a profound constitutional change with incalculable consequences. What is the business of a court of law? To make law or to do justice according to law? This question should be given a clean answer. If the law and justice of the case require the court to give a decision which its members think will not make good law for the future, I think that the court should give the just decision and refer the future to a lawmaking body.

18 L. Jaffé, *English and American Judges as Lawmakers* (1969).
19 Ibid., p. 35.

See to same effect M. D. A. Freeman, 'Standards of Adjudication, Judicial Law-making and Prospective Overruling,' 26 *Current Legal Problems*, 1973, pp. 166, 200–7. But see also Robert Traynor, 'Quo Vadis, Prospective Overruling: A Question of Judicial Responsibility', 28 *Hastings L. Jrnl.* 1979, 533–68, which supports the case for prospective overruling: and G. Tedeschi, 'Prospective Revision of Precedent'. 8 *Israel Law Review*, 1973, p. 173. Tedeschi suggests that 'prospective revision' is a better term than 'prospective overruling', since if it is prospective it does not technically amount to overruling. The concept of prospective decisions has been used by the English courts on occasion in the context of remedies in administrative law – for instance by granting a declaration prospectively. The principal reason is to avoid administrative chaos. See Clive Lewis, 'Retrospective and Prospective Rulings in Administrative Law', *Public Law*, Spring 1988, pp. 78–105; Harry Woolf, *Protection of the Public – A New Challenge* (Stevens, 1990) pp. 52–55. See also J.F. Avery, 'Decisions with Prospective Effect: A less Drastic Solution for the House of Lords' (1984) *British Tax Review* 203.

See also the majority decision of the High Court of Australia in *R.* v. *McKinney* (1991) 171 C.L.R. 468 laying down *for the future* a new and rigorous requirement of judicial warning to juries about the danger of convicting on disputed and uncorroborated confessions to police. Similarly the European Court of Justice in Luxemburg in the second *Defrenne* case (*Defrenne* v. *Sabena* [1976] E.C.R. 455) affirmed the principle of equal pay for equal work for men and women but applied it prospectively only because applying it retrospectively would have created impossible burdens for both public and private institutions.

Question

Do you think that, on balance, prospective overruling has enough merit to justify the English judges experimenting with it?

(c) Better information for judges about the policy implications of law-making

If the judges are now supposed to engaged increasingly in a more creative role of judicial law-making, how can they inform themselves of the policy implications of alternatives offered to them? As has been seen above (p. 275), the English courts do not permit counsel to call evidence about the social and economic implications of existing or proposed future formulations of the law. Nor can counsel cite to the court written reports on such issues. In *Miliangos* Lord Simon suggested that if courts 'are to undertake legislative responsibilities, something might be done to equip them better for the type of decision-making which is involved. Official advice and a balanced executive view might be made available by a law officer or his counsel acting as amicus curiae' ([1975] 3 W.L.R. 792). Is this suggestion viable? Could one expect the law officers to provide such a service? If so, would the service be likely to be truly 'objective', or would it tend to put only or mainly the official view? Could there be a system for permitting others to come before the court (whether orally or through some form of written submission) to argue the policy issues? In the United States it is very common to have issues of law argued not simply by the parties but by other interested groups and bodies through *amicus curiae* written briefs. The institution is described in the piece that follows:

Ernest Angell, 'The Amicus Curiae: American Developments of English Institutions', 16 *International and Comparative Law Quarterly*, 1967, p. 1017

> The *amici* whose names appear in the printed columns of reported decisions fall into three general categories. First, there are, as in the English practice, the legal representatives of the government, federal or state, counties, municipalities, government agencies and bodies. Secondly, there are private organisations of professional or other occupational membership; employers, business, commercial and industrial entities; labour unions; government and private industry employees by occupational class; bar associations and many others. In this category there should be included, though less common, a business unit which does not appear as part of an organised group and, rarely, an individual person. Thirdly, there are innumerable private associations, in general formally organised, which purport to speak for non-occupational, non-governmental, broad public interests; churches and religious bodies; minority groups such as Negroes (22 million in the United States) and Jews (5 million) civil libertarians, pacifists – the range is almost unlimited... .
>
> *Some reasons for the multiplicity of appearances of amicus curiae in American courts:* avoiding dogmatic assertion of any single factor, one can state that several have disparately combined, without overall shaping by the courts. What does appear to be the most obvious is the American legal habit of presenting printed or typed 'briefs',[20] to marshal the acts and cite the pertinent authorities of cases, statutes and texts: (1) at the conclusion of a trial and often in support of a motion on evidence or for interlocutory remedy; and (2) universally on appeal to the reviewing court. In the absence of special leave granted to counsel for the *amicus* to make oral argument, the judges thus avoid the necessity of listening to expanded oratory of the intervenor, but do have the advantage of being able to study his written argument which may range beyond the industry and legal knowledge of counsel for the parties of record. Some judges give only perfunctory attention to oral pleading from any but the most persuasive advocates and rely much more heavily on the written word.

20 See p. 360 below.

The universality of the written brief seems to have been born from the enormous sheer volume of American law – the decision of well over 100 federal courts and of several hundred courts of the 50 states; statutes, rules and regulations beyond the possibility of count; innumerable texts, the 'model' codes of the American Law Institute and 100 or so law 'journals' or law 'reviews' published by bar associations, learned societies and the many schools of law. No judge or lawyer can know or without immense labour pinpoint *ad hoc* anything more than a small fraction of the 'law' in America, compared with the wider familiarity of the English barrister with his own far more restricted volume of law. American counsel for a party of record may overlook what the court later finds to be the key point at issue and the available authorities. Our judges need more frequent and informed advice from the barristers before them; sometimes, perhaps frequently, this comes from the 'friend'... .

Finally, the growth has been favoured by the proliferation in our society of the private non-profit organisations which exist to promote at the bar or courts, before legislatures and in public opinion, the interests of a class group and their convictions about the values of some social interest – the Red Indian, the conscientious objector, tighter control over excesses of the 'free press', the economic interest of railway clerks. Newspapers, magazines, television and radio abound with the highly vocal claims of conflicting legal interests put forward by organised groups alert for every occasion to speak publicly.

The courts cannot operate in an Olympian remoteness from the social scene; they must perforce listen to what class interest claims are laid upon the bench for judicial digestion. Moreover, the judges seek information and informed opinion by inviting such appearances by those believed to be able to render such assistance – by no means confined to law officers of government. It has become inevitable that the threads of argument spun by these intervening 'friends' are woven into the fabric of formal decisions, sometimes visible to the inquiring eye outside the judicial chamber and, occasionally if more rarely, openly acknowledged in the formal opinion... .

Procedure
...the court rules provides that *amicus* briefs may be filed merely with the consent of counsel for the formal parties to the cases then pending; if consent is refused – as sometimes happens – then a motion may be made and the court passes upon this, generally granting it.

Note – Amicus curiae

The concept of the *amicus* in English practice is mainly confined to the role of the Attorney-General. In *Adams* v. *Adams* [1970] 3 All E.R. 572 it was held that the Attorney-General has the right of intervention in a private suit whenever it may affect the prerogatives of the Crown. Certainly he had locus standi at the invitation of the court or with leave of the court. He also had a right of intervention at the invitation or with the permission of the court, where the suit raised any question of public policy on which the executive might have a view which it might desire to bring to the notice of the court (at 576–7, per Simon P.)

The concept is, however, also used in other circumstances. One example is the intervention of The Law Society. For a typical instance see for instance *R.* v. *Central Criminal Court, ex p. Francis and Francis* [1989] A.C. 346 regarding access for the police to solicitors' papers or *Wallersteiner* v. *Moir (No. 2)* [1975] 1 All E.R. 849, in which it appeared as guardian of the rules of etiquette of solicitors in a case raising the propriety of contingency fee arrangements. Another example was *Ridehalgh* v. *Horsefield* [1994] 3 W.L.R. 462 a test case on wasted costs orders.

The Motor Insurers' Bureau has on occasion been permitted to intervene in cases between insurance companies and insured persons where the decision might affect the amount the Bureau would have to pay out in the future.

In *Gillick* v. *West Norfolk and Wisbech Area Health Authority and D.H.S.S.* [1985] 3 All E.R. 402 the House of Lords had to rule on the problem of contraceptive advice given by doctors to girls under sixteen. Mrs Gillick challenged the legality of a D.H.S.S. circular to doctors stating that in some circumstances it might be legitimate to give such advice to under sixteen-year-olds. The parties to the case were Mrs Gillick and the D.H.S.S. No one was there to represent the position of minor girls. The Children's Legal Centre applied to the House of Lords before the hearing to be allowed to instruct counsel specifically to make arguments on behalf of children.

The Centre presented three alternatives. One was to lodge a written case and to make oral submissions at the hearing; the second was to instruct counsel as *amicus curiae* in the normal sense; the third was to submit a written case only. The House of Lords rejected all three alternatives without a hearing and without giving any reasons. For a discussion of the matter see Jenny Levin, 'Interested Parties', *Legal Action*, October 1985, p. 10.

In 1988 however the House of Lords granted a petition on behalf of the UK insurance market to file a written brief in a forthcoming appeal. The Court of Appeal's decision in *Phoenix General Insurance Co. of Greece* v. *A.D.A.S.* [1987] 2 W.L.R. 512 has caused consternation in the insurance world. The petition was brought by a solicitor, Mr Donald O'May, senior partner of Ince & Co., who had long argued for the extension of *amicus* briefs in commercial cases to those affected by issues even if they were not parties.[1]

Another increasingly important development is the role of the Commission for Racial Equality and the Equal Opportunities Commission in promoting litigation and in arguing cases raising issues within their field of concern. In *Social Research Council* v. *Nassé*, for instance, counsel for both Commissions appeared in their own right in the Court of Appeal. In the House of Lords the Law Lords at first objected but then allowed it with the consent of the other parties. (Information supplied by counsel.)

---

1   See *Law Society's Gazette*, 6 January 1988, p. 3.

See also *Attorney-General's Reference No. 2 of 1979* [1979] *Criminal Law Review*, 585, in which the Law Commission submitted a memorandum on the law of burglary to assist the court. In *R* v. *Khan (Sultan)* [1996] 3 All E.R. 289 the National Council for Civil Liberties was permitted to participate with written legal submissions on the admissibility of a tape recording resulting from a listening device fixed to the outside of the defendant's house. In the proceedings brought at the end of 1998 to have General Pinochet extradited to Spain, Amnesty International was permitted to intervene in the proceedings and the Medical Foundation for the Care of Victims of Torture and several other organisations were allowed not only to submit written arguments and evidence to the courts but to be represented by Professor Ian Brownlie QC as counsel able to take part in the oral argument.[2]

One problem with the role of *amici* is that procedure in English cases is almost entirely oral. If the concept of *amici* were to be developed, would there be value in permitting legal argument to be presented in written form in 'briefs', as in the United States? The difference between the two systems was discussed in 1962 by the late Professor Delmar Karlen of New York University, rapporteur of an Anglo-American exchange of jurists to examine each other's system:

Delmar Karlen, 'Appeal in England and United States', 78 *Law Quarterly Review*, 1962, p. 371

Papers on appeal

An outstanding difference between the two nations is the fact that 'briefs' are required in the United States, whereas in England they are not. The brief is a full-dress argument in writing often running to fifty or more printed or mimeographed pages in length. It states the facts, outlines the claimed errors in the proceedings below, and cites and discusses the authorities claimed to justify reversal or affirmance. The appellant serves his brief on the other side well in advance of the time for oral judgment, and the respondent then serves his answering brief on the appellant, again well in advance of oral argument. Sometimes the appellant serves a reply brief.

In England such a document is virtually unknown. The closest approach to it is the 'case' normally required from both sides in the House of Lords and Privy Council. This, however, is a very abbreviated paper, seldom running to more than six or seven pages in length, and is intended only as a preliminary outline of the extended oral argument to be made later. It does not discuss authorities in detail, or argue the propositions of law to be relied upon. Relatively few cases are cited (although this may be attributable more to the English

2   For further consideration of public interest intervention with other recent examples see Rosalind English' Wrongfooting the Lord Chancellor: Access to Justice in the High Court' 61 *Modern Law Review*, 1998, 245,250–54.

theory of precedent than to the form which papers on appeal take). In the other appellate courts of England, no written arguments of any kind have traditionally been used [though the Court of Appeal has recently adopted the practice of asking for skeleton arguments – see pp. 367-71 below (ed.)].

In both England and the United States, the judges are furnished with a record on appeal. It consists of the notice of appeal, pleadings and other formal documents, the judgment below, and so much of the evidence as may be relevant as to the questions raised on appeal. There is this difference, however. In England, there is almost always a reasoned (though often extemporaneous) opinion by the judge below, outlining the evidence, the authorities relied upon, the decision and the reasons therefor. In the United States, such a document is frequently lacking. If the case has been tried by jury, as many cases are, in place of a reasoned opinion, there will be simply the judge's instructions to the jury, without any citation of the authorities upon which his propositions of law are based. If the case has been tried without a jury, there ordinarily will be only formalised findings of fact and conclusions of law, again without the citation of authorities. Sometimes there is a reasoned opinion below, as where the case has gone through an intermediate stage of appeal, but this is the exception rather than the rule.

In England, the record on appeal is almost always mimeographed. In the United States, it often has to be printed at a great increase in cost. The practice, however, varies from one court to another, some courts permitting mimeographing or other relatively cheap forms of duplication.

The Evershed Committee considered but rejected the idea of introducing something akin to the American written brief:

(d)   Should English appeal courts consider written argument?

Final Report of the (Evershed) Committee on Supreme Court Practice and Procedure, 1953, Cmnd 8878

572... .it seemed to some of us, at first sight, that the American system possesses certain marked advantages over the procedure for hearing appeals in this country, at any rate from the point of view of the saving of costs. These apparent advantages may be briefly summarised as follows:

(*a*) Since the grounds of appeal are precisely stated and the authorities relied on are cited in the written 'brief', there is no room for surprise. Not only are the members of the court apprised at once of the point that is to be decided, but the other side are fully aware, before the hearing, of what is going to be said against them.

(*b*) Formulation beforehand of the precise grounds of the appeal makes it possible in many cases to eliminate much of the evidence, both oral and documentary, which came before the trial Judge but which is not relevant to the particular question that forms the subject of appeal. This enables considerable economies to be made in the transcribing of evidence and duplication of documents.

(*c*) The 'brief' constitutes a permanent record of the argument on either side, which the judges can take away and consider at leisure. They are not so dependent therefore, on the notes which they are themselves able to make during the hearing or on their fleeting recollection of counsel's oral argument.

(*d*) Above all, at the cost of preparing the written argument, there is, at any rate in all but the smallest cases, an immediate economy in relation to the time occupied in the hearing of the appeal. As already pointed out, the consumption of time, involving as it does the payment of refresher fees to counsel, is the most expensive feature of our English appellate procedure.

573. Whatever may be thought to be the advantages of the American system of 'briefs', however, we found singularly little enthusiasm for it amongst the witnesses whose opinions we sought. The members of the Court of Appeal whom we consulted were emphatically opposed to the adoption of such a system in this country as also were the representatives of the Bar Council and Law Society. We also had the advantage of hearing evidence from Mr Justice Frankfurter, of the United States Supreme Court, as well as from Mr John W. Davis, who was able to speak with a wealth of experience of appellate work in the United States Court. We gained the impression from these witnesses that they were by no means whole-heartedly in favour of the American system of conducting appeals, but that they rather envied the system prevailing here of unrestricted oral argument. They appeared to regard the American 'brief' system, with its strict limitation of the time for oral argument, as a necessary evil forced upon them by the pressure of appellate work, the volume of which is so great that it would be simply impossible to get through it if unrestricted oral argument were permitted.

574. After giving the matter our careful consideration we have had little doubt in coming to the conclusion that the American system would provide in this country a less satisfactory system for conducting appeals than that now prevailing. Furthermore, we are satisfied that the American system would be quite unsuitable for adoption in this country in view of the different conditions prevailing here and would not be likely to lead to any marked reduction in the costs of appeals. Our reasons for arriving at these conclusions are briefly as follows:

(*a*) We are satisfied that there are real and substantial advantages in our system of unrestricted oral argument, whereby every point in a party's case is thoroughly sifted in the process of discussion between counsel and the members of the court. Furthermore, our system enables the members of the court to work together as a team, each member having the advantage of hearing the questions put by the other members and of weighing the answers of counsel thereto. Under this system, it is thought, there is a far greater chance of the court arriving at a common conclusion, so that in the majority of cases the parties have the advantage of a unanimous decision, and the court's decision on the question in issue carries all the greater authority.

(*b*) By contrast, the system prevailing in the United States leads to a higher proportion of dissenting judgments. It has seemed to us that the members of the appellate court, reading the 'briefs' and documents for themselves, and without the advantage of hearing unrestricted oral argument together, must tend to bring their individual minds to the case rather than work as a team.

(c) Under the American system there is likely to be much greater delay in reaching a decision. Having regard to the time which must be allowed for filing the 'briefs' – first that of the appellant, then that of the respondent, and possibly a 'brief' in reply by the appellant – a considerable time must elapse before the case can be brought on for hearing. What is perhaps more serious is the fact that the court can rarely deliver judgment at once, on the termination of the oral argument. The oral argument having been necessarily abbreviated, the members of the court must go away and digest the written argument and evidence, by reading it to themselves after the hearing, before they can form their opinions and are ready to give judgment. In the appellate courts of the United States almost every judgment must be reserved, and we were informed that it is not uncommon for a substantial time to elapse, often extending to many months, before the judgments are delivered.

(d) Perhaps the strongest objection to the introduction in this country of anything resembling the American system for conducting appeals arises from the fact that here the legal profession is divided into two branches. The system works in America largely because the profession is differently organised. The American lawyer is a member of a firm and has at his disposal an office staff of trained lawyers. The lawyer who is conducting the case can thus be relieved of the spadework of preparing the written 'brief' which a more junior member of the firm's staff can do. It is not difficult to fix a fair inclusive fee to cover the whole conduct of an appeal including both the preparation of the 'brief' in the office and the oral argument in court. If a similar system were adopted in this country, it is not to be thought that solicitors would find it possible, even if it were otherwise desirable, to prepare the 'briefs' in their offices. Few solicitors' offices in this country would have the staff to do so; and in any case it would be unfair to counsel who would be instructed to conduct the oral argument that he should have no hand in preparing the written 'brief'. In practice it would be inevitable that counsel would be employed to settle the 'brief'. The time which counsel would spend on doing so would not usually be less than, and might often far exceed, the time which under the present system would be occupied in conducting the oral argument. The fees charged by counsel for preparing a written 'brief' would necessarily be governed to a large extent by the time occupied, and it seems to follow inexorably that substantial fees would have to be charged. It is true that a somewhat smaller fee than that now paid would possibly be sufficient to cover the abbreviated oral argument, and there would be no refreshers. At the same time it is to be remembered that counsel would have to get up the case twice – once for the purpose of preparing the 'brief', and again for the oral argument, for which purpose he would have to be prepared for any point that might be raised against him in court. Bearing in mind this additional burden on counsel, we do not think that any marked reduction in counsel's fees could be expected. On the contrary, the overall total of counsel's fees for the preparation and hearing of an appeal might well be greater than it is at present.

575. For these reasons we do not think that the introduction of a system of written 'briefs' such as that prevailing in the United States would be likely to

lead in the end to any material saving of costs, and bearing in mind the other objections to which we have referred we are not disposed to recommend the adoption of any such system in this country.

A written brief in an English case

Rondel v. *Worsley* [1966] 3 W.L.R. 950 (Court of Appeal)

The plaintiff sued a barrister for negligence in the conduct of his defence at the Old Bailey. His statement of claim was struck out by Lawton J. as disclosing no cause of action. He applied to the Court of Appeal for leave to appeal. At that time he was acting in person. His application asked for permission to formulate another statement of claim and to get a solicitor to help him with it. In view of the importance of the matter, leave to appeal was given. After obtaining leave the plaintiff was assisted voluntarily by a solicitor (the writer) who prepared for the consideration of the court a typewritten document of 116 pages setting out the arguments and authorities in support of the contention that barristers were liable for negligence. The members of the court agreed to receive the brief, and when the hearing began on 13 June 1966, Lord Denning M.R. referred to it as a very valuable document and said that the court had read it.

Commenting in the course of his judgment on the written brief, however, Lord Justice Danckwerts said:

> There are two other matters on which I want to comment and which I trust will not be allowed to occur in future cases.
> The solicitor acting for Rondel was allowed to present to us a typewritten document of 116 pages, in which he set out the legal argument on behalf of the plaintiff's case, something in the style of the briefs which are allowed under the quite different procedure of the courts in the United States of America. Secondly, at the conclusion of the arguments by counsel on behalf of the defendant, Rondel was allowed to read nine typewritten pages, in the form of a reply which had obviously been prepared for him, notwithstanding that the arguments on his behalf had been presented by counsel instructed by the Official Solicitor, who were ready to make such arguments in reply as were proper. Both these matters were wholly irregular and contrary to the practice of the court and in my opinion should not be allowed as a precedent for future proceedings. It appears that counsel was in fact available to appear for Rondel without a fee, and the course mentioned above was deliberately adopted (p. 968).
> [Neither of the other two judges referred to the matter.]

In spite of these strictures, the most recent trend is slightly towards an increase in the written material available to the courts – especially in the Court of Appeal and the House of Lords.

The new approach in the House of Lords was outlined by Lord Diplock in an appeal decided in March 1982:

M. V. Yorke Motors v. *Edwards* [1982] 1 All E.R. 1024

LORD DIPLOCK (at 1025): The length of time required for counsel's opening addresses at hearings of appeals to the House of Lords has been significantly reduced by the practice adopted over the last seven years under which all the members of the Appellate Committee who will be sitting on an appeal will have read in advance at least the judgments in the courts below and the written cases lodged by the parties. This practice of which the purpose is to reduce the length and consequently the cost of appeals to the House of Lords is one of which by now the Bar should be well aware. Signs are, however, now appearing that this awareness may be giving rise to a tendency to expand the written cases lodged by the parties so as to incorporate and develop in them detailed written arguments supported by lengthy citations from and references to numerous authorities, much on the same lines as the written 'briefs' submitted by the parties in appeals to appellate courts in the United States which have resulted in oral argument playing a relatively insignificant role in the decision-making process adopted by appellate courts in that country.

The practice of this House whereby members of the Appellate Committee read in advance the judgments in the courts below and the parties' written cases is not intended to reduce the importance of the role played by oral argument in the decision-making process. Its purpose is to add to the cogency of the oral argument by eliminating the necessity for vocal exposition of facts already stated in the judgments below and the reading out of those judgments in extenso. Counsel are thus enabled from the outset to concentrate their arguments on what are the real issues in the appeal. A written case lodged by a party, which itself contains long and elaborate argument and citations from and references to numerous authorities, does nothing to serve this purpose that is not better done by a written case that follows the guidance contained in r. 22(i) of the Directions as to Procedure applicable to Civil Appeals to the House of Lords (the Blue Book 1981, p. 16). On the contrary, it defeats one of the principal objects of the practice by adding substantially to the costs of the appeal which the shortening of the oral hearing is designed to reduce.

Rule 22(i) has remained substantially unchanged since before the period when it became the uniform practice of *all* members sitting on an appeal to have read in advance of the hearing the judgments below and parties' written cases and at the outset of the hearing to inform counsel of this fact. The instant appeal provides an appropriate occasion for indicating the form which a party's written case should take pursuant to this rule in order to be of greatest assistance at the hearing of the appeal.

It should be borne in mind that the members of the Appellate Committee will have also read the judgments in the courts below. The case should, accordingly, start with a statement of what the party conceives to be the issues that arise on the appeal. In an appeal to this House, these are generally questions of law or (as in the instant case) of the exercise of a judicial discretion, although occasionally a party may want to challenge a finding of fact. It should generally be possible to describe each issue (if there be more than one) in not more than a sentence or two. If there are issues decided adversely to the party in the court below that he does not intend to pursue on the appeal, this should be stated plainly. Similarly, if it is intended to seek leave to take on the appeal a point that was not taken below, the nature of the point should be identified with sufficient specificity; and if it is intended to invite the House to overrule or depart from a previous decision of its own, this should be expressly stated.

The case should set out the heads, but no more than the heads, of the argument on each of the issues which it is intended should be advanced by counsel for the party at the oral hearing to challenge or support, as the case may be, the decision on that issue of the court from which the appeal is brought. Detailed or elaborate argument adds unnecessarily to the costs of preparing the case and is seldom helpful or time saving at the oral hearing. Reference to authorities relied on in support of the argument on any issue should be limited to key authorities (seldom numbering more than one or two on any one issue) which lay down the principle which it is contended is applicable, and the particular passage or passages in the judgments in which the principle is stated and should be identified and, unless unduly lengthy, may helpfully be quoted verbatim. But references to numerous other cases in which that principle has been previously applied by the courts to particular facts which it is claimed may be regarded as presenting some analogies to the facts of the case under appeal, are usually out of place in the written case and, I may add, more often than not turn out to be time wasting in oral argument also. Where, however, it is intended to rely, as persuasive authority, on cases decided by courts in other countries or legal writings such as the American Restatement, it is of assistance to their Lordships if specific reference is made to these in the written case.

My Lords, I have thought it right to make these observations in the instant appeal because it provides, in the case lodged by the appellant, an example of the spread of the tendency which I have deprecated towards preparing written cases in the style of American 'appellate briefs' and, in the case lodged by the respondent, an example of a written case drafted in the succinct manner which I have indicated, not only is called for by the Directions as to Procedure applicable to Civil Appeals to the House of Lords but also is most helpful to the members of the Appellate Committee in their preparation for the oral hearing. The appellant's case runs to no less than $39\frac{1}{2}$ single spaced foolscap pages of detailed argument involving very long citations from judgments of the two cases relied on as key cases, and references to more than a score of other English authorities none of which was of more than peripheral relevance. The respondent's case was only one-sixth of that length; but it contained by way of heads of argument all that was required to render it unnecessary to call on counsel for the respondent at the conclusion of the oral argument. The short duration of the oral argument, $1\frac{1}{2}$ hours, cannot in my view be ascribed to the elaborate way in which the argument for the appellant had already been developed in his written case. It was a short oral argument because the point decisive of the appeal, once it was identified, as it had been in the respondent's written case, was intrinsically a short one. It would have taken no longer to argue if the appellant's case had been drafted in the same style as the case for the respondent and in consequence had been of similar length.

The House of Lords, in other words, wanted something less than an American-style written brief but rather more than it was normally getting. In April 1983 the new Master of the Rolls, Sir John Donaldson, issued a Practice Note in which he set out the Court of Appeal's approach to the same issue:

Practice Note (Presentation of Appeals) [1983] 2 All E.R. 34

As is well known, the judges of the Court of Appeal have been seeking new ways in which appeals can be presented and decided more quickly and at less expense to the parties. One innovation which has proved very successful in more complex appeals is the submission by counsel of what have been called 'skeleton arguments'.

It would be quite inappropriate to use a practice direction in this context since whether skeleton arguments should be submitted, what form they should take and how they should be used will depend on the peculiarities of the appeal concerned. However, it may assist both branches of the profession if I mention the result of such experience as we have had of their use.

Skeleton arguments are, as their name implies, a very abbreviated note of the argument and in no way usurp any part of the function of oral argument in court. They are an aide-mémoire for convenience of reference before and during the hearing and no one is inhibited from departing from their terms. Nevertheless experience shows that they serve a very real purpose.

Before the appeal is called on, the judges will normally have read the notice of appeal, and the respondent's notice and the judgment appealed from. The purpose of this prereading is not to form any view of the merits of the appeal, but to familiarise themselves with the issues and scope of the dispute and thereby avoid the necessity for a lengthy, or often any, opening of the appeal. This process is assisted by the provision of skeleton arguments, which are much more informative than a notice of appeal or a respondent's notice, being fuller and more recently prepared.

During the hearing of the appeal itself, skeleton arguments enable much time to be saved because they reduce or obviate the need for the judges to take a longhand note, sometimes at dictation speed, of the submissions and authorities and other documents referred to. Furthermore in some circumstances a skeleton argument can do double duty not only as a note for the judges but also as a note from which counsel can argue the appeal.

The usual procedure is for the skeleton argument to be prepared shortly before the hearing of the appeal at the same time as counsel is getting it up. It should contain a numbered list of the points which counsel proposes to argue, stated in no more than one or two sentences, the object being to *identify* each point, not to argue it or to elaborate on it. Each listed point should be followed by full references to the material to which counsel will refer in support of it, i.e. the relevant pages or passages in authorities, bundles of documents, affidavits, transcripts and the judgment under appeal. It should also contain anything which counsel would expect to be taken down by the court during the hearing such as propositions of law, chronologies of events, lists of dramatis personae and, where necessary, glossaries of terms. If more convenient, these can of course be annexed to the skeleton argument rather than being included in it. Both the court and opposing counsel can then work on the material without writing it down, thus saving considerable time and labour.

The document should be sent to the court as soon as convenient before the hearing or, if for some reason this is not possible, handed in when counsel rises to address the court. It is however more valuable if provided to the court in advance. A copy should of course at the same time be sent or handed to counsel on the other side.

It cannot be over-emphasised that skeleton arguments are not formal documents to the terms of which anyone would be held. They are simply a tool to be used in the interests of greater efficiency. Experience shows that they can be a valuable tool. The judges of the court all hope that it will be possible to refine and extend their use.

Finally, even in simple appeals where skeleton arguments may be unnecessary, counsel should provide notes (preferably typed) of any material such as I have mentioned which would otherwise have to be taken down by the court more or less at dictation speed, thereby saving considerable time and labour.

A further nudge in the direction of written arguments on points of law was given in the final *Report of the Review Body on Civil Justice* (Cm. 394, 1988). It referred to the recent Guide to Commercial Court Practice on the conduct of a hearing which, inter alia, encouraged counsel to provide written summaries of legal propositions and facts and to avoid prolonged reading aloud of documents and authorities. It would be inappropriate, the Report said (para. 264), for wholesale adoption in trials generally of this system. But it pointed towards the need to establish for general purposes a number of matters including 'judicious use of written argument and avoidance of lengthy quotation from written material' (ibid.). An important aspect of this issue is the potential saving of time in court if counsel can assume the court has already read a precedent cited in a written argument as compared with the need to read it aloud in open court. A huge amount of time is consumed in oral argument about points of law in simply reading aloud great chunks of decided cases.

But it would seem that Lord Donaldson at least seemed to think that the balance between oral and written argument in the Court of Appeal was about right. In his 1986 review of the legal year (*New Law Journal*, 17 October 1986, p. 990), the Master of the Rolls said:

The basis of the 1982 procedural reforms was a realisation that time spent in court was extremely expensive, because it occupied not only the judges, but also counsel, solicitors and sometimes the parties. Accordingly, it was thought that, even if there was no overall saving in the time taken to hear any given appeal, a change whereby part of the process could be undertaken by the judges reading in their rooms, instead of being read to in court, should effect a reduction in the cost of the proceedings to the parties. A secondary advantage would accrue if, as seemed likely, such a division between time spent in and out of court would lead to some slight reduction in the time occupied by each individual appeal. The latter expectation was based upon the fact that judges, like anyone else, can absorb written material more quickly if they read it to themselves than if it is read aloud to them. In the event there is every reason to believe that both advantages have been achieved, although it is difficult to measure the precise extent of the achievement.

In the light of four years' experience, the question has now to be asked whether more should be done to shift the process of hearing an appeal from oral argument in court to private study in the judges' rooms. There is no doubt that it could be done.

The United States judiciary do it. They rely heavily on written 'briefs' prepared by the parties, they use legally qualified assistants ('law clerks') and they impose time limits on oral argument in court.

The fact that in this country we have a specialist corps of advocates in the Bar, upon whom the judiciary can and do rely to do much of the work done by judicial law clerks in the United States, and that we have a long tradition of oral argument differentiates our position from that of the United States. It is, therefore, no criticism of that system if I say that in my opinion we have in general gone as far as we should in reducing court time. The judges' present aim is to enter court for the hearing of the appeal already knowing the background facts, the point or points in issue and the essence of the arguments to be advanced by the parties … If we were to go further, I think that we should lose the undoubted advantage of a dialogue between bench and Bar in detecting, refining and resolving the crucial point or points in the appeal and, although we should undoubtedly decrease the expense of time spent in court, we should considerably increase other costs in that the written arguments prepared by counsel would have to be far more elaborate …

This is not to say that the system works perfectly in all cases. We have always recognised that there are a few cases in which written skeleton arguments may be unnecessary and others in which some degree of flesh may legitimately be put upon the bones, although obesity is never justified. Flexibility and tailoring the method of presentation to particular appeals is of the essence of the system. From this it follows inexorably that counsel may sometimes get the balance wrong, but in general the system works well. If I had one criticism to make, it would be that some skeleton arguments are submitted to the court too late. Judges, like counsel, have to plan their work and their personal lives. It is highly disruptive of both if a skeleton argument is delivered late in the afternoon of the day before an appeal is due to be heard first thing in the morning. Furthermore, the absence of the argument when the judge was reading the papers will probably have made his task substantially more difficult and time-consuming.

In March 1989, Lord Donaldson took the next step by issuing a *Practice Note* ([1989] 1 All E.R. 891) requiring skeleton arguments in all cases as from June 1989. They would have to be lodged by both sides not less than four weeks before the date of the scheduled hearing. Lord Donaldson said this was not a first step toward the system operated in American appellate courts of having written briefs supplemented by brief oral argument. But skeleton arguments supplied to the court well in advance would enable the judges to prepare for the appeal and also to consider the parties' estimates of time. In May 1990, Lord Donaldson issued a further *Practice Note* ([1990] 2 All E.R. 318) reducing the period within which the skeleton arguments have to be lodged from 4 weeks to 2 weeks – at the request of the Bar. But he gave notice that the new rule would be enforced more strictly than the 4-week rule. Cases where skeleton arguments had not been lodged in time would be listed for counsel to explain the reason.

But the 14-day rule proved problematic. A new Practice Note[3] provided that normally the deadline is 14 days, but in heavy cases the court can order extended time. In that case the appellant's advocate must serve his skeleton argument on the respondent's advocate within 28 days of the date of entry of the case into the list of forthcoming appeals. Within 28 days of getting the skeleton, the opponent must serve his own. Within 21 days of receipt of the respondent's, the appellant's advocate may serve a further skeleton argument. Within 28 days of the respondent serving his skeleton argument on his opponent, both must serve copies on the court.

But a much more radical change in regard to skeleton arguments came in February 1999 with a new Practice Direction [1999] 1 All E.R. 186 requiring that they be delivered with the appeal bundle of documents within 14 days after the appeal has appeared in the list of forthcoming appeals. Writing in *The Times* (26 January 1999) to protest about this new rule Mr David Pannick QC said this meant they had to be filed months before the hearing. This would mean the case would have to be prepared twice over, once to prepare the skeleton argument and once for the hearing. More important, they would decline in quality and focus and will not provide as much assistance to the court as a skeleton argument filed close to the hearing date. ('No doubt the previous 14-day rule was based on Dr Johnson's principle that "when a man knows he is to be hanged in a fortnight, it concentrates his mind wonderfully".'.) Replying, Lord Woolf, the Master of the Rolls, said that early skeleton arguments were needed because of the new rule requiring leave to appeal in almost all cases. They were also needed as part of the new approach to case management. ('They are essential for the monitoring and management of appeals from the time of receipt. The Court of Appeal in a modern civil justice system must manage its workload.')[4]

In 1991, Professor Robert Martineau, an American scholar, published research comparing English law with American appellate procedures. He sat over a period of months in the Court of Appeal, Civil Division. He had great experience of the American appellate process. He came expecting to find our appellate advocacy of a calibre distinctly superior to that in the United States. To his surprise he found that it was not. 'Most English barristers' he said, 'are not effective appellate advocates'. It took an inordinate time for counsel to identify what their appeals were about, what

3   [1995] 3 All E.R. 850, 856–59.
4   *The Times*, 2 February 1999.

the issues were and what were their contentions. Most appeals began at 10.30 a.m. 'It was often 2.30 or 3 p.m. before [the author] could ascertain what the key issues were'. By contrast, in the U.S., it only required 15 minutes to ascertain the key issues and some 30 minutes to come to a conclusion. The English oral tradition, he suggested, 'rather than forcing counsel to focus on the key facts and legal arguments, has allowed [barristers] to argue *ad infinitum* and often *ad nauseam* without the discipline of the written word or a time limit'.

Professor Martineau strongly urged the merit of the US system combining a written brief with severely restricted oral argument. English advocates and judges ridiculed the idea that oral argument could be reduced to half an hour or so for each side and remain a useful tool. But in his view it gave the best result both in terms of efficiency and effectiveness – 'oral argument based on a written brief becomes an intense exercise in advocacy in which the lawyers and the judges immediately confront the key issues of dispute that require resolution by the judges'.[5]

Time limits on oral argument The courts have not yet adopted the American approach to time limits but they are moving in that direction. Applications for leave to appeal in the Court of Appeal, Civil Division are allowed 20 minutes for oral argument. A renewed application for leave is allowed 30 minutes.[6] Since 1987 counsel have had to give estimates of time they believe the case will take. The 1995 Practice Note states that 'the court and its listing officers place considerable reliance on advocates' time estimates' (ibid., 853). The 1997 Bowman *Review of the Court of Appeal (Civil Division)* said that although there were no formal limits on oral arguments in some cases, especially heavy cases, 'the CA does seek to impose limits' based on the parties' estimates (p. 88): 'It is the experience of the CA that time limits are often over-estimated and that where the CA imposes time limits, they are usually not exceeded' (ibid). The Bowman Report said:

> The oral tradition is an important part of the legal system of England and Wales. We fully support that and believe that there must always be a right to oral argument on appeal. We are also satisfied that there is no need to impose strict mandatory time limits on oral argument in appeals. We know that this would not receive widespread support. However, we do consider that there is a greater need to impose appropriate time limits for individual appeals, although we are not suggesting that they should be anywhere near as short as those imposed in the United States. That would be entirely opposed to the oral tradition of England and Wales. In Ontario there was a member of the provincial

5   Robert Martineau, *Appellate Justice in England and the United States*, William Hein, 1991. For an article on the book see M. Zander, 'A brief encounter', *New Law Journal*, 12 April 1991, p. 491.
6   *Practice Note* [1995] 3 All E.R. 850, 852.

Court of Appeal with particular responsibility for overseeing time limits. It is
that sort of judicial oversight that we would like to build on in our jurisdiction.

Bowman recommended that appeals should normally require leave
(implemented by *Practice Note* [1999] 1 All E.R. 186) and thought that in
most cases the Lord Justice who granted leave to appeal could estimate a
time limit for oral argument. Otherwise it should be done by a member of
the court hearing the appeal or by one of the new supervising Lords
Justices proposed by the Bowman Report. The court should not necessarily
accept the estimates given by the parties.

Bowman also suggested that there were some cases where with
agreement of the parties and of the Court, it should be possible for an
appeal to be decided on the papers alone – with no oral argument at all.
(P. 89.)

In 1991 the House of Lords issued a *Procedure Direction* [1991] 3 All
E.R. 608 that, subject to any directions during the hearing, counsel would
be 'expected to confine the length of their submissions to the time indicated
in the estimates'. But in practice these time estimates are not strictly adhered
to and formal time limits have otherwise not been imposed.

Counsel in the House of Lords have to give an opponent advance
notice of 'heads of arguments' which are much the same as skeleton
arguments – see *Procedure Note* [1991] 3 All E.R. 609. But this is nothing
new in the House of Lords where the parties have for centuries been
required to prepare a printed case.

(e) Interaction between the judge and the advocate

It is an axiom of the adversary system that the judge sits more or less
silently as a kind of umpire whilst the battle rages between the lawyers in
the case. But while this model may be broadly accurate in regard to the
process of establishing the facts, it hardly does justice to the role of the
judge in the process of establishing the law. Here the judge tends to be
very much more active. He sees it as his job to challenge the propositions
of law advanced by counsel and to test them by detailed questioning and
probing. The higher in the courts system, the more the exchanges between
counsel and the court are apt to resemble a seminar, with the judges firing
questions at counsel.

In a curious way the result of this process is that the contest is in a
sense between counsel and the court rather than between the lawyers for
the two sides. Lord Kilbrandon expressed this in Alan Paterson's book
The Law Lords based on interviews with judges of the House of Lords.
From the dialectic between Bench and Bar which resembled nothing so
much as 'conversation between gentlemen on a subject of mutual interest',

'the judge is forced to come to terms, openly and explicitly, with the views of counsel; to present, in short, his own assessment of them and, where necessary, his counter-argument' (p. 50). Often, in fact, the judges are using their exchanges with counsel to advance their own thoughts in order to attempt to persuade one or more doubters amongst their brother judges.

Paterson has pointed out (p. 82) that these exchanges between counsel and the Bench are not recorded in the way that the questioning of witnesses and the summing-up or judgments are taken down, by tape-recorder or shorthand writer. The law reported in The Law Reports gives an abbreviated version of counsel's arguments and may include some of the judicial interventions. But this is far from the whole of the oral exchanges that take place. The result is that only those who are present can gauge what really happened between counsel and the judges and to what extent the lawyers for the winning party had a role in the process that led to the court finding for their side. Paterson comments (at pp. 82–3):

'Inevitably, this means that significant aspects of the decision-making process in the Lords are lost to posterity. Judicial interjections which change the course of appeals go unreported... . Equally the persuasive influence of counsel's submissions, the pictures they paint, the baited analogies they proffer, the avenues they close in their arguments – all these are left neglected. Worst of all, the lack of proper transcripts helps perpetuate the notion amongst academic scholars that the real work of the Law Lords and the only important aspect of appeals ... are the speeches produced at the end of the day. This concentration on the end product, to the exclusion of the process by which it was arrived at, is intellectually dangerous and academically unsound.'

For further reading see also Simon Lee, *Judging Judges* (Faber & Faber, 1988).

CHAPTER 8

Other sources of law

The two main sources of law – legislation and judicial decisions – dominate the field of law-making within the UK system. But there are other sources of law for the UK of which the most important is European Community law. The chapter deals also with textbooks and custom as sources of law and with various forms of quasi-legislation.

1. EUROPEAN UNION LAW[1]

Community law became part of the UK system as from 1 January 1973, the day on which the United Kingdom became a member of the European Communities. On the international plane this was by virtue of joining the relevant treaties – the Treaty of Paris of 1951 establishing the European Coal and Steel Community and two Treaties of Rome of 1957 establishing Euratom and the European Economic Community. It is the last named EEC Treaty that is mainly in question. Under the Maastricht Treaty of 1992 the EEC was renamed the European Community.

The EEC system took effect internally as part of UK law by virtue of the European Communities Act 1972 which made EEC law part of internal law. Thus section 2(1) of the 1972 Act provides that 'all such rights, powers, liabilities, obligations and restrictions from time to time created or arising by or under the Treaties, and all such remedies and procedures from time to time provided for by or under the Treaties, as in accordance with the Treaties, are without further enactment to be given legal effect or used in the United Kingdom shall be recognised and available in law, and be enforced, allowed and followed accordingly; and the expression 'enforceable Community right' and similar expressions shall be read as

---

1 I am indebted to my colleague Mr Damian Chalmers for guidance on the EU law section. He should not however be blamed for any blemishes or errors.

referring to one to which this subsection applies.' The effect of section 2(1) was to make directly effective Community law immediately part of national law – notwithstanding that national law conflicts with Community law. Section 2(2) provided that implementation of any Community obligation could be done by Order in Council.

Section 2(4) of the 1972 Act requires the courts in the United Kingdom, in their interpretation of both present and future statutes, to give full effect to section 2. It states '… any such provision (of any such extent) as might be made by Act of Parliament, and any enactment passed or to be passed … shall be construed and have effect subject to the foregoing provisions of this section …'.

Section 3 states that questions as to the validity, meaning and effect of the treaties is to be determined in accordance with the jurisprudence of the European Court of Justice. ('… for the purposes of all legal proceedings any question as to the validity, meaning or effect of any Community instrument, shall be treated as a question of law, and if not referred to the European Court, be for determination as such in accordance with the principles laid down by and any relevant decision of the European Court.')

(a)   The institutions of the Community

The institutions of the Community are (1) the *Council* (formerly called the Council of Ministers), which is the most powerful body of the Community. It is composed of one ministerial representative from each member state. The appropriate Minister for the subject under discussion attends the meeting. The Council has the right to legislate but in most cases it can only act on proposals made by the Commission. Such proposals can become law by a qualified majority vote – voting is on a weighted basis with the larger countries having more votes. (2) The *Commission*, which consists of one or more national from each of the member states, though they are supposed to act independently of their national origin as members of the Community's executive. The Commission is responsible for formulating policy on a day-to-day basis. By contrast, the Council meets less frequently. (3) The *European Parliament* (formerly the Assembly), which is a parliamentary body. As from 1994 the number of Members of the European Parliament (MEPs) has been 626–including 87 for the UK. Originally its members were chosen by national parliaments from amongst their own members but from 1979 onwards the members have been elected directly by the national populations. The European Parliament is primarily a forum for debating Community policies and problems. In theory it has ultimate control over the Commission, as it can by a vote of censure force the members of the Commission to resign. (In March 1999 the entire Commission resigned to forestall such a censure vote.) (4) The *Court of Justice* (formerly the European Court of Justice) at Luxembourg, which has one judge from each of the member states plus one additional judge. There are currently 15 judges. They can sit in chambers of three or five as well as in plenary session. The Court uses the power to sit in chambers a great deal. To relieve some of the burden of the huge case-load the Single European Act in 1987 provided for a second court, called the Court of First Instance (CFI), which also has fifteen judges. Like the ECJ it can sit in chambers of three and five judges. It deals with a limited range of cases mainly dealing with disputes regarding staff and competition matters.

The Court has two principal functions. One is to decide points of Community law which come up in the course of litigation in national courts. Under Article 234 (formerly Art. 177) of the Rome Treaty, any court *may* refer a point of law that arises before it to the European Court for decision.[2] (In England this has even been done by a magistrates' court.) If the point comes up in a court that is the final court of appeal, then under Article 234 there is an obligation to refer it to the Luxembourg court.[3] The litigation is then suspended while the European Court decides the issue. The case then continues in the national forum in the light of the European Court's ruling on the point of Community law.[4]

The Court's second chief function is to determine actions brought by Community organs, member states or individuals alleging breaches of obligations under Community law. If one state wishes to bring another before the Court it must first approach the Commission. Only if the Commission does not succeed in resolving the issue can the state go to the Court. Individuals cannot take proceedings against states, but an individual affected by an act of the Council or the Commission – say a Commission decision – can apply to the Court to have it quashed. The Court does not enforce its own decisions. It is left to each state to provide machinery to enforce judgments against individuals or companies. Until Maastricht, there was no machinery for enforcing judgments against states. This was left instead to the pressure of membership of the Community, which seems so far to be sufficient to secure compliance with the small

2   See, for guidelines, *Bulmer* v. *Bollinger* [1974] 2 All E.R. 1226 at 1234–6, per Lord Denning; *Customs and Excise Commissioners* v. *Aps Samex (Hanil) Synthetic Fiber Industrial Co. Ltd* [1983] 1 All E.R. 1042 ; *R* v. *International Stock Exchange, ex p. Else* (1993) Q.B. 534.

3   Where leave to appeal to the House of Lords is refused, this includes the Court of Appeal – see *R. Hagen* v. *Fratelli, D. & G. Moretti S.N.C. and Molnar Machinery Ltd* [1980] 3 C.M.L.R. 253.

4   At one time it was argued that the UK courts were too reluctant to use the power to refer cases to the European Court. But in recent years it would seem that this is no longer the case. See Alec Stone Sweet and T.L.Brunell, 'The European Court and the National Courts: A statistical analysis of preliminary references 1961-95', *Jrnl. of European Policy*, 1998, 66.

number of decisions concerning states.[5] Under Maastricht, however, there is provision for fines of Member States in the form of lump sums or penalty payments to be imposed on states. In 1996 and 1997 proceedings to impose fines were started by the Commission against several states though in the end they were not pursued and by early 1999 no state had yet been fined. There is no limit set to the level of fines but the Commission has issued a memorandum on the size of fines.[6] The factors to be taken into account are the seriousness and duration of the offence and what is needed as a deterrent.[7]

There are several different ways in which national law is affected directly by membership of the EU.

(b) Community law and the UK system

1. The Treaties

Some of the provisions of the Treaties are directly applicable law in the UK, which means that they require no action by any UK authority to be fully effective as law. Not all the provisions of the Treaties are of this kind, but some are what the European Court has called 'complete and legally perfect'. They include for instance provisions prohibiting new (or preventing the extension of) discriminatory customs duties and internal taxes on other member states' products or prohibiting new (or the tightening of old) import quotas. Some are provisions that create direct rights of individuals. It is for the Court to determine which treaty articles are directly applicable. In doing this the Court looks at the clarity and conciseness of the article, the degree to which it envisages further acts by the Community or member states for its implementation, and the degree of discretion given to member states in deciding how to implement it. It is the norm for Treaty provisions to be held directly applicable.

Examples of treaty provisions that have been held to be directly applicable are Article 28 (formerly Art. 30) which prohibits quantitative

---

5   In February 1979, for instance, the Court held that the UK was obliged to comply with an order requiring tachographs (the 'spy in the cab') to be installed in over half a million lorries. Under EEC law, tachographs were supposed to be installed by 1 January 1978. The British government informed the Commission that it would 'neither be practical nor politic' to comply with that deadline. The Commission then brought the UK before the court which ruled that there was a breach of Community law and ordered the UK to comply. There were confident predictions in the press that the British government would defy the order but on 5 March 1979, less than a month after the order, the government announced that it would comply.

6   O.J., 1996, Case 242/6 and O.J., 1997 Case 63/2.

7   See also Case 121/97 *Commission v. Germany*, O.J., 1997, C166/7.

restrictions on imports, Article 39 (formerly Art. 48) prohibiting discrimination based on nationality in employment, Articles 81 and 82 (formerly Arts. 85 and 86) prohibiting anti-competitive practices and Article 141 (formerly Art. 119) on equal treatment of men and women in employment.

These directly applicable rights and obligations created by the Treaty, as well as secondary legislation made under it, take precedence over national provisions and as was held by the European Court in the case of *Simmenthal* ([1979] ECR 777) 'by their entry into force render automatically inapplicable any conflicting provision of national law'.

This principle was applied by the European Court in *R.* v. *Secretary of State for Transport ex parte Factortame & Ors* [1991] 3 All E.R. 769; [1990] 3 CMLR 1. The United Kingdom had passed an Act, the Merchant Shipping Act 1988, the purpose of which was to protect the British shipping industry, in particular against Spanish fishermen. The Spanish fishermen claimed that the Act was in breach of the applicable Treaty provisions prohibiting discrimination on grounds of nationality. They challenged the Act in the European Court but pending the decision of the Luxembourg Court they also brought proceedings in the English courts to get an interim injunction to stop enforcement of the 1988 Act. The Divisional Court granted the interim injunction ([1989] 2 CMLR 353) but both the Court of Appeal ([1989] 2 CMLR 353) and the House of Lords ([1989] 2 All E.R. 692) held that the English courts had no jurisdiction to grant such an interim injunction to suspend the operation of an Act of Parliament. However the question whether the national system had to provide an interim remedy in such a situation was referred by the House of Lords under Article 177 to the European Court. The European Court held that: 'the full effectiveness of Community law would be … impaired if a rule of national law could prevent a court seized of a dispute governed by Community law from granting interim relief in order to ensure the full effectiveness of the judgment to be given on the existence of the rights claimed under Community law.' It followed that a court which in those circumstances would grant interim relief were it not for a rule of national law, was obliged to set that rule aside.

Thus where the tests for such interim relief are satisfied, an English court is required temporarily to set aside even a statute alleged to violate Community law. See further, N. P. Gravells, 'Disapplying an Act of Parliament Pending a Preliminary Ruling: Constitutional Enormity or Community Law Right?', *Public Law*, 1990 p. 568; J. Steiner, 'Coming to Terms with EEC Directives', 106 *Law Qtly. Rev.*, 1990, pp. 2, 144.

Under Article 249 (formerly Art. 189) of the EC Treaty it is provided that 'in order to carry out their task, the Council and the Commission shall in accordance with the provisions of this Treaty make regulations, issue Directives, take decisions, make recommendations or deliver opinions'.

2.   Regulations

Article 249 provides that regulations 'shall have a general application' and 'shall be binding in every respect and directly applicable in each Member State'. Regulations require no national legislation to implement them. They take effect on the day specified, or in the absence of such date on the twentieth day following their publication in the Official Journal.[8]

3.   Directives

Article 249 provides: 'A Directive shall be binding as to the result to be achieved upon each Member State to which it is addressed but shall leave to the national authorities the choice of form and method'.

Directives have become the most usual channel for the translation of Community law into national law. There are many hundreds of Directives in force. Unlike a Regulation, a Directive does not normally in itself alter the national law. The Directive will, however, always state the date by which national systems must have implemented it. The Member State is left with a discretion only as to how it will implement the Directive. If it is not properly implemented, however, it may be treated as directly applicable.

The technical term is that a directive can have vertical (as opposed to horizontal) direct effect. This means that if the directive is clear, precise and unconditional it can have direct effect in the sense that it can be utilised by an individual against the state when it has failed to implement the directive properly or in time.[9] It cannot be relied on by an individual however until the time limit given for implementation has expired. The Court permitted an individual to use a directive in order to bring proceedings against the state requesting that her tax returns be calculated in accordance with the directive.[10] But the direct effect of a directive can only be pleaded against the state which has failed to implement it and not against a non-State entity or individual.[11]

On the other hand, the definition of State entity is not narrow. It covers bodies and organisations subject to the control and authority of the state even though they have no responsibility for the failure to implement the directive.[12] However, the guidance given to national courts as to what is and what is not a State entity or organ for this purpose lacks clarity.

---

8   See Case 39/72 *Commission* v. *Italy* (1973) ECR 101, [1973] CMLR 439.
9   See *Van Duyn* v. *Home Office* Case 41/74 (1974) ECR 1337; Case 148/78 *Pubblico Ministero* v. *Tullio Ratti* (1979) ECR 1629, [1980] 1 CMLR 96.
10 Case 8/81 *Becker* v. *Finanzamt Munster-Innenstadt* (1982) ECR 53, [1982] 1 CMLR 499.
11 *Marshall* v. *Southampton and South West Hampshire Area Health Authority* (Teaching) Case 152/84 [1986] ECR 723; [1993] 4 All E.R. 586; Case C-91/92 *Dori* v. *Recreb* (1994) ECR I 3325.
12 See for instance Case 188/89 *Foster* v. *British Gas* plc (1990) ECR 3313.) See also *Dori* v. *Recerb* above; Case 168/95 *Arcaro* [1996] ECR I-4705.

Although the Court has refused to allow direct horizontal enforcement by an individual pleading a directive against a non-state entity or individual, it has, confusingly, developed a principle requiring national law to be interpreted in such a way as to conform to directives.[13] *Marleasing* decided that a non-implemented directive could be relied on to guide the interpretation of national law in a case between individuals, even where the national law predated the directive. But the duty to conform to the directive where possible does not apply where such an interpretation is impossible.[14] The extent of this doctrine is uncertain.[15]

The European Court's decision in *Francovitch* v. *Republic of Italy*[16] took this doctrine further still by holding that an individual can sue the state for damages when it has failed to provide rights required under Community Directives. An Italian company went into liquidation, leaving F and other employees with unpaid arrears of salary. Italy had not set up a compensation scheme for employees in such circumstances as was required by a Community Directive. F sued in the Italian courts. The Court held that although the Directive was not sufficiently precise to have direct effect it gave a right to damages if (1) the Directive gave rights to individuals; (2) the content of such rights could be identified in the Directive; and (3) there was causal relation between the Member State's violation of its obligation and the damage suffered by the individual. It held that F was entitled to damages. The implications of this ruling are very wide.

However this doctrine has been refined since the decision in *Francovitch*. States are not responsible in damages whenever their breach of EU law results in loss to individuals. Damages would only be payable if the breach is serious (did the Member State 'manifestly and gravely disregard' its obligations).[17] Examples include: 1) Failure to transpose a Directive;[18] 2) Breach of an obligation that is so clear that no other

---

13 Case C-106/89, *Marleasing SA* v. *La Comercial Internacionale de Alimentacion SA* (1990) ECR I-4135, [1992] 1 CMLR 305.
14 Case C 334/92 *Wagner Miret* v. *Fondo de Garantia Salariel* (1993) ECR I-6911. And see also Case 80/86 *Kolpinghuis Nijmegen BV* (1987) ECR 3969, [1989] 2 CMLR 18; C-168/95 *Arcaro* (1996) ECR I-4705.
15 See for instance, Case C-1994/94 *CIA Security International SA* v. *Signalson SA and Securitel SPRL* (1996) ECR I-2201.
16 Cases C-6/90 and C-9/90 *Francovich and Bonfaci* v. *Italy* (1991) ECR I-5357, [1993] 2 CMLR 66.
17 Cases 46/93 *Brasserie du Pecheur* v. *Germany* and Case 48/93 *R* v. *Secretary of State, ex p. Factortame* (1996) ECR I –1029.
18 Case 178–179/94 – Cases 188–190/94 *Dillenketjen* v. *Germany* (1996) ECR I – 4845.

interpretation is reasonable.[19] 3) Breach of an obligation established by settled case law.[20] 4) Breach of an interim order of the Court.[1]

4. Decisions

Decisions may be directly applicable depending on how they are framed. Under Article 249 (formerly Art. 189) 'decisions shall be binding in every respect for the addressees named therein'.[2] They can be directed at individuals or companies as well as member states.

There are many kinds of decisions. One sort is a decision authorising a Member State or individuals to do something. An example would be granting an undertaking or exemption under Article 81(3) (formerly Art. 85(3)) from the cartel prohibition of Article 81(1). Some decisions place obligations on those to whom they are addressed. An example would be a decision requiring a Member State to modify a particular state regime because it infringes a prohibition in the Treaty. Other decisions are merely declaratory.

5. International agreements

The Community has legal personality and can enter into formal legally binding agreements. The ECJ has held that in certain circumstances such agreements can be directly effective in the national systems of Member States.[3]

6. Decisions of the Court of Justice

Under Article 220 (formerly Art. 164), the Court of Justice is required to 'ensure that in the interpretation and application of the Treaty the law is observed'. One important way in which the Court has fulfilled this function is through preliminary rulings on matters referred to it by national courts under Article 234 (formerly Art. 177) of the Treaty.

Decisions of the European Court interpreting Community law have direct effect in the United Kingdom, and take precedence over anything in UK law, including statutes, that may be contrary to such interpretation. It is an absolute principle of membership of the Community that in case of conflict, Community law takes precedence over national law. This point

19 Case 323/93 *Queen* v. *HM Treasury, ex p. British Telecom* (1996) ECR I-1631.
20 See *Brasserie du Pecheur*, above.
1 See *Factortame*, above.
2 For an example see Case 9/70 *Franz Grad* v. *Finanzamt Traunstein* [1970] ECR 825, [1971] CMLR 1.
3 For an example see Case 104/81 *Haupzollamt Mainz* v. *Kupferberg* (1982) ECR 3641, [1983] 1 CMLR 1; cp Case 21–24/72 *International Fruit Co* v. *Productschap voor Groenten en Fruit* (1972) ECR 1219, [1975] 2 CMLR 1.

was first established in the great case of *Van Gend en Loos* (Case 26/62 (1963) E.C.R 1). The plaintiff had challenged a Dutch law as contravening an article of the Rome Treaty. The Dutch and Belgian government argued that the European Court had no jurisdiction to decide whether the provisions of the EEC Treaty prevailed over Dutch legislation and that the solution to the problem was one exclusively for the national courts. The Court rejected this argument and held that a provision of Community law 'produces direct effects and creates individual rights which national courts must protect' (at 16). The individual has no direct access to the European Court but if he takes action in the national courts these courts are required to follow the decisions of the European Court on a question of Community law. If the court is in doubt over the question it *can* refer the question to the Luxembourg court under Article 234 (formerly Art. 177) and if it is a hearing in a final final Court of Appeal, it *must* do so.

The Court expressed its basic philosophy in the judgment in *Costa* v. *E.N.E.L.* (6/64 (1964) E.C.R. 585 at 593): by contrast with ordinary international treaties, the EEC Treaty has created its own legal system which, on the entry into force of the Treaty, became an integral part of the legal systems of the Member States and which their courts are bound to apply. By creating a Community of unlimited duration, having its own institutions, its own personality, its own legal capacity and capacity of representation on the international plane, and more particularly, real powers stemming from a limitation of sovereignty or a transfer of powers from the States to the Community, the Member States have limited their sovereign rights, albeit within limited fields, and have created a body of law which binds both their nationals and themselves.

The issue came up squarely in the *Simmenthal* case (1978) E.C.R. 629, in which the Court held unambiguously that it was the duty of national courts to apply directly applicable Community law *even in preference to subsequently enacted national law*. There could be no more dramatic illustration of the effect of joining the Community. (See also the *Factortame* case above.)

7. Recommendations

Recommendations have no binding force and are therefore not directly a source of law. But national courts are required to interpret their own law in the light of Recommendations, especially where the national law is implementing the Recommendation or where the Recommendation 'perfects' a Directive.[4]

---

4   Case 322/88 *Grimaldi* v. *Fonds des Maladies Professionelles* (1989) ECR 4407; Case 188/91 *Deutsche Shell –Hauptzollamt Hamburg-Harburg* (1993) ECR I – 363.

8. Opinions

Opinions likewise have no legal force. Article 249 (formerly Art. 189) states 'Recommendations and opinions shall have no binding force'.

See generally T.C. Hartley, *The Foundations of European Community Law* (4ᵗʰ ed. 1998, Oxford); D. Chalmers, *European Union Law* Vol. 1 *Law and European Union Government* (1998, Ashgate, Aldershot); P. Craig and G. de Burka, *European Union Law* (2nd ed. 1998, OUP); S. Weatherill and P. Beaumont, *European Community Law* (3rd ed. 1999, Penguin); L. Neville Brown, *The European Courts* (1997, Cartermill, London); R. Dehousse, *The European Court of Justice* (1998, Macmillan).

(c) Parliamentary scrutiny of European legislation

Proposals for Community legislation are formulated by the Commission. They are usually discussed in detail with officials in each country and with technical experts and interest groups. (It has been said that the Commission is sometimes better at consultation with national interest groups than the UK government.) The proposals are then sent to the Council of Ministers which must approve them before they become law. The European Parliament is also consulted. Detailed technical legislation implementing measures previously agreed by the Council of Ministers can be made directly by the Commission.

The importance of Community legislation is clear. As the 1992 Hansard Society report *Making the Law* said (p. 124):

> the whole corpus of EC law is influencing the development of UK law in many fields. The requirements, demands and implications of EC laws must be fully considered at every stage.

Not that all areas of the law are affected. Criminal law, law relating to education, children, local authority organisation and finance, health services and most fiscal law remain largely within the control of national parliaments. But in major areas of the law, especially those affecting trade, industry, agriculture, employment, the environment and financial services, Community law is of great significance.

Technically and constitutionally, the making of Community law does not require the approval of Parliament. However both Houses of Parliament have set up special machinery to assist in the process of keeping abreast of proposed Community legislation. It would seem that this is the most searching and systematic method of parliamentary scrutiny in any member country.[5]

5   This view is expressed in a comparative survey by K. M. Newman, counsel to the Chairman of Committees and Legal Adviser to the European Select Committee ('The Impact of National Parliaments on the Development of Community Law', 1987).

Thus the House of Commons first addressed the issue in the two reports of a committee chaired by Sir John Foster (H.C. 143 and H.C. 463, 1972–73). One of the major recommendations of the Foster Committee was that a committee should be established to examine proposals from the European Communities with the object of informing the House as to any which raised issues of legal or political importance and to make recommendations. Such a committee was first set up in 1974. Its terms of reference were:

> To consider draft proposals ... and to report their opinion as to whether such proposals or other documents raise questions of legal or political importance, to give their reasons for their opinion, to report what matters of principle or policy may be affected thereby, and to what extent they may affect the law of the United Kingdom, and to make recommendations for the further consideration of such proposals and other documents by the House.

Note that these terms of reference did not give the Committee any scope to express views on the merits of the proposal. A report of the Committee in 1985–86 suggesting that its terms of reference should be widened so as to enable it to go into the merits of proposals of particular importance[6] had a negative response from the government.[7] Value judgments and political decisions are for the House of Commons after the Committee has identified the legal and political issues worthy of debate.

The Committee, usually referred to as the Scrutiny Committee, consists of 16 members, nominated for a Parliament, and is able to appoint specialist advisers. From the outset the government undertook to deposit with Parliament copies of all proposals submitted to the Council of Ministers for decision and not to agree to any such proposal in the Council until each House of Parliament has had a chance to consider it. If exceptionally the Minister does give consent in Brussels before Parliament has given its approval he is supposed to explain the circumstances to the House as soon as practicable. This undertaking was embodied in a resolution of the House of Commons in 1980.

The text of such proposals is normally deposited with Parliament within two days of its receipt in London and the Minister responsible submits an explanatory memorandum within two weeks thereafter explaining the implications. If the proposal is significantly changed during negotiations in Brussels, the Minister puts in an up-dating memorandum. The Select Committee generally meets once a week to consider such papers. It can call witnesses to give it oral or written evidence. It then produces reports

---

6　Second Report from the House of Commons Select Committee on European Legislation, 1985–86.

7　Observations by the government on the [said] Report – col. 123 of HC Official Report, 15 April 1987.

highlighting issues that it considers raise questions of legal and/or political importance with its recommendations.

The House of Lords too has a Committee to consider how to proceed – the Maybray-King Report of July 1973. It too proposed the establishment of a committee – but its terms of reference were wider than those for the Commons:

> To consider Community proposals whether in draft or otherwise, to obtain all necessary information about them, and to make reports on those which, in the opinion of the Committee, raise important questions of policy or principle, and on other questions to which the Committee consider that the special attention of the House should be drawn.

These terms of reference do not inhibit expression of views as to the merits or otherwise of proposals.

The House of Lords Select Committee on the European Communities has a membership of 24 members who meet fortnightly. It works through standing sub-committees,[8] each of 2–4 Committee members plus 8–12 co-opted members and specialist advisers. (From time to time additional sub-committees are set up.) The sub-committees typically take written and oral evidence from Ministers, experts and interest groups which is printed with the Committee's reports.

The process consists of examination of EC Commission proposals. Some 800 are brought forward each year. The appropriate government department prepares an explanatory memorandum summarising the proposal and indicating its legal, financial and policy implications, the procedure to be followed in negotiations and the likely timetable for its consideration by the Council of Ministers.

The Select Committee cannot deal with all the 800 or so proposals. The Chairman therefore sifts out those that require the Committee's attention. Those that do are remitted to the appropriate sub-committee. About half of all proposals are remitted to a sub-committee. Usually the sub-committee simply takes note without further inquiry. About one-tenth of proposals are the subject of a Report to the House. Sometimes, for fast-moving issues, the Committee uses the technique of a letter to the Minister.

About half of the Committee's Reports include a recommendation for debate in the House. These usually take place on a neutral 'take note' motion.

The reports of the House of Lords sub-committees are highly regarded throughout the EC. Sometimes the sub-committee discusses the issue under consideration with the European Commission's officials. It can

---

8   A – Finance, Trade and Industry and External Relations; B – Energy Industry and Transport; C – Environment and Social Affairs; D – Agriculture and Food.

influence Community legislation at an earlier stage than the House of Commons Committee.

The Hansard Society's 1992 Report *Making the Law* suggested (para. 414) that the new House of Lords Delegated Powers Scrutiny Committee (p. 98 above) might be able to play a role in vetting bills and delegated legislation to check whether they comply with Community Law. Parliamentary Counsel could not be expected to do this job; it had to be done systematically by experts (para. 560).

Implementation The Hansard Society's Report also highlighted the problem of implementation of EC Directives both in terms of drafting and substance. In regard to drafting (paras. 562–65), there was sometimes a conflict between the broad and general terms of the Directive and the narrow and precise terms of the UK statute giving it effect. In terms of substance there had been 'a tendency either to over-implement or to under-implement directives' (para. 555). Thus the Directive about food safety appeared to have been incorporated into UK law 'with far greater precision and regulation to the detriment of the affected industries than may have been conceived by the original Community draftsman' (ibid.). There was a need for all Acts and statutory instruments implementing European Directives to be accompanied by explanatory memoranda giving the essential Community background (para. 557).

In 1988/89 the House of Commons Select Committee on Procedure in its Fourth Report (*The Scrutiny of European Legislation*) made proposals for improving the Scrutiny Committee's machinery. The Government published its response in 1990 (Cm. 1081). Thus, the Committee proposed that its terms of reference be extended to broader issues. The Government replied that broad issues should in general be considered by the Lords Committee rather than the Commons Committee. But it agreed that the Commons Committee could consider 'horizontal' issues, namely ones recurring in various documents. The Government also agreed to supply the Committee with pre-legislative Commission working documents.

The *Report of the (Jellicoe) Select Committee on the Committee Work of the House of Lords* (HL Paper 35–I, 1991–92) made several proposals regarding the work of the Scrutiny Committee. It warmly commended the work of the Committee but thought that a smaller proportion of documents should be sifted for detailed scrutiny and that its reports should be shorter and sharper (para. 189). It recommended that there should be more liaison between the Committee and the European Commission and the European Parliament (para. 191). It urged a more flexible sub-committee structure with the number of peers involved in the work of sub-committees to be reduced from around 80 to around 50. The number of Committee members should be reduced from 24 to 12–15. The House 'took note' of the Jellicoe Report in a lengthy debate on 3 June 1992 – cols. 904–1010. The Commons

Select Committee on European Legislation reported on the scrutiny arrangements in July 1996 (27th Report, 1995–96) and its recommendations were endorsed by the Commons Select Committee on Procedure in March 1997 (3rd Report, 1996–97).

In its manifesto the Labour Opposition made a commitment to overhaul the scrutiny arrangements and in January 1998, after coming to office, it made proposals to the Select Committee on Modernisation of the House of Commons. That Select Committee reported to the House in June 1998 (7th Report, 1997–98, HC 791).

In November 1998, the Labour Government published a new report on ways of improving Parliamentary scrutiny of EU business. ('The Scrutiny of European Business', Cm 4095). It endorsed the proposals regarding scrutiny of EU business made by the Select Committee on Modernisation. The Government would provide an Explanatory Memorandum to assist the Scrutiny Committees assess the documents with which they were presented. In the House of Commons, for the majority of documents, this would normally be in one of the European Standing Committees. There would be scope for specialist Select Committees to be more closely involved in the scrutiny process and the Scrutiny Committee would be able to seek the views of Departmental Select Committees. The rule that Government should not implement EU proposals until both Houses had completed their scrutiny should apply to a wider range of contexts.

See generally E. Denza, 'Parliamentary Scrutiny of Community Legislation', 14 *Statute Law Review*, 1993, pp. 56–63; T. St. J. M. Bates, 'European Community Legislation before the House of Commons', 12 *Statute Law Review*, 1991, pp. 109–34.

2. TEXTBOOKS

According to orthodox theory, textbooks fall into two categories – those that are authoritative and those that are not. Authoritative writers are those who are dead, and in particular a select band of hallowed names such as Bracton, Glanvil, Littleton, Coke, Hale and Blackstone. Most practitioners go through their entire professional lives without ever having occasion to cite any of these giants.[9] But if their views are brought to the attention of a court, they have an extra patina of respectability not available to lesser writers. On the other hand, it is questionable whether in practice their views are treated as any more persuasive – this depends on what they said and what other authorities counsel has been able to deploy. These names certainly evoke in English lawyers a Pavlovian respectful

9   For examples of modern cases which dealt with these great names see however *Button* v. *D.P.P.* [1966] A.C. 591 or *L.* v. *K.* [1985] 1 All E.R. 961.

response. But this does not mean that their views are more likely to be followed.

The rule that an author must be dead before he could be cited as authority was said to be based on the somewhat feeble ground that until then it could not be known whether he might change his mind. (On that basis no living judge ought to have been cited either.) In practice lawyers circumvented the rule by the simple device of citing a living author and then saying they were adopting his views as part of their argument. But in recent years the courts have taken a more relaxed attitude and counsel would not today be reprimanded for boldly presenting the work of a living author in support of his proposition. There are a number of scholars whose books and articles are regularly honoured by being cited both by counsel and by the judges in their decisions.[10]

But the contribution of scholars does not have the same role in the English law-making process that it has in many other countries. In the United States or on the continent of Europe, for instance, no self-respecting practitioner would present an argument to the court on a point of law without directing the court's attention to the views of the leading academic commentators. The decisions of the Supreme Court of the United States as well as those of lower courts cite a mass of academic authority as a matter of course.

The difference is probably due to the relatively low esteem in which academic lawyers have traditionally been held in the English legal profession. For centuries the only two English universities, Oxford and Cambridge, did not even teach English law. They taught only Roman and Canon law, which were irrelevant to practitioners. Those who went into the profession as barristers learnt their law first at the Inns of Court and then in practice. Blackstone is said to have inaugurated the teaching of English law at the universities with his famous course on the Common Law from 1753, but in reality the teaching of the subject lapsed after his resignation. In 1800 the Downing Chair of the Laws of England was founded in Cambridge, but the subject did not flourish there either. When in 1846 a Select Committee inquired into the state of legal education in this country, it reported that 'no legal education worthy of the name is at this moment to be had'.[11] Whereas in Berlin, for instance, there were fourteen professors teaching some thirty branches of law to hundreds of students, in Oxford

---

10 Professor Rupert Cross's book on *Evidence*, Dicey on *Conflicts of Law*, Rayden on *Divorce*, Maxwell on *The Interpretation of Statutes*, Archbold on *Criminal Pleading, Evidence and Practice*, and Dymond on *Death Duties* are familiar examples.

11 *Report of the Select Committee on Legal Education*, 1846 vol. X, British Parliamentary Papers, p. lvi, para. 3.

and Cambridge there appeared to be neither lectures, nor examinations, nor for that matter any students.[12]

The Select Committee's Report led to changes. In 1852 Oxford established a B.C.L. degree and in 1855 Cambridge started an LL.B. degree. Law faculties were created at London University and in provincial universities as they were set up. By 1908 there were eight law faculties. But they had to struggle to establish their academic respectability. It was still a moot point whether law was a fit subject for university legal education. (That this particular canard dies hard may be judged from the fact that Lord Diplock told the annual meeting of the Society of Public Teachers of Law in 1966 that he had serious doubts on the question.[13] Lord Diplock was at the time not only chairman of the Council of Legal Education of the Inns of Court, but also chairman of the Institute of Advanced Legal Education at London University!) The acid test of whether law was suitable for inclusion in university courses was whether it was 'liberal'. A distinction was drawn for this purpose between liberal education on the one hand and practical, technical or vocational training on the other. The essence of the difference between the two, it was thought, lay in the different content of each. Thus Roman law, jurisprudence and legal history were ideal subject-matter for liberal education, whilst company, tax or labour law manifestly were not. The closer the subject came to being concerned with the affairs of the ordinary man or, worse, the market place, the less it qualified as 'liberal'. Common law subjects such as contract and tort and even property law were somehow exempted, even though they plainly had practical importance.

The fallacy that liberality of pursuit is limited to certain subject-matter is not a new one. A hundred years after Newton's *Principia*, Oxford and Cambridge were still making virtually no contribution to scientific thought because they refused to accept that science was a proper subject for study. In the medieval university the seven liberal arts were grammar, rhetoric, dialectic, geometry, music, arithmetic and astronomy. After the Renaissance the emphasis shifted to the language and literature of the Hebrews, the Romans and above all of the Greeks. More recently the classics have receded, as the concept of liberal education has expanded to embrace the imaginative and philosophical literature of modern Europe. Today none but the most sheltered humanist would deny that science has an honoured place in this great tradition.

The view that regards the content of liberal education as crucial ignores the fact that the most liberal subjects can be and often are taught in a narrow, pedantic and scholastic manner which is the very antithesis of the spirit of liberal education. It is not the content at a particular place or time

12 Ibid., para. 2.
13 *Journal of the Society of Public Teachers of Law*, 1966, p. 193.

which is fundamental, but rather the way in which that content is imparted. As Samuel Alexander said: 'Liberality is a spirit of pursuit not a choice of subject.' If a subject is one in which principles can be discovered and reasons for facts can be related to the principles, then such a subject can be made the basis for liberal education. A practical subject, such as company law, can be taught in one of two ways – either as a means to achieving technical proficiency, or alternatively as a means of studying the problems of business organisation as a phase of human experience to be appreciated and understood as part of the economic and social problems of a wider society.

As a result of their worries about the liberality of the subject-matter, the university law schools for decades failed to teach some of the most ordinary practical subjects which today we take for granted. The result was that even the minority of practitioners who had read law at the university tended to regard their academic law studies as largely irrelevant to their professional work. They barely read the academic journals and, when they did, they found their prejudices amply confirmed. Worse, the teaching of the subjects that were supposed to be liberal was frequently arid, technical and dull. The legal academic world, with few exceptions, was detached from the concerns of the real world and was understandably ignored by both practitioners and judges.

In the past three decades this has all been changing. The law faculties are teaching subjects of importance to practitioners; books and articles in academic journals are of direct relevance to them; both teaching and textbooks are improved; practitioners have normally read law at university;[14] contact between the two worlds is more common and more on the basis of mutual respect instead of the old mutual disparagement.

This is borne out by statistics produced by Professor Alan Paterson as to the times that the work of living authors is cited in the House of Lords. In 1955 Appeal Cases, there were only seven references by counsel to textbooks written by authors who were then alive, and two to articles. In the Law Lords' speeches there were six references to textbooks and none to articles. By 1961 the position had changed only marginally. In that year counsel cited textbooks by living authors only eleven times. But by 1971 there had been a threefold increase (compared with 1955) in the number of

14 Between 1970 and 1978 the proportion of new solicitors who were law graduates rose from 40 per cent to 60 per cent – an astonishing rate of increase (*Report of the Royal Commission on Legal Services* 1979, Cmnd 7648, para. 38.13, p. 609). In 1989, of those admitted to the Rolls as solicitors, 73 per cent were law graduates, 14 per cent were non-law graduates and the remainder were miscellaneous categories including 10 per cent who were overseas lawyers, most of whom would have been law graduates. In 1998, the proportion of home law graduates had fallen to 45 per cent, the number of home non-law graduates had risen to 29 per cent and the proportion of overseas lawyers 6 per cent. (Source: Law Society's *Annual Statistical Report*.)

such references by counsel and the Law Lords themselves. The author of the study said that such references were now a commonplace and that 'in some recent cases in the House of Lords the welter of academic references on both sides of the Bar has reached floodlike proportions which would have astounded their counterparts of twenty years ago'.[15]

In this developing relationship it is probable that the courts will increasingly welcome the contributions of scholars as a useful additional source of guidance and support. But given the long tradition of distance between the profession and the academic community, it would be surprising if scholars came to exercise the same influence on the development of the law that they do in many other Western countries. An article by Dr F. A. Mann in the *Law Quarterly Review* in 1973 led to two re-hearings before the House of Lords and altered the view of the majority (ibid., p. 17). But this kind of impact is very rare. Dr Alan Paterson, for instance, said that 'there seems little evidence that the Law Lords regard pronouncements of living academic writers (as a group) as having even persuasive authority. Their practice seems to be to accord such writings merely "permissive" status' (op. cit., pp. 18–19).

For a rare fulsome encomium see however the remarks of Lord Bridge in his speech in *Shivpuri* [1986] 2 All E.R. 334. In explaining how he had come to change his view as expressed in the then recent House of Lords decision in *Anderton* v. *Ryan*, he indicated that he had been considerably influenced by an article by the late Professor Glanville Williams:

> I cannot conclude this opinion without disclosing that I have had the advantage, since the conclusion of the argument in this appeal, of reading an article by Professor Glanville Williams entitled 'The Lords and the Impossible Attempts, or Quis Custodiet Ipsos Custodies?' [1986] CLJ 33. The language in which he criticises the decision in *Anderton* v. *Ryan* is not conspicuous for its moderation, but it would be foolish, on that account, not to recognise the force of his criticism and churlish not to acknowledge the assistance I have derived from it. [P. 345.]

Even the judge who is also a scholar feels the difference between the two forms of creativity. Lord Justice Megarry expressed this with his usual felicity when commenting on the authority of his own textbook which had been cited to him by counsel in a case:

> I would add one comment, in amplification of certain observations that I made when during the argument counsel cited a passage from the 3rd edition of Megarry & Wade's *Real Property*. It seems to me that words in a book written or subscribed to by an author who is or becomes a judge have the same value as words written by any other reputable author, neither more nor less. The

process of authorship is entirely different from that of judicial decision. The author, no doubt, has the benefit of a broad and comprehensive study of his chosen subject as a whole, together with a lengthy period of gestation, and intermittent opportunities for reconsideration. But he is exposed to the perils of yielding to preconceptions, and he lacks the advantage of that impact and sharpening of focus which the detailed facts of a particular case bring to the judge. Above all, he has to form his ideas without the aid of the purifying ordeal of skilled argument on the specific facts of a contested case. Argued law is tough law.... . I would therefore give credit to the words of any reputable author in book or article as expressing tenable and arguable ideas, as fertilisers of thought, and as conveniently expressing the fruits of research in print, often in apt and persuasive language. But I would do no more than that; and in particular I would expose those views to the testing and refining process of argument. Today, as of old, by good disputing shall the law be well known.[16]

3. CUSTOM

There are several separate meanings of the word 'custom' as a source of law. The first is *general custom* in the sense of common usage. It seems possible that after the Norman Conquest this was a real source of some law. As the country was gradually reduced to centralised order by the judges travelling around the country, they must have based at least some of their decisions on the common custom of the realm. According to Sir Frederick Pollock, 'The common law is a customary law if, in the course of about six centuries, the undoubting belief and uniform language of everybody who had occasion to consider the matter were able to make it so.' Coke described custom as 'one of the main triangles of the laws of England', and for Blackstone, general customs were 'the universal rule of the whole kingdom and form the common law in its stricter and more usual signification'. But these claims are likely to be more poetic than historically accurate. In fact a high proportion of the so-called customs were almost certainly invented by the judges.

An article in the *Law Quarterly Review* in 1893 claimed, for instance, that there was 'a very strong presumption that the common law originated in the judicial adoption of the common customs of the realm'.[17] The kind of evidence cited for the proposition, however, hardly bears the weight of the argument. Thus the man who so negligently looked after his house that it caught fire and the fire spread to his neighbour's house was liable 'by the law and custom of the realm'. But what sort of custom was this? Is the plea that it was customary for every man to look after his own property so that fires did not arise and spread? Or is it rather that when such fires

16 *Cordell* v. *Second Clanfield Properties Ltd* [1968] 3 W.L.R. 864, 872.
17 Greer, 'Custom in the Common Law', 9 *Law Quarterly Review*, 1893, pp. 157–60.

occurred the house owner was customarily held liable? The custom, in other words, was of the courts rather than of the people. Similarly, it is said that the law regarding the liability of carriers and innkeepers was founded on the custom of the realm. But what was the nature of the custom? Did the common carriers voluntarily pay their customers when goods entrusted to them were lost or damaged? It seems unlikely. Or did the populace demand that the rule be so? Even making the large and somewhat improbable assumption that the public did make such a demand, this hardly amounts to a popular custom but merely to popular pressure for a rule.[18] Although therefore, no doubt, general custom may have played some part in the early development of the law, it seems probable that even at that time the judges were the true originators of a good deal of the custom of the realm.

The second main meaning of custom as a source of law is in the sense of *local custom* in contrast to the common law. From early times the judges, for obvious reasons, established a series of rigorous tests or hurdles that had to be met by anyone claiming the benefit of some exception to the common law. The judges were trying to impose the Westminster brand of justice and did not look benevolently on too many local variations. There were seven main tests for a local custom.

(1) It must have existed from 'time whereof the memory of man runneth not to the contrary', or from time immemorial. This concept was arbitrarily defined by statute to mean from 1189. If proof could be brought that the custom did not exist in 1189, it was rejected. Thus in *Simpson* v. *Wells* (1872) it was shown that the appellant could not have a customary right to set up a refreshment stall on a public footway as he claimed from 'statute sessions', because these were first authorised in the fourteenth century. More recently Mr Justice Lawton rejected a claim by a barrister that there was a customary rule that barristers could not be sued – on the ground that dicta in a case in 1435 suggested that at that time a barrister might be sued![19]

(2) The custom must have existed continuously since 1189 – any proved interruption defeated the claim.

(3) The custom must have been enjoyed peaceably without opposition.

(4) It must have been felt to be obligatory.

(5) It must be capable of being defined precisely – a requirement of certainty.

(6) Customs must be consistent one with another.

18 I am indebted for these examples and the analysis presented to E. K. Braybrooke, 'Custom as a Source of English Law', 50 *Michigan Law Review*, 1951, pp. 71, 74.

19 *Rondel* v. *Worsley* [1966] 2 W.L.R. 300, 307. However, he was able to find other reasons to uphold the immunity.

(7)   Finally they must be reasonable – if it could be proved that it would
       have been unreasonable in 1189, again the claim would fail.

These formidable qualifying conditions gave the judges ample powers
to reject any local custom they regarded as unsuitable for recognition.

Inevitably, claims to local custom in modern times are rare. They do
occur, however, from time to time. In *Egerton* v. *Harding* [1974] 3 All E.R.
689, for instance, the courts upheld a customary duty on one of the parties
to fence land against cattle straying from the common. Another case in the
same year concerned the alleged right of the mayor, bailiff and burgess
and others to indulge in lawful sports including shooting on land in the
centre of the borough of New Windsor:

New Windsor Corporation v. *Mellor* [1974] 2 All E.R. 510 (Chancery
Division)

The respondent caused certain land in the centre of the borough of New
Windsor to be registered in the register of town or village greens maintained
by the registration authority under s. 3 of the Commons Registration Act
1965, claiming that the inhabitants of the borough had by custom acquired
the right to indulge in lawful sports and pastimes on it. The borough
objected to the registration and an inquiry was held by the Chief Commons
Commissioner. The evidence before the Commissioner showed that in
1651 a lease of the land had been granted by the borough for 40 years, the
lease containing a covenant by the lessee that it should be lawful for the
'Mayor Bailiffs and Burgesses and ... all and every person and persons to
have access' to the land 'as well as to exercise and use shooting or any
other lawful pastime for their recreation at all convenient times'. The lessee
also covenanted to set up a pair of butts 'for the inhabitants of the ... town
to shoot at' and to repair and maintain them, and not to do anything which
might be 'hurtful to the shooting or any other pastime then to be exercised
for recreation of the people'. Further leases of the land for 40-year terms,
containing similar covenants, were granted in 1704 and 1749. In 1819 the
corporation granted a three-year lease, the lease being made subject to the
right 'of the Native Bachelors of Windsor in exercising all lawful sports
games and pastimes' over the land, and, in 1822 a similar lease 'subject to
the rights and privileges of the Bachelors of Windsor who are entitled to
use the [land] for all lawful recreations and amusements'. After the Inclosure
Act 1813 the borough held the land by virtue of their statutory title under
that Act. Following an inclosure award in 1819, they held it free from any
rights of common of pasture or turbary, but still subject to any rights to
use it for lawful sports and pastimes to which it was formerly subject. The
land was used annually for 'revels' until the 1840s. There were also in
evidence extracts from newspaper reports and reports of meetings, a

newspaper extract of October 1875 recording that the land had been used for sports by a large number of people and that the mayor had vetoed the holding of the sports, on wrong advice given to him by the town clerk on the legal effect of the inclosure award. From 1875 onwards the borough refused to recognise that the inhabitants had any right to use the land for recreation and accordingly it was no longer used for that purpose. At the time of the respondent's registration the land had for some years been used partly as a school sports ground and partly as a car park. It was listed in the development plan for the borough as the site for a multi-storey car park. On the evidence the Commissioner confirmed the registration, holding that a customary right to indulge in lawful sports and pastimes on the land had been acquired by the inhabitants of the locality from time immemorial and that the land was therefore 'town or village green' within ss. 1 and 22(1) of the 1965 Act. The borough appealed, contending, inter alia, (i) that the evidence did not support the conclusion of long usage since there was no direct evidence of any user and the Commission had found that there had been no such user since 1875, and (ii) that the user was incapable of existing as a custom since, from the terms of the covenants in the 1651 lease, the user was not confined to the inhabitants of the borough, i.e. the 'Burgesses', but extended to 'all and every other person', i.e. persons residing outside the borough.

Foster J. stated:

Long usage
There was, in my judgment, ample evidence on which the Commissioner could come to the conclusion that there had been long usage, and I, for my part, on that evidence would have come to the same conclusion.

That the claim had been made as of right
The Commissioner came to the conclusion that the user has been as of right, in view of the leases granted, subject to the right and to the events in 1819 and 1822, to which I have referred. In my judgment, his conclusion was right.

That the right claimed is capable of existing as a custom
It is well established that to create a custom the user must have been, by the inhabitants of an area, defined by reference to the limits of some recognised division of land such as a town... . This raises the question of construction of the words used in the lease of 1651. The Commissioner held that the words 'all and every other person or persons' and the words 'the people' must be read in their context and the covenant to set up a pair of butts 'for the inhabitants of the said town' to shoot at shows that those wide expressions should be limited to the inhabitants of the town. He therefore concluded that the custom was confined to the inhabitants of a particular locality.

Counsel for the borough submitted that the word 'burgesses' included all the inhabitants of the town, and reliance was placed on the definition of 'burgesses' in Wharton's Law Lexicon: 'Generally the inhabitants of a borough or walled town'. In Stroud's Judicial Dictionary, 'Burgesses' is defined as referring to men of trade. Earlier in the lease there are found the words 'Mayor Bailiffs Burgesses and their Successors', showing that the words 'Mayor Bailiffs and Burgesses' refer to the body corporate rather than to every person living in the town. It might well be ultra vires for the corporate body to provide benefits for persons not living within its boundaries, and it may be, but this is pure surmise, since there is only an extract from the lease, and after the words 'all and every other person or persons' there may have followed some words such as 'being inhabitants of the town', which occur later. I have, however, come to the conclusion that the Commissioner was correct in confining the expressions used to the inhabitants of the town.

Does the custom arise from time immemorial?
Counsel for the respondent submitted that once the first three points were established the court should be astute to find that the origin of the custom was from time immemorial, and he relied for his submission on three cases: *Cocksedge* v. *Fanshaw*,[20] *Malcomson* v. *O'Dea*[1] and *Johnson* v. *Barnes*.[2] Counsel for the borough referred me to a statute of Henry VIII[3] which was not cited to the Commissioner, to show that the origin of the usage stemmed from that statute and not from time immemorial. If it could be shown that the right to use Bachelor's Acre stems from a statute passed after 1189, then the claim of a custom would be defeated (see *Simpson* v. *Wells*).[4]

Section 4 of that statute is in these terms:

'… (4) and also that Butts be made on this Side the Feast of St. *Michael* the Archangel next coming, in every City, Town and Place, by the Inhabitants of every such City, Town and Place, according to the law of ancient Time used; (5) and that the Inhabitants and Dwellers in every of them be compelled to make and continue such Butts, upon Pain to forfeit for every three Months so lacking, xx.s (6) and that the said Inhabitants shall exercise themselves with Long-Bows in shooting at the same time, and elsewhere in holy Days and other Times convenient.'

But from the terms of s. 4(4) the words 'according to the Law of ancient Time used' show that the making of butts was not started by virtue of that Act. The provisions do not negative the right having existed from time immemorial.

The Court should therefore be astute to find the origin from time immemorial and, in my judgment, the Commissioner was right to do so. For these reasons, in my judgment the appeal fails and I propose to dismiss it.

In 1992 the High Court held that anglers had a customary common law right to dig on the foreshore for worms as bait. The right to fish in tidal

---

20   (1779) 1 Doug. KB 119.
1   (1863) 10 H.L. Cas. 593.
2   (1872) L.R. 7 CP 592.
3   33 Hen. 8 c.9.
4   (1872) L.R. 7 Q.B. 214.

waters, dating back to Magna Carta, included the ancillary right to dig for bait. But the right did not cover digging for bait for sale or other commercial purposes.[5]

The question has been much canvassed as to whether a local custom is law regardless of the court's decision. If this is so, the court recognises the custom because it is already law. This represents the late Professor Rupert Cross's view.[6] But there is an inevitable circularity about the argument. If the custom is not recognised, it was not law; if it is recognised, it was. It seems more accurate to posit that the custom is authenticated by the judicial decision which upholds it. Professor Cross objected that this is the equivalent of saying that a statute is not law until it has been interpreted by a judge. But the two cases are very different. A statute is undeniably law – every word is law and there is no possibility of argument about it. The document is tangible and certain and the contents are known even if the meaning is in dispute. There could never be litigation testing whether a statutory provision is a law. By contrast, the fact that there is litigation over the existence of the custom indicates that there are serious doubts as to whether a court will uphold the claim. An alleged custom, the validity of which is as yet unrecognised by a court, may be more than half way to being a law; but it lacks the accolade of recognition without which it is merely a claim.

Much the same is true of *mercantile custom*, which is often cited in the books as another instance of custom as a source of common law. The practices of merchants, it is said, were recognised by the courts and became rules of law because they were felt by the courts to be binding. But this is again to pay excessive regard to the rhetoric, and not to focus on the likely reality of the situation. The point has been made by a learned commentator, E. K. Braybrooke:

> If we take as typical of the custom of merchants the rule that if A draw upon B a bill payable to C, B (if he accept the bill) is bound thereby to pay C, we may readily see expressed in this rule the result of a long-continued course of practice among merchants; the crux of the matter is that acceptors of such bills have in the past acknowledged their liability to pay the payee, though there may be no privity of contract between them. All that remains to be done is for the courts to enforce this customary rule by allowing C to succeed in an action against B. But is the matter quite as simple as it looks? If acceptors of bills have customarily acknowledged their liability in the past, is it not because by all acknowledged *rules of contract* they are bound to A in any case. Certainly it may be the custom of merchants to *make* contracts of this kind; but how can the mere existence of this custom persuade a court to grant an action to the payee, in contradiction to its fundamental theories of the law of contract? This

custom of merchants is a more complex affair than appears at first sight. The development of the bill of exchange in the form summarised above owes at least as much to the theories of lawyers as to the usages of merchants; and the notion of the direct liability of the acceptors to the payee is the end-product of a complex process of juristic reasoning on the part of ... lawyers... . The adoption of mercantile customs by the common law courts was the product of a deliberate decision, motivated by a desire to extend the jurisdiction of those courts, not by any belief that the law-creating effect of popular custom compelled them to apply the rules of the law merchant professed to be based on such custom.[7]

When, in 1657, Chief Justice Hobart said 'The custome of merchants is part of the common law of this kingdom, of which the judges ought to take notice',

the operative part of the statement was not the semi-fictional statement that the custom of merchants was part of the common law of the kingdom but the assertion that the judges would take notice ... of it.[8]

The same was true, Braybrooke suggested, of the famous cases of the nineteenth and twentieth centuries concerning the attitude of the common law courts to mercantile custom:

We find this fact of deliberate adoption readily deducible from the decisions... . We may indeed see in the history of mercantile custom a reflection of the pattern which we may suppose the history of the general custom of the realm to have followed. No doubt at some early time the complex of popular and feudal practices and usages which was in fact, and not in name merely, the common custom of the realm, furnished a rich storehouse of rules and standards and principles from which the judges might draw the materials to lay down the foundation of fundamental rules and principles on which the common law was built. But once these fundamental rules and principles are established the same habit of mind which endows popular custom with what authority it possesses endows them with perpetual life; they become fixed, unalterable, fundamental. The general customs of the realm lose their law-creating force; they can no longer prevail against the fundamental rules which were their own creation... . But the tradition that the common law is no other than the common custom of the realm survives as a fossilised doctrine long after it has ceased to correspond fully with the facts. Its survival may indeed become a source of embarrassment to those whose charge it is to lay down the common law; and so, we may conjecture, the doctrine becomes converted into a rule of pleading whose object is to prevent the judges, who are repositories of the common law, from possible

---

7   E. K. Braybrooke, 'Custom as a Source of English Law', 50 *Michigan Law Review*, 1951, pp. 84–5, 86.
8   Ibid., p. 87. There follows some discussion of the cases, which has been omitted here. (Ed.)

coercion by evidence of a strong current of popular usage which they are unwilling to accept.[9]

What Braybrooke wrote of general, local and mercantile custom seems more convincing than the conventional theory that the courts were meekly following in the wake of the people in recognising the existence of the custom. It is the court, not the people, that exercises the decisive voice. In this sense it is possible to acknowledge that custom is, and always has been, a vital source of law. In a multitude of ways the courts are constantly referring to the actions and practices of the community as a point of reference in order to determine either rules or the application of existing rules. Thus in the whole field of negligence, which forms the staple diet of many judges, the court has to determine whether the conduct of the parties fell above or below the reasonable standard of performance required at any given time in the field in question. If the issue, for example, is whether a surgeon is negligent, the court hears expert evidence as to the practice of surgeons in regard to the procedure in question. It then decides that what was done by the defendant surgeon is acceptable and therefore free from liability, or not acceptable and therefore subject to liability. In making that judgment the court will bear in mind amongst other things the state of development of medical knowledge, the difficulty and cost of taking the precautions that were not taken in that case, the differences that may exist between the level of practice to be expected in a London teaching hospital as against a small provincial one and a host of similar considerations. The practice of the community will be fed into the process of decision-making as one of the factors to be taken into account. The court will not accept the particular procedure of surgeons as representing an acceptable standard unless it thinks it consistent with what can fairly be expected at that stage of development of medical practice. Custom in the sense of what the community does is therefore a potent living source of law in the sense that the courts draw upon it and rework it into the daily application of the common law. In this way the law is constantly renewed by contact with the life of the community and reflects back to the citizens the law's evaluation of what they do. Here again Benjamin Cardozo has expressed the reality:

Benjamin N. Cardozo, *The Nature of the Judicial Process* (1921) pp. 62–3

It is, however, not so much in the making of new rules as in the application of old ones that the creative energy of custom most often manifests itself today. General standards of right and duty are established. Custom must determine whether there has been adherence or departure. My partner has the powers

9   'Custom as a Source of English Law', 50 *Michigan Law Review*, 1951, pp. 87–8.

that are usual in the trade. They may be so well known that the courts will notice them judicially. Such for illustration is the power of a member of a trading firm to make or indorse negotiable paper in the course of the firm's business. They may be such that the court will require evidence of their existence. The master in the discharge of his duty to protect the servant against harm must exercise the degree of care that is commonly exercised in like circumstance by men of ordinary prudence. The triers of the facts in determining whether that standard has been attained must consult the habits of life, the everyday beliefs and practices, of the men and women about them. Innumerable, also, are the cases where the course of dealing to be followed is defined by the customs, or, more properly speaking, the usages, of a particular trade or market or profession. The constant assumption runs throughout the law that the natural and spontaneous evolutions of habit fix the limits of right and wrong. A slight extension of custom identifies it with customary morality, the prevailing standard of right conduct, the *mores* of the time.

But it is the judge who decides – not the people nor the custom.

4.   QUASI-LEGISLATION, CODES OF PRACTICE, CIRCULARS, ETC.

The concept 'quasi-legislation' seems to have been identified first by R. E. Megarry in an article in 1944 – 'Administrative Quasi-legislation', 60 *Law Quarterly Review*, 1944, p. 125 – in which he pointed to law-which-is-not-law such as tax concessions and Practice Notes.

Since then there has been an explosion in the type and range of such semi-law-making. In a book on the subject published in 1987, Professor Gabrielle Ganz referred to 'an exponential growth of statutory and extra-statutory rules in a plethora of forms. Codes of practice, guidance, guidance notes, guidelines, circulars, White Papers, development control policy notes, development briefs, practice statements, tax concessions, Health Services Notices, Family Practitioner Notices, codes of conduct, codes of ethics and conventions are just some of the guises in which the rules appear' (G. Ganz, *Quasi-Legislation: Recent Developments in Secondary Legislation* (1987), p. 1).

In 1986 Dr Robert Baldwin and Mr John Houghton wrote a major article on the phenomenon – 'Circular Arguments: The Status and Legitimacy of Administrative Rules', *Public Law*, 1986 pp. 239–84. They suggested that there were at least eight different categories.

(1) *Procedural rules* E.g. rules for the guidance of applicants for licences to the Gaming Board; Prison Rules laying down disciplinary rules for prisoners; the Codes of Practice under the Police and Criminal Evidence Act 1984, etc.

(2) *Interpretative guides* Official statements of departmental or agency policy, explanations of how terms or rules will be interpreted or applied, expressions of criteria to be followed, standards to be applied or considerations to be taken into account.

(3) *Instructions to officials* Prison Department Circulars, Standing Orders and Regulations; Home Office Circulars to magistrates' courts; Home Office Circulars to Chief Constables; the D.H.S.S. 'L' Code, etc.

(4) *Prescriptive/evidential rules* E.g. the Highway Code, breach of which can be taken into account by a court; the Secretary of State's Code on Picketing under the 1980 Employment Act can be taken into account by the courts; under the Employment Protection Act 1975 the ACAS codes have evidential status; so too do the Codes under the Police and Criminal Evidence Act, which therefore have dual status.

(5) *Commendatory rules* Commendatory rules simply or mainly recommend a course of action. An example are the guidance notes issued by the Health and Safety Commission and Executive advising on how safety objectives may be achieved. They overlap with prescriptive rules in that some rules of evidential significance might also be considered commendations – e.g. the ACAS industrial relations codes. Another example of growing importance is that of specimen directions to juries formulated by the Judicial Studies Board for the guidance of judges which are increasingly cited by the courts. They are only available to the judges.[10]

(6) *Voluntary codes* The City Code on Takeovers and Mergers or the Press Complaints Commission are typical examples. Usually they are designed to stave off government regulation. Businesses often have voluntary labelling, codes of ethics and of good practice.

(7) *Rules of practice, management or operation* A new policy or enforcement practice would come under this heading. Extra-statutory concessions made by the Commissioners for Inland Revenue are in point. They are listed in a booklet. So for instance the Revenue have agreed not to charge tax on cash payments to miners in lieu of free coal or on removal expenses borne by an employer where the employer has to change his residence to take up new employment. Similarly an allowance is given for an employee who has to bear the cost of upkeep of tools for his work.

10 For the argument that they should be published and thereby available to practitioners and scholars see R. Munday, 'The Bench Books: Can the Judiciary Keep a Secret?', *Criminal Law Review*, 1996, p. 296; the reply by Lord Justice Kennedy, *ibid.*, p. 529 and Dr Munday's riposte, *ibid.*, p. 530.

From time to time the courts have expostulated about this practice. In *Absalom* v. *Talbot* [1943] 1 All E.R. 589 at 598, Scott L.J. said: 'No judicial countenance can or ought to be given in matters of taxation to any system of extra-legal concessions. Amongst other reasons, it exposes Revenue officials to temptation, which is wrong, even in the case of a service like the Inland Revenue, characterised by a wonderfully high sense of honour. The fact that such extra-legal concessions have to be made to avoid unjust hardships is conclusive that there is something wrong with the legislation.' See, to like effect, *I.R.C.* v. *Frere* [1965] A.C. 402 at 429, per Lord Radcliffe; *Gleaner Co. Ltd* v. *Assessment Committee* [1922] A.C. 169 at 175, per Lord Buckmaster; *Bates* v. *I.R.C.* [1968] A.C. 483 at 516 per Lord Upjohn; *Vestey* v. *I.R.C. (No. 2)* [1979] 2 All E.R. 225 per Walton J.; [1979] 3 All E.R. 976 (H.L.). See further M. Nolan, 'The Unsatisfactory State of Current Tax Law', *Statute Law Review*, 1981, pp. 149–50; G. W. Thomas, 'The Constitutionality of Extra-Statutory Concessions', *Law Society's Gazette*, 27 June 1979, pp. 637–8; John Alder, 'The Legality of Extra-Statutory Concessions', *New Law Journal*, 21 February 1980, p. 180.

(8) *Consultative devices and administrative pronouncements* This is a safety-net category that absorbs other pronouncements which do not fit into any of the previous groups but which have a significance beyond the individual case. One type of this category are consultative statements inviting comments on draft outlines or agency or departmental policy.

The attitude of the courts towards these various manifestations of rule-making has varied. To some they have given legal effect; to others they have denied it. Sometimes the same rules have legal effect for one purpose but not for another. (See four cases interpreting the Immigration Rules: *ex parte Bibi* [1976] 1 W.L.R. 979; *Ex p. Hosenball* [1977] 1 W.L.R. 766; *Ex parte Ram* [1979] 1 W.L.R. 148; *Ex p. Kharrazi* [1980] 1 W.L.R. 1396.) Often the courts give the benefit of the doubt to the administrators by denying the rule legal effect. (See commentary by Baldwin and Houghton, op. cit., pp. 245–56.)

Among the important issues raised by such rule-making are the issues of control – by parliament and by the courts – and the issue of consultation in such rule-making.

Mode of Trial Guidelines for magistrates' court were issued by the Lord Chief Justice in 1990 by way of a Practice Direction ([1990] 3 All E.R. 979). A revised version was issued by the Criminal Justice Consultative Council in 1995 but not as a Practice Direction and not published in any law reports. At the same time the 1990 Practice Direction was not amended or withdrawn. For the argument that this will not do, see S. White, 'The Antecedents of the Mode of Trial Guidelines' [1996] *Criminal Law Review*, p.471.

See generally, Ganz, op. cit.; Baldwin and Houghton, op. cit.; D. G. T. Williams in 'Statute Law and Administrative Law', *Statute Law Review*, 1984, pp. 164–5; Campbell, Lord, 'Codes of Practice as an Alternative to Legislation', *Statute Law Review*, Autumn 1985, pp. 127–32; Alec Samuels, 'Codes of Practice and Legislation', ibid., Spring 1986, pp. 29–34; T. St John N. Bates, 'Parliament, Policy and Delegated Power', ibid., Summer 1986, pp. 120–23; Laurence Lustgarten, *The Governance of Police* (1986), pp. 105–6 (on the impact of Home Office Circulars to Chief Officers of Police). See also the House of Lords debate on Codes of Practice: House of Lords, *Hansard*, 15 January 1986, cols 1075–1104.

CHAPTER 9

The process of law reform

I. HISTORICAL

The problem of keeping the law abreast of changing circumstances afflicts every system in every age. A brief history of the response to the problem in this country was given by Sir Michael Kerr, former Chairman of the Law Commission, in a lecture in 1980:

Lord Justice Kerr, 'Law Reform in Changing Times', 96 *Law Quarterly Review*, 1980, pp. 515, 517–8

SOME OF THE LANDMARKS

As long ago as 1593 (and one could start earlier) Francis Bacon introduced a project in Parliament for reducing the volume of statutes, which were 'so many in number that neither the common people can practise [*sic*] them nor the lawyers sufficiently understand them.' This task was committed to all the lawyers in the House of Commons, but nothing came of it. In 1607 James I invited Parliament to scrape the rust off the laws so that they 'might be cleared and made known to the subjects.' The idea was to reconcile conflicting decisions, discard obsolete material and prepare an authoritative restatement of the law. In his 'Proposition touching the Amendment of the Law' in 1616, Bacon himself, by then Lord Chancellor, again called for digests of the common law and statute laws with 'law commissioners' to revise them and keep them up to date, but again nothing was done... .

Brougham's great speech on law reform on 7 February 1828, no doubt deserves to be considered as the greatest single landmark in our non-history of systematic law reform before 1965. The speech lasted 6 hours and 3 minutes, and he is reported to have sustained himself by consuming a hatful of oranges, 'which were all the refreshment then tolerated by the custom of the House.'...

He ended with the greatest peroration in our legal history, paradoxically one of Lord Denning's favourite quotations, although it exhorted reform by legislation:

'It was the boast of Augustus ... that he found Rome of brick, and left it of marble... . But how much nobler will be our Sovereign's boast, when he shall have it to say, that he found law dear, and left it cheap; found it a sealed book – left it a living letter; found it the patrimony of the rich – left it the inheritance of the poor; found it the two edged sword of craft and oppression – left it the staff of honesty and the shield of innocence,'

and then moved that

'an humble Address be presented to His Majesty praying that he will graciously be pleased to issue a Commission for inquiring into the defects, occasioned by time and otherwise, in the Laws of this realm of England, as administered in the Courts of Common Law, and the remedies which may be expedient for the same.'

After a speech of this length it is not surprising that the Solicitor-General proposed an adjournment of the debate. It was resumed three weeks later and Brougham's motion was duly accepted, but again led to no result.

After Brougham had become Lord Chancellor in 1830 the same fate befell a 'Royal Commission on the Consolidation of Statute Laws' which he set up in 1833. The Commission reported in 1835 but nothing was done to implement its recommendations. A further 20 years on, in 1853, when Lord Cranworth became Lord Chancellor, he wrote to the Chancellor of the Exchequer within three weeks of taking office to ask him for the necessary funds and facilities from the Treasury to appoint five Commissioners to compose a 'Board for Consolidating and Digesting the Statute Law.' He only asked for £3,400 per annum, a room, messenger, and 'two or three copies of the Statutes with Stationery, etc.' But again nothing came of it. In 1965, when a further 115 years of statutes and decisions had piled up, Lord Gardiner, the then Lord Chancellor, was armed with a copy of Lord Cranworth's letter during the House of Lords debate on the Law Commissions Bill!

Nevertheless, Brougham's great speech and the many other pressures for reform during the first half of the nineteenth century left their mark, and the next hundred years did see a great deal of reform, but wholly piecemeal. The ancient system of causes of action and pleadings was simplified in 1852 and the common law and equity were fused in 1873. A number of important statutes codifying parts of the criminal law were passed in the 1860s; and towards the turn of the century there were codifying Acts dealing with negotiable instruments, arbitration, partnership, sale of goods and marine insurance. The law of property was finally reformed in 1925. But each initiative was piecemeal and in a strictly limited field; at no time was there any machinery for systematic reform across the board.

The penultimate development in this brief survey of over three and a half centuries, in which only a few of the milestones have been mentioned, was a halting step towards a new regime: the establishment of two standing committees to advise on the reform of civil and criminal law topics as referred to them from time to time by the Lord Chancellor and Home Secretary of the day. In 1934 Lord Chancellor Sankey set up the Law Revision Committee, revived after the war in 1952 by Lord Simonds as the Law Reform Committee; and in 1959 the

Home Secretary, (the late) Lord Butler, set up the Criminal Law Revision Committee. Both did and are doing invaluable work, and many of our important law reform statutes during the last decades, civil and criminal, are due to their efforts. But both Committees are composed of members who give their services voluntarily part-time: judges, academics, barristers and solicitors meeting at intervals, usually after court hours. Moreover, the Committees only deal with specific topics referred to them by successive Lord Chancellors and Home Secretaries; they have no initiative of their own. Their establishment was therefore a step forward only to the extent that they marked the first formal recognition that some permanent machinery outside government was necessary to keep the law abreast of the time. Historically it was a typical compromise; a half-way house towards real change.

The idea of a permanent body to keep the whole of the law under review was articulated in 1921 in New York by the great American judge Benjamin Cardozo, later to become a Justice of the Supreme Court:

> The courts are not helped as they could and ought to be in the adaptation of law to justice. The reason they are not helped is because there is no one whose business it is to give warning that help is needed... .We must have a courier who will carry the tidings of distress... .Today courts and legislature work in separation and aloofness. The penalty is paid both in the wasted effort of production and in the lowered quality of the product. On the one hand, the judges, left to fight against anachronism and injustice by the methods of judge-made law, are distracted by the conflicting promptings of justice and logic, of consistency and mercy, and the output of their labours bears the tokens of the strain. On the other side, the legislature, informed only casually and intermittently of the needs and problems of the courts, without expert or responsible or disinterested or systematic advice as to the workings of one rule or another, patches the fabric here and there, and mars often when it would mend. Legislature and courts move on in proud and silent isolation. Some agency must be found to mediate between them.[1]

2.   THE LAW COMMISSIONS

Cardozo's call led in due course to an experiment in 1923 and to the setting up in 1934 of the New York Law Revision Commission.[2] Thirty years later Cardozo's plea was echoed in Britain by Gerald Gardiner QC in *Law Reform Now*, a book published in 1963 which Gardiner co-edited with Professor Andrew Martin. In the next year Gerald Gardiner (by then Lord Gardiner) became Lord Chancellor in Harold Wilson's first government. He took the post only on condition that his idea for a Law Commission was implemented,

---

1   'A Ministry of Justice,' 35 *Harvard Law Review* (1921), pp. 113–14.
2   See John W. Macdonald, 'The New York Law Revision Commission', 28 *Modern Law Review*, 1965, p. 1.

and shortly after the Government came into office a White Paper was published:

(a)   The White Paper

White Paper, 'Proposals for English and Scottish Law Commissions,' 1965, Cmnd 2573

One of the hallmarks of an advanced society is that its laws should not only be just but also that they be kept up-to-date and be readily accessible to all who are affected by them. The state of the law today cannot be said to satisfy these requirements. It is true that the administration of justice in our courts is highly regarded, and rightly so, in other countries beside our own; and it is also true that the spread of the ideas of personal liberty and respect for the rule of law which have been of such importance in the development of Western civilisation has been profoundly influenced by the importance which our law attaches to these concepts. But the very fact that English and Scottish law have a history stretching back for so many centuries is one of the reasons why the form of the law is now in such an unsatisfactory state.

England and Wales
English law today is contained in some 3,000 Acts of Parliament, the earliest of which dates from the year 1235, in many volumes of delegated legislation made under the authority of those Acts, and in over 300,000 reported cases. Although Parliament has been actively at work for so many years, much of the law is still to be found in the decisions of the courts operating in fields which Parliament has not entered. It is true that the law on certain subjects has from time to time been largely restated in codifying statutes, but these are few and far between and date mostly from the end of the nineteenth century. The result is that it is today extremely difficult for anyone without special training to discover what the law is on any given topic; and when the law is finally ascertained, it is found in many cases to be obsolete and in some cases to be unjust. This is plainly wrong. English law should be capable of being recast in a form which is accessible, intelligible and in accordance with modern needs... .

There is at present no body charged with the duty of keeping the law as a whole under review and making recommendations for its systematic reform.[3] Each Government department is responsible for keeping under review the state of the law in its own field and from time to time Royal Commissions or independent committees are set up to examine and make recommendations on particular subjects. There are standing bodies such as the Lord Chancellor's

---

3   For a review of the then-existing machinery of law reform, see E. C. S. Wade, 'The Machinery of Law Reform', 24 *Modern Law Review*, 1961, pp. 3–17; *Law Reform Now* (eds. Gardiner and Martin 1963), Chapter 1; J. H. Farrar, *Law Reform and the Law Commissions* (1974), Chapters 1 and 2 and Appendices A, B, C, and D, setting out the achievements of the respective bodies. (Ed.)

Law Reform Committee,[4] whose task it is to review such small fields of the civil law as may from time to time be referred to it, while a similar task is performed in the case of the criminal law by the Home Secretary's Criminal Law Revision Committee. While valuable work has been done by these means and important changes in the law have been made as a result of the recommendations of these and other bodies, this work has been done piecemeal and it is evident that comprehensive reform can be achieved only by a body whose sole task it is and which is equipped with a professional staff on the scale required.

The Government therefore propose, subject to the approval of Parliament, to set up a Law Commission for England and Wales. This will consist of five lawyers of high standing appointed by the Lord Chancellor with an adequate legal staff to assist them. The Commissioners will be required to keep the whole of English law under review and to submit to the Lord Chancellor programmes for the examination of different branches of the law with a view to its reform. The programmes will include recommendations on the best means of carrying them out. When a programme has been approved by the Lord Chancellor after consulting other Ministers concerned it will be laid before Parliament. It may be appropriate for some of the detailed projects for reform contained in the programmes to be undertaken by the Commissioners, for others to be referred to the Law Reform Committee or the Criminal Law Revision Committee, and others again to be undertaken by the Government department concerned; or, particularly, where important social questions may arise, for a topic to be referred to a Departmental Committee or a Royal Commission by, or at the instance of the appropriate Minister. The detailed proposals for reform prepared by the Commissioners or by those other bodies will be published, and if they are accepted by the Government the necessary legislation will be introduced.

The Commissioners will also be charged with the duty of pressing forward the task of consolidation and statute law revision. The object of the latter is to prune the statute book of dead and obsolete enactments, while consolidation consists of the bringing together in one Act of all the enactments on a particular branch of the law. It is true that some progress has been made with these tasks since the war, but much remains to be done.

It is generally agreed that in the field of law reform much valuable guidance can be obtained from the experience of other countries like the United States, the Commonwealth countries and the countries of Western Europe which have had to face problems similar to our own. While in some respects the insularity of English law has been one of the sources of its strength, there is no doubt that in other directions it is a source of weakness. There is much to be gained from comparative legal studies and this will be one of the tasks of the Law Commissioners. It is intended that the Commissioners should provide Government departments which are contemplating legislation with the research and advisory facilities which will be available to the Commissioners and this may well be of particular importance in enabling departments to take account

---

4   See Michael C. Blair, 'The Law Reform Committee: The First Thirty Years', *Civil Justice Quarterly*, 1982, p. 64. (Ed.)

of relevant Commonwealth and foreign experience. It is not, of course, proposed that the Commissioners should duplicate the work done by other bodies such as the British Institute of International and Comparative Law.

The Law Commissioners will be appointed by the Lord Chancellor for periods to be agreed upon at the time of their appointment. This will enable distinguished lawyers to be appointed to the Commission for a term of years before returning to work in their own field, whether on the Bench, in the practising legal profession or at the universities. It is likely that similar arrangements will be made in the case of some of the staff of the Commission so as to enable full advantage to be taken of the valuable work being done at the present time by academic lawyers in the field of law reform. The task of the Commission will be immense and will not be completed for many years.

The Commissioners will be required to make an annual report to the Lord Chancellor, which will be laid before Parliament.

The White Paper was published in January 1965 and the Law Commissions Bill was introduced the same month. It received the Royal Assent on 15 June and the names of the first Law Commissioners were announced the following day.[5]

Each Commission consists of five lawyers, appointed in the case of the English Commission by the Lord Chancellor and, in the case of the Scottish, by the Secretary of State for Scotland and the Lord Advocate. The chairman has so far always been a judge.

The duties and functions of the Law Commissions are set out in s. 3:

(b)   The Law Commission Act 1965

3. (1) It shall be the duty of each of the Commissions to take and keep under review all the law with which they are respectively concerned with a view to its systematic development and reform, including in particular the codification of such law, the elimination of anomalies, the repeal of obsolete and unnecessary enactments, the reduction of the number of separate enactments and generally the simplification and modernisation of the law, and for that purpose –

(a) to receive and consider any proposals for the reform of the law which may be made or referred to them;

(b) to prepare and submit to the Minister from time to time programmes[6] for the examination of different branches of the law with a view to reform,

5   (On the background and for an analysis of the Act, see Lord and G. Dworkin, 'The Law Commissions Act 1965', 28 Modern Law Review, 1965, p. 675. For a fascinating study of the history of the establishment of the Law Commission thirty years later and based therefore on the departmental papers see S.M. Cretney, 'The Law Commission: True Dawns and False Dawns', 59 Modern Law Review, 1996, pp. 631–57.

6   This has been done five times.

including recommendations as to the agency (whether the Commission or another body) by which any such examination should be carried out;

(c)   to undertake, pursuant to any such recommendations approved by the Minister, the examination of particular branches of the law and the formulation, by means of draft Bills or otherwise, of proposals for reform therein;

(d)   to prepare from time to time at the request of the Minister comprehensive programmes of consolidation and statute law revision, and to undertake the preparation of draft Bills pursuant to any such programme approved by the Minister;

(e)   to provide advice and information to government departments and other authorities or bodies concerned at the instance of the Government with proposals for the reform or amendment of any branch of the law;

(f)   to obtain such information as to the legal system of other countries as appears to the Commissioners likely to facilitate the performance of any of their functions.

(2) The Minister shall lay before Parliament any programmes prepared by the Commission and approved by him and any proposals for reform formulated by the Commission pursuant to such programmes.[7]

The nature of the new machinery was described by the first chairman of the English Law Commission, Mr Justice Scarman (later Lord Scarman):

Sir Leslie Scarman, *Law Reform — the New Pattern* (1968), pp. 11–16

The Commission is an advisory body; Parliament is to be the source of any new law that may arise from proposals of the Commission. The Commission has been called into being to advise the government and Parliament, first in the planning of law reform; secondly, in the formulation of detailed proposals for the reform of the law. The theory that underlies the Act is that law reform should be the province of the legislature; that the legislature requires specialist advice in the planning and formulation of law reform; and that this advice should be provided by a body independent of the executive and of Parliament.... .

It is clearly contemplated by the Act that, once the Lord Chancellor has approved a programme prepared by the Commission for the purpose of law reform, both the programme, and any proposals made by the Commission in the light of the programme, shall become public property. There is therefore a

7   There have been only two publicised instances of the use of the power of veto. One instance was an inquiry into damages. But the Pearson Royal Commission on personal injuries was later set up instead. The second was on administrative law. The Commission in its Fourth Annual Report recommended that a Royal Commission or similar body should make 'a comprehensive review of the principles and procedures of this important branch of the law' (para. 65). But the Lord Chancellor did not agree. Instead he asked the Law Commission to report on a limited part of the subject – the remedies for the judicial control of administrative acts. (Ed.)

significant difference between government legislation and legislation based upon proposals by the Commission. It is the practice of governments to keep secret their detailed legislative proposals until the appropriate Bill is introduced. Law Reform Bills introduced pursuant to a Commission proposal are likely, however, to follow the draft of a Bill already published with the Commission's proposal.

A plain implication of these provisions of the Act is that proposals for the reform of the law, though made to the legislature, ought to be kept outside the field of political controversy. They are to be carefully considered by an expert body before the introduction of legislation. The public is to be given an opportunity of debating them – also before the introduction of legislation. And, finally, when Parliament itself has to consider them, it should have the benefit of expert advice and prior public discussion.

Two further features of the Commission should be mentioned. It holds an initiative in the reform process, and it is more than a mere committee, whose existence may be terminated by the stroke of a Minister's pen. It is an institution, having a statutory existence. Neither the anger of a Minister nor the rebellion and resignation of Commissioners can destroy it. It exists until Parliament by enactment delivers the coup de grace. These two features merit a little reflection. Prior to the Act, law reform usually began with an investigation undertaken either by an ad hoc body, set up with clearly defined terms of reference, or by a standing committee, to whose attention specific topics would be referred from time to time. A good example of the ad hoc committee is the Goddard Committee, which in 1953 produced a report on Civil Liability for Animals. It could act only within its terms of reference and was dissolved upon submission of its report. The standing committee, in the field of law reform, has a long and honourable history. Modern examples of it are the Lord Chancellor's Law Reform Committee, established in 1959. Both these committees are active to-day. But neither of them has any power to propose topics for examination with a view to reform. They act only within specific terms of reference and are liable to dissolution at a stroke of their Minister's pen. I have already commented on the Law Commission's statutory existence. Equally important, however, is its right and duty to originate proposals in the field of reform. These proposals are embodied into a programme which, once it survives the veto of the Lord Chancellor, must be published, and confers upon the Commission independence of action within its limits.

(c) The method of working

The Law Commission published its First Programme of work on 19 July 1965, only a month after it was appointed. It covered an enormous range under seventeen subject heads, including codification of the law of contract, of the law of landlord and tenant, and of family law. The codification of criminal law was added in 1967. In addition to such vast projects it also proposed to tackle some minor matters. It has always maintained a balance between large-scale and small-scale issues. In November 1965 it outlined its proposals for a programme of statute law reform to improve the arrangement, accessibility and form of the statute book. This proposed chiefly consolidation (the bringing together into one statute of provisions that are scattered among many statutes) and statute law revision (the repeal of obsolete or unnecessary statutory provisions) (see p. 63 above). Further law reform programmes were published – 1968, 1973, 1989,1991 and 1995.

In 1999 the legal staff of the English Law Commission was sixteen civil service lawyers, five parliamentary draftsmen, and (fifteen) research assistants. Use was being made also of a considerable number of part-time consultants.

The Commission's method of working has been described by a former Law Commissioner:

Mr Norman Marsh, 'Law Reform in the United Kingdom: A New Institutional Approach', 13 *William and Mary Law Review*, 1971, p. 263

The process can best be illustrated by following the course of a project of the Law Commissions from the time that it appears as an item in an approved Programme until the stage when the completed report on the item is laid before Parliament with a draft Bill giving effect to the recommendations made in the report.

First, a detailed Working Paper with provisional recommendations, usually including information about the relevant legal position in other countries,[8] is prepared by a small team in the Law Commission, headed by one or two Commissioners. After the Working Paper has been discussed at length by the Commission as a whole and, as a result, often rewritten or amended, it is distributed in an edition of about 1500 copies, not only to the various interests in the legal sphere – the judiciary, practising and academic lawyers (the latter two categories have set up special committees to deal with Law Commission papers) – but also to many lay organisations particularly interested in the subject-matter. Further, it is sent, as a matter of course, to the relevant government departments and to the national press, both general and legal.[9] It is worthy of note that the Commissions, although they welcome informal oral consultations, do not hold anything in the nature of formal hearings. On the

8   The Law Commissions are required by s. 3(1)(f) of the Act to obtain information on the relevant law of other countries.
9   The legal 'weeklies' generally print a summary of the Working Paper which the Commissions are careful to provide. Working Papers occasionally feature in the general press. Final reports, however, are given very considerable coverage in the national 'dailies', sometimes with 'leader' articles commenting on them. The Law Commissions take considerable pains to prepare appropriate press summaries which may bring out the salient issues of interest to lay readers. In general, it may be said that the Law Commissioners have attached great importance to keeping their work before the general public and the individual Commissioners speak quite frequently on the subject at meetings, over the radio and in the form of articles for the legal and general press. Their underlying thought has been that law reform is a cause which must be kept in the public eye if it is to achieve practical results.

whole their experience is that the most satisfactory results are obtained from carefully prepared Working Papers which are not content to ask questions but which also set out in detail the basic material from which answers can be given, with some guidance as to the provisional thinking of the Commissioners, and a survey of other possible solutions with their accompanying advantages and drawbacks. It has been found that although this technique involves much work, in the long run it spares the Commission many irrelevant and time-wasting suggestions.

After an interval of perhaps six months to a year the comments received on the Working Paper are considered, first by a specialist team within the Commission who, with or without a general consultation with the Commission as a whole depending on the tenor of the comments received, proceed to prepare a draft Report. This Report, generally at this stage without an accompanying draft Bill, is debated by the whole Commission and sent back for any necessary amendments and the addition of the Bill, which is supplied by Parliamentary draftsmen attached to the Commission, in often prolonged consultation with the Commissioners and their staff. The Report as presented to the Lord Chancellor (in the case of the Law Commission for England and Wales) will not only outline the present law in the area covered by the Report and set forth the recommendations therewith, together with the implementing draft Bill, but it will also deal in detail with the process of consultation, including the names of those consulted and (unless there is some problem of confidentiality) the views they have expressed. The Law Commissions see the ultimate object of the elaborate process of consultation as assisting Parliament on matters of often great technical detail which can seldom be adequately investigated in the course of Parliamentary debate. This assistance is ineffective unless the scope and nature of the consultation is clearly set out on the face of the Report.

The English Commissioners are assisted by a total staff of about 50, of whom slightly over half are trained lawyers. The Scottish Law Commissioners have a relatively small staff. The resources which have been made available to the Law Commission, although not particularly striking by comparison with, for example, the departments concerned with law reform in some European Ministries of Justice, are considerable by earlier British standards. The Law Commission has thereby undoubtedly been helped to produce, within five years, a large number of Working Papers and final reports, a fact which, even apart from their content, is not without importance. A new institution, in a sense on trial, has been seen by Parliament and the public as capable of producing results.

A more recent description of its working methods given by the then Chairman stated that the Commission worked on law reform through four teams. Each team was led by a Commissioner and usually consisted of three lawyers and three recently graduated research assistants. The draftsman was normally not brought into the project until well into the third year – after the Commission had decided its response to the Consultation Stage. The draft Bill together with the draft report was considered by the whole Commission. After publication there might be further consultation between the Commission and the relevant government department. The new head of Parliamentary Counsel's office had said that wherever possible he would use the draftsman employed by the Law Commission 'to avoid the unnecessary delay and duplication of resources which have often happened in the past' ((Mr Justice Brooke, 'The Role of the Law Commission in Simplifying Statute Law', 16 *Statute Law Review*, 1995, pp. 1–3).

(d) The Law Commission and consultation

Dr Peter North, himself a former Law Commissioner, has raised for consideration whether the Law Commission does not devote too much time and effort to the process of consultation, which he suggested was often more for form's sake than valuable in terms of its results.

Dr North argued that the process rarely achieved its objectives. These he identified as (1) the discovery of factual evidence as to the current operation of the law; (2) the provision of detailed technical advice; (3) the creation of a democratic legitimacy for any ultimate solution; (4) the assessment of the weight of public opinion on social issues; and (5) to flush out the potential opposition. He was sceptical on all five counts:

Peter North, 'Law Reform: Processes and Problems', *Law Quarterly Review*, 1985, p. 338

3. Effectiveness of Consultation

I am highly sceptical whether all or any of the legitimate purposes of consultation are adequately achieved in this country so far as law reform is concerned and, from my limited experience of other jurisdictions, I have little confidence about success there either. Some examples might illustrate the problems. Detailed technical advice on law reform measures from professionals requires a significant commitment of time from the consultee and a careful detailed analysis of the problems and their potential solutions by the law reformers. There is a real danger that the consultation document which is so prepared as to identify that on which detailed advice is sought is so long that the commentators do not have time to master it. 'Use shorter discussion papers' is the obvious response. Unfortunately, that produces shorter answers.

There is no doubt that individual requests for views – and modern word processors can make them seem more individual than they really are – produce a far better rate of response than making available large numbers of copies of papers coupled with a generalised request for views. The academic legal community provides a good illustration of this. My experience of eight years as a Law Commissioner was that the institutional response from academic lawyers to general requests for views made by the Commission was little short of appalling and usually a waste of taxpayers' money. Every law school in the country is sent a copy of every Law Commission Working Paper and some are sent a number of copies. This costs several hundreds of pounds each time. It has produced very little indeed of benefit to the Commission – though it may have provided free copies for financially hard pressed university law libraries; but that is not the function of the Law Commission nor of its budget. On the other hand, direct requests for assistance from academics, such as through membership of working parties, acting as consultant on the formulation of views by a committee of the Society of Public Teachers of Law, or directly as consultants to the Commission have been far more productive.[10] Financial constraints are such that serious consideration may, I believe, need to be given by the Law Commission to abandoning the wide generalised distribution of consultation papers in favour of a far more selective approach.

I think that, no matter how widespread the circulation of consultation material, and the recent distribution by the Central Office of Information on behalf of the Law Commission of 45,000 short pamphlets dealing with the question whether the Land Registry should be open for public inspection is as widespread as the law reform agencies in this country have gone, any claim to some form of democratic legitimacy is spurious. Equally, such consultation techniques go little way towards enabling an accurate assessment of public opinion to be made. To do that requires sophisticated and expensive opinion polling. What pamphlets may produce is a substantial response – but it is not necessarily statistically relevant. For example, when the Law Commission consulted on whether the crime of blasphemy should be abolished without replacement,[11] the relevant pamphlet produced about 1,000 letters and petitions with some 20,000 signatures in favour of retaining the offence. This was, numerically, a vastly greater response than that in favour of abolition. The fact that it came as a result of an orchestrated campaign of response only shows that a large number of people were sufficiently concerned to respond. It is not yet known what the Law Commission will recommend on this issue; but what if they were to decide to recommend the abolition of blasphemy without replacement? What then would have been the purpose of the widespread consultation? The numerical weight of opinion as expressed to the Commission would have been ignored – in favour of what? There was no other survey of public opinion. Presumably the intellectual weight of the arguments put by some consultees would have been such as to convince the Commission. So even the spurious legitimacy of the broad response to their pamphlet would, on such an hypothesis, have been rejected by the Commission.

Is the answer to have large-scale opinion sampling surveys? There is no doubt that such surveys are expensive and time consuming. Public funds of the kind available to law reform bodies will not stretch to support large surveys. For example, it was estimated some six years ago that a survey of the expenditure pattern of 16- and 17-year olds, relevant to the Law Commission's work on minors' contracts, would cost getting on for half a million pounds. It might be asked whether survey work can be done much more cheaply without a significant

10 For an examination of the contribution of academic lawyers to law reform, especially of the criminal law, see Smith (1981) 1 *Legal Studies* 119. On the academic lawyer as activist reformer, see Zander (1979) 42 M.L.R. 489.

11 Working Paper No. 79 (1981).

rise in the risk of inaccuracy. Is it fair to suggest that those whose preference it is to conduct surveys feel it necessary in the interests of academic respectability as to size of sample and the like to design bigger exercises than a law reform agency may demand? Is there a case for saying that such bodies should be prepared to take the risks of, for example, using a smaller sample which costs half as much and takes half as long? The significance of its taking half as long is not to be ignored. Empirical research and survey work takes a long time to set up, to conduct and to assess. It could take the whole period that a law reformer, perhaps under time pressure from outside, is willing to devote to the complete project. Forward planning has not, in this country, been an obvious skill shown in law reform projects over the last 20 years and there is a current tendency to move away from major projects spread over a decade or more in favour of specific shorter term completable reviews. It is important with such a change of approach not to ignore the need for long term planning, better than it has so far been shown to be, of the basic research necessary to underpin the proposals of the law reformer.

4. Excessiveness of Consultation

It is assumed to be axiomatic that consultation on law reform as on many other matters is desirable. As quoted earlier, Lord Scarman described the invention of the working paper as 'perhaps the greatest contribution to the public life of the nation made by the Law Commission.'[12] In other words that part of the process was seen as more important than any of the end results, the law reform proposals or legislation, stemming from the process. Not only does that seem to be a rather extravagant claim, it also ignores the difficulties created by widespread consultation. Consultation brings problems in its wake. They may be counted as less than its virtues, but counted they should be.

Formal consultation is time consuming. In the experience of the Law Commission one third at least of the minimum period necessary for taking a law reform project through from start to finish is devoted to the consultation process. This period can be shortened by less formal consultation. A paper produced for private circulation to a selected readership in smaller numbers is likely to be about as effective as a paper publicly available through H.M.S.O. – especially if the views of each recipient are individually sought.[13] But there is a price to be paid. Someone excluded from the charmed circle of consultees will complain of the hole and corner way in which little discussed and ill thought out proposals are being foisted on the British public, or use other similarly mild language.

Consultation breeds bureaucracy. Views are sought from a wide range of bodies and from an increasing variety of bodies. Consultees have to devise procedures for responding. This means more committees and more staff to

---

12 Lord Scarman, 'Law Reform – the British Experience', Nehru Memorial Lectures, (1978).
13 *E.g.* Consultation Paper on the Recognition of Foreign Nullity Decrees and Related Matters (1983); see Law Commission Eighteenth Annual Report, 1982–3, Law Com. No. 131, para. 2.62.

service them and thus more expense for the membership of the bodies – all to enable the public sector to do its job more effectively. One effect of this burgeoning bureaucracy is that consultation tends inevitably and increasingly to be with an organisation's officials or standing committees rather than more directly with its membership. There is a danger that the experience of the official or the members of a small and hard worked committee may not mirror the experience of the wider membership. That creates a risk of policy proposals, formulated on the basis of the consultation, being rejected by the members when finally published or, as is more common, at the later stage of debate in Parliament, when amendment is politically harder to achieve.

Is there too much consultation? The law reformer might find it hard to think that there could ever be too much of what he assumes to be a good thing. The recipient of the consultation documents may think differently. Those whom law reformers consult are also often consulted by other bodies, ad hoc commissions and committees and by Government itself. The regular recipients of this constant barrage of paper are showing signs of wilting under the burden. There is clear evidence of consultee resistance. It takes different forms – complaints about the size or complexity of consultation material, the fact that regular consultees take longer to comment than in the past, or the fact that their comments are less thorough or complete than used to be the case.

One reason for less effective consultation by law reform bodies may be because of wider government consultation. If it is to continue to be (as it seems to have become) general practice for Government to use, for example, a Law Commission white paper report as a green paper for a further round of consultation not only within the public service, as one would expect, but also with those who have already been consulted outside the public sector, is it any wonder that their enthusiasm for the first round of consultation is limited? This creates a vicious circle. If government conducts widespread consultation, those whom they consult will tend to reserve their comments and efforts for this later stage. This means that the law reform agency's proposals are less able to take into account the views and expertise of the bodies whose views they seek but do not get, thus making it the more important for government to consult fully before reaching a final decision – and so the spiral goes on.

For similar scepticism about the representativeness of consultation see Stephen Cretney, 'The Politics of Law Reform', 48 *Modern Law Review*, 1985, pp. 505–6.

An experienced former member of the Law Commission's staff said that in his view, although Working Papers were valuable, they were not as valuable as all that. Sources of opposition were not always identified. Government departments in particular often did not reveal their criticisms until after the publication of the final report when they could no longer be accommodated. Nor in his experience did the views of those consulted normally have much impact. Usually their positions were well known in advance and had in fact already been allowed for in the writing of the Working Paper. The main value of the Working Paper, in his estimation, was to give the ultimate report greater strength politically through its evidence of consultation. Also it reduced the danger that the Commission would proceed in ignorance of some relevant matters of fact or law.[14]

3.   THE LAW COMMISSION AND SOME PROBLEMS OF LAW REFORM

Delivering the Third Nehru Lecture in India in 1979, Lord Scarman (chairman of the Law Commission from 1965 to 1972) said that although the institution had achieved much there were several identifiable problems.

(1)   The Law Commission as an adviser to government

Too much of the time of the Law Commission was taken up in responding to requests for advice and assistance from official agencies. The Commission had prepared its first programme in 1965, its second programme in 1968 and its third programme in 1973. [As has been seen, further programmes were produced in 1989, 1991 and 1995.] The Commission had the right to put anything it wanted into its programme. The Lord Chancellor could exercise a veto but he could not tell the Commission what to put into its programme. ('The programme is part and parcel of the Commission's independence.')

But there were other ways in which the Commission could become involved in work. It was under a duty to 'receive and consider any proposals for the reform of the law which may be made or referred to it' (s. 3(1)(a)). It was also bound 'to provide advice and information to government departments and other official bodies concerned with the reform or amendment of any branch of the law' (s. 3(1)(e)). In its Thirteenth Annual Report the Commission had said 'a much greater proportion of our work now comes from special references'. In other words, Lord Scarman told his Indian audience, 'the government is largely determining what work the Commission will undertake'. Again, the Thirteenth Report gave details of such references – five draft EC conventions or directives, four draft conventions of the Council of Europe, two Hague conventions on Private International Law topics, one Commonwealth topic and one United Nations draft convention. All of this no doubt was important work. 'But it is departmental stuff, not law reform.' If such references multiplied, 'the Law Commission will cease to be the watchdog of all the law and run the risk of becoming something resembling a law research division of a Ministry of Justice'. Departmental encroachment – though flattering – was 'a bear's hug'. 'It could squeeze the breath out of the Commission, leaving it neither

14   R. T. Oerton, *A Lament for the Law Commission* (1987), p. 64.

the time nor the energy for the work of law reform conceived in the comprehensive terms of s. 3 of its statute.'

Questions

1.   Should the Law Commission be given a power to decline ministerial requests for assistance?
2.   If not, is there any other way in which the Law Commission could preserve itself from time-consuming work of little general consequence?

(2)   Law Commission confined to lawyers' or technical law reform

The topics addressed by the Law Commission have perhaps been mostly a little dull – by comparison at least with the rather spicier issues tackled by the comparable body in Australia. The Australian Law Reform Commission has dealt, inter alia, with complaints against the police, criminal investigation, alcohol, drugs and driving, consumer insolvency, human tissue transplants, defamation, sentencing and privacy. Moreover almost all of the Australian Commission's reports have been wholly or largely implemented or are actively under consideration.[15]

In his 1979 Delhi lecture, Lord Scarman said that Departments of State were 'only too relieved to turn to the Law Commission to lighten the darkness of common market conventions or private international law'. But they 'resist strongly intrusion by the Commission into fields where they believe they have a commanding expertise'. Company law, labour law, tax law, constitutional and administrative law 'are kept firmly away from the Commission'. Apart from its paper on divorce reform,[16] the Commission had on the whole 'been steered away from socially or politically controversial questions'. The future of the law was bleak 'if the institution established to keep under review all the law may not examine some branches of the law merely because they lie in an area of political or social controversy'. Not that all law reform should be channelled through the Law Commission. The Lord Chancellor's Law Reform Committee, the Home Secretary's Criminal Law Revision Committee, Royal Commissions and departmental committees all had a role to play. The Commission's greatest

---

15   See Michael Kirby, *Reform the Law* (1983), pp. 16–18. Kirby was the highly effective chairman of the Commission until his appointment as presiding judge in the Federal Court of Appeal at the end of 1984.
16   In 1966 the Lord Chancellor asked the Law Commission to advise on the various alternatives in divorce law reform. The Commission's Report ('Field of Choice') offered no proposals, but implicitly the logic of the analysis strongly supported the concept of divorce based on marital breakdown without proof of fault. This became the method adopted in the Divorce Reform Act 1969.

successes had been in family law, criminal law and consumer protection, and in the statute law revision programme. There was no reason why it could not tackle socially sensitive areas. The Scottish Law Commission had been asked to advise on the constitutional implications of devolution. Lord Scarman suggested that 'By using carefully its working paper and consultative technique, [the Law Commission] can tackle controversial issues, and take the heat out of them.'

Sir Michael Kerr, who was chairman after Lord Scarman, said in 1980 that the Commission had not dealt with various topics which were left entirely to government departments including tax, labour law, company law, civil procedure, criminal procedure and sentencing 'and many other specialised fields, quite apart from matters which are purely in the fields of general social and economic policy' (*Law Quarterly Review*, 1980, p. 526). In September 1984, however, the Law Commission was responsible for organising a major seminar on civil procedure to consider what needed to be done in this field (see 19th *Annual Report*, 1983–4, pp. 2–3). (This led to the establishment by the Lord Chancellor's Department of the Civil Justice Review.) But according to Sir Michael Kerr, the boundaries to what the Commission could inquire into were not set by lawyers' law or by the controversial nature of the topic. They were set, he suggested, 'by the logistics of what is possible within a relatively small organisation. Above all, however, the Commission's work of reform must inevitably be restricted to proposals which have some realistic prospect of implementation by Parliament within the limits of the Government's programmes and of parliamentary procedures. These logistic difficulties pose the greatest problems in practice. Unfortunately, law reform is not a purely forensic exercise, as perhaps it should be; like politics it is no more than the art of the possible' (at p. 526).

Questions

1. Is there any real distinction between lawyers' law reform suitable for the Law Commission and political or general law reform that requires a broader approach?
2. Should the Law Commission be used for controversial law-reform projects?
3. Should there be a law-reform supremo to decide who inquires into what? If so, should the power to decide this be given to a minister or to the Law Commission?

(3) Judicial law-making in the light of the existence of the Law Commission

When the Law Commission was set up, some took the view that this spelled the end for judicial law-making. One distinguished observer who expressed this opinion at an early stage was Lord Devlin:

Lord Devlin, 'The Process of Law Reform', 63 *Law Society's Gazette*, 1966, pp. 453–62

There can be no doubt that the institution of the Law Commission marks a great step forward in the process of law reform. It has immediately and easily assumed command of the first stage of the process and its institution, taken in conjunction with other measures, holds out hope of widening the bottleneck in the second stage so that there is a much needed flow of beneficial reform. Its command of the first stage will mean that the importance of judicial law-making, which has been dwindling now for a century or more, will probably almost entirely vanish but without, I hope, dimming the name and reputation of Lord Denning, who will stand for future generations as the last great judicial innovator.

The trouble about judicial law reform was never, as it is with parliament, lack of time but lack of opportunity – that and the multiplication of courts of appeal. When Lord Mansfield laid down the law, new law was created more or less from the moment he said it. But since his time the delay before a point of principle reaches the House of Lords may be so long as to outdistance by ten times or more the parliamentary process. With the Law Commission speeding the work of statutory reform and codifying the law, the day of the judicial law-maker is brought quite to an end.

Realisation of the concept of codification (as will be seen below), is still in the future. In the meantime, contrary to Lord Devlin's view, there is not much evidence that the existence of the Law Commission has significantly altered the judges' attitude to law reform. They appear to be no less ready to undertake a role in the improvement of the law than before the Law Commissions were set up.

Moreover, law reform by judges is not to be dismissed as necessarily second-class by comparison with that of the legislature. Professor H. K. Lücke of the University of Adelaide made this point in an important article:

Adjudication is the judge's most important function and the responsibility which it casts upon him is a personal and a heavy one. Like all human activity, adjudication must become routine to some extent, but it is difficult to see how the sense of occasion which affects every trial, civil or criminal, and to which barristers so readily testify, can ever be completely lost on the judge himself. Law, which grows out of adjudication, stems from a situation of judicial engagement much intensified by both proximity and the judge's special responsibility. Nothing comparable could exist in the remote atmosphere of ministries of justice, law reform commissions, or even of parliaments where statute law is prepared and made. A rule or principle which grows out of live adjudication differs from a legal opinion formed *in abstracto* in much the same way as a live performance differs from a mere rehearsal, real combat from a manoeuvre, the final race from a mere practice run.

All this is unmistakably reflected in a fundamental feature of common law jurisprudence: hard, binding law emerges from judgments only to the extent to which the judge's faculties are sharpened and engaged by his duty to adjudicate a real dispute.[17]

The value of the common law as the method of developing the law slowly was emphasised by Lord Reid in a speech to teachers of law:

> Finally, may I make some comparison between the common law and statute law. I am tempted to take as an analogy the difference between old-fashioned, hand-made, expensive, quality goods and the brash products of modern technology. If you think in months, want an instant solution for your problems and don't mind that it won't wear well, then go for legislation. If you think in decades, prefer orderly growth and believe in the old proverb more haste less speed, then stick to the common law. But do not seek a middle way by speeding up and streamlining the development of the common law.[18]

But clearly, judges cannot be regarded as sufficient law reformers. The reasons were considered by a former Law Commissioner.

Norman Marsh, 'Law Reform in the United Kingdom: A New Institutional Approach', 13 *William and Mary Law Review*, 1971, p. 263

> Five considerations, some of which, if not entirely new, have at least intensified in recent years, and others, more or less inherent in a system of judge-made law, suggest that English law cannot, at least for the future, rely on that system as the main instrument of law reform.
>
> First, it is no longer possible for the judge in modern English society to make those bold assumptions about family life and about relations between landlord and tenant, employer and employee, citizen and the State which underlie many reforms of a seemingly legal character. On the one hand, he lives in an era where many value assumptions are being challenged; on the other, he does not enjoy quite the unquestioned prestige, the charismatic authority, enjoyed by his Victorian forbears. As the House of Lords recognised, after a decade or more of attempted judicial innovations designed to provide protection in the matrimonial home for the deserted wife, and after an even longer period of judicial experiments aimed at protecting the economically weaker party to a contract from unfair exemption clauses, reform of the law may raise issues which in present conditions are more appropriately dealt with by the legislature.
>
> Secondly, judge-made reforms are dependent on the issue coming before the courts, and more particularly on the issue reaching an instance which places the court in a position to overrule, ignore, or distinguish any awkward precedents which stand in the way of reform. This chance element is accentuated by another factor, namely, the respective means of the parties to the litigation in

---

17 'The Common-Law: Judicial Impartiality and Judge Made Law', 98 *Law Quarterly Review*, 1982, pp. 29, 62.
18 'The Judge as Law Maker', *Journal of the Society of Public Teachers of Law*, vol. 12, N.S., 1972, p. 28.

question. Between the litigant who qualifies for legal aid and the man, or more often the corporation or government body, for whom costs matter less than a satisfactory legal result, there is a large group of potential litigants deterred by lack of means from fighting a case through the courts and, if necessary, to the House of Lords. Sometimes it may profit a litigant with a business in which the same issue may reoccur, to settle a case in spite of a favourable ruling in, say, the Court of Appeal, in order to prevent a possible reversal in the House of Lords. Indeed, this is rather more likely since the House of Lords assumed power to overrule its own decisions. In such circumstances the average party to a case is likely to prefer the cash in hand to the doubtful distinction of running a large financial risk in the interests of a possible reform of the law.

A third and even more important consideration may be summed up by a slight modification of a well-known aphorism: hard cases make not so much bad as unsystematic, incoherent and therefore, from the point of view of the law as a whole, uncertain law. In other words, the hard case invites an equitable decision, which is not bad in itself, but requires a broader base of principle than the judge in that particular case is entitled to provide. If he does reach a decision, he only prepares the way for a further spate of litigation which may ultimately have to be stemmed by legislation… .

Fourthly, it must be remembered that the reforming decision, which is welcomed by the critical academic lawyer, long familiar and impatient with some outdated but hitherto accepted piece of conventional legal wisdom, may be extremely unjust to the unsuccessful party. The latter is, in effect, the victim in a case of retrospective law-making. The danger of injustice by departing from the expected patterns of judicial behaviour was emphasised by the House of Lords when they announced in 1966 that they would no longer be necessarily bound by their own previous decisions. They would, they said, 'bear in mind the danger of disturbing retrospectively the basis on which contracts, settlements of property and fiscal arrangements have been entered into and also the especial need for certainty as to the criminal law.'

There is a fifth consideration which it would, in the context of English law, seem natural to bear in mind when assessing the potentialities of the judiciary as a source of law reform. It concerns, of course, the important part played by stare decisis in the English legal system. Clearly there is less scope, at least for rapid change, where that principle prevails than by the clean-sweeping enunciation by the legislature of some new general principle.

A sixth consideration, not referred to by Mr Marsh, is that the courts are likely to be relatively ill-informed as to the background to the problem that is said to require reform. The court relies normally on the arguments presented by counsel for the parties. It has no opportunity to consult with other persons, interested bodies, government departments or experts, as to what kind of reform would be most beneficial.

On the other hand, if the court abdicates responsibility for improving the law, nothing may happen. Legislatures and government departments normally have more than enough to occupy their time and may not find time for a proposed project of reform. In particular they may lack both the time and the energy to conduct the necessary researches to formulate reform proposals that are well designed to meet the problem. It is this above all which justifies the existence of a full-time law reform body such as the Law Commission.

See further on this issue the reflections of another Law Commissioner Dr Peter North, 'Is Law Reform Too Important to be Left to Lawyers?', *Legal Studies*, 1985, p. 119, especially pp. 126–9.

4. IMPLEMENTATION OF LAW-REFORM PROPOSALS

It is often said that law reform proceeds at a very leisurely pace and in particular that the reports of law-reform bodies are implemented very slowly, if at all. But it is by no means clear that these beliefs are well founded.

Dr Helen Beynon considered the point in her research on the role of independent advisory commissions and committees. In a sample of 136 reports published between 1950 and 1975 she found that 87 (or 64 per cent) were implemented in full, and another 16 (or 12 per cent) were implemented in part. Only 24 per cent were not implemented at all.[19] The sample consisted of 7 reports of Royal Commissions, 68 of Departmental Committees, 18 of the Law Reform Committee, 10 of the Criminal Law Revision Committee, 3 of the Private International Law Committee and 30 of the Law Commission.

Nor were the delays as great as is often supposed. Of the reports in the sample that were substantially implemented, no less than 65 per cent had been implemented within two years and a further 17 per cent within two to four years. (Ibid., Table VI, p. 171.)

The productivity of the Law Commission has been remarkable. Mrs Justice Arden, the then Chairman, said in October 1997 that of the 157 reports published until then, 101 had been implemented in whole or in part. The process of weeding out of obsolete enactments has also had considerable success.

Between 1965 and 1980, some 2,300 obsolete enactments had been repealed at the instance of the Law Commission, including 947 whole Acts (M. Kerr, 'Law Reform in Changing Times', 96 *Law Quarterly Review*, 1980, p. 525). See for details Law Commission annual reports.

Nevertheless, there has been some concern about implementation of Law Commission reports. Thus, Sir Michael Kerr, former chairman of the Commission, made it clear in his 1980 lecture that this issue concerned him.

---

19 Dr H. Beynon, *Independent Advice on Legislation*, unpublished Ph.D., Oxford University, Table IV, p. 176.

Sir Michael Kerr, 'Law Reform in Changing Times', 96 *Law Quarterly Review*, 1980, p. 532

> The difficulties of implementation stem from our parliamentary procedures and the notorious problem of securing time in legislative programmes, which are usually greatly overcrowded. As mentioned earlier, this problem has been largely solved for the technical Bills which lead to Statute Law Repeals and Consolidation Acts. Since these do not effect any change of substance in the law, Parliament has been content to leave their consideration to a joint committee of both Houses without any further debate. However, there is at present no special procedure of any kind for law reform Bills. Unless a Minister or his department is willing to make a bid for a Law Commission Bill in the parliamentary programme, and succeeds in getting a place, the Commission has to rely on Private Member Bills. But Private Members are usually more interested in Bills with a greater social impact than law reform... .
>
> It is clear that the problem of combining the concept of the Law Commissions Act with our traditional parliamentary procedures is an endemic weakness of the whole scheme. The Commission is at present examining the question whether anything might be done to overcome this so as to give greater administrative and political impetus to the implementation of its recommendations. Thus, if a new joint select committee, or one of the present select committees, were to take on the task of considering law reform Bills, taking evidence from the Government departments mainly concerned with them, and were to report its conclusions to Parliament, then Ministers, Government departments and Members of both Houses might be readier to try to ensure that a place may be found in the programme for Bills to which there are no real policy objections. The present position, however, apart from the possibility of Private Members' Bills in a few cases, is that the Commission's best chances of having its proposals implemented lie in the relatively short slack periods immediately before and after General Elections, or during periods of a 'hung' House of Commons, as in recent years, when controversial legislation is avoided and law reform provides an anodyne stop-gap. But this is clearly not a long-term solution, and something will have to be done if an ever increasing accumulation of unimplemented measures is to be avoided.

But in October 1980, at the end of a two-day Civil Service College seminar on law reform, Sir Michael Kerr admitted that he now doubted whether changes in parliamentary procedure were needed. Professor Stephen Cretney, a former Law Commissioner, in his Inaugural Lecture at Bristol University in October 1984, also doubted whether parliamentary reform was appropriate.[20] In the period 1965–82 the Law Commission had produced 58 reports making law-reform proposals. Of these, no fewer than 78 per cent had been implemented. It was true that over half of the more recent reports had not been implemented but he did not think that this was

---

20 'The Politics of Law Reform – a View from the Inside', *Modern Law Review*, 1985, p. 493.

necessarily a matter for complaint. There was often a substantial political element concealed even in apparently technical law-reform proposals, and government departments and governments were entitled and indeed bound to have regard to this when deciding whether to implement the proposals. In Cretney's view many of the reports that were unjustifiably impeded or held up came within the purview of the Home Office and the Department of the Environment (which had opposed the establishment of the Law Commission in the first place). But it was understandable that a department with daily involvement in the detailed administration of the law in a particular area should be reluctant to cede responsibility for the formulation of law-reform proposals to any outside body, however eminent. He did not therefore think that the problem of non-implementation was as serious as some had suggested.

Dr Peter North writing at about the same time agreed with Professor Cretney that there was nothing intrinsically wrong with a decision by government not to implement a particular Law Commission proposal. What he objected to was when the government failed to respond at all or within a reasonable time to a proposal. This was only rarely the case with the Lord Chancellor's Department but it did occur with the Home Office and the Department of the Environment.

Dr North thought there were a number of different steps that could be taken that would help.

(1)   One would be to implement Freedom of Information legislation as an impetus for prompt and open decision-making on law-reform matters as on all matters of government.
(2)   Another would be to publish legislation in draft for comment.
(3)   A third would be to change the rule so that legislation which has not completed its parliamentary passage by the end of the session should be allowed to survive, rather than having to start afresh in the new session. The rule should be changed at least for law-reform bills.
(4)   A fourth would be to extend the remit of the Home Affairs Select Committee of the House of Commons to include the Lord Chancellor's Department's law-reform responsibilities.[1] [Implemented in 1991.]

See further the view of Gavin Drewry in a paper given to the May 1986 Law Commission–QMC Colloquium on law reform in which he suggested that the key to a better implementation rate for law-reform proposals would be 'adequate public consultation' before a decision is taken as to whether to implement the proposal. The place for such debate should be Parliament.

---

1   See P. North, 'Law Reform: Processes and Problems', *Law Quarterly Review*, 1985, pp. 338, 356–67.

Such pre-legislative scrutiny could pave the way for subsequent parliamentary proceedings but would not pre-empt them.

His preference for the appropriate machinery would be for a joint committee, say, of five members of each House, required to keep under review all proposals of both the English and the Scottish Law Commissions and able also to consider at its discretion proposals from other sources such as JUSTICE. It would take evidence from the Commissions and the sponsoring department and would invite submissions from interested parties and from academic and other expert opinion. It would liaise with the relevant specialist select committees of both Houses. The joint committee would report annually to Parliament.[2]

The Hansard Society's 1992 Report on the Legislative Process (*Making the Law*) said there appeared to have been a slow-down in implementation of the Law Commission's Reports and the number of unimplemented reports grew longer and longer. In 1990 no Law Commission bill had been introduced and in 1991–92 there was no government bill to introduce Law Commission bills though two had been introduced by private Members.

The Jellicoe Committee (HL 35–1, 1992) had recommended that uncontroversial Law Commission bills should go to special standing committees in the Lords after Second Reading where evidence could be taken but debate thereafter might then be abbreviated. The Lord Chancellor had accepted the suggestion and the Hansard Society's Report welcomed this proposal. The 27th Annual Report of the Law Commission for 1992 said that the Law Commission stated that it too welcomed the proposal.[3] But this would not get bills through the Commons more quickly. The Hansard Society Report said it would be normal for uncontentious Law Commission bills to go, as in the past, to Second Reading Committee but there would seem to be no point in having them go to Special Standing Committees 'as there would seem to be no need to hear further evidence on these bills' (para. 500, p. 119). Timetabling of bills (see pp. 84–86) would seem to be a possible solution.

For a pessimistic view of the success of the Law Commission see R. T. Oerton, *A Lament for the Law Commission* (1987). Mr Oerton was one of the team of senior lawyers who had been with the Law Commission for many years who were sacked as an economy measure in 1982. Understandably, he was bitter about this and the bitterness shows. But his account of the work of the Commission from the inside is fascinating

2   Gavin Drewry, 'The Legislative Implementation of Law Reform Proposals', *Statute Law Review*, Autumn 1986, pp. 161, 171–2.

3   The Hansard Society Report said (para. 499, p. 119): 'Although we find this slightly curious – since these bills probably need less evidence than most because of the extensive consultations by the Law Commissions – it may be that such special procedures would reassure any critical peers and enable later stages of the bills to be unimpeded and to require little time.'

and there is much in his book which throws valuable light on the problems of the law-reform process.

For the complaint by an outgoing Chairman of the Law Commission that the House of Commons does not take reform of the criminal law seriously see Henry Brooke, 'The Law Commission and Criminal Law Reform' (1995) *Criminal Law Review*, p. 911. A spectacular example of the Law Commission not anticipating opposition was the angry right-wing campaign led by the *Daily Mail* against the Family Homes and Domestic Violence Bill which was based on the Commission's *Report on Domestic Violence and Occupation of the Family Home*. It had been thought that the Bill would be uncontroversial but it received a fearful media drubbing as 'a charter for live-in lovers'. In the event, the Bill was withdrawn by Lord Mackay in November 1995 though it was reintroduced in the next session with minor amendments and became Part IV of the Family Law Act 1996.[4]

A severe attack on the Law Commission was launched by a distinguished law reformer, Dr Alec Samuels, formerly of Southampton University – 'The Law Commission: Do We Really Need It?', *New Law Journal*, 8 August 1986, p. 747. His conclusion was that we do not – that the whole show should be wound up and taken over by the Lord Chancellor's Department. For a reply see the spirited retort by the same R. T. Oerton, 'The Law Commission: In Need of Support', *New Law Journal*, 7 November 1986, p. 1071. He agreed with many of Alec Samuels' criticisms but thought that the solution of the Lord Chancellor's Department taking over the functions of the Law Commission was equivalent to allowing a tiger in a zoo that has savaged a small boy to be allowed to eat him.

See also J. H. Farrar, *Law Reforms and the Law Commission* (1974); Sir Ralph Gibson, 'The Law Commission', 39 *Current Legal Problems*, 1986, p. 57; the bibliography at the end of Dr Cretney's article in *Modern Law Review*, 1985, p. 515; and G. Zellick (ed), *The Law Commission and Law Reform* (Sweet and Maxwell, 1988).

5.   THE LAW COMMISSION AND CODIFICATION

As has already been seen, codification was specially referred to in s. 3 of the Law Commissions Act as one of the chief duties of the Law Commissions. The nature of the duty and of its implications was explored in a lecture in 1966 given by Mr Justice Scarman (as he then was) at Hull University.

---

4   See S.M. Cretney, *Modern Law Review*, 1996, pp. 632–33.

Sir Leslie Scarman, 'A Code of English Law?', Hull University, 1966

No one could suggest, without taking leave of his senses, that the present shape of English law is either simple or modern ... English law lacks coherent shape, is inaccessible save to those with the training, the stamina, and the time to explore the jungle of case and statute law, and is unmanageable save by the initiated. It retains the mystical, priestly quality of early law: it has survived into the modern world only because of the tremendous quality of its high-priests – the judges who, from their seats of judgment, have from time immemorial – often in prose of striking beauty and clarity – declared its principles and solutions.... .

But it may be that the quality of our judge-made law – its flexibility, its certainty, its capacity to develop in response to the stimuli of actual life conveyed through the channel of litigation to the minds of the judges – is such that its unmanageable bulk must be accepted. Can it be said that the refined gold of the common law is not to be had without the dust, darkness, and encumbrances of the mineworkings? I would not pretend in the time at my disposal to attempt an assessment of the value of our judge-made law, save to say that the achievements of the judges are immense. They have created one of the two great systems of jurisprudence existing today in the western world. Blessed as we have been with an unbroken legal development over a period of 600 years, we find in our judge-made law a wonderful consistency of legal thought and action, and a remarkable capacity for adjustment to changing social conditions. The risk exists that codification might well shatter it. Yet, if this is right, law reform by legislative process, even when it does not lead to codification, should in logic be abandoned as a danger to the unity of the common law. But no one suggests the need for so conservative an approach. And there are clear indications that under the strain of our times the courts, notwithstanding the quality of their work, can no longer be accepted as sufficient instruments for the reform or modernisation of the law.... .

The basic weakness of a system of law which relies upon judicial precedent for its development is that it is not the primary function of courts or judges to legislate. This criticism may be put somewhat differently: development by judicial precedent is development of the law by lawyers – a practice against which man has protested with more or less success since the dawn of civilisation. One is back in the priestly atmosphere which bemuses and bewilders the ordinary citizen, which outraged Bentham. Codification is, however, a true law-making process – not merely an incidental benefit thrown up by another process, that of adjudication. It provides for study, research, consultation, planning – all essential to orderly development: it looks forward to the shape of things to come as well as back to the achievements of the past. Further, in an English context, it is a process which enables the layman's voice to be heard in the process of law-making. The community and its experts are involved: and the final stage is critical discussion of the proposed code in and outside Parliament during its passage into law. Codification as a process is thus responsive to modern ideas, and can be so managed as to be deliberate, scientific and representative. And as a process it can be kept in continuous action. It is true that a code begins to grow old, to become obsolete as soon as it is enacted. But if there be machinery for its continuous review, a code becomes not the last but the first stage in codification. The coalition of enacted code, judicial interpretation, probing and application, and continuous review by a commission such as the Law Commission Act creates, should ensure that codification continues, after as well as at the moment of the enactment of the code, to meet the endless challenge of simplification and modernisation... .

Let us assume it can be done. What would its impact be on the common law? We must face it: the impact would be immense. First, in the use of precedent. It would be inconceivable, upon the view I have put forward of the nature and objects of a code, that precedent earlier in date than the enacted code could be used as a source of law. It would, I suppose, be permissible to refer to earlier case law if it should be relevant to discover what the earlier law was: otherwise, with the enactment of the code, the curtain would drop for all save legal historians upon the earlier case law. Secondly, in the function of the judges. They would be interpreters of the law as found in the code. No doubt, as in France, a considerable judge-made jurisprudence carrying great authority would arise: for, as Aristotle once remarked, 'no piece of legislation can deal with every possible problem'.

The MacMillan Committee on Income Tax Codification (Cmnd. 5131, 1936) described the relationship of code and judges in these words (p. 17):

> 'Nothing short of omniscience would suffice to enable the draftsman to conceive and provide for every possible contingency ... It is not practicable to pursue any given topic to its last details. There must always remain a margin within which the process of judicial interpretation and application is left to operate.'

Thus the judges would retain a vital legislative function when confronted with situations with which the code had failed to deal. Both as legislators, therefore, and as interpreters, their part in developing as well as applying the law would continue to be of immense importance. They would also fulfil a vital function as critics in continuous session.

...[I]t will be the judges who will find the weaknesses, the ambiguities, the gaps, and so provide the opportunities and the incentive for keeping the code in 'efficient working order'.

They would, however, have to be freed of the rigidities of our present 'stare decisis' rule; for though precedent would have a persuasive role to play of great importance, it could not be allowed to become sovereign. Code and persuasive precedent can co-exist to the advantage of law. Further, a code will require a 'fair, large and liberal' interpretation: the priorities now obtaining among the many rules of statutory interpretation, that at present our law offers, according to context, to the judge, would call for re-assessment. Further, it will be necessary to consider whether new aids to interpretation should not be made available: for example, a Law Commission memorandum or commentary on the code.

All this may at first sight appear to portend legal revolution. But it is not so very drastic if viewed against the background of the legal development of the past 100 years. Much of our criminal law, our company law, our law as to competition and consumer protection, our planning and property law, our tax law is already embodied in statute: our judges already spend a great part of their time upon the interpretation of statute law. Even before the Law Commission Act, our law was on the move towards codification: a universal codification would not be such a strange new world as some lawyers fear.

The observations that I have made do not enable a decisive answer to be given to the question – will English law become a codified system? I have endeavoured only to suggest grounds for believing that codification of our law – in part, if not in whole – is both desirable and possible. A final answer can be given only when its problems and implications have been subjected to more scientific study than has yet been thought necessary.

On a different occasion in 1966 Sir Leslie Scarman also considered the form or style of the proposed codes:

Mr Justice Scarman, 'Codification and Judge-made Law', Birmingham University, 1966

… I come now to the question – what sort of code is likely to come – one replete with detailed provisions or one confined to general declarations? The history books provide few examples in modern times of the short general code. The German civil code is more typical – 2,385 sections – than the Swiss, which is a short generalised code. What should we choose?

It is pertinent to remember we are codifying piecemeal – preparing codes, not one Digest of all the law. It is likely that the character of each code will be determined not so much by theoretical considerations as to the nature of codified law but by the subject-matter of the particular branch of law being codified. Nevertheless, any codification may find itself impaled upon the horns of a dilemma. If it is to be simple and easily understood, it will in eschewing detail attract so much subsequent case law that it will rapidly lose any practical importance as a source of law: the history of Articles 1382–86 of the French civil code is an object lesson. It was such a fate that Bentham had in mind when he called for codification in great detail: for it was his view that:

> 'the code having been prepared, the introduction of all unwritten [i.e. not enacted] law should be forbidden.'

But, if the code be detailed, will it not lose the qualities of brevity, intelligibility, and accessibility to which the advocates of codified law attach importance?

The escape from the dilemma is to be found, I suggest, by concentrating attention on subject-matter. Complex social conditions, of course, necessitate complex laws. It is disingenuous to ask of law that it should be simple, when its subject-matter is not. The problem becomes one of degree. In certain branches of the law, e.g. contract, property, the criminal law, the ordinary citizen requires guidance. He enters into business agreements: he buys and sells; he owns property; he has to determine his personal conduct in society. In these fields it is not merely the judge who wants to know how to decide his case; it is the ordinary citizen who, without recourse to litigation, has to regulate his dealings and his conduct. In such branches of the law the code must condescend to detail, thus ensuring that its provisions are not overlaid by judicial decision which, by and large, will be accessible only to the legal profession. But where the law is concerned more to provide a remedy than to chart a course, e.g. in the law of negligence or, I would suggest, in a properly developed administrative law, less detail is needed, and a wider discretion may be left to judicial decision. But, whatever the degree of detail, the code must be such that in its field of application it is in practice as well as in theory the authoritative and exclusive source of law.

If one of the alleged virtues of codified systems is that they are easier to use than the common law system, the experience of practitioners is relevant. One who practised both in Germany and in England was the late Dr Ernst Cohn, who compared the two systems:

Dr Ernst Cohn, 'The German Attorney', *International and Comparative Law Quarterly*, 1960, pp. 586–7

Codification renders the task of the practising lawyer very much easier than it is in an uncodified system. No code solves more than some problems. Freedom of interpretation and casuistry must remain and do remain. But only a very bad code would fail to deal clearly and succinctly with the vast majority of the day-to-day problems that are the bread and butter of the routine lawyer's life. These codes have been ably commented upon by numerous authors during the last sixty years. Commentators vary in size from a little one-volume pocket edition to huge standard works approximating in size our 'Halsbury'. But it is believed that a good selection of pocket commentaries together with a more elaborate edition of one or two codes, plus the last fifteen years of the leading legal periodical, *Neue Juristische Wochenschrift*, and the current official Statute Book will do for the needs of a large percentage of attorneys in all but a fairly small number of cases, in particular if this 'library' is supplemented by some of the better-class students' textbooks from his university days.

By the term 'codification' I mean, of course, what may well be styled the 'radical codification' which is the only form of codification known to the Continent of Europe. This type of codification differs from what is designated by the same term in this country by the fact that it will make recourse to all the accumulated mass of earlier material – whether statutes or decisions or other works of authority – completely unnecessary except perhaps in a case of the most extraordinary character. This radical codification furthermore differs from the common law type of codification by its attempt at laying down principles of a sweepingly wide and general character, rather than deciding in a binding manner typical cases as do so many common law statutes. This seemingly abstract type of code has the beneficial effect of drawing into its net a far larger number of actual cases. A practitioner who has grasped the rules of the first book of the German Civil Code and those of the first part of the second book of the German Civil Code is thereby alone well equipped to deal satisfactorily with an astonishingly large number of everyday problems. A question which would require a common law practitioner to search in books of reference for one or several quarters of an hour could be solved by his Continental colleague completely satisfactorily in as many minutes.

Dr Cohn's view has, however, been challenged.

H. R. Hahlo, 'Here Lies the Common Law', 30 *Modern Law Review*, 1967, p. 241

Whether codification renders the routine work of legal practice and adjudication easier is a question on which opinions differ. Dr E. J. Cohn, who has practised in Germany and England, asserts ... that

'There can be no doubt at all ... that codification renders the task of the practising lawyer very much easier than it is in an uncodified system'

and that

'A question which would require a common law practitioner to search in books of reference for one or several quarters of an hour could be solved by his Continental colleague completely satisfactorily in as many minutes'

referring in support to an article by Mr E. Moses on 'International Legal Practice'.[5]

Other lawyers with experience of practice, both on the Continent and under an uncodified system, have been heard to assert, with equal assurance, that the task of a French, Dutch or German lawyer in arguing a legal point is not substantially easier than that of his English, American or Scottish colleague, and that there are as many points of controversy in modern Continental systems of law as there are in the common law.

Ex cathedra statements of this sort, even if supported by an 'of course' or 'no doubt', are in the nature of things capable of neither proof nor disproof. Since a code wipes out the past, it generally obviates the need for historical research going back in time beyond the date of the code and, to this extent, it makes legal work easier, but how many cases arise, after all, in any system of law, in which deep historical research is required? In an uncodified as well as a codified system, it is rarely necessary to go beyond the last thirty years of law reports.

Dr Cohn, after having told us that codification 'renders the task of the practising attorney very much easier ...', goes on to say that the German codes 'have been ably commented upon by numerous authors during the last sixty years. Commentaries vary in size from a little one-volume pocket-edition to huge standard works approximating in size our *Halsbury*.' He then informs us that a library consisting of 'a good selection of pocket commentaries together with a more elaborate edition of one or two codes [one of the 'huge' standard works?], plus the last fifteen years of the leading legal periodical, *Neue Juristische*

5   (1935) 4 *Fordham Law Review*, p. 244.

Wochenschrift [which contains, apart from articles, extensive case notes], and the current official Statute Book ... supplemented by some of the better-class students' textbooks ...' will 'do for the needs of a large percentage of attorneys in all but a fairly small number of cases.'

Reading this, one cannot help wondering whether practice on the Continent can really be so very much easier than in England. How much more by way of materials does an English lawyer require in all 'but a fairly small number of cases?'

Professor Hahlo listed a variety of reasons for the belief that codification was unlikely to be a remedy for the alleged ills of the common law system:

The immediate effect of the introduction of a code, so far from making the law more certain, is to create a lengthy period of increased legal uncertainty. True, many hitherto doubtful issues will have been settled, but the reformulation of the old rules and the adoption of new rules, added to the systematisation of the law, are bound to open up new disputes. For each head of controversy that has been cut off, there will arise, hydra-like, one or more new ones. And it will only be decades later, after the code has become overlain with a thick encrustation of case law, that the old measure of legal certainty (or uncertainty) will be restored... . But it is not only the growing body of case law which will soon provide the nakedness of the infant code with a wardrobe rivalling in its variety and complexity that of the common law prior to codification. Almost as soon as the ink is dry the need for legislative amendments will become manifest.

... In addition to the growing body of case law, there will soon be an ever growing body of amending legislation, followed in due course by judgments explaining the amending legislation, and amendments upon the amendments.

How long this process can continue before the need for wholesale code revision arises, depends upon the tempo of social and economic change and the readiness of the legislature and the profession to undertake the enormous task of redrafting the code. That, sooner or later, wholesale revision will be required, is certain – and sooner rather than later in a time such as ours, when the rate of social change is far quicker than it was when the Continental codes were drafted, and is accelerating at a rate undreamt of by our forbears. There is no turning back once the law is codified, you have to go on codifying. Like the sorcerer's apprentice, the codifier is forever pursued by the spirits he evoked from the deep... .

It is of the nature of law that the bulk of it should be certain, but that there will always be a fuzzy zone of uncertainty around the edges. It is also of the nature of law that it stands perpetually in need of revision if it is to remain in keeping with changing conditions. To think that law could be rendered either more certain or more stable by codification, is to blame a certain form of law for attributes which are in fact inherent in the nature of law, whatever form it may take... . Codification of a country's law must be paid for, and the price is heavy.

First of all, there is the work of preparing the code which, if Continental experience is any guide, will keep the best legal brains in England and Scotland busy for the next twenty or thirty years.

Secondly, there is the need for re-learning the law. Only one who has never worked with a code can believe that codification is nothing but a formal change, requiring no fundamental adjustments in approach and method. A code is not just a large statute, it is a different species of law, demanding different techniques, and these techniques have to be learnt by the legal profession. Even where a rule of the common law is merely restated, the fact that it is now laid down in writing and forms part of a system of interrelated rules, affects its meaning and scope. Legal textbooks have to be rewritten. Judges, practitioners and academic lawyers have to learn an entirely new system, a task likely to tax the capacity of some of the older members of the profession to the limit... .

Another portion of the price to be paid, to which reference has been made earlier, is the increased legal uncertainty which follows in the train of any new major piece of legislation, and ends only when its meaning and effect have been clarified by the courts. How long this period is going to last in England it is, of course, impossible to foretell. Much will depend on the method of codification and the type of code chosen.

Each one of the great Continental codes, from Napoleon's *Code Civil*, came into life complete and fully-formed. The Law Commission has chosen to proceed on the instalment system of codification. Starting with the general part of the law of contract, it proposes to proceed, step by step, to the codification of other branches of the law – special contracts, the law of obligations, a family code... .

The choice between codification in one piece and codification on the instalment system is somewhat like choosing between having all one's teeth out in one go or one by one. For better or worse this particular choice has been made. A choice which has still to be made by the Law Commission is what type of codification to adopt.

On the one side, there is the pattern of the *Code Civil*, which eschews definitions and favours broad principles, leaving it to the courts to fill in the gaps. On the other, there is the pattern of the far more detailed and definitive German civil code.[6] Broad general principles leave the law flexible and permit the courts considerable latitude in doing justice within the framework of the code, but they leave the law uncertain until the courts have had time to build up a body of case law. Detailed rules provide a greater measure of certainty and, hence, predictability, but leave the courts less space in which to manoeuvre... .

The English civil code will have no resemblance in form to the common law. Modelled on Continental codes, it will consist of definitions and principles, systematically arranged. The Law Commission, no doubt, hopes to preserve the substance of the common law, whilst changing its form, but in law, more than in any other field, substance and form go together. Once the common law is codified, it will, of necessity, cease to be the common law, not only (rather obviously) in form, but also in substance.

The effect on the role of English law in the world may turn out to be profound. It is of the essence of a codified system that any legal inquiry takes its starting point from one or more specific provisions in the code. The result

---

6   On the various types of codes, see also F. H. Lawson (1960) 2 *Inter-American Law Review*, at pp. 2–3.

is that no country which does not have identical code provisions can derive much benefit from its case law. Once English law is codified, the legal-cultural tie between England and other countries governed by the common law will become attenuated. The courts of the various American states, of the common law provinces of Canada, of Australia and of New Zealand, unless they decide to take over the new English civil code *en bloc*, will discover that they no longer derive the same assistance from English cases as before... .

If this be true, it does not appear unlikely that as a result of codification, the influence of English law outside the United Kingdom will decrease, and that, so far from becoming entrenched in its position as a world system, it will suffer a *capitis deminutio*, being reduced in status from that of the senior member of the Anglo-American common law family to that of a purely national system, governed by just one more code among many.

Considerable scepticism about the alleged advantages of codification was also expressed by Professor Aubrey Diamond in a lecture published three years before he himself became a Law Commissioner.

Professor Aubrey Diamond, 'Codification of the Law of Contract', 31 *Modern Law Review*, 1968, p. 361

Various reasons have been given over the years why codification is desirable. The case for codification in England at this time rests on the following arguments.

1. Accessibility of the law to the legal profession
On several occasions Lord Gardiner has stressed the inaccessibility of the law: over 3,000 separate Acts of Parliament, dating from about 1235, contained in 359 different volumes, ninety-nine volumes of subordinate legislation; and well over 350,000 reported cases.

The Lord Chancellor may be right in believing that this is the real case for codification, though it is important not to get carried away by the practical difficulties of the common law. One must not think that the mass of reports and statutes is all that daunting to the practitioner, whatever the effect it may have on the student.

The truth is that there are many practitioners who rarely open a law report more than two years old. Apart from keeping up to date with the latest *Weekly Law Reports* or *All England Law Reports* they will rely for their law on Halsbury's *Laws of England* (forty-two volumes, including index volumes, and a two-volume cumulative supplement), specialist textbooks and books of precedent forms and *Halsbury's Statutes* (forty-seven volumes up to and including the loose-leaf volume for 1967, and two volumes of supplement). Probably they will also take *Current Law* and one or more journals.

Even for those lawyers who do refer to case reports in their daily practice, the figure of 350,000 cases gives a false impression. It is difficult to know how much cases really are used. In an attempt to find out, we may analyse the 434 cases reported in the three volumes of the *All England Law Reports* for 1965. In those 434 cases 3,865 cases were cited in judgments or referred to in argument.

This gives an average of 8.9 authorities to a case, but like most averages this does not give a true picture. In thirty-six cases no authorities were cited, and in 108 cases – one-quarter of the total – two or less authorities were referred to. At the other extreme, there were forty-eight cases in which twenty or more authorities were referred to, the highest number being ninety-two (in *National Provincial Bank* v. *Ainsworth*,[7] the case of the deserted wife's equity). In 130 reported cases (30 per cent), ten or more authorities were referred to.... More than three-quarters of them (2,959 cases, 76.6 per cent) were reported in this century and nearly a half (1,766 cases, 45.7 per cent) were reported since 1945. Only 12.9 per cent (502) date from before the Judicature Acts (1875 or earlier), and only 1.7 per cent (sixty-seven cases) from before 1800. There was one Year Book case (in 1470). This scarcely gives the appearance of an antique law (remember that the Civil Code of France dates from 1804).

It is of interest, incidentally, to see that included in the 3,865 cases are thirty unreported cases, sixty-five Scottish cases, thirty-seven Australian, twelve Irish, twelve Canadian, ten American, four New Zealand, three Northern Irish and two South African cases, and one Indian case.[8]

A similar survey of the ten years from 1957 to 1966 enables us to compare the cases on the law of contract with those on codified branches of the law. During this period I found thirty cases that seemed to me to be based fairly and squarely on provisions in the Sale of Goods Act, the Bills of Exchange Act or the Marine Insurance Act. In those thirty cases some 388 authorities were referred to, giving an average of 12.9 authorities per case, appreciably greater than the overall average for 1965 (which of course included cases on recent statutes). (The authorities cited in individual cases ranged from two to forty-nine). In the same period there were fifty-six cases on points of contract law that would probably be incorporated into a code: here a total of 968 authorities were referred to, an average of 17.3 authorities per case ... the statistics suggest, and common sense tells us, that a code does make the law more accessible than the uncodified common law.

2. Accessibility of the law to the public
If a code makes the law more easily accessible to the legal profession, it thereby makes the law accessible to the public.... English lawyers have never laid much stress on lay knowledge of the law. They have preferred the esoteric nature of our legal system.

... Nevertheless, some recent social surveys have been undertaken to discover how far the English are acquainted with particular legal rules. One survey, sponsored by the Latey Committee on the Age of Majority, investigated the familiarity of people aged between 16 and 24 with the incapacities of youth; the other, conducted under the auspices of the Consumer Council, sought to evaluate public knowledge of consumer rights under the law of sale of goods, codified for over seventy years.... [W]hereas 94 per cent knew the minimum age for being served in a public-house, only 22 per cent knew that under the Sale of Goods Act the retailer can be made liable for faulty goods. The

7   [1965] 2 All E.R. 472, H.L.
8   This breakdown does not include cases cited in Privy Council Appeals.

results demonstrate that the subject-matter of a rule contributes more to its becoming widely known than the form of the law or, perhaps, that we are more interested in pubs than in shops.

3. Improvement of the law

The real case for codification, I believe, is that it facilitates law reform. We can improve the content of the law when we create the new code; and we can improve it later by revising the code.

There are two kinds of codes. One merely seeks to reproduce the existing law, to translate case-law into statute-law without radical change; the other aims to produce a new set of principles, as the Uniform Commercial Code does. The Law Commission intend the new contract code to be of this second kind: 'The intention is to reform as well as to codify.'[9]

DIFFICULTIES OF CODIFICATION

Commendable as these objectives are, it would be foolish to ignore the difficulties that lie in the way of successful codification. These centre on the problems of statutory interpretation and the limitations of draftsmanship.

(a) Judicial conservation

A code is intended to replace the earlier common law. How can one ensure that the judges, brought up on the common law and familiar with it, will wipe out their knowledge of the cases from their memories and concentrate on the statutory words? This has been a very real problem that has not always been successfully dealt with.

The Civil Code of California, passed in 1872, declared in section 4 that:

'4. The rule of the common law, that statutes in derogation thereof are to be strictly construed, has no application to this code... .'

But the very next section, section 5, was not wholly in harmony with that sensible rule of interpretation.

'5. The provisions of this code, so far as they are substantially the same as existing statutes or the common law, must be construed as continuations thereof, and not as new enactments.'

Exactly what was the purpose of this section is far from clear. The California courts were understandably uncertain whether they ought to have regard to prior common law authorities until 1884, when Professor J. N. Pomeroy published a series of articles on the method of interpreting the Code. He pointed out that many provisions in the Code were meaningless except to a person educated in the common law, and argued that the Code provisions 'are to be regarded as simply declaratory of the previous common law and equitable doctrines and rules, except where the intent to depart from those doctrines and rules clearly appears from the unequivocal language of the text.' This approach

9   The Law Commission, First Annual Report, 1965–6 (Law Com. No. 4), para. 31.

was soon adopted by the Californian courts, and consequently the prior common law remained a living source of the law.

Exactly the same question arose at the same time in England, where the Bills of Exchange Act had been passed in 1882. Chalmers had included in section 97(2) the following provision:

'The rules of the common law, including the law merchant, save in so far as they are inconsistent with the express provisions of this Act ..., shall continue to apply to bills of exchange.'

In 1885 the case of *Re Gillespie, ex p. Robarts*[10] came before Cave J. In ignorance, no doubt, of Pomeroy's articles in California, he followed the same method: 'The first question is, whether previous to the Bills of Exchange Act 1882, damages of this kind could be recovered.... Then comes the Bills of Exchange Act 1882, and the first provision to which it is important to call attention is section 97(2).... It therefore follows, unless there is something in the Act expressly inconsistent with the ancient law, that the right to prove for damages of the kind which I have spoken of still exists.'[11]

All six members of the Court of Appeal applied the same technique in *Vagliano Brothers* v. *Bank of England*[12] four years later. Lord Esher M.R., dissenting in his conclusions, said: 'In order to arrive at the true interpretation of [the Bills of Exchange Act], I think it is necessary to consider not merely what was the law at the time of the passing of the Act, but what were the principles on which the different cases which declared the law were founded.'[13] The majority, as distinguished a Bench as one could hope to find, agreed that one must start with the prior law. In the House of Lords[14] Lord Bramwell (and perhaps Lord Field) adopted the same approach. Fortunately the majority thought differently – fortunately because otherwise a code would in no way have served to make the law more accessible, but instead would merely have adopted an additional stage in a consideration of the authorities.

It was in this case that Lord Herschell gave us the classic statement of how to interpret a codifying statute:

'I think the proper course is in the first instance to examine the language of the statute and to ask what is its natural meaning, uninfluenced by any consideration derived from the previous state of the law, and not to start with inquiring how the law previously stood, and then, assuming that it was probably intended to leave it unaltered, to see if the words of the enactment will bear an interpretation in conformity with this view.'[15]

---

10 (1885) 16 Q.B.D. 702.
11 Ibid, at p. 704.
12 (1889) 23 Q.B.D., 243, C.A.
13 Ibid., at p. 247.
14 *Bank of England* v. *Vagliano Brothers* [1891] A.C. 107, H.L.
15 Ibid., at p. 144.

But he went on to open the door to previous decisions 'if, for example, a provision be of doubtful import'[16] and it is an unusually well-drafted statute that admits of no doubts. In practice, judges often look at the pre-code cases: this is particularly noticeable in cases on the Marine Insurance Act 1906,[17] while there are several cases on the law of sale of goods where the Act is not even mentioned.[18]

The truth is that it is very difficult to prevent judges from applying the law they know, and have learnt to love, instead of the new and strange statute.

The real difficulty is in envisaging a completely self-contained code. According to the Law Commission: 'The object of a code is, in our understanding, to set out the essential principles which are to govern a given branch of the law.' A court, they go on, 'is expected to discover in the code the principles from which the answer to a particular problem can be worked out.'[19]

This is certainly the theory of continental codes,[20] but it would be a radical departure for a common law code.[1]

As we have seen, one thing is certain. The existing English 'codes' have not wiped out the old law. In Chalmers' *Sale of Goods Act* nearly half of the cases cited still date from before the Act, and even in the more modern narrative works as many as 20 per cent of the cases are from before the Act.

(b) Professional prejudice
It is not necessary to dwell on the undoubted prejudice against legislation felt by common lawyers. A leading legal periodical will discuss the implications of a decision by a puisne judge but has no regular feature giving similar attention to new statutes. There are still people who distrust a code because it is impossible to foresee everything: but one seldom hears the common law criticised because only things that have already happened come before the courts. The notion of the completeness of the common law is today universally acknowledged to be a legal fiction, but its habits of thought remain.

(c) The problem of drafting
David Dudley Field saw clearly the problem: 'There should be neither a generalisation too vague nor a particularity too minute, in the Code... .'[2]

---

16 Ibid., at p. 145.
17 See, e.g., *British & Foreign Marine Insurance Co. Ltd* v. *Sanday & Co.* [1916] 1 A.C. 650, H.L., per Lord Loreburn at p. 656, Lord Atkinson at p. 660, Lord Parmoor at p. 667 and Lord Wrenbury at pp. 672–3; and *Yorkshire Insurance Co. Ltd* v. *Nisbet Shipping Co. Ltd* [1961] 2 All E.R. 487, per Diplock J. at p. 492.
18 See, e.g., *McDougall* v. *Aeromarine of Emsworth Ltd* [1958] 3 All E.R. 431; *Victoria Laundry (Windsor) Ltd* v. *Newman Industries Ltd* [1949] 2 K.B. 528. C.A.
19 The Law Commission and the Scottish Law Commission: Published Working Paper on The Interpretation of Statutes, 1967, p. 45.
20 See e.g., A. T. Von Mehren, *The Civil Law System*, pp. 60, 64 and generally.
1   Cf. A. P. Sereni, 'The Code and the Case Law', in *The Code Napoleon and the Common-Law World*, pp. 58–9.
2   *First Report of the Commissioners of the Code to the New York Legislature,* 1858, cited Honnold, *The Life of the Law*, at p. 109.

The trouble is that there is a difference between case-law and statute-law. In case-law we are concerned with ideas, in statutes we are concerned with words. The Statute Book is littered with phrases that have become battlegrounds – 'arising out of and in the course of the employment', 'absolutely void', 'debt, default or miscarriage of another person'. This problem of fixing the right level of abstraction is really: how much discretion should be left to the judge? Some of the difficulties arising from existing codes such as the Sale of Goods Act are due to excessive detail caused by Chalmers' attempt to codify the existing, but still developing, law. What started as the germ of a judicial idea, which might have been distinguished or overruled, became statute-law, binding on all courts including the House of Lords.

(d) Restriction on legal development

The most telling objection to a code in a common law jurisdiction is that it limits the development of the law. The common law grows and changes. Statute-law is static until it is changed by the legislature. 'It is the function of courts,' says a modern master of the common law, 'to mould the common law and to adapt it to the changing society for which it provides the rules of each man's duty to his neighbour.'[3] But courts do not see it as their function to mould statute-law or to adapt it to our changing society.

Part of the problem lies in the lawyer's approach to an Act of Parliament. He does not see it as a creative force in the formation of new law, but rather as an interference with the 'natural' development of the law by the judges. Hence the notion that Acts of Parliament must be strictly construed and the extraordinary presumptions that a statute leaves the common law unchanged. Lawyers do not argue by analogy from statutes as they do from judgments, and many would think it wrong to do so. The late James Landis, Dean of the Harvard Law School, expressed this in a paragraph that cannot be bettered:

> 'When the highest tribunal of England in 1868 decided that the land-owner who artificially accumulates water upon his premises is absolutely liable for damages caused by its escape[4] that judgment had an enormous influence throughout Anglo-American law…. Had Parliament in 1868 adopted a similar rule, no such permeating results to the general body of Anglo-American law would have ensued. And this would be true, though the Act had been preceded by a thorough and patient inquiry by a Royal Commission into the business of storing large volumes of water and its concomitant risks, and even though the same Lords who approved Mr Fletcher's claim had in voting "aye" upon the measure given reasons identical with those contained in their judgments. Such a statute would have caused no ripple in the process of adjudication either in England or on the other side of the Atlantic….'[5]

---

3   Diplock L.J. in *Indyka* v. *Indyka* [1966] 3 All E.R. 583, 591.
4   *Rylands* v. *Fletcher* (1868) L.R. 3 H.L. 330. (Footnote in original.)
5   'Statutes and the Sources of Law,' in *Harvard Legal Essays*, 1934, p. 213 at p. 221. The whole of this valuable essay repays careful study.

If we could devise a way to stimulate the judicial mind, to distinguish between statutes laying down limited solutions to limited problems and those containing in them more widely applicable truths, progress might be made.

(e) Accretion of case law
It may be that on the day the code is passed one can look at the Queen's Printer copy of the statute and say: 'That, and that alone, is the English law of contract.' But there is no reason to think that lawyers will stop regarding judicial decisions as binding authorities, whether on a common law rule, an ordinary statute, or a codifying statute, and once the judges start to interpret the code it will no longer be possible to rely on the statutory words alone. Thus recent books on the law of sale of goods, though based substantially on the Sale of Goods Act 1893, refer to between 400 and 850 cases decided since the Act was passed. In this way the accessibility of the law, to the profession and to the public, is inevitably marred.

This is unavoidable. Neither judicial nor academic commentary on the code can be prevented. Attractive though the idea may seem, it would not be possible to emulate the *c. Deo auctore* which forbade commentaries on Justinian's *Digest* (and which was not long observed).[6] The approach of Cardozo J. is more realistic: '... code is followed by commentary and commentary by revision, and thus the task is never done.'[7]

CONCLUSION
If the new code is well done lawyers will be in the Lord Chancellor's debt for generations, and like the first Lord Chancellor Gardiner he will be in office a hundred years after his death. If it is not well done, Sir Frederick Pollock's sane and balanced comment will offer a crumb of comfort to the Chancellor and his Law Commission: 'It is strange how little harm bad codes do.'

Most progress in the field of codification has so far been made in the area of family law. This was the subject of a lecture by one of the Law Commissioners much involved in the process:

Stephen Cretney 'The Codification of Family Law', 44 *Modern Law Review*, 1981, p. 1

Gradual codification
The Commission's fundamental assumption has been that reform of the substance of the law must necessarily precede codification; the reformed statutory provisions are then brought together by the legislative process of

6   Carolina once 'absolutely prohibited' any form of 'comments and expositions on any part' of the law (though I am not clear whether this applied to judges): 'The Fundamental Constitutions of Carolina', art. 80, in 5 *The Federal and State Constitutions, Colonial Charters, and Other Organic Laws* (ed. F. Thorpe) 2782 (1909), cited Mellinkoff, *The Language of the Law*, p. 209.
7   Cardozo, 'A Ministry of Justice' (1921), 35 *Harv. L. Rev.* 113.

consolidation. Our codification process is gradual, but this does not mean that it lacks the systematic approach which is one of the main characteristics of the codification process.

Mr Cretney outlined the considerable number of reports and bills for which the Law Commission had been responsible in the family law field on engagement, capacity to marry, the marriage ceremony, the financial consequences of marriage and divorce, divorce law, children, the international aspects of family law and the position of illegitimate persons. With the last it might be possible to claim that the Family Law Code would be complete.

Is it true codification?
And yet ... ever since I became a member of the Law Commission in October 1978 I have had a recurrent nightmare, in which I am exposed to questioning by an evidently sceptical inquisitor carried here on one of those incoming (or is it now advancing?) tides from a country with a more firmly established tradition of codification. In this nightmare, I recount to him the Law Commission's achievements in the field of family law over the past 15 years; but he remains strangely unimpressed. 'Change', he says, 'I certainly see; progress – in the social sense – perhaps; but what real progress have you made towards codification? The *Code Napoléon* was initially drafted by four men in four months, and completed in four years; whilst even that model of exhaustive scientific codification, the German Civil Code, took only 13 years to appear in draft. You talk to me about progress, but after 15 years, all that I can see in this area of your civil law is a heap of disconnected and ill-related statutes. To begin with (he might say) I cannot understand why your reforms are carried through in the piecemeal fashion you have described. Surely that is bound to lead to anomalies?'

The Parliamentary process and codification
With this question I have no difficulty. All that I need to do is to send my inquisitor for instruction into British political institutions and parliamentary procedures. He would learn from this how entirely unrealistic it would be to suppose that a comprehensive legislative code of Family Law could ever be passed into law in this country as a single venture. For much of the subject matter would be highly controversial, and would clearly engender long Parliamentary debate. Parliament is properly concerned that no outside body should usurp its sovereignty over even the details of legislation. Every clause in a Bill is thus open to debate, and indeed to amendment; and any member of either House may put forward any new clause he likes, provided that only that it is within the scope of the Bill... .

Our codification therefore necessarily proceeds by way of instalments, all the relevant reformed legislation being in due course collected into a single statute under the special consolidation procedure. The working out of this strategy can be seen in the Matrimonial Causes Act 1973 which consolidates three major reforming measures, the Divorce Reform Act 1969, the Matrimonial Proceedings and Property Act 1970 and the Nullity of Marriage Act 1971 – all in their different ways controversial. The great advantage of the consolidation procedure is that a consolidation measure becomes law with virtually no debate and with only such amendments, if any, as are necessary to secure that it is a 'true' consolidation. Hence, practically no Government time is required, and the Government's legislation programme is unaffected.

What consolidation can and cannot achieve

Consolidation is thus a necessary final stage in our codification process, but it can achieve only the limited objective of bringing together in one Act all the enactments on a particular branch of the law. Draftsmen no longer feel it necessary to use precisely the same wording as the legislation being considered, but it is axiomatic that a consolidating measure must not change the law. Indeed, all consolidation measures are carefully scrutinised by a Joint Committee which subjects the draftsman to a searching examination. The purpose of the scrutiny (it has been authoritatively stated)[8] is 'to provide that measure of parliamentary control over Bills which is consistent with the parliamentary doctrine that nothing must be enacted which changes existing law without full scrutiny in Parliament... .'

To the principle that consolidation measure must not change the law there is an important, albeit limited, exception:[9] a procedure now exists for consolidation with amendments pursuant to Law Commission recommendations, but the changes in the law which can be effected under this procedure are limited to those desirable to secure a *satisfactory consolidation* of the relevant subject-matter. The Joint Committee has to be satisfied that the Commission's proposals go no further than is necessary to achieve this objective, and it has been stated that the procedure should not be used to introduce any substantial change in the law or one that might be controversial – indeed, nothing that Parliament as a whole would wish to reserve for its consideration.[10] Consolidation, on the one hand, and reform (or even rationalisation) on the other remain mutually incompatible concepts;[11] the consolidation procedure cannot be used to re-state the common law, and it cannot be used to remove doubt and obscurity from the law.[12]

---

8 See 'Consolidation and Statute Law Revision' by Lord Simon of Glaisdale and J. V. D. Webb [1975] Pub. L. 285, 297.

9 Under the Consolidation of Enactments (Procedure) Act 1949 'corrections and minor improvements' as defined in s. 2 of that Act may be made in a Consolidation Bill. The scope of this exception is narrow: see [1975] Pub. L. 285, 293–4; and *Farrell* v. *Alexander* [1976] Q.B. 345, 366, *per* Lawton L.J.

10 See the Report of the Joint Committee on Consolidation Bills on the Bill for the Rent Act 1977.

11 There may however be occasions when the courts hold that the clear and unambiguous language of a consolidating measure has changed the law: see generally the discussion of the correct approach to the construction of a consolidation Act in *Farrell* v. *Alexander* [1977] A.C. 59.

12 See e.g. s. 13 Child Care Act 1980, reproducing the exact wording of the Children Act 1948 as amended by the Children Act 1975. The Child Care Bill, as originally ordered by the House of Lords on 22 March 1979 to be printed, used clearer language under which no offence would be committed by a parent who removed a child who had been in the care of a local authority throughout the preceding six months in cases where the Local Authority had passed a resolution vesting in

Parliamentary control over legislative detail

The special procedure for consolidation is thus valuable, but its scope is limited. We lack any comparable special arrangements for dealing with law reform measures, even those of a purely rationalising nature. It is, of course, right and proper that the control of Parliament over our law should be preserved; but a price inevitably has to be paid for the insistence that this control be exercised, in relation to almost all legislation, through the present procedures involving repeated line by line debate. Furthermore, one might perhaps question whether those procedures are, in relation to technical matters of law reform, wholly adequate to achieve truly effective control. We could all give examples of cases where Parliament lacked the information and background effectively to question the provisions of a Bill; and it is not surprising that in some cases (for example where provisions relating to succession or other complex and technical matters of that kind are involved) the interest of members has (in the absence of representation from some pressure group) not always seemed to be fully engaged. At least where Law Commission Reports are under consideration, concerned members can and do inform themselves in detail about all the Bill's provisions, however technical they may be; in other cases Members of Parliament may lack the necessary briefing to ask the right questions... .

But I fear that this explanation of codification process *à l'Anglaise* leaves the inquisitor in my nightmare somewhat less than satisfied. 'What you have told me is very interesting,' he says with exquisite courtesy but perhaps less than total conviction. 'Nevertheless with the greatest possible respect, I fear that it indicates that you do not fully comprehend the objectives of codification. Of course, I can well see that it would be possible to bring this pile of laws which you show me with such pride within the covers of a single volume, but this would still not constitute a code of family law in the sense in which the expression is understood amongst civilised nations. For what you put forward as an embryonic code is little more than a jumble of procedures, couched almost entirely in terms of remedies rather than rights, moving directly from the information of marriage to divorce or death, pausing only to give the parties the right to apply to a court for protection from violence. How can you be content with a so-called code which will perhaps in due course tell one how to get married, but will say little or nothing of the legal consequences of marriage and the mutual rights and duties of the spouses, and of parent and child? Of course,' my inquisitor goes on, 'I am well aware of the obstacles in the past placed in the way of reform on scientific principles by the continued dominance of your legal system by guilds of craftsmen, but surely a body specifically committed to systematic development of the law should do better.'

Was it not curious, for instance, that family law dealt so sparsely with the rights of spouses? Thus a wife was given a right to save half of any housekeeping money that she was given but she had no right to have a housekeeping allowance.

---

itself (under s. 3 of the 1980 Act) the rights only of the other parent. The exact wording of the 1948 Act as amended was substituted by the Joint Committee on Consolidation Bills in order to preserve the possibility of a different construction: see generally Minutes of Evidence, 31 October 1979 (H.C. 256).

A spouse had a statutory right to benefit from improvements to the property but no statutory right to benefit by virtue of a contribution to the costs of acquisition.

The truth of the matter is that each of these rights was conferred as a more or less instant response to pressure to deal with what was perceived to be a pressing social evil in need of urgent reform – the antithesis of the process of orderly and systematic codification. It is not surprising that if one were to stitch all the provisions together one would not even get a decent patchwork quilt.

Conclusion
How far can I hope to have satisfied my inquisitor about our achievements in relation to codification? Certainly I hope that he would regard the assertion that 'no material progress' has been made towards this end as somewhat exaggerated. Provided one is prepared to adopt a distinctively English style of codification, it can perhaps fairly be claimed that we have the main structure of a code dealing with the law of husband and wife. I have however perhaps said sufficient to give some idea of the difficulties (arising, for example, from the distinctive nature and traditions of our legislative process and system of government) which would prevent the Law Commission from having full control of the 'coach of law reform' even if it had the resources which would be required. A complete family law code is indeed still 'a long way off'.

I must admit that I am not myself unduly perturbed by this fact. For codification is surely a means to an end, and not an end in itself; the end is the proper development and reform of the law. Codification is a goal at which we should aim; if only because such an objective should necessarily involve that our reforming law be clear, logical, and above all consistent. In 1965 it may well have seemed that codification was to be the primary justification for the Commission's existence; but, in my view, experience has shown that the Commission's most useful function has been to deal, sometimes on an ad hoc and pragmatic basis with perhaps limited areas of the law where reform has been shown to be necessary. Its distinctive contribution to the development of the law has in fact been to open up to serious public analysis and discussion the implications of reform, and the formidable difficulties of policy which are often involved.

The rather dismal history of codification by the Law Commission was traced in a lecture by a former chairman of the Commission:

Sir Michael Kerr, 'Law Reform in Changing Times', 96 *Law Quarterly Review*, 1980, pp. 527–9

… The experience of the Law Commission so far has certainly been that codification in the Continental sense is quite impracticable. It was first attempted in relation to Item I of the Commission's First Programme in 1965, 'Codification of the Law of Contract'. During the first six years of the Commission's existence this was one of its main priorities. Virtually all of our law of contract is governed by the common law; there are hardly any statutes. The Commission's objective was accordingly to produce a code of principles and rules which would cover the whole of the law of contract and to enact this in a single statute. However, by 1972 it had become clear that this was simply not practicable. Thus, it proved impossible to agree as between England and Scotland what should be the unified rules of contract for the whole of the United Kingdom. It then also proved impossible to produce a code for English law alone. It was found that agreement could not be reached on the formulation of rules and propositions to replace the immense body of case law in this field, as distilled in our text books, covering innumerable permutations of situations which a code would inevitably leave at large. In the result, this attempt at codification had to be suspended indefinitely,[13] and at present it has no prospect of realisation. What has been substituted for it is the objective of reforming specific parts of our law of contract by statutory reformulation where this seems particularly necessary.[14] Instead of having one all-embracing code of rules, as in other countries, we will therefore in the foreseeable future have no more than a number of statutes superseding those parts of our law of contract which appear to be in particular need of reform, leaving the rest to the common law as before.

Very much the same fate befell the original scheme for the 'Codification of the Law of Landlord and Tenant', which was Item VIII of the Law Commission's First Programme. In the early years an attempt was made, with the assistance of outside specialists, to formulate a code. An experienced barrister did a great deal of work to evolve a set of propositions and rules intended to codify the whole of the present law of landlord and tenant apart from the Rent Act legislation.[15] However, it soon became clear, both inside the Commission and in consultation with others, that, at any rate for the present, any exercise on these lines had no realistic prospect of implementation by legislation. Here again, therefore, the Commission had to compromise[16] by concentrating on the statutory restatement of a number of aspects of the law where reform appears particularly desirable, and this work is now proceeding.[17]

The same problem faces the Commission in relation to the Criminal Law. There is hardly any legal system in the world without a comprehensive Criminal Code, but there is none in this country. The Commission is committed to the ultimate codification of the Criminal Law. With the assistance of the Criminal Law Revision Committee we are now well on the way towards the statutory restatement of all common law offences. This would be regarded as a self-

13 See Eighth Annual Report, 1972–3, paras. 3 to 5, Law Com. No. 58.
14 E.g. the doctrine of consideration, the parol evidence rule, the law concerning minors' contracts, and parts of the law of insurance.
15 The late L. A. Blundell, Q.C. The code would have contained about 880 propositions, of which over 650 had been fully drafted by him before his death. The work was then suspended indefinitely.
16 Eighth Annual Report, 1972–3, paras. 3 to 5. Law Com. No. 58.
17 The Law Commission published a Report and draft Bill on *Obligations of Landlords and Tenants* (1975) Law Com. No. 67; an unpublished draft Report on *Covenants against Dispositions, Alterations and Change of Use* is at present under consideration by the Department of the Environment; and the Commission will shortly produce a draft Report on *Termination of Tenancies* for consideration by this and other Departments.

evident necessity in virtually every other legal system, where it would be unimaginable that it should be left to the courts to decide *ex post facto* whether or not some particular course of conduct had or had not been criminal. We are now gradually approaching the stage when there will be a number of detailed statutes which, between them, will define all offences. However, this will still be a very long way from having anything in the nature of a comprehensive Criminal Code, such as exists in virtually all other jurisdictions, including the Commonwealth.

However progress toward a code of criminal law has been considerable. The Law Commission accepted assistance from the Society of Public Teachers of Law. From 1981 onwards a team headed by Professor Sir John Smith QC with Professor Edward Griew and Professor Ian Dennis prepared a draft Code. Their Report, published in 1985, formulated the general principles governing criminal liability – jurisdiction, burden of proof, fault and the like. (See the May 1986 issue of the *Criminal Law Review* the whole of which was devoted to the draft Code. See also Ian Dennis, 'The case for Codification', 50 *Journal of Criminal Law*, 1986, pp. 161–77.) For criticism of the drafting of the Code see F.A.R. Bennion, 'The Law Commission's Criminal Law Bill: No Way to Draft a Code' *Statute Law Review,* 1994, pp. 108–15.

Following publication of the 1985 draft Code, eight groups of lawyers around the country, each headed by a circuit judge, were asked to scrutinise in detail some part of the draft Code and to report back to the Law Commission. In addition many comments were received from other persons and bodies. In April 1989 the Law Commission published the Criminal Code as its final report – *A Criminal Code for England and Wales* (vols. 1 and 2) (Law Commission No. 177, 1989). Part I covered the general principles of liability. Part II contained specific offences grouped into five chapters dealing with offences against the person; sexual offences; theft, fraud and related offences; other offences against property; and offences against public peace and safety. These offences, it was said, would cover 90–95 per cent of the work of the criminal courts. (For comment see A. T. Smith, 'Legislating the Criminal Code: The Law Commission's Proposals' [1992] *Criminal Law Review*, 396.)

The Code was laid before Parliament but it was thought that it could not all be digested together. In its 1990 *Annual Report* the Commission said: 'work on the Code could best be furthered by means of a series of reports recommending the reform or restatement of areas of specific crimes along the lines envisaged in the Code Report, together with the reformulation in "Code" terms of general principles relevant to the offences in question' (para. 2.15).

The area chosen for the first such treatment was that of offences against the person. The Commission's proposals regarding this offence were published in March 1992 in the form of a Consultation Paper containing a bill. The accompanying press release said that the bill 'builds on and uses the concepts and terminology contained in the Commission's Code that was published in 1989. If enacted, it would be an important step forward in the process of, eventually, putting the whole of the criminal law into a single code.' The Consultation Paper was different from most put out by the Law Commission since it did not canvass alternative options but simply put forward a bill with an extensive commentary.

However, the criminal law code made no progress. At the annual Mansion House Dinner for H.M. Judges in July 1998 the Lord Chief Justice, Lord Bingham, devoted part of his speech to this topic. It was published under the title 'A Criminal Code: Must we Wait for Ever?' (1998) *Criminal Law Review*, pp. 694–96.

6. CAN MORE BE DONE TO INVOLVE THE COMMUNITY IN THE PROCESS OF LAW REFORM?

The Law Commission pioneered the use of Working Papers which are widely circulated to experts and interested bodies as a means of stimulating responses to draft law reform proposals. But although the recommendations are often mentioned briefly in the law press, this method of consultation has not made much impact on the general public. In a paper delivered in September 1979 at Warwick University, at the annual meeting of the UK National Committee on Comparative Law, the then chairman of the Australian Law Reform Commission, Mr Justice Kirby, outlined efforts made by his commission to broaden the process of consultation.

(a) Consultative documents

One method used was to employ a range of lay consultants. On every project a team of such consultants was set up – mainly on a voluntary basis. The willingness of experts to come forward without remuneration was 'a heartening reflection of the interest in the community in law improvement'. The choice of consultants was broad and so far as possible reflected very different interests. So in a project on the introduction of class actions in Australia, the President of the Consumers' Association sat down with representatives of business and industry. In the project on the recovery of debt the Director of the Finance Conference took part with persons experienced in helping and counselling the poor. In the project on laws governing transplants, medical experts were balanced by a professor of philosophy and two theologians. For the reform of defamation laws, no fewer than thirty consultants had been appointed including journalists, newspaper editors and managers, and academics. The end result was 'a remarkable collection of inter-disciplinary talent which has greatly enriched the thinking of the law commissioners.'

Another technique still well within the accepted traditions of law-reform bodies was the use of discussion papers in briefer form than the full Working Papers, designed to be read by lawyers and laymen who did not have time to read the fuller document. Such discussion papers were normally limited to 20–30 pages, were written in somewhat less technical form, and concentrated on the issues of general policy.

Attempts were also being made to translate this document into even briefer and simpler form suitable for disadvantaged, migrant and less well-educated groups 'whose legitimate interest in law reform may be as great as that of the educated middle class'.

The practice had also been developed of circulating large numbers of copies of regular four-page summaries of discussion papers.[18]

The Australian Commission was continuing to experiment with 'a number of consultative documents of varying length, technicality and sophistication to ensure that communication with different groups is achieved'.

(b) Public hearings

A bolder approach had been that of the public hearing at which experts, lobby groups, interested bodies and institutions as well as the ordinary citizen could come forward to express their views on the Commission's tentative proposals for reform of the law. Such hearings had now become a regular feature of the work of the Commission. They were widely advertised in the press and on the radio and television. Specific invitations were addressed to bodies and individuals who had already submitted written evidence. The dates were usually fixed four to five months ahead of time.

The public hearings were conducted informally. There was no need for the person making a submission to have produced a written document – though some did. The procedure was inquisitorial, with the chairman of the hearing taking the witness through his statement. Commissioners would then put questions. Legal representation was not permitted. Sometimes when a particular federal authority was closely concerned, it was allowed to ask questions of some witnesses, and subsequently to comment on

18 This has been tried in the UK too, but not always with very impressive results. Professor Stephen Cretney said in October 1984 that even on an issue of such great popular concern as the ownership of family property, on which the Scottish Law Commission had gone to great trouble to publicise its views by means of pamphlets that were widely distributed (for instance to citizens' advice bureaux and public libraries), only forty or so comments had been received.

individual submissions. There were no rules of evidence. Hearings were normally in daytime but trials were being made of evening hearings in addition.

Public hearings were arduous and time-consuming but they had proved more useful than many had supposed likely. Normally they were well attended and they served a variety of ends. It was useful to have the different parties and interests involved to come together to express their viewpoints and to hear the viewpoints of others. The ordinary citizen could personalise his own problems and thereby often throw new light on the issues under consideration. The various interest groups could to some extent orchestrate their participation by bringing forward witnesses to different arguments.

Mr Justice Kirby said that considering the time and effort already devoted to the problem, 'surprisingly enough, public hearings often identify aspects of a problem which have simply not been considered by the Commission'. But apart from the argument of utility there was also a point of principle:

> The business of reform is not just a technical exercise. It is the business of improving society by improving its laws, practices and procedures. This involves a consideration of competing values. Lawyers inevitably tend to see social problems in a special way, often blinkered by the comfortable and familiar approaches of the past, designed in times less sensitive to the poor, deprived and minority groups in the community. There is a greater chance of avoiding lawyers' myopia if a window is opened to the lay community and the myriad of interests, lobbies and groups that make it up.... . Increasingly there is an awareness that a theoretical say through elected representatives is not always adequate because of the pressures of party politics and heady political debates. What is needed is new machinery which realistically acknowledges the impossibility of hearing everybody but affords those who wish to voice their grievances and share their knowledge the opportunity to do so.

It was appropriate to note that cases of abuse of the process were rare. 'The fears of irrelevant and long-winded submissions or of hordes of unbalanced or nuisance witnesses has not been borne out.'

(c) Use of the media

Mr Justice Kirby said that newspapers, radio and television had all come to play an important part in the process of better consultation. The reality was that 'the printed word is no longer the means of mass communication for the ordinary citizen'. The caravan had moved on. The electronic media were the means by which most people received news and information and considered topics of public interest and concern. Law-reform bodies had to become skilled in using these techniques. Commissioners took part in television debates, radio talk shows and national programmes with audiences in millions. The Prime Minister and the Governor-General of Australia had both acknowledged the effectiveness of this departure. Brief but accurate and well-presented news releases helped the media to report the activities of the Commission.

(d) Surveys and questionnaires

The Commission had used surveys and questionnaires in a variety of projects. In the study of federal offenders it had administered a survey to federal prosecutors to elicit information about prosecution practice. For the project on child welfare laws, a survey was being conducted in which the police were being asked for facts and views about prosecution decisions. Children coming before the courts would also be interviewed. In the project on sentencing, the Commission had asked all judges and magistrates to fill out a questionnaire that took about an hour and a half to complete. The response rate was nearly eighty per cent. The Commission was also seeking prisoners' views and experiences in a questionnaire that was being sent sealed and uncensored direct to the Commission from prisoners in all federal prisons. Commissioners were currently engaged in visiting the remotest parts of Australia in order to try to discover the views of aboriginals on the laws that affected them. The difficulties of communication were daunting but if the procedures of consultation meant anything, 'they require an effort that goes far beyond tokenism and that reaches out to those who will be affected by a reform proposal'. Statistics and social surveys provided a means by which the inarticulate and disadvantaged could speak to law-makers.

Conclusion

All these varying methods were ways of assisting the clearer public articulation of issues and arguments for and against law reform proposals. The whole process raised the quality of the public debate about law reform. It also mirrored the growing openness of government, law-making and public administration in Western societies. Another benefit was the possibility that the social education involved in explaining the defects in the law might help to generate a perception of injustices that would otherwise be shrugged off, overlooked or, worst of all, not even perceived. Finally, Mr Justice Kirby argued:

> A lasting value of law reform commissions may be that by involving the community and the legal profession together in the improvement and

modernisation of the law, they contribute to the stability of society. The rule of law, that unique feature of the Western communities, is, after all, only worth boasting of if the rules which the law enforces are just and in tune with today's society.

Note

Of the various techniques referred to by Mr Justice Kirby, only some have been tried in the UK. The Law Commission has used academic consultants but almost all have been lawyers. The National Association of Citizens' Advice Bureaux occasionally produces evidence based on the collective experience of its vast case-load which bears on law-reform proposals. There have been a few – very few – examples, of surveys undertaken in connection with law-reform projects. One example was the Law Commission's survey of the incidence of binding over (19th Annual Report of the Law Commission, 1983–4, paras 2.16–2.17.) But there have been no experiments with public hearings organised by the Law Commission or for that matter other law-reform bodies.

Law reform is seen by both lawyers and non-lawyers to be a topic of interest mainly to lawyers. Thus the House of Commons is normally virtually empty when law-reform matters are under discussion.

Index